D0948627

DATABASE DESIGN AND DEVELOPMENT

DATABASE DESIGN AND DEVELOPMENT
An Essential Guide for IT Professionals

PAULRAJ PONNIAH

IEEE PRESS

A JOHN WILEY & SONS, INC., PUBLICATION

Published by John Wiley & Sons, Inc., Hoboken, New Jersey.
Published simultaneously in Canada.

For general information on our other products and services please contact our Customer Care Department within the U.S. at 877-762-2974, outside the U.S. at 317-572-3993 or fax 317-572-4002.

Wiley also publishes its books in a variety of electronic formats. Some content that appears in print, however, may not be available in electronic format.

Library of Congress Cataloging-in-Publication Data:

Ponniah, Paulraj.
    Database design and development: an essential guide for IT professionals/Paulraj Ponniah.
        p.   cm.
    "A Wiley-Interscience publication."
    Includes bibliographical references and index.
    ISBN 0-471-21877-4 (cloth)
    1. Database design.   2. Database management.   I. Title.

    QA76.9.D26P58 2003
005.74—dc10
                                                                                2002192402

Printed in the United States of America.

10 9 8 7 6 5 4 3 2 1

In loving memory
of
my dear parents.

CONTENTS

PART VII   ADVANCED DATABASE TOPICS   551

APPENDICES   685

PREFACE

Are you a programmer, systems analyst, network specialist, project leader, or any other type of information technology professional? Alternatively, are you a student aspiring for a career in information technology? Then you definitely need to know how database systems are designed and developed. You have to understand the fundamentals of database systems clearly.

As you know, in today's business environment, companies depend on their databases to provide crucial information essential for running their businesses. Gone are the days of file-oriented data systems. Now database systems form the centerpiece of the growing and maturing electronic commerce. Database and Web technologies have merged. Over the years, commercial database products have become sophisticated and robust.

In this transformed computing environment, knowledge of database systems can no longer be confined only to specialists such as data analysts and database administrators. All IT professionals need basic knowledge of database technology and its applications. This book comes to you as an essential guide on database design and development, covering all the necessary topics in proper measure, written especially for IT professionals—present and future.

THE SCENARIO

In every industry across the board, from retail chain stores to financial institutions, from manufacturing organizations to government departments, and from airline companies to utility businesses, database systems have become the norm for information storage and retrieval. Whether it is a Web-based application driving electronic commerce or an inventory control application managing just-in-time inventory or a data warehouse system supporting strategic decision making, you need an effective and successful technology to store and retrieve data. It is no wonder that companies have adopted database technology without reservations. The modern relational database system, proven to be eminently suitable for data management, has become more and more pervasive.

Over the recent years, vendors of all leading database products have released more sophisticated and powerful software versions. Database management systems such as DB2, Informix, Oracle, SQL Server, and Sybase have all expanded with several useful features. Database management systems have become the centerpiece of e-business. Numerous books feature commercial database products.

THE ROLE OF IT

In this scenario, the information technology department of every organization has a primary responsibility. The department has to support and keep the database systems running. Without the database system, the day-to-day business of the organization will come to a grinding halt.

Therefore, all IT staff must understand the workings of database systems. It is not enough to have just a handful of specialists knowledgeable in database technology. All applications in the enterprise now work with databases. Every IT professional, therefore, must know the basics of the technology. Everyone must learn how database systems are designed and developed. Every IT professional must understand the fundamental principles.

WHAT THIS BOOK CAN DO FOR YOU

This book provides you with necessary information on the basics of database technology. It covers all the essential topics carefully with proper emphasis as required by each topic. If you are new to the fundamentals of database technology, this book is an essential pre-requisite before you determine the next steps toward specialization in the database field. If you are already familiar with the technology, this book is a suitable refresher to reinforce your grasp of the subject.

More specifically, here is a summary of what this book can do for you:

Specially designed for IT professionals

Specifically intended for IT professionals like you, this book builds on what you already know. The book takes into account the background, knowledge, and terminology of IT professionals; it presents the topics in a suitable direct style.

Comprehensive with just the necessary details

The book deals with every significant topic needed by IT professionals looking for the fundamentals. It encompasses database concepts, terminology, planning, implementation, and administration; the book also includes significant technology trends.

Suitably organized

The book follows an organization most apt and logical for IT professionals concentrating on the fundamentals. It is the type of organization these professionals is most familiar in their day-to-day work experience. Beginning with an overview of basic concepts, the book moves on to an overview of the database system development process, then to the important topic of data modeling, on to design, then to implementation, and concludes with ongoing maintenance and growth.

Feature highlights

Every chapter opens up with chapter objectives and concludes with a chapter summary. At the end of each chapter, you find a set of review questions and exercises. These features make the book eminently suitable for self-study or for use as a textbook in a college course.

Exposure to real-world situations

Throughout the book, each concept or technique is illustrated with real-world examples. An appendix is devoted to the review of leading commercial database management systems.

Preparation for database specialists

Although intended as a first course on the fundamentals, the book provides sufficient coverage of each topic so that you may easily proceed to the next phase of specialization for specific roles such as data modeler, database designer, data analyst, data administrator, or database administrator.

ACKNOWLEDGMENTS

The authors listed in the reference section at the end of the book greatly enhanced my understanding and appreciation for database technology. I am deeply indebted to the authors for their insights and observations; I wish to express my sincere thanks to them.

I must also record my appreciation for the several professional colleagues who had worked with me on various database projects during my 25-year consulting career. Also, thanks are due to the many students in my database classes over the years. Interactions with my students and colleagues have enabled me to shape this book according to the specific needs of IT professionals.

PAULRAJ PONNIAH, Ph.D.

Milltown, New Jersey
November 2002

PART I

BASIC DATABASE CONCEPTS

CHAPTER 1

THE DATABASE APPROACH

CHAPTER OBJECTIVES

- Understand how the database approach is different and superior to earlier data systems
- Examine how information demand and technology explosion drive database systems
- Trace the evolution of data systems and note how we have arrived at the database approach
- Comprehend the benefits of database systems and perceive the need for them
- Survey briefly various data models, types of databases, and the database industry

Consider the following scenarios:

- You meet someone in a computer store. As a knowledgeable IT professional, you want to help this person. He says he is looking for *database* software to keep the names and addresses of his customers to do his mailings and billings. But what he really needs is a mail-merge program.
- You call your travel agent to make your airline reservations for the vacation you have been waiting for all year. The agent responds by saying that she cannot do that just now because the *database* is down. She really means that the reservations computer system is not working.
- Here is one more. You call your cellular phone company to complain about errors on the latest billing statement. The phone company representative says

Database Design and Development: An Essential Guide for IT Professionals by Paulraj Ponniah
ISBN 0-471-21877-4   Copyright © 2003 by John Wiley and Sons, Inc.

that the *database* must have printed some incorrect numbers. What the representative really implies is that the billing application has miscalculated the charges.

In our modern society most people know the term *database* without understanding its full and clear meaning. Even in information technology circles, not everyone knows the concepts in reasonable detail. What is a *database*? Is it data? Is it software? Is it the place where you store data? Is there something special about the way you store data? Is it how you store and retrieve data? What exactly is a database system? What are the features and functions? Many more such questions arise.

Today, almost all organizations depend on their database systems for the crucial information they need to run their business. In every industry across the board, from retail chain stores to financial institutions, from manufacturing enterprises to government departments, and from airline companies to utility businesses, database systems have become the norm for information storage and retrieval. Database systems form the centerpiece of the growing and maturing electronic commerce. Database and Web technologies have merged.

The Information Technology department of today's organization has a primary responsibility: The department has to support and keep the database systems running. In this transformed computing environment, knowledge of database systems is no longer confined only to specialists such as data analysts and database administrators. Are you are a systems analyst, programmer, project leader, or network specialist? Then you also need to know the basics of database systems. You also need to grasp the significance of the database approach. All IT professionals need to study the basic principles and techniques of database design and development.

First, let us begin to understand how we got to this stage where most organizations depend on their database systems for running the business. Let us trace the evolution of data systems and see the essential need for the database approach. Let us understand what exactly the database approach is. Let us briefly survey the database industry and grasp the significance of the developments.

EVOLUTION OF DATA SYSTEMS

How were companies running their business before computers came into use? Even at that time, organizations needed information to execute the business processes, sell goods and services, and satisfy the needs of customers. Manual files supported business operations. Accounting personnel performed manual calculations and prepared invoices. Payroll departments manually wrote the checks. Business operations were reasonably satisfactory.

So, what happened? How did we get to the computer database systems of today? When computers were introduced in the 1960s, computer file systems replaced the manual files. This marked a significant leap in the way data was stored and retrieved for business operations. What has been really happening from that time until now, when database systems have become the norm? What prompted the progress toward database systems?

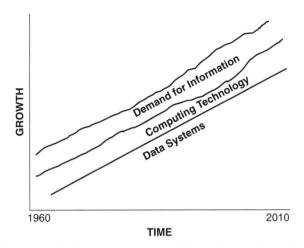

Figure 1-1   Technology growth and demand for information.

From the 1970s onward, two striking and remarkable phenomena were distinctly observed. Refer to Figure 1-1 indicating these two major developments.

First, demand for information has escalated in every organization. Organizations have steadily become global and widespread. Organizations have to contend with fierce competitive pressures. They need vast and complex information to stay in business and make a profit. Second, the past three decades have witnessed a huge, explosive growth in information technology. Processors have become faster, cheaper, and smaller. Operating systems have become powerful and robust. Data storage media have expanded tremendously in capacity; data storage prices have tumbled. Network and communication technology can now connect any remote site without difficulty. Application programming and people-machine interface have dramatically improved.

The escalating demand for information and the explosive growth in information technology have worked hand in hand to bring about the evolution to database systems. Ever-increasing demand for information drives the need for better methods of storing and retrieving data, for faster ways of processing data, and for improved methods of providing information. The demand for more and better information drove the technology growth. Progress in technology, in turn, spurred the capability to provide different types of information, not just to run day-to-day operations of an organization, but also to make strategic decisions.

Let us first examine the pertinent aspects of the technology explosion as related to data systems, because these are what we are specifically interested in. Then let us discuss the escalating demand for information that has prompted better and improved data systems.

Technology Explosion

If you have been in the information technology area for 5–10 years, you are certainly an eyewitness to the explosive growth. Growth is not confined to any one sector. All aspects of the technology have been improving tremendously. Here are some specifics:

- Twenty-five years ago, there were only 50,000 computers in the whole world; now more than 500,000 are installed every day.
- More than 60% of American households have at least one computer; more than 50% have e-mail and Internet access.
- Growth of the Internet and the use of the Web have overshadowed the PC breakthrough of the 1970s; at the beginning of 2000, about 50 million households worldwide were estimated to be using the Internet; by the end of 2005, this number is expected to grow 10-fold.
- About 7 years ago, there were only 50 websites; now 100,000 are added every hour.
- Databases in the terabyte range are becoming common; a few years ago, even the gigabyte range was unusual.
- In the mid-1960s, programmers in large corporations had to write programs that had to run on 12K machines; today even your personal computer at home has 10,000 times larger memory.

Growth has not been isolated here and there in hardware and software. We notice explosive growth in all sectors of information technology. Let us proceed further to look at specific areas of information technology that are related to data systems.

Data Storage Devices   Have you seen an 80-column card that very early computer systems used to store data? Each column in a card had holes punched to represent a single character. So a card could hold up to 80 characters. Keypunch operators typed data and program code into the cards. In the next stage, computer systems stored data on magnetic tapes. Initially, magnetic tapes of 800 BPI (bytes per inch) were used. Then we moved on to higher densities of 1600 BPI and 6250 BPI. For a brief while, paper tapes with punched holes were used as the storage medium. Special-purpose paper tape readers were used to read data from paper tapes.

It was a large leap forward when disk drives began to replace the earlier data storage media. Disk drives in mainframes consist of sets of large circular disks arranged in parallel with a common spindle. Sophisticated disk drives have come to stay as the common storage device of choice. Today's data servers use RAID (redundant array of inexpensive disks) technology as the advanced fault-tolerant storage system. Data storage devices have progressed tremendously from the primitive punched cards to the sophisticated RAID systems.

Three-and-a-Half-Inch Disk Drives   You are very familiar with the three-and-a-half-inch disk drives in your home computer system. Just review the progress in the capacities of these disk drives. See how the capacities kept doubling every year. Note the following details:

1992	1 gigabyte
1993	2 gigabytes

1994   4 gigabytes
1995   9 gigabytes
1997   18 gigabytes
2000   50 gigabytes

Computer Applications   Over the years, the types of computer applications have changed and progressed from mere bookkeeping applications to multimedia and data mining applications. Some of you might remember the days when the computer department was known as the data processing department. Applications in those days just processed data in elementary ways to produce some reports. The technology explosion resulted in a grand transition of computer usage from simple to increasing sophistication. Review the following details.

Data Processing Applications (DP). In the early days of computing, computer departments built applications just to replace clerical labor. Mostly, these applications performed simple accounting and financial functions. These applications produced straightforward reports. Speed and accuracy of the computer in performing calculations were the primary factors. Computer systems stored and retrieved data from magnetic tapes and earlier versions of disk drives. Applications used sequential or flat files to organize data.

Management Information Systems (MIS). In the next stage, growth of technology manifested itself in applications that went beyond accounting and finance to supporting the entire core business of an organization. Applications began to appear to process orders, manage inventory, bill customers, pay employees, and so on. Organizations depended on their management information systems for their day-to-day business. Storage and retrieval of data mostly depended on hard disks. Many applications adopted the use of database technology.

Decision-Support Systems (DSS). Further technology growth in processor speed, storage media, systems software, and database techniques pushed the application types to systems that supported strategic decision making. These applications are not meant for supporting day-to-day operations of a business but for providing information to executives and managers to make strategic decisions. In which markets should the company expand? Where should the next distribution warehouse be built? Which product lines should be discontinued? Which ones should be boosted? These applications dealt with sales analysis, profitability analysis, and customer support. Decision-support systems made use of improved storage facilities and newer features of database technology.

Data Warehousing (DW) and Data Mining (DM) Systems. In recent years, with the enormous progress in processor scalability, mass storage, and database methods, organizations are able to forge ahead with their applications, especially in building data warehousing and data mining systems. These recent decision-support systems, much more sophisticated than earlier attempts, require large volumes of data and complex analytical techniques. These systems need large databases specially designed and built separately from the databases that support the day-to-day operational systems.

Data Systems   What is the effect of the technology explosion on the way data is organized? Over the years, how were businesses organizing data? We just looked at the way applications have progressed from simpler types toward increasing sophistication. What about data systems?

Manual-Type Records.   Very early computer applications worked with data stored on punched cards and paper tapes. Keypunch operators prepared data on these primitive media from manual files and records. Computer applications read data from cards and tapes to prepare reports.

Sequential Files.   Improved storage media such as magnetic tapes and early disk drives enabled application developers to organize data as sequential (or flat) files. Each file contained data records of the same type arranged sequentially one after the other, usually in the order in which they were created. Sorting techniques allowed data records to be resorted in a different sequence.

Databases.   Increased sophistication in data storage techniques on hard disk drives and enhancements to operating systems enabled random and quick access of data. Data systems moved to a wholly new level. Applications were able to store data in databases and retrieve data sequentially and randomly.

Demand for Information

Of the two major factors that mutually contributed to the database approach to computing, so far we have considered the explosive growth of technology. Let us now turn our attention to the other factor, namely, the escalating demand for information. It is not just more information that organizations need. The demand for information includes several dimensions.

Consider how billing requirements and sales analysis have changed. In the early years of computing, organizations were happy if they could bill their customers once a month and review total sales by product quarterly. Now it is completely different. Organizations must bill every sale right away to keep up the cash flow. They need up-to-date customer balance and daily and cumulative sales totals by products. What about inventory reconciliation? Earlier systems provided reports to reconcile inventory or to determine profitability only at the end of each month. Now organizations need daily inventory reconciliation to manage inventory better, daily profitability analysis to plan sales campaigns, and daily customer information to improve customer service.

In the earlier period of computing, organizations were satisfied with information showing only current activity. They could use the information to manage day-to-day business and make operational decisions. In the changed business climate of globalization and fierce competition, this type of information alone is no longer adequate. Companies need information to plan and shape their future. They need information, not just to run day-to-day operations, but to make strategic decisions as well.

What about the delivery of information now compared to the early days of computing? Today, online information is the norm for most companies. Fast response times and access to large volumes of data have become essential. Earlier computer systems just provided reports, mostly once a month, a few once a week, and a small number once a day.

Organizations have come to realize that information is a key asset to be carefully managed and used for greater profitability. In summary, demand for information by today's enterprises contains the following attributes:

- More information
- Newer purposes
- Different information types
- Integrated information
- Information to be shared
- Faster access to information

Waves of Evolution

As we have seen so far, information technology, along with and because of the escalating demand for information, has made giant strides in the past few decades. Evolution to higher levels is evident in every aspect of information technology. The evolution has taken place in distinct waves. Refer to Figure 1-2.

Note carefully the evolution of information technology in the three major areas. First note how the very methods of computing technology have progressed from mainframes to client/server architecture. The centrally administered mainframes have made room for the client/server configuration in which each set of machines can perform specialized tasks.

What about the way in which humans interface with computers? In earlier days, we punched data on cards and fed them to be read by the early computers. Then came the CRTs (cathode-ray terminals) where textual data could be typed into the computer through the use of keyboards. Point-and-click GUIs (graphical user interfaces) proved to be a major improvement. Now, interfacing with computers through

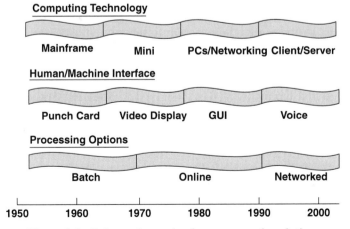

Figure 1-2   Information technology: waves of evolution.

the human voice is gaining ground. What a major transition from punch cards to direct voice input!

In the early days of computing, transactions were batched together for processing at the end of a stipulated period. For example, you could not invoice each sale as it happened. You had to collect and batch all the sales for a month and run the batched sales through the invoicing application. We moved to online transaction processing in the next wave. Now transactions are transmitted and processed over LANs (local area networks) and WANs (wide area networks).

File-Oriented Data Systems

As the demand for information continued to increase, organizations began to adopt improved file systems to store and access data. The file-oriented data systems essentially mimicked the manual file systems. The computer files corresponded to the paper files. In a filing cabinet, you store file folders and each file folder contains file records. Similarly, the computer systems use electronic files containing records. For example, a customer file would contain records, with each record containing data about a single customer. In the beginning, these computer files were primarily used for accounting applications. As we shall discuss in some detail, file-oriented systems have serious limitations. Therefore, organizations needed to go to better and improved methods for data storage and access.

File-oriented systems started out by using sequential or flat files. When you need to retrieve the 100th record from a sequential file, you have to read and bypass the first 99 records before you can get to record number 100. This is a very serious shortcoming. Therefore, slightly better methods of retrieval evolved. This was the transition to improved file-oriented data systems. Let us review how storage and retrieval methods apply to a customer file.

Sequential File. Customer records are stored in the sequence in which they are entered into the file. Record retrieval is sequential. For the file to be processed in any other sequence, it must be sorted in the required sequence.

ISAM File. This is the indexed-sequential access method. The customer records in the data file are stored sequentially, similar to the sequential file method. However, another index file is created, for example, with the customer numbers and the physical addresses of the records. When the record of a specific customer is needed, as done previously, you do not have to read the records of the data file one after the other until you find the record you are looking for. You can read the smaller index file, find the record you are looking for, and then use the physical address of the data record stored in the index file.

VSAM File. This is based on virtual storage access method, a major improvement over ISAM files. VSAM files provide for indexed access. Also, this method provides for storing and retrieving records directly from the customer file without an index file. In the direct method, the address where a customer record is stored may be calculated from the customer number with a specialized algorithm.

WHY DATABASE SYSTEMS?

We traced the evolution of data systems. We grasped the essentials of the explosive growth of information technology. We noted the escalating demand of organizations for information. We observed how growth in information technology and the increased demand for information worked hand in hand. Increasing demand for information spurred the growth of information technology. Growth of information technology, in turn, enabled organizations to satisfy the increasing demand for information.

Let us summarize the driving forces for organizations to adopt database systems. A major reason is the inadequacy of the earlier file-oriented data systems. We shall review the limitations and see how database systems overcome the limitations and provide significant benefits.

The Driving Forces

Among others, four major forces drove organizations to adopt database systems. Figure 1-3 illustrates these four major forces.

Information as a Corporate Asset. Today, companies strongly realize that information is a corporate asset similar to other assets such as cash, plant and equipment, or inventory. Proper management of key assets is essential for success. Companies understand that it is essential to manage information as a key asset. They understand the need to find improved methods for storing, retrieving, and using information.

Explosive Growth of Computer Technology. Computer technology, especially data storage and retrieval systems, has grown in a phenomenal manner. Without growth in this sector, it is unlikely that we could have progressed to database systems that need sophisticated ways of data storage and retrieval.

Escalating Demand for Information. We have noted the increase in demand for information by organizations, not only in volume but in the types of information as

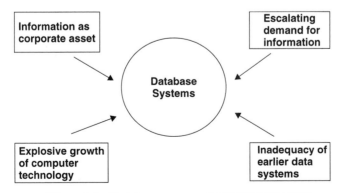

Figure 1-3 Database systems: the driving forces.

well. If companies did not need more and newer types of information, there would have been no impetus for development of database systems. The earlier data systems might have been satisfactory.

Inadequacy of Earlier Data Systems. Suppose the earlier data systems were able to meet the escalating demand for information. Then why bother to find better methods? But the fact is that these earlier systems were grossly inadequate to meet the information demands. Storage and management of large volumes of data were not adequate. Finding and retrieving information were extremely difficult. Protecting the information asset of a company was nearly impossible with the earlier data systems. Why was this so? How were the earlier systems inadequate? In what ways could they not meet the information demands? Understanding the limitations will give you a better appreciation for database systems.

Inadequacy of Earlier Data Systems

Assume that you work for a company called Progressive Book Distributors in the early 1970s. Your company purchases books from various publishers and sells them to retail bookstores and book clubs. The computer applications in your company would work with sequential files because those are the types of data systems available at that time. Here is a list of possible sequential computer files in your company.

Customer master file   Every time a new customer comes on board, a record is created in the file, with a new customer number, in the order in which the customers are added.

Book master file   As each new book is added to the inventory, a record is created in the file, with ISBN identifying each book.

Salesperson file   As each new salesperson is hired, the person is given an identification number and data about him or her is added to the file.

Sale transaction file   Each sale is recorded with the date of the sale.

Publisher file   As each new publisher is included, a record is created in the file, with a new publisher number, in the order in which the publishers are added.

Payment transaction file   Payments received from customers are recorded with the date of the payment.

Refer to Figure 1-4 showing the fields and sample data for each file.

What types of information is your company's staff looking for? Do they need to print an invoice for customer Allbooks Book Store for the sale on January 10, 2002? Do they want the total sales of all books from publishers Ron Fairchild during the month of December 2001? Do they want a list of all customers in New York state? In today's computing environment, no one will think of these requests as difficult or impossible. This was not the case with file-oriented applications of the early 1970s. File-oriented data systems have serious limitations.

Let us take just one specific example of printing statements to customers for sales. This had to be done in a batch mode at the end of a reasonable interval such as at

CUSTOMER MASTER FILE			
CustNo	CustName	Address	Country
1000	Allbooks Book Store	5757 Westheimer, Houston, TX 77057	U.S.A.
1010	Akito Books	Chiyoda-ku, Tokyo 100	Japan
1040	Robert Smith Ltd.	10 Bonds St., London W1A 2AA	U.K.
2050	Sally Orobetz	8 Hazelton Ave., Toronto, Ontario M5R 2E1	Canada

BOOK MASTER FILE			
ISBN	Title	Author	PubId
2093356790	DB Design	Carey	100
2101155897	DW Fundamentals	McMillan	200
1558712215	Art Appreciation	Stewart	300
3456765432	Existentialism	Ernst	400

PUBLISHER FILE		
PubId	PublisherName	Country
100	Ron Fairchild	USA
200	Crosley	U.K.
300	Summer Hill	Canada
400	Ully Wille	Germany

SALESPERSON FILE			
SalRepId	SalRepName	Office	Comm%
10	Williams	Chicago	13
20	Harreld	London	12
30	Swamy	Toronto	9
40	Katzman	Munich	10

SALE TRANSACTION FILE					
SalDate	CustNo	SalRepId	ISBN	Qty	Amount
6-Apr	1000	10	2093356790	10	799.50
10-Apr	1010	20	2101155897	10	699.50
19-Apr	1040	30	1558712215	20	1,000.50
24-Apr	2050	40	3456765432	10	750.00

PAYMENT TRANSACTION FILE			
PymtDte	CustNo	PayMethod	Amount
13-Apr	1000	Amex	600.00
22-Apr	1010	Visa	500.00
24-Apr	1040	Check	800.00
30-Apr	2050	Visa	650.00

Figure 1-4 Progressive Book Distributors: files.

the end of a month. All the sales transactions and payment transactions for the month had to be batched together and processed in a batch mode.

Figure 1-5 indicates a flowchart of the jobs that must be run to produce the billing statements.

Even an initial review of the flowchart reveals that there are too many sorts for just producing simple billing statements. That is because each file is kept in a sequence that is not useful for the processing logic of the entire application. The whole concept of batch processing is very inflexible. Suppose in the middle of the month you need the billing statements for just a few select customers. There is no easy way of doing this. You have to run the complete batch process in the middle of the month and then separate out the statements you need.

File-oriented systems are inadequate to face the challenges of increasing demand for information. Especially when companies care for information as a key asset, the earlier file-oriented data systems possess severe limitations. Let us discuss the important limitations so that we can appreciate how database systems overcome these shortcomings.

Uncontrolled Data Redundancy In file-oriented systems, each application has its own set of files. Each application creates and stores data just for the use of that application. For example, in a bank, there could be three separate applications— one for checking accounts, one for savings accounts, and another one for loan

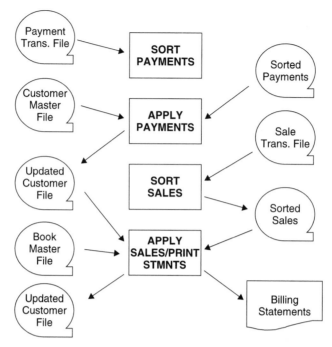

Figure 1-5   Flowchart for billing application.

accounts. If a bank customer has a checking account, a savings account, and a loan account, data about that customer such as name and address are kept separately in each of these applications. There is unnecessary and uncontrolled duplication of the same data in the bank's computer files. Similarly, the possibility of data duplication exists in the inpatient and outpatient accounts of a medical center. In an auction business, data duplication is possible in sellers' and buyers' accounts.

Obviously, data duplication results in wasted storage space. In the bank example, it is very likely that many customers have both checking and savings accounts. In auction businesses, dealers of art and other such items are customers recorded in both sellers' and buyers' account applications. In these cases, the wastage of storage space can be enormous. Multiple input of same data item also requires extra time and resources that could be applied for other, useful purposes.

Inconsistent Data   Data redundancy or duplication of data in your computer files can cause serious inconsistency in the data. Suppose a bank customer has both checking and savings accounts. If that person's name, address, or both are different in the two accounts, then the data about that customer are inconsistent in the bank's files. Which set of data is correct? It is possible that the name of that customer in one system is correct and the address as recorded in the other application is correct. Inconsistency of data is a direct result of data duplication.

Field sizes and formats of the same data item might be different in the various applications. In the checking and savings accounts, there could be just one long field for the address to be recorded in textual format. The loan account, being a later application, could have separate fields for street address, city, state, and zip code.

Such variations are likely causes for data integrity problems. Variations in names and addresses may cause erroneous printing of names and addresses on documents mailed to customers.

Inflexibility   When an application cannot adapt to changing requirements, we say that the application is inflexible. By the very nature of sequential files, a file-oriented system can process transactions only in batch mode. That is, transactions are accumulated and processed as batches. You cannot print an invoice for a single customer for a single sale. Sequential files allow retrieval of data records, one at a time, in sequence. Such files do not possess the flexibility to meet new and changing information requirements.

Suppose you are interested in finding and listing all the purchases made by customers in Japan for the past three months. Or you want a list of all customers in a certain zip code range. It is very difficult to satisfy such ad hoc queries in a file-oriented system without reprogramming.

Limited Data Sharing   Consider two typical applications, namely, order processing and inventory control. Each of these applications needs data on products. But data on products are repeated in each of these two applications when the business depends on file-oriented data systems. There is no sharing of data on products between the two applications. If product descriptions of certain products are changed, these changes must be made in both applications.

Difficult Data Integration   Let us get back to the bank example with separate customer files in the checking, savings, and loan applications. If you wanted to combine data from these applications and send consolidated statements to customers showing the transactions in all three accounts, it would be nearly impossible with file-oriented data systems. You would have to run special programs to extract banking transactions from each application. Then you would have to come up with methods for matching customer accounts from each application and consolidate the transactions in a single statement, which is not an easy task. The proliferation of files and duplication of data continue as each new application is implemented with its own set of files.

Poor Enforcement of Standards and Controls   Standards relate to data names, formats, value restrictions, and access controls. When duplicated data are spread across many applications, it is extremely difficult to enforce standards. For example, if the standard in your company is for the customer name field to be 35 bytes, then you will have to impose this standard, not in one place, but in many applications that store customer names. Suppose you have to include a business rule that the employee daily wage rate must be between 0 and 100; you may have to stipulate this rule in at least two different applications, namely, payroll and human resources.

Problems with the resolution of homonyms and synonyms deserve special attention. File-oriented data systems are likely to have problems with these.

Homonyms.   If a single field name represents two or more objects in different applications, it is called a homonym. For example, the field name *balance* may represent the checking balance in the checking accounts application. The same field name *balance* may also represent the savings balance in the savings accounts application. In this case, the term *balance* is a homonym. In file-oriented data systems, it is hard to control homonyms.

Synonyms. If different field names in different applications represent the same object, these names are known as synonyms. As an example, consider how a student may be referred to in a college data system. In the student registration system, the student may be referred to by the field name *student-number*. On the other hand, in the majors and graduation system, the student may be referred to by the field name *candidate-number*. The terms *student-number* and *candidate-number* are synonyms. In file-oriented data systems, controlling synonyms is difficult.

Excessive Program Maintenance   How is program maintenance a problem in file-oriented systems? Consider the coding of computer programs in file-oriented applications. These programs are usually written in third-generation languages like COBOL. A program in languages like COBOL contains two distinct sections. One section of the program, namely, FD or file definition section, has the structures of the files used in the program embedded within the program itself. The other section has the processing logic. Data structures and processing logic are interconnected and combined together in the program. This means that reference to data is not independent of the processing logic. There is no data independence.

What is the effect of the lack of data independence in file-oriented systems? Consider all the computer programs that use the customer file for processing. In each of these programs, the structure of the customer file is embedded within the program itself. What happens when a new field such as cellular phone number is added to the customer record? Every one of the programs using the customer file need to be changed and recompiled, irrespective of whether the program uses the cellular phone number field or not. Lack of data independence results in excessive program maintenance.

Productivity Losses   Two main factors cause reduction in productivity while using file-oriented systems:

- The same data need to be maintained in multiple places.
- Because of lack of data independence, multiple programs need to be changed frequently.

Database Systems Meet the Challenges

As the demand for information escalated, it became urgent to overcome the limitations of file-oriented data systems. With these limitations, companies could not meet the requirements of increased demand for information. They needed a different approach to storing, retrieving, and managing data. They could not afford the productivity losses. They could not waste space because of data duplication in file-oriented systems.

Specialists at Rockwell and General Electric began to work on better methods for managing data. These methods attempted to overcome the limitations of file-oriented systems. Data and processing logic had to be separated so as to improve programmer productivity. The new approach of using databases instead of conventional flat files addressed the challenges for meeting the increased demand for information. The database approach overcame the limitations of the earlier data systems and produced enormous benefits. Let us review the specific benefits and understand in what way the database approach is superior to the earlier data systems.

Minimal Data Redundancy   Unlike file-oriented data systems where data are duplicated among various applications, database systems integrate all the data into one logical structure. Duplication of data is minimized. Wastage of storage space is eliminated. Going back to the bank example, with a database, customer data is not duplicated in the checking account, savings account, and loan account applications. Customer data is entered and maintained in only one place in the database.

Sometimes, in a database, a few data elements may have to be duplicated. Let us say that product data consist of product number, description, price, and the corresponding product line number. All the fields relating to product line data are kept separately. Whenever the details of products and product lines are needed in applications, both data structures are retrieved from the database. Suppose a heavily used product forecast application needs all the details of the product from product data and just the product line description from the product line data. In that case, it will be efficient for the product data to duplicate the product line description from the product line data. Thus, in some instances, data duplication is permitted in a database for the purpose of access efficiency and performance improvement. However, such data duplications are kept to a minimum.

Data Integrity   Data integrity in a database means reduction of data inconsistency. Because of the elimination or control of data redundancy, a database is less prone to errors creeping in through data duplication. Field sizes and field formats are the same for all applications. Each application uses the same data from one place in the database. In a bank, names and addresses will be the same for checking account, savings account, and loan applications.

Data Integration   In a database, data objects are organized into single logical data structures. For example, in file-oriented data systems, data about employees are scattered among the various applications. The payroll application contains employee name and address, social security number, salary rate, deductions, and so on. The pension plan application contains pension data about each employee, whereas the human resources application contains employee qualifications, skills, training, and education. However, all data about each employee are integrated and stored together in a database.

So, in a database, data about each business object are integrated and stored separately as customer, order, product, invoice, manufacturer, sale, and so on. Data integration enables users to understand the data and the relationships among data structures easily. Programmers needing data about a business object can go to one place to get the details. For example, data about orders are consolidated in one place as order data.

Data Sharing This benefit of database systems follows from data integration. The various departments in any enterprise need to share the company's data for proper functioning. The sales department needs to share the data generated by the accounting department through the billing application. Consider the customer service department. It needs to share the data generated by several applications. The customer service application needs information about customers, their orders, billings, payments, and credit ratings. With data integration in a database, the application can get data from distinct and consolidated data structures relating to customer, orders, invoices, payments, and credit status.

Data sharing is a major benefit of database systems. Each department shares the data in the database that are most pertinent to it. Departments may be interested in data structures as follows:

Sales department—*Customer/Order*

Accounting department—*Customer/Order/Invoice/Payment*

Order processing department—*Customer/Product/Order*

Inventory control department—*Product/Order/Stock Quantity/Back Order Quantity*

Database technology lets each application use the portion of the database that is needed for that application. User views of the database are defined and controlled. We will have more to say about user views in later chapters.

Uniform Standards We have seen that, because of the spread of duplicate data across applications in file-oriented data systems, standards cannot be enforced easily and completely. Database systems remove this difficulty. As data duplication is controlled in database systems and as data is consolidated and integrated, standards can be implemented more easily. Restrictions and business rules for a single data element need to be applied in only one place. In database systems, it is possible to eliminate problems from homonyms and synonyms.

Security Controls Information is a corporate asset and, therefore, must be protected through proper security controls. In file-oriented systems, security controls cannot be established easily. Imagine the data administrator wanting to restrict and control the use of data relating to employees. In file-oriented systems, control has to be exercised in all applications having separate employee files. However, in a database system, all data about employees are consolidated, integrated, and kept in one place. Security controls on employee data need to be applied in only one place in the database. Database systems make centralized security controls possible. It is also easy to apply data access authorizations at various levels of data.

Data Independence Remember the lack of data independence in file-oriented systems where computer programs have data structure definitions embedded within the programs themselves. In database systems, file or data definitions are separated out of the programs and kept within the database itself. Program logic and data structure definitions are not intricately bound together. In a client/server environment, data and descriptions of data structures reside on the database server, whereas the code for application logic executes on the client machine or on a separate application server.

Reduced Program Maintenance   This benefit of database systems results primarily from data independence in applications. If the customer data structure changes by the addition of a field for cellular phone numbers, then this change is made in only one place within the database itself. Only those programs that need the new field need to be modified and recompiled to make use of the added piece of data. Within limits, you can change programs or data independently.

Simpler Backup and Recovery   In a database system, generally all data are in one place. Therefore, it becomes easy to establish procedures to back up data. All the relationships among the data structures are also in one place. The arrangement of data in database systems makes it easier not only for backing up the data but also for initiating procedures for recovery of data lost because of malfunctions.

THE DATABASE APPROACH

What are the implications when an organization makes the transition from file-oriented systems to database systems? When an organization changes its approach to management of data and adopts database technology, what are the significant effects in the way business is conducted? What happens when an organization embraces the database approach?

Let us find answers to such questions. We will discuss the way applications are designed and implemented with database systems. We will explore the basic concepts of the database approach. We will also review some of the types of databases and how these are used.

We have reviewed the benefits of database systems and established how they are superior to the earlier file-oriented data systems. We caught a glimpse of the features of database systems that produce several benefits. Database systems reduce data redundancy, integrate corporate data, and enable information sharing among the various groups in the organization. Now you are ready for an initial, formal definition of a database.

Database: A Formal Definition

Let us examine the following definition:

> A database is an *ordered collection* of *related data elements* intended to meet *the information needs* of an organization and designed to be *shared* by multiple users.

Note the key terms in the definition:

Ordered collection.   A database is a collection of data elements. Not just a random assembly of data structures, but a collection of data elements put together deliberately with proper order. The various data elements are linked together in the most logical manner.

Related data elements. The data elements in a database are not disjointed structures without any relationships among them. These are related among themselves and also pertinent to the particular organization.

Information needs. The collection of data elements in a database is there for a specific purpose. That purpose is to satisfy and meet the information needs of the organization. In a database for a bank, you will find data elements that are pertinent to the bank's business. You will find customer's bank balances and ATM transactions. You will not find data elements relating to a student's major and examination grades that belong in a database for a university. You will not find a patient's medical history that really belongs in a database for a medical center.

Shared. All authorized users in an organization can share the information stored in its database. Integrated information is kept in the database for the purpose of sharing so that all user groups may collaborate and accomplish the organization's objectives.

Data-Driven, Not Process-Driven

When an organization adopts a database approach to managing corporate data, the very method of designing and implementing applications changes. Traditionally, when you design and implement an application with file-oriented data systems, you use a process-driven approach. That method changes with database systems. You shift your design and implementation method to a data-driven approach. Figure 1-6 shows the difference between the two methods.

In both methods, you begin with the definition of requirements. However, there is an essential difference between the two methods. In the process-driven method,

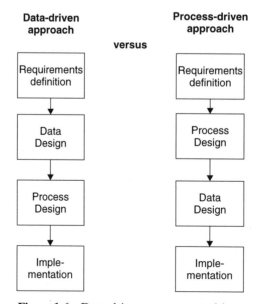

Figure 1-6   Data-driven, not process-driven.

you collect requirements for the outputs and the processes and then determine the inputs. Determination of the inputs leads to the design of the data files.

In the data-driven method, you gather requirements about the business objects that are pertinent to the business. You collect the data required to be included about these objects. Then you design the database to support the business. After this, the design of the initial processes follows.

Right away, you can see the advantage of the data-driven approach. Although you are interested in supporting the initial processes, because you have designed the database to contain all data relevant to the business, you will find it easy to add further processes later on. Data-driven approach provides enormous flexibility to provide for new and additional processing requirements at a later time. In practice, companies adopting the database approach use a combination of both methods, although the data-driven method dominates the application development phases.

Basic Concepts

You are now beginning to appreciate the significance of the database approach. You are discerning the major benefits of developing and using applications in a database environment. Before proceeding further, let us review a few fundamental concepts and become familiar with some key terminology.

Data Repository   All data in the database reside in a data repository. This is the data storage unit where physical data files are kept. The data repository contains the physical data. Mostly, it is a central place of storage for the data content.

Data Dictionary   The data repository contains the actual data. Let us say that you want to keep data about the customers of your company in your database. The structure of a customer's data could include fields such as customer name, customer address, city, state, zip code, phone number, and so on. Data about a particular customer could be as follows in the respective fields: Jane Smith/1234 Main Street/Piscataway/NJ/08820. There are two aspects of the data about customers. One aspect is the structure of the data consisting of the field names, field sizes, data types, and so on. This part is the structure of the data for customers. The other part is the actual data for each customer consisting of the actual data values in the various fields.

The first part relating to the structure resides separately in storage, and this is called the data dictionary or data catalog. A data dictionary contains the structures of the various data elements in the database. It also contains the relationships among data elements. The other part relating to the actual data about individual customers resides in the data repository. The data dictionary and the data repository work together to provide information to users.

Database Software   Are Oracle and Informix databases? Oracle and Informix are really the software that manages data. These are database software or database management systems. Database software supports the storing, retrieving, and updating of data in a database. Database software is not the database itself. The software helps you store, manage, and protect the data in a database.

Data Abstraction   Consider the example of customer data again. Data about each customer consist of several fields such as customer name, street address, city, state, zip code, credit status, and so on. We can look at customer data at three levels. The customer service representative can look at the customer from his or her point of view as consisting of only the fields that are of interest to the representative. This may be just customer name, phone number, and credit status. This is one level. The next level is the structure of the complete set of fields in customer data. This level is of interest to the database designer and application programmer. Another level is of interest to the database administrator, who is responsible for designing the physical layout for storing the data in files on disk storage.

Now go through the three levels. The customer service representative is just interested in what he or she needs from customer data, not the entire set of fields or how the data is physically stored on disk storage. The complexities of the other two levels may be hidden from the customer service representative. Similarly, the physical level of how the data is stored on disk storage may be hidden from the application programmer. Only the database administrator is interested in all three levels. This concept is the abstraction of data—the ability to hide the complexities of data design at the levels where they are not required. The database approach provides for data abstraction.

Data Access   The database approach includes the fundamental operations that can be applied to data. Every database management system provides for the following basic operations:

- READ data contained in the database
- ADD data to the database
- UPDATE individual parts of the data in the database
- DELETE portions of the data in the database

Database practitioners refer to these operations by the acronym CRUD:

- C—Create or add data
- R—Read data
- U—Update data
- D—Delete data

Transaction Support   Imagine the business function of entering an order from a customer into the computer system. The order entry clerk types in the customer number, the product code, and the quantity ordered. The order entry program reads the customer data and allows the clerk to sight verify the customer data, reads product data and displays the product description, reads inventory data, and finally updates inventory or creates a back order if inventory is insufficient. All these tasks performed by the order entry program to enter a single order comprise a single order entry transaction.

When a transaction is initiated it should complete all the tasks and leave the data in the database in a consistent state. That is, if the initial stock is 1000 units and the order is for 25 units, the stock value stored in the database after the transaction is

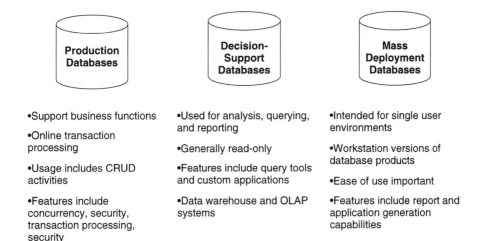

Figure 1-7   How databases are used.

completed must be 975 units. How can this be a problem? See what can happen in the execution of the transaction. First, the transaction may not be able to perform all its tasks because of some malfunction preventing its completion. Second, numerous transactions from different order entry clerks may be simultaneously looking for inventory of the same product. Database technology enables a transaction to complete a task in its entirety or back out intermediary data updates in case of malfunctions preventing completion.

How Databases Are Used

You now realize the use of databases for supporting the core business of an organization and enabling day-to-day operations. These are production databases that support the operational systems of an enterprise. More recently, with increasing demand for information, databases fulfill another important function. Databases provide support for strategic decision making in an organization. Such decision-support databases are designed and implemented separately and differently. Production databases and decision-support databases are large-scale databases for the several users within organizations.

Individuals and single departments may also use private databases. For example, a specialty department may want to send targeted mailings to specific customers and to keep these customers in a separate database. Individual business analysts may keep data and research results in a separate database just for their use. These are mass deployment individual databases.

Figure 1-7 shows the separation of databases by their uses and describes some of the features.

OVERVIEW OF DATA MODELS

A data model represents the data requirements of an organization. You can diagrammatically show a data model with symbols and figures. Data for an organization reside in a database. Therefore, when designing a database, you first create a data model. The model would represent the real-world data requirements. It would show the arrangement of the data structures.

Database software has evolved to support different types of data models. As we try to represent real-world data requirements as close as possible in a data model, we come up with a replica of the real-world information requirements. It turns out that we can look at data requirements and create data models in a few different ways. At this stage, let us survey a few leading data models. Over time, different vendors have developed commercial database management systems to support each of these common data models.

Hierarchical

Let us examine the data requirements for a typical manufacturing company. Typically in manufacturing, you have major assemblies, with each major assembly consisting of subassemblies, each subassembly consisting of parts, each part consisting of subparts, and so on. In your database for the manufacturing company, you need to keep data for the assemblies, subassemblies, parts, and subparts. And the data model for manufacturing operations must represent these data requirements.

Think about this data model. This model should show that an assembly contains subassemblies, a subassembly contains parts, and a part contains subparts. Immediately you can observe that this data model must be hierarchical in nature, diagramming the assembly at the top with subassembly, part, and subpart at successive lower levels.

In the business world, many data structures are hierarchical in nature. You can notice a hierarchy in department, product category, product subcategory, product line, and product. You can trace a hierarchy in division, subdivision, department, and employee. Figure 1-8 illustrates one such model showing the hierarchy of customer, order, and order line item. A customer may have one or more orders, and an order may have one or more line items, perhaps one line item for each product ordered.

Let us review the key features of the hierarchical model by referring to Figure 1-8.

Levels. Each data structure representing a business object is at one of the hierarchical levels.

Parent-Child Relationships. The relationship between each pair of data structures at levels next to each other is a parent-child relationship. CUSTOMER is a parent data segment whose child is the ORDER data segment. In this arrangement, a child segment can have only one parent segment but one parent segment may have multiple child segments. You may want to separate orders into phone orders and mail orders. In that case, CUSTOMER may have PHONE ORDER and MAIL ORDER as two child segments.

Root Segment. The data segment at the top level of the hierarchy is known as the root data segment (as in an inverted tree).

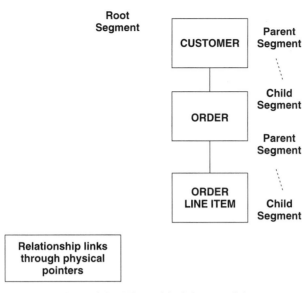

Figure 1-8 Hierarchical data model.

Physical Pointers. How are the orders of a particular customer linked in the implementation of the hierarchical data model? These linkages are by means of physical pointers or physical storage addresses embedded within physical records in the database. Physical pointers link records of the parent segments to those of the child segments by means of parent-child forward or backward pointers. Similarly, forward and backward physical pointers link records of the same segment type.

Network

The hierarchical data model represents well any business data that inherently contains levels one below the other. We have just discussed how the manufacturing application deals with hierarchical levels of plant inventory with assemblies broken down into lower-level components. The hierarchical data model suits this application well. However, in the real world, most data structures do not conform to a hierarchical arrangement. The levels of data structures do not fall into nice dependencies one below another as in a hierarchy. In the hierarchical data model, you have noticed that each data segment at any level can have only one parent at the next higher level. In practice, many sets of related elements may not be subjected to such restrictions.

Let us consider a common set of related data elements in a typical business. The data elements pertain to customers placing orders and making payments, salespersons being assigned, and salespersons being part of sales territories. All of these data elements cannot be arranged in a hierarchy. The relationships cross over among the data elements as though they form a network. Refer to Figure 1-9 and note how it represents a network arrangement and not a hierarchical arrangement. Observe the six data elements of sales territory, salesperson, customer, order, order line item, and payment as nodes in a network arrangement.

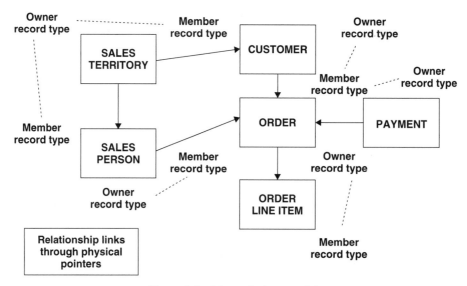

Figure 1-9   Network data model.

The network data model overcomes some of the limitations of the hierarchical data model. The network data model is more representative of real-world information requirements than the hierarchical model. The network data model can represent most business information.

Let us go over the key features of the network model by referring to Figure 1-9.

Levels. As in most real-world situations, no hierarchical levels exist in the network model. The lines in a network data model simply connect the appropriate data structures wherever necessary without the restriction of connecting only successive levels as in the hierarchical model. Note the lines connecting the various data structures with no restrictions.

Record Types. In the network data model, each data structure is known as a record type. For example, the CUSTOMER record type represents the data content of all customers. The ORDER record type represents the data content of all orders.

Relationships. The network data model expresses relationships between two record types by designating one as the owner record type and the other as the member record type. For each occurrence of an owner record type, there are one or more occurrences of the member record type. The owner record type may be reckoned as the parent and the member record type as the child. In a sense, the owner record type "owns" the corresponding member record type. Each member type with its corresponding owner record type is known as a set. A set represents the relationship between an owner and a member record type.

Multiple Parents. Look at the ORDER member record type. For ORDER there are two parents or owner records, namely, CUSTOMER and PAYMENT. In other words, for one occurrence of CUSTOMER, one or more occurrences of ORDER exist. Similarly, for one occurrence of PAYMENT there are one or more occurrences of ORDER. By definition, a hierarchical data model cannot represent this kind of data arrangement with two parents for one child data structure.

Physical Pointers. Just as in the case of the hierarchical data model, related occurrences of two different record types in a network model are connected by physical pointers or physical storage addresses embedded within physical records in the database. Physical pointers link occurrences of an owner record type with the corresponding occurrences of the member record type. Within each record type itself the individual occurrences may be linked to one another by means of forward and backward pointers.

Relational

This book will provide you with in-depth discussions about the relational model. This data model is superior to the earlier models. Dr. E. F. Codd, the celebrated father of the relational model, stipulated the rules and put this model on a solid mathematical foundation. At this stage, however, we want to introduce the relational model as a superior data model that addresses the limitations of the earlier data models.

The earlier hierarchical data model is suitable for data structures that are naturally hierarchical, with each data structure placed at a certain level in the hierarchy. However, in the business arena, many of the data structures and their relationships cannot be readily placed in a hierarchical arrangement. The network data model evolved to dispense with the arbitrary restriction of the hierarchical model. Nevertheless, in both of these models, you need physical pointers to connect related data occurrences. This is a serious drawback because you have rewrite the physical addresses in the data records every time you reorganize the data, move the data to a different storage area, or change over to another storage medium. The relational model establishes the connections between related data occurrences by means of logical links implemented through foreign keys. Figure 1-10 illustrates the relational data model.

Let us note the key features of the relational data model by referring to Figure 1-10.

Levels. Just like the network data model, no hierarchical levels are present in the relational model. The lines in a relational data model simply indicate the relationships between the appropriate data structures wherever necessary without the restriction of connecting only successive levels as in the hierarchical model. As in the network model, note the lines connecting the various data structures with no restrictions.

Relations or Tables. The relational model consists of relations. A relation is a two-dimensional table of data observing relational rules. For example, the CUSTOMER relation represents the data content of all customers. The ORDER relation represents the data content of all orders.

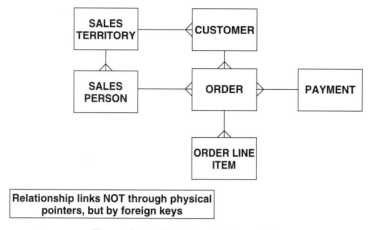

Figure 1-10   Relational data model.

Relationships. Consider the relationship between CUSTOMER and ORDER. For each customer one or more orders may exist. So this customer occurrence must be connected to all the related order occurrences. In the relational model, physical pointers do not establish these connections. Instead, a foreign key field is included in the ORDER data structure. In each of the order occurrences relating to a certain customer, the foreign key contains the identification of that customer. When you look for all the orders for a particular customer, you search through the foreign key field of ORDER and find those order occurrences with identification of that customer in the foreign key field. We will deal with this topic in more detail in later chapters.

No Physical Pointers. Unlike the hierarchical or the network data models, the relational model establishes relationships between data structures by means of foreign keys and not by physical pointers.

Object-Relational

Take the case of the State of California Department of Water Resources (DWR), which manages the waterways, canals, and water projects in that state. DWR maintains a library of more than half a million pictures. Users access this library several times a day. A user requests a picture by content: "Show me Lake Cachuma" (a Santa Barbara County reservoir with a low water level). Despite an index system of captions and keywords, retrieval of the right picture within a reasonable time is virtually impossible with the current relational database systems. Nor are purely object-oriented data systems totally adequate to handle the challenge. As the demand for information continues to grow, organizations need database systems that allow representation of complex data types, user-defined sophisticated functions, and user-defined operators for data access.

Object-relational database management systems (ORDBMS) present viable solutions for handling complex data types. The object-relational model combines the ability of object technology to handle advanced types of relationships with features of data integrity, reliability, and recovery found in the relational realm. We will cover object-relational database systems in greater detail in Chapter 20.

TYPES OF DATABASES

By now you are convinced of the significance of information for an organization. You know that information is a key corporate asset and that it has to be managed, protected, and used like any other major asset. The corporate database that holds an organization's data is the underlying foundation for corporate information. Organizations are also faced with questions regarding how and where to hold the corporate data.

Where should an enterprise hold its data? Should all the corporate data be kept centrally in one place? If so, what are the advantages and disadvantages? Or should the corporate data be divided into suitable fragments and the pieces kept at different locations? What are the implications of this arrangement?

Organizations primarily adopt one of two approaches. If the entire database is kept in one centralized location, this type of database is a centralized database. On the other hand, if fragments of the database are physically placed at various locations, this type of database is a distributed database. Each type has its own benefits and shortcomings. Again, whether an enterprise adopts a centralized or a distributed approach depends on the organizational setup and the information requirements. Let us review the two types.

Centralized

Figure 1-11 illustrates a centralized database.

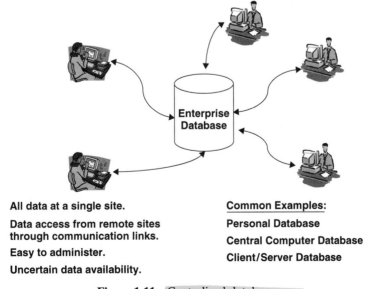

All data at a single site.

Data access from remote sites through communication links.

Easy to administer.

Uncertain data availability.

Common Examples:

Personal Database

Central Computer Database

Client/Server Database

Figure 1-11 Centralized database.

Personalized databases are always centralized in one location. If your company has a centralized computer system, then the database must reside in that central location. In the client/server architecture, the database resides on a server machine. The entire database may be kept on a single server machine and placed in a central location.

When all corporate data is in one place in a centralized database, companies find it easier to manage and administer the database. You can control concurrent accesses to the same data in the database easily in a centralized database. You can maintain security controls easily. However, if your company's operations are spread across remote locations, these locations must access the centralized database through communication links. Here, data availability depends on the capacity and dependability of the communication links.

Distributed

Figure 1-12 shows how fragments of a corporate database are spread across remote locations.

Global organizations or enterprises with widespread domestic operations can benefit from distributed databases. In such organizations computer processing is also distributed, with processing done locally at each location. A distributed database gets fragmented into smaller data sets. Normally, you would divide the

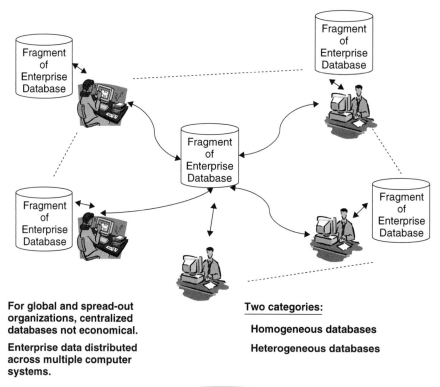

For global and spread-out organizations, centralized databases not economical.

Enterprise data distributed across multiple computer systems.

Two categories:

Homogeneous databases

Heterogeneous databases

Figure 1-12   Distributed database.

database into data sets on the basis of usage. If a fragment contains data that are most relevant to one location, then that data set is kept at that location. At each location, a fragment of the enterprise data is placed based on the usage.

Each fragment of data at every location may be managed with the same type of database management system. For example, you may run Oracle DBMS at every location. In that case, you run your distributed database as a homogenous database. On the other hand, if you elect to manage the data fragments at different locations with different DBMSs, then you run your distributed database as a collection of heterogeneous database systems. Heterogeneous arrangement provides extra flexibility. However, heterogeneous distribution is difficult to coordinate and administer.

SURVEY OF THE DATABASE INDUSTRY

So far we have reviewed the basic concepts of the database approach. You have understood the forces that drove the transition from file-oriented systems to database systems. We discussed in detail how the escalating demand by organizations for information and the explosive growth of computing technology mutually contributed to the rise of database systems. We also looked into the types of databases.

We should now conclude with a brief survey of the database industry. Where is the industry now? How did it get here? You will find such a survey useful because it will provide you with the context and the foundation for further study. You have been introduced to the leading data models. As you walk through a brief history, you will grasp the significance of one data model following the earlier one. A list of the leading commercial database management systems will give you an appreciation of the spread of database systems. You will also get a quick glimpse of the future direction of database technology. We will be returning to these topics in later chapters. At this stage, let us just do a brief survey.

Brief History

Although the initial movement toward database systems began in the 1960s, software sophistication and widespread use of database systems began in the mid-1970s. More and more organizations began to adopt database technology to manage their corporate data. Figure 1-13 provides you with a historical summary of the database industry. The figure highlights the major events and developments in the various decades.

Generalized Update Access Method (GUAM) contained the first trace of the forerunner to the hierarchical database systems. In early 1960s, Rockwell developed this software to manage the data usually associated with manufacturing operations. IBM picked this up and introduced Information Management System (IMS) as a hierarchical database management system.

Integrated Data Store (IDS), developed at General Electric, formed the basis for database systems on the network data model. Database Task Group (DBTG) of the Conference on Data Systems and Languages (CODASYL) began to produce standards for the network model. CODASYL, a consortium of vendors and

Rockwell develops GUAM software for hierarchical data structures.	Dr. E.F. Codd of IBM Research writes paper on the relational data model.	IBM's IMS continues to be enhanced for the hierarchical model.	Every leading database vendor offers a relational database product.	DB vendors provide for newer data types.
IBM develops IMS database software. Charles Bachmann heads team at GE that develops IDS based on network data structure. CODASYL is established. DBTG is formed as a sub-group for database software standards. First generation of commercial database products.	Codd stipulates his rules for the relational model and proposes data manipulation languages. System R project at IBM's San Jose laboratory. SQL is developed as part of the System R project. Commercial products begin to appear on the market.	Database software products for the network model gain strength. Newer products for the relational model introduced by IBM, Oracle, and other vendors. Relational model becomes accepted as a superior model. SQL gains importance as the standard.	SQL-92 becomes the accepted standard. The relational model becomes the preferred data model. Database technology becomes the cornerstone for data warehousing, data mining, and Web applications. OODBMS and ORDBMS emerge as solutions to address increasing complexity.	Spatial databases introduced. Databases support ERP, DW, DM, OLAP, and CRM applications.
1960	1970	1980	1990	2000

Figure 1-13   Database industry: historical summary.

leading businesses, serves as a group to establish standards. Among the many standards established, a major contribution by CODASYL is the set of standards for COBOL, a leading programming language. In the late 1960s, vendors started to release the first generation of commercial database systems supporting the network data model. Cincom's TOTAL database management system is a primary example.

The 1970s ushered in the era of relational database technology. Dr. Codd's foundational paper on the relational model revolutionized the thinking on data systems. The industry quickly realized the superiority of the relational model, and more and more vendors began to adapt their products to that model.

During the 1980s, the use of database systems gained a lot of ground and a large percentage of businesses made the transition from file-oriented data systems to database systems. All the three leading data models—hierarchical, network, and relational—were quite popular, although the relational model was steadily gaining ground.

Essentially the 1990s may be considered as a period of maturity of the relational model and the emergence of that data model as the leading one. Companies considered moving their data to relational databases from hierarchical and network databases. Also, vendors started to incorporate the features of both relational and object technologies in their products. Object-relational database management systems (ORDBMSs) hit the market.

Now in the new millennium, the usage of database technology is spreading into newer areas. Properly designed databases serve as a chief component in data warehousing (DW), enterprise resource planning (ERP), data mining (DM), on-line analytical processing (OLAP), and customer relationship management (CRM) applications.

Leading Commercial Databases

In Appendix E, you will find broad reviews of major commercial database systems. At this point, let us list some of the leading systems in alphabetic sequence of the product names:

ACCESS
DATACOM/DB
DB2
FOXPRO
IDMS
INFORMIX
INGRES
ORACLE
PARADOX
SQL SERVER
SYBASE
SYSTEM 2000

Peek into the Future

Chapter 20 covers the trends in database technology in extensive detail. The following list indicates some of the specific developments.

Very large databases. Modern commercial database management systems can support very large volumes of data in the terabyte range. Data access and manipulation do not pose problems. As databases store data for corporate data warehouses and for on-line analytical processing applications, the sizes of databases will continue grow rapidly.

User-defined data types. Newer applications for global organizations need special data types. One example is the spatial data type where data values consist of areas and volumes. In addition to standard data types, DBMSs have begun to enable database users to define their own data types with special characteristics.

Complex data manipulation. The current set of data manipulation functions such as sum, difference, average, and the like are no longer adequate when your users want to utilize the database for complex calculations. While performing analysis, they might need to calculate moving averages. Modern database software products provide the ability to perform complex data manipulations.

Intelligent database servers. The trend already includes automatic execution of programs based on exception conditions detected from the data in the database. Future database management systems will contain a substantial extent of logic for intelligent triggers to initiate automatic operations.

Wider use for decision support. Improved database technology spurs the spread of decision- support systems such as data warehousing, data mining, and on-line analytical processing.

Merging with Web technology. The database has become the centerpiece of Internet and intranet applications. The merging of database technology with Web technology will become even stronger and serve newer purposes.

CHAPTER SUMMARY

- Two remarkable phenomena together have caused the evolution of database systems: (1) escalating demand for information at every organization, and (2) explosive growth of computing technology.
- For nearly three decades, there has been tremendous growth in every sector of computing technology, especially in data storage devices and in the software to manage enterprise data.
- Organizations began to need not only more information but also different types of information for newer purposes than merely running day-to-day operations.
- Major forces driving the evolution of database systems: information considered as key corporate asset, explosive growth of computer technology, escalating demand for information, and inadequacy of earlier data systems.
- Benefits of database systems compared to file-oriented systems: minimal data redundancy, integration of corporate data, preservation of data integrity and consistency, data sharing, ease with which uniform standards can be established, better enforcement of security controls, reduced program maintenance through data independence, and simpler backup and recovery of data.
- Common data models: hierarchical, network, and relational.
- In an organization, data may be kept in a centralized location or suitable fragments of data may be spread across several physical locations. Organizations may opt for centralized or distributed databases.

REVIEW QUESTIONS

1. What is your understanding of the term *database*? Describe it in two or three sentences.
2. List three areas of technology growth that had direct positive effects on data systems. Briefly explain the positive impact.
3. What are ISAM and VSAM files? Why are they better than sequential files?
4. Name and briefly describe the major driving forces for database systems.
5. List and explain any three problems with file-oriented systems.
6. What are homonyms and synonyms? Explain why file-oriented systems may have problems with these.
7. List and describe any three benefits of database systems in comparison with file-oriented systems.

8. What is a data dictionary? Describe its purpose.

9. Briefly describe the features of a network data model. How are relationships represented in a network data model?

10. Is the relational data model better than the earlier data models? Give your reasons.

EXERCISES

1. Match the columns:

1. data redundancy	A. foreign keys for relationships
2. inconsistent data	B. data storage
3. data independence	C. large data volumes
4. data integration	D. used for storing data
5. data repository	E. structure definitions
6. data dictionary	F. easy to administer
7. decision-support database	G. wasted storage space
8. relational data model	H. unified view of corporate data
9. centralized database	I. data separated from program logic
10. punched card	J. errors on customer documents

2. "Escalating demand for information and explosive growth of computing technology together enabled the evolution of database systems." Discuss this statement, giving your reasons for agreeing or disagreeing.

3. You are hired as the project leader for a new database project at a local bank. The bank wants to convert the existing file-oriented systems to a database system. Your department head wants you to write a note to the Executive Vice President listing the expected benefits of the proposed database system in comparison with file-oriented systems. Write a one-page note.

4. Compare the features of the hierarchical, network, and relational data models. Explain how related data elements are linked in each model.

5. A manufacturer of electronic components has two factories in two different states. The company has a central warehouse at a location where the head office is situated. There are five sales offices in five different regions of the country. Discuss whether the company should have a centralized database or distributed databases. List the advantages and disadvantages of each approach.

CHAPTER 2

OVERVIEW OF MAJOR COMPONENTS

CHAPTER OBJECTIVES

- Understand the various aspects of the database environment
- Examine the overall architecture of the database environment
- Identify the different components that make up the database environment
- Note the distinction between DB and DBMS
- Study the functions and features of each component

What is the database approach? You have gained an insight into how the database approach for storing, retrieving, and managing data is superior to the earlier file-oriented approaches. We have discussed the evolution of database systems in detail. Organizations could not tolerate the limitations of file-oriented systems because of escalating demand for information. Explosive growth of computing technology, especially in the area of data systems, acted as a strong catalyst for development of the database approach. Over the past decades, different types of data models—hierarchical, network, and relational—have evolved to offer tremendous benefits to organizations. More and more commercial databases emerged in the marketplace.

Most organizations have adopted the database approach. To manage corporate data and satisfy information needs, companies have created database environments within their organizations. The database environment exists to support the organization's business. Figure 2-1 traces the typical progression to a database environment in an organization. Note the differences between the database environment and the earlier environments.

If a database environment is established in an organization to support the information requirements, what must the environment be composed of? What is a

Database Design and Development: An Essential Guide for IT Professionals by Paulraj Ponniah
ISBN 0-471-21877-4   Copyright © 2003 by John Wiley and Sons, Inc.

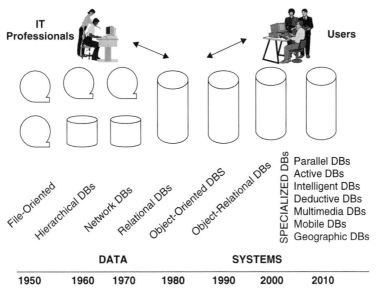

Figure 2-1 Progression to database environment.

database environment? What are the various pieces in the environment? Obviously, corporate data must be a key component. What else? What is the complete setup? What are the components? What are their features? What functions do they serve? Let us examine these questions and understand the composition and significance of a database environment.

WHAT MAKES UP A DATABASE ENVIRONMENT?

Consider an organization running file-oriented applications. The applications depend on the data content in sequential or flat files. These files primarily constitute the data system for the organization, and in such a system no special sophistication is required. No special storage mechanisms are necessary. The operating system itself mostly supports data storage and data access facilities. Basic hardware, data storage, and operating system alone establish the data environment. You do not need anything too special. Such an environment provides information potential on a moderate scale.

Contrast the file-oriented environment with the database environment. The newer database environment provides data access in ways totally unmatched in the file-oriented environment. On-line, real-time retrieval of substantially large result sets is fairly common. Random and indexed access to data replaces the slow and inefficient sequential access. The new environment clearly recognizes the value of information as a key corporate asset and therefore protects the data. For similar reasons, the environment also controls the access privileges and prevents unauthorized data retrieval. The new environment enables users to share information and collaborate smoothly to achieve corporate goals.

So, in this new environment providing database functions, you require robust data storage mechanisms. The operating system alone cannot support data retrieval and presentation. Simple methods of data backup and recovery are not adequate. Complex data structures have to be properly defined. Data delivery systems must be properly tuned to provide instant data access and retrieval. The environment must be open to hundreds or thousands of users. It should be able to handle concurrent transactions seeking to access the same pieces of data and still ensure the integrity of the data. Powerful processors, robust data repository, enhanced operating systems, improved networking capabilities, specialized database software—all of these become necessary components of the database environment.

We have mentioned just the software and hardware components necessary in the database environment. Software and hardware components, however important they may be, are not enough to make the database work. We need the people components. We need procedures for people to carry out the various functions. Who are these people? Users on one hand and database practitioners with special skills on the other hand. The database environment, therefore, also consists of people and procedures. Let us look at the overall architecture of the database environment and then discuss each component in sufficient detail.

Overall Architecture

How do you determine the architecture of a building? You look at the building blocks. You notice the arrangement of the components in the structure. These building blocks, together with their arrangement, make up the overall architecture of the building. Similarly, what is the overall architecture of a database environment? What are the pieces that make up the architecture? How are they put together and arranged to become a cohesive whole?

Essentially, a database environment includes the storage of data. The data repository, important as it is, constitutes just one piece in the overall architecture. You need specialized software to manage and make use of the data. You need hardware to store and process the data. You already know about the people component. You are also aware of the procedures necessary to guide the storage, management, and use of data. Figure 2-2 illustrates the overall architecture of a database environment in an organization. Note the individual components and observe how they are connected.

Before we discuss hardware, software, and people in detail, let us quickly go over the functions of the individual components as seen in Figure 2-2.

Data repository. Stores the organization's data in databases. This is a primary component, essential in every database environment.

Data dictionary. Contains the definition of structures of the data stored in the data repository. As mentioned previously, keeping the structure definitions apart from the actual data provides a level of independence in the database environment.

DBMS. Database Management System is specialized software needed to manage storage, use, and protection of the data stored in the database.

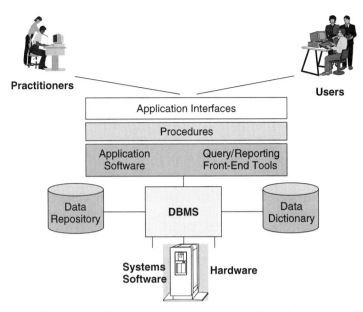

Figure 2-2 Database environment: overall architecture.

Systems software. Includes the operating system, network operating system, and utility programs that are needed to support and work with the DBMS.

Hardware. Comprises the processors, storage devices, and network connections. Hardware is part of the underlying infrastructure.

Application software. Suite of application programs to perform various business processes of the organization by making use of the database. The application programs provide users with interfaces to the database.

Front-end tools. These are query tools, report writers, and other front-end tools that supplement the application programs for data access and usage.

Procedures. Relate to instructions and guidelines for use by database practitioners and end users. These are needed to streamline the operations in the database environment.

Application interfaces. These include hardware and software components at the client workstation to connect to the database through application programs, query tools, or report writers.

Practitioners. Nothing happens in the database environment until database practitioners perform their various functions and responsibilities. Database practitioners include data administrators, database administrators, analysts, and programmers.

Users. The fundamental goal of a database environment is to satisfy the information needs of the end users. The user population extends to the entire organization in need of information for performing their day-to-day tasks.

When you review the components in the overall architecture, you will notice that these fall into three major groups: (1) hardware, (2) software, and (3) people and procedures. Let us now briefly examine the general features of these three groups that make up the database environment. In later sections of this chapter, we will get into the details of the functions and features of individual components.

Hardware Infrastructure

Hardware components form the basic infrastructure over which the functions of the database environment take place. First of all, you need hardware storage to store the data and the structure definitions. Then you need the processors and the computer memory components to retrieve, process, and update the data by using the structure definitions. You require communication links to connect the database to the user machines. Figure 2-3 shows parts of the hardware infrastructure.

Note the choice of hardware platforms. Database environments may exist in a mainframe, mini-computer, or client/server configuration. Modern database systems use storage devices that operate using the RAID (Redundant Array of Inexpensive Disks) technology. You will get a detailed description of RAID in Chapter 12. The client machines and the communication links are also part of the hardware infrastructure.

Supporting Software

If hardware forms the infrastructure for the database environment, software provides the supporting layer for the environment to function. Software controls and enables the storage and use of data. Figure 2-4 presents the software group of components.

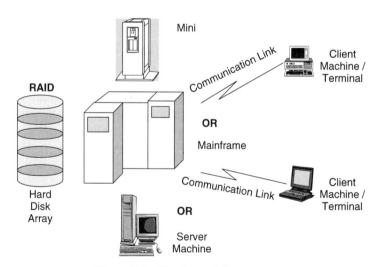

Figure 2-3   Hardware infrastructure.

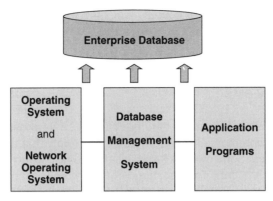

Figure 2-4 Supporting software.

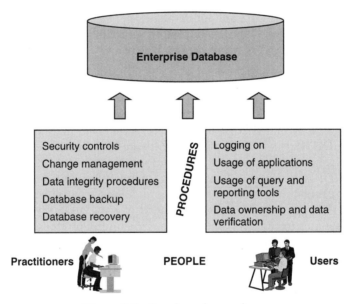

Figure 2-5 People and procedures.

Observe the major pieces of supporting software. The operating system piece includes the basic software such as DOS, Windows, or UNIX plus the network operating system. The database management system is the selected DBMS running the database environment. The suite of application programs forms a significant part of the software component.

People and Procedures

This group of components makes things happen in the database environment with the aid of the underlying hardware infrastructure and the supporting software. Standards are set through manual and automated procedures. Figure 2-5 shows the people and procedures component of the database environment.

Note the two major groups of people associated with the database environment. Each group needs a set of procedures. Observe the types of procedures applicable to each group.

DATABASE AND DBMS

Is Oracle a database? Is Informix a database? Is DB2 a database? Frequently, when we talk about such commercial products, we tend to imply that these products themselves are databases. Someone asks you what database your company uses. You probably respond by mentioning the name of the commercial product used in your company.

It is crucial to have a clear understanding of the term *database*. This book is about database design and development. What do we mean by *database*? When we discuss the term *database*, what is the scope of our discussion? Commercial products such as Oracle, Informix, and DB2 are not databases per se. They are software products that support the storage and management of databases. Let us explore the differences between databases and database software.

DB and DBMS—Not Synonymous

Database Management System (DBMS) is a collection of software components. It is a set of programs that enables us to create, access, and maintain a database. In other words, DBMS is a general-purpose software to define databases, build them, and manipulate the data content. Oracle, Informix, DB2, and similar products are examples of DBMSs. *Database*, on the other hand, refers to the data itself. Let us come up with broad definitions.

Database. Relates to the data and the data structure definitions stored according to the designed data model with the following features: shared, persistent, secure, valid, consistent, nonredundant, and independent of application logic.

DBMS. Software that provides services to access and use the database, incorporating the following features: control of concurrent transactions, recovery from malfunctions, security against unauthorized data access, reliability in data access, efficient storage management, and effective language interface for data structure definition and data access.

Why Use a DBMS?

Consider data management in a file-oriented system. Here, the sequential or indexed files provide the data content. The applications manipulate the data contained in these files. When you want to list information about a customer in your organization, you read the particular customer record from the customer sequential file. Simple file access software and an operating system—just these are all the software needed for the data access. The same set of software also enables you to rewrite the updated record or mark outdated records for deletion. Nothing more is expected from the set of software components for data management.

Contrast this simplicity with the sophistication required in database software. Realization of the significance of information as a key corporate asset drove the evolution to database systems. If information is a significant asset, then it has to be managed well and safeguarded with utmost care. Database software, therefore, has to be much more than a mere data access mechanism; it has to perform many other complex functions. This type of complexity warrants specialized software, and that specialized software is the set of sophisticated programs collectively known as the database management system (DBMS). The DBMS enables us to represent the data structures, relationships, and constraints.

In a later section of this chapter, we will look inside the DBMS and examine the individual components. At this point, you need to convince yourself of the need for the specialized set of software called DBMS by reviewing the major functions.

Language Interfaces   You must already have guessed the need for two types of languages in the database environment. For defining data structures, you need a data definition language (DDL). For performing data access operations of retrieving, updating, and deleting data, you need another type of language. Data manipulation language (DML) serves the requirements of data access.

DBMS provides support for DDL and DML. Each particular DBMS works with a specific DDL, and using that data definition language you can define the data structures in the data dictionary. The DBMS interprets the syntax and semantics of the language and records the data structure definitions in the data dictionary. Again, each particular DBMS works with a specific DML to enable access to data. The DBMS translates the DML commands into data access instructions. In later chapters, we will discuss DDL and DML for relational DBMSs in detail.

Storage Management   Storage management involves support for sophisticated data retrieval and update requests. Among the thousands of customers in your database, you may want to get a list of all customers in the state of Wisconsin, who have bought for more than $10,000 during the past six months, and who have no past due balances. The storage management component of the DBMS must provide for complex data requests.

Specifically, the storage manager performs the following functions:

· Simplifies and facilitates access to data
· Provides interface with the operating system to access data
· Translates the data manipulation language (DML) commands to low-level file access instructions for storing, retrieving, and updating data
· Works with the structure definitions in the data dictionary to store and find data
· Manages space allocations on permanent secondary storage

Transaction Management   What is a transaction in a database environment? Assume you are an order entry operator and you are in the process of entering an order from one of your customers for 100 units of Product A. Usually, the order entry application program works in the following manner. You enter the customer number, date, order location, shipping details, and 100 units for Product A. The application program reads the quantity in stock for Product A from the database and displays 10,000 units. You indicate that you want to complete the order. The program changes the stock quantity to 9,900 units and updates the database accordingly. As far as the database is concerned, your order entry transaction consists of a read of the record for Product A containing 10,000 units and an update of the record to store the revised number of 9,900 units.

In a database environment, many data entry operators like you will be entering orders simultaneously. Some of these operators may be entering orders for Product A at the same time you are entering your order. The DBMS must be able to handle such concurrent transactions and ensure that each transaction leaves the database in a consistent state. The following components in the DBMS perform transaction management functions.

Transaction manager. Institutes proper controls for transactions and coordinates their execution within a database. Enables each transaction to start, perform database accesses, commit the updates permanently in the database, and complete the execution properly.

Integrity manager. Ensures correctness, accuracy, and validity of the data in the database through edit and data validity constraints.

Concurrency control manager. Enables concurrent transactions to update the same database record correctly by using appropriate locking mechanisms. DBMS has special lock, unlock, and deadlock control modules to assist in concurrency control.

Security Management Protecting the information resource is a major function of DBMS. All the applications supporting the various business processes in the organization depend on the data resources in the corporate database. The database acts as the foundation for running the day-to-day business. The major asset of corporate information must be safeguarded.

Security management involves preventing unauthorized access to the organization's database. Outsiders must be kept away from the database. Several security methods are available for preventing unauthorized access. The second aspect of security management deals with providing proper access privileges to those who should be allowed to use the database. Some parts of the database should be available for access to selected groups only. For example, corporate payroll data should be available only to the payroll department and a few other selected personnel.

Recovery Management What happens to the database when hardware or software malfunctions happen? Suppose you lose data because of a disk head crash. Maybe an application program or system software corrupts the data content and affects the consistency of the database. How do you deal with database failures? How do you recover lost data or bring the database back to a consistent state?

Recovery of a database returns it to a consistent state after any kind of failure. Two modules of the DBMS—log manager and recovery manager—enable recovery after failures. Log manager saves database updates on another data set, called the log file, while updates take place in the database. Recovery manager uses the log file and brings the database to a consistent state.

Multilevel Data Independence Remember that one of the significant advantages of the database approach relates to data independence. In the earlier file-oriented systems, data definitions and application logic were intricately interwoven within application programs. Every time data structures changed programs had to be modified, causing serious productivity problems. This is not the case in a database environment. DBMS provides data independence. Let us see how.

DBMS supports a three-schema architecture that separates the level of details about the data as indicated below.

Internal level. Deals with physical storage; describes details of storage and access mechanisms. At this level, DBMS keeps track of the files, records, blocks, and physical locations.

Conceptual level. At this level, DBMS keeps the structure of the whole database for the entire user community. This level concentrates on entities, relationships, constraints, and user data access operations. Details of physical storage are hidden from this level.

External level. User views of individual user groups form this level. From this level, only the data covered by specific user views are available for individual user groups. For example, the user view of the accounting group may consist of just parts of customer and billing data.

The DBMS separates out the three level schemas. Requests for data go through a mapping between the external level to the conceptual level and then between the conceptual level and the internal level. So, what do these levels have to do with data independence? Very simply, a change of the schema at one level need not result in a change at another level.

You may rearrange or modify the conceptual level schema. For example, you may add some new fields to customer data. This change will affect only those user views where the new fields are required. All other user views need not be modified. The ability to change the conceptual schema without changing the external schema or the application programs refers to logical data independence. Also, you may shift the physical files and move them to new storage media without having to change the conceptual or external schemas. This is physical data independence. With a three-schema architecture, the DBMS provides for logical and physical data independence.

DBMS Classifications

In any database environment, DBMS forms the most significant software component. We have briefly looked at the major functions of DBMS. We have reviewed the reasons why you need a specialized set of software modules in a database environment. If every DBMS serves the same purposes, are all DBMSs the same? Will any DBMS work in every environment?

Although all DBMSs have similar functions and features, they are not all the same. There are subtle but significant differences. DBMSs may be broadly classified based on the following criteria:

- Meant for single user or multiple users
- Physically linked (hierarchical, network) or logically linked (relational)
- Whether based on inverted file structure with interfile connections
- Whether restricted to specific data models (hierarchical, network, relational, object-relational)
- Intended for centralized or distributed databases
- Based on the type of data distribution (homogeneous, heterogeneous, or federated)
- General purpose or special purpose

Languages and Interfaces

Let us now elaborate on the means by which database practitioners and users interact with the database. They require interface mechanisms to access the database. The database administrators need languages to manage the database; users need languages to access the database. Figure 2-6 indicates the interface mechanisms for interacting with the database.

Let us examine the different types of languages and interfaces and study their functions. Each type serves a distinct function.

Data Definition Language (DDL)   Database administrators use DDL to define the data structures and store the definitions in the data dictionary also known as the data catalog. DDL provides language syntax for defining the conceptual and external schemas. Specifically, DDL includes features to define the following:

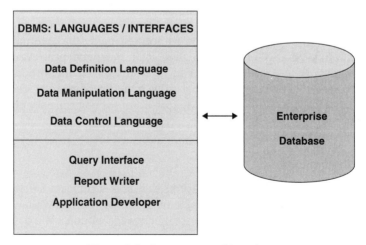

Figure 2-6   Languages and interfaces.

- Tables, segments, or files
- Each data item and groups of data items
- Data item properties such as type, encoding, and length
- Range of values for data items, wherever necessary
- Edit rules and error checking rules
- Key fields to identify structures independently
- Relationships between tables, segments, or files
- Unique names for data components
- Privacy locks

Data Manipulation Language (DML)   Programmers and analysts use DML to provide data access to users. When you want to write programs to retrieve data from the database, update data, or delete data, you have to use a data manipulation language. DMLs contain commands for performing individual data retrieval and update operations. In practice, DDL and DML usually get integrated into a single language interface. For example, Structure Query Language (SQL), which has become the standard for relational DBMSs, includes both DDL and DML components.

On the basis of the way the language enables programmers to state their data requests, DMLs may be placed in two distinct groups.

Procedural.   When a programmer uses a procedural DML, he or she will have to write the specific commands and individual steps in proper sequence to perform the database operation. The programmer will have to give detailed instructions on how the data retrieval task must be done. You have to write the detailed procedure specifying the sequence of the explicit instructions. A procedural DML details how to perform the data access operation, step by step.

Nonprocedural.   On the other hand, when a programmer uses a nonprocedural language, he or she need not list the individual instructions and the sequence in which they have to be executed to complete the data retrieval process. It is not necessary to write detailed procedures. The language is nonprocedural. A nonprocedural DML just mentions what data are to be retrieved. The implementation of the language takes care of how the data retrieval will be carried out. Nonprocedural languages are easier to learn and use.

Data Control Language (DCL)   Database administrators have the responsibility for protecting databases from unauthorized access. They need a language to control access to the database. First, unauthorized personnel must be kept away from the database. Second, even for the authorized users, database access must be provided only for those parts of the database each group is entitled to. Even if a group is authorized to access certain parts of the database, access privileges may vary. Some in the group may only retrieve and view the data. Others might be allowed to add data, and yet a few others may be authorized to update or delete data.

Database administrators use DCL to grant or revoke access privileges to users. Granting access privileges could involve granting privileges to the entire database or only to some parts. Access privileges also cover privileges to retrieve, add, update, or delete data. When circumstances change, database administrators may also need to revise the initial authorizations and revoke the privileges. DCL provides commands extending to various types of granting and revoking data access privileges.

Query Interface   A database query is a request for information. A query may take the form: "Display all the customers in the country of Switzerland who bought products from Japanese manufacturers during the prior month." Or the query may just relate to one customer: "Display the last three orders from customer 1234." When a programmer or a user submits a query, the query interface interprets, optimizes, executes the query, and displays the result.

Report Writer   This is another interface between the programmer or user and the database. Many types of report writers exist. At a minimum, a report writer allows a programmer to construct a report with proper headings, page breaks, and totals. It also includes a method for submitting the reports for execution and printing them.

Application Developer   The application developer comprises software for creating applications. Mostly used by programmers, the application developer enables them to combine input forms, reports, menus, submenus, and application logic to create program modules and then to pull all of these together as specific applications that can be used by various groups of users.

FUNCTIONS AND FEATURES

We have looked at the individual components that make up the database environment in an organization. Briefly, we have seen the hardware, software, and people components. You have observed how the various pieces fit together and support the environment. You have gained a broad understanding of database management systems and the necessity for such sets of specialized software.

Each component in the environment serves a special purpose. Each component is required to perform certain functions. To serve its designated purpose, each component is equipped with specific features. For example, the modern storage devices have fault-tolerant features that help the continued functioning of the database despite hardware malfunctions. If you want to appreciate why the various components exist in the database environment, you have to study the functions and features. Let us go over the major components and examine their functions and features.

Hardware

Hardware, of course, forms the underlying basis of the infrastructure. The collection of physical devices for storing and processing of data in the database constitute the hardware in the environment. Remarkable progress in hardware components during the last few decades has promoted the use of database systems. Apart from the physical storage devices, other pieces of hardware support the processing and transmission of data. Note how these pieces are especially important in a database environment.

Processor. Processors have become more powerful, faster, and cheaper. In a database environment, the processors in the client workstations and the application servers have to be powerful and fast. The processors in the client machines perform instructions to present data to the users in many new and sophisticated ways. The fast and powerful processors in the application servers must process complex requests for data from the database. In a three-tier client/server architecture, data storage and retrieval functions are separated out of application servers and the database resides on separate database server machines.

Main Memory. When data are fetched from a database for processing, they are initially brought into memory buffers and then moved through the processors. In a database environment, you deal with movement of large volumes of data through the memory buffers. Proper buffer management is essential. When a request is made for data, the memory buffers are searched first to see whether the requested data are already in the memory buffers as a result of prior data retrievals. If the data are already found in the memory buffers, then the data could be accessed and used much faster. Main memory that can accommodate many large buffers is conducive to the performance of a database environment.

Input/Output Control. Computer systems use I/O (input/output) mechanisms to move data into and out of the computer's main memory from secondary storage. A typical sequence followed by I/O control for movement of data runs like this: select the storage device, wait until the device is ready, transfer a piece of data from the device I/O buffer to the processor's accumulator, transfer the data from the accumulator into a memory location, reckon the next memory location, go back, and repeat the steps until all requested data is moved into memory. When you deal with high volumes of data in a database environment, you need sophisticated I/O control to improve performance.

Tape Storage Devices. Content of databases is backed up regularly and used for recovery if and when malfunctions destroy databases, fully or partially. Also, periodically, parts of old data are archived and saved, sometimes at remote locations. In small and medium-sized database environments, magnetic tapes serve as the medium for backing up and saving the data. Although data can be stored and retrieved sequentially, this restriction is not a handicap for content backup and storage. In the modern database environment, compact tape cartridges are widely used.

Communication Links. In earlier database environments of organizations, most of the processing was done locally around a centralized database. Communication links transferred data between the centralized database and the PCs or computer terminals—all mostly at a single site. Today's database environments are different. Distributed databases have become common. Client/server systems have spread rapidly. Data communications move high volumes of data from distributed databases to different locations, from the database server to the client workstations, and from the central computer to remote sites. Communication links with sufficient capacity and speed are essential to handle all the data movement.

Storage of Data

Without the storing of data on secondary storage devices, there is no database. How you use secondary storage and how you are able to retrieve data from it affects the performance of the database environment. The storage component contains all data related to the environment, even including screen formats and report formats.

Data Repository. The repository includes all the data values that are part of the database. If your database contains information about customers, orders, invoices, products, and employees, then you store data values of individual customers, orders, invoices, products, and employees in secondary storage. Two special features are important for data repository. The secondary storage must provide for fast access to data so that data requests may be processed speedily. Modern storage media used for databases are robust and fast. Secondly, data storage must be fault tolerant. Data storage mechanisms should ensure that the database operations continue even when some malfunction affects parts of the storage. RAID technology applied to today's data storage allows you to store copies of data redundantly so that even if one part gets corrupted, the database operations continue from the duplicate set of data.

Storage of Structure Definitions. The data storage component also relates to the storage of the structure definitions in the data dictionary. These definitions are also stored on physical storage as files and records. Structure definitions specify the composition of each data element as well as the mappings between external, conceptual, and internal schemas. Again, speed is of the essence for the storage devices holding the data dictionary. This is more so because the data dictionary has to be accessed first for every data access.

Operating System Software

As we have seen, the collective software component constitutes the specialized database management system (DBMS), operating system software, and application programs. Operating system software, among other things, acts as the layer between database management system and hardware. When a user requests some data from the database, the database management system processes the request. From the data dictionary, it determines what data are requested and where the data are stored in physical storage. Then DBMS requests the operating system software to fetch the data from physical storage. The operating system software, in turn, interacts with physical hardware to retrieve the data.

Review the following functions of the operating system software in the database environment.

Hardware Management. The operating system manages allocation and control of hardware resources for processing database requests. When multiple users initiate their requests for data, the operating system prioritizes and sequences the requests and allocates CPU and other hardware resources to the several database transactions. To accomplish these functions, the operating system uses hardware timers and interrupts.

Process Management. The operating system executes database and other operations as processes. A process is the lowest executable level of software. Say that one of your users makes a request for data retrieval from the database. This is a process for the operating system. If another of your users makes a request for his or her data retrieval, that is another process. The operating system manages all such processes by allocating resources, initiating and completing the processes, and resolving deadlocks when processes compete simultaneously and wait for the same resources.

Memory Management. The operating system coordinates the movement of data in and out of the primary and cache memory of a computer. It maintains the free memory space. It manages the memory hierarchy. Main memory is divided into pages, and the memory manager of the operating system allocates memory pages for the execution of the individual processes.

File Management. An important function of the operating system, file management, controls and coordinates the structure and storing of data on secondary storage. Files stored on disk drives and tape devices are under the control of the file manager. Files are collections of data that are moved to and from main memory. The file manager enables applications to create, delete, and insert data into files or alter the contents of files. Suppose a file is mostly accessed in a sequential manner. Then the data blocks of the file must be kept sequentially in disk storage on adjacent cylinders. Ealier mainframe operating systems allowed the systems programmers to control the placement of a file on specific cylinders. However, this control placed a burden on the systems programmers to calculate and allocate the cylinders needed for each file. Also, volatile files had to be reorganized frequently. But, modern operating systems make disk organization transparent to the programmers and manage the organization internally.

Input/Output Management. This area covers the setting up and maintaining of logical channels or paths between processor tasks and workstations. The functions encompass channel allocation and deallocation, channel setup, channel coordination, and remote data movement. Error detection and correction over the channels are also part of I/O management. Physical links are initiated, and the data transfer is controlled.

Network Control. Network management software manages the flow of data over communications media. This is especially critical in distributed database environments. Major functions of network management include message routing, naming schemes, addressing of nodes, protection against potential deadlocks of competing data movements, media access control, error detection and correction, and communications setup.

Fault Detection and Recovery. The operating system monitors the overall system for malfunctions, faults, and failures. When you consider a busy database environment with thousands of users needing information, fault detection and recovery assumes crucial importance. The operating system relies on hardware agents to detect errors. Once the software monitors of the operating system detect errors, the errors are localized and resolved.

Database Software

By now, you are fully aware that everything in the database environment hangs together by the specialized set of software components known as the database management system (DBMS). Database software enables you to create, maintain, and manage the database environment. As we have noted, DBMS is an integrated collection of software modules with each component designated for special purposes. In the last section of this chapter, we will delve into a DBMS and examine each component in detail.

Users

Who are the users in a database environment? It is clear that the database in an organization exists solely to serve the needs of the users at various levels, in different locations, and performing distinct functions. We can classify the users into a few groups on the basis of their data requirements, levels of their computer skills, and the frequency of their data access.

Casual Users. This group uses the database occasionally from time to time. The types and content of the needed data differ each time. Usually, middle- and upper-level executives fall into this group. Casual users, being somewhat naïve of database features, need special considerations for providing data access. This group of users is comfortable with predefined queries and reports where they can enter simple parameters to make the data requests. You have to provide these users with simple menu-driven applications.

Regular Users. The database in a production environment serves as the information repository for the regular users to perform their day-to-day functions. This group of users—whether from the accounting department entering customer orders, from the marketing department setting monthly quotas for the salespersons, or from the inventory control department reconciling physical inventory—constantly retrieve data and update the database. These users are familiar with what data are available and how to make use of the data. They work with programs that retrieve data, manipulate data in many ways, and change data to current values. You have to provide these users with customary menu-driven online applications and standard reports on a daily basis.

Power Users. These users do not require well-structured menu-driven applications to access the database. They can write their own queries and format their reports. For the power users, you have to provide general guidance about the query and reporting tools and let them have a road map of the database contents. Some power users may even construct their own menu-driven specialized applications.

Specialized Users. Business analysts, scientists, researchers, and engineers who are normally part of research and development departments need the database for specialized purposes. These users know the power and features of database systems. They write their own applications. Users of computer-aided design (CAD) tools also fall into this group. These users need special database tools and utilities.

Individual Users. Some users in your organization may justify maintaining stand-alone, private databases for individual departments. Departments working with very highly sensitive and confidential data may qualify for personal databases. Software packages with easy graphics and menus meet the requirements of this group of users.

Practitioners

We refer to the entire group of IT personnel who create and maintain databases as database practitioners. These people keep the database environment functioning and enable the users to reap the benefits. Broadly, we can classify database practitioners into three categories: those who design, those who maintain, and those who create the applications. Let us review the individual roles.

Business analysts. Work with senior management, conduct special studies, and interpret management's direction for information requirements. Interact with other database practitioners.

Data modelers. On the basis of information requirements, create semantic data models with popular modeling techniques. Use computer-aided software engineering (CASE) tools to create data models.

Database designers. Develop user views of data, integrate the views, and create the logical design for the database to be implemented with the selected commercial DBMS. Use CASE tools to generate the outputs of the logical design process.

Systems analysts. Determine the process requirements of the various user groups and write application specifications. Work with the programmers in testing and implementing applications.

Programmer/analysts. Translate applications into program code. Test and implement applications. Also, write programs to convert and populate databases from prior file systems.

Database administrators. Exercise overall control and manage the database. Perform key functions in the database environment including the following:

- Assist in acquiring additional hardware and system software.
- Recommend and assist in obtaining the DBMS.
- Create the physical model from the logical model and enter data dictionary definitions.

- Perform the physical organization and implementation.
- Authorize access to the database.
- Monitor and coordinate database usage.
- Perform ongoing maintenance functions.
- Provide consultation to other practitioners.
- Define backup and recovery mechanisms.
- Improve performance.

Methods and Procedures

How do methods and procedures fit into the discussion of the components of the database environment? These are not tangible components. Can methods and procedures be really considered as components? Without proper methods and procedures, any database environment will slip into confusion and chaos. Some procedures are essential just for making the database stay up and running. Users and practitioners both need good methods and procedures.

Procedures may be manual and automated. Here is a brief list of their purpose and features.

Usage. Users need clear and concise procedures on how to make use of the database. They must have plain and understandable instructions on how to sign on, initiate the menus, navigate through submenus, and use the various functions provided by the applications.

Queries and Reports. Casual and regular users must have a list of available predefined queries and reports along with instructions on how to supply the parameters and run them. Power users require guidelines on how to format and print reports.

Routine Maintenance. Routine maintenance consists of monitoring usage of storage, allocation of additional space whenever necessary, keeping track of access patterns, and looking out for problem areas. The database administrators must have proper procedures to perform the routine maintenance functions.

Structure Change Management. Do not imagine that after the initial implementation of the database in your organization the data structures remain static. Business conditions keep changing continuously, and the data structures must change accordingly. Every organization must have detailed procedures on how to initiate structure changes, review and approve the changes, and implement the changes.

Backup and Recovery. Your users cannot afford to be without the database for long periods. In the event of a disaster, database administrators must be able to recover from the malfunctions and restore the functioning of the database. Clearly defined and tested procedures will resolve disruptions. Backup and recovery procedures stipulate the type and frequency of backups, the planning and testing of recovery, and proper methods for recovering from malfunctions with the backed up data.

Database Tuning. As the volume of data increases the number of users multiplies, and as the usage rises database performance tends to degrade. Database administrators must constantly monitor performance and find ways to tune the database. Tuning procedures help them with instructions on how to locate areas that slow down and to apply techniques for improving performance.

How Databases Are Used

Figure 2-7 summarizes the functions and features of a database environment by illustrating how the users interface with the database for their data requirements and how database practitioners interact to perform their roles.

Note the Methods and Procedures shown on the right next to Users and Practitioners. As discussed just above, both groups of people refer to methods and procedures for interacting with the database. One the other side of the figure, note the DBMS component. All interaction with the database passes through the database management system. Look at the other blocks in the middle of the figure. These software components enable users and practitioners to achieve their objectives in the database environment.

Applications. Systems analysts and programmers develop and implement applications. Regular users interact with the database through applications.

CASE tools. Data modelers create models with CASE tools. Database designers complete the logical design through CASE tools. Database administrators may use CASE tools to create schemas for defining data structures in the data dictionary.

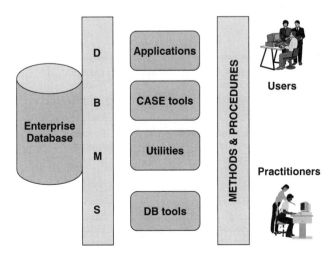

Figure 2-7 How databases are used.

Utilities. Database administrators use a comprehensive suite of utility programs to perform their maintenance and tuning functions.

DB tools. Programmer/analysts make use of query and reporting tools to create components of applications. Power users and specialized users create their own queries and reports with the aid of these tools.

INSIDE A DBMS

We have discussed the significance and capabilities of the database management system (DBMS). You know that it is a collection of specialized software modules. Database administrators cannot implement, control, and manage databases without the DBMS. Every request for data from the user groups must go through the DBMS. Power users need the facilities of the DBMS to create and run their database queries. DBMS stands in the center of an organization's database environment.

Let us now take a look inside the DBMS. Let us find out what components form the software collection and examine each component. Over the years, the features and functions of DBMSs have been broadened. Today's DBMSs do not just provide data access; they contain a powerful and versatile set of tools. Making the toolkit a part of DBMSs is a major step forward. Figure 2-8 shows how the various software modules inside a DBMS may be grouped as major components. We will study each of these components.

Database Engine

The kernel or heart of the DBMS is the database engine. From this central position, the database engine coordinates all the other components. When you review every other component, you will note their specific tasks. The engine has the special responsibility of coordinating the tasks performed by the other components. Because of this coordination, every database operation gets completed correctly and

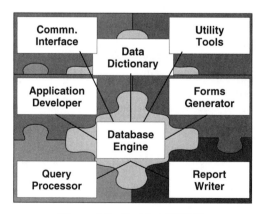

Figure 2-8 Inside a DBMS.

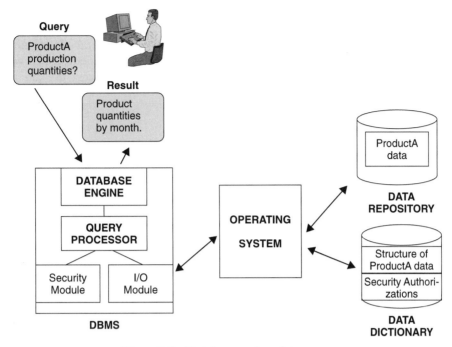

Figure 2-9 Database engine: data access.

completely. The other components depend on the database engine to store data and other system information so that their tasks may be carried out.

In the following subsections, review a few of the major features of the database engine component and note how this component interacts with other components.

Data Access   Suppose you, as a programmer, create a query for one of your user groups that needs production data of products from the database of your organization. When your users run this query, the DBMS must coordinate the tasks to be carried out by its various components. Once the structures of the product data and production data are determined, the DBMS interacts with the operating system to retrieve the requested data. Database engine component is responsible for storing data, retrieving data, and updating data in the database.

Figure 2-9 demonstrates how the engine component processes the query request by coordinating the functions of other components.

Note the interaction with the data dictionary. When your query requests for the production quantities of Product A, the query need not specify that the quantity for the product is numeric, is 8 bytes long, and starts in position 24 of the product record. All of this information is stored in the data dictionary. The query just names the quantity field and specifies Product A by name. Data dictionary definitions enable the query to find the location of the required data.

Does the user executing the query have authorization to access the data specified in the query? The database engine component coordinates the services of the security module to verify the authorization. When the location of the requested data is determined from the data dictionary, the engine component coordinates the tasks of the Input/Output module to work with the operating system to actually fetch the data from secondary storage.

To run a program for updating quantities for Product A, the database engine has to invoke the services of other modules for transaction management, concurrency control, and logging and recovery management. As we have seen, the database engine exercises control and coordination for every data storage, retrieval, and update operation.

Business Rules   Business rules ensure data integrity and data validity. Can you have negative numbers in the field for product cost or product price? In the employee record, can the days worked in a year plus the vacation days exceed 366? In a bank loan system, can the minimum interest rate be more than the maximum rate for a variable loan? All such discrepancies are resolved by enforcing of business rules by the database engine component.

Edit and business rules are stored in the data dictionary along with the structure definitions. The database engine component enforces the rules while storing or updating data. Some rules other than the ones mentioned above may be more involved.

For example, consider a program used for assigning employees for special projects. When an employee is assigned to a project and an authorization report is printed by the program, the employee can start on the project. Only employees who have undergone extensive training programs may be assigned to special projects. When an employee is assigned to a special project before he or she completes the required training programs, the system must provide warnings. This is not just a matter of having a few edit rules. Here you require a more complex software module to check whether the employee has completed the training. Such modules are stored in the database itself and are triggered when someone tries to print an authorization report for an employee lacking training.

Database Performance   The database engine component is also responsible for the speed of database operations. When a database request arrives, the database engine component is able to determine the needs of each database request, to figure out which modules must be brought into action, to specify the efficient order of the actions, and to coordinate the actions rapidly. The efficiency and the pace of database operations rest on the makeup of the database engine.

Now turn your attention to the volumes of data accessed by individual transactions. A request for the name and address of a customer produces a small result set. If you want the names of all customers in San Francisco, you are looking for more data in the result set. If you require the names of all customers in the whole of the western region, now the data volume of the result set is even larger. The database engine must be able to scale up to accommodate data requests producing large result sets.

Data Dictionary

In an earlier section, we considered the data dictionary as one of the components in the overall architecture of a database environment. In that discussion, *data dictionary* refers to the storage of structure definitions—the storage repository of structure definitions. Apart from this storage repository itself, within a DBMS you have software components to link the data dictionary repository with other software components. That data dictionary interface software is considered a distinct component within a DBMS.

Let us now examine all aspects of data dictionary—both the storage of structure definitions and the software interface to the data dictionary storage.

Consider a distinct difference between database systems and file-oriented systems. The difference lies in the way data is accessed. Database systems enable you to access physical data in a more abstract manner. You do not have to specify the physical layout of the data structure of how data is stored, nor do you need to indicate where exactly the data is to be found on secondary storage media. This provides you with enormous flexibility and ease in writing programs with database operations. The data dictionary is a fundamental component providing this capability. In most relational databases, the data dictionary comprises a set of system tables. It is a like a directory system. The data dictionary is also known as metadata—data about data.

Particularly, the data dictionary performs the following tasks:

- Keeps the definitions of all data structures and relationships
- Describes data types of all stored data items
- Specifies field sizes and formats of data items
- Holds information on space allocations and storage locations for all data
- Enables the database engine to keep track of the data and store it in the assigned places
- Maintains indexes
- Stores report and screen definitions

Query Processor

Power users, who know more about computer capabilities and usage, write queries to retrieve information from the enterprise database. You, as a programmer or analyst working within the Information Technology department, formulate and write queries to be used by other user groups. Specialized users like business analysts, engineers, and scientists also write their own queries for their information requirements.

To write queries, you need a language to communicate your request to the computer system. Each commercial vendor adopts a standard query language or develops its own proprietary language for creating queries. SQL (Structured Query Language) has become the standard for relational DBMSs. Each relational database vendor enhances the standard SQL and adds a few features here and there, but the essential features of SQL remain in every commercial DBMS. You write queries with SQL and run them in your database environment.

Let us say you write the following query in SQL for the marketing VP in your company, who wants to plan a marketing campaign for promotional mailings to a certain segment of the customer base:

```
SELECT *
     FROM CUSTOMER
          WHERE CUSTOMER_ZONE = 'North' and
               CUST_BALANCE > 10000
```

You submit the query for execution and printing of the customer list for the VP. What happens in the DBMS when your query is presented to it for execution? The database engine coordinates the services of the query processor to go through different steps and produce the results for the query. Figure 2-10 shows the steps of the query execution.

Note the processing of the query through the following key steps:

- Database engine initiates the execution.
- Data dictionary determines the data elements needed.
- Security module checks data access authorizations.
- Query processor verifies language syntax.
- Query optimizer subcomponent examines the query and creates an optimal execution plan.
- Query processor works with the database engine to execute the optimal plan.
- Database engine interfaces with the operating system to retrieve the requested data.
- Query processor presents the data.

When you write and submit a query for execution, the query component takes over and produces the result set. Apart from using direct queries, you also request information through other means. You may use a form or screen to initiate the data request. Data retrieval may also be through applications. The query processor component is involved when you make data requests through other such methods.

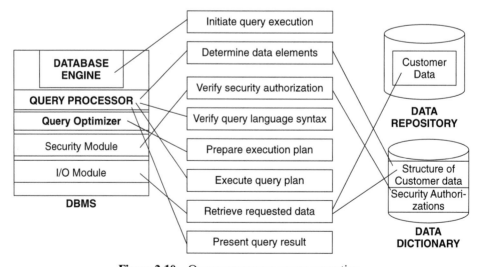

Figure 2-10   Query processor: query execution.

Forms Generator

The forms generator component in the DBMS enables you to create screen layouts or forms for data input and data display. Data input and data display are the two equally important purposes served by forms. You want to display the details of a customer order to your user. You need a layout to display the various data elements such as the order number, date, method of shipment, products ordered, price, and so on. Forms may also include graphics and images. You may want to display the picture of the employee in a form containing employee information.

Figure 2-11 indicates the modules used for forms design and execution. Leading commercial DBMSs offer facilities within the forms generator to create self-contained small applications.

The following elements are present in the forms generator component of many DBMSs, serving several purposes:

Navigator. Presents all the elements that may be combined to create a small application with forms.

Trigger. Function executed when some condition or activity occurs on a form.

Alert. Used to provide warnings or messages on the form to the user for a response.

Block and item. In a form, a block corresponds to an individual structure in the database, for example, customer data structure. An item refers to an individual piece

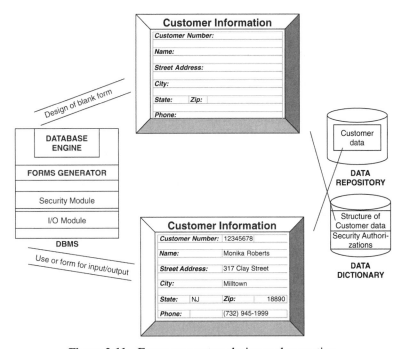

Figure 2-11 Forms generator: design and execution.

of data or data field. Blocks and items on the form are the places where data is input or displayed.

Relationship. Represents the associations between separate blocks and items. Presents all the elements that may be combined to create a small application with forms.

Editor. Window for viewing and maintaining large data structures.

Lists of values. List of permissible values for individual fields.

Parameters. Used to pass values from form to form.

Property sheets. Contain the characteristics of individual data elements on the form.

Layout editor. Enables form objects to be laid out on a canvas to create the format of a form.

Report Writer

In earlier file-oriented data systems, reports were the only means of providing information to users. Also, all batch processing and printing of reports happened overnight. In today's database environment, most data retrieval and data manipulation occur on-line in an interactive manner. As we have seen, the query processor and forms generator components provide online facilities for data access. So, what is the need for report writers?

Although most information access is on-line, a good deal of information delivery still remains in the medium of printed reports. Reports may first be viewed online before selecting and printing only the ones needed on hard copy. Nevertheless, these are reports, and the use of reports is not likely to be eliminated altogether. Power users and specialized users have needs to format and generate their own reports. All applications generally include a substantial suite of daily, weekly, and monthly reports. You can create reports to show detailed and summary data. Reports can show results of complex calculations; they can print multilevel totals.

Figure 2-12 illustrates design and execution of reports. Note how the report writer interfaces with the query processor to retrieve the necessary data. After the query processor delivers the requested data, the report writer formats and prints the report.

Here are a few significant capabilities of report writers in modern DBMSs:

- Easy interface with query processor to retrieve data based on complicated retrieval conditions
- Sophisticated layout editors to format intricate reports
- Methods for storing individual report preferences
- Quick construction of tabular reports
- Creation of summary and detailed reports

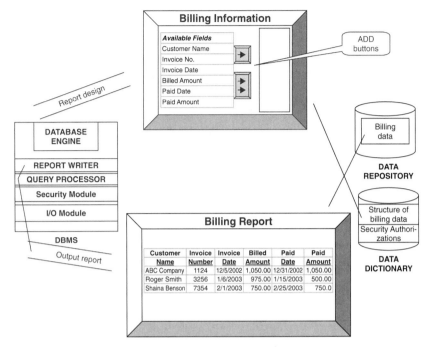

Figure 2-12   Report writer: design and execution.

- Incorporation of report break levels and subtotals
- Usage of subqueries during execution of reports
- Customizing reports with boilerplate graphics and text
- Generation of specialized formats: mailing label, form letter, matrix
- Dynamic reports using dynamic query parameters

Applications Developer

We have discussed the components of query processor, forms generator, and report writer. The outputs of these components form the basis for developing applications for the users. An application consists of forms, reports, and underlying queries. The set of forms and reports provides the users with the capabilities to input, retrieve, and manipulate data in the database. In a sense, an application is a complete package to serve the needs of the users for performing their specific day-to-day tasks. Sales entry, order processing, inventory control, payroll, employee project assignment, and general ledger are examples of applications built with forms, reports, and queries.

The applications developer or applications generator component assembles the outputs of other components to develop coherent systems to support specific functions in the organization. The applications developer components enable the use of menus, submenus, and navigation among various execution options. Small applications consist of just a handful of forms and reports. With the powerful applications developer in modern DBMSs, you can put together a small application easily and quickly. Application developers contain several tools to develop even the most complex of applications within a reasonably short time.

Communications Interface

Some database management systems have separate modules for establishing and managing communications among databases running on different computer systems and under multiple operating systems. The databases may be distributed among various locations.

Communications interface modules interact with the operating system and network software to initiate and manage the connections. They manage the data flow across databases; they promote true global data sharing.

Another aspect of the communications interface is the link with traditional programming languages. Programs written in traditional languages like COBOL or C++ are able to establish links with the database through the communication interface, which in turn interacts with the query processor.

Utilities

No modern database management system is complete without a comprehensive set of utility programs and interface modules. Most commercial vendors have enhanced their DBMSs and equipped them with rich sets of utility tools. This set of tools and interface modules is commonly known as the toolkit portion of database software. The toolkit is primarily intended for database administrators to perform their various functions. Database environments are much more broad and complex than file-oriented systems. Data sharing also implies proper authorization for data retrieval and update. Organizations cannot afford to be without their databases even for a short time. Quick recovery from disasters and malfunctions is mandatory.

Figure 2-13 presents the types of utility tools and interface modules.

Observe how the set of utilities supports the following broad areas:

- Access control
- Preservation of data integrity
- Performance improvement
- Recovery from malfunctions
- Interfaces to languages, programs, and other database systems

CHAPTER SUMMARY

- Most of today's organizations have adopted database environments for their information needs.
- The database environment encompasses several components, not just the data and the software to manage it. The environment includes the following: data repository, data dictionary, DBMS, systems software, hardware, application

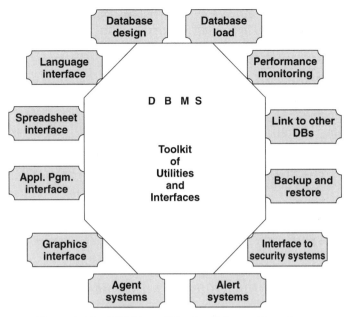

Figure 2-13   DBMS: toolkit of utilities and interfaces.

programs, front-end tools, procedures, people interface, database practitioners, and, importantly, the users.

- Database and DBMS do not mean the same thing. Database refers to the stored data and the definition of its structures. DBMS is the collection of software modules to create, access, maintain, and manage a database.
- Unlike a file-oriented environment, specialized software as a DBMS package is needed because of sophistication in the areas of language interface, storage management, transaction management, and so on.
- Languages needed for database practitioners and users to interact with the database: data definition language (DDL), data manipulation language (DML), and data control language (DCL).
- Each component such as hardware, operating system software, DBMS, and the others possesses specific features and performs definite functions.
- Looking inside a DBMS you will find distinct software modules that perform precise functions and provide specific services in a database environment.

REVIEW QUESTIONS

1. List any six major components of a database environment. Why do you think components other than data storage and database software are also included as part of the environment?
2. Explain the distinction between database and DBMS.

3. Unlike in a file-oriented environment, specialized software (DBMS) is absolutely necessary in a database environment. Give any four reasons why this is true.

4. What is multilevel data independence? How does DBMS provide this independence?

5. What are the major hardware components that support a database environment?

6. Describe any three functions of operating system software in a database environment.

7. How can you classify the users in a database environment? List the requirements of any two of the user groups.

8. "The database engine is the heart of the DBMS." Is this so? Explain briefly.

9. List any four types of services provided by the data dictionary.

10. What are forms? What is the role of the forms generator in the DBMS?

EXERCISES

1. Indicate whether true or false:
   A. People and procedures are part of a database environment.
   B. DML contains features for defining data structures.
   C. The external level schema defines files, records, blocks, and physical locations.
   D. In a database environment, large volumes of data pass through memory buffers.
   E. Tape storage devices are not useful for database backup.
   F. CASE tools may be used for data modeling.
   G. Sometimes the data dictionary is also used for storing the actual data.
   H. The applications developer component in the DBMS is independent and does not use the outputs from other components.
   I. Fault-tolerant data storage generally keeps duplicate sets of data.
   J. The database engine component is responsible for the speed of database operations.

2. Manual and automated procedures are part of the overall database environment in an organization. Discuss the types of procedures needed by database practitioners and end users.

3. What is transaction management in a database environment? Describe the DBMS components that perform transaction management.

4. Discuss the role of operating system software in a database environment. What functions must this software provide?

5. You are one of the power users in your company's database environment. How would you plan to use the database and what services do you expect to be provided for you?

PART II

DATABASE DEVELOPMENT PROCESS

CHAPTER 3

SIGNIFICANCE OF THE DATABASE ENVIRONMENT

CHAPTER OBJECTIVES

- Appreciate the significance of information as a key asset for an organization
- Understand the context in which the database system is critical
- Review who the users are and what types of information they need
- Grasp the benefits of information sharing and note how the database system enables sharing
- Clearly see why database systems are indispensable for modern enterprises

When an organization launches a database system, it takes on a systematic development effort. The effort includes substantial planning and feasibility studies. Because of the significance of the database system, a concerted method is needed for a successful implementation. For many organizations, a database project is something entirely new and not resembling anything previously undertaken. In Chapter 4, we will study the organized methodology applied to development of database systems. We will walk through the various development phases. Many different skills are needed for the development effort. You will note each activity and task required to bring about a transformation of an organization to be dependent on its database system.

Why do you have to go through such elaborate, detailed, and methodical effort to develop a database system? Why do organizations expend all the energy and resources to create a database environment? Is the effort necessary, and is the payback worthwhile? Most certainly, yes. A database environment is absolutely

Database Design and Development: An Essential Guide for IT Professionals by Paulraj Ponniah
ISBN 0-471-21877-4   Copyright © 2003 by John Wiley and Sons, Inc.

essential for the effectiveness and, sometimes, even for the very survival of an organization. Let us view the database environment in the context of the organization that it serves. Where exactly does the database fit in the organization? And for what purpose? If the database exists for the purpose of providing information to the users within the organization, who are these users? What types of information do they want? If the database environment enables information sharing, what benefits accrue to the users? Is a database system indispensable for today's enterprise? If so, why and how? Let us find answers to such questions.

ORGANIZATIONAL CONTEXT

Consider why a database environment must exist in an organization. Each organization has its goals and objectives, the very reason for its existence. People in the organization perform various functions to achieve the goals and objectives. A banking company exists to provide banking services to customers. A medical center exists to provide health care services to patients. A manufacturing company exists to make products and sell them. Primarily, in each of these companies, a database system is there to support the core business of the company by making the necessary information available.

Companies need information to run their businesses. The database system provides that information. Simplistic as this may sound, the relevance of a database system in an organization needs to be explored and appreciated. At this stage, while we are preparing to study the development of database systems, the contextual place of a database system in an organization is especially critical. We need to appreciate the reasons for the special efforts for developing database systems. First, let us observe what happens in each organization and how the database system is tied to what happens there.

Core Business

Notice the numerous activities in a company. For example, look at the activities in a car rental business. Different departments are engaged in various activities. Consider one department in this company. What are the activities in the department that manages the fleet? This department studies the demand for different types of cars. The department examines the usage and status at individual branches. It places orders to replace cars that need to be retired soon. All these and many more activities within the fleet management department happen for the purpose of supporting the core business of the car rental company, which is renting cars to customers. Take another department in the company. The servicing department's activities are focused on keeping each car in top condition. Each car must be thoroughly checked after each rental and maintained. Again, the activities of the servicing department, although different from those of fleet management, are still happening for the purpose of supporting the core business of the car rental company, namely, renting cars to customers.

Consider another organization, say, a medical center. Here the core business is treating patients—inpatients and outpatients. The pharmacy department in the medical center keeps stock of the required drugs and dispenses them to the patients in the wards and to the outpatients. The laboratory examines blood samples, performs tests on the samples, and provides results to the physicians and surgeons. In all of their activities, although varied, the pharmacy and the laboratory support the core business of the medical center, which is patient care.

However we might expand the list of companies for consideration, we will observe that each company has a core business and that the diverse activities of various departments in the company are performed for the purpose of supporting the core business. All activities center upon the core business.

Here is a sample of the core businesses of a few types of organizations:

- *Retail grocery store*—buy groceries from vendors and sell to retail customers
- *Stock brokerage*—buy and sell stocks and bonds for individuals and institutions
- *Auction company*—enable customers sell and buy goods through auctions
- *Computer consulting*—provide consulting services
- *Airlines*—provide air transportation to customers
- *Car dealership*—buy and sell cars
- *Department store*—buy and sell consumer goods
- *University*—provide higher learning to students

How does the core business of an enterprise get done? How does the core business of buying and selling cars get done by a car dealership? How is the core business, namely, patient care, of a medical center accomplished? Each department in the enterprise performs processes to achieve the objectives of the enterprise to get the core business done. Let us examine the processes and see the connection to the database system.

Primary Processes

When you consider organizations and their core businesses, it ultimately comes down to the fact that each core business is somehow related to providing either services or goods. The type of service depends on the individual organization. A medical center provides health care services; a banking institution makes financial services available. Similarly, the nature of the goods is determined by the individual organization. An automobile manufacturer makes cars and trucks; a pharmaceutical company produces drugs and medical accessories.

The core business is to provide goods or services. To whom? To customers. How does an organization accomplish the provision of goods or services? Who in the organization is part of this activity of providing goods and service? Everyone. The functions of each person and every department are directed toward accomplishing the purpose of the core business. Many distinctive processes carried out by the departments support the core business. These primary processes fulfill the purpose of the core business. Figure 3-1 illustrates this principle of core business accomplished through business processes within the organization.

Let us take a concrete example. Consider the case of an airline company. Providing air transportation to customers is the core business. One of the organizational units of the airline company is the ticketing department or the ticketing counter at the airport. This unit is involved with many processes that support the

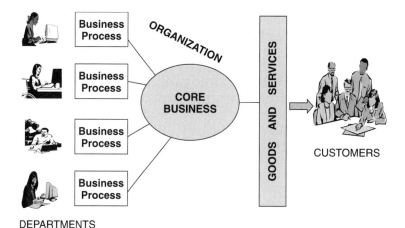

Figure 3-1   Business processes supporting core business.

core business. One primary process is ticketing and seat reservation. Review the tasks in this business process:

- Ascertain the customer's present travel requirements
- Find suitable discounted plans
- Check possible routing options and connecting flights
- Verify seat availability
- Reserve seats on selected flight routes
- Record meal and other preferences
- Issue ticket
- Collect airfare
- Print itinerary

The ticketing and seat reservation process consists of tasks performed—all part of the core business of providing air transportation to customers. You may continue your review with other processes such as passenger check-in, luggage handling, promotional campaigns, aircraft maintenance, crew scheduling, frequent flyer operations, and so on. Apart from the primary processes, an organization conducts secondary or incidental processes. In a major organization, you will find hundreds of different processes, all of them, however, performed under the overall purpose of the core business.

Information as a Major Asset

Go back to the example of the airline company and the process of ticketing and seat reservation. How does the company carry out this process? To accomplish this process, the organization makes use of assets and resources. Look at the terminal building and the ticketing counter itself. Observe all the equipment and materials needed to perform this process. What about the people needed to complete the

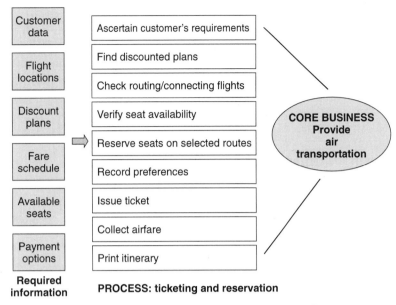

Figure 3-2   Information for ticketing and seat reservation process.

process? The people, buildings, equipment, and materials are all part of the assets and resources necessary for performing the process. Given these assets and resources, can the process be completed? Is anything else essential for carrying out the process?

Now examine the individual tasks of ticketing and seat reservation process. Let us say that the customer wants to make a trip from New York to Miami on a Monday. Are there any promotional discount plans? Now the ticketing agent must find and offer a suitable discount plan, if available. Although the agent has the desk, equipment, and other resources, he or she needs information about the available discount plans. Only with proper information, can the agent find and offer a suitable discount plan.

Next proceed to the task of checking possible routing options and connecting flights. To perform this task, the agent needs information about the different routing options and connecting flights on Mondays. After going through the routing options and flight times, let us say that the customer has picked a specific routing option. Go further to the next task in the process: verifying seat availability. What information does the agent need to complete this task? Of course, the agent must have information about seat availability in each leg of the journey. Our review continues with all the tasks of the process. You will note that the agent needs different types of information for every task of the process. Figure 3-2 shows information needed for the ticketing and seat reservation process. Notice the various types of information necessary for the process.

We have considered just one process in the airline company. Even for this one process, various types of critical information are essential to finish the process. What about the numerous other processes in the company, all geared to provide air transportation to customers? Each of the processes is carried out through several tasks.

Each of the tasks requires information. We observe an emerging pattern. To carry out the various processes, the company needs resources and assets such as buildings, equipment, materials, people, and money. But that is not all. The company also needs information to accomplish its processes. Information is a major asset like any other tangible and intangible assets of the company to be used for performing the multitude of processes. The key asset of information supports an organization's core business.

DB System in the Organization

Return to the example of the airline company. We noted the information essential for performing the ticketing and seat reservation process. Reviewing the tasks once again, let us mark the elements of information needed to complete each task of the process:

- Ascertain the customer's present travel requirements—*customer information, departure and destination locations, travel date*
- Find suitable discounted plans—*available discount plans*
- Check possible routing options and connecting flights—*possible legs of the journey, connecting flights, and times*
- Verify seat availability—*seat availability in each segment*
- Reserve seats on selected flight routes—*customer seating preferences, vacant seats in each flight segment*
- Record meal and other preferences—*available preferences and options*
- Issue ticket—*customer information, fare schedule, taxes, airport dues, etc.*
- Collect airfare—*payment options, customer payment preferences, payment type, date, amount*
- Print itinerary—*customer information, flights and times, special preferences, assigned seating, and booking status*

Following this method of ascertaining the information needs for each task in a process, we will be able to put down the needs for the tasks in all the processes. The result will be a large compilation of all the elements of information needed in the company to support its core business through various processes. The large collection of information needs will constitute a variety of information types. How do you organize all of the elements of information? How do you store the seemingly disparate pieces of information, manage these, and provide quick access for carrying out individual tasks? This is where the database system of the company comes into the picture. The database system organizes all the information into cohesive data structures, stores data efficiently, manages and maintains data storage, and affords data access whenever information is needed to perform a specific task. Figure 3-3 indicates how the database system of an airline company supports the core business and its processes.

Let us recapitulate the concepts regarding the place and purpose of the database system in an organization. Let us summarize briefly how the database system fits into the context of an organization.

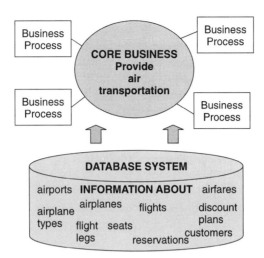

Figure 3-3   DB system supporting core business in airline company.

- Every organization is engaged in a core business.
- The organization achieves the purposes of its core business through primary processes.
- Each process is carried out through a set of related tasks.
- Apart from other resources and assets, each task requires information for its performance.
- Putting all the processes and the component tasks together, an organization needs a large collection of information elements.
- Information is, therefore, a major asset for an organization.
- The database system in an organization exists to provide the information needs in all the processes.

INFORMATION REQUIREMENTS

Information is a key asset absolutely essential for performing the business processes in an organization. By this time, you should be convinced of this significant principle, which is almost axiomatic. We have also seen how the database system in an organization supplies the much-needed information. As the complexities of business grow resulting in the demand for sophisticated types of information in high volumes, a database proves to be the optimal means for information delivery. Well, if the database delivers information, to whom is it supplying information? To the users—the employees and agents working to execute processes for the achievement of the organization's core business.

Who are these people needing information? Where are they situated? What functions do they perform within the organization? What are their responsibility levels? To fully appreciate the significance of the database environment in an organization, we need to explore these questions. What are the information requirements of users

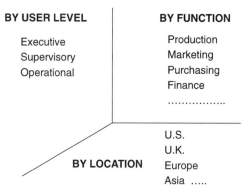

Figure 3-4 Community of users.

at different responsibility levels, performing various distinct functions, and located in multiple places?

Figure 3-4 indicates how the user community in an organization may be divided into groups in three different ways. This kind of division helps us understand the differences in the types of information various user groups require and to note the differences in methods of information delivery to them.

Remember that information is required to carry out the business processes. So, if you want to understand the information requirements of each user group, you must review the processes and the relevant tasks performed by each group.

At User Levels

Dividing users into groups based on their responsibilities in an organization seems to be the most natural method for forming groups. Note the division of users into three groups based on their responsibility levels: executive, managerial, operational. If you are an operations person, you work with current data to carry out your processes. You process a customer order, make an airline reservation, send an invoice, issue payroll checks, or balance inventory. You perform the processes that run the day-to-day business. On the other hand, the processes carried out by the other two levels are not so directly connected to the everyday operations.

Supervisory processes relate to monitoring operations and exercising control. Supervisors need information in the form of summaries and exception reports. Executives establish long-term plans, set the overall direction, and make strategic decisions. Their processes need historical data revealing trends and business conditions. Executive processes must have data that can be used for analyzing past performance and future trends.

Here is a summary of information requirements and how the enterprise database serves the needs:

For operational level. Current data on all the entities relevant to the organization. Examples of such business entities: customer, supplier, order, invoice, aircraft type, employee, and so on. Users at the operational level need data at the lowest level of detail. They require data about an individual customer, a single order, a particular invoice, a single sale, or seat availability in a specific flight to complete their business processes. The organization's database serves this group of users with detailed, current data.

For supervisory level. Current data in summarized formats. Supervisory staff needs information on the overall functioning of their departments. Supervisors require periodic reports summarizing the data about their departments. They are responsible for making sure that everything in their departments is done right and on time. Supervisors monitor the various processes that take place in their departments and control the way their processes get completed. A supervisor in a sales department must have weekly and monthly summary reports on the performance of salespersons against targets. If some event happens that is out of the ordinary, the supervisor has to know about it to take corrective action. The organization's database serves this group with summary data and triggers to alert to exceptional events.

For executive level. Executives are not concerned with the details of how each process in every department gets done. They do not need detailed data about every order, every shipment, or every invoice. Nor do they need summary reports at short, regular intervals. Most of the information necessary for executives is not routine or regularly scheduled. Information must enable them to analyze the overall performance of each major division and of the organization as a whole. For spotting trends, planning the organization's direction, and formulating company policies, executives make use of historical data in addition to current data. The organization's database serves this group of users with large volumes of past and current data, summarized as needed in ad hoc fashion.

In Functional Divisions

We have noted a primary method of dividing users into three groups based on their level of responsibilities. At each responsibility level, users work within functional divisions. If one of your users is a supervisor, he or she performs the business processes as part of a specific department. He or she is a supervisor in the accounting division, the marketing division, or the product division. Within a major division, the user is a supervisor of a single unit, say the order processing department within the accounting division. The types of business processes differ from division to division. The information needs, therefore, vary from division to division. Grouping users by functional division proves to be a helpful method.

What is the significance of the enterprise database when we group users by functional divisions? How does it serve users in various functional divisions? Although there are operational level users in all divisions, the types of processes they complete require different categories of data. For example, an operational level user in the accounting division may create invoices to be mailed out to customers. An operational level user in the marketing division may compile quarterly sales targets to be sent to salespersons. An operational level user in the production department may assemble production flow statistics to be sent to the production manager. All three users need detailed data from the database. However, what each user needs from the database varies according to his or her function. Similar differences in data requirements apply to supervisory and executive level users attached to diverse divisions.

Viewed from the context of functional divisions, the organization's database system supplies the information needs of users in the following ways:

- Provides each department within each division with data specific to each process in that department.
- Enables every department to perform its processes.
- If necessary, allows one department to use data collected by another.
- Collectively, provides data for processes of all functions of the organization.
- In essence, affords data for the carrying out the core business of the organization.

At Geographic Regions

Today's organization has a worldwide presence. As the world has become smaller because of improved communication facilities and rapid transportation methods, it is easy for businesses to expand globally. It is not uncommon for many companies to have offices in the U.S., the U.K., Europe, and Asia.

In a global company with worldwide offices, where are your users? Who are the users that need to be serviced by the company's database? One user may be located in Chicago, another in London, one in Paris, another in Milan, and yet another in Hong Kong. All users in the company need information to perform their various processes. Although the processes may be similar to the ones performed by users in operational, supervisory, and executive levels in domestic companies, the information needed in a global organization by the same type of users is conditioned by local requirements. The user in Hong Kong is more interested in the customers from China. The user in Paris depends on the information about sales to French customers to complete his or her process.

Information needs of users in various geographic regions of a company may be classified into two categories as indicated below.

Local Information Consider a user in the accounting division of the Paris office of a company with worldwide branches. To prepare an invoice to cover a sale to a French customer, the user needs information about that French customer, the product, units supplied, the price, shipping charges, and French tax rates. When you examine these pieces of information, you will note that these are not needed by a user in Hong Kong to prepare an invoice for a Chinese customer.

Names and addresses of customers in France, shipping charges within France, and French tax rates are examples of local information for the users in the French region. In the same way, names and addresses of customers in China, shipping charges within China, and Chinese tax rates are examples of local information for the users in the Chinese region. Users in each geographic region require local information to perform their business processes. The nature and extent of local information varies from region to region. Some regions may require a substantial volume of local information, more than other regions.

Global Information In the example of local invoicing considered above, product information comprises product codes, product descriptions, stock keeping units, unit prices, and any standard discounts. Whether a company's product is supplied to a French customer or a Chinese customer, the product code, description, stock keeping unit, and unit price are usually the same. These pieces of information are not specific to individual regions, but they apply to all users globally throughout the company. This is global information.

Global information includes pieces of information common to all users in all geographic regions. In a company with international customers, customer information may be both global and local. Global information includes information about all international customers who buy from many geographic locations of the company. Information about local customers is part of the local information for that region. In an airline company, international flight schedules are part of global information. In an international bank, money transfer methods are part of global information. In a worldwide fast-food franchise, the ingredients in the proprietary recipe are global information.

In companies with users in multiple geographic regions, the organization's database environment provides both local and global information to the users for performing their business processes.

Providing Information

You have noted that an organization's database environment provides information to users at different levels of responsibilities, in various functional divisions, and at many geographic regions. It seems that the database supplies to a very wide user base. This is true. When you consider the users grouped by the three major categories, there must be a vast collection of information in the organization's database. How does the database enable each segment of users to perform its processes? How is the information provided?

Whether the users are part of different functional divisions or operate in multiple geographic regions, they are basically operational, supervisory, or executive users. Therefore, if we consider how the database caters to the needs of the users categorized by user levels, we will cover the needs of all users. We can do so by examining the types of computer applications used by the users at the different responsibility levels. Broadly, we can classify computer systems into operational and informational systems.

Operational Systems. These systems make the wheels of business turn. Such systems are used to run day-to-day operations of the company. They support the basic business processes such as taking an order, processing a claim, making a shipment, generating an invoice, receiving cash, or reserving an airline seat. Examples of operational systems are the checking account system in a bank, the factory shop-floor system in a manufacturing business, the reservation system in an airline company, the credit-checking system in a credit bureau, and the sales system in a retail grocery chain.

Informational Systems. These systems let the users watch the wheels of business turn. Such systems are used for analyzing the results of the operations and for making strategic decisions. They enable users to get answers to requests such as: "Show me the top-selling products," "Show me the problem regions," "Tell me why," "Let me see other related data," "Show me the highest margins," and "Alert me when a region sells below targets." Examples of informational systems include marketing management information systems, credit analysis, credit card fraud detection, profitability analysis, and market share analysis.

The database environment supports operational and informational systems with appropriate data. Users at different responsibility levels use these systems for performing their business processes.

- Operational level users perform all their processes with operational systems.
- Supervisory level users mostly make use of summary information provided by operational systems. Occasionally, informational systems supply some information to supervisory users.
- Executive level users almost totally rely on informational systems. Usually, informational systems are fed by separate databases especially designed for analysis.

INFORMATION SHARING

We have already seen that information sharing is one of the major advantages of database systems. Sharing takes place among the various groups of users. In earlier days of computing, each user group within an organization created its own files and no other group could share the information contained in those files. The reason for this is obvious. File-oriented systems were developed and built to serve individual departments. An order entry system was implemented to support only the processes of the order entry department. Even though the files created in the order entry system contained order data that could be of use to the marketing department, data about the orders could not be shared. All of this changed with the introduction of database systems. The organization's database stores the data created by all departments in an orderly and combined fashion.

In a database system, all of the enterprise data is in one place. People in the organization need not go to different storage areas or files to get information. Applications developed in a database environment center on the database. Each department has equal access to the database. This ability to share information has brought about a shift in the very thinking of the people in the different departments. Database systems have altered ideas about ownership of data. Order entry departments no longer consider data about customer orders to be their exclusive property. Now, data entered into organization's database by any department becomes available to all departments. Figure 3-5 illustrates information sharing in a database environment.

Why Share Information?

Go back to the order entry example. Orders come into the order entry department. While processing an order, that department verifies customer credit, checks stock,

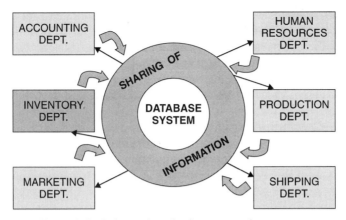

Figure 3-5   Information sharing among departments.

ascertains the appropriate shipping method, and determines prices and discounts. The order entry clerk then records all the data about the order in the company's database. Why must the data entered by the order entry clerk be shared with other departments?

Effective Customer Service   When the customer has a question regarding prices or the status of the order, the order entry department has to provide answers. When part of the order must be back ordered because of out-of-stock condition, the order entry department ensures that the back-ordered items are shipped later. If the order entry department is responsible for the complete processing of each order, why is it necessary for order data to be shared with other departments? After all, does not the order entry department carry out every process relating to orders? If so, what use do other departments have for order data?

In today's business conditions, it is not entirely true that the order entry department performs every process relating to orders. With strong emphasis on customer service, many departments need to have information about orders. Modern businesses place a lot of importance to customer service—for very good reasons. Good and prompt service to customers makes a company stand out among the competition. Consider order data against this business background. When a salesperson contacts his or her customer, the salesperson needs information about what and how much the customer had ordered, information about the status of all recent orders, and information on when the back orders are likely to be fulfilled. If a customer wants clarification on the prices and discounts of an order, the customer service department needs access to order data to provide a proper response. The company warehouse needs data about each order to prepare the shipments. Many departments need to share order information to offer unified service to every customer.

Data Recording and Data Usage   Think about the core business of any organization. You know that each department in every division performs specific business processes; all of these processes contribute to the overall core business. The diverse processes—all together—make up the entire core business. To perform each of these processes, users need information from the enterprise database.

Another fact, equally important, is that while performing each of the processes, users also record fresh data in the database. For example, to complete the order entry process, the order entry clerk needs product data from the database. While processing an order, the clerk in turn creates and records order data. This twofold aspect of using data and recording data affords a sense of unification among the processes and makes the core business of the organization a cohesive whole.

Information—Common Asset   You are already very much aware that information is a major asset for an organization. Assets and resources in an organization are needed to run the business. Plant and equipment are utilized for production of goods. Cash is used to pay the company's bills. Compare information to the other assets in the organization. The other assets are used for specific purposes by specific departments. The production department makes use of plant and equipment for manufacturing products. The accounting department pays bills with cash. Information, as an asset, differs from other types of assets. Corporate information in the company database is not made of separable parts. It is a unified whole set of data, ordered and integrated, for the purpose of supporting the company's core business. The company database contains information common to all—created by all and used by all. Information is a common corporate asset that must be shared easily by all divisions and departments.

Major Benefits

Before we consider the major benefits of information sharing, let us be clear about what the information is that users are sharing. Who records the information in the corporate database in the first place? As you know, each department is responsible for certain business processes. While performing the specific processes each department creates data, and this data gets recorded in the database. In effect, all users share information that is recorded through the performance of the various business processes.

Let us now summarize the major benefits of information sharing within an organization.

Synergy of Collective Information.   When data are combined in a database environment, the effect is synergistic. In other words, the combined data are more valuable than the sum of individual parts. In a file-oriented system, each department creates and uses data in its own files. The order entry department uses the data in its files, the marketing department the data in its files, and the production department the data in its files. When you put order data, marketing data, and product data in the database, each department still has access to its own files. But more than that, each department has access to other files as well. The benefits each department derives from its own data are complemented by the advantages of having access to other files. This concept of data integration means that the benefits from the collection of all parts of the data are more than sum of the benefits from each single part of the data.

Complete Information.   Because of information sharing, each department has access to complete information about each business entity and business process.

When a customer order is received, the order entry department initiates recording of order data. The order fulfillment department adds fulfillment data. The shipping department records shipment data. All of these data complete the information on an order. When users share information through a database, they have complete information about each order.

Consistent Information. When you record each data element only once and store it in only one place in the database, you reduce data redundancy. What is the advantage of eliminating data redundancy? When one department is looking for information about a particular invoice, every other department looking for information about that invoice will find the same information. If the total amount of the invoice is $2000, everyone retrieving that information from the database will find the amount to be $2000. In a database environment, all users will share consistent information. Chances of errors in reporting and calculations are greatly reduced when users share information that is consistent.

Better Customer Service. Sharing of complete and consistent information results in better customer information. When a customer contacts the customer service department, the service representative has access to complete information about the order relating to which the customer has questions. The service representative also has access to prior orders, the customer's buying patterns, and the customer's outstanding balances. The service representative can help the customer with proper responses because of information sharing.

Support for Business Processes. We come back to the business processes that various departments perform to carry out the mission of an organization. Clearly, each department requires information to complete its processes. Processes cannot be performed without information. A substantial part of the information needed for completing a particular process comes from other processes performed elsewhere in the organization. Sharing of information enables users to complete all the business processes.

Enabling Uniform Applications. Information sharing is a first step toward uniform computer applications to support the different business processes. All information in a database environment comes from the organization's database. Nonredundant data are stored with uniform standards in the database. The formats are uniform; the naming conventions are standardized. In a database environment, the database feeds data to all applications. Applications are developed around the database. Therefore, it is easier to develop uniform applications for various groups of users. Inventory control and order entry applications can easily have the same input formats, similar output reports, and standard navigation in the user interface.

Promotion of Collaboration. Information sharing promotes an atmosphere of collaboration among the several divisions and departments. All share the same data. Turf wars over data ownership are greatly minimized. Both information sharing and uniform applications motivate users across departments to come together and collaborate. When users complete processing through collaboration, productivity increases and shows up in improved profitability.

Information Sharing Schemes

To relate users to the database environment in an organization, we suggested above some ways for dividing them into groups. Users fell into natural groups based on their responsibility levels, business functions, and locations. Data sharing involves each group making use of data created by other groups. If a group in the accounting division creates data about invoices and stores the data in the database, other groups in the marketing and planning divisions share this data. When you examine the contents of the database, you will note that various user groups create specific segments of the database either by recording or updating data in the course of their processes.

When each user group needs data from the database to perform its business processes, the content and format of the data are relevant. Some user groups need very detailed data; others want summaries. Some user groups require data about single business objects such as customer, order, or invoice; others must have data about multiple objects. Data content and format are essential factors facilitating information sharing.

How does the database enable information sharing? How do data content and format play significant roles in information sharing? What are the information schemes? How exactly does information sharing happen? We will go back to the ways in which we grouped users and consider each method of grouping and note how information sharing takes place within each set of groups.

Among Functional Departments   This is where organizations gain the most advantage from information sharing. This was also the primary problem area in file-oriented systems with data files restricted to each functional department. When information is shared among departments performing distinct functions, all for carrying out the objectives of the core business, organizations obtain the greatest benefits.

Let us consider the customer service department—a department crucial for customer retention. This department, by itself, does not create and enter too much data into the database. Perhaps the department records basic data on each customer contact. On the other hand, it needs data created and entered by other departments to perform customer service functions. Imagine a customer calling the customer service department to check on his or her orders and to ask other questions about some specific products. The customer service department must be able to respond and provide the following types of information: breakdown of sales to the inquiring customer, product stock, back order status, billing clarifications, and so on. Some of the information relates to detailed data, and a few other types of information are based on summary data. Where does the customer service department get information to serve the customer? The department relies on data created by other departments. It has to share the information produced by other departments.

Figure 3-6 illustrates information sharing in a specific case.

Note how the customer service department makes use of data created by other departments. Also, observe the types of data entered into the database by these other departments and how the types of data enable the customer service department to perform its processes.

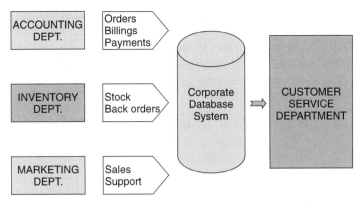

Figure 3-6   Information sharing for customer service.

Among User Levels   We considered three responsibility levels of users—operational, supervisory, and executive. Generally, all users fit into these three broad categories. Information sharing signifies that data created by one user group are shared by another group. What is the implication of information sharing among user levels? Is this sharing different from other sharing schemes?

Information sharing among operational, supervisory, and executive levels tends to be one-way: Executives make use of data entered by supervisory and operational levels, and supervisors utilize data stored by operational-level users. Operational-level users share the data created by them with supervisors and executives, and supervisors, in turn, share their data with executives. This is because operational-level users are responsible for entering the bulk of the data in the enterprise database.

Supervisors perform processes for monitoring and controlling business operations. For these processes, they need summary data that are derived from the detailed data created by operational-level users. Special procedures within applications summarize data in the manner required by supervisory staff.

Executives mostly need very high-level summaries to see how the division as a whole is performing. Data produced by operational staff must be summarized further to meet the needs of executives. In addition, executives have their business analysts working on special projects. These special projects require both summary and detailed data.

Across Geographic Regions   We have noted that in an organization spread across multiple regions, corporate information may be segmented into global and local categories. Local information at a region refers to the information restricted to the business processes at that region. Each region generates its own local information. Local information of one region may not be useful to any other region. What we have reckoned as local information is generally not shared across geographic regions.

Let us proceed to look at what is considered global information in multiregional organizations. Customer data is usually part of global information. In a worldwide company or even a domestic company with many regions, customers residing in one region do purchase different goods and services from different regions of the same company. Each region generates data about the customers in that region.

Regional units may specialize in distinct types of products and services. If so, product data would also be part of global information. Each region produces data about the products and services created in that region. A specific product made in one region may be sold to customers in a second region. The second region must, therefore, be able to share data about that product with the first region.

Sharing of global information forms the major part of information sharing across geographic regions. The categorization of information into global and local depends on the organizational setup and business conditions of each organization. The type of data considered to be global information in one company may be deemed to be local information elsewhere. Nevertheless, in each company the types of data reckoned as global information in that company get to be shared by users across geographic regions.

DB System as Enabler

Let us recall the definition of a database system.

> A database is an *ordered collection* of *related data elements* intended to meet *the information needs* of an organization and designed to be *shared* by multiple users.

As an ordered collection of related data elements meeting the information needs of an organization, the database system enables information to be shared among groups of users. The following points amplify the role of the database system in information sharing.

Common Data Pool. The database provides a common storage pool to keep all of an organization's data. When the database is centralized, all data are kept in one location. Even a distributed database is a still a common set of the organization's data conveniently placed at different sites.

Integrated Data. Before data are placed in a database, redundancies and duplications are removed. Integration of data prevents inconsistencies from creeping into the database. When user groups share integrated data, they work with one set of data and present unified and consistent information to customers.

Uniform Access. Database systems promote uniform applications that standardize methods of data access and usage. With standard data access methods, users find it easier to get information from processes other than their own. Uniform data access reduces user training.

Simplified Sharing. In file-oriented systems, information sharing proved to be extremely difficult. Users had to contend with disparate data formats, variations in computing platforms, and differences in file access methods. Database systems have simplified information sharing to a very large degree.

Figure 3-7 depicts the facets of information sharing in an organization and clearly presents the role of the database system enabling information sharing.

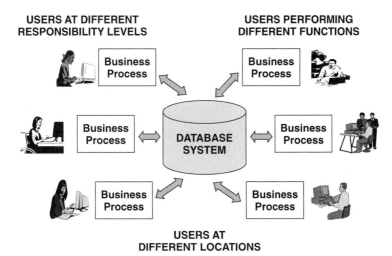

Figure 3-7 Information sharing: DB system as enabler.

PIVOTAL ROLE OF THE DATABASE SYSTEM

Let us pause and review our discussions so far. The database system in an organization supports the numerous business processes that take place there to achieve the objectives of the organization's core business. You have noted that the database system is indispensable for the business processes.

The database system provides the information essential for the successful performance of business processes. Users at different responsibility levels, in various functional departments, and at multiple locations—all need information from the database to complete their business processes. Modern enterprises depend on collaboration among departments; the database system makes collaboration possible by enabling departments to share vital information among themselves.

Data Storage

The database in an organization serves as the primary repository for corporate information. In a company, data in different formats may be held within individual departments in private files and spreadsheets. The accounting department may keep budget numbers in departmental files. The marketing department may hold sensitive information about some key clients in their individual files. Nevertheless, the vast bulk of the organization's data resides in its corporate database.

Note the following aspects of storage of data and observe how the corporate database supports the organization by storing data.

Data about business objects. The organization's database stores data about all the business objects that are relevant to the organization. For a medical center, the database stores data about patients, physicians, diseases, diagnosis, treatments, medications, patient visits, patient stays, and so on. For a banking institution, the database collects data about customers, checking accounts, savings accounts, loans, bank withdrawals, deposits, money transfers, and so on. For each type of organization, the database in that organization gathers data about its pertinent objects.

Data for business processes. It is worthwhile to repeat that the database stores data for the purpose of being useful for completing the business processes of the organization. Where are the data stored for completing a reservation of an airline seat? Where are the data stored for completing an auto insurance claim? Where are the data recorded for completing stocktaking in an industrial warehouse? In the databases of the respective organizations.

Suitable for all user levels. The database in an organization stores data in various summary and detailed formats suitable for users at the operational, supervisory, and executive levels.

Valid and consistent data. Data stored in a database are free from duplications and inconsistencies. The database keeps a data element in only one place. Every data element conforms to established standards and conventions. Thus the organization's database holds valid and consistent data.

Easily accessible data. Data in the enterprise database are meant for sharing among various groups of users. Therefore, the database keeps data as easily accessible to all groups as possible.

Secure data. Database administrators carefully safeguard the enterprise database because information contained in it forms a key corporate asset. The database, therefore, stores data in a secure and protected environment.

Scalable and expandable. As the number of users and the usage increase, the database can be expanded in size. Also, storage can be scaled up to faster and more sophisticated media.

Information Delivery

You do not store data in your organization's database to preserve it and keep it safe in a protected environment. Of course, your users value the information greatly and would like the database storage to be guarded well. Nevertheless, a database exists for the purpose of delivering information to the users to conduct their day-to-day operations and perform their business processes. Proper information delivery is crucial to these processes.

The enterprise database system plays a significant role in delivering information to user groups. It has to make information available in the ways users want it, in the places they need it, and for the purposes for which they require it. Note the following points with regard to information delivery and the role of the database system.

One place for information. Unlike earlier file-oriented systems, a database system sets up one place from which information may be fetched or delivered. The database approach eliminates variations and ambiguities as to sources of information for various business processes. Information needed for all business processes resides in one logical place, although under certain conditions individual data files may be stored in multiple physical locations as in the case of distributed databases.

Information delivery tools. The database system comes with its own set of tools for information access and delivery. Query processors and report writers enable easy information access.

Empowering users. In a database environment, sophisticated users can write their own queries and format their own reports. Such users gain control over their information access; to a large extent, they need not depend on the information technology department to get information for them.

Promotes information delivery. The manner in which data structures get organized in the database makes information available by easy combinations of different structures. If you need information to process insurances claims, you can combine data on insurers, policies, covered contingencies, and damages. If you want information to reserve an airline seat, you can combine data on customers, flight schedules, seat availability, rates schedules, and available discounts. This synergy of the data content promotes information delivery.

Foundation for Applications

In a database environment, the data repository forms the underlying basis for developing applications. All applications receive data from the database; data also are recorded and updated through applications. The database appears to sit in the middle surrounded by the various applications. In fact, the database shapes the input and display of data in the applications.

Consider the following factors that make the database environment the foundation for applications.

Input and display of data. Suppose you display customer name and address in the order entry application as well as in the product shipment application. Because customer name and address in both applications come from the same database, the formats, sizes, and data types will be same. Similarly, when you input customer name and address through the marketing application or update the data from the customer service application, you use the same formats, sizes, and data types. The database environment creates uniformity in data input and display across all applications. Departments and users are no longer divided by their applications.

Standardization of applications. You know that it is easier to apply standards and controls in a database environment. You can standardize data names, relationships among data elements, and data input and display formats. You can also establish

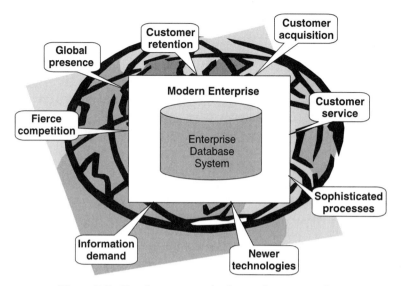

Figure 3-8   Database system in the modern enterprise.

data edits and controls. Standards and controls within a database enable applications to be standardized as well.

Easy cross-training. When an organization has standardized applications, cross-training of users among different applications becomes easy. Users may be made more mobile between departments, and productivity is likely to increase. This benefit is more pronounced in organizations with user groups in multiple locations.

Indispensable for Modern Enterprise

You cannot visualize any modern enterprise existing without a database system. The database has assumed a pivotal role in today's businesses. Contemporary organizations cannot function if they do not integrate and store their data in efficient databases. Figure 3-8 summarizes the features of the modern enterprise and matches them with its information requirements.

   Note the following features of modern enterprises:

- Global presence
- Stiffer competition
- More service-oriented businesses than production-oriented businesses
- Importance of customer acquisition and retention
- Higher customer expectations
- Newer and more sophisticated business processes
- Need to exploit and manage newer technologies
- Ever-increasing demand for information

CHAPTER SUMMARY

- Every organization has a core business; several primary processes support the core business.
- Information is a major asset for an organization to complete the processes and accomplish its core business.
- The database system stores and manages the organization's data and provides indispensable information to accomplish the core business.
- The users in an organization may be divided into groups based on responsibility levels, functional units, and geographic regions. The database system provides information to each group of users to carry out its business processes.
- Information sharing in an organization has major benefits; it promotes effective customer service, supports all business processes, enables uniform applications, and creates an atmosphere for collaboration. The database system acts as a primary enabler for information sharing.
- The pivotal role of the database system in an organization covers the areas of data storage, information delivery, and computer applications. Modern organizations cannot survive without database systems.

REVIEW QUESTIONS

1. What do you understand by core business of an organization? Give an example of an organization and its core business.
2. What are business processes in an organization? Give an example of a business process and explain how it supports the overall core business of an organization.
3. List any two primary processes in a medical center. Describe the elements of information supplied by the database system of the medical center to complete these processes.
4. What are the three common levels of responsibility of the users in an organization? What types of information are needed at each level?
5. What do we mean by local and global information in an organization? Give examples.
6. Give any two reasons why information sharing is important in an organization. Explain the reasons.
7. How does the database system enable information sharing among users in different geographic regions of an organization?
8. "The enterprise database system plays a significant role in delivering information to user groups." Describe any two factors justifying this statement.
9. How does a database system promote uniform applications in an organization?
10. "A database system is indispensable for modern enterprises." Do you completely agree? If so, give any two reasons. If not, explain your position.

EXERCISES

1. Match the columns:

1. primary business processes	A. promotes collaboration
2. supervisory users	B. create own queries and reports
3. global information	C. support core business
4. informational systems	D. devoid of inconsistencies
5. collective information	E. need information for control
6. information sharing	F. common for all users
7. integrated data	G. need trend analysis
8. power users	H. analyze operational results
9. standards and controls	I. synergistic effect
10. executive users	J. easy in database environment

2. The core business for a car dealership is buying and selling cars. List some of the major processes supporting this core business. Describe the elements of information needed for two of these processes.

3. You are the new project manager for the database project at a large department store launching its first database. Your CIO has asked you to write a memo to the Executive VP on initiating the project. List the major benefits of a database system in the memo.

4. Describe the ways in which information can be provided to executives and supervisors from the database system of a large retail grocery chain.

5. The database system in an organization promotes information sharing. Discuss how the database system enables information sharing. List the major benefits of information sharing.

Chapter 4

DATABASE DEVELOPMENT LIFE CYCLE

CHAPTER OBJECTIVES

- Understand the need for a careful and systematic approach to database development
- Examine the steps and tasks in the database development life cycle (DDLC)
- Learn why proper planning is absolutely essential for database development
- Study how requirements are defined and how the design phase is completed
- Observe and appreciate the tasks necessary to complete the implementation and for ongoing maintenance of the database system

At this point, you greatly appreciate the pivotal role of the database system in an organization. The success of modern organizations rests on the effectiveness of their database systems. The database system in an organization provides information critical for achieving the goals of the organization, for fulfilling its core business, and for driving the primary processes. The importance of the organization's database system cannot be overstated.

If the database system of an organization is of paramount importance, then its design and development must be substantially significant as well. If so, how should an organization go about establishing its database system? Obviously, with a lot of care and attention. We will discuss the activities and tasks required to create a sound database system for an organization. We will begin with an overview of the required steps; next, we will walk through each of the steps in sufficient detail. When we have completed the discussion, you will have gained a broader understanding of the design and development process.

Database Design and Development: An Essential Guide for IT Professionals by Paulraj Ponniah
ISBN 0-471-21877-4   Copyright © 2003 by John Wiley and Sons, Inc.

MAJOR DEVELOPMENT STEPS

For a moment, think of an organization running its business with file-oriented systems. All the data that support the business reside on sequential or flat files. There is no flexibility, no data sharing. Each user group has its own set of files; you note data proliferation to a great extent. You find disparate islands of data—all of which are meant to support one core business of the organization. The same elements of data may be found in different files, and these duplicate versions of the same data elements could result in gross data inconsistency.

Now imagine the same organization running its business with a database system. This environment is quite the opposite of one with file-oriented systems. First, you observe data integration with completely reduced data duplication. Removal of data redundancies produces a major improvement and projects a uniform image of the company to the outside world. Every document sent to customers and business partners shows the same values for any data element.

Information sharing resulting from a database system is a major change in the organization. Users are no longer confined to their own individual sets of files. Each group of users does not try to protect its data turf. Data in the database system are everyone's data; the integrated whole is for the benefit of the entire organization; the data serve the core business of the organization as a single entity. The transition of an organization from data proliferation to information sharing constitutes a major step.

So how does the changeover from individual data files to an integrated database system occur in an organization? How does the transition from an environment of isolated data islands to one of information sharing happen? With a lot of planning, of course. Companies need to plan and think through all the aspects of the change. The transition requires a systematic and coordinated effort. The development of a database system calls for a proven approach with distinct and purposeful steps. Businesses adopt a life cycle approach to database development. In a life cycle approach, you pay attention to each individual step and make the steps proceed in a standard, productive manner. The approach deals with all the necessary steps in the life of a database system from beginning to ongoing phases.

Starting the Process

Let us go back to when data systems and applications were developed in a file-oriented environment. Consider developing applications for the order processing department in an organization. You study the various functions performed for completing the processing of orders. You gather the data required to complete each task of these functions. Then you put all the required data into one or more sequential files, and these files make up the data system for the department. Here you use a function-oriented approach to developing the data system. In a function-oriented approach, the focus is on the functions. If the functions change or if you need to add more functions, the composition of the data system changes too, sometimes quite extensively.

However, it is different in a database system. This type of data system is designed to cater to current information needs and be able to extend easily to accommodate changes in the requirements and to meet additional ones. You do not focus on the

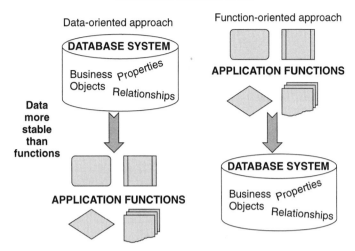

Figure 4-1 Data-oriented versus function-oriented approach.

applications first but look at the overall data requirements of running the business. What are the business objects? What are the relationships among the objects? You store all relevant data about the business objects and then use the data to run the applications. This approach is different—it is data-oriented as opposed to being function-oriented.

Adopt a Data-Oriented Approach

Figure 4-1 illustrates this essential difference. At the very outset, we need to appreciate the significance of the difference in the development of the new data system. The success of database development rests on the adoption of a data-oriented approach.

Establish a Framework for Development

Because of the tremendous importance of the database system in an organization, you must create and work with a structured framework for its development. Figure 4-2 shows a framework for database development. You must adapt and use such a framework.

Begin Development Project with an Initiation Report

A carefully prepared project initiation report defines the scope of the database development, the methodology, the basic data content, and the overall project schedule. The report sets the direction and provides the development parameters.

The following are standard contents of an initiation report for a database development project:

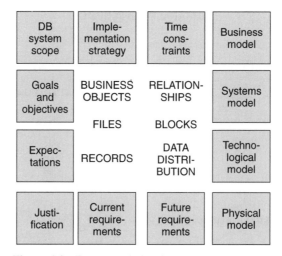

Figure 4-2 Framework for database development.

- Scope of the proposed database system
- Goals and objectives
- Values and expectations
- Justification
- Key business objects for the organization
- Core business and primary processes
- Supporting data elements
- Implementation strategy
- Tentative schedule
- Project authorization

Design and Development

How does a manufacturing company produce a product? The company initiates the process, performs the design, and gets the blueprints ready; then it develops and transforms the design into a finished product. Although it appears simplistic, design and development make up the processes for the manufacture of a product. This metaphor may be extended to the establishment of a database system. After the initiation phase, design of the database system takes place; then the design forms the basis for the development of the system. Figure 4-3 provides an overview of database design and development.

To design the database system, you have to gather the information requirements to support the various processes that make the core business of the organization happen. What are the requirements? What should the data residing in the organization's database be about? Remember that this is a data-oriented approach and the primary focus is on the data requirements. Ascertain the business entities or things of interest to the organization. Is your organization a banking institution? If so, some of its business entities are customer, checking account, savings account, and

| Requirements | Analysis and Design | Storage allocations | Application testing | Production |

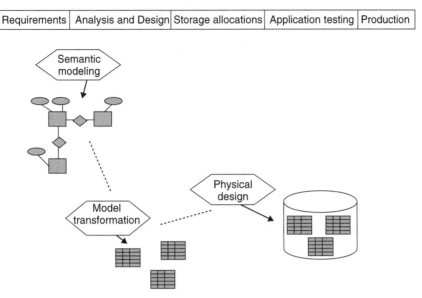

Figure 4-3 Database design and development.

loan account. Is your organization a medical center? Then a few of its entities are patient, physician, diagnosis, and treatment procedures. Whatever the nature of your organization's core business, you list the business entities and determine the information desired about each of these entities. In the case of the banking institution, a customer is related to one or more checking accounts. While considering the business entities, you note such relationships between sets of entities. These relationships must be ascertained to understand how information will be retrieved from the database system and used.

Let us say that you have determined the entities and the relationships. What do you do with them? How do you represent them in the database, and how do you store information about them? How do you design your database system? Design is broken down into two phases based on what actually happens in the design process itself.

Logical Design. True, data is stored in the database as files and records. But what about the structure of the data? What are the pieces of data within each structure? How do the various elements of the structure relate to one another? What are the connections? In the first design phase, you formulate these data structures, their arrangement, and their relationships. You come up with the conceptual view of the database. You use boxes and lines to represent this conceptual view as a logical design diagram. This design is not at the level of how data is stored as files, records, and fields. It is at a higher level that can be understood easily by the users—a level that can be used as a means for communication among the database practitioners and between the database practitioners and the user groups.

Physical Design. Once the logical design is firmed up, it has to be transformed into the design of the physical files and records because that is how data can be in physical storage. Each component of the logical design is mapped into one or more physical design components. Physical design deals with data storage, data retrieval, data updates, and methods for improving data access performance. Where you want to keep the data, how you intend to lay out the data on the storage media, how you establish the relationships at the storage level—these make up the components of the physical design.

Development and Implementation

When the logical design and physical design phases are completed, you are ready to develop and implement the database. The database administrator has the responsibility of completing the development and implementing the database. He or she defines the data structures, relationships, business rule constraints, storage areas, and performance improvement techniques in the data dictionary.

The database is then populated with data. If the transition in an organization is from a file-oriented system to a database system, then data from the previous files are extracted and converted. Special database utility programs and specially written conversion programs are used to load data in the new database.

Steps and Tasks

The life cycle approach comprises systematic and well-defined steps or phases to complete the design and development of a database system. Each step comprises specific major activities; each activity contains individual tasks. Although the project progresses from step to step, it is not necessary to complete all the activities of one step to proceed to the next. Parts of the steps may be performed in parallel. Sometimes it becomes necessary to repeat and refine some of the steps in an iterative manner.

Figure 4-4 shows the major steps of the database development life cycle (DDLC). Note the sequence of the steps from the bottom to the top. Note how the figure illustrates that the steps may be performed in parallel. While some aspects of requirements definition are still to be completed, the design step may commence. Also, observe the indication of the iterative nature of design and development. When you complete a portion of the design, you may want to go back to the requirements definition phase to review and refine a few aspects of the data requirements.

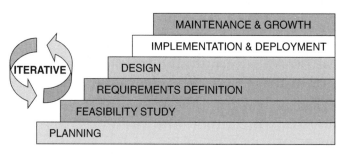

Figure 4-4   DDLC: major steps or phases.

In the rest of this chapter, we will be studying each step or phase of DDLC in sufficient detail. However, at this point, let us highlight the objective for each step.

Planning. Review the organization's long-term plan; plan specifically for the database system.

Feasibility study. Study the state of readiness; establish the costs and benefits.

Requirements definition. Define the business objects or entities; determine data requirements.

Design. Complete logical design; transform it into physical design.

Implementation and deployment. Populate database; train users; get database ready for applications.

Maintenance and growth. Perform ongoing maintenance; plan for growth of the database system.

Roles and Responsibilities

Who are the people responsible for database design and development? Who are the people doing the design and implementation phases? Who gathers the data requirements? What are their roles? What types of specialized skills are needed in the major design and development effort? To a limited extent, we have already looked at the roles of database practitioners and database users. Now, we will define the roles more precisely. First, a few points about the specialized skills that are necessary in a database project.

Specialized Skills For a company, the launching of a database system for the first time is a major undertaking. The transition is from a file-oriented data system to a completely different approach to storing, accessing, and using data. The company needs to modify its very attitude and practices about data usage. The people responsible for designing and developing the database system need a whole new set of skills for proceeding through the DDLC phases. Database design and development demands different techniques and poses greater challenges.

Here is an indication of specialized skills needed for the various phases:

Planning. Ability to interpret the organization's long-term plan and apply it to the database plan.

Feasibility study. Skills to assess the resource requirements, calculate costs, and determine tangible and intangible benefits.

Requirements definition. Analytical skills to identify business objects and related data, knowledge of interviewing techniques, and ability to collect and present requirements in a complete and correct way.

Design. Knowledge of data modeling; training in CASE tools, in-depth understanding of selected DBMS, and knowledge of system software, data storage methods, and media.

Implementation and deployment. Experience in data conversion and storage space allocation; knowledge of remote and on-site deployment techniques.

Maintenance and growth. Knowledge and experience in data security, data integrity, and data recovery.

User Roles The participation of users in the database design and development project must extend throughout the project. In each phase, users have important roles to fulfill. No database project can succeed without the intimate participation of users. Database practitioners and users must work in close cooperation in every phase. Although database practitioners take primary responsibilities in the design and implementation phases, users have definite tasks in these phases as well as the other phases.

Figure 4-5 indicates how and where users must be made to participate in a database project. Carefully note the roles and responsibilities in each phase. We must emphasize that database design and development is not the sole responsibility of

Planning & Feasibility Study

> Provide goals, objectives, expectations, information during preliminary survey; grant active top management support; interpret business plan; assess benefits.

Requirements Definition

> Actively participate in meetings for defining requirements; identify all application screens and reports used; provide documents; identity processes; define control reports; define data access patterns; discuss special information needs.

Design

> Review semantic data model; review conventional model tables and relationships; define business rules; provide standards and procedures.

Implementation

> Actively participate in user acceptance testing; test screens and reports; test queries; test report writer options; provide input for indexing options.

Deployment

> Verify audit trails and confirm initial data load; match deliverables against stated expectations; arrange and participate in user training; provide final acceptance.

Maintenance & Growth

> Provide input for enhancements; test and accept enhancements; present performance problems.

Figure 4-5 DDLC: user participation.

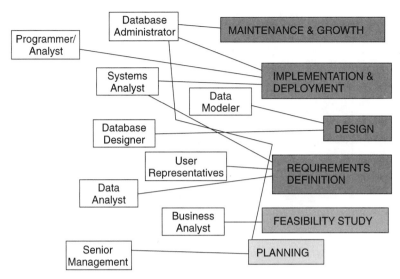

Figure 4-6   DDLC phases: participation of users and practitioners.

the information technology department of an organization. User participation, involvement, and acceptance of responsibility will result in a successful database system.

Roles of Database Practitioners   Now let us bring out the cast of characters. Who are the database practitioners and what are their roles? What are the phases in which they perform the tasks of design and development? These questions are best answered by means of two figures.

First, Figure 4-6 relates database practitioners and users to the phases where they are most active in fulfilling assigned tasks. Note how some practitioners participate in more than one phase.

Next, Figure 4-7 separates out design and development into data and process areas. In each of the two areas, practitioners and users assume specific roles. Note the types of activities in the two areas and some of the techniques adopted for performing the activities.

Management and Control

We have discussed information as a key resource for modern organizations. You have understood that the success and sometimes the very survival of many organizations rest on the information obtained from their database systems. Almost all of today's organizations depend on their database systems to run their day-to-day business. Because the database system is an indispensable resource, it has to be managed with utmost care and attention. Organizations must manage and control how their database systems provide storage of information, how they are accessed, and who may access data.

In the effort to manage and control this key resource, organizations face a few new challenges. These challenges are new and different because the management

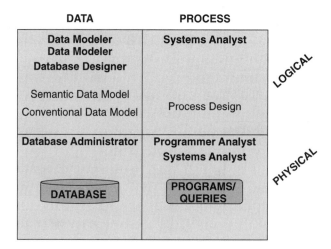

Figure 4-7 Data and process: design and development roles.

of earlier file-oriented systems was much simpler. Here are some of the major challenges:

- The database is more open to everyone in the organization than the separate files in the earlier data systems. Openness and information sharing necessitate better control of security. The database system must be made secure by preventing unauthorized access by insiders and outsiders. Only authorized users must be allowed to use relevant portions of the database system.
- In a database environment, many users may be attempting to access and update the same data elements simultaneously. This is likely to cause erroneous updates and compromised data integrity. Preserving data integrity in a database system is a big challenge.
- If the database system is crucial for an organization, then it should be available to users at all times when they need information. The database system must provide uninterrupted service with no unscheduled downtime. Whenever hardware or software malfunctions occur, the database must be restored to a stable state and become available for use quickly.
- In a dynamic business environment, changes happen all the time. The database system must be amenable to such changes. If business conditions warrant newer elements of data, the database must accommodate changes and additions to the data structures. If the number of database transactions increases and more users begin to access the database, the system must be able to scale up.

Who is responsible for management and control of the database system? Although user representatives and database practitioners share the responsibility to some extent, the database administrator bears the primary responsibility. In smaller organizations, one person may assume the role of database administration. In larger organizations, an entire group of professionals perform the database administration function. Here is a brief list of the management and control functions carried out by the administrators:

- Grant or revoke database access privileges to users.
- Arrange periodic backups of database content.
- Manage storage allocation.
- Install software upgrades.
- Collect data access statistics and monitor usage.
- Fine-tune the database as necessary.
- Oversee data integrity provisions.
- Recover database from hardware and software malfunctions.

Chapter 14 extensively discusses the administration functions in a database environment. You will learn a great deal more about the functions of the data administrator and the database administrator in that chapter.

PLANNING FOR THE DB SYSTEM

Before we begin a database project, we have to assess how the management and users understand data systems in the context of the organization. What do they think about the utility of data systems to support the core business and the business processes? If they are from a file-oriented environment, their views are likely to be narrow and limited. The planning process broadens their views about data systems and moves them forward to appreciate the benefits of information sharing. Planning involves senior management and therefore provides a means for them to express their support and sponsorship.

Planning sets the direction and scope for the database project. The project will be a new type of project for those organizations launching a database for the very first time. Even for those companies that are expanding their database systems or migrating from one commercial database system to another, the project may offer new challenges. The planning process identifies the challenges; it also brings out the opportunities afforded by database systems.

We can think of the planning process as containing two distinct subphases. In one subphase, you study and interpret the impact of the organization's long-term plan on the proposed database system. If the company is planning for expansion into three new territories within the next two years, what types of data must be included in the database? The other subphase of planning relates to the actual planning for the database system based on the current requirements. The two subphases are important to complete the planning because you must combine current and future requirements in the design.

The planning process, naturally, is the first phase or step in DDLC. Although some limited portion of the next phase may be started while planning is being completed, generally organizations tend to complete the planning phase before proceeding to the other phases. Planning sets the tone and direction of the entire project, and this is important for the conduct of the other phases. How long should planning last? It depends on the situation in each organization. If your organization is one for which a database project is completely new, then the people doing the planning must carefully review all relevant issues and take the time to complete the planning process. Nevertheless, as a general rule, the planning phase should not last longer than four to six months.

The planning phase ends with a clear report that can be used and referred to in later phases. This planning document serves as a guide and reference throughout the project. It articulates the management's view and understanding of a database system; it states the expectations; it communicates the opportunities. The planning document, as soon as it is completed, confirms the management's commitment to the database project.

Scope of Overall Planning

Planning a database system translates into planning for the current and future information requirements of the users in several organizational units performing different business functions and residing at various geographic locations. They need information about business objects that are relevant to the organization's goals and objectives. The organization's long-term business plan provides input for the planning phase. Again, the business plan is grounded in the company's core business. The blend of all these planning objects is the overall database plan for the project.

Figure 4-8 illustrates the overall planning process. Note how the organization's business plan provides input for the planning process. Observe the elements of the core business that go into the planning. Note how the business plan and the factors of the core business lead into the user requirements and how all of these are tied together in the database plan.

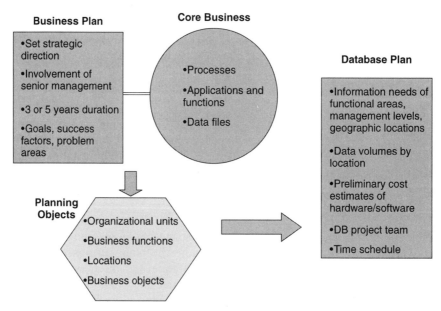

Figure 4-8   Overall planning.

Who Does the Planning?

The senior executives of an organization think through the future opportunities and challenges. Every year most organizations come up with a long-term plan for 3–5 years; some even prepare 10-year plans. The senior management takes the primary responsibility for producing the long-term plans. The CEO of the organization is intimately involved and usually directs the planning. Some institutions have separate planning departments to collect data for the planning process and coordinate the overall planning effort.

What has the long-term business plan to do with the database project? The proposed database for the organization is not meant to be static. Once implemented, the database system will have to grow and accommodate requirements relating to the foreseeable future. It should be able to conform to the direction and goals set forth in the long-term business plan. It must be able to anticipate the data requirements for the next three to five years.

We have already noted that one subphase of project planning deals with interpreting the organization's long-term plan and applying it to the database project. The other subphase is the consolidation of all requirements and preparation of the database plan. Generally, organizations carry out these two subphases by assigning responsibilities as noted below.

- Senior Managers of the IT Department review the long-term plan, estimate the data that would be required to support the long-term goals and objectives, and highlight the business areas that would need the support from the proposed database system. The CIO and CTO are likely to be part of the group of the organization's senior executives who created the long-term plan. Therefore, these executives contribute greatly in the interpretation of the long-term plan for the purpose of relating it to the database project.
- Usually, companies form a special team within IT to prepare the database plan. This team consists of the heads of data administration, database administration, database design, and application development. Some others with specialized skills in relevant hardware and software may also be included in the planning team.

Impact of the Business Plan

We have emphasized the significance of applying the long-term business plan to the database project. How exactly does the business plan impact the proposed database system? First of all, what do long-term business plans contain? We will briefly review the normal contents of a long-term business plan and then see how each element in the plan can affect the planning for the database.

Among other components, here are the major contents of a long-term business plan:

- Scope and duration of the plan
- General goals
- Specific objectives

- Special opportunities
- Challenges, internal and external
- People responsible for executing parts of the plan

Now let us consider each of these major components and see how it applies to planning the database project.

Scope and duration. These set the boundaries in terms of geographic and logical extents as well as in terms of time. You will know who will need data in the future, what types of data, and when.

General goals. These are broad statements of what the organization wishes to do in the future. For example, an organization may intend to strengthen certain product lines and drop a few lines in the future. Or an organization may express a general theme of cost cuts. It may emphasize an overall improvement in product shipments. It may underscore progress in customer service. General goals do not come with definable targets. What can we do about general goals in the database systems? Use general goals to identify areas of special emphasis and ensure that the database covers these areas. If improvement of customer service is emphasized as a general goal, make sure that the database would contain data elements to support this business function.

Specific objectives. These take the form of directives with set targets. For example, a specific objective of an organization may be increasing the market share by 5 percent within three years or a 6 percent increase in overall sales within five years. Specific objectives tend to be aggressive and definite. Defined action items also accompany specific objectives. For example, the objective of increased market share may be accomplished through expansions in the western and central regions. Look for specific objectives in the organization's long-term business plan. These are not like general goals. Those formulating the database plan must take the specific objectives seriously and ensure that the proposed database system supports these specific objectives completely. Pay special attention to the action items. If an expansion in the market in the central region is set forth as an action item, then plan to have the database include additional stores and offices in that region.

Special opportunities. The long-term business plan may detect certain trends and spot opportunities that are likely to result from these trends. For example, if your organization is a financial institution, the lowering of interest rates is expected to increase the number of loans that can be offered. Assess the expression of these opportunities in the business plan and then plan to accommodate the data requirements in the database system. If the number of loans is expected to increase, plan to include all data elements that will make loan processing easier and faster.

Challenges. The proposed database system can help the organization in overcoming some of the challenges the organization faces or is likely to confront in the near future. For a pharmaceutical company, conforming to the requirements of the Food and Drug Administration (FDA) and providing mountains of data for product approvals may pose a great challenge. Your proposed database system can be robust and flexible enough to store, sort out, and provide data for FDA approvals.

People. These are the people in the organization responsible for carrying out the directives in the long-term business plan. When you interpret the business plan, you might need additional information as to the proposed data requirements. You then go to the people who are charged with the execution of parts of the business plan.

The Database Plan

The database plan covers what must be done in the remaining phases of DDLC. It sets the tone for the project; spells out the key activities necessary for the success of the project, and provides a planning document to guide the rest of the project. Study the following highlights of the activities for preparing the database plan and for suggestions on its content.

- Classify your users by responsibility levels, business functions, and geographic regions. Include the overall, very general nature of the data requirements for each user group.
- Adopting a data-oriented approach, consider the business objects and intrinsic data about them. These are the data that will be stored in the proposed database system.
- Make preliminary estimates of data volumes. These will help you determine storage capacities and access paths.
- On the basis of broad assumptions, prepare very general estimates of hardware and system software requirements.
- Take input about future data requirements from the long-term business plan.
- Gather data requirements on current functions, applications, and files.

The issuance of a database plan report marks the conclusion of the planning phase. This planning document gathers the discussions and decisions of the phase; it sets the tone and momentum for the remaining phases. Here is a typical outline for a database plan report:

- Introduction
- Scope
- Specific Objectives
- Key Issues and Assumptions
- Expectations
- Overview of Data Requirements
- General Implementation Strategy
- Tentative Schedule

Critical Planning Issues

While preparing the database plan, the staff preparing the plan must be continuously watchful for special challenges and critical issues. Database design and development is not a common or easy project. Several new challenges will arise, and sufficient awareness and planning for the contingencies are necessary. Let us briefly go over a few of the major issues.

Data Ownership   If your organization is making the transition from a file-oriented data system to a database system, then you will be faced with resolution of data ownership conflicts. Even when a database project consists of conversion from one type of database system to another, some data ownership conflicts remain. Who owns the data in the database? Which user groups are responsible? You know that the database is for information sharing. No one group has exclusive ownership. Then who is responsible for data quality? For example, many user groups would be adding and updating customer data. Which user group owns customer data? Your planners must recognize potential data ownership conflicts and review general principles applicable to your organization.

Specialized Skills   As already mentioned, implementation and maintenance of database systems require specialized skills. You need people trained in data administration, database administration, data modeling, database design, database management systems, and programming in a database environment. The database plan must consider issues relating to recruitment and training of personnel throughout the entire DDLC.

Project Vulnerability   For most organizations, when they undertake a database project they are breaking into new ground. They have not faced many of the issues and challenges posed by a database project. Possibilities exist for failures, delays, and cost overruns in such a novel project. Planners ought to recognize the possibilities for failures and suggest preventive measures and remedial action. For example, if project failure is possible because of the spread of user groups over many locations, planning must specifically address how to bring about cooperation and collaboration.

New Overhead Costs   Be prepared for additional overhead costs. Some of these costs may be for additional hardware infrastructure; some may be for enhancing the operating system software; a large chunk of additional overhead costs may be for people with new specialized skills. Plan for such new overhead costs.

Issues for Large Projects   Large projects pose particular challenges. A large database project covers numerous user groups, extremely big data volumes, a huge number of anticipated database transactions, and data about several business objects. Many database professionals and user representatives participate in a large project. When the size and scope of a project is huge, communication among the designers, developers, administrators, and user representatives may be a source of potential problems. Coordination and control could be difficult. Staff retention for the entire duration of the project is another area for concern. Recruitment and retraining may delay the project. Planners ought to be aware of the special problems and challenges related to large projects and indicate methods to address and contain the problems. They may also suggest how the project may be divided into manageable parts in each phase of DDLC.

FEASIBILITY STUDY

The database project has been initiated, the database plan has been completed, and the plan report has been issued. Are you then ready to jump into the requirements and design phases? Should you simply proceed into each phase? Are there any more essential activities before going ahead full steam?

The project initiation denotes the formal beginning of the project—an announcement of the intention for a database system. The planning phase defines the scope of such a database system and lays down the planning issues. However, your organization does not yet know how ready it is for a database system.

Before proceeding with the project, you need to assess this readiness. No organization is completely ready for a new database system—the hardware and software platform may need revisions and enhancements, sometimes very extensive ones. People would need to be trained in specialized skills. Therefore, between the planning phase and the other design and development phases, there must be definitive activities to assess readiness. This set of intervening activities makes up the feasibility study phase of DDLC.

Purpose and Extent

What happens during the feasibility phase of a database project? Usually, business analysts with assistance from database administrators conduct the feasibility study phase. Sometimes, the responsibility for the phase is assigned to the project manager who runs the database project with a few IT professionals assisting him or her. As the name of the phase indicates, this is a study phase. They look at the organization as a whole, the IT resources, and user readiness to assess what more has to be done before a database system could be implemented in the organization. This phase is critical because getting immersed in a database project without proper readiness assessment may result in project failures. Some organizations may even decide to put off implementing a database system until they are ready for it.

We will now walk through the objectives, activities, and crucial issues of the feasibility study phase.

Objectives Assessment of readiness for a database system implies taking inventory of the resources already available in the organization. The business analysts must evaluate each resource and determine whether it is adequate for the proposed database system. If the resource is lacking in functions and features, then the analyst must estimate what it will take to enhance the resource. For example, if the server hardware needs upgrades, the types of upgrades must be estimated and specified.

When an organization implements a database system, many new types of resources become necessary. The feasibility study phase reviews the available resources and lists the new types of resources the organization will have to procure.

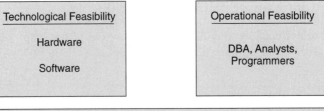

Figure 4-9 Feasibility study phase: three areas.

Broadly, the objectives of this phase include specifications of the enhancements to the already available resources and recommendations on the purchase of additional resources. Also, the study phase lists the action items for accomplishing the recommendations to improve the readiness of the organization.

Three Types of Feasibility We may think of the feasibility study phase as studies in three areas—technological, operational, and economic. This helps break down the activities of the phase into convenient and natural sets. To complete the activities in each area, business analysts rely on the help of different groups of database practitioners and user representatives.

Figure 4-9 presents the three areas for feasibility study. Note the components that analysts will have to study in each area. Analysts use assistance from the information technology department for the study of technological feasibility and operational feasibility. Analysts work with IT personnel and user representatives for the study of economic feasibility. Outside agencies also provide information to complete the feasibility study phase.

Action Items Out of the feasibility phase comes a comprehensive list of action items. Business analysts may adopt the division of action items to correspond to the study in the three areas—technological, operational, and economic. Whatever format the list may take, it is important to include all the needed enhancements to existing resources and all the additional resources to be obtained.

Timing The listing of action items must be accompanied by recommendations on when each action item must be completed. For example, if one of the action items recommends adding two data modelers to the team, this action will be useless unless the data modelers are recruited or trained before the design phase commences. Indication of the timing for each action is absolutely essential.

Technological Infrastructure

Business analysts first look at the technological infrastructure to assess its adequacy for the proposed database system. Technological infrastructure includes both hardware and systems software. This is the platform on which the database system will operate. Business analysts size up the proposed data volumes and the estimated number of transactions to study whether the available infrastructure can support the database system. The technological feasibility study involves taking an inventory of existing hardware and systems software; the study usually results in recommendations for additional hardware and upgrades of the systems software.

Hardware   Consider the hardware environment for the proposed database system. The database will usually reside on a database server machine. Database management system (DBMS) software will run on the server machine. How big and powerful the server machine has to be depends on the size and use of the database. If the data content were large, you would need ample storage and a choice of better media for storing the data. If rapid data access were critical, you would need faster storage media. In a database environment where information is shared, keeping the database available at all times becomes crucial. Therefore, storing data in fault-tolerant storage media is desirable. Most database systems use RAID (redundant array of inexpensive disks) storage technology. This technology provides duplicate versions to be stored with mirroring techniques. We will focus more on this technology later, but for now just note that many aspects and options must be considered for database storage.

What about the applications for the users to draw on the wealth of data stored in the proposed database? Applications in a database environment tend to be more sophisticated than those in a file-oriented environment. Database applications multiply quickly. Because these applications are more standardized and uniform, their spread to many user groups becomes easier. Where should the applications run? On the client machines? If the proposed applications in your organization are expected to be more involved, large, and widespread, the business analysts doing the feasibility study may consider running the applications in the middle tier on separate application servers. This option will also make deployment of the applications easier.

Now turn your attention to client machines. How many additional client machines does your organization need? What about the speed and capacity of each machine? The business analysts need to take an inventory of the client machines in each user department and assess the number and types of additional machines required.

Study of the hardware configuration also includes review of the communication network links. This is very important if the user groups are spread out in multiple geographic regions domestically or internationally. Will the network configuration be adequate to deliver data from the proposed database? What about the public carriers? What about the sufficiency of the bandwidth? Will the Internet be a delivery medium in your database environment? These are some of the major questions the business analysts must consider.

Systems Software   Database management system software (DBMS) interacts with the operating system for accessing data from the database. Every query or application data request gets executed by the DBMS, which in turn depends on the operating system for input and output operations. The operating system must be robust enough and compatible with standard commercial database management systems. In a database environment, security, reliability, and scalability are important considerations in the choice of operating systems. The business analysts, with the help of other database practitioners, ascertain the necessary capabilities of the required operating systems. The analysts make recommendations for version upgrades to the existing operating system or for a new and more powerful system.

The business analysts must also look closely at the existing network operating system. Now with a database system, network traffic patterns and data transfer volumes are likely to change drastically. This is especially true in a distributed database environment. Will the current network operating system be up to the task in the proposed environment? Can it be upgraded or augmented with third-party tools? Or should the current network operating system be replaced with a better and more suitable system?

Skills Review

Review of skills and listing of recommendations form the key activities of the operational feasibility study. Business analysts must proceed systematically to list the necessary skills demanded by the database project. Next, they must take an inventory of the skills currently available in the organization. On the basis of the information gathered in these tasks, the business analysts make recommendations for actions to make up the deficiencies.

Necessary Skills   The first part of the operational feasibility study entails making a list of all the skills necessary for the successful completion of the project. The business analysts must seek the help of others, including the project manager and the database administrator, to determine the types of skills needed for each phase of DDLC. If the database administrator function is not fully staffed yet, this fact goes on the list first. Each phase needs different kinds of special skills. You need people with different types of experience and training in the various phases. At this point, do not make a list of the types of persons needed but only the types of skills needed. For example, in the design phase, you would need data modeling skills. In the requirements definition phase, you would need interviewing skills.

After determining the types of needed skills, the business analysts can translate and relate these skills to the qualifications of the types of people needed for the project. Sometimes, you may be able to find people with multiple skills who can be assigned to more than one type of activity. A person well versed in logical database design may also be able to lay out the physical files and records.

People Inventory   What is the availability of people for the database project in your organization? Do you have analysts who are experts in interviewing techniques? Are there data modelers? Do you already have database administrators? Do you have programmers experienced in writing data conversion programs? The business analysts have the task of noting the skills and experience of each person already assigned to the project. This must be done in sufficient detail so that the right person may be given the right assignment.

If some people possess more than one skill that can be used in the project, this can be effective in a project of reasonable size. In large projects, allocation of different assignments to the same person may not be practical.

Matching Up   Once the business analysts have a list of the skills necessary for the project and an inventory of the available personnel, the next task is one of matching up the skills with the people. If the project manager is not directly involved in the feasibility study, this task calls for his or her participation. The project manager and the business analysts determine how the skills and the people match up best and estimate the deficiencies.

Wherever people are not present to handle specific skills, suitable people must be found for the project. Here are the three common options for filling the deficiencies:

Training insiders. First look at the prospects inside the organization. Some qualified candidates within IT or within the rest of the organization would welcome a transfer to the database project. If these candidates can be tested for their aptitude, they could be trained before being assigned to the project. Some programmers without any database experience can be trained easily and quickly. If the project schedule is flexible enough, selecting and training loyal insiders can rank as the best and easiest option.

Recruiting outsiders. What do you do if there are not enough qualified people inside the organization who can be trained for the database project? Then, of course, you have to recruit from outside. If this is a viable option for your organization, sufficient lead time for recruitment must be built into the project schedule.

Hiring consultants. Consultants can always fill the gap wherever suitable talent is not available from within or outside the organization to be included as employees on the project. Nevertheless, consultant assignments must be very specific in terms of tasks and time. While the particular tasks are carried out, some employees may be trained for those tasks. The assignments of the consultants terminate as soon as the specific tasks are done.

Estimation of Costs

While conducting the technological feasibility study, the business analysts estimate the additional hardware and software requirements. The operational feasibility study produces a list of what is needed for training, recruiting, and assigning people to the various phases of the object. In effect, these two activities in the feasibility study phase result in a list of technical and people resources. How much is it going to cost to get these resources? How long in the project are these resources likely to be used? Which of the costs are one-time costs, and which of these are ongoing?

The first part of the economic feasibility study determines the major costs of the project. Every database project has one-time costs incurred before the implementation of the database system. Costs for some items such as personnel continue for ongoing maintenance of the system even after implementation. It is easier to estimate the costs by separating the costs into one-time and ongoing costs. By so dividing up the costs, you are not likely to omit any costs. Some items like database software have an initial one-time cost to purchase the item and then ongoing cost to maintain the item after implementation.

One-Time Costs Let us make a list of the common one-time costs. Although most of the items on the list are standard for every database system, the project in your organization may include a few new items. Review the list and adapt it to suit your database system.

Hardware. Include all necessary upgraded servers—additional memory, storage, and processor power. Add enhancements to client machines. Estimate additional communication equipment and cabling. Use quotations from vendors to prepare cost estimates.

Systems Software. Most of the time, later versions of existing operating systems will be able to handle the requirements of a database system. Estimate version upgrade. If your organization needs to go to another more robust operating system, then systems software costs could be substantial. Also, include the costs of any specialized utility tools such as backup programs or file reorganization software.

Database Software. This is perhaps the largest portion of one-time costs, almost in the same range as costs for major enhancements to hardware. Estimate costs for database software by obtaining quotations from a few vendors of leading DBMSs. Also, include cost of any necessary CASE tools in this category.

Communications Software. A database system in a distributed environment presupposes a strong communications system. If this is the case for your organization, allocate costs for upgrades to the existing network operating system or even for a more sophisticated replacement that can control potential increase in communication traffic.

Training. Training costs relate to training any IT personnel being transferred to the database project and to training other people from other departments suitable for the project. It would cost more to train people from other departments, but these training costs would offset recruitment costs if people would otherwise have to be recruited from outside.

Recruitment. Include search and recruitment fees for getting qualified people for the database project. People with specialized skills in database techniques and concepts attract larger recruitment fees.

Studies. In addition to the initial feasibility study, other studies become necessary in a database project. If your system needs elaborate data modeling because of its enormous size, then you would need studies to assess and purchase a good CASE tool. Another study may be warranted to select a new network operating system. In all projects, a special study is needed for examining the options and selecting the proper DBMS.

Materials and Supplies. Do not overlook costs for supplies and materials. Make a provision for these costs in your estimation.

Ongoing Costs Once a specific item is purchased, that item attracts ongoing costs. Hardware will have to be maintained; software upgrades will be essential; personnel costs continue. Ongoing costs begin during the various phases of the project itself. When the project is completed and the database system is deployed, many of the costs continue. Personnel costs to administer and manage the database system continue beyond the implementation phase.

Estimate ongoing costs for the following items:

- Hardware maintenance
- Software upgrades
- People
- Support system
- Training
- Materials and supplies

Assessment of Benefits

Not all of the benefits of a database system are derived directly. In other words, it is hard to estimate many of the intangible benefits although such benefits empower the users and produce great positive impact on the business. Unlike the estimation of costs, assessment of benefits poses difficulties. The general method consists of coming up with estimated numbers for tangible benefits and explicitly expressing every intangible benefit in the feasibility study report.

A database system results in cost savings in several areas. Make a list of the cost savings. Compare your current data environment with the proposed environment and assess all possible cost savings. How will the proposed database system make collaboration among the various departments easier? What synergies will result from information sharing? How will the proposed system improve customer service? How easy will it be to get all information from one data source? Consider such questions to produce a list of intangible but significant benefits.

Intangible Benefits

Data consistency. A database system contains consistent data values. For a particular data item, the same data value exists irrespective of who retrieves the data. Your organization will present consistent data values in the documents sent to customers and business partners.

Data integrity. It is possible for a database system to enforce edits and checks for data entered into the database. The database system expects to store more reliable and correct data.

Data availability. Data backups and recovery procedures are more standardized in a database environment.

Stricter controls. You can control data access better in a database system. Database management systems provide better methods for granting and revoking access privileges.

System flexibility. Changes to business conditions occur rapidly and unexpectedly. If your organization can react to changes quickly and take appropriate action, it will have a competitive edge. A database system provides flexibility for adapting to changing business conditions.

Information sharing. A database system promotes information sharing and results in closer collaboration among users.

Better standards. In a database system, it is easier to establish standards on data names, edit rules, data types, field lengths, data access patterns, and so on.

Timely information. A database system provides timely and up-to-date information on business objects.

Improved productivity. Because of standardization and ease of use, you will notice improved productivity in the way users are able to access and use data from a database. Many data operations are provided through query and reporting tools that are part of the database management system. This eliminates the need to write programs for these purposes. Programmer productivity increases in a database environment. Sometimes it is possible to estimate cost savings relating to improved programmer productivity.

Better management decisions. Integrated and accurate data in one place in the organization's database, allowing easier and faster data access, enable better management decisions. Managers and supervisors can obtain timely reports of data needed for managing and controlling their resources.

Cost Savings

Minimal data duplication. As you know, hardly any duplication of data exists in a database management system in comparison with file-oriented data systems, where you observe a proliferation of duplicate data. Elimination of data duplication means less overall storage space for storing an organization's data content. Estimate the cost savings from using less storage space.

Fewer error corrections. Minimal data duplication also results in less effort to correct errors or updates to data. If the same data, say a customer's name and address, are duplicated across many applications, any changes to the name and address must be applied in several places. However, in a database system, the name and address of a single customer is stored only once; therefore, any corrections to this name and address need to be made only once in only one place. Try to come up with a reasonable estimate on the possible savings due to reduction in error corrections.

Less programming. Application programs do not require elaborate coding for data retrieval and update operations; the database management system will interpret simple data access coding and complete the operations. Moreover, separate programs are not needed for writing most queries and reports. Query tools and report writers will do the job.

Reduced training costs. As we have seen above, applications can be standardized in a database environment. So it becomes easier to train users across applications. This brings about a general reduction in training costs.

Weighing the Options

Before the business analysts reach the end of the technological and operational feasibility study activities, they collect enough material to list and evaluate the options. Consider physical hardware, especially the database server machines. Should you upgrade the existing servers, or switch to a new brand, more powerful but also more expensive? Weigh the available options at each decision point and make recommendations.

The feasibility study phase concludes with the publication of a comprehensive report. The study phase not only answers whether the organization is ready for a database system at all but also makes an assessment of the organization's preparedness. Make suggestions on the available options. Show the costs and benefits for each option.

Here is a list of standard contents for a feasibility report:

- Introduction and scope
- How costs and benefits are estimated
- Assumptions derived from planning
- Hardware
  - Current status
  - Proposed enhancements
- System Software
  - Current status
  - Proposed upgrade
- Database Management System
  - Major features needed
  - Options and vendors
  - Recommendation
- Costs
  - One-time
  - Ongoing
- Benefits
  - Intangible
  - Cost savings

- Final Recommendations
  - List of options
  - Suggested recommendations

REQUIREMENTS DEFINITION

Proper definition of information requirements drives the design and deployment of the database system. The earlier planning phase sets the tone and direction for the project. The feasibility study phase provides the justification and examines the options for the project. But it is the requirements definition phase that lays the foundation for the system. The importance of requirements definition as a driving force cannot be overemphasized. Every organization launching a database system must pay special attention to how the requirements definition phase is conducted.

In this phase you observe the overall business, you understand the core business, you examine the primary processes, you find out who needs what data to run which processes, and you determine the complete information requirements. You study the data volumes and data access requirements to estimate storage space and the exact type and features of the database software. Note the following summary list of major tasks during the requirements definition phase:

- Study overall business operations.
- Observe business processes.
- Understand business needs.
- Interview users.
- Determine information requirements.
- Identify data to be collected and stored.
- Establish data access patterns.
- Estimate data volumes.
- Document the information requirements.

Who is involved in requirements definition? Practically, everyone on the project may have some input, but usually one or more data analysts, ably supported by a team of systems analysts, initiate and control this phase. In every task, the user representatives must participate actively. Technical know-how will have to come from the database administrator.

Data analysts and systems analysts working on requirements must have had training and experience in gathering requirements and documenting requirements according to accepted standards. They have to work closely with user groups and understand their information needs; this requires training in interviewing and documenting techniques. They must know how to work with users to collect the information needs and have the gathered type of information requirements confirmed by the users. Representatives for users at different responsibility levels, in various functional units, and at several geographic locations—all must make the phase successful. These analysts must also have access to existing systems and documents.

Although information requirements are derived by observing business functions and processes, the approach must be clearly data-oriented. In other words, the emphasis is not on how the functions and processes are carried out but on what data are required for performing the business functions and processes. This is a new mind-set for analysts who had previously worked on designing and deploying applications. In applications, you are designing the "how" of the processes. But in a database system, you are designing the "what" of the data requirements. So keep requirements definition for a database system data-oriented. Come up with the elements of data required for each process and for each function.

At the end of the phase, the analysts pull all the data requirements together and consolidate them. This aggregation step eliminates any duplicate statements of requirements and aggregates all data required for individual business objects. A requirements definition document is produced to conclude the phase.

Requirements Gathering Methods

It may appear that the requirements definition phase is a formidable effort because of its extreme importance. Many project teams think of the project as mainly consisting of design and implementation. However, requirements drive these later phases, and without properly defined requirements the phases that follow cannot be successful. If requirements definition is so significant, are there standard methods that can be applied universally?

Undoubtedly, each organization will have its own special requirements and these special requirements may warrant innovative techniques. Nevertheless, most requirements gathering methods follow a set pattern. You now know the purpose of this phase and what is expected at the end of the phase. But how do you reach the desired end and document the information requirements?

A summary list of the major standard methods follows. In the subsequent subsections, we will elaborate on a few of the important ones.

Interviews. This is a common technique. Personal interviews cannot be replaced by other methods. Still, one-on-one interviews produce the best results.

Group sessions. When it is convenient and desirable to meet a user group as a whole, group sessions work well. Here you save time by not interviewing the people in the group one by one.

Observation of processes. The combination of all processes within an organization makes up the entire business. So if you review each process beginning to end, you will be able to get a handle on what information is needed at the several points along the way.

Review of applications. The current computer applications are used to run the business now. These applications store, retrieve, and update data. The storage, retrieval, and update techniques may not be satisfactory. That is one of the main reasons for moving to a database system. However, much can be learned from the data elements used by the existing applications.

Study of documents. Existing documents give ample indications as to the type and content of the data needed for the organization to run the business. Planning and policy documents indicate long-term data needed for achieving the company's business goals. Reports printed from current applications form a valuable source for requirements gathering. Layouts of the current files are good starting points to determine the information requirements. Procedure documents for individual processes indicate what data are required to perform the processes.

Conducting User Interviews

The first question is, Whom do you interview? Who are the users of the proposed database system? Broadly, we may classify the users as follows:

> Senior executives and division heads
> Departmental managers
> Operational staff
> Business analysts
> IT staff maintaining computer files

Senior executives will give you a sense of the direction and scope for the database system. You can derive information requirements for future expansions and changes in business strategies. Departmental managers can provide information about the type of control and exception reports they would need and the data content of those reports. Interviews with operational staff will produce the bulk of what you need in this phase. That is where most of the emphasis must be placed. Business analysts can tell you the types of data they use for conducting studies and producing results for the executives. A lot of data requirements will be available from IT people such as systems analysts, programmers, and operations staff who maintain the current applications and their computer master files and transaction files.

When you gather data requirements from each group, separate the requirements by business objects. The requirements you collect will comprise of the following:

- Data elements
- How and who uses the data elements
- When and where the data elements are used
- Business rules governing the data elements
- Data volumes

You may consider the interview process as consisting of the following steps:

- Decide on the list of persons to be interviewed.
- Prepare for interviews.
- Conduct interviews using appropriate techniques.
- Document interview findings.
- Follow up and confirm interview write-ups.

You will have to go to various user groups and IT personnel to gather information requirements. Analysts adopt two basic techniques for meeting with people and gathering requirements, (1) interview, one-on-one or in small groups, and (2) joint application development (JAD) sessions. Note the following thoughts on individual interviews and group sessions. We will consider JAD sessions in a separate subsection.

Interviews

- Up to two or three persons at a time
- Easy to schedule
- Good approach when details are many and intricate
- Some users prefer one-on-one interviews
- Need adequate preparation to be effective
- Always require preinterview research
- Users also must be encouraged to prepare for the interview

Group Sessions

- Groups of 20 or fewer persons at a time
- Useful only after obtaining a baseline understanding of requirements
- Not good for initial data gathering
- Effective for confirming requirements
- Sessions need to be well organized

Interview Techniques   Interview sessions, when properly conducted, take up a lot of the project time. Therefore, interviews must be planned, organized, and managed well. Before the analysts begin the interview process, the project team must make sure that the following major tasks are completed:

- Provide further training in interviewing techniques to the selected analysts.
- Assign specific roles to the members of the interviewing team (lead interviewer, scribe, and so on).
- List the persons to be interviewed.
- Prepare a broad schedule of interviews.
- Note the expectations from each set of interviews.
- Complete preinterview research.
- Prepare interview questionnaires.
- Prepare users for interviews.
- Conduct a brief kick-off meeting of all users to be interviewed.

To a large extent, the effectiveness of the interviews rests on the preinterview research. This task provides you with the necessary background information on which the requirements definition may be built. Here is a list of a few topics for preinterview research before interviewing a specific business unit:

- History and organization of the business unit
- Number of employees and their roles and responsibilities

- Locations of the users
- Preliminary purpose of the business unit in the organization
- Contribution of the business unit to the overall core business
- Secondary purpose of the business unit
- Relationship of the business unit to other business units

Here are some tips on the types of questions for the interviews:

Major business processes. What are the business processes for which your unit is completely responsible (example: completely responsible for the process of preparing invoices to customers)? What are the business processes that your unit is not completely responsible for but participates in with other business units? Briefly describe each process your unit is involved in.

Current information sources. Do your processes generate all the information needed by your unit? If not, what are the sources of information you need for your business processes? Which reports do you use for running your business?

Timeliness of information. Do your processes require real-time data? What are they? Which are the on-line data types? Which types of data used are a day old, a week old, or a month old? Does your unit need historical data? If so, for what purposes?

Major computer applications. What are the computer applications used in your unit? Which are the important reports? Which are the input screens? What are the types of data input by your unit? Which display screens are important to your unit?

Data volumes. How much of the data your unit generates is stored in the computer files? Give volume estimates. How much of the data your unit uses, but does not generate, is stored? Give volume estimates.

Document each interview with a write-up adopting the following general outline:

1. Profile of the person or persons interviewed
2. Background and objectives
3. How the unit is managed and controlled
4. Business processes
5. Business objects
6. Data requirements related to each business object
7. Current computer screens used
8. Current computer reports used
9. How success of the business unit is measured

JAD Methodology   If you are able to collect a lot of baseline information up front from documents, group sessions may be a good substitute for individual interviews. In this method, you are able to get a number of interested users meet together in groups. On the whole, this method could result in fewer group sessions than individual interview sessions. The overall time for requirements gathering may prove to be less and therefore the project may be shortened. Also, group sessions may be more effective if the users are dispersed in remote locations.

Joint application development (JAD) techniques were successfully used to gather requirements for application projects in the 1980s. Users of computer systems had grown to be more computer savvy, and their direct participation in the development of applications proved to be useful.

As the name implies, JAD is a joint process with all concerned groups getting together for a well-defined purpose. It is a methodology for developing computer applications jointly by users and IT professionals in a well-structured manner. JAD centers on discussion workshops lasting a certain number of days under the direction of a facilitator.

JAD consists of a five-step approach:

Project Definition

Complete high-level interviews.

Conduct management interviews.

Prepare management definition guide.

Research

Become familiarized with the business units and systems.

Document user information requirements.

Document business processes.

Gather preliminary information.

Prepare agenda for the sessions.

Preparation

Create working document from previous phase.

Train scribes.

Prepare visual aids.

Conduct presession meetings.

Set up venue for sessions.

Prepare checklist for objectives.

JAD Sessions

Open with review of agenda and purpose.

Review assumptions.

Review current applications.

Review data requirements.

Discuss timeliness of required information.

Examine data volumes.

Resolve all open issues.

Close sessions with lists of action items.

Final Document

Convert the working document.

Map the gathered information.

List all current data sources.

Identify all future data requirements.

Assemble and edit the document.

Conduct review sessions.

Get final concurrence from users.

Establish procedure to change requirements.

The success of a project using the JAD approach depends on the composition of the JAD team. The size and mix of the team will vary based on the scope and extent of the proposed database system. The typical composition, however, must have certain roles present on the JAD team. For each of the following roles, usually one or more persons are assigned.

Executive Sponsor   Person controlling the funding, providing the direction, and empowering the team members

Facilitator   Person guiding the team throughout the JAD process—usually the project manager or lead analyst

Scribe   Person designated to record all decisions

Full-Time Participants   Everyone involved in making decisions about the database system

On-Call Participants   Persons affected by the project, but only in specific areas

Observers   Persons who would like to sit in on specific sessions without participating in the decision making

Observation of Processes

Almost all of the data requirements will be collected through one-on-one interviews or through group sessions. This step of observing the business processes serves two purposes. First, this step enables you confirm the data requirements gathered through interviews. Second, the step provides an opportunity for you to collect any requirements that were missed during the interviews.

You know that every business process within the organization generates data that must be stored for use by the same process itself or by other processes. Furthermore, most processes make use of data generated by other processes. What exactly do these two concepts mean—generating data and making use of data by a process?

Consider the process of settling an automobile claim by an insurance company. This is a primary process for the claims processing business unit of the company. The process begins with the receipt of an automobile claim from one of the policyholders. The person or persons in the company responsible for processing the claim get some data from outside and enter them into the computer system. These are the data generated by the process to be stored in the database. At the same time, the

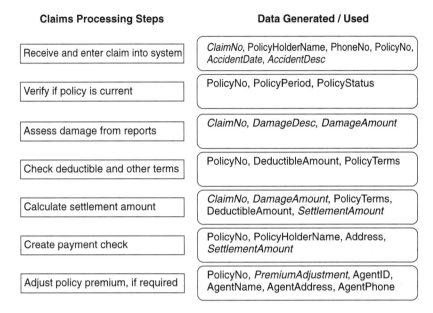

NOTE: Data generated by this process shown in *italics*.

Figure 4-10   Claims processing: data requirements.

process needs to make use of some data elements generated by some other business unit. Figure 4-10 illustrates data generated and used by this process. Note each step of the process and observe the data generated and the data used at each step. Also, see how the data requirements are tied to business objects that are relevant to the company.

When you finish confirming the requirements through the observation of business processes, your requirements definition solidifies. Any vagueness in the requirements determined through interviews is removed. We have two more steps that accomplish similar confirmation of requirements: review of applications and study of documents. Let us go over these two steps before finishing the requirements definition phase.

Review of Applications

During the interviews, you would have completed a list of all the current computer applications that support the various business processes. In fact, you would have noted all the applications reports and screens that are especially important to the user groups. Now in this step you will use the compiled list of applications, reports, and screens to review the data requirements. This step is another step to augment the requirements gathering through interviews.

While reviewing the current applications, you are not interested in how the users navigate through the menus and screens. That goes with the design of applications. In DDLC, you are finding out what data are required to support the applications.

You are not generally concerned with the application structure. Review the applications not for functions, but for data requirements.

Review of applications consists of examining the following for data content and relationships:

- Input screens
- Screens only for display of information
- Reports
- Business rules covering relationships among business objects
- Edit rules for individual fields

Study of Documents

Again, this is another step to confirm the requirements gathered through interviews. For the interviews you need the involvement and participation of the user groups. You have to work around their daily responsibilities and to schedule time for the interviews. However, you can study existing documents without too much involvement from the users. Scheduling the study of documents involves only the analysts performing the activities of the requirements definition phase.

Documentation from User Groups   What information can you obtain from the existing documents? In many organizations with old computer systems, not much documentation is readily available. You will have to piece together several individual documents to the complete the picture. If you have documents recording the screen formats and report layouts, study those in detail. These documents will complete the information about the data currently used by the various departments. If you have additional documents on the rules and edits, go through those as well.

Documentation from IT   Go to the people in IT responsible for maintaining the files of the current applications. These are the technical support persons who are responsible for backing up the files and expand space for files, and so on. Collect the layouts of all the files. Study of the layouts will yield valuable information about the data that support the current applications. In IT, programmers and systems analysts are assigned to support specific applications. If you have an order processing application, find the analysts and programmers supporting this application. Obtain all relevant documents for your study.

Consolidating Information Requirements

We have reviewed a few methods for collecting and confirming data requirements for the proposed database system. You understand that interviewing users and IT professionals is still the best method for gathering requirements. Now we are at the stage of consolidating everything that has been collected and formalizing the data requirements. In a large project in which many analysts are working on the activities of the requirements definition phase, they would have accumulated many pieces of information. How do you aggregate and make sense of everything that has been collected?

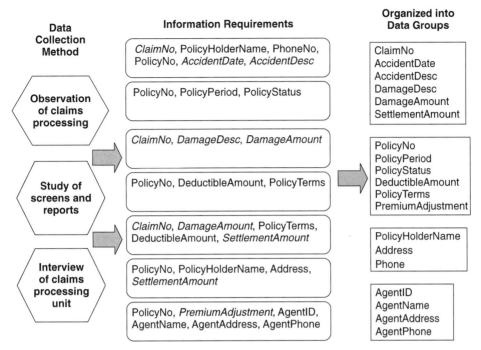

Figure 4-11   Claims processing: organizing data groups.

The consolidation step is intended to organize the collected requirements in a way that would make sense and be useful for the design phase. So what are the tasks in this step? Let us say that you have collected requirements from the interviews with the users in the claims processing unit and also gathered requirements by studying the screen formats and the report layouts of the claims processing application. You would have collected most of the information through the interviews and additional information through the study of the screens and reports. How do you consolidate and record what you have collected? Figure 4-11 illustrates the method for organizing the information collected and recording these by business objects. Observe how the data groups are formed for the process of settling claims.

The outcome of this step is the organized data groups. Each data group relates to a single business object, and each data group has been derived from the information gathered for a single process through the standard methods.

Requirements Definition Document

Publishing a requirements definition document signals the end of the requirements definition phase. The analysts combine all the information collected through different methods and prepare the document. After a draft is prepared, it must be reviewed and confirmed by the users. This is absolutely essential to ensure that you have not overlooked any data requirement. Also, the review and confirmation task corrects any misunderstandings and clarifies ambiguous requirements.

Here is a suggested outline for the requirements definition document. Amend and adapt the outline to suit your database project.

1. **Introduction.** State the overall scope and purpose of the project. Include broad project justification. Provide an executive summary for each subsequent section.

2. **Requirements collection methods.** Describe the methods used for collecting requirements. List departments and business units interviewed. List documents studied and applications reviewed.

3. **Interview summaries.** Include summaries for all key interviews. If you used JAD methodology, attach JAD documentation.

4. **Data groups.** Provide information requirements in the form of data groups compiled in the previous consolidation step. Pay special attention to this section as it forms the foundation for the design phase.

5. **Future information requirements.** Include the requirements gleaned from those interviewed and inferred from the planning documents.

6. **Other information requirements.** In this section, put down other requirements such as data volumes, remote locations, data access patterns, data conversion needs, and business rules.

7. **User expectations.** Record all special expectations in terms of data timeliness, data integrity, problems, and opportunities.

8. **User review and sign-off.** Describe the procedure used for getting the requirements reviewed and signed off on by the users. Also, indicate how users may request changes to the requirements definition and how the changes would be accepted for inclusion.

THE DESIGN PHASE

As noted above, the outcome of the requirements definition phase drives the design phase and the subsequent phases. Very specifically, the design phase transforms the requirements collected in the previous phase into a design for the proposed database system. All the materials and information gathered in the requirements definition phase are used to produce the design. The product of the design phase generally takes the form of a design diagram together with descriptions and explanations.

In the design phase, you find answers to questions such as, How is the data required by the users to be organized and structured? How is the data going to be stored in physical storage? What are the file layouts? What are the data structures? When you produce the design for a database system, you do so at two levels—one at the level of physical storage and the other at a higher level showing just the data structures. As you know, this type of separation of the design provides data independence. Changes at one level need not propagate into changes at the other level.

Later chapters deal with the design of a database system in more detail. Chapters 5, 6, and 7 elaborate the topic of data modeling that is part of the design process. Chapters 8, 9, and 10 deal with design specifically with regard to the relational model, which is a major focus of this book. Chapters 11 and 12 also relate to the design phase. Therefore, at this stage, when we are discussing the entire database development life cycle (DDLC), we will be fairly brief about the design phase. Enough will be said later. So just try to note the general concepts of design here.

Design Objectives

Before we briefly describe the activities of the design phase, let us understand the main objectives of this phase. We want to represent the information requirements in a format that can describe how data structures are perceived, how the structures are related, and how data are to be stored. Data are stored for access and usage. The ability to navigate through the structures and retrieve data must also somehow be portrayed in the design. The design must express the data content.

Here is list of major objectives for the design, both at the level of physical storage and at the higher level indicating the data structures:

- Show data content in detail.
- Represent data relationships.
- Indicate how data structures may be accessed easily.
- Denote information sharing.
- Introduce data independence.
- Secure and safeguard data.
- Establish data integrity and consistency.
- Allow easy data management and administration.

Logical Versus Physical Design

As noted above, the design phase produces two levels of design. Design at the two levels represents two levels of data abstraction. At one level, you design the data structures and arrange them in a manner that expresses their relationships. If your database consists of data only on customers and orders, then the data structures in one level of abstraction will represent the logical view of the data. This is the logical design. At the other level of the design, you will indicate the files, blocks, records, fields, data types, field lengths, keys, indexes, and so on. This level of design that relates to physical storage is the physical design.

The following summarizes the distinction:

Logical design. This is a high-level view of data contained in the entire database. This is a conceptual view of the whole database. It consists of data structures and their relationships. Consider how each user group looks at the data in the database. A particular user group may be interested in only a few data elements from customer data and most of the data elements in the order data. Then, from outside, the view of the database for the user group consists only of the required data elements from customer and order data. This set of data elements is the external view for that user group. Therefore, in the design process, we come up with sets of external views for the various user groups. The combined external views constitute the logical design.

Physical design. The logical design shows the data structures; the physical design represents how data relating to these structures are stored on physical storage. The physical design takes the design closer to hardware. While performing physical design, you have to consider physical hardware features. The physical design step is the transformation of the logical design into a design in terms of hardware.

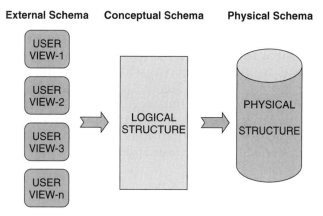

Figure 4-12 Logical versus physical design.

Figure 4-12 indicates the output from the logical design and physical design steps. "Schema" means a way of indicating the output of the design phase. "External schema" constitutes the set of external views of various user groups. "Conceptual schema" represents the structures of the database as a whole. Finally, "physical schema" consists of the files and records as stored in hardware. Creation of the external schema and the conceptual schema are generally reckoned as logical design activities; whereas production of the physical schema is the physical design step.

Go back to the example of the process of settling an auto insurance claim. Imagine that your proposed database just has the data required to perform this process. We will describe the external, conceptual, and physical schema for the database of an auto insurance company in the next three subsections. For the sake of keeping it simple, we will deal with only a few data elements.

The External Schema

Try to understand what exactly "external schema" means and why it is noted as *external*. Imagine that some user group is looking at the data structures represented in the database from outside, from a standpoint external to the database. What would that user group like to see in the database? The group is interested in several data elements inside the database, most probably not all of it. When that group looks at the database, for the group the database is a collection of data elements that are important to it; that set of data elements is the group's view of the database.

The external schema is the collection of such views of different user groups. Figure 4-13 clarifies the concept further with an example from the database of an auto insurance company. Note the separate user views that make up the external schema.

The Conceptual Schema

This is another level of the design. Let us step back to the concept of external schema. We described the external schema as the collection of data views of

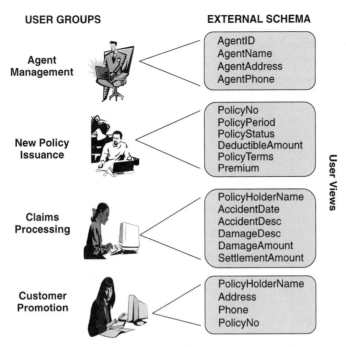

USER GROUPS   EXTERNAL SCHEMA

Agent
Management

AgentID
AgentName
AgentAddress
AgentPhone

New Policy
Issuance

PolicyNo
PolicyPeriod
PolicyStatus
DeductibleAmount
PolicyTerms
Premium

Claims
Processing

PolicyHolderName
AccidentDate
AccidentDesc
DamageDesc
DamageAmount
SettlementAmount

Customer
Promotion

PolicyHolderName
Address
Phone
PolicyNo

User Views

Figure 4-13   Auto insurance database: external schema.

individual user groups looking at the database from outside. Now let us ask the questions. What if there is a user group interested in every data element in the database? What will be the data view of such a user group? Of course, the view will comprise the entire database. The view comprising the whole database represents the concept of the complete database. It is known as the conceptual schema.

Now compare the two notions of external schema and conceptual schema. The external schema comprises individual views of the database by separate groups of users; the conceptual schema encompasses the whole database.

You must have already guessed it: the conceptual schema may be derived from the external schema by combining the various data views of individual user groups. It turns out that aggregation of the external schema is a good method for designing the conceptual schema.

Figure 4-14 shows the conceptual schema for the insurance database. Observe closely how the conceptual schema evolves out of the external schema. See clearly the similarities and differences between the two levels of design.

The Internal Schema

If the external schema and the conceptual schema represent views of the database from outside, the internal schema may be thought of as looking at the database from inside. From outside, the database is perceived as a collection of data structures and their relationships. How does the database look on the inside? If you look inside the database as it resides on physical storage, how does it appear? For this reason, the internal schema also goes by the name of physical schema.

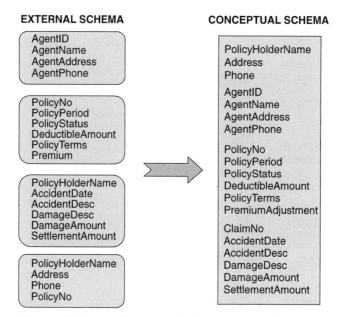

EXTERNAL SCHEMA

AgentID
AgentName
AgentAddress
AgentPhone

PolicyNo
PolicyPeriod
PolicyStatus
DeductibleAmount
PolicyTerms
Premium

PolicyHolderName
AccidentDate
AccidentDesc
DamageDesc
DamageAmount
SettlementAmount

PolicyHolderName
Address
Phone
PolicyNo

CONCEPTUAL SCHEMA

PolicyHolderName
Address
Phone

AgentID
AgentName
AgentAddress
AgentPhone

PolicyNo
PolicyPeriod
PolicyStatus
DeductibleAmount
PolicyTerms
PremiumAdjustment

ClaimNo
AccidentDate
AccidentDesc
DamageDesc
DamageAmount
SettlementAmount

Figure 4-14 Auto insurance database: conceptual schema.

Figure 4-15 shows the components of the internal schema for the insurance database. Note that the internal or physical schema is made up of data files, index files, records, fields, and so on. Also, note how the internal schema is a translation of the conceptual schema to the level of physical hardware. In physical storage, data exist as files and records.

IMPLEMENTATION AND DEPLOYMENT

Before you can implement the database of your organization and deploy it for use, you must know what you are implementing. This knowledge comes from the design. We have noted the two types of design necessary for a database—logical and physical. We have also recognized the need for design at these two levels. We have seen how the external schema and the conceptual schema for the database result from the logical design process. Transformation of the conceptual schema into the internal schema results from the physical design process. Once you have the design at the two levels, you are ready for implementation and deployment of the database. Essentially, implementation consists of getting the data storage areas and files ready and placing initial data in these storage files. Deployment relates to making the database available to the users once the initial data is in.

Database administrators perform most of the activities in the implementation and deployment phase. Analysts also participate in this phase, but the primary responsibility rests with database administrators. Figure 4-16 indicates the major activities in this phase. Note how the responsibilities for the activities are shared.

Part V of this book covers topics on implementation and deployment of relational databases in greater detail. Therefore, at this stage of enumerating DDLC

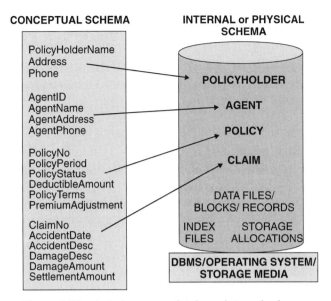

Figure 4-15   Auto insurance database: internal schema.

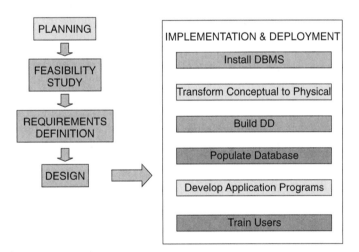

Figure 4-16   Implementation and deployment phase.

phases, we will just highlight the major activities. This will prepare you to appreciate the flow of the phases from requirements to design and then to implementation and deployment.

Conceptual to Internal Schema

Implementation of a database takes place at the physical level. When you implement a database, you are preparing for its usage at the level of physical storage and hardware. As you know, the internal schema represents the database at this level. Implementation of a database is, in effect, establishing the physical files in accordance with the internal schema. How do you get to the internal schema? You get to the internal schema by transforming the data structures of the conceptual schema into the components of the internal schema.

The internal schema deals with the database at the level of hardware, operating system, and database software. Therefore, you need to take into account the following while formulating the internal schema:

- Features of the selected database management system (DBMS)
- Interface mechanism of the DBMS with the operating system
- Hardware configuration, especially the features of the storage devices

Refer back to Figure 4-15 and note the mapping between the conceptual schema and the internal schema. Also, observe how other factors influence the design of the internal schema.

DBMS Installation

Several considerations go into the selection of the proper DBMS and the right version that suits the needs of the organization. To select the appropriate DBMS, you check for flexibility, you make sure you can scale up, you verify compatibility with the operating system, and you examine features relating to easy data access. Once the selection is made, the project team procures the database software and the database administrator installs the DBMS.

A list of major installation tasks follows. These tasks are elaborated in later chapters.

- Ensure compatibility of DBMS with operating system.
- Obtain installation support from database vendor.
- Determine options to be installed (base product, language options, distribution options, etc.).
- Verify availability of disk space and memory for chosen options.
- Set installation parameters.
- Follow installation menu options and install DBMS.

Building the Data Dictionary

The data dictionary is a set of files to record the structure of the database. Before you can make use of the database, you must define the structure of the database in the data dictionary. The database software continually refers to the data dictionary for data manipulations. If you submit a query for customer names and addresses, the database software refers to the files in the data dictionary to find the field structure for customer name and address and also to find where customer names and addresses are stored. So before you can use the database, you must build the files that make up the data dictionary.

The database administrator defines the structure of the database in the data dictionary. The DBMS itself provides tools and procedures to enter this information into the data dictionary. The database administrator uses the conceptual schema to define the overall structure of the database, the external schema to define individual data views, and the internal schema to define the storage spaces and to tie the data structure to physical storage.

Populating the Database

What has taken place so far in the database development life cycle? The requirements definition was completed, and the requirements drove the subsequent phases. The logical design activities were finished. The logical design was translated into the physical design. The data dictionary files have been built. The storage space is ready. The data dictionary has all the entries necessary to define the data structures and relationships. What next? Next comes the activity of placing data in the database so that users can make use of the data.

You place data in the database in two stages. Is your database being converted from some other data system? Are you making the transition from a file-oriented data system? Or are you converting to a later database model? In any case, you will have to convert the data over to the new database system. This is the initial loading of data. Initial loading is usually done through utility programs provided in the DBMS package. Some organizations may opt to load initial data by using third-party tools. Generally, populating the database consists of the following major tasks:

- Extract data from the old data system and create extract files.
- Verify extract files for correctness and data consistency.
- Prepare data in the extract files by sorting and merging as needed.
- Create load files from the sorted and merged extract files to conform to the target database structures.
- Use DBMS load utility or third-party utility programs to populate database with initial data.

Developing Application Interfaces

Loading initial data is the first activity for placing data in the database. This is just the initial data from the old system. Once the database is up and ready for use, day-to-day business transactions can begin to store data in the new database. Ongoing transactions may add, update, or delete data from the database. This is the next activity in populating databases. Users now take over the task of manipulating data.

However, users need applications designed and built to be able to access data from the database. The applications needed to run the business processes must have interfaces to connect to the new database. Although applications may be thought of as part of the overall database environment, design and development of applications fall outside the scope of DDLC. The DDLC phases cover the design and development of databases; application design and development is usually accomplished through a similar life cycle approach—system development life cycle (SDLC).

MAINTENANCE AND GROWTH

The database development life cycle (DDLC) does not end with deployment of the database system and the users beginning to use the system. The development life cycle continues beyond deployment. The database has to be kept up—24/7 in many organizations—and continually maintained. The database administrator continues to monitor the performance of the database and initiates measures to tune the database whenever necessary. He or she continues to check space utilization and the usage of other resources such as processors and communication lines. After the deployment, the project enters a continuous phase of maintenance and growth.

Compare the maintenance and growth stage of a database system with that of an earlier data system. Maintaining the database system and coping with its growth require more effort and specialized skills. The types of maintenance activities are different and more involved. In the earlier phases of DDLC, you find many database professionals taking the various responsibilities. During this phase, however, the roles of analysts, designers, and programmers are diminished; the database administrator takes the primary responsibility. During this phase, the following are the major functions of the database administrator:

- Ongoing monitoring of the database with the aid of usage statistics
- Tuning the database for performance
- Planning and executing tasks related to the growth of the database
- Managing changes to the structure and physical characteristics of the database

Here we have just highlighted the functions during the maintenance and growth phase. Chapter 17 is completely devoted to ongoing maintenance, and we will discuss more details in that chapter.

Administration Tools

You have noted that during the maintenance and growth phase, the database administrator and a few other database professionals are charged with many responsibilities. It is a dynamic environment, and these professionals must stay on top of so many facets of the database system. How are they able to perform their intricate functions? Fortunately, modern database management systems (DBMSs) provide appropriate tools to carry out these functions. This feature of the modern DBMS is even referred to as the toolkit feature. Today's commercial DBMSs come equipped with adequate toolkits. Even where the DBMS is lacking a specific tool, you can find third-party providers offering the missing tools.

DBMSs come with a complete set of DBA commands for the database administrator to evoke the functions of the toolkit. Commonly, the toolkit component of a DBMS contains tools and utility programs to perform the following functions:

- Load additional data as needed
- Import data from outside data sources
- Export data to outside data systems
- Create log files for recovery
- Supply usage statistics
- Backup database files
- Recover database after any type of malfunction

- Manage users and provide authorization for data access
- Manage disk space
- Create indexes for faster data retrieval or drop indexes that are no longer necessary
- Tune the database

Ongoing Monitoring

Monitoring the database is a primary daily function for the database administrator. Every day, the database administrator checks the space utilization reports produced through database utilities. The administrator must make sure that none of the database files is close to running out of space. If a file runs out of space during normal daily operations, users will be prevented from adding records to the file. For those users, the database becomes useless until the situation is rectified. Database administrators try to prevent such mishaps by keeping watch over space utilization through database statistics.

Database administrators continually monitor usage by the various user groups. They constantly monitor usage patterns to determine how each data structure is being accessed. Is there a need to establish new and faster paths for retrieval? Are there peak times when excessive usage overloads the system? Is there a steady increase in the number of users?

Another aspect of ongoing monitoring relates to database security. Database administrators must continue to prevent unauthorized access. They must monitor against illegal attempts at data retrieval and guard against hackers. This is especially significant where the database is open to the organization's business partners or even to the general public. Database administrators constantly scrutinize who uses the database and which files they normally use.

Database administrators continually monitor the database by analyzing database statistics produced by the DBMS utilities. These statistics enable them to take the necessary steps to tune the database whenever necessary and to facilitate smooth and uninterrupted growth of the database.

Performance Tuning

If the database project is successful and the implementation satisfactory, you will notice a marked increase in the number of users. More people will understand the ease with which they can obtain information from the organization's database. They will realize how information sharing could be effective in each individual process. Enthusiasm will increase rapidly.

More users mean more database transactions. The number of daily transactions accessing the database usually doubles within the first six months. The increase in the number of transactions is produced through standard applications as well as ad hoc queries for information from the database. At the outset, power users may begin with simple queries; but, as they become adept at using the database, they will execute more and more complex queries.

An increasing number of users, a rising number of transactions, and an increased query sophistication—all of these slow database access down over time. Retrieving information from the database becomes difficult and time-consuming. The task of fine-tuning recognizes the performance problems of the database and sets out to improve performance. The database administrator, in coordination with the applications analysts and programmers, adopts measures to fine-tune the database. Essentially, the purpose of tuning the database is to make it faster and easier to retrieve information from the database.

Database administrators have a variety of options and methods for tuning a slow and lethargic database. They examine statistics collected by the DBMS and take appropriate action. The following is a list of the major methods:

- Create or drop index files to suit the changes in data access patterns.
- If there are multiple index files for the same data file, force the system to use the right index for retrieval.
- Revise memory buffer management as number of transactions increase.
- Revise how records are blocked within a file.
- Place records that are retrieved together closer to one another in storage.
- Change storage medium if necessary.

Managing Growth

Growth in the database system is inevitable in an organization. The database environment is dynamic. You must anticipate more users and more database transactions with the passage of time. Databases grow in size. That is, you will need more storage space. Databases tend to grow in complexity. As changes in business conditions occur, existing data structures will be revised and newer data structures will be added to your organization's database. Databases tend to get distributed. As users disperse to newer locations, data must be provided to them at the additional locations.

Managing database growth occupies the continued attention of the project team. All IT professionals responsible for the upkeep of the database environment share the responsibility to plan and manage the growth. Here are a few tips to manage growth of the database system:

- Be prepared for growth. Immediately after the requirements definition phase, start planning for growth.
- Establish a small team of IT professionals charged with the responsibility of monitoring growth and making recommendations.
- Archival of old data frees up storage space for current data. Have a regular schedule for archival of infrequently used data.
- Reorganize disk files at regular intervals to consolidate fragmented empty spaces.
- Wherever feasible, use data compression techniques.
- Adopt parallel processing hardware and software techniques, especially if your database environment has to support a large volume of ad hoc queries.

- At regular intervals of about 12 months, review your processor capacity to handle the increased number of transactions. Upgrade if necessary.

CHAPTER SUMMARY

- Because of the importance of database systems, organizations must build them with a lot of care and attention.
- Right at the outset, adopt a data-oriented approach and establish a framework for the development.
- The database development life cycle (DDLC) consists of the following phases or steps, not necessarily in sequential order: planning, feasibility study, requirements definition, design, implementation and deployment, maintenance and growth.
- Database practitioners from IT and user representatives have distinct roles in database development.
- Proper definition of requirements is critical because it drives the design and the other phases.
- The design phase consists of producing the logical design (data structures, relationships, etc.) and physical design (files, records, etc.).
- Database administrators play key roles in database implementation, deployment, and maintenance.

REVIEW QUESTIONS

1. What do you understand about a data-oriented approach for database development?
2. Name the phases or steps of DDLC. Describe very briefly the types of tasks in two of these phases.
3. Who normally does the planning for the database system in an organization? What are the planning responsibilities?
4. What are the three general areas for feasibility study? Why are they important?
5. Describe the types of costs associated with a database system.
6. List any six major tasks in the requirements definition phase. Describe any one of these tasks.
7. What is the distinction between logical and physical design? Why are these two levels of design necessary?
8. What are some of the tasks for populating the new database with initial data? Describe briefly.
9. "DDLC does not end with the initial deployment of the database." Do you agree? Explain.
10. What is tuning the database for performance? Why is this necessary?

EXERCISES

1. Indicate whether true or false:
   A. The DDLC approach enforces a systematic method for database development.
   B. In every database project, the steps of DDLC must be followed strictly in sequence.
   C. The company's business plan indicates future information requirements.
   D. The feasibility study phase defines the requirements.
   E. JAD is an appropriate methodology for a small company with a few users.
   F. The logical design deals with how data are actually stored in the database.
   G. The conceptual schema is an aggregation of the external schema.
   H. The data dictionary is built after the database system is deployed.
   I. Fine-tuning the database is an exclusive responsibility of the database administrator.
   J. Disk space management is an ongoing administrative task.

2. You have been hired as the database administrator for a medical center that is implementing a new database system from scratch. Consider each phase of the development life cycle and describe your expected role in each phase.

3. A company manufacturing parts for appliances proposes to move from a mainframe hierarchical database system to a client/server relational database system. As the project manager, examine briefly your main challenges in this major transition.

4. If you are the chief user representative for the database development effort in a large global organization, what contributions are you expected to make in the requirements definition phase?

5. You are the senior database designer in the database project for a local bank. What are your responsibilities in the design phase?

PART III

CONCEPTUAL DATA MODELING

CHAPTER 5

DATA MODELING BASICS

CHAPTER OBJECTIVES

- Understand what exactly a data model is
- Learn why a data model is necessary
- Observe how a data model represents information requirements
- Study how data design is derived from a data model
- Examine how data views are integrated into a data model

Data modeling is an integral part of designing a data system. It has gained importance as more and more businesses have moved into database systems. In a large database project, the data modelers are a distinct group of database practitioners. Professionals responsible for data modeling create models of the data that must reside in the organization's database. They are not concerned with the particular database management system. The data model is independent of the target DBMS. Third-party vendors offer good CASE tools to aid in the creation of data models.

The technique of modeling is nothing new. If a company is building an intricate product, it first creates a model of the product. The model is not the product itself; it is a representation or replica of the product. However, for the model to be a true representation it must display all the major features of the product itself. Building models is common in manufacturing.

Compare the building of a database system to the manufacture of a product. Something intricate is being built in both cases. The idea of building a data model is similar to the creation of a model for the product to be manufactured. The data model serves as a replica of the information content in the proposed database system.

Database Design and Development: An Essential Guide for IT Professionals by Paulraj Ponniah
ISBN 0-471-21877-4   Copyright © 2003 by John Wiley and Sons, Inc.

WHAT IS A DATA MODEL?

Let us make the idea of a product model more specific and concrete. Assume that an automobile manufacturer wishes to manufacture the 2003 version of Splendid. The engineers begin with general concepts of the major components; they start with an overall notion of how the components must fit together. From these very general concepts, they put together a representation of how the automobile looks and possesses the required features; they create a 2003 model for Splendid. The model is refined and utilized to come up with the actual design of the automobile.

Relate this analogy to database development. Here we are building a database system. The requirements definition provides a collection of concepts about the information content; the definition gives indications about the data structures, their relationships, and constraints within the structures. The data model is a representation of the collection of these concepts about the information content. Just as the automobile model symbolizes the form and features of the actual automobile, the data model indicates the actual data structures and relationships of the data content.

A data model provides a method and a means for describing real-world information requirements in a form that can be designed and implemented as a computer database system. The method abstracts the characteristics of real-world information; the method enables us to capture the gist and meaning of the required data.

Take a particular example. Let us say that we want to create a data model for a university database. This model must represent the data structures necessary in that database. It should show the characteristics of the structures. The model has to indicate the data elements, relationships, and any constraints. In a university database, one data structure relates to the real-world information content about STUDENT. Even before defining any notation on how to show representations in a model, let us see how real-world information about STUDENT gets represented in the data model for STUDENT. Figure 5-1 shows the creation of this data model from real-world information content.

Why Create a Data Model?

We have noted that you create a data model based on the data requirements gathered and defined. In the requirements definition phase, you adopt various

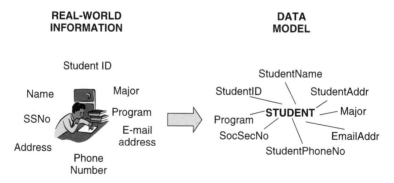

Figure 5-1   STUDENT: real-world information to data model.

methods to collect the information requirements to be implemented in the organization's database system. We have also indicated that these requirements drive the design of the database system. So where does the data model fit in? Why do you need to create a data model for the information requirements and to derive the design from the data model?

In the Chapter 4, we discussed the logical design of a database system. The logical design indicates the data structures and relationships; it shows how the various data elements hang together and are perceived. In a relational database system, these are perceived as two-dimensional tables. On the other hand, in a hierarchical database system, these are reckoned as data segments arranged in a hierarchical, top-down fashion. In a network database system, the arrangement is in the form of data nodes connected to form a network.

The logical design for a relational database system shows the data structures as tables, for a hierarchical database system as data segments, and for a network database system as data nodes. The logical design indicates the structures according to the conventional models—relational, hierarchical, or network. Now, see where the generic data model fits in. It is the preliminary step in the logical design activity. You create a generic data model that simply represents the real-world information requirements without regard to the conventional model of the final, target database. This step produces a replica of what real-world information must be found in the final database, not necessarily according to any conventional model.

Creation of a generic data model as the preliminary step offers several benefits. Here is a list of the major benefits:

- Provides independence so that any real-world information may be freely represented without any restrictions from conventional models
- Captures the essence of the data structures
- Represents real-world objects and their data characteristics
- Defines how real-world objects are related
- Plain and simple representation; easily understandable
- Is at a basic level so that creation and refinement are easy
- Is a very effective method for data abstraction

Real-World Information Requirements

The term "real-world information" has been used a few times, and you may be wondering what exactly it means. Let us clarify. Information or data about the external objects must be present in the database. The database is the internal representation of the data about the external objects. These objects exist in the outside world or the real world, whereas data about these objects exist inside the database. The database residing inside a computer system, therefore, is the internal manifestation of what exists outside in the real world.

Let us go back to the case of the university database. What does the internal university database represent? It indicates the information requirements about the objects present in the real world. What is the real world as far as the information requirements for the university is concerned? What are the objects in this part of

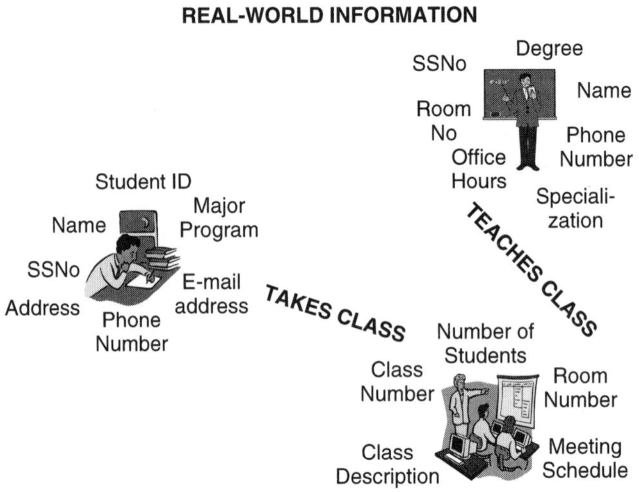

REAL-WORLD INFORMATION

Figure 5-2   University database: real-world information requirements.

the real world that is of concern to the university? Figure 5-2 indicates a few of the objects in the real world for the university. Note the information requirements about these objects. These information requirements must be reflected in the generic data model.

How do you determine the real-world information requirements? The analysts on the database project for the university collect the requirements in the requirements definition phase. We covered that phase of DDLC in great detail. Recall how the information requirements are recorded in the requirements definition document as data groups. The collection of the data groups along with the descriptions of relationships and constraints forms the real-world information requirements for the university.

Data Model as the Replica

We have noted the meaning of real-world information requirements. The following are the requirements that must be satisfied by the proposed database. The database must be implemented to serve the users, providing them with information as required by them. The database must be designed so that it will contain data as required by the users. And the design may be derived from a generic data model that represents the information requirements.

The data model, therefore, is a replica or representation of the information requirements. Examine the information requirements defined in the definition phase of DDLC. Create a model—a data model—from the information requirements. That data model will then be a replica or representation of the information requirements. Figure 5-3 illustrates how a data model is created from the information requirements. Refer back to the Figure 5-2 and observe how the information requirements about objects in the university's real world are represented in the data model.

DATA   MODEL

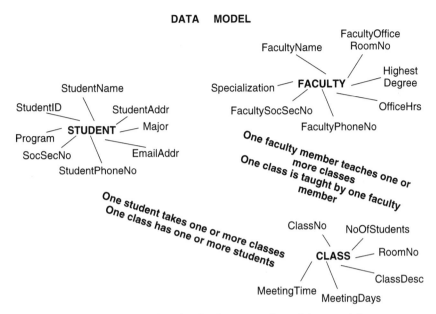

Figure 5-3   University database: creation of data model.

You would also have noticed that to create a data model you need distinct building blocks. Just as you need building blocks or parts to build a model for the manufacture of a product, you require building blocks to construct a data model. Later we will inspect different sets of notations for the building blocks commonly used in data modeling.

Data Model Components

Let us review the characteristics and functions of a data model. The data model is a replica or representation of the information requirements. It must truly reflect the real world of the organization as far as the data requirements are concerned. The data model should provide the meaning and gist of the information content in the proposed database. Whatever components are used to build the data model, when you observe and study the model, you must be able to understand clearly the nature and characteristics of the proposed database. You must be able to discern the types of data and the data structures from the data model.

How should the data model look, and how should it be put together? To match the proposed database correctly, we have to use appropriate building blocks to create the data model. Each building block has to serve a specific role in the overall purpose of representing the real-world information requirements. Also, the combination of all the building blocks and their arrangement must indicate clearly how elements of real-world information interact with one another. Finally, an appropriate symbol will be required for each building block of the data model, as well as a notation to show the relationships.

Based on this discussion, notations or symbols are needed to represent the following in the data model:

- Objects or things about which information must be stored in the database
- Notations for special object types
- Inherent characteristics or properties of each object
- Notations to classify characteristics
- Method to uniquely identify a particular instance of an object
- Indication of relationships among the objects
- The nature of each relationship
- In each relationship between two objects, indication as to how many of one object are related to how many of the other
- Notation to indicate special relationships
- Any constraints on the elements of data

Figure 5-4 presents the types of components or building blocks that are required to create a data model. Compare the components shown in the figure with the points mentioned above and examine whether these components make up a complete list to reflect real-world information requirements in a data model.

DATA MODELING CONCEPTS

By now, you have a fairly clear picture of what a data model is and why a data model becomes necessary as a preliminary step for the logical design. You understand what is meant by real-world information requirements and how the data model must truly reflect these requirements. You have noted the principle that a data model is a replica of the real-world information requirements. Also, you have realized that

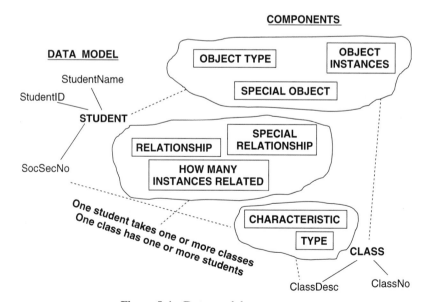

Figure 5-4   Data model components.

appropriate components or building blocks are necessary for the data model to be a true and correct replica.

We will briefly discuss some basic concepts of data modeling. When we consider the real-world information content, the first thing that strikes you is the vastness of data that exist. Even in the case of the real world relating to a university, the potential information content is enormous. You know that STUDENT is an object about which information must be stored. But how much information about the object called STUDENT must be stored? Everything there is about each student? Even after arriving at what information about STUDENT must be stored, how do you relate STUDENT and its characteristics to the data model components and represent them? After the data model is created, how do you proceed to the logical design? Let us examine these issues and find the answers.

The progression is from reality to data model and then from data model to design. Figure 5-5 illustrates the movement from reality to design.

Representation of Information Requirements

Let us work with a specific scenario, look at the information content, and examine the process of representing the information requirements in a data model. Take the case of an emergency room in a medical center and the services rendered there. Assume that you are asked to create a data model to represent the information requirements for billing for emergency room services.

Naturally, the first step is to observe the objects and processes in the emergency room and to collect information requirements for the stated purpose. The information requirements are for the purpose of supporting one process, namely, billing for emergency room services.

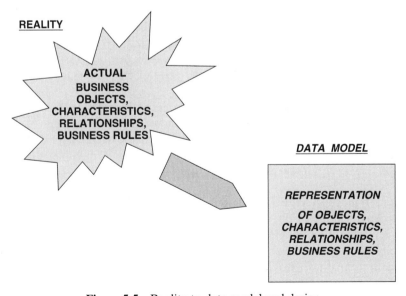

Figure 5-5 Reality to data model and design.

Start by observing the objects in the real world, in this case, the emergency room. The data model must represent the information requirements of this real-world situation. What do you see? What are the objects in the emergency room? In fact, there are many objects, and each object has a set of data relating to it. Begin with the patients in the emergency room waiting for their turn. There is a bunch of data about each patient. Then you see the nurses in attendance. Data elements about the object called NURSE may be enumerated. Next, you notice the physicians attending to patients in the booths behind the waiting area. The object called PHYSICIAN has a set of data relating to it. Then you look around and see the walls and ceiling and the overall lighting. What about the data about the walls and ceiling—the color of the walls and the height of the ceiling? You also hear the supposedly soothing music that comes over the PA system.

There is no need to push the observation farther. Two aspects of the information content of the real world become clear. When you observe the real world for information content, first you notice the existence of a large number of objects about which data are available. Second, you also realize that for each object there exists an abundance of data. Here is the predicament. What do you do with the abundance of data in the real-world situation? How do you represent the real-world information content in a data model?

Filtering Out Irrelevant Data

When you observe the real-world objects and the extent of data about these, how do you translate these into a data model? We mentioned that a data model is a replica or representation of real-world information requirements. A data model is a representation, but with one qualification. It is a representation only insofar as it is relevant to the purposes of the database.

Go back to the scenario of the emergency room. What is the stated purpose of the database in this case? Ability to support billing for emergency services. The types of uniforms worn by the nurses, the color of the walls in the waiting area, the height of the ceiling, the nature of the music heard, and the overall number of doctors in attendance—are these germane to the process of billing for emergency services? Not really. However, if the purpose is to assess the customer service in the emergency room, then the color of the walls, the state of cleanliness, and the nature of the music may all have a bearing.

What, therefore should a data model reflect? Not the entire information content of the real world, only those data elements that are relevant. In the emergency room situation, the data model for billing must exclude data elements such as the nurses' uniforms, wall colors, and ceiling heights. Remember, though, these could have been legitimate and relevant data if the purpose of the database had been different.

Figure 5-6 illustrates this filtering process for creating the data model for billing for emergency services. Note the data items that are excluded and observe how only those relevant to the billing process are included.

Usually, most of the filtering out of irrelevant data happens during the requirements definition phase itself. When you collect information requirements, you observe the primary business processes, review current applications, and examine

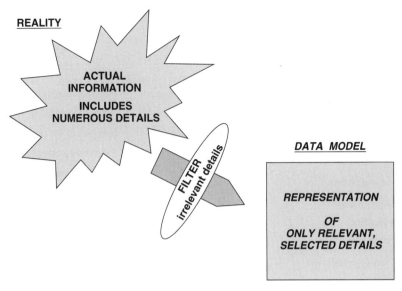

Figure 5-6   Filtering out of irrelevant data.

existing documents. While performing these tasks, automatically only the relevant data are indicated as information requirements.

Mapping of Components

Once you have filtered out the irrelevant information, how do you proceed to create the right data model? After you complete the filtering process, you are left with only the objects and only the relevant elements of data about each object to be included in the data model. You have noted that a data model is built with suitable building blocks or components. These components or building blocks must represent each and every element of the selected information requirements. So the next step for creating the correct data model is to map the information requirements to individual building blocks of the model.

Go back to the model to be built for emergency services billing. In this context, also review the data model components indicated in Figure 5-4. The information content for emergency services billing must be mapped to such components. Figure 5-7 shows how the mapping is done. Note each element of information requirements and the corresponding component of the data model.

Data Model to Data Design

Requirements definition, filtering out of irrelevant details, creating the data model—these are the steps up to the data model. The data model you have created with some standard building blocks is now ready for the next step in the development process. The data model truly represents the information content of the proposed database. How do you get to database implementation from the data model?

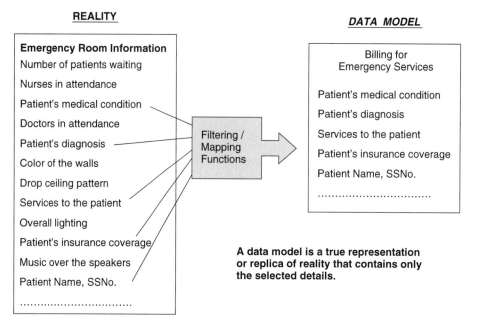

Figure 5-7 Mapping of data model components.

The next step is to formulate the logical design of the proposed database. As you know, the logical design consists of the conceptual view of the database. We referred to the output of the logical design step as the conceptual schema of the database. The conceptual schema provides a representation of the entire database, its structure, the relationships among the data structures, and any constraints. Well, how does the conceptual schema differ from the data model you have created up to this step? The essential difference lies in their basic nature. The data model created up to this step is a generic model built with building blocks independent of any conventional models. Remember that the conventional data models are the hierarchical, network, and relational models. In these models, the data structures and relationships are portrayed with certain defined arrangements—as hierarchical segments, network nodes, or two-dimensional tables.

Let us summarize the steps up to this point:

1. Requirements definition
2. Filtering out of irrelevant details
3. Creation of generic data model
4. Transformation into selected conventional model (hierarchical, network, relational, etc.)

Before we discuss the types of data models and describe their patterns, let us introduce the placement of these models in the database development life cycle. Figure 5-8 shows the phases in which the different types of models are created. Just note the different types of models indicated in the figure. The essential nature of each type is described in the next section.

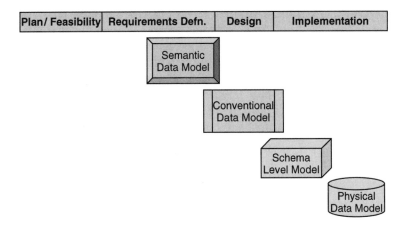

Figure 5-8   Data modeling in DDLC.

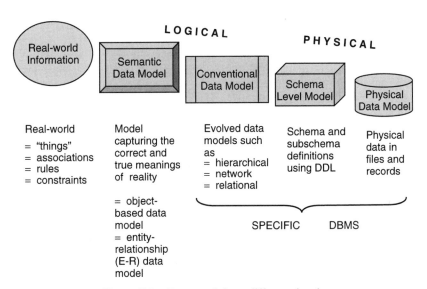

Figure 5-9   Data models at different levels.

PATTERNS OF DATA MODELING

At this point, two aspects of data modeling call for your attention. First, you realize the importance of data modeling in the database development process. You know the benefits and understand the reasons for creating a data model. You need to be clear about the purpose and the place of data modeling in the development life cycle. Second, you need to grasp the essential differences between the patterns of data models mentioned in our discussion.

Figure 5-9 distinguishes the placement of the types of data models at different levels.

Note the data models at the different levels from the semantic data model to the physical model. All of these are data models. Why? Remember that a data model is a representation of real-world information and not the actual real world itself. Each of the models indicated in the figure is a representation of real-world information at a particular level, but they are all representations; they are all data models. Let us describe the distinguishing features of each pattern. Pay special attention to understanding where each pattern fits in, why it is necessary, and how it contributes to the goal of implementing the proposed database.

High-Level Data Model

Let us begin at a level where none of the specifics of predefined arrangement of data structures comes into consideration. This is a level at which the data model is as generic as possible. In other words, once you have a data model at this high level, then making the transition to any type of conventional model is easy and straightforward. From a generic model, you can branch out to any of the conventional models, namely, hierarchical, network, or relational. That is the advantage of creating the generic, nonspecific model first.

Some database authors refer to the data model at the highest level as a semantic data model. A semantic model conveys the essential meaning of the data to be stored in the proposed database. This data model is created with commonly accepted building blocks or components. The following is a list of the essential features of the semantic data model:

- Contains relevant, selected details
- Correctly reflects the information requirements by excluding unnecessary details
- Truly conveys the meanings of all relevant "things" in reality
- Exactly represents the associations between "things" in real-world situations
- Correct data model of a real-world system
- Proper mapping of real-world information requirements
- Convenient means for communicating proposed information content to users

Object-Based Modeling Technique

Enough has been said about the semantic, generic data model. You have noted its nature, its characteristics, and its place in the database development cycle. You also understand that the semantic model is built with certain components. Now let us briefly turn our attention to the major techniques for building the semantic model. Two techniques are commonly used: the object-based modeling technique and the entity-relationship modeling technique. When you use either of the techniques, the result is a semantic data model of the proposed database. The techniques are similar and have many common features. They even share common notations or symbols to denote the building blocks or components. Chapters 6 and 7 cover the principles and components used in these two techniques. At this stage, we will just introduce the two techniques and broadly describe them.

First, let us consider the object-based modeling technique. In a real-world situation, every organization deals with business objects. You may even say that the organization's business processes are mere involvement with business objects. In the case of a university, the business objects include STUDENT, PROFESSOR, CLASS, COURSE, REGISTRATION, ASSIGNMENT, TEXTBOOK, and so on. For an airline business, the business objects include PASSENGER, AIRCRAFT, RESERVATION, ROUTE, MANUFACTURER, AIRPORT, AIRPLANE, FLIGHT, and so on.

Object-based modeling technique recognizes and builds on the fact that business processes involve such business objects. It rests on the premise that if your model reflects relevant information about business objects and how they interact with one another, then the model will truly represent the information requirements. Therefore, by adopting the object-based modeling technique, you produce a generic data model composed of the following:

- Business objects
- Characteristics of each object
- Interaction or linkage between pairs of objects
- Number of occurrences in linked pairs
- Method for identifying each unique occurrence of an object
- Special types of object sets
- Linkages within object sets

Entity-Relationship Modeling Technique

The entity-relationship modeling technique is similar to the object-based modeling technique and produces similar results. The main difference is that the two techniques were developed independently for the same purpose. Their evolutions take separate paths. In the object-based modeling technique, representation of information content is centered upon the concept of business objects. Here, in the entity-relationship (E-R) modeling technique, as the name of the technique explicitly indicates, the replica of information requirements is based on business entities and their relationships.

What are called entities in the E-R modeling technique are the objects in the object-based technique. However, a few subtle differences exist. The object-based technique recognizes special types of object sets called supersets and subsets. We will describe these in Chapter 6. The E-R modeling technique had to be enhanced later to include such entity sets. On the other hand, the E-R modeling technique includes concepts such as weak entities. The E-R model technique, more widely used, is built with well-defined and accepted graphics.

By adopting the entity-relationship modeling technique, you can create a generic data model consisting of the following:

- Business entities
- Properties of each entity type
- Relationship between pairs of entities

- Number of occurrences in related pairs
- Method for identifying each unique occurrence of an entity type
- Special entity types

Data Modeling Aids

In practice, how do you create a semantic or generic data model? You know that you need symbols to denote each component you want to use to build the model. The proper arrangement of appropriate symbols constitutes a data model diagram. A data model diagram gives you a graphic picture of the model. When you look at the data model diagram, you observe what the objects are, how they are linked together, and what the characteristics of each object are.

Graphic Tools. You may use any commercial graphic tool to draw the standard symbols and connecting lines to produce a data model diagram. This is still a useful method for creating data model diagrams, but it has limitations. It produces a static diagram; any revisions must be made by adding, changing, or deleting the symbols. Moreover, the diagram itself cannot be used directly to proceed to the next phases of the database development life cycle.

CASE Tools. Computer-aided software engineering (CASE) tools overcome many of the limitations of the plain graphic tools for drawing data model diagrams and creating semantic data models. CASE tools produce the data model diagrams and also keep the model components stored. Revisions may be made easily. Most CASE tools enable you to take the model to the next step. You can create the semantic model and transform it into a conventional data model and then into the physical model for the target commercial database system. This process is called forward engineering of the data model. Some CASE tools also have backward engineering capabilities, with which you can take a physical schema of an Oracle database and convert it back into a semantic model.

DATA VIEWS

In Chapter 4, while discussing the design phase of DDLC, we referred to the external schema. Recall that the external schema relates to the views of the database content by individual user groups. The external schema depicts the database as user groups perceive or view it from the outside—an external view.

What are these external perceptions of the database? What do the external perceptions hold? How do the users see the database? What is the relevance of these external views to data modeling? These external views are also referred to as *data views* or *user views*.

The concept of data views is critical in the development of a database system. It forms the underlying basis for creating a data model, which in turn leads us to the design. Later on, you will also learn about the role of data views in providing security to the database system. We will now explore the significance of data views and their role in data modeling and logical design. We will present different aspects of

MARKETING: DATA VIEW

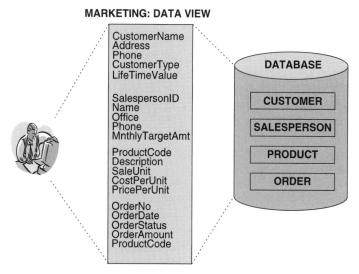

Figure 5-10 Data view: marketing department.

the concept of data views so that you may get a good grasp of its meaning and significance.

What Are Data Views?

Let us begin with a simple explanation. A data view represents one view of the database by a single user group. Figure 5-10 provides a simple explanation of data views. See how the users in the marketing department would view the database of a supermarket chain. The set of data in the database they are interested in constitutes their view of the database.

What we see here is that a data view is the description of a specific data set—a data set relevant to a single user group. As seen in the figure, the data set consists of those data elements the marketing department is interested in and needs to perform its business processes. Also, note that the specific data set for the marketing department does not just relate to data of a single business object. The set includes data elements from more than one business object.

Collection of Information Requirements

Recall how information requirements are gathered. The analysts review the processes, examine the existing documents, and interview user groups. The output from the requirements definition phase contains a collection of data sets or data groups. Each data set or data group supports a specific process.

Let us say that you are gathering information for the data system of a medical center. Take examples of two processes: providing services to patients in the emergency room and billing Medicare for services to patients. For each of these processes, you need data. Each process requires a set of data for its completion. Each data set forms a part of the overall information requirements of the medical

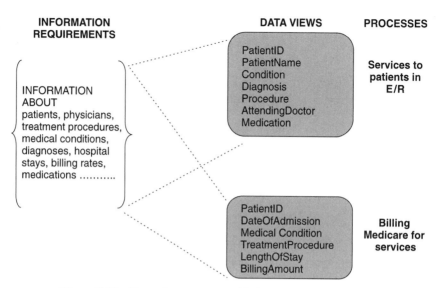

Figure 5-11   Data views as parts of information requirements.

center. A single data set constitutes one particular view of the entire collection of data. Figure 5-11 indicates how each data set forms a part of the information requirements.

Several processes, similar to the two described here, form the entire business of the medical center. You have seen that each process requires a data set or a data view. When you put all these separate views together, you arrive at the entire set of information requirements. Therefore, you may perceive the combination of all the data views as the collection of information requirements for an organization.

Windows into the Data System

Move on to another way of understanding data views. Imagine the database system to be structure like a building with many windows. If you look into the database system through a single window, you are likely to see a specific set of data elements. If you look through a second window, you will see another set of data elements. A third window will provide you with a view of yet another set of data elements. Just pause to note that some of the data elements observed through one window may overlap with a few of the elements seen through another window. A second significant note is that the windows do not represent the actual data; they are just means for looking at sections of the data itself.

Let us understand how this analogy relates to data views. Get back to our university database. This database supports the various processes performed at the university. As examples, take two processes such as course registration and assignment of final grades. Consider the computer screens and reports that enable these two processes to be performed. The screens and reports for each process contain a set of data elements from the university database. What the user is looking at from the screens and reports of a particular process is a set of data elements from the database. This is like looking into the database system through a specific window. The view of data for the process is the view of data through a specific window.

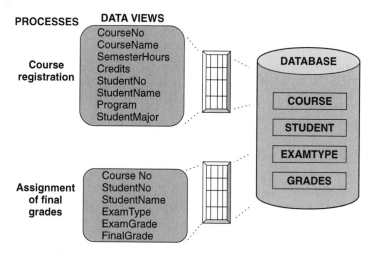

Figure 5-12   Data views as windows into database.

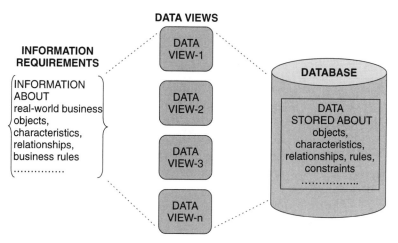

Figure 5-13   Data views: two perceptions.

Figure 5-12 illustrates this comparison of data views with windows into the university database system. Notice the data elements for the two processes seen through the two windows.

Data Views: Two Perceptions

You have now perceived data views from two sides of the entire database development process. Let us summarize our discussion of data views so far using two approaches. On one side, you have seen the real-world information requirements as a collection of individual data views. From the other side, you have perceived data views as windows into the completed database system. Figure 5-13 demonstrates the two perceptions of data views from both sides.

What you understand now is that data views relate to the real-world information on one side and to the completed database system on the other side. The objective of a database development project is the implementation of a database system that matches with the information requirements. Now you see the connection and role of data views in the development process.

VIEW INTEGRATION

Data views offer a useful link from real-world information requirements to the finished database system. You can assemble the data views from the side of real-world information, consolidate them, and derive the proposed database system. How are these data views assembled? What is the process? The combining of the data views results in a consolidated data model for the proposed database system. Let us now discuss this topic.

We have established the connection between data views and data model. The data model is derived from the data views. Go back to the real-world information. This, as we have seen, is a collection of individual user views. You get the resultant data model by combining the separate user views. How can you accomplish this and produce the entire data model? Analysts adopt one of two distinct approaches depending on the circumstances and skills of the data modelers. Here are the two approaches or methods:

Merge individual user views. You take all the individual user views, merge these user views, and then create the complete data model from the complete set of merged data views.

Integrate partial data models. You create a partial data model with standard building blocks for each user view and then integrate these partial data models into the complete data model.

Figure 5-14 illustrates the two approaches showing three user views. The principle can be extended to any number of data views.

Merging Individual User Views

This approach for creating the consolidated data model by merging individual user views generally consists of the following major tasks. Amend and adapt this list to suit your database project.

1. Take each user view and group the data elements by business objects.
2. Within each user view, identify the relationships among the data groups.
3. Take three or four user views at a time and combine the data groups eliminating duplicate elements.
4. For each such combination, mark the relationships among the data groups.
5. Repeat tasks 3 and 4 until all user views are combined.
6. Separate out objects and their characteristics.
7. Establish relationships among objects.

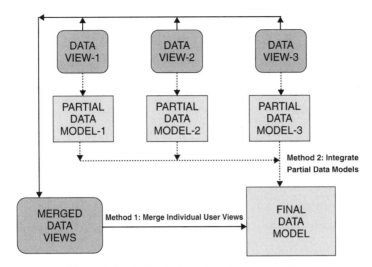

Figure 5-14   View integration: two approaches.

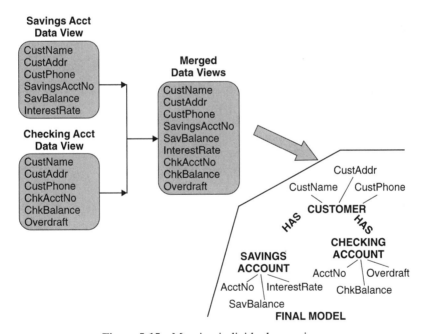

Figure 5-15   Merging individual user views.

8. Indicate how an instance of each object will be uniquely identified.
9. Create complete or global data model from the complete set of objects and relationships.

Figure 5-15 describes the approach of merging individual user views for a banking example. Notice how each task is indicated and how the tasks work together to produce the final, global data model.

Integrating Partial Data Models

In this approach, you do not wait to apply data modeling techniques until all the requirements are merged. You create a mini-model or partial data model from a few related user views. How do you form these sets of related user views? Usually, user views of a department or a natural user group can be combined to form a related group. This approach for creating the consolidated data model by integrating partial data models generally consists of the following major tasks. Amend and adapt this list to suit your database project.

1. Combine the data elements of related user views (usually those of a department or user group).
2. Eliminate duplicate data elements.
3. Separate out objects and their characteristics for the combined set of elements.
4. Establish relationships among objects.
5. Create a local or mini data model for the objects and relationships for the first combination.
6. Repeat tasks 1 through 5 until local data models are created for all combinations.
7. Integrate all the local models, two at a time.
8. Indicate how an instance of each object will be uniquely identified.
9. Review the final, global data model created from the partial model for completeness.

Figure 5-16 describes the approach of integrating partial or local data models for the banking example. Observe how each task is shown in the figure and how the tasks work together to produce the final data model.

Enhancement and Validation

As soon as you produce the global or complete data model with either of the two methods, your data model is almost ready to complete the logical design. Before you use the data model, you have to review the data model to ensure completeness. This is the time to enhance the data model by removing discrepancies and to validate the model.

Generally, enhancement of the data model includes the following tasks:

1. **Reconcile naming conflicts**. If two or more different names are used to refer to the same data element, then these names are synonyms. Review the data model and reconcile synonyms. If the same name is used to refer to two or more data elements, then the name is a homonym. Reconcile homonyms.
2. **Resolve conflicts between data element types**. If a data element in the model refers to an object in one place and to a characteristic of another object in a different place, then there is conflict between the two types of data elements. Resolve such discrepancies.

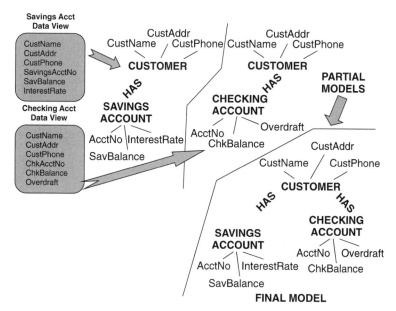

Figure 5-16   Integrating partial data models.

3. **Ensure correct value sets for each characteristic.** If a characteristic of an object has a defined set of values in one user view and a different set of values in another user view, this characteristic cannot be taken as the same characteristic for the object. If the characteristic *employee height* is given in inches in one user view and in centimeters in another user view, then there is a discrepancy if the two user views are merged without reconciling the units of measurement. Review the data model and ensure that the value sets for each characteristic are correct.

4. **Resolve discrepancies in the constraints.** Suppose that, in one user view, the relationship between employee object and department object is such that one employee may belong to only one department. On the other hand, another user view such as project assignments may allow one employee to be involved in multiple departments, that is, assigned to projects of multiple departments. This is a discrepancy in the constraint on the relationship. Resolve such discrepancies.

One more task remains before the global model is finally complete and ready. This is the task of validating the data model with the users. Usually, user representatives knowledgeable in the organization's business processes are selected to perform the review of the data model. The project team walks the user representatives through the global data model, reviewing each object, each relationship, and each type of constraint.

Consolidated Data Model

After enhancement and validation, the global data model must be reviewed one last time to check for any data redundancies. After verification and modification to set right any data redundancies, the data model is ready for completing the logical design.

Let us summarize the steps and tasks from requirements definition to preparing the consolidated data model.

- Filter out unnecessary details; collect the selected data requirements.
- Adopt one of the following methods to create the global data model:
  - Merge user views
  - Integrate partial data models
- Enhance the global model.
- Validate the global model.
- Review the global model to ensure that redundancies have been removed.
- Create the final consolidated data model.

Figure 5-17 summarizes these steps. Note the flow of the tasks from one step to the next.

CHAPTER SUMMARY

- A data model is the representation or replica of real-world information.
- A data model is built with defined and accepted building blocks or components.
- Before a data model is built from information requirements, irrelevant details must be filtered out.
- A generic or semantic data model captures the true meaning of real-world information.

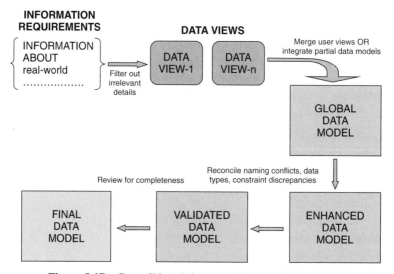

Figure 5-17 Consolidated data model: steps for creation.

- There are two techniques for creating a generic or semantic data model: (1) the object-based modeling technique and (2) the entity-relationship modeling technique.
- Data views form the underlying basis for creating a data model; data views can be perceived as a collection of information requirements and as windows into the database system.
- There are two methods for data view integration: (1) merging individual user views and (2) integrating partial data models.

REVIEW QUESTIONS

1. Give a simple definition of a data model. Explain the connection between real-world information and the data model.
2. State any four reasons for creating a data model during DDLC. Is creating a data model absolutely essential?
3. What do you understand by "real-world information"? What would real-world information be for a banking organization?
4. Data model components need notations or symbols to represent them. List any such five data model components.
5. What is filtering out of irrelevant data? How is this important in data modeling?
6. What is your understanding of a generic, semantic data model? How does it differ from a conventional data model as specified in the text?
7. Name the two common modeling techniques for creating a semantic data model. What are the differences between the two techniques?
8. How do CASE tools aid data modeling?
9. Explain briefly the role of data views in data modeling.
10. What is view integration? Briefly describe any one method for view integration.

EXERCISES

1. Match the columns:

1. real-world information	A. technique for creating semantic data model
2. semantic data model	B. reconcile naming conflicts
3. special object type	C. window into data system
4. E-R modeling	D. expresses true meaning of data
5. CASE tools	E. integrated from partial data models
6. data view	F. based on data models
7. merging user views	G. represented by data model

    8. data model enhancement   H. allow forward engineering of data model

    9. logical database design   I. technique to create partial data models

    10. consolidated data model   J. a data model component

2. As the project manager, write a memo to the Executive VP of information technology explaining the significance of data modeling and justifying the purchase of a CASE tool.

3. As the senior data modeler in the database project for an insurance company, describe the business objects you would consider in your data model.

4. Describe with examples from a banking business how data views represent both a collection of information requirements and windows into the proposed data system.

5. You are a senior analyst responsible for view integration in the database project of a department store. Which method will you choose? Describe how you will proceed to produce the consolidated data model.

CHAPTER 6

OBJECT-BASED DATA MODEL: PRINCIPLES AND COMPONENTS

CHAPTER OBJECTIVES

- Understand the essentials of the object-based modeling method
- Examine and study each component of the data model
- Discuss special types of object sets represented in the data model
- Explore relationships among object sets in detail
- Study means for creating an object-based data model

Before proceeding further, let us recapitulate what we have covered so far on data modeling so that you can grasp the significance and place of the object-based data model in logical design. By now, you understand clearly that a data model is a representation or replica of the portion of real-world information that is relevant to the organization. We reviewed the concept of data views. These are user views of data to be present in the proposed database. All data views, merged and aggregated, form the basis for the data model.

We also discussed different levels of the data model. The semantic data model, capturing the true meaning of real-world information and created from the integration of user views, is said to be at the highest level of integration. Two techniques are generally employed to create a semantic data model: the object-based data modeling technique and the entity-relationship data modeling technique. These techniques are equally effective.

Database Design and Development: An Essential Guide for IT Professionals by Paulraj Ponniah
ISBN 0-471-21877-4   Copyright © 2003 by John Wiley and Sons, Inc.

OVERVIEW OF OBJECT-BASED MODELING

Data modeling deals with creating data models to represent real-world information. Object technology relates to the treatment of business objects, their relationships, and how they interact with one another. Object-based data modeling is a method or discipline that combines the concepts of data modeling and object technology.

You make use of both concepts and arrive at a method to represent real-world information. That is, you look for business objects in the real world, relate real-world information with the business objects, and use this association to build a data model. Obviously then, the modeling method centers on the business objects. Figure 6-1 expresses this merging of the two concepts in object-based data modeling.

A Generic Data Model

First of all, the object-based data model is a generic data model. Let us examine the significance and implications of this statement. What are the types of databases that are being implemented in organizations? You hear about an organization using a specific database product from a particular vendor. For example, the database could be an Oracle database, an Informix database, or a Microsoft SQL Server database. Or the database could be an IBM IMS database.

Oracle, Informix, and SQL Server databases are based on the relational model. The relational model is a data model in which all data are perceived as two-dimensional tables. On the other hand, the IMS database is based on the hierarchical model. The hierarchical model is also a data model but is a model in which all data are perceived as hierarchical data segments with parent-child relationships. The relational model and the hierarchical model are specific models based on defined conventions on the arrangement of the components. These two models are specific conventional models.

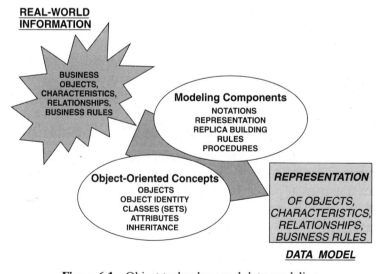

Figure 6-1   Object technology and data modeling.

In contrast, the object-based data model is a broad type of model that can be transformed into any type of conventional model dictated by nature of the commercial database management system to be implemented. In the object-based data model, no preset or predefined arrangement of data structures exists. The data model is generic, applicable to all types of information content.

Benefits of Object-Based Data Model

Being generic, the object-based data model provides a number of benefits to analysts and designers for creating a truly representative data model. Let us review the major advantages. The model is closer to the way business processes are executed.

Universal model. The model is able to reflect all types of real-world information. Also, you can represent all aspects of information—the business objects and everything relevant to each type of object.

True replica. Because it is able to represent every relevant aspect of real-world information, the data model can be a true and correct representation of real-world information.

Free from restraints. The conventional models adopt certain specific ways of representing data. Through these models, you need to perceive real-world information in predefined ways in the form of a particular arrangement of data structures. The object-based data model has no such restrictions.

Easily transformable. Once you create an object-based data model, you can easily transform it into any of the conventional data models.

Intuitive. In the object-based data model, you observe as components just what you notice as different aspects of real-world information. Therefore, learning the modeling technique becomes easy.

Introduction to Components

When you create a data model and produce a data model diagram, you need symbols or notations to denote the various components. In Chapter 5, when we introduced data modeling, we did not use any formal notations. There, the intention was to introduce the basic concept of data modeling. So let us now go over the notations.

Although you might see some variations in the notations, mostly these are standardized. Figure 6-2 presents the components and their standard notations.

Note how these components cover the various aspects of real-world information. Also, realize how, with a just a handful of components, you can represent the entire spectrum of real-world information. With a limited number of building blocks or components, you are able to represent any set of information with all its variations and complexities.

Object Set. The rectangular box denotes a set of object instances. Each box in a data model diagram represents the set of certain object instances. The name of the

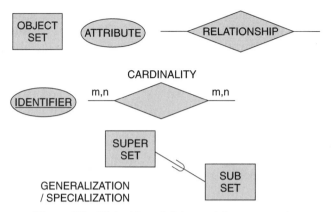

Figure 6-2   Object-based data model: components.

business object is written inside the box. For example, if a box indicates the STUDENT object, it symbolizes the set of all students in the university. You may visualize each student as being represented by a single point within the box. Then the complete set of points represents the entire set of students.

Attribute.   The ellipse or oval indicates an attribute or inherent characteristic of an object. The name of the attribute goes inside the ellipse. If an ellipse denotes the attribute *First Name*, then the name of this attribute is written inside the ellipse and the ellipse is attached to the box that represents the STUDENT object.

Identifier.   Inside the box representing the business object STUDENT, you assume the presence of multiple points, each denoting a single student. Each is an instance of the object in the object set. How do you uniquely identify any particular instance of the object set? How do you find the first name of a specific student? You need a method to identify a specific student instance and then find the name attribute for that instance. The values of certain attributes of an object may be used to identify instances of the object uniquely. For example, values of the attribute *Social Security Number* can uniquely identify individual instances of the object STUDENT. Social Security Number 101-38-4535 uniquely points to a particular instance of the object STUDENT. The identifier, being an attribute, is also represented by an ellipse with the name of the attribute written inside. Because it is a special type of attribute, the name written inside the ellipse is underlined or underscored.

Relationship.   In the real-world information for a university, a student enrolls in a class of a particular course. Here STUDENT and CLASS are business objects. Henry Porter enrolls in the database class meeting on Tuesday nights. The instance "Henry Porter" of STUDENT object is related to the instance "Tuesday DB class" of CLASS object. A diamond, with two lines joining the two related object boxes, denotes relationships. The name of relationship itself, "enrolls" in this case, is written inside the diamond.

Cardinality. Consider the object instances "Henry Porter" and "Tuesday DB class." Henry Porter must have enrolled for other classes such as Systems Analysis and Design, Data Structures, and so on. That means that one instance of the object STUDENT is related to many instances of the object CLASS. Similarly, on the other side, one instance of "Tuesday DB class" of the object CLASS is related to many instances of the object STUDENT. In other words, many students are enrolled for the "Tuesday DB class." The indication of numbers of instances of one object relating to number of instances of another object is known as the cardinality of the relationship. Cardinality of a relationship is shown as numbers near the lines of the diamond symbol for the relationship. The variables "m, n" indicate a many-to-many relationship between two object sets.

Generalization/Specialization. Think about the business object STUDENT. The object set representing STUDENT includes all students in the university. Both graduate students and undergraduate students are part of the STUDENT object set. The set of graduate students is one part of the STUDENT object set; the set of undergraduate students is the other part. Both graduate students and undergraduate students share most of the attributes of the object called STUDENT. However, graduate students may have attributes such as undergraduate degree and undergraduate major that do not apply to undergraduate students. What you observe is that the set of graduate students is a subset of the superset STUDENT. GRADUATE and UNDERGRADUATE are subsets; STUDENT is the superset. Subsets and supersets commonly occur in real-world situations. Look at supersets and subsets from another angle. A subset is a specialization of a superset; the superset is a generalization of the subsets. As shown in Figure 6-2, a special mark like a "U" is placed on the line linking the subset to the superset to indicate that the superset contains the instances of the subset.

Mapping of Real-World Information

We have mentioned that the object-based data model is an intuitive model, a true model, and a model that represents all types and variations of real-world information. With the aid of just the defined set of components and their notations, you are able to represent any collection of information requirements.

Let us take specific examples of business processes in real-world situations of different types of organizations. Note the following details indicating how you can represent information requirements with the principles of object-based data modeling. At this introductory stage, let us describe how portions of the data model diagram would be completed without getting into any complex issues. We just want to map the elements of real-world information to the components and notations of the data model.

Airline Reservation

Business Objects Show object boxes for PASSENGER, AIRLINE, and FLIGHT.

Attributes Show attribute ellipses for characteristics of the above three objects.

Identifiers Show attribute ellipses for following identifiers, underlining the attribute names within the ellipses:

PASSENGER: Passenger Number (or Record ID assigned)

AIRLINE: Airline Code (AA, BA, AI, etc.)

FLIGHT: Flight Number (preassigned)

Relationships Indicate relationships, with diamond shapes, between FLIGHT and AIRLINE, PASSENGER and FLIGHT.

Cardinalities Number to show cardinalities at either side of the diamonds for the above relationships.

Generalization/Specialization None required.

Taking a Customer Order

Business Objects. Show object boxes for CUSTOMER, ORDER, and PRODUCT.

Attributes Show attribute ellipses for characteristics of the above three objects.

Identifiers Show attribute ellipses for the following identifiers, underlining the attribute names within the ellipses:

CUSTOMER: Customer Number (system-assigned)

ORDER: Order Number

PRODUCT: Product ID (preassigned)

Relationships Indicate relationships, with diamond shapes, between CUS-TOMER and ORDER, ORDER and PRODUCT.

Cardinalities Number to show cardinalities at either side of the diamonds for the above relationships.

Generalization/Specialization None required.

Student Registration

Business Objects Show object boxes for STUDENT, COURSE, CLASS, and TERM.

Attributes Show attribute ellipses for characteristics of the above four objects.

Identifiers Show attribute ellipses for the following identifiers, underlining the attribute names within the ellipses:

STUDENT: Student ID or Social Security Number

COURSE: Course ID

CLASS: Class Number or Section Number

TERM: Semester ID

Relationships Indicate relationships, with diamond shapes, between COURSE and CLASS, TERM and COURSE, STUDENT and CLASS.

Cardinalities Number to show cardinalities at either side of the diamonds for the above relationships.

Generalization/Specialization If necessary, show superset STUDENT and subsets GRADUATE STUDENT and UNDERGRADUATE STUDENT.

Product Inventory Verification

Business Objects   Show object boxes for PRODUCT, PRODUCT LINE, DEPARTMENT, and WAREHOUSE.

Attributes   Show attribute ellipses for characteristics of the above four objects.

Identifiers   Show attribute ellipses for the following identifiers, underlining the attribute names within the ellipses:

PRODUCT: Product ID
PRODUCT LINE: Product Line Number
DEPARTMENT: Department Code
WAREHOUSE: Warehouse ID

Relationships   Indicate relationships, with diamond shapes, between DEPART-MENT and PRODUCT LINE, PRODUCT LINE and PRODUCT, WARE-HOUSE and PRODUCT.

Cardinalities   Number to show cardinalities at either side of the diamonds for the above relationships.

Generalization/Specialization   None required.

Patient Service at Doctor's Office

Business Objects   Show object boxes for PHYSICIAN, PATIENT, DIAGNO-SIS, and TREATMENT.

Attributes   Show attribute ellipses for characteristics of the above four objects.

Identifiers   Show attribute ellipses for following identifiers, underlining the attribute names within the ellipses:

PHYSICIAN: Social Security Number or Certification Number
PATIENT: Patient Number (assigned)
DIAGNOSIS: Diagnostic Code
TREATMENT: Procedure ID

Relationships   Indicate relationships, with diamond shapes, between PHYSI-CIAN and PATIENT, PATIENT and DIAGNOSIS, PATIENT and TREAT-MENT.

Cardinalities   Number to show cardinalities at either side of the diamonds for the above relationships.

Generalization/Specialization   None required.

Deposit to Checking Account

Business Objects   Show object boxes for ACCOUNT, CHECKING ACCOUNT, CUSTOMER, and DEPOSIT.

Attributes   Show attribute ellipses for characteristics of the above four objects.

Identifiers   Show attribute ellipses for following identifiers, underlining the attribute names within the ellipses:

ACCOUNT: Account Number
CHECKING ACCOUNT: Account Number

CUSTOMER: Customer Number (preassigned)
DEPOSIT: Transaction Number

Relationships Indicate relationships, with diamond shapes, between CHECKING ACCOUNT and CUSTOMER, CHECKING ACCOUNT and DEPOSIT, CUSTOMER and DEPOSIT.

Cardinalities Number to show cardinalities at either side of the diamonds for the above relationships.

Generalization/Specialization Show notations to indicate superset ACCOUNT and subset CHECKING ACCOUNT.

Medical Insurance Claims Processing

Business Objects Show object boxes for INSURED, POLICY, AGENT, and CLAIM.

Attributes Show attribute ellipses for characteristics of the above four objects.

Identifiers Show attribute ellipses for the following identifiers, underlining the attribute names within the ellipses:
INSURED: Social Security Number
POLICY: Policy Number
CLAIM: Claim Number (assigned)
AGENT: AGENT ID (assigned)

Relationships Indicate relationships, with diamond shapes, between INSURED and POLICY, AGENT and POLICY, CLAIM and POLICY.

Cardinalities Number to show cardinalities at either side of the diamonds for the above relationships.

Generalization/Specialization None required.

Example of a Model Diagram

From the above real-world information requirements and their mapping to the object-based data model, you have a glimpse of how the model is created and the model diagram drawn. Note, however, that we have just introduced the principles; we have not gone into too many details or dealt with any complexities in the real-world business situations. Nevertheless, you now have a more concrete notion about how a model represents real-world information.

The subsequent sections of this chapter elaborate on the individual model components. Before getting into a discussion of the details, let us take a specific example of real-world information about a small group practice of surgeons, review a data model diagram, and note the components. The description of the group practice operations and information requirements follows:

Three orthopedic surgeons, Dr. Samuel J. Laufer, Dr. Andrew Bowe, and Dr. Lisa Sanderson, have joined together to form Orthopedic Associates P.A. They want to install a computer system for their group practice. They also want to use a database for their information requirements. Initially, the database is required to support just the billing function.

Group Practice Operations   The three surgeons are equal partners in the group practice. Irrespective of how many patients each surgeon attends to, they share the net income equally.

There are two receptionists, a business manager, and three nurses.

Patients   About 20% of patients are repeat patients. The rest are new referrals. Patient visits are usually by appointment. The receptionists are responsible for scheduling the appointments for the surgeons. Patients may be allotted to the surgeons based on the availability of the surgeons and the daily schedule. Sometimes, patients may opt to see a particular surgeon, although this is not encouraged.

Billing   The business manager is responsible for billing for each visit. On the basis of the diagnosis and treatment, the doctor or sometimes the nurses write down the fee for the visit. Services may include some surgical procedures performed in the premises and various types of tests. Third-party providers such as Blue Cross/Blue Shield, other insurance companies, Medicare, or Medicaid are billed. Wherever the third-party providers do not cover a the cost of a visit fully, the balance is billed to the patient. Third-party providers are invoiced for each visit. The patients receive a monthly statement showing any opening balance, the visits during the month, the amounts billed to third-party providers, payments received from the providers, amounts billed to the patient, payments received from the patient, and any balance due. Third-party providers may include one or more invoices in one payment. A patient may make a partial payment against a billing statement.

Initial Information Requirements

- Send billing invoices to third-party providers.
- Send monthly statements to the patients.
- Receive payments from third-party providers.
- Receive payments from patients.
- At the end of each month, print a list of the names of patients seen by each surgeon.

The first version of the database is intended to support only the initial information requirements. Therefore, the data model has to be created *just for the initial information requirements*.

Figure 6-3 presents a data model diagram for the initial information requirements. As desired, it is intended to represent only the information relevant to patient services and billing. It is important to note that other irrelevant details are filtered out before the model is created.

Carefully observe the notations or symbols in the model diagram and the components represented by these symbols.

Business Objects   Note the rectangular boxes denoting the objects. Only the objects involved in the initial information requirements are included. You do not see an object for EMPLOYEE because this is not required for the initial information requirements. Also, note the bigger box representing the object VISIT.

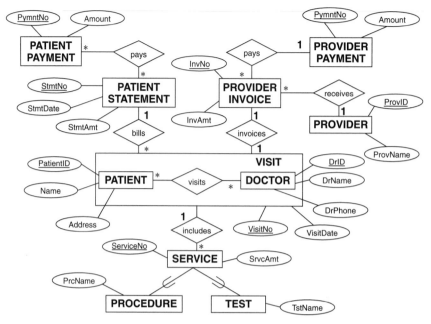

Figure 6-3 Model diagram: medical practice.

This is an aggregate object. See the explanation of aggregate objects in a later subsection.

Attributes Review the ellipses attached to each object. These are the inherent or intrinsic characteristics of the objects. Each attribute is a basic property of the object to which it is connected. Note also that only the characteristics that are relevant to the initial information requirements are included.

Identifiers Note the ellipses containing attribute names that are underlined. Each such ellipse denotes the identifier for the particular object.

Relationships Look at all diamonds and the lines connecting pairs of objects. These are the direct relationships. What are direct relationships? Consider the object PROVIDER PAYMENT. Of course, this payment pertains to a visit by a patient. Nevertheless, the payment is directly related only to invoice sent to the third-party insurance provider. The relationship of a payment from a provider to the patient is an indirect relationship. The model diagram only needs to show the direct relationships. The indirect relationships may be derived from the direct relationships displayed in the diagram.

Cardinalities Note the numbers marked along the relationship lines. Number to show cardinalities at either side of the diamonds for the above relationships. An asterisk (*) indicates that many instances of the object participate in the relationship. Note the cardinalities between the objects PROVIDER and PROVIDER INVOICE. One instance of the object PROVIDER may be related to many instances of the object PROVIDER INVOICE.

Generalization/Specialization   Note the superset SERVICE and the subsets PROCEDURE and TEST. SERVICE is a generalization of PROCEDURE. On the other hand, TEST is a special type of SERVICE.

BUSINESS OBJECTS

In an object-based data model, as the name itself implies, the business object is the primary building block. The preliminary step for creating a data model rests on the identification of the business objects for a given set of information requirements. After the identification of business objects, the rest of data modeling follows.

You need to clearly understand the concept of a business object and the methods for identifying business objects and to explore how the objects relate to one another. You need to differentiate between an object set and an instance of an object set. You need to examine the nature of objects and see what different types of objects exist.

We have been discussing characteristics of objects and named these "attributes." What are these attributes for an object? Consider the object EMPLOYEE. An employee has a definite street address and is attached to a department. Are both *address* and *department* attributes of the object EMPLOYEE? If not, why not? You need to understand how characteristics qualify to become attributes of objects in a data model.

Object Sets and Instances

Sets   Pursue the example of the object EMPLOYEE. As you know, a rectangular box indicates the object EMPLOYEE in a data model with the name of the object written inside the box. It is worthwhile repeating what we mentioned above about what the box actually represents. It does not just represent a single employee. It indicates the entire set of employees in the organization. The importance of the concept of an object set becomes clear when we study the concept of relationships.

Thus the object set EMPLOYEE represented by a box is the collection of all individual employees. Within the box, imagine the single points as denoting individual employees. The box contains a set of such points.

Instances   Each point represents an instance or individual occurrence of the object EMPLOYEE. If you examine a single point in the box, that point would denote a particular employee. If there are 500 employees in the organization, then 500 individual points make up the box that represents the object EMPLOYEE. Each of the 500 points represents a specific employee.

Examples:

Object Set	EMPLOYEE
Instances	John Doe, Mary Smith, Jane Williams, Maryanne Rogers
Object Set	CUSTOMER
Instances	Harold Epstein, Bill Richardson, Walker Electricals, Inc., Jerry Philips and Sons, Inc.
Object Set	PRODUCT
Instances	Coat, slacks, shirt, dress, socks, hat, gloves
Object Set.	INVOICE
Instances.	No.1234 dated 10/15/2002, No.2345 dated 12/23/2002, No.3456 dated 1/10/2003
Object Set	BUILDING
Instances	121 Main Street, 33 Park Avenue, 101 Center Boulevard, 25 Ray Road

Types of Objects

We have gone through several examples of business objects and their instances. You now have a fairly good understanding of objects represented in a data model. You have seen that EMPLOYEE is a business object. You have also noted that PRODUCT, INVOICE, and BUILDING are objects as well. What then are objects? What are the various types of objects? How do you differentiate between one type of object and another?

A person, as in the case of EMPLOYEE, is an object. A BUILDING is a material object. In the case of INVOICE, it is neither a person nor a material. When you refer to the object INVOICE, you do not indicate the piece of paper on which the invoice details are printed and sent to the customer. The piece of paper is a manifestation of a single instance of the object INVOICE. What then is the object INVOICE? It is a concept that covers the billing to a customer for services or products.

Listed below are the common types of objects:

Person	EMPLOYEE, STUDENT, PATIENT
Place	STATE, COUNTRY, REGION
Material	MACHINE, PART, PRODUCT, BUILDING
Event	SALE, VISIT, APPOINTMENT
Concept	ACCOUNT, COURSE, INVOICE

Recognizing Object Sets

Let us say that you have the responsibility for examining the information requirements of a department store and creating an object-based data model. As you very well know, business objects are the fundamental building blocks for creating the model. So, by inspecting the requirements definition, you must first recognize the business objects that are relevant. How do you accomplish this initial task?

By carefully going through the requirements definition, you will discern the relevant real-world information tied to people, places, materials, events, and concepts. As mentioned above, information requirements for each process tend to be grouped in terms of the relevant things. Initially, note all such things with which the business processes are concerned.

Let us quickly do this exercise for a department store. From the information requirements, you will recognize the things or objects for the business. The store buys and sells products; PRODUCT therefore, is a relevant business object. The store sells products to customers; CUSTOMER becomes a relevant object. The store invoices customers for the products sold; therefore, INVOICE is a relevant object. As you continue the inspection of the information requirements for the department store, one by one, you will recognize all the objects for the business and come up with a complete list.

Occasionally, you may run into a situation in which it may not be clear whether a data element must be recognized as a business object to be shown distinctly in the model or must be indicated as just an attribute of another object. For example, in the case of the data model for the department store, consider the data element *product line*. Each product is part of a product line. The question arises: Should product line be considered as an attribute of the object PRODUCT or be represented as a separate object PRODUCT LINE? If the information requirements demand that the characteristics of product line such as line description, date of introduction of product line, and so on be shown in the model, then product line must be represented as a distinct object. If the information content dictates that only the name of the product line be known, then product line becomes an attribute of the object PRODUCT.

Attributes

Every business object possesses certain properties or characteristics that are relevant to the information requirements. These characteristics describe the various instances of an object set. For example, *last name* McKeown describes an instance of the object EMPLOYEE. Similarly, if that employee was hired on 10/1/1985, *hire date* is another attribute describing that instance of the object.

Figure 6-4 shows the attributes of an object STUDENT. Note the names of the attributes written inside the ellipses or ovals. Observe how these are characteristics or descriptors of the individual instances of the object set.

So, what are attributes? Attributes of an object are characteristics, properties, or descriptors. Let us explore the meaning and significance of attributes further.

Inherent Characteristics   Consider the data elements StudentID, StudentName, SocSecNo, StudentPhone, StudentMajor. These data elements are associated with the object STUDENT. They are innate, natural, or inherent properties of STUDENT. Next, think of a particular course for which a student has enrolled. CourseNo is also a data element associated with the object STUDENT. If so, is CourseNo also an attribute of the object STUDENT? Compare the two data elements StudentName and CourseNo. StudentName is a natural characteristic of the object STUDENT, whereas CourseNo does not indicate a basic property of the object. CourseNo does not describe some intrinsic property of STUDENT but only

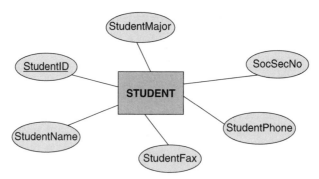

Figure 6-4   STUDENT object: attributes.

StudentID	StudentName	SocSecNo	StudentPhone	StudentMajor	StudentFax
111245	Kristin Rogers	214-56-7835	516-777-9584	Networking	516-777-9587
121365	Rob Smith	123-44-5546	718-312-4488	Web Design	
123456	Mary Williams	101-54-3838	212-313-1267	Networking	212-313-1267
234754	Shaina Gonzales	213-36-7854	212-126-3428	Social Science	
388910	Andrew McAllister	311-33-4520	718-567-4321	Engineering	718-567-4322
400500	Kassy Goodman	512-22-8542	732-346-5533	Programming	732-346-5538
511675	Rob Smith	111-22-3344	908-212-5629	Liberal Arts	908-212-5630

Figure 6-5   STUDENT object: sample attribute values.

its relationship with another object called COURSE. Therefore, CourseNo does not qualify to be an attribute of STUDENT.

Unique Values for an Instance   Take a few samples of the attributes for the object STUDENT as shown in Figure 6-5.

Look at the set of values shown in one row of the figure. These values for the attributes StudentID, StudentName, SocSecNo, and StudentPhone relate to one student, a specific instance of the object STUDENT. These attributes do not relate to any random instance of the object; they relate to one particular student.

Let us say that this student is Rob Smith. Then these attributes are characteristics of Rob Smith. If you observe a specific instance of the object STUDENT, namely Rob Smith, then you will note a unique set of values for the attributes. This unique set of values describes Rob Smith. In the data model, each instance of an object possesses a unique set of values for its attributes.

Changeable Values   We have noted that each instance of an object is described by a unique set of values for its attributes. Review the unique set of values for the attributes describing the instance represented by Mary Williams in Figure 6-5. Let us say that Mary marries John Pearson and changes her name to Mary Pearson. Also, she changes her phone number. What are the implications?

What you notice is that although each instance is described by a unique set of values for its attributes, these values may change over time. The values for StudentName and StudentPhone would change, but the instance would still refer to the same student. Again, after the changes, a unique set of values for the attributes describes the student Mary Pearson. It is important to note that values of the attributes for an object instance may change, but the instance itself remains the same.

Null Values   Suppose the object STUDENT has another attribute, StudentFax. What about the values of this attribute for the various object instances? If Mary Pearson has a fax machine, then that fax number will be the value for StudentFax for her.

On the other hand, if Rob Smith does not have a fax machine, then what about the value for StudentFax for Rob Smith? We then say that the attribute StudentFax for Rob Smith has a *null* value. If an object instance has no value for one of its attributes, then this attribute has a null value for that instance. Null values are not blanks or spaces. Null value for an attribute in an object instance indicates the absence of a value for that attribute in that instance.

Null values for attributes play a significant role in databases. The value of an attribute for a particular instance of an object may be set to null if a value is not available, is missing, or is genuinely absent. In a database, as you will see later, null values may not be permitted for certain attributes. Using appropriate language commands, you can check for null values in attributes for object instances.

Attribute Domains   Let us now consider the example of a different object and its possible attributes.

Object: EMPLOYEE
Attributes: EmployeeID, SocSecNo, EmpName, EmpZip, Salary, HireDate

Examine the values of each of these attributes. You will note that the values for a particular attribute are from a definite set of values. For example, the values of EmployeeID may be any number with six digits. That means that the set of values from which the value of EmployeeID for a particular instance of the object EMPLOYEE is derived is the set of numbers from 000000 to 999999. This is the domain of values for the attribute EmployeeID.

The domain of an attribute is, therefore, the set of legal or allowable values for that attribute. In the case of EmployeeID, the attribute domain is the set of numbers from 000000 to 999999. Attribute domains are sets based on natural limitations as for numbers or characters of the alphabet. Mostly, business rules determine attribute domains.

Each attribute has its own domain for its values. Here are some examples of domains for the above attributes:

EmployeeID   Set of numbers from 000000 to 999999
SocSecNo   Set of legal 9-digit Social Security Numbers
EmpName   Any text up to 45 characters
EmpZip   Set of legal zip codes

Salary   Currency value from 000000.00 to 999999.99

HireDate   Legal values for date greater than January 1, 1900

Identifiers for Instances

Go back to Figure 6-5 displaying sample attributes for object STUDENT. You have noted that the set of values in each row describes a single instance. But do you know which set describes a particular instance? If asked "what is the address of Rob Smith?", how can you find the address from the database? You can go through all instances of the object STUDENT and check for the name value Rob Smith and then find the value for the address. What if there are three students in the university with the same name Rob Smith? Which Rob Smith are we referring to?

You need a method to identify a particular instance of an object. Obviously, values of an attribute may be used to identify particular instances. You tried to do that by looking for STUDENT instances with value "Rob Smith" for the attribute StudentName. However, you could not say for sure that you found the correct student because of the possibility of duplicate values for this attribute. On the other hand, if you had used values of the attribute StudentID, you could uniquely identify the student. What is the address of the student with StudentID 123456? It is Mary Williams; nobody else has that StudentID. Therefore, values of the attribute StudentID can be used to uniquely identify instances of STUDENT.

Attributes whose values can be used to uniquely identify instances of an object are known as identifiers. They are also known as keys for the object. Now, review the attributes for the object STUDENT. StudentName, StudentPhone, or Student-Major cannot be used to identify instances uniquely. This is because these may have duplicate values in the set of instances for the object. Therefore, any attribute that is likely to have duplicate values does not qualify to be a key or identifier for an object.

How about the attributes StudentID and SocSecNo? Either of these attributes qualifies to be a key for STUDENT. Such attributes are called *candidate keys*. One of the candidate keys is chosen to be the identifier for the object. The *primary key* of an object is a candidate key selected as the identifier for the object. For some objects, one attribute alone will not be enough to form the identifier. You may have to use a combination of two or more attributes as the identifier. In such cases, the primary key is a *composite key*.

Refer back to our discussion of null values for attributes. Can an attribute with null values qualify to be a key? If null values are permitted for an attribute, then many instances of the object may have null values for this attribute. That means this attribute is useless for identifying those instances for which the attribute has null values. Attributes for which null values are allowed cannot be used as keys.

Here are a few tips on selecting a primary key:

- Obviously, exclude attributes for which null values are allowed.
- If possible, prefer a single attribute to a combination of multiple attributes.
- Select an attribute whose values will not change for the life of the database system.

- Choose an attribute whose values do not have built-in meanings. For example, if part of the key for an object PRODUCT represents the warehouse code, the key value will have to change if the product is no longer stored in the original warehouse.

RELATIONSHIPS BETWEEN OBJECTS

Consider an order entry process. This is a typical process in most organizations. Examine the information requirements. Apart from others, three business objects feature prominently in the information requirements. The information requirements are about CUSTOMER, ORDER, and PRODUCT. Each object has its own set of attributes. If your data model represents just the three objects and their attributes, then the model will not be a true representation of the information requirements. Of course, in the real-world situation, you have these three objects. But that is not the whole story. These three objects do not just remain in seclusion from one another. The business process of order entry takes place on the basis of associations between the three objects. Accordingly, the data model must reflect these associations.

Customers place orders; orders contains products. At a basic level, the object CUSTOMER and the object ORDER are associated with each other. Similarly, the object ORDER and the object PRODUCT are linked to each other. As you know, such links and associations are represented as relationships in data model diagrams.

Role of Relationships

Let us inspect the associations among the three objects CUSTOMER, ORDER, and PRODUCT. Figure 6-6 shows a data model diagram with these objects.

First, observe the relationship between CUSTOMER and ORDER. The relationship symbol indicates that the relationship exists because in the real-world situation a customer *places* an order. The action of placing an order forms the basis for the relationship. A relationship name is an action word—usually a single verb. Relationships indicate interaction between objects. They represent associations between objects and the types of action that govern the associations.

Next, review the relationship between ORDER and PRODUCT. Here the action is not as apparent; nevertheless, it is the action of an order containing products. The association of ORDER with PRODUCT rests on the fact that orders are for products, that is, orders contain products. The verb or action word in this case is *contains*.

Look at the relationship symbol between CUSTOMER and ORDER. Does the symbol indicate the linkage between the two boxes representing the two objects or individual object instances within each of the two boxes? Figure 6-7 illustrates this important distinction.

The relationship indicated between two object boxes is actually the association between specific instances of one object and particular occurrences of another object. Take a little time to grasp the significance of the meaning and role of relationships symbolized in data model diagrams. The connection shown between two

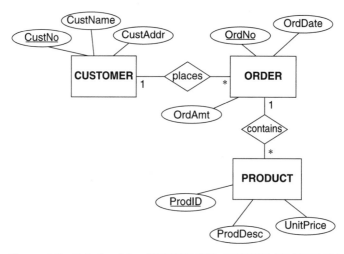

Figure 6-6 Relationships: CUSTOMER, ORDER, PRODUCT.

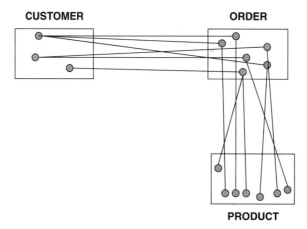

Figure 6-7 Relationships: links between instances.

object boxes simply indicates that the instances are related with one another. The name of the relationship as written within the diamond applies to each link between instances.

Cardinality in Relationships

You now clearly understand that relationships between two objects indicate the associations of instances of one object with instances of a second object. Let us take the example of the relationship between the objects CUSTOMER and ORDER. The relationship exists because a customer places one or more orders. Examine this relationship. Let us say that customer Techchoice, Inc. has placed four orders and that the order numbers for these orders are 1234, 3456, 4567, and 5678. What does this relationship between CUSTOMER and ORDER mean for this example? The explicit association is between customer Techchoice, Inc., an instance of the object CUSTOMER, and orders 1234, 3456, 4567, and 5678, instances of the object ORDER. So far, this is clear enough.

Now, the question arises: If instances of the objects CUSTOMER and ORDER are related, how many instances of the object ORDER can be associated with one instance of the object CUSTOMER? The answer to this question depends on the business rules of the real-world situation. In our example, one customer may place just one order or may place many orders. There is no restriction. That means one instance of the object CUSTOMER is related to many instances of the object ORDER. These numbers, referring to how many instances of one object may be related to how many of the other object, express the cardinality of the relationship.

Cardinality of relationships between two objects as shown in a data model indicates how many instances of the first object may be related to how many instances of the second—whether the number of instances is *one* or *many*. So three possibilities exist for the expression of the cardinality of a relationship: one-to-one, one-to-many, and many-to-many. We will explore these three types further.

One-to-One Relationship Take an example of the objects INVOICE and PAYMENT. Although not practical, suppose a business rule in the organization states that each invoice must be paid in full by a single payment because of accounting restrictions. In this case, the relationship between the objects INVOICE and PAYMENT is a one-to-one relationship. The cardinality is 1:1. Figure 6-8 illustrates this one-to-one relationship.

Note the associations indicated between instances of one object with instances of the other object. Observe how only one instance of INVOICE may be connected to a particular instance of PAYMENT. Similarly, only one instance of PAYMENT may be linked to a specific instance of INVOICE. This is a one-to-one relationship—one instance to one instance from either side of the relationship in the model diagram.

One-to-Many Relationship Refer back to the example of the relationship between CUSTOMER and ORDER. Here the relationship is a one-to-many relationship. The cardinality is 1:* (asterisk indicating *many*). Figure 6-9 shows this one-to-many relationship.

Let us go over the associations between the objects instances, one by one. From the side where the object CUSTOMER is shown, select customer instance A. This customer A placed orders numbers 2, 5, and 7. So the relationship observed from CUSTOMER side is: one customer instance related to many order instances. Note the * (asterisk) placed closer to the ORDER object on the relationship line.

Now look at the relationship associations from the ORDER side. Note that order number 1 from this side is linked to only one customer, namely B, on the CUSTOMER side. So the relationship observed from ORDER side is: one order instance is related to one customer instance. Notice the number 1 placed closer to the CUSTOMER object on the relationship line.

One invoice is paid by one payment.
One payment pays one invoice.

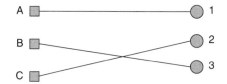

Figure 6-8 Relationship cardinality: one-to-one.

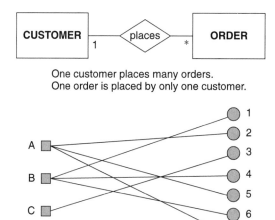

Figure 6-9 Relationship cardinality: one-to-many.

Observing from the CUSTOMER side, one instance of the object CUSTOMER is related to many instances of the other object ORDER. Again, observing from the ORDER side, one instance of object ORDER is related to only one instance of the other object CUSTOMER. So is the relationship one-to-many, or many-to-one? It appears to be both. Conventionally, this type of relationship is only referred to as a one-to-many relationship, and not the other way round.

Many-to-Many Relationship Consider an example of the relationship between the objects EMPLOYEE and PROJECT. Let us say that an employee may be assigned to several projects. Also, a project may have many employees. What is the nature of the association between instances of EMPLOYEE and PROJECT? Figure 6-10 presents this many-to-many relationship where the cardinality is *:*.

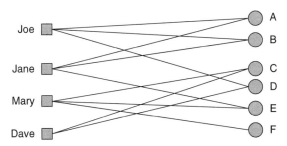

One employee is assigned to many projects.
One project has many employees.

Figure 6-10   Relationship cardinality: many-to-many.

Go over the association indicated between instances of the two objects. Look at the associations from the EMPLOYEE side. Employee Joe is assigned to projects A, B, and D. That is, one instance of EMPLOYEE is related to many instances of PROJECT. Now, observe the associations from the PROJECT side. Project B is associated with Joe and Jane. This means one instance of PROJECT is related to many instances of EMPLOYEE. Note the asterisks placed at both ends of the relationship line to indicate this many-to-many relationship.

Minimum and Maximum Cardinalities   Go back and look at the cardinality indicators such as 1 or * placed on the relationship lines in the model diagram. Analyze the meaning of these indicators. What do they indicate? These indicators tell us about the number of instances of an object that can be related. Related to how many instances of the other object? Let us review the meanings from the above figures.

Figure 6-8: "1" placed closer to object INVOICE   Indicates that a maximum of one instance of the object INVOICE can be related to one instance of the other object PAYMENT.

Figure 6-9: "" placed closer to object ORDER*   Indicates that a maximum of many instances of the object ORDER can be related to one instance of the other object CUSTOMER.

Figure 6-10: "" placed closer to object EMPLOYEE*   Indicates that a maximum of many instances of the object EMPLOYEE can be related to one instance of the other object PROJECT.

At this point, you realize that the cardinality indicators we have used so far really indicate the maximum cardinalities. Is there something known as a minimum cardinality in a relationship between objects? If so, what is the significance of minimum cardinality? First, let us formally define maximum and minimum cardinalities.

Maximum cardinality. Maximum number of instances of one object that are related to a single instance of another object.

Minimum cardinality. Minimum number of instances of one object that are related to a single instance of another object.

Figure 6-11 shows two relationships, one between SUPERVISOR and EMPLOYEE and the other between EMPLOYEE and PROJECT.

Review the cardinality indicators marked on the relationship line between SUPERVISOR and EMPLOYEE. Each set of indicators has two parts. The first part indicates the minimum cardinality; the second part indicates the maximum cardinality. Whenever cardinality indicators are shown as a set of two indicators, they denote the minimum and maximum cardinalities, respectively. If only one indicator is shown in a relationship, then assume it to be the maximum cardinality indicator, the minimum cardinality indicator being omitted. Interpret the cardinality indicators between SUPERVISOR and EMPLOYEE.

Indicators next to SUPERVISOR

Minimum 1:   A minimum of one instance of SUPERVISOR associated with one instance of EMPLOYEE.

Maximum 1:   A maximum of one instance of SUPERVISOR associated with one instance of EMPLOYEE.

Indicators next to EMPLOYEE

Minimum 1:   A minimum of one instance of EMPLOYEE associated with one instance of SUPERVISOR.

Maximum *:   A maximum of many instances of EMPLOYEE associated with one instance of SUPERVISOR.

What do these cardinality indicators really mean? Which aspects of real-world information do these indicators represent? Note carefully that the indicators next

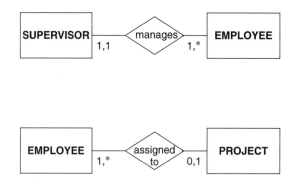

Figure 6-11   Relationships: maximum and minimum cardinalities.

to one object indicate the number of the instances of that object associated with one instance of the other object.

Looking at the above cardinality indicators, what can you say about the real-world information portrayed by the data model? How many employees does one supervisor can have under his or her supervision? For the answer, look at the cardinality indicators next to the other object, EMPLOYEE. What do you see? A minimum cardinality of 1 and a maximum cardinality of *. This means a supervisor must supervise at least one employee but may supervise many employees. Now ask the other question. How many supervisors does one employee report to? To answer this question, look at the cardinality indicators "1,1" next to the other object, SUPERVISOR. These indicators represent the real-world condition that each employee must report to one supervisor and an employee cannot report to more than one supervisor.

Continue with the other relationship in the figure between EMPLOYEE and PROJECT. A project must have at least one employee; furthermore, a project may have many employees. From the other point of view, an employee may be assigned to only one project and not more. Also, some employees may be associated with no project (note minimum cardinality of "0") at all.

Let us summarize maximum and minimum cardinalities with one more example involving three objects. In particular, note carefully how the minimum cardinality indicator expresses the optional or mandatory participation of object instances in a relationship. Figure 6-12 displays three objects, CUSTOMER, ORDER, and PRODUCT, and indicates their relationships.

CUSTOMER and ORDER are in a one-to-many relationship; ORDER and PRODUCT are in a many-to-many relationship. Note the minimum cardinality of "1" or "0." Read the explanation given in the figure and understand how "1" as the minimum cardinality indicates the mandatory nature of the relationship and how "0" as the minimum cardinality denotes its optional nature.

Aggregate Objects

Let us suppose you are modeling the information requirements for a dental office. Two objects in your data model will be PATIENT and SERVICE. Now consider

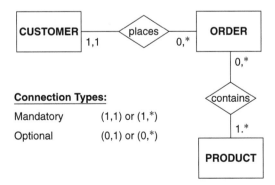

Figure 6-12   Optional and mandatory participation in relationship.

the instances of the object PATIENT. This object set contains all patients who come for dental service. The instances of the object SERVICE comprise all services received by patients at the dental office. These include services such as oral exams, X rays, amalgams, tooth extractions, prosthodontics, crowns, endodontics, and periodontics.

Typically, the cost for a certain service received by a particular patient depends on the type of insurance coverage the patient has. If patient Robert Bridges gets complete upper dentures, cost for him is $595, whereas patient Diane Silverstein is charged $475 for the same service. Different types of insurance policies cover the patients, hence the variation in the service costs.

Is *Cost* an attribute of the object SERVICE? You find that values of *Cost* are not dependent just on particular instances of this object alone. What are the values of *Cost*? The $595 and $475 indicated above are values of the attribute *Cost*. For complete upper dentures to Robert, the value of the *Cost* attribute is $595; for the same service to Diane, the value is $475. What does that mean? The values of the attribute *Cost* depend on pairs of instances from PATIENT and SERVICE put together as shown in the following examples:

(Robert Bridges, complete upper dentures)	$595
(Diane Silverstein, complete upper dentures)	$475
(John Rawlins, plastic crown)	$498
(Ruth Goldberg, plastic crown)	$325

Review the above examples. Robert, Diane, John, and Ruth are instances of the object PATIENT. Complete upper dentures and plastic crown are instances of the object SERVICE. What can you say about the pairs shown in parenthesis? How can you represent this kind of real-world information in your data model? You may consider these as instances of the two objects PATIENT and SERVICE put together—instances of an aggregate object comprising the two individual objects.

Figure 6-13 illustrates this concept of an aggregate or composite object. A relationship viewed as an object gives rise to the notion of an aggregate object.

An aggregate object behaves like any other object. A rectangular box represents an aggregate object also. The aggregate object PATIENT-SERVICE is shown as a large box surrounding the two objects whose relationship produces the aggregate.

Figure 6-14 presents the aggregate object called SHIPMENT. Here the aggregate is made up of three objects that participate in a three-way relationship. Note the larger box representing the aggregate object encompassing all the three participating objects.

From these two figures, note the following features of aggregate objects that are common to all types of objects:

Attributes. An aggregate object has specific attributes representing real-world information.

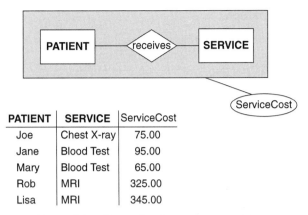

Figure 6-13 Example of an aggregate object.

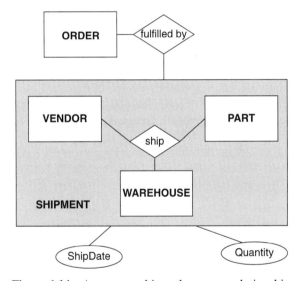

Figure 6-14 Aggregate object: three-way relationship.

Relationships. An aggregate object may have relationships with other single objects or other aggregate objects depending on the real-world information portrayed by the data model.

Under what circumstances do you have to show aggregate objects in your data model diagram? If you find that a certain characteristic such as cost or date depends on combinations of object instances, then an aggregate must be shown with that characteristic as an attribute of the aggregate object. Again, if you note that instances of some object are related to combinations of instances of other objects and not to instances of single objects, then you need an aggregate object to show the combination. Look at Figure 6-14 again for such a relationship.

Degrees of Relationships

Before we leave the topic of relationships, let us explore one final aspect of relationships. From the examples seen so far, you note that objects are related in twos or threes. That is, instances of two objects are associated with each other, or instances of three objects are associated to form a combination. Figure 6-15 indicates three types of relationships. Note the associations between instances of the same object, between instances between two objects, and among instances of three objects.

The degree of a relationship is the number of object sets that participate in the relationship. If three objects participate in a relationship, its degree is 3. Occasionally, the real-world information being modeled may require relationships of degrees 4, 5, or higher. Generally, the binary relationship is the most common type.

GENERALIZATION AND SPECIALIZATION

A true data model must reflect every aspect of real-world information. Do you agree? If there are peculiarities about certain business objects, then the model must represent those special conditions. If some relationships are different from regular relationships, then the data model must portray those special relationships. A realistic data model should display everything about the set of real-world information requirements. Frequently, you will find that some of the attributes and relationships are the same for more than one object. The object-based data modeling technique handles this special condition very well. Generalization and specialization of object sets is a powerful feature of this technique.

Take the case of modeling the real-world information for a medical center. One of the main business objects to be modeled is the PATIENT object. Think about

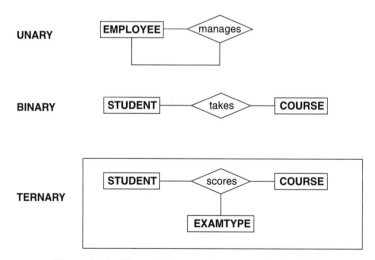

Figure 6-15   Unary, binary, and ternary relationships.

coming up with a model for this object. Modeling any object requires considerations of the possible and relevant attributes for the object. Also, you must consider the relationships that instances of this object have with instances of other objects. As you proceed to model the object PATIENT, you realize that there are inpatients, outpatients, and emergency room patients. Your model must include all these patient types. Now examine these patient types for attributes. You note that all three of these types of patients have common attributes such as PatientID, PatientName, Address, Diagnosis, and so on. But you also realize that each set of patients has attributes that are not common to the other two sets of patients. For example, inpatients have attributes such as AdmissionDate, DischargeDate, LengthOfStay, TypeOf Meals, and so on that are not shared by outpatients and ER patients. Furthermore, inpatients are related to another object in the model, namely, ROOM. They may be transferred from one room to another.

You see that there is something special about the three sets of patients in the way they share their attributes and in the manner in which some attributes are specific to each set. Clearly, all patients in the medical center cannot be modeled with one object PATIENT. Then what are the options? You can opt to model the patients with three separate objects INPATIENT, OUTPATIENT, and ERPATIENT. If you make this choice, then your model will repeat several attributes and perhaps relationships for each of the three objects.

Step back and look at the four objects PATIENT, INPATIENT, OUTPATIENT, and ERPATIENT. It appears that an object PATIENT is a supertype of object and that the other three are subtypes whose attributes and relations may be derived from the supertype object. You will find it best to use these four objects in your data model to truly represent the real-world information in the case of the medical center. Figure 6-16 explains the need for this method of representation in the model.

What you have noted is the concept of generalization and specialization in a data model. This concept enables special types of objects to be represented in a data model. As you examine the information requirements of any business, you will

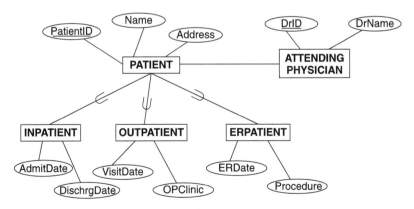

Figure 6-16   PATIENT object: supertype and subtypes.

observe these types of objects. Two main reasons warrant the indication of generalization and specialization in a data model:

- Although each subtype object may share most of its attributes with all the other subtypes, certain attributes may apply only to that subtype.
- Only the instances of certain subtype objects may participate in some relationships.

In practice, how do you note these special object types while modeling the information requirements? You may adopt the top-down or the bottom-up approach. You may look at several objects and realize that these may be subtypes of some supertype object. Conversely, you may examine an object and find that it would break down into subtype objects. Let us summarize these two routes:

Generalization. Create object boxes for every possible type of business object. Examine objects and see whether some of these may be subtypes of some other object. Suppress the differences between the subtypes, identify the common attributes, and generalize to define the supertype object.

Specialization. Create object boxes for only the high-level business objects. That is, ignore any possible variations in the set of attributes for instances within each high-level object. In the case of the medical center, first you would come up with the PATIENT object. Then examine the instances within the object and note the differences in the sets of attributes for the instances. Separate out the instances that possess the same set of instances as a special subtype object for PATIENT.

Supersets and Subsets

Object sets that are supertypes are also known as supersets; similarly, subtype object sets are also called subsets. Figure 6-17 presents a few examples of supersets and subsets.

Note each superset and the corresponding subsets. Taking any particular example, while modeling the information requirements you could model by the generalization method from the subsets or by the specialization method from the superset.

Generalization Hierarchy

Refer back to Figure 6-16 showing the subsets and the superset representing patients in a medical center. As certain attributes for a subset are derived from the superset, the superset and its subsets form a hierarchy in the arrangement of these objects in a data model. The hierarchical, top-down arrangement with the superset object box above the subset boxes gives an indication of how the superset provides the attributes common to the subsets in real-world situations.

Figure 6-16 shows two levels of the hierarchy, PATIENT at the higher level and the other three objects one level down. Sometimes, you will come across more

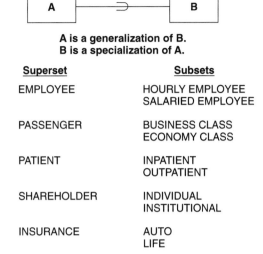

**A is a generalization of B.
B is a specialization of A.**

Superset	Subsets
EMPLOYEE	HOURLY EMPLOYEE SALARIED EMPLOYEE
PASSENGER	BUSINESS CLASS ECONOMY CLASS
PATIENT	INPATIENT OUTPATIENT
SHAREHOLDER	INDIVIDUAL INSTITUTIONAL
INSURANCE	AUTO LIFE

Figure 6-17   Supersets and subsets: examples.

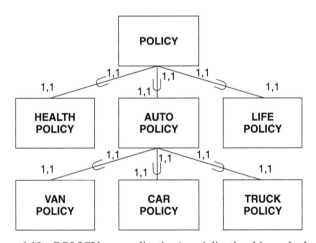

Figure 6-18   POLICY: generalization/specialization hierarchy levels.

than two levels in the generalization/specialization hierarchy. Figure 6-18 shows three levels in the hierarchy for POLICY, showing levels of subsets for insurance policies.

What about the instances in the superset and each of the subsets? The set of instances within the supertype object is a collection of all the instances in the lower-level subtype objects. If a particular instance is present in subtype AUTOPOLICY, then that instance also exists in the supertype POLICY. Note the cardinality indicator "1,1" between the supertype and each subtype object.

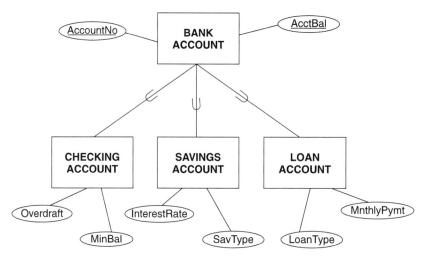

Figure 6-19   Subsets: inheritance of attributes.

Inheritance of Attributes

A significant feature of a superset and its subsets is the inheritance of the attributes by each subset from the superset. These are the attributes that are common to all the subsets. In the case of the objects for a medical center as discussed above, all the subsets share common attributes such as PatientID, PatientName, Address, and Diagnosis. Because the subsets share these attributes, there is no point in repeating these as attributes of each of the subsets. In a data model diagram, you may, therefore, show these as attributes of the superset. The principle of inheritance of attributes by the subsets from the superset implies that each of the subsets has these attributes. In addition, each subset may have other attributes specific only to that subset.

Figure 6-19 illustrates the principle of inheritance of attributes by the subsets. Note the common attributes shown at the superset level. Also, observe the attributes specific to individual subsets.

Inheritance of Relationships

Let us take an example of a company leasing vehicles to customers. A lease agreement covers a particular leasing arrangement with a customer. Examining the information requirements, you can come up with two initial objects, namely, VEHICLE and AGREEMENT. Of course, there would be other objects. But let us consider these two objects for now. Over a period of time, the same vehicle would relate to different lease agreements. That is, when a vehicle comes out of one lease agreement, it would be leased to another customer or to the same customer with a new lease agreement. You note that a direct relationship exists the objects AGREEMENT and VEHICLE.

Examine the instances of the object VEHICLE. Do all the instances have the same attributes? You quickly notice that cars, trucks, and vans that are leased have common attributes. More importantly, each of these three types has specific attrib-

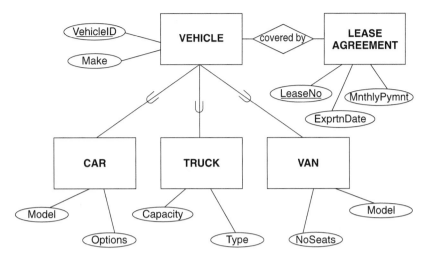

Figure 6-20   Subsets: inheritance of relationships.

utes not shared with the other two types. You have now come across the situation of superset and subsets in the information requirements. VEHICLE is the superset and CAR, TRUCK, and VAN are the subsets.

What about the association of the instances of VEHICLE with instances of AGREEMENT? In the same way, do instances of CAR have associations with instances of AGREEMENT? They do, because cars are covered by lease agreements. You note that if the superset VEHICLE has a relationship with another object, AGREEMENT, then its subset CAR also has the same relationship with the same object AGREEMENT.

Figure 6-20 illustrates this principle of inheritance of relationships by the subsets from the superset. Note that each of the subsets inherits the relationship with the object AGREEMENT.

Special Cases

In real-world situations, you will run into a few special cases of specialization. Usually, these special cases deal with the presence of particular instances in just one subset or in more than one subset. Let us examine these special cases. We will describe each special case with an example. Each example shows the links between instances in the superset and instances in the subsets. The notations to represent the special cases in a data model diagram vary. You need not be unnecessarily confused with variation in the notations. Please pay attention to the concepts; concepts are more important than notations.

Exclusive Subsets   Figure 6-21 describes this special case. In this case, an instance of the superset can be an instance of only one of the subsets. The subsets are exclusive.

Nonexclusive Subsets   Figure 6-22 shows nonexclusive subsets. In this case, an instance of the superset can be an instance of more than one subset. The subsets are nonexclusive.

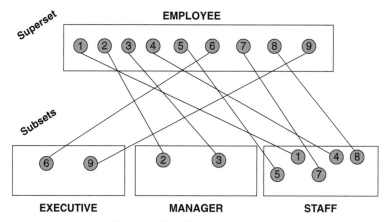

Figure 6-21   Exclusive subsets.

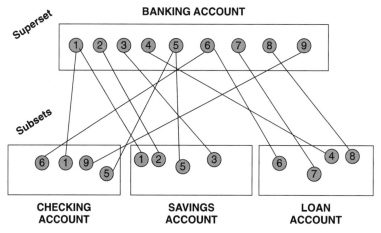

Figure 6-22   Nonexclusive subsets.

Total Specialization   Figure 6-23 illustrates the special case in which every instance of the superset must be an instance of some subset. That means the list of subsets is total or complete. The model includes all possible subsets known at the time of design. Total specialization implies exhaustive specialization; all possible subsets are considered.

Partial Specialization   Figure 6-24 shows an example of partial specialization. Here, some instances of the superset are not found in any of the subsets. That means that the list of subsets is not exhaustive; all possibilities are not accounted for in the subsets. The list of subsets is only partial.

In a particular data model, you are likely to see combinations of these special cases. The following are the possible combinations:

- Exclusive, total specialization
- Nonexclusive, total specialization

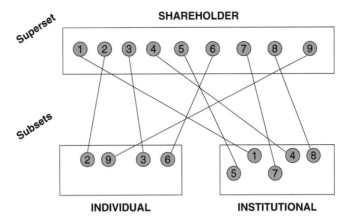

Figure 6-23 Total specialization.

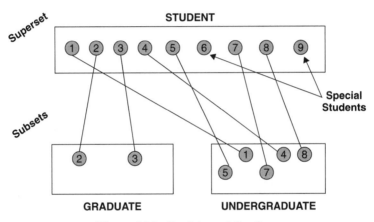

Figure 6-24 Partial specialization.

- Exclusive, partial specialization
- Nonexclusive, partial specialization

SPECIAL OBJECT TYPES AND RELATIONSHIPS

We have discussed various examples of objects and their relationships. The object sets you represent by a rectangular box in a data model diagram are all business objects relevant to the information requirements of the real world portrayed by the model. You have also noted, through many examples, that instances of one object may have associations with instances of another object. If so, you draw lines connecting the two associated objects, indicating the relationship by a diamond shape in between with the name of the relationship written inside the diamond. By now, you know all of this clearly.

We also went through special cases of objects that are related in a particular way. One object appeared to be contained within another or one object seemed to be inheriting attributes and relationships from another object. This is the concept of generalization and specialization. You have also noted examples of supersets and subsets.

We now want to consider a few remaining concepts about special object types and relationships. This would complete the types of objects and relationships you commonly come across in real-world information requirements. As you know, a data model must be a true replica of everything relevant in the real world.

Conceptual and Physical Objects

Assume that you are asked to model the information requirements for an airline company. Very quickly, you realize that AIRCRAFT must be one of the objects in your data model. Now examine the requirements of the company with regard to the object AIRCRAFT. The company's fleet consists of many aircraft. Each of these aircraft has a serial number, a given number of seats, the date it was placed in service, the chief mechanic responsible to service it, and so on. The company needs to keep track of all the planes in its fleet. Notice also that the company uses different types of aircraft like Boeing 747, MD 11, Airbus 321, and so on. The company needs to keep track of the aircraft types used in its fleet as well. What are Boeing 747, MD11, Airbus 321, and so on? Are these aircraft? No, these are types of aircraft, not the physical aircraft themselves. In this case of information requirements for the airline company, you find two types of related objects. One is the object AIRCRAFT and the other is the object AIRCRAFT TYPE.

Now consider the information requirements for a library. The library has to keep track of the individual copies of the books so that it will know which particular copy is out with a member. Each copy is marked with a call number. Furthermore, the library must also have a catalog of books available for members. These are not the actual copies of the books but the titles. So, in this case, you see the need for two related objects in your data model: BOOK and BOOK COPY. The two are not the same. The instances within each object are different. In the case of the object BOOK, the instances are the individual titles; for the object BOOK COPY the instances are individual copies of the books.

Just one more example. An appliance store needs to keep track of individual units of each appliance. Also, the store has to maintain a list of the types of appliances available in the store. Here you note the need for two related objects in the data model: APPLIANCE UNIT and APPLIANCE TYPE.

Physical Objects   The objects like AIRCRAFT, BOOK COPY, and APPLIANCE UNIT are examples of physical objects. A physical object refers to tangible objects that you can see, touch, or feel. These are physical things. You need to have physical objects in your data model, whenever the information requirements call for keeping track of individual, physical things.

What about the instances within a physical object? Each instance represents a particular physical thing. The instances within the object AIRCRAFT are the physical aircraft in the company's fleet. If the company owns 100 aircraft, 100 instances exist within the object set. In the same way, if the library has a total inventory of

10,000 physical copies of various books, the object set BOOK COPY contains these 10,000 instances.

Conceptual Objects   AIRCRAFT TYPE, BOOK, and APPLIANCE TYPE do not represent any tangible things. You cannot touch or see an AIRCRAFT TYPE. What you can see is a physical aircraft that is of the Boeing 747 type. So these are not examples of physical objects. The objects represented by these are conceptual; these are conceptual objects.

What kinds of instances does a conceptual object set contain? These instances are not physical things. Each instance within the object set BOOK refers to a particular title in the library. The library may have the book, *A Brief History of Time* by Stephen Hawking. This title will be an instance of the conceptual object BOOK. If the library holds four copies of this book, then you will have four corresponding instances in the physical object BOOK COPY.

Data Model Diagrams   Figure 6-25 presents the data model diagrams for the three examples discussed.

Note the relationships between the conceptual object and the corresponding physical object in each example. Also, observe the cardinality indicators and understand the association of the instances.

Recursive Relationships

EMPLOYEE is a fairly common object in many real-world information requirements. Think about the instances for this object set. Every employee in the organization will be represented by an instance. In the set of instances, you will find workers who supervise other workers. An instance representing a supervisor associates with those instances of employees under his or her supervision. What you find here is instances of an object associating with instances of the same object. Associations recur within the same object. These are recursive associations, and this type

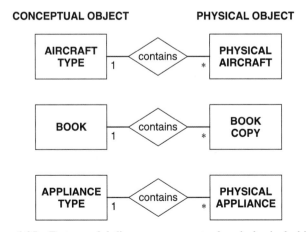

Figure 6-25   Data model diagrams: conceptual and physical objects.

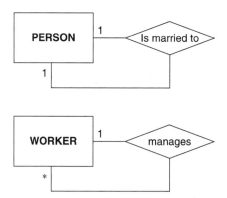

Figure 6-26   Recursive relationships.

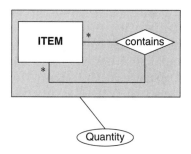

Figure 6-27   Assembly structure.

of association is a recursive relationship. Your data model must be able to indicate recursive relationships.

Figure 6-26 shows examples of recursive relationships.

Note how the relationship line from an object is linked back to itself. Cardinalities may vary with recursive relationships just like they do with regular relationships. Observe the different sets of cardinality indicators represented in the figure.

Assembly Structures

What is a bill of materials structure? You come across bill of materials processing (BOMP) in manufacturing. In manufacturing of automobiles, an assembly of a major part consists of several subassemblies; each subassembly in turn may be broken down further. Assembly structures are cases of recursive relationships in which the associations recur at many levels.

Figure 6-27 displays an example of an assembly structure.

Notice the attribute Quantity shown in the diagram for the object ITEM. This attribute Quantity does not represent quantities of individual instances of the object. Quantity indicates units for the various recursive associations. How many units are there for the combinations of item number 1 with item numbers 4,5, and 6? It is an attribute of an aggregate object consisting of just one object ITEM.

REVIEW OF OBJECT-BASED DATA MODEL

As we conclude our discussion, let us recapitulate what we covered on this important topic. Object-based data modeling is a natural, intuitive method of representing real-world information requirements. In the real world, most commonly you notice business objects. This modeling technique provides components to represent business objects, their characteristics, and their interactions.

Summary of Components

You can create a true data model for any set of real-world information requirements by using the following basic components, showing these with standard notations or symbols:

Object Set. To represent a business object.

Attribute. To represent an inherent or intrinsic characteristic of an object.

Identifier. An attribute or set of attributes whose values will uniquely identify individual instances of an object.

Relationship. Direct association between instances of objects.

Cardinality Indicators. Set of values to denote the minimum and maximum number of instances that may participate in relationships between objects.

Generalization/Specialization. To represent a superset and its subsets.

Comprehensive Data Model Diagram

Figure 6-28 presents a data model diagram for manufacturing operations.

Carefully note each component in the diagram. Study the various object sets, relationships, and cardinality indicators and also observe the special cases. Even though the data model represents many aspects of real-world information requirements, note that the whole model is constructed with only the basic components listed above.

CHAPTER SUMMARY

- Object-based data modeling based on both object technology and data modeling is an effective method focusing on business objects.
- The object-based data model is a generic model that has several advantages: universal model, true replica, free from restraints, easily transformable, and intuitive.
- The components or building blocks of the data model are object set, attribute, identifier, relationship, cardinality indicators, generalization/specialization.

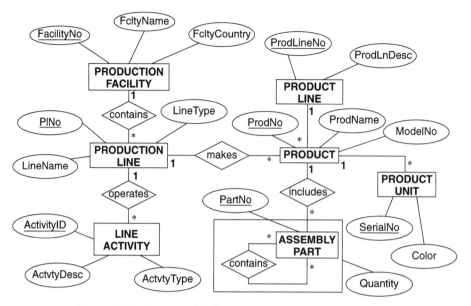

Figure 6-28   Data model diagram: manufacturing operations.

- With just these components, you can represent any collection of real-world information in the data model.
- Some object sets are subsets of other object sets. Generalization/specialization deals with supersets and subsets. Subsets inherit attributes and relationships from a superset.
- Physical objects represent physical things that can be seen or touched, for example, a copy of a book; conceptual objects indicate nontangible things, for example, "book."
- In a recursive relationship, instances of an object are associated with other instances of the same object.

REVIEW QUESTIONS

1. Explain how an object-based data model is a generic data model.
2. Name the components of the object-based data model and list the standard symbols or notations used to construct the model.
3. Distinguish between object sets and object instances. Give an example.
4. Describe the different types of objects, with an example for each type.
5. What is your understanding of null values for attributes? When are null values used?
6. "Relationships are really associations between instances of objects." Explain this with an example.
7. What do maximum and minimum cardinality indicators represent? What is an optional relationship?

8. What is an aggregate object? Give an example.

9. What is your understanding of total specialization? Explain with an example. Do you think total specialization is common in data models?

10. Describe the notion of conceptual objects and physical objects with an example.

EXERCISES

1. Indicate whether true or false:
   A. The object-based data modeling technique produces generic models.
   B. An identifier for an object set must not include more than three attributes.
   C. Cardinality indicators denote the number of object sets that are in a relationship.
   D. The maximum cardinality indicator denotes whether a relationship is optional or mandatory.
   E. The attributes of an object include only the intrinsic or inherent characteristics of that object.
   F. Two or more attributes of an object may share an attribute domain.
   G. The many-to-many relationship is actually a one-to-many relationship from either side of the relationship line.
   H. Aggregate objects may have attributes but not relationships.
   I. If some instances of the superset are not found in any of the subsets, then this is partial specialization.
   J. All recursive relationships are one-to-many relationships.

2. As a data modeler for a company manufacturing automobile parts, review any one of the business processes in your company. Identify the objects, relationships, and so on supporting this process. Create a partial data model diagram showing these components.

3. You are a member of the database project team responsible for analyzing information requirements for a grocery store and identifying the business objects to be included in the data model. Describe how you will proceed with your task. List the business objects you would identify.

4. Consider data modeling for an auction business. Customers in an auction business fall into different categories. Consignors bring items for sale; buyers purchase items at auction; property owners bring items for appraisal of values; subscribers subscribe to auction catalogs. Can you apply the principles of generalization/specialization to customers in this business? If so, describe the superset and the subsets. If not, explain the reasons.

5. You are a Senior Data Modeler for a local bank. Create a data model to cover the major banking operations. State your assumptions on the types of processes included in your data model.

CHAPTER 7

ENTITY-RELATIONSHIP DATA MODEL

CHAPTER OBJECTIVES

- Study entity-relationship (E-R) data modeling as another technique to create a semantic model
- Understand the principles and concepts of E-R modeling
- Discuss the components of the E-R data model
- Explore special types of business entities and relationships
- Examine an entity-relationship diagram

Database practitioners and experts refer to a data model that captures the true meaning of real-world information requirements as a semantic data model. Such a model truly represents the semantics or real meaning and implications of what you need to model from the relevant real-world information. We have studied the object-based data modeling technique as a technique for creating a semantic data model. Now we want to study another popular technique for building a semantic data model: entity-relationship (E-R) data modeling.

As you review the concepts, principles, and components of the E-R data model, you will notice a number of similarities with the object-based data model. Both achieve the same purpose; both are intended to produce similar results; both reflect the true meaning of information requirements. As we proceed with our discussion, wherever essential, we will compare the two techniques and point out the correspondences.

Because of the similarities, we need not go over again the basic principles and examples of the mapping of real-world information to the components of the model.

Database Design and Development: An Essential Guide for IT Professionals by Paulraj Ponniah
ISBN 0-471-21877-4   Copyright © 2003 by John Wiley and Sons, Inc.

These are basically the same for both modeling techniques. We will therefore concentrate on presenting the various components and their notations used to draw the E-R data model diagram. Because the two data modeling methods were developed independently, the notations or symbols used for the components are somewhat different. However even in the notations, you will note many resemblances.

Study this chapter for the purpose of reinforcing the concepts already learned in the discussion of object-based data modeling. Note the variations in certain notions. Also, observe how the E-R data model includes additional notations to represent individual types within a particular component.

INTRODUCTION TO E-R MODEL

First of all, note that the E-R data model is another generic model similar to the object-based data model. You will recall how a generic model is free from the rules and restrictions of conventional models such as hierarchical, network, and relational models. As you know, these conventional models call for information requirements to be perceived in certain given ways and their relationships to be established according to defined conventions. Being a generic model, the E-R data model can apply to all types of nuances in information requirements. Again, because it is a generic data model, the E-R model is amenable to being transformed to any particular conventional model based on the implementation of your database system.

The E-R data modeling technique is a widely used method. You have a choice of many data modeling tools to create the model. Because of its popularity and widespread use, the notations and symbols are more standardized. This modeling technique provides a wider range of notations to represent variations within each component.

Basic Concepts

By way of introduction to the basic concepts and principles of E-R modeling technique, note the following points:

Mainstream approach. Most data modelers and practitioners seem to prefer the E-R modeling technique, probably because of the availability of several CASE tools to support the technique.

Things and associations. Examining any set of information requirements, you discover that these are really about things and their associations—things that are of interest to the business and associations that are relevant to the business processes. The E-R modeling technique recognizes this underlying premise.

Entities and relationships. As the name of the technique signifies, the entity-relationship modeling technique focuses on entities and relationships as natural concepts. Entities are the things the business is interested in, and relationships are the associations among the things.

Description of information. The data modeling technique describes real-world information in terms of entities, their attributes, and the relationships among the entities.

Graphics and rules. You draw an entity-relationship diagram (ERD) according to appropriate rules by using well-defined graphical symbols.

Theoretical foundation. The modeling technique rests on a solid foundation on the principles of entities, attributes, and relationships.

Means for communication. An E-R model proves to be a useful and easily understood means for communication among the IT professionals on the database project as well as with user representatives.

Data Modeling Process

E-R data modeling seems to be a natural way of looking at real-world information without being particularly guided by business processes. Following up on this realization, Figure 7-1 illustrates how E-R data modeling derives the components, one by one, as a result of natural observation of real-world information.

The figure essentially illustrates the process of creating an E-R model. Carefully note the boxes on the left side of the figure showing how each observation seems to follow naturally from the previous one. Let us see how this process of creating an E-R model works from one observation to the next. This is how the model is created from observations made of the information requirements.

Consider a typical organization without getting into too much detail. Let us record the flow of observations and the derivation of the components.

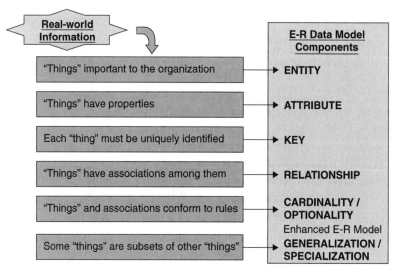

Figure 7-1 Deriving E-R data model components.

Certain "things" are important to the organization. List these things and derive these as entities of DEPARTMENT, EMPLOYEE, CUSTOMER, ORDER, and INVOICE.

Each of these "things" has properties. Mark these properties or characteristics and derive these as attributes of each of the entities DEPARTMENT, EMPLOYEE, CUSTOMER, ORDER, and INVOICE. For example, note that EMPLOYEE has characteristics such as EmployeeName, EmployeeAddress, and SocSecNumber. Derive these as attributes of EMPLOYEE.

Each case or occurrence of a "thing" must be uniquely identified. Select one or more attributes in each entity so that the values of these attributes may be used to uniquely identify an occurrence of an entity. Select SocSecNumber as the identifier or key for EMPLOYEE.

"Things" have associations among them. Derive relationships among entities from the associations. CUSTOMER places ORDER. Derive a relationship between the two entities from this association.

"Things" and associations conform to rules. One customer may place one or more orders. There may some customers who have not placed any orders. Rules govern the association between CUSTOMER and ORDER. From such rules, derive the cardinality and optionality of the relationship.

Some "things" are subsets of other "things." Individuals and institutions may be customers to the organization. From this concept, derive INDIVIDUAL and INSTITUTION as subsets of CUSTOMER.

In earlier versions of E-R modeling, the natural sequence had stopped with the component "Cardinality/Optionality" mentioned above. Deeper observation of real-world information requirements reveals the existence of supersets and subsets as special types of entities. Therefore, the E-R data model was enhanced later to include generalization and specialization.

Major Components

The components of the E-R model are practically the same as the object-based data model. Both being techniques for building a semantic data model, you would almost expect the building blocks to be the same. Therefore, as we describe the components here or below in the chapter, you will note the special features of the E-R model. Over the years, more precise notations have been included to indicate special aspects of real-world information requirements.

Figure 7-2 presents the graphical notations or symbols for the various components.

We mentioned above that E-R data model provides representations for different variations within a component. For example, real-world information contains variations in attributes. Sometimes, an attribute may be a composite of other attributes. Mostly, an attribute has a single value for one occurrence of an entity. However, you also come across an attribute having multiple values for one occurrence of an

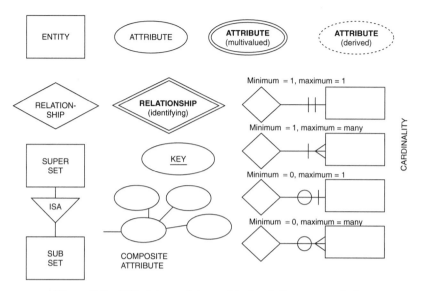

Figure 7-2   E-R data model: graphical notations or symbols.

entity. Note the different notations in the figure to denote single-valued, multivalued, derived, and composite attributes. Also, observe the notations for the two types of relationship. You will also note that symbols for supersets, subsets, and cardinality indicators are different from the ones used in the object-based data model covered in Chapter 6.

ENTITIES

Consider a banking institution. For this organization, real-world things exist that are of interest. The bank is interested in customers; it renders banking services to each customer. The real-world thing called CUSTOMER is of interest to the bank. Customers open bank accounts. These bank accounts may be checking, savings, or loan accounts. As such, real-world things such as CHECKING ACCOUNT, SAVINGS ACCOUNT, and LOAN ACCOUNT are also of interest to the organization. If you examine the bank's operations, you will notice other real-world things that are of interest to the bank.

In creating an E-R data model, you start by observing real-world things that are of interest to the organization in the course of its operations. You are not really examining individual processes; you are just listing the things, both tangible and intangible. These real-world things are the entities that need to be included in the data model. This is similar to recognizing business objects and including them in an object-based data model.

While studying entities in the E-R data model, observe the similarities with the object-based data model. Observe how entity types and entities match up with object sets and object instances.

Entity Definition

Entities are real-world "things" of interest to an organization. Note the following businesses and a few of the things of interest to the particular organizations:

Airline: AIRCRAFT, AIRCRAFT TYPE, MANUFACTURER, PASSENGER, FLIGHT

Pharmacist: CUSTOMER, PRODUCT, PRESCRIPTION, SUPPLIER, BILL

Car Wash: WASH TYPE, WASH, EQUIPMENT

Farm Market: PRODUCE, SUPPLIER, SALE

Orchard: TREE, VARIETY, SPECIES, ORCHARD, CUSTOMER

Observe the following features of an entity:

Independent existence. Notice that in each case, an entity in the real world has independent existence. That means an entity does not depend on the presence of another entity for its existence. The entity PASSENGER exists irrespective of whether it is related to another entity called FLIGHT. There could potentially be prospective passengers who have not been associated with any flights at all. Still, the entity exists in the database system.

Distinguishable. In the real world, one entity is distinguishable from another. That means that one passenger named Tom James is distinguishable from another passenger named Joe Rawlins. Each entity is unique, and you can differentiate one entity from another.

Physical and Conceptual Entities. When you review the examples of entities listed above, you observe that some of the things may be seen or touched—things that are tangible. When you examine the others on the list, you realize that some of the other things cannot be really seen or experienced. These are not tangible. Nevertheless, both categories are things that are of interest to an organization. Make sure you include both types as indicated below in your data model.

Things with physical existence. An employee, a specific automobile, a particular building, an explicit machine, and a particular aircraft are examples of this type.

Things with conceptual existence. Examples include a university course, a visit to the doctor, an invoice sent to a customer, a bank account, and a type of aircraft.

Entity Types

So far in our discussion we have indicated one particular thing of interest to an organization as an entity. An entity is a single thing. One customer is a "thing" that an organization is interested in. Of course, there would be thousands of customers for an organization. So database practitioners make a distinction and refer to the notion that refers to the collection of entities as an entity type. Entities are individual "things," whereas entity types refer to the group of entities.

Figure 7-3 illustrates the two notions of entity types and entities.

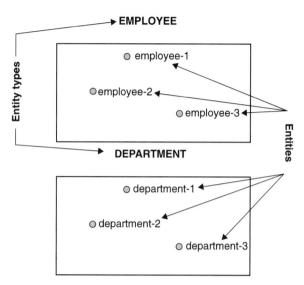

Figure 7-3 Entity types and entities.

Note the two examples shown in the figure:

Entity Types—EMPLOYEE, DEPARTMENT
Entity—Individual occurrences of each entity type

Entity Sets

You now understand the meaning of the two terms "entity" and "entity type." Take the example of the entity type EMPLOYEE. Assume that there are 5000 employees in the database at a given time. This is the set of employee entities in the database at that time. "Entity set" refers to the entire group of entities of an entity type in the database at a given time.

Figure 7-4 explains the concept of entity set.

Note the sets of employee and department entities shown in the figure. In practice, the name of the entity type also refers to the entity set. See how the entity type EMPLOYEE refers to the set of employee entities. A rectangular box denotes an entity type in the E-R data model.

Weak Entity Types

Consider the real-world situation of customers placing orders and orders containing one or more detail lines. Each detail line in an order contains the data about a product ordered. For this small set of real-world information requirements you can come up with three entity types as shown in Figure 7-5.

Now think about these three entity types, especially about the existence of entities of these types. An entity of CUSTOMER can exist whether a corresponding entity of ORDER exists or not. Each customer entity is uniquely identified inde-

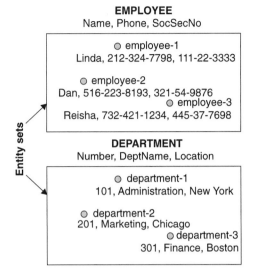

Figure 7-4   Entity sets.

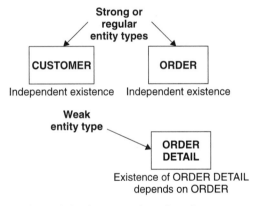

Figure 7-5   Strong and weak entity types.

pendently. Similarly, each order entity is uniquely identified by an order number and therefore, can exist without dependence on entities of other entity types.

Contrast this with the case of the entity type ORDER DETAIL. An order detail is not uniquely identifiable unless it is related to the corresponding order to which it is an order detail. That is, an order detail entity has no independent existence apart from an order entity. The ORDER DETAIL entity type depends on the ORDER entity type for its existence.

ORDER DETAIL is called a weak entity type. CUSTOMER and ORDER are known as regular or strong entity types. A weak entity type depends on another regular entity type for its existence. Weak entities depend on the corresponding strong entities for identification. We will review weak entities further in later sections.

ATTRIBUTES

In the discussion on entities and entity types, you must have observed that a group of entities were put together and called an entity type because these entities are similar. Customer entities are grouped together as the entity type CUSTOMER for the reason that the entities share common characteristics. If one customer entity possesses the characteristics of name, address, and phone, then another customer entity also has these characteristics; yet another customer entity also shares these characteristics. Common characteristics or attributes determine whether a number of entities or "things" may be grouped together as one type.

The E-R data model represents inherent characteristics of entity types as attributes in the same way as the object-based data model indicates properties of object sets. Therefore, our discussion of attributes can be brief, just highlighting the representation and serving as a refresher.

Attribute Specification

Inherent characteristics or basic properties of an entity type are defined as attributes for that entity type. What is the function of attributes? Attributes describe an entity type. Consider the attributes for the entity type CUSTOMER shown in Figure 7-6.

The figure presents four attributes for CUSTOMER. Look at the following values of the attributes for one customer or a single entity:

CustomerName:	John A. Harreld
CustomerAddress:	2401 Merry Boulevard, Branchburg, NJ 08810
CustomerPhone:	(908) 722-8419
CreditCode:	AAB

The values indicate the particular customer entity you are interested in. The values describe the specific customer and distinguish that customer from others.

Similar to the attributes represented in an object-based data model, the attributes in an E-R data model also possess the following features:

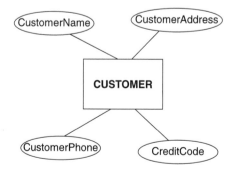

Figure 7-6 Attributes for CUSTOMER entity type.

Unique values. Each entity within an entity type has a unique set of values for the attributes. The values for CustomerName, CustomerAddress, CustomerPhone, and CreditCode for John A. Harreld form a distinct set that pertains to this customer entity. This, however, does not mean that a value for any attribute is not repeated for other customers. Other customers may also have the value "AAB" for Credit-Code.

Changeable values. As mentioned for the object-based data model, the values of a particular customer entity may change over time. John A. Harreld may change his phone number to (908) 887-6123.

Null values. An attribute may have a null value when the actual value is unknown, unavailable, or missing.

Values and Domains

As you already know, each attribute of the various entities of an entity type gets its values from a set of allowable values. This set of legal values forms the domain of values for the attribute. Figure 7-7 displays examples of attributes and respective domains for the entity type EMPLOYEE.

Note how the domain for each attribute consists of a set of allowable values. Notice how the two attributes DateOfBirth and DateOfHire share the same domain. A domain of values may apply to several attributes of an entity type. However, each attribute takes its values from a single domain.

Attribute Types

In most cases, a particular attribute of a single entity has only one value at any given time. For example, the attribute ProjectDuration for a single entity of the entity type

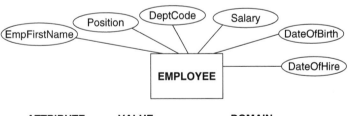

ATTRIBUTE	VALUE	DOMAIN
EmpFirstName	Susan	Character: size 25
Position	Manager	Character: size 30 (Manager, Programmer, Analyst, etc.)
DeptCode	D62	Character: size 3, range D01–D99
Salary	95000	Numeric: 6 digits, range 0-995000
DateOfBirth	01JAN1955	Valid date, range 01JAN1920–
DateOfHire	16SEP1986	Valid date, range 01JAN1920–

Figure 7-7 Attributes and domains for EMPLOYEE entity type.

PROJECT has a value of 90 days. At any given time, this is the only value for that attribute. However, in real-world situations, you will come across attributes that may have more than one value at the same time. You will also notice other types of variations in attributes.

In this subsection, we describe such variations in the types of attributes. As you know, a semantic data model such as the E-R data model must reflect real-world information correctly. The E-R model provides for representation of different attribute types. Let us go over a few examples.

Single-Valued and Multivalued Attributes   Note the following examples of single-valued and multivalued attributes. Observe the values of attributes for a single entity. These are the values at a given point in time.

Single-valued

Entity type:	EMPLOYEE
Attribute:	EmployeeJob
Attribute value for single entity:	Salesperson
Entity type:	EMPLOYEE
Attribute:	EmployeeDOB
Attribute value for single entity:	24JAN1975

Multivalued

Entity type:	AUTOMOBILE
Attribute:	ExteriorColor
Attribute values for single entity:	Beige, Gold (two-tone color)
Entity type:	CUSTOMER
Attribute:	CustomerPhone
Attribute values for single entity:	732-888-1234, 732-888-3456, 732-889-5566

Figure 7-8 illustrates how single-valued and multivalued attributes are represented in a data model diagram with different notations for the two types.

Simple and Composite Attributes   This is another variation in attribute types. In real-world information, you will notice that some attributes may be divided further into smaller units. The smaller units are known as simple or atomic attributes, whereas the larger units are called composite attributes. Most of the attributes in real-world information, however, are simple attributes. Your data model has to represent these variations. Note the examples presented below.

Composite

Entity type:	CUSTOMER
Composite attribute:	CustomerAddress
Component simple attributes:	Street, City, State, Zip

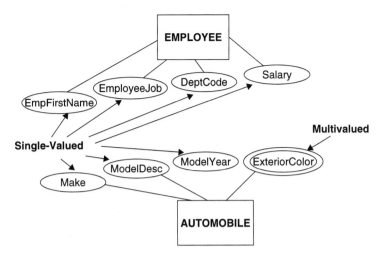

Figure 7-8   Single-valued and multivalued attributes.

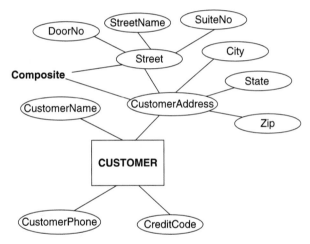

Figure 7-9   Composite attribute.

Entity type:	EMPLOYEE
Composite attribute:	EmployeeName
Component simple attributes:	FirstName, LastName, MidInitial

Simple

Entity type:	LOAN ACCOUNT
Simple attribute:	LoanAmount
Entity type:	EMPLOYEE
Simple attribute:	SocialSecNumber

Figure 7-9 shows the notations used for representing composite attributes. Note how the composite attribute branches into the simple attributes that are its components. Especially observe how the attribute Street may be broken down further into simple attributes.

Attributes with Stored and Derived Values In later phases of database development, you will transform the data model into the physical structure of how data gets stored in the database. From our discussion of attributes, you must have realized that the physical data stored in the database consist of values of the attributes of the complete set of all the entities. Stored data are really values of the attributes. If you have a CUSTOMER entity type with CustomerName, CustomerAddress, and Phone as the attributes, then your database stores the values of these attributes for all the customer entities in your organization. These are attributes whose values are stored in the database.

Sometimes you would want to calculate and derive values from the values of one or more attributes and to store the derived values in separate attributes. These are attributes containing derived values. Look at the following examples.

Attributes with derived values

Entity type:	EMPLOYEE
Derived attribute:	LengthOfEmployee
Attribute derived from:	EmployeeStartDate (and today's date)
Entity type:	PRODUCT
Derived attribute:	ProfitMargin
Attributes derived from:	UnitPrice and UnitCost

Figure 7-10 illustrates how a derived attribute is represented in an E-R data model.

Candidate and Primary Keys

In the discussion of object sets and object instances of object-based data model, we studied how certain attributes of an object set may be used to uniquely identify the instances. These were called identifiers. In the same manner, entity-relationship model has provisions to represent key attributes. All the points discussed on keys in Chapter 6 apply to the E-R model as well. You also know that underlining the

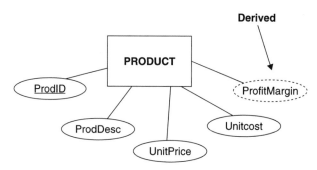

Figure 7-10 Derived attribute.

attribute name in a data model diagram indicates that the attribute is the primary key. Here is a brief summary of the main points:

Candidate key. One or more attributes whose values uniquely identify individual entities.

Primary key. One of the candidate keys selected to serve as the unique identifier for the entity type.

Composite key. A candidate key that consists of two or more attributes.

Considerations for Choosing Primary Key

Attribute length. Choose the shortest of the candidate keys.

Number of attributes. Prefer a key with a single attribute to a composite key.

Certainty of uniqueness. From the candidate keys, select the one that is more likely to contain unique values during the life of the database system.

Built-in meanings. Avoid any candidate key where values of parts of the attribute have built-in meanings, e.g., the attribute ProductNumber, where the values of part number indicate the production batch in the manufacturing plant.

RELATIONSHIPS

Let us reconsider information requirements for a university. Note the obvious fact that students register for courses. You observe that a particular student registers for several courses. Student Karolyn Stone registers for the courses Database Design, Data Warehousing, and Web Page Design. This is a relationship of that particular student Karolyn Stone with the three courses.

On the flip side of the relationship, you also note that many students register for one particular course. You find that for the course on Database Design, other students such as Samuel Wang, Tabitha Peters, and Monika Gonzales have also registered. So you notice the relationship between the course Database Design and the four students.

We have been through relationships and their features in sufficient detail while discussing the object-based data model. You know how instances of one object set may have relationships with instances of one or more object sets. Now let us highlight some key points in the way the E-R data model deals with relationships. Note the slight differences in the notations used in the E-R data model.

Association Between Entities

Go back to the above example of students and course. Let us review the example in the context of the E-R data model and use the terms that apply to this model.

Entity type: STUDENT

Entities: Karolyn Stone, Samuel Wang, Tabitha Peters, and Monika Gonzales

Entity type: COURSE

Entities: Database Design, Data Warehousing, Web Page Design

Associations: Karolyn Stone with Database Design

Karolyn Stone with Data Warehousing

Karolyn Stone with Web Page Design

Associations: Database Design with Karolyn Stone

Database Design with Samuel Wang

Database Design with Tabitha Peters

Database Design with Monika Gonzales

Note the above associations and express these in E-R model terminology. Carefully examine the two sets of associations. What is the observation? In the first set of associations, an individual entity Karolyn Stone of entity type STUDENT associates with other individual entities Database Design, Data Warehousing, and Web Page Design of the other entity type, COURSE. If entities of one entity type associate with entities of another entity type, you express these associations in a E-R data model diagram by joining the rectangular boxes representing the two entity types with a relationship line. Although the two entity types are linked together to express the relationship, remember that the associations are actually between individual entities of these two entity types.

Figure 7-11 indicates how the above relationship is represented in an E-R diagram. Look at the associations between individual entities illustrated in the figure. As you know from our study of object-based data modeling, this is a many-to-many relationship. Observe the notation in the figure to denote a many-to-many relationship. This notation has acquired the name "crow's feet." Compare this notation with the notation used in object-based data model for a many-to-many relationship. Usage of a specific notation is just a matter of convention and acceptance. In practice, you will come across different sets of notations in common usage. Appendix C covers diagramming conventions and symbols.

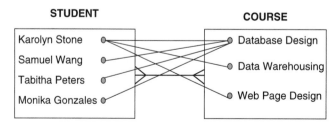

Figure 7-11   Relationship between entity types.

Degree of a Relationship

The degree of a relationship in the E-R data model is defined in the same way as in object-based data model. The degree of a relationship refers to the number of entity types that participate in the relationship. A three-way relationship is a ternary relationship, two-way a binary relationship, and one-way a unary relationship. A unary relationship is also known as a recursive relationship, because the entities of the same entity type associate with one another.

Figure 7-12 illustrates the concept of relationship degrees. It presents relationships whose degrees are three, two, and one. You may visualize relationships with higher degrees, although they are not common in real-world information requirements. Binary relationships are the most common relationships in the real world.

Cardinality in Relationships

It may be worthwhile to refer back to our detailed discussion of cardinality in relationship expressed in the object-based data model. The discussion covered one-to-one, one-to-many, and many-to-many relationships. Also, the notions of maximum and minimum cardinalities should be reviewed. The same principles and concepts apply to the E-R data model as well. We do not propose to repeat the discussions here. However, let us note the notations used for representing these two relationship types in the E-R data model.

Figure 7-13 shows the notations for representing these relationship types. Note the minimum and maximum cardinality indicators placed near each entity type.

Optional and Mandatory Conditions

Recall how the minimum cardinality indicator expresses the optional or mandatory nature of a relationship. Placing a "0" as the minimum cardinality indicator near an

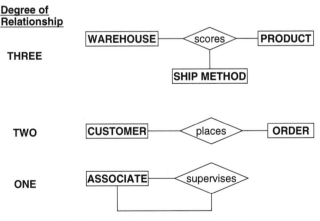

Figure 7-12 Degrees of relationships.

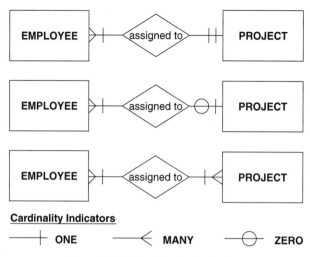

Figure 7-13 Cardinality indicators.

entity type indicates that some of the entities of that entity type may not participate in the relationship. That means that the relationship is optional for that entity
type. Let us explore the notion of optional and mandatory nature of relationships
further.

Consider a real-world situation of employees working in departments. Normally,
every employee is assigned to a department and every department will have
employees. But this may not always be true. Newer employees may not be assigned
to a department yet; some employees on special assignments may not be part of the
conventional departments. On the other hand, some special departments may have
been created for costing raw materials and equipment with no human resources
being part of the departments. In this case, such departments do not have employees associated with them. Your data model must be able to represent such exceptional conditions found in real-world information requirements. Follow along to
learn how these conditions are represented in the data model.

Four cases arise based on the exception conditions. Figure 7-14 illustrates the first
two cases and Figure 7-15 the next two cases. Note the minimum and maximum cardinality indicators shown in each case. Also, note each dotted line indicating that
the relationship on that side is optional.

Let us review these four cases in some detail. As you will observe, the minimum
cardinality indicator denotes the optional or mandatory nature of the relationship—
whether it is partial participation or full participation in the relationship by the specific entity type. Pay special attention to the figure while we discuss the four cases
in detail.

Case 1

A department must have at least one employee, but it may have many employees.
Note minimum cardinality indicator 1 and maximum cardinality indicator * near
EMPLOYEE entity type.

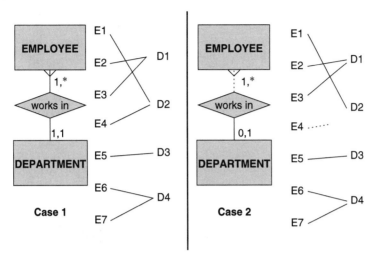

Figure 7-14   Relationship: optional and mandatory conditions—Part 1.

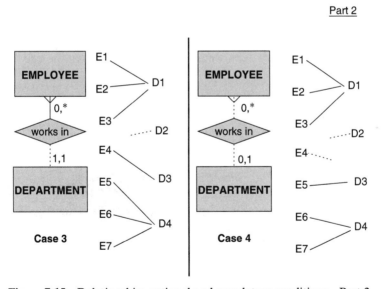

Figure 7-15   Relationship: optional and mandatory conditions—Part 2.

Meaning of minimum cardinality indicator 1   Each department entity is associated with at least one employee entity. That is, the minimum number of employee instances associated with one department entity is 1. Note the solid relationship line next to DEPARTMENT indicating that the relationship on this side is mandatory and that every department entity participates in the relationship.

Meaning of maximum cardinality indicator *   A department entity may be associated with many instances of employee.

An employee must be assigned to at least one department, and he or she can be assigned to only one department. Note minimum cardinality indicator 1 and maximum cardinality indicator 1 near DEPARTMENT entity type.

Meaning of minimum cardinality indicator 1   Each employee entity is associated with at least one department entity. That is, the minimum number of department instances associated with one employee entity is 1. Notice the solid relationship line next to EMPLOYEE indicating that the relationship on this side is mandatory and that every employee entity participates in the relationship.

Meaning of maximum cardinality indicator 1   An employee entity can be associated with one instance of department at most.

Case 2

A department must have at least one employee, but it may have many employees. Note minimum cardinality indicator 1 and maximum cardinality indicator * near EMPLOYEE entity type.

Meaning of minimum cardinality indicator 1   Each department entity is associated with at least one employee entity. That is, the minimum number of employee instances associated with one department entity is 1. Notice the solid relationship line next to DEPARTMENT indicating that the relationship on this side is mandatory and that every department entity participates in the relationship.

Meaning of maximum cardinality indicator *   A department entity may be associated with many employee entities.

Every employee may not be assigned to a department; if assigned, he or she can be assigned to only one department. Note minimum cardinality indicator 0 and maximum cardinality indicator 1 near DEPARTMENT entity type.

Meaning of minimum cardinality indicator 0   Some employee entities may not be associated with any department entities. Not every employee entity is associated with a department entity. That is, the minimum number of department instances associated with one employee entity is 0. Not every employee entity participates in the relationship. Notice the dotted or broken relationship line next to EMPLOYEE entity type, indicating that the relationship on this side is optional and that not every employee entity participates in the relationship. A broken or dotted line denotes partial participation in the relationship.

Meaning of maximum cardinality indicator 1   An employee entity can be associated with one instance of department at most.

Case 3

Every department may not have employees; if a department has employees, it can have many employees. Note minimum cardinality indicator 0 and maximum cardinality indicator * near EMPLOYEE entity type.

Meaning of minimum cardinality indicator 0   Some department entities may not be associated with any employee entities. Not every department entity is associated with employee entities. That is, the minimum number of employee instances associated with one department entity is 0. Not every department entity participates in the relationship. Note the dotted or broken relationship line next to the DEPARTMENT entity type, indicating that the relationship on this side is optional and that not every department entity participates in the relationship. A broken or dotted line denotes partial participation in the relationship.

Meaning of maximum cardinality indicator *   A department entity may be associated with many employee entities.

An employee must be assigned to at least one department, and he or she can be assigned to only one department. Note minimum cardinality indicator 1 and maximum cardinality indicator 1 near DEPARTMENT entity type.

Meaning of minimum cardinality indicator 1   Each employee entity is associated with at least one department entity. That is, the minimum number of department instances associated with one employee entity is 1. Note the solid relationship line next to EMPLOYEE, indicating that the relationship on this side is mandatory and that every employee entity participates in the relationship.

Meaning of maximum cardinality indicator 1   An employee entity can be associated with one instance of department at most.

Case 4

Every department may not have employees; if a department has employees, it can have many employees. Note minimum cardinality indicator 0 and maximum cardinality indicator * near EMPLOYEE entity type.

Meaning of minimum cardinality indicator 0   Some department entities may not be associated with any employee entities. Not every department entity is associated with employee entities. That is, the minimum number of employee instances associated with one department entity is 0. Not every department entity participates in the relationship. Note the dotted or broken relationship line next to DEPARTMENT entity type, indicating that the relationship on this side is optional and that not every department entity participates in the relationship. A broken or dotted line denotes partial participation in the relationship.

Every employee may not be assigned to a department; if assigned, he or she can be assigned to only one department. Note minimum cardinality indicator 0 and maximum cardinality indicator 1 near DEPARTMENT entity type.

Meaning of minimum cardinality indicator 0   Some employee entities may not be associated with any department entities. Not every employee entity is associated with a department entity. That is, the minimum number of department instances associated with one employee entity is 0. Not every employee entity participates in the relationship. Note the dotted or broken relationship line next to EMPLOYEE entity type indicating that the relationship on this side is optional and that not every employee entity participates in the relationship. Broken or dotted line denotes partial participation in the relationship.

Meaning of maximum cardinality indicator 1   An employee entity can be associated with one instance of department at most.

SPECIAL CASES

In our discussion on object-based data modeling, we have already covered supersets and subsets. The concept of generalization and specialization was added to the E-R model at a later date. The enhanced entity-relationship (EER) model includes the concept of superentity and subentity types.

We will now devote some time to special considerations of the E-R data model. We have already touched on weak entity types; we will now elaborate on this. What about the concept of aggregate object sets in the object-based data model? Is there anything comparable in the E-R data model? What is a gerund? What is the place for a gerund in data modeling? Let us discuss this and other such special cases.

Modeling Time-Dependent Components

Think of the values of attributes stored in the database. Normally, the values stored are the current values. What values do you find for the Address attribute of the CUSTOMER entity type? The current address of each customer. As a customer's address changes, the new address replaces the old address in the database. In the same way, what values will be stored in the ProductUnitCost and ProductUnitPrice attributes of the PRODUCT entity type?

Assume that just the current costs and current prices are stored in the database for the products. What happens if an old invoice to a customer has to be recalculated and reprinted? What happens when you want to calculate the profit margin for the past quarter using the unit cost and unit price? If there had been no intervening price or cost changes, you can perform these tasks without any problems. What you notice is that ProductUnitCost and ProductUnitPrice are time-dependent components and that your data model must include historical entity types to keep track of the changes.

Figure 7-16 indicates how historical entity types are included in the data model. Note why ProductNo and EffectiveDate are used together to form the primary key for the historical entity types.

Identifying and Nonidentifying Relationships

Refer back to Figure 7-5 describing a weak or dependent entity type. Let us now explain the relationship among the entity types shown in that figure. ORDER DETAIL was shown to be a weak entity type depending on ORDER entity type

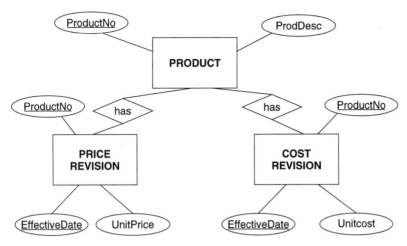

Figure 7-16   Time-dependent model components.

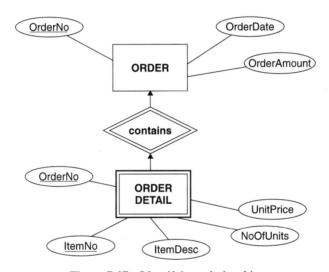

Figure 7-17   Identifying relationship.

for its existence. This implies that you cannot have an order detail entity unless a corresponding order entity exists. Without an order entity an order detail entity cannot exist in the database. It is meaningless to think of stray and loose order detail entities existing in the database. Figure 7-17 shows the relationships between two entity types presented in Figure 7-5. Notice the notations used in the diagram to distinguish the components.

Note the following points about the two entity types:

Weak entity type. An entity type that is existence-dependent on another entity type. ORDER DETAIL is a weak entity type. It depends on ORDER entity.

Identifying entity type. A weak entity is identified by being related to another entity type called the identifying or owner entity type. ORDER is the identifying entity type.

Primary key. A weak entity does not have a primary key by itself. Usually, weak entities are identified by partial identifiers or discriminators just to distinguish them within the owner entity. For ORDER DETAIL, ItemNo is a partial identifier. The full primary key of a weak entity type usually consists of the concatenation of the primary key of the owner entity type with the partial identifier of the weak entity type. Note the primary key for ORDER DETAIL—OrderNo and ItemNo concatenated together.

Identifying relationship. The relationship between a weak entity type and its identifying or owner entity type is known as an identifying relationship. Observe the relationship notation shown between ORDER DETAIL and ORDER.

Attributes of Relationship Types

In the discussion of the object-based data model, we studied aggregate object sets. Recall that relationships between objects sets give rise to aggregate object sets. Such aggregate object sets behave in the same way as regular object sets. An aggregate object set may have attributes and relationships with other regular or aggregate object sets.

This notion of aggregate object sets is also found in the E-R data model. A relationship object type in E-R modeling corresponds to an aggregate object set in object-based modeling. Figure 7-18 shows an example of relationship object type. Note the attributes for the relationship object type WORKSON shown in the diagram.

When to Use a Gerund

What is a gerund? The relationship entity type described above is sometimes called a gerund. In English grammar, the word "writing" is a gerund; it is derived from the verb "to write" but behaves like a noun. Similarly, if a relationship behaves like an entity type, that relationship may be termed as a gerund.

Consider a three-way many-to-many relationship among three entity types: CUSTOMER, PRODUCT, and WAREHOUSE. This relationship arises out of the real-world situation of shipping products to customers from different supply warehouses. A diamond symbol normally represents this relationship. However, in reality, the relationship appears to be an entity type. It is a gerund. When do you, as a data modeler, represent a relationship as a gerund? You need to represent a relationship as an entity type if the relationship truly has specific attributes or the relationship, by itself, has relationships with other entity types.

Figure 7-19 illustrates the gerund SHIPMENT, based on the relationships among CUSTOMER, PRODUCT, and WAREHOUSE.

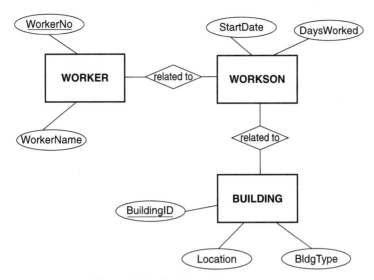

Figure 7-18   Relationship entity type.

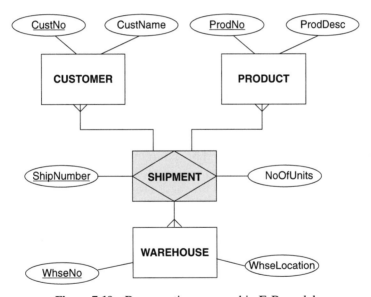

Figure 7-19   Representing a gerund in E-R model.

Generalization and Specialization

All the points covered in our discussion of generalization and specialization in the object-based data model apply to the E-R data model. Instead of repeating the discussion here, it will be worthwhile to refer back to Chapter 6.

We just want to highlight the difference in the notations. Figure 7-20 contains a partial E-R data model showing an example of generalization and specialization. Note the notations used according to E-R data model conventions.

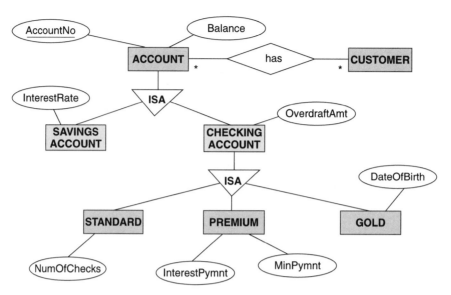

Figure 7-20   E-R model: generalization and specialization.

THE ENTITY-RELATIONSHIP DIAGRAM

This section pulls together everything we have covered on E-R data modeling and summarizes the topic with a comprehensive entity relationship diagram (ERD). Before we review the diagram and note the components, let us revisit the components and their notations. As mentioned above, in practice, you will observe some minor variations in the notations used by different data modelers. Which set will be your standard set? You would want to conform to the notations adopted by a CASE tool you are required to use in your database project.

Review of Components and Notations

Figure 7-21 highlights many of the standard components and notations used in entity-relationship modeling. Carefully review the notations or symbols.

The following is a recapitulation of components:

Entity Type
    Strong
    Weak

Attribute
    Simple, single-valued
    Composite
    Multivalued
    Derived

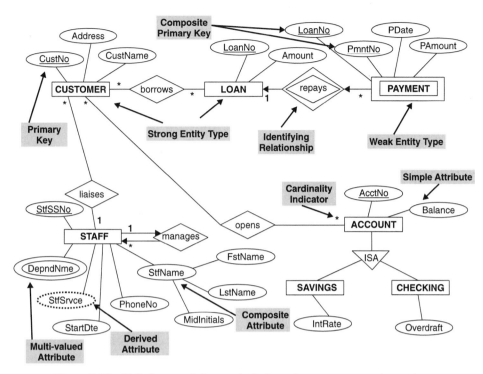

Figure 7-21   E-R data model: recapitulation of components and notations.

Primary Key
    Single attribute
    Composite

Relationship
    Names
    Cardinality indicators
        Maximum
        Minimum
    Identifying and nonidentifying
    Optional and mandatory conditions
    Gerund

Sample ERD

Let us bring all the principles and concepts of E-R data modeling together and create a data model for the information requirements for a university. Assume that the data model has to represent only the teaching aspects of the university. Ignore other information relating to receivables, payables, salaries, administration, employees, and so on.

Consider the following requirements to be included in the model:

1. Each course offered may be taught in different classes. For example, the Database Design course may have a Tuesday night class and a Thursday night class.
2. A faculty member may teach one or more classes.
3. Different faculty members may be assigned to teach different classes of the same course.
4. Each faculty member decides on the number of exams for the class he or she teaches. Student scores are assigned for each type of examination or test.
5. A specific textbook is assigned to a course.
6. A student may be enrolled in one or more courses.
7. Each class meets in the same room during a semester.

Figure 7-22 presents an ERD for the given information requirements. Note that the diamond-shaped relationship notation is not shown in this ERD. This is an acceptable practice. Although the relationship notation is not explicitly shown, the implied relationships are expressed by the lines connecting entity type boxes.

Highlights of Sample ERD

Study the ERD carefully. Note all the entity types and observe the relationships. What do the cardinality indicators represent? Are there any composite attributes? Go back to the list of components and notations shown in Figure 7-21. How many of these can you identify in Figure 7-22?

Compare the information requirements with the ERD. Does the ERD reflect the information requirements adequately?

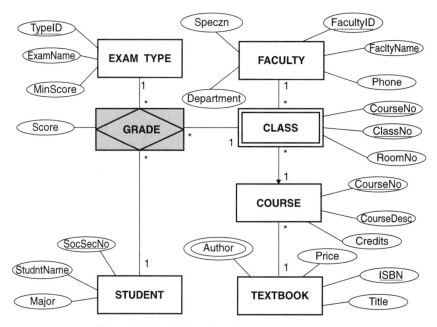

Figure 7-22   ERD: university teaching aspects.

Let us highlight certain points about the ERD to indicate how it matches with the stated information requirements.

- For each course, there may exist one or more classes. Note the one-to-many relationship between COURSE and CLASS.
- The relationship between COURSE and CLASS is an identifying relationship. CLASS depends on COURSE for its existence. CLASS is a weak entity type.
- Observe the one-to-many relationship between TEXTBOOK and COURSE. Although a specific textbook is assigned to a course, the relationship allows the possibility of the same textbook being used for more than one course.
- Why is the attribute *Author* shown as a multivalued attribute? This is to provide for multiple authors for the same textbook.
- The entity type EXAM TYPE includes examinations such as Mid-Term, Quizzes, Assignments, Laboratory Work, Final, and so on.
- The entity type GRADE represents the three-way relationship among CLASS, STUDENT, and EXAM TYPE.
- Although faculty members teach specific courses, the teaching assignments are for teaching particular classes of these courses. Note the direct relationship between FACULTY and CLASS.
- The attribute *Score* refers to the score for a given student, in a certain class, and for a particular examination type.

CHAPTER SUMMARY

- Like object-based modeling, entity-relationship modeling is another generic data modeling technique. E-R data modeling seems to be a natural way of looking at real-world information.
- Many data modelers prefer E-R data modeling because several CASE tools support it.
- Components or building blocks of E-R data model: entity type, attribute, primary key, relationship, cardinality indicators, generalization/specialization. The E-R data model provides additional notations to indicate variations in the components.
- An entity type represents all similar entities; on the flip side, an entity is an instance or occurrence of an entity type.
- Attribute types: single-valued and multivalued, simple and composite, derived.
- One of the candidate keys is chosen as the primary key for an entity type. A composite key consists of more than one attribute.
- Relationship between two entity types expresses the associations between entities of one entity type and entities of the second entity type. The cardinality indicators denote how many instances of one entity type may be associated with one instance of the other entity type.
- The minimum cardinality indicator represents optional or mandatory nature of a relationship.

- A weak entity type depends on another entity type for its existence.
- The notion of generalization and specialization in the E-R model is similar to the same concept in the object-based data model.

REVIEW QUESTIONS

1. "The E-R data modeling technique focuses on entities and relationships as fundamental model components." Explain.
2. Define the terms entity, entity type, and entity set.
3. What are physical and conceptual entities? Give two examples for each.
4. Describe attributes and value domains with three examples.
5. What is a composite attribute? Can a composite attribute itself be part of another attribute? If so, can you think of an example?
6. Describe the considerations for choosing the primary key for an entity type.
7. What is the degree of a relationship? Give two examples.
8. Give an example of a situation that needs modeling time-dependent components.
9. What is an identifying relationship? Explain briefly with an example.
10. What is a gerund? Why would you use a gerund in a data model? Give an example.

EXERCISES

1. Match the columns:

1. domain	A. three-way relationship
2. composite attribute	B. one or more simple attributes
3. relationship	C. time-dependent
4. ternary relationship	D. not absolutely essential in a model
5. minimum cardinality	E. no independent primary key
6. historical entity type	F. unary relationship
7. weak entity type	G. has distinct notation in E-R model
8. recursive relationship	H. association between entities
9. derived attribute	I. allowable values for attribute
10. primary key	J. indicates optionality of relationship

2. As a data modeler for a car dealership, identity the major entity types. List the attributes and primary keys for two of the entity types.
3. The health care coverage for employees in your company extends to employee dependents. Create a partial E-R data model to represent the health insurance coverage. (Hint: use identifying and nonidentifying relationships.)
4. Consider the relationship between the entity types WORKER and BUILDING. Assume variations in business rules with optional and manda-

tory conditions governing the relationship. Describe the different cases that might arise. In each case, show the minimum and maximum cardinality indicators for the relationship.

5. You are a senior data modeler for an airlines business. Consider all the major business processes. Create an E-R data model to represent the information requirements. Use proper notations to indicate the various components.

PART IV

THE RELATIONAL DATA MODEL

CHAPTER 8

RELATIONAL DATA MODEL FUNDAMENTALS

CHAPTER OBJECTIVES

- Understand how the relational model is a superior conventional data model
- Study the components of the relational data model in detail
- Review the significance of data integrity and how this model provides proper constraints
- Learn about data manipulation in the relational model and examine generic languages
- Survey two common methods for relational model design

In Chapter 1, you had a very brief introduction to the relational data model. Before the introduction of this data model, databases were developed based on the hierarchical model first and then based on the network model. We also mentioned that although these two models overcame most of the limitations of earlier file-oriented data systems, a few drawbacks still remained. However, a landmark paper written by Dr. E. F. Codd in 1970 completely changed the database scene. People began to view data and databases in a different way. The era of relational database systems started, and organization after organization began to adopt the new, superior model.

In the previous chapters, you have been studying semantic data modeling. You went through the details of two methods for creating a semantic data model—object-based data modeling and entity-relationship data modeling techniques. A semantic data model represents the true meaning of the information requirements of an organization. As explained in Chapter 5, a conventional model portrays how data in the database are to be perceived. As mentioned before, the hierarchical,

Database Design and Development: An Essential Guide for IT Professionals by Paulraj Ponniah
ISBN 0-471-21877-4   Copyright © 2003 by John Wiley and Sons, Inc.

network, and relational data models are conventional data models. These dictate the view and arrangement of data in the database. A conventional data model is based on a set of standards or conventions developed in a certain way and accepted. The hierarchical model views data in a database as arranged in a hierarchical, top-down fashion; the network model views as arranged in a network configuration.

On one side, the semantic data model—a generic data model—represents the information requirements of an organization. On the other side, the conventional data model represents how data stored in the database are perceived. Each of the three conventional data models has its own way of perceiving the arrangement of data. Now, if your organization wants to implement a hierarchical database, you take your semantic data model and transform it into a conventional, hierarchical model and implement the hierarchical database. You take similar routes from the semantic data model to the implementation of your database if your organization wants to have a network database or a relational database. The big advantage of creating a semantic data model first is this—being generic, the semantic data model can be transformed into any type of conventional data model.

STRUCTURE AND COMPONENTS

The relational model uses familiar concepts to represent data. In this model, data are perceived as organized in traditional, two-dimensional tables with columns and rows. The rigor of mathematics is incorporated into the formulation of the model. It has its theoretical basis in mathematical set theory and first-order predicate logic. The concept of a relation comes from mathematics and represents a simple two-dimensional table.

The relational model derives its strength from its simplicity and the mathematical foundation on which it is built. Rows of a relation are treated as elements of a set. Therefore, manipulation of rows may be based on mathematical set operations. Dr. Codd used this principle and provided with two generic languages for manipulating data organized as a relational model.

A relation or two-dimensional table forms the basic structure in the relational model. What are the implications? In requirements gathering, you collect so much information about business objects or entities, their attributes, and relationships among them. All of these various pieces of information can be represented in the form of relations. The entities, their attributes, and even their relationships are all contained in the concept of relations. This provides enormous simplicity and makes the relational model a superior conventional data model.

Strengths of the Relational Model

Before we proceed to explore the relational model in detail, let us begin with a list of its major strengths. This will enable you to appreciate the superiority of the model and help you understand its features in a better light. Here is a summary of the strengths:

Mathematical relation. Uses the concept of a mathematical relation or two-dimensional table to organize data. Rests on solid mathematical foundation.

Mathematical set theory. Applies the mathematical set theory for manipulation of data in the database. Data manipulation uses a proven approach.

Disciplined data organization. Resting on solid mathematical foundation, data organization and manipulation are carried out in a disciplined manner.

Simple and familiar view. Provides a common and simple view of data in the form of two-dimensional tables. Users can easily perceive how data are organized; they need not be concerned with how data are actually stored in the database.

Logical links for relationships. As you will recall, hierarchical and network data models use physical links to relate entities. If two entities such as CUSTOMER and ORDER are related, you have to establish the relationship by means of physical addresses embedded within the stored data records. In striking contrast, relational model uses logical links to establish relationships. This is a major advantage.

Relation: The Single Modeling Concept

As mentioned above, a relation or table is the primary data modeling concept in the relational mode. A table is collection of columns that describe a thing of interest to the organization. For example, if COURSE is a conceptual thing of interest in a university, then a two-dimensional table or relation will represent COURSE in the relational data model for the university. Figure 8-1 shows a plain two-dimensional table whose format represents an entity or object.

Note the following features about a relation or two-dimensional table:

- The relation is a table, representing data about some entity or object.
- The relation is not just any random table, but one that conforms to certain relational rules.
- The relation consists of a specific set of columns that can be named and an arbitrary number of rows.
- Each row contains a set of data values.

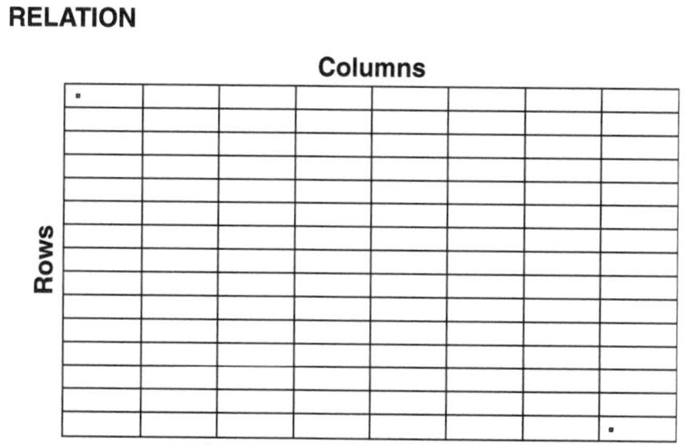

RELATION

Figure 8-1 Relation or two-dimensional table.

EMPLOYEE Relation

Columns

SocSecNumber	EmployeeName	Phone	Position	DeptCode
.				
				.

Rows

Figure 8-2 Employee relation: attributes.

- Table names and column names are used to understand the data. The table or relation name indicates the entity type; the column names indicate its characteristics.

Columns as Attributes

Figure 8-2 presents a relation representing the entity type EMPLOYEE.

Make note of the following about the columns in a relation as illustrated in the figure.

- Each column indicates a specific attribute of the relation.
- The column heading is the name of the attribute.
- In the relational model, the attributes are referred to by the column names and not by their displacements in a data record. Therefore, no two columns can have the same name.
- For each row, the values of the attributes are shown in the appropriate columns.
- For a row, if the value of an attribute is not known, not available, or not applicable, a null value is placed in the specific column. A null value may be replaced with a correct value at a later time.
- Each attribute takes its values from a set of allowable or legal values called the attribute domain. A domain consists of a set of atomic values of the same data type and format.
- The number of columns in a relation is referred to as the degree of the relation.

Rows as Instances

Rows, also referred to by the mathematical name of tuples, indicate the occurrences or instances of the object represented by a relation. In a relation, each row represents one instance of the object. Each column in that row indicates one piece of data about the instance.

EMPLOYEE Relation

Columns

	SocSecNumber	EmployeeName	Phone	Position	DeptCode
Tuples OR Rows	214-56-7835	Robert Moses	516-777-9584	Programmer	501
	123-44-5546	Kassia Raj	718-312-4488	Analyst	
	101-54-3838	Andrew Rogers	212-313-1267	Manager	408
	213-36-7854	Samuel Prabhu	212-126-3428	Controller	201
	311-33-4520	Kaitlin Jones	718-567-4321	Assistant	
	512-22-8542	Carey Smith	732-346-5533	Senior VP	301
	111-22-3344	Amanda Lupo	908-212-5629	Executive VP	101
	122-65-5378	Tabitha Williams	215-576-4598	DBA	501

Figure 8-3 Employee relation: tuples.

Figure 8-3 shows the rows or tuples for the EMPLOYEE relation.

If there are 5000 employees in the organization, the relation will contain 5000 rows. The number of tuples in a relation is known as the cardinality of the relation. For an EMPLOYEE relation with 5000 rows, the cardinality is 5000.

Now, because a relation is considered as a mathematical set, this EMPLOYEE relation is a set of 5000 data elements. Manipulation of data in the EMPLOYEE relation, therefore, becomes a set operation. Later on, you will study set operations and learn how to apply these in working with data in a relational model.

Each row represents a particular employee. Look at the row for the employee Carey Smith. Note the value shown under each column in this row. Each of the values in the columns describes the employee Carey Smith. Each value represents one piece of data about the employee. All data for the employee are contained in the specific row.

Primary Key

As mentioned above, in a relation, each tuple represents one instance of the relation. In an EMPLOYEE relation with 5000 rows, each row represents a particular employee. But, how can we know which row represents an employee we are looking for? To identify a row uniquely, we can use the attribute values. We may say that if the value of the attribute EmployeeName is "Carey Smith" that row represents this particular employee. What if there is another Carey Smith in the organization? You need some attribute whose values will uniquely identify individual tuples. Note that the attribute SocSecNumber can be used to identify a tuple uniquely.

Given below are definitions of identifiers in a relation:

Superkey. A set of attributes that uniquely identifies each tuple in a relation.

Key. A minimal set of attributes that uniquely identifies each tuple in a relation.

Composite key. A key consisting of more than one attribute.

Candidate key. A set of attributes that can be chosen to serve the key.

DEPARTMENT Relation

DeptCode	DeptName	DeptLocation
101	Administration	New York
201	Finance	Chicago
301	Marketing	Atlanta
303	Sales	Boston
408	Production	Detroit
501	Information Technology	San Francisco

LOGICAL
LINKS

EMPLOYEE Relation

SocSecNumber	EmployeeName	Phone	Position	DeptCode
214-56-7835	Robert Moses	516-777-9584	Programmer	501
123-44-5546	Kassia Raj	718-312-4488	Analyst	
101-54-3838	Andrew Rogers	212-313-1267	Manager	408
213-36-7854	Samuel Prabhu	212-126-3428	Controller	201
311-33-4520	Kaitlin Jones	718-567-4321	Assistant	
512-22-8542	Carey Smith	732-346-5533	Senior VP	301
111-22-3344	Amanda Lupo	908-212-5629	Executive VP	101
122-65-5378	Tabitha Williams	215-576-4598	DBA	501

Figure 8-4 Department and employee relations: relationship.

Primary key. One of the candidate keys actually selected as the key for a relation.

Surrogate key. A key that is automatically generated for a relation by the computer system, for example, CustomerNumber, generated in sequence by the system and assigned to CUSTOMER rows. Surrogate keys ensure that no duplicate values are present in the relation.

Relationships Through Foreign Keys

You have noted above that the relational model is superior to other conventional data models because it does not use physical links to establish relationships. The relational model uses logical links. How is this done? What is a logical link?

Figure 8-4 presents two relations, EMPLOYEE and DEPARTMENT. Obviously, these two relations are related to each other because there are associations between employees and departments. One or more employees are assigned to a particular department; an employee is assigned to a specific department.

Observe the links shown between tuples in the EMPLOYEE relation to corresponding tuples in the DEPARTMENT relation. The DeptCode attribute in the EMPLOYEE relation is called a foreign key attribute. Note especially the value of the foreign key attribute and the value of the primary key attribute of the related row in the other relation.

Let us summarize how relationships are established in the relational data model.

- Relationships in the relational data model are established through foreign keys, not physical pointers.
- The logical link between a tuple in the first relation and a tuple in a second relation is established by placing the primary key value in the tuple of the first

relation as the foreign key value in the corresponding tuple of the second relation. The first relation may be referred to as the parent relation and the second as a child.

- If tuples of a relation are related to some other tuples of the same relation, then the foreign key attribute is included in the same relation. This is a recursive relationship. For example, in an EMPLOYEE relation, some tuples representing employees may be related to other tuples in the same relation representing supervisors.
- Foreign key attributes need not have the same names as the corresponding primary key attributes.
- However, a foreign key attribute must be of the same data type and length of the related primary key attribute.

In the above figure, you notice that some tuples show null values for the foreign key attributes. What is the significance of the null values?

Optional Relationship Consider a tuple in the EMPLOYEE relation with a null value in the foreign key column. This shows that the specific tuple is not linked to any tuple in the DEPARTMENT relation. This means that this particular employee is not assigned to any department. He or she could be a new employee not yet assigned to a department or an employee on special assignment not tied to a specific department. A null value in the foreign key column indicates the nature of the relationship. Not all employees need be associated with a department. Null values in the foreign key column indicate an optional relationship between the two relations.

Mandatory Relationship In the EMPLOYEE relation, suppose that null values are not allowed in the foreign key. This requires specific discrete values to be present in all the tuples of this relation. Every tuple in the EMPLOYEE relation, therefore, points to a related tuple in the DEPARTMENT relation. In other words, every employee must be related to a department. If null values are not allowed in the foreign key, the relationship between the two relations is a mandatory relationship.

Relational Model Notation

Figure 8-5 gives an example of relational tables. Figure 8-6 presents a standard notation used to represent this relational data model.

Note the following description of the notation:

- The notation for each relation begins with the name of the relation. Examples—WORKER, ASSIGNMENT, BUILDING, SKILL.
- For each relation, the column names are enclosed within parenthesis. These are the attributes for the relation.
- Primary key attributes are indicated with underscores. Examples—BuildingID, SkillCode.
- Statements immediately following the notation of a relation indicate the foreign keys within that relation. Example—Foreign keys: SkillCode references SKILL.

WORKER Relation

WorkerNo	Name	HourlyRate	SkillCode	SupvId
1111	Morris	24.50	ELE	
1287	Vitale	20.00	MAS	
3917	Nagel	18.00	ROF	
4467	Hart	20.50	ELE	1111
5179	Grasso	22.50	PLM	

BUILDING Relation

BuildingID	Address	Type	Status
H245	135 Green Street	House	S1
H267	212 Tices Road	House	S4
O123	295 Hillside Avenue	Office	S2
O156	15 Camner Terrace	Office	S3
T451	23 Oaks Drive	Townhouse	S5

SKILL Relation

SkillCode	SkillType	WklyHrs
MAS	Masonry	35
FRM	Framing	40
ROF	Roofing	35
ELE	Electric	35
PLM	Plumbing	40

ASSIGNMENT Relation

WorkerNo	BuildingID	StartDate	DaysWorked
1111	H245	15-Mar	10
1287	O123	15-Feb	8
5179	T451	1-Mar	7
4467	O156	15-Apr	15
1287	H267	1-Apr	9

Figure 8-5 Relational tables.

WORKER (WorkerNo, Name, HourlyRate, SkillCode, SupvID)
Foreign Keys: SkillCode references SKILL
                     SupvID references WORKER

ASSIGNMENT (WorkerNo, BuildingID, StartDate, DaysWorked)
Foreign Keys: WorkerNo references WORKER
                     BuildingID references BUILDING

BUILDING (BuildingID, Address, Type, Status)

SKILL (SkillCode, SkillType, WklyHrs)

Figure 8-6 Relational data model: notation.

- The foreign key statement includes the name of the foreign key and the name of the parent relation.
- Note the foreign key SupvID indicating a recursive relationship.

DATA INTEGRITY CONSTRAINTS

It is essential that a database built on any specific data model must ensure the validity of the data. The data structure must be meaningful and be truly representative of the information requirements. Constraints are rules that make sure proper restrictions are imposed on the data values in a database. The purpose is to regulate and ensure that the data content is valid and consistent. For example, to preserve the uniqueness of each tuple in a relation, the constraint or rule is that the primary key has unique values in the relation. Another example is a domain constraint that requires that all values of a specific attribute be taken from the same set or domain of permissible values.

As mentioned above, a relational data model consists of tables or relations that conform to relational rules and possess specific properties. We will now discuss the constraints and properties that ensure data correctness and consistency in a relational data model. First, let us establish the reasons for ensuring data integrity. A database is said to possess data integrity if the data values provide a correct and valid representation of the characteristics of the entities or objects. Data integrity includes consistency of data values. Data values derived from one business process must match up correctly with the same values derived from another process.

Why Data Integrity?

Let us summarize the reasons for data integrity and examine how the relational data model must ensure data integrity.

- Each tuple must represent one specific entity. There must be no ambiguity in identification of the tuple for each specific entity.
- The values in all tuples for any single attribute must be of the same data type, format, and length. There must not be variations, confusion, or unpredictability in the values for every attribute.
- The columns must be identified only by names and not by position or physical order in a relation.
- A new row may be added anywhere in the table so that the content does not vary with the order of the rows or tuples in a relation.
- The model should express relationships correctly and without any room for exceptions.
- The data model must consist of well-structured relations with minimum data redundancy.
- Data manipulations in a relational database must not result in any data inconsistencies.

First, we will consider the basic relational properties that support data integrity and data consistency. Next, we will address three special cases that further enhance data integrity.

Basic Relational Properties

Here is a list of the significant relational properties that govern the relations in a relational model:

Row uniqueness. Each row or tuple is unique—no duplicate rows with the same set of values for the attributes are allowed. No two rows are completely identical.

Unique identifier. The primary key identifies each tuple uniquely.

Atomic values. Each value of every attribute is atomic. That is, for a single tuple, the value of each attribute must be single-valued. Multiple values or repeating groups of attributes are not allowed for any attribute in a tuple.

Domain constraint. The value of each attribute must be an atomic value from a certain domain.

Column homogeneity. Each column gets values from the same domain.

Order of columns. The sequence of the columns is insignificant. The sequence may be changed without changing the meaning or use of the relation. The primary key may be in any column, not necessarily in the first column. Columns may be stored in any sequence and, therefore, must be addressed by column names and not by column positions.

Order of rows. The sequence of the rows is insignificant. Rows may be reordered or interchanged without any consequence. New rows may be inserted anywhere in the relation. It does not matter whether rows are added at the beginning, middle, or end of a relation.

Entity Integrity

Consider the relation EMPLOYEE. The rows in the relation represent individual employees in an organization. The rows represent real-world entities. Each row represents a specific employee. Similarly, a row in the relation CUSTOMER stands for a particular customer. In other words, each tuple or row in a relation must be uniquely identified because each tuple represents a single and distinct entity. The entity integrity rule in the relational data model establishes this principle for an entity.

But, how is a specific row or tuple in a relation uniquely identified? As you know, the primary key serves this function. The primary key value of each tuple or row uniquely identifies that row. Therefore, the entity integrity rule is a rule about the primary key that is meant to identify rows uniquely. The rule applies to single relations.

> *Entity identity rule:* No part of the primary key of any tuple in a relation can have a null value.

Figure 8-7 presents three relations, EMPLOYEE, PROJECT, and ASSIGN-MENT. The relations EMPLOYEE and PROJECT have primary keys with single attributes; two attributes make up the primary key for the ASSIGNMENT relation. The figure explains how violation of the entity identify rule affects the integrity of the data model.

Note the null values present in a few rows; because of these rows the entity integrity rule is violated in the relation. If two or more rows have null values as primary key values, how can you distinguish between these rows? Which row

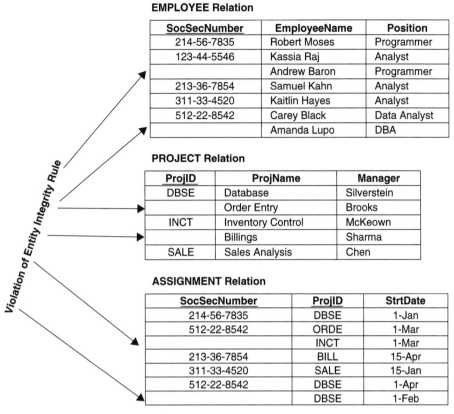

EMPLOYEE Relation

SocSecNumber	EmployeeName	Position
214-56-7835	Robert Moses	Programmer
123-44-5546	Kassia Raj	Analyst
	Andrew Baron	Programmer
213-36-7854	Samuel Kahn	Analyst
311-33-4520	Kaitlin Hayes	Analyst
512-22-8542	Carey Black	Data Analyst
	Amanda Lupo	DBA

PROJECT Relation

ProjID	ProjName	Manager
DBSE	Database	Silverstein
	Order Entry	Brooks
INCT	Inventory Control	McKeown
	Billings	Sharma
SALE	Sales Analysis	Chen

ASSIGNMENT Relation

SocSecNumber	ProjID	StrtDate
214-56-7835	DBSE	1-Jan
512-22-8542	ORDE	1-Mar
	INCT	1-Mar
213-36-7854	BILL	15-Apr
311-33-4520	SALE	15-Jan
512-22-8542	DBSE	1-Apr
	DBSE	1-Feb

Violation of Entity Integrity Rule

Figure 8-7   Entity integrity rule.

denotes which specific entity? In the case of the relation ASSIGNMENT, even if only part of the primary key contains null values for any rows, the entity integrity rule is violated.

Referential Integrity

You have noted that foreign keys establish relationships between tables or relations. The value placed in the foreign key column of one table for a specific row links to a row with the same value in the primary key column in another table. Figure 8-8 shows two relations, DEPARTMENT and EMPLOYEE.

Note how the values in the foreign key column DeptNo in the EMPLOYEE relation and in the primary key column DeptNo in the DEPARTMENT relation link related rows in the two relations. In the figure, employee Charles is assigned to department Accounting and employee Eldon is assigned to Marketing. What about employee Mary, who is supposed to be assigned to department D555, but the database does not have department D555? Look at the row for employee Paul. This row has a null value in the foreign key column. Is this allowed? What do null values in foreign key columns indicate? You know that null values in foreign key columns

EMPLOYEE Relation

EmpNo	EmpName	Phone Ext.	DeptNo
E10	Charles	418	D200
E20	Mary	236	D555
E30	Eldon	179	D300
E40	Paul	522	

DEPARTMENT Relation

DeptNo	DeptName	Location
D100	Engineering	West
D200	Accounting	South
D300	Marketing	East

Figure 8-8 Referential integrity rule.

denote optional relationships. That means that employee Paul is not assigned to any department.

When one relation is related to another through foreign key values, the references of the relationship must be clearly indicated. There should not be any ambiguities. A foreign key value must clearly indicate how that row is related to a row in the other relation. The referential integrity rule addresses the establishment of clear references between related tables. The referential integrity rule, therefore, applies to sets of two relations.

> ***Referential integrity rule:*** The value of a foreign key in a table must either be null or be one of the values of the primary key in the related table.

Functional Dependencies

Let us use the EMPLOYEE, PROJECT, and ASSIGNMENT relations shown in Figure 8-7 to examine the concept of functional dependency. Functional dependency in a relation arises because the value of one attribute in a tuple determines the value for another attribute. Let us look at some examples.

In the EMPLOYEE relation of Figure 8-7, note the tuple with key value 213-36-7854. This determines that the tuple represents a distinct employee whose name is Samuel Kahn and whose position is Analyst. Now, look at the tuple with key value 311-33-4520. This key value uniquely identifies an employee whose name is Kaitlin Hayes and whose position also happens to be Analyst. Let us inspect the dependencies.

Which attribute's values determine values of other attributes? Does the value of the primary key uniquely and functionally determine the values of other attributes?

- Key value 213-36-7854 uniquely and functionally determines a specific row representing Samuel Kahn with position Analyst.
- Key value 311-33-4520 uniquely and functionally determines a specific row representing Kaitlin Hayes with position Analyst.

Let us ask the questions the other way around. Does the value of the attribute Position uniquely and functionally determine the value of the primary key attribute?

- Attribute value Analyst does not uniquely determine a key value—in this case, it determines two values of the key, namely, 213-36-7854 and 311-33-4520.

What you see clearly is that the value of the primary key uniquely and functionally determines the values of other attributes, and not the other way around.

Let us express this concept with a functional dependency notation

FD: SocSecNumber $\rightarrow$ EmployeeName

FD: SocSecNumber $\rightarrow$ Position

In the ASSIGNMENT relation, two attributes, SocSecNumber and ProjectID, together make up the primary key. Here, too, the values of the other attribute in the tuple are uniquely determined by the values of the composite primary key.

FD: SocSecNumber, ProjID $\rightarrow$ StrtDate

The discussion of functional dependencies leads to another important rule or constraint for the primary key of a relation.

Functional dependency rule: Each data item in a tuple of a relation is uniquely and functionally determined by the primary key, by the whole primary key, and only by the primary key.

DATA MANIPULATION

What is the motivation for creating a database system for an organization? Why do you examine all the information requirements, create a data model to reflect the information requirements, and build a database system based on the designed data model? Of course, the reason is to provide users with the ability to access the data, share it, and use it to perform the various business processes. The database is meant for usage—read data, change data, add data, and also delete data from the database as needed.

The structure of the relational model in the form of two-dimensional tables rests on a solid mathematical foundation. Can mathematical principles and methods based on the set theory be used to retrieve data from a database built on the relational model? How can you manipulate data? Are there sound languages to interface with the database and work with the data in the database?

Dr. Codd, who formulated the structure and rules of the relational model, also provided methods for data manipulation in a relational database. He suggested languages for doing so. We will now examine these languages and appreciate the robust mathematical foundation on which the languages stand.

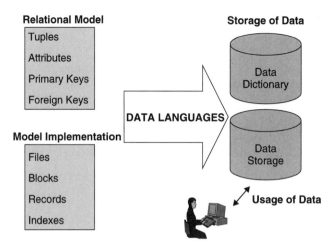

Figure 8-9   Role of data languages.

Role of Data Languages

Figure 8-9 illustrates the role of data languages. You know that data in a relational database are perceived in the form of tables. From the users' or programmers' points of view, the database contains data in the form of two-dimensional tables. Data languages for the relational model, therefore, must relate to data in the form of tables.

To use the data from a relational database, first the structures of the tables must be defined in the data dictionary. Only then will you be able to manipulate the data based on the definition of the structures. For example, if you are looking for all the customers in Alaska from your relational database, to retrieve information about the customers the DBMS must know the structure of the CUSTOMER relation. The structure of the CUSTOMER relation must have been defined first.

Two types of languages are necessary for the relational data model:

Data definition language (DDL). To define the relations, attributes, primary keys, foreign keys, data types, attribute lengths, and so on.

Data manipulation language (DML). To perform the data manipulations such as reading data, updating data, adding data, or deleting data.

Data Manipulation Languages

For data manipulation, Dr. Codd suggested two generic languages, both based on mathematical principles. Because data are perceived as organized in the form of tables, any data manipulation in the relational model can be reduced to operations on rows and columns of tables. The two languages provide well-defined methods to work on rows and columns of tables.

These are the two languages:

Relational Algebra. Consists of mathematical operations on rows and columns of one or more relations. Each operation in a series of operations produces a resulting relation. A data manipulation solution comprises a set of these operations performed on relations in a definite sequence.

Relational Calculus. Applies data manipulation conditions to rows and columns of relations. A data manipulation solution does not contain a series of operations but has a single solution statement to produce the necessary result.

Both relational algebra and relational calculus are generic languages. Popular languages included in commercial database management systems implement elements of these generic languages. In these generic languages, Dr. Codd has stipulated the semantics and syntax and has shown how these can be applied to perform data manipulation. Commercial vendors build their language implementations based on the two generic languages. Structured Query Language (SQL) is one such implementation based on the generic languages, mostly based on relational calculus. We will look at SQL in Chapter 13.

Let us now examine the provisions in these two languages. Remember that these are generic languages. That means that no programs are written using the syntax and semantics of the native operations in these languages. No program code is directly written to contain relational algebra and relational calculus commands or operations. However, the commercial data manipulation languages are built based on the operations and commands of the two generic languages. Therefore, to understand how data manipulation is made possible in a relational data model, you need to gain a good understanding of the two generic languages. We will now explore the major operations and constructs of the two languages. Note the underlying principles. Study the various operations and understand how they produce the required results.

Relational Algebra

In relational algebra, you have operations that work on relations. Some operations work on a single relation and others on two relations at a time. A solution for data retrieval consists of a set of operations performed in a certain order. When all the operations are performed in sequence, the final result is obtained. For example, the final result may be the retrieval of all orders for a specific customer.

Note, however, that the result is always a relation. In the case of the retrieval of orders for a specific customer, the result is the set of orders satisfying the given condition. The result is therefore a relation consisting of columns representing the attributes of the ORDER relation and only those rows satisfying the condition of belonging to the specific customer. In any case, the result consists of a relation with rows and columns.

Sometimes, the resulting relation may contain just one column and many rows, may contain many columns and just one row, or may contain just one column and just one row. In every case, the result is still a relation.

Relational algebra consists of the following nine major operations:

SELECT
PROJECT

	PatientNo	PatientName	DateAdmit	DateDischarged
PATIENT	1134	Bruce Greenberg	2-Jan	11-Jan
Relation	1389	Sheryl Rodericks	10-Jan	26-Jan
	2107	Miranda Poko	22-Jan	1-Feb
	2298	Pedro Pomales	2-Feb	18-Feb
	2576	Bob Totten	11-Feb	25-Feb
	3158	Peter Tora	14-Feb	14-Mar
	3255	Gary Goran	6-Mar	10-Mar
	3380	Pia Dorsey-Adams	15-Mar	22-Apr
	4157	Anthony Brett	22-Apr	24-Apr
	6199	Milton Kalma	25-Apr	27-Apr

	PatientNo	PatientName	DateAdmit	DateDischarged
Result of	1389	Sheryl Rodericks	10-Jan	26-Jan
SELECT	2298	Pedro Pomales	2-Feb	18-Feb
operation	3158	Peter Tora	14-Feb	14-Mar
	3380	Pia Dorsey-Adams	15-Mar	22-Apr

	PatientName	DateDischarged
	Bruce Greenberg	11-Jan
	Sheryl Rodericks	26-Jan
Result of	Miranda Poko	1-Feb
PROJECT	Pedro Pomales	18-Feb
operation	Bob Totten	25-Feb
	Peter Tora	14-Mar
	Gary Goran	10-Mar
	Pia Dorsey-Adams	22-Apr
	Anthony Brett	24-Apr
	Milton Kalma	27-Apr

Figure 8-10 Relations for SELECT and PROJECT operations.

ASSIGNMENT

UNION

INTERSECTION

DIFFERENCE

PRODUCT

JOIN

DIVIDE

Let us examine each of these operations with the aid of examples. To study the following three operations, we will use the relations or tables shown in Figure 8-10.

Select

Features and function

- Operates on a single relation.
- Selects specific rows from a relation on the basis of given criteria.
- The result is a relation containing rows and columns as indicated below:
  - Rows—only the selected rows from the original relation
  - Columns—same columns as in the original relation

Example

Data request   From PATIENT relation, find all the patients who have stayed in the medical center for more than 15 days.

Relational algebra solution
SELECT (PATIENT : (DateDischarged − DateAdmit) > 15)

Note the syntax for the operation in relational algebra. The keyword SELECT is used to indicate the operation.

Project

Features and function

- Operates on a single relation.
- Selects specific columns from a relation on the basis of given criteria.
- The result is a relation containing rows and columns as indicated below:
  - Rows—same rows as in the original relation
  - Columns—only the selected columns from the original relation

Example

Data request   From PATIENT relation, list only the names of patients and their discharge dates.

Relational algebra solution   PATIENT [PatientName, DateDischarged]

Note the syntax for the operation in relational algebra. There is no need for a keyword. The selected columns are indicated within the square brackets. In this case, the result is a relation containing the same number of rows as the number of patients in the database and two columns.

Assignment

Features and function

- Simple operation; not really an operation in the sense of other operations.
- Assigns the result of some set of operations to the resulting relation.

Example

Data request   From PATIENT relation, find all the patients who have stayed in the medical center for more than 15 days. Assign the result of the operation to a relation called PATIENT-15.

Relational algebra solution
PATIENT-15:= SELECT (PATIENT : (DateDischarged − DateAdmit) > 15)

Note the symbol := used to perform the assignment of the result and name the resulting relation as PATIENT-15. There are no keywords.

Union

Features and function

- Operates on two relations.
- Combines two relations.
- Both relations must be union-compatible; that is, they must have the same columns.
- The result is a single relation containing rows and columns as indicated below:
  - Rows—all the rows from both relations, duly eliminating any duplicate rows
  - Columns—same columns as in either of the original relations

Example

In the database of a medical center, there are two relations representing data about the doctors. One relation, SUPVRDOCTOR, represents data about doctors with supervisory responsibilities who have other doctors reporting to them. The other relation SUBDOCTOR represents data about every doctor who reports to another doctor. Figure 8-11 shows these two tables with data in the rows and columns.

Data request   List all the attributes of all the doctors in the medical center. Call the result relation ALLDOCTOR.

SUBDOCTOR Relation

DrID	DrName	Specialty	DrPhone	SuprDrID
10	Kim Maggio	Family Practice	918-756-0831	25
14	Monika Isaac	Neurology	609-238-3377	45
23	Marcus Kulper	Internal Medicine	732-613-9313	36
37	Ira Goldman	Psychiatry	609-246-0331	13
39	Lawrence Stark	Radiology	918-613-1988	45
45	Robert Martin	Surgery General	609-924-9248	25
36	Elaine Hsu	Urology	908-535-5228	25
13	Leroy Richardson	Oncology	908-322-5566	25

SUPVR DOCTOR Relation

DrID	DrName	Specialty	DrPhone	SuprDrID
25	Roger Smarts	Neurology	609-238-5100	
45	Robert Martin	Surgery General	609-924-9248	25
36	Elaine Hsu	Urology	908-535-5228	25
13	Leroy Richardson	Oncology	908-322-5566	25

Figure 8-11   SUBDOCTOR and SUPVRDOCTOR relations.

ALLDOCTOR Relation

DrID	DrName	Specialty	DrPhone	SuprDrID
10	Kim Maggio	Family Practice	918-756-0831	25
14	Monika Isaac	Neurology	609-238-3377	45
23	Marcus Kulper	Internal Medicine	732-613-9313	36
37	Ira Goldman	Psychiatry	609-246-0331	13
39	Lawrence Stark	Radiology	918-613-1988	45
45	Robert Martin	Surgery General	609-924-9248	25
36	Elaine Hsu	Urology	908-535-5228	25
13	Leroy Richardson	Oncology	908-322-5566	25
25	Roger Smarts	Neurology	609-238-5100	

Explanation of
UNION operation

Figure 8-12   UNION operation.

Relational algebra solution
ALLDOCTOR:= SUPVRDOCTOR ∪ SUBDOCTOR

Note the syntax for the operation in relational algebra and the symbol U indicating the union operation. The union operation combines the data from the two relations, eliminating duplication. Note that some doctors, who report to others and also have doctors reporting to themselves, will be in both relations. The union operation in relational algebra is similar to the union function in mathematical set theory. Note the solution shown in Figure 8-12.

Intersection

Features and function

- Operates on two relations.
- Identifies common rows in two relations.
- Both relations must be union-compatible; that is, they must have the same columns.
- The result is a single relation containing rows and columns as indicated below:
  - Rows—only those rows that are common to both relations
  - Columns—same columns as in either of the original relations

Example

Refer to Figure 8-11 for the discussion of this operation.

Data request   List all the attributes of only those doctors who have doctors reporting to them and who themselves report to other doctors. These are the doctors who are both subordinates as well as having supervisory responsibilities. Call the result relation DOCTOR.

DrID	DrName	Specialty	DrPhone	SuprDrID
45	Robert Martin	Surgery General	609-924-9248	25
36	Elaine Hsu	Urology	908-535-5228	25
13	Leroy Richardson	Oncology	908-322-5566	25

DOCTOR Relation

**Explanation of
INTERSECTION operation**

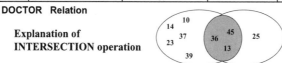

DrID	DrName	Specialty	DrPhone	SuprDrID
10	Kim Maggio	Family Practice	918-756-0831	25
14	Monika Isaac	Neurology	609-238-3377	45
23	Marcus Kulper	Internal Medicine	732-613-9313	36
37	Ira Goldman	Psychiatry	609-246-0331	13
39	Lawrence Stark	Radiology	918-613-1988	45

SUBORDDOCTOR Relation

**Explanation of
DIFFERENCE operation**

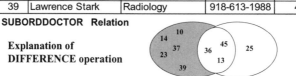

Figure 8-13   INTERSECTION and DIFFERENCE operations.

Relational algebra solution
DOCTOR := SUPVRDOCTOR ∩ SUBDOCTOR

Note the syntax for the operation in relational algebra and the symbol ∩ indicating the intersection operation. The intersection operation finds only those entities that are common to both relations. Intersection operation in relational algebra is similar to intersection function in mathematical set theory. Note the solution shown in Figure 8-13.

Difference

Features and function

- Operates on two relations.
- Identifies the rows in one relation that are not present in the other relation.
- Both relations must be union-compatible; that is, they must have the same columns.
- The result is a single relation containing rows and columns as indicated below:
  - Rows—only those rows that are in the first relation but not in the second
  - Columns—same columns as in either of the original relations

Example

Refer to Figure 8-11 for the discussion of this operation.

Data request   List all the attributes of all doctors who report to some other doctors but have no one reporting to them. These are the doctors who are subordinates without any supervisory responsibilities. Call the result relation SUBORDDOCTOR.

Relational algebra solution
SUBORDDOCTOR : = SUBDOCTOR — SUPVRDOCTOR

Note the syntax for the operation in relational algebra and the symbol — indicating the difference operation. The difference operation finds only those entities in the SUBDOCTOR relation but not present in the SUPVRDOCTOR relation. These are subordinates that do not have any supervisory responsibilities at all. Note the solution shown in Figure 8-13.

Also note that the result will not be same if you reverse the order of the two relations in the difference operation.

(A—B) is not the same as (B—A). (SUPVRDOCTOR — SUBDOCTOR) represents the doctors who only have supervisory responsibilities and do not report to any other doctor at all.

Product

Features and function

- Operates on two relations.
- Produces the scalar product between the two relations.
- By itself, the product operation has no meaning in business functions. But the product operation is an essential interim operation for the more important join operation.
- The result is a single relation containing rows and columns as indicated below:
  - Rows—formed by concatenation each of row of one relation to each row of the other relation
  - Columns—all the columns of both relations put together

Example

Refer to Figure 8-14 for the discussion of this operation. Note the two relations A and B.

Data request   Find the product relation C between two relations A and B.
Relational algebra solution   C := A $*$ B

Note the syntax for the operation in relational algebra and the symbol $*$ indicating the product. Observe how the rows for relation C are formed from the rows of A and B.

Let us generalize the product operation.

If relation A has m columns and p rows, and relation B has n columns and q rows, then the result relation C will have $(m+n)$ columns and $(p*q)$ rows.

RELATION A

X	Y
12	25
13	28

RELATION B

S	T
34	56
38	99
45	84

RELATION C

X	Y	S	T
12	25	34	56
12	25	38	99
12	25	45	84
13	28	34	56
13	28	38	99
13	28	45	84

Figure 8-14   PRODUCT operation.

Join

Features and function

- Operates on two relations that have common columns.
- Connects data across two relations based on values in common columns.
- Types of join operations: natural join, theta join, outer join.
- The result is a single relation containing rows and columns as indicated below for a natural join of relations A and B with a common column with name c:
  - Take the product of A and B
  - The resulting relation will have two columns for c
  - Eliminate all rows from the product except those rows where the value for column c in one relation is the same the value for column c in the other relation
  - Apply project operation to eliminate one of the two common c columns from the result relation

Example

Refer to Figure 8-15 for the discussion of this operation. Note the two relations PATIENT and BILLING.

Data request   List the billing data for all discharged patients. Call the result relation DISCHRGPATIENT.

Relational algebra solution
DISCHRGPATIENT := JOIN (PATIENT, BILLING)

Note the syntax for the operation in relational algebra and the keyword JOIN indicating the join operation. Note the steps and also the rows and columns in the final result. The data about patient discharges is in the PATIENT relation. The BILLING relation contains data about patient billing. We need to

PATIENT Relation

PatientNo	DischargeDate
1234	10-Feb
2345	22-Feb
3456	5-Mar

BILLING Relation

BldPatientNo	BilledCharges
1234	150.00
2345	225.00
1234	315.00
2345	195.00

DISCHRGPATIENT Relation --- three types

	PatientNo	DischargeDate	BldPatientNo	BilledCharges
Result of equijoin	1234	10-Feb	1234	150.00
	2345	22-Feb	2345	225.00
	1234	10-Feb	1234	315.00
	2345	22-Feb	2345	195.00

	PatientNo	DischargeDate	BilledCharges
Result of natural join	1234	10-Feb	150.00
	2345	22-Feb	225.00
	1234	10-Feb	315.00
	2345	22-Feb	195.00

	PatientNo	DischargeDate	BilledCharges
Result of outer join	1234	10-Feb	150.00
	2345	22-Feb	225.00
	1234	10-Feb	315.00
	2345	22-Feb	195.00
	3456	5-Mar	

Figure 8-15   JOIN operation.

connect these pieces of data across the two relations based on equal values in PatientNo columns that are common to both relations. Natural join operation accomplishes this task.

Also note the other two types of join operations illustrated in Figure 8-15.

Divide

Features and function

- Operates on two relations.
- The divide operation is the reverse of the product operation.
- The result is a single relation containing rows and columns as indicated below:
  - Rows—rows in one relation matching with every row in another relation
  - Columns—all and only columns of the first relation, but not of the second

Example

Refer to Figure 8-16 for the discussion of this operation. Note the three relations A, B, and C.

Divide relation B by relation C, giving A as the result relation. The following conditions apply:

(B)
ASSIGNMENT
Relation

EmployeeNo	ProjectNo
89	1
89	2
44	3
53	1
53	2
55	2
55	3
55	7
55	8
77	9
77	7
87	7
87	9
21	9
21	8
55	8

(C)
JONESPROJ
Relation

ProjectNo
1
2

(A)
JONESEMP
Relation

EmployeeNo
89
53

**Divide relation B by relation C
giving relation A**

Figure 8-16   DIVIDE operation.

Columns of C must be a subset of columns of B.
Columns of A are all and only those columns of B that are not columns of C.
Place a row in A, if and only if it is associated with every row in C.

Data request   Find all employees who worked on every project Jones had worked on. Name the result as relation JONESEMP (see Figure 8-16).

Relational algebra solution
JONESEMP := ASSIGNMENT / JONESPROJ

Note the syntax for the operation in relational algebra and the symbol / indicating divide operation. Observe how the rows for the result relation JONESEMP are formed. Note that columns of JONESPROJ are a subset of columns of relation ASSIGNMENT. Columns of the result relation JONESEMP are all and only those columns of ASSIGNMENT that are not columns of JONESPROJ.

Relational Calculus

This is the second generic language proposed for manipulating data in a database conforming to the relational data model. As you have seen, relational algebra consists of distinct operations. To arrive at a required solution relation, you use the operations one after another in a specific sequence. Commercial database vendors provide equivalent commands or statements for the relational algebra operations in their language implementations.

Relational calculus is markedly different. Here, no separate and distinct operations exist similar to the relational algebra operations. Relational calculus expresses a solution relation in a single statement. Database vendors implement the typical relational calculus statement in their database languages.

SALESPERSON Relation

SalespersID	SalesperName	SupvrID	OfficeCity
15	Peterson	42	Boston
21	Espinoza	38	Trenton
23	James	42	Boston
27	Warren	38	Toronto
35	Rolland	38	Montreal
38	Demetrius		Quebec
42	McPherson		Boston

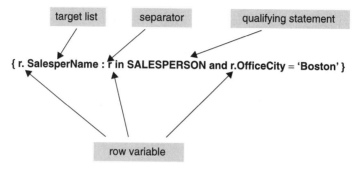

Figure 8-17   Relational calculus statement.

Let us take an example. Refer to Figure 8-17.

Data request   What are the names of the salespersons attached to the Boston office?

We mentioned that relational calculus provides single solution statements. First, let us try to write the solution statement in plain English.

Solution to contain

SalesperName
    from rows in SALESPERSON relation,
    only from certain rows from SALESPERSON relation,
        a row in SALESPERSON to qualify to be part of the solution
        it must satisfy the condition that
            OfficeCity from that row must be Boston.

A relational calculus solution statement is similar to this plain English statement. Instead of expressing the solution in a long-winding way as the above statement, relational calculus statement is more succinct and standardized. See the solution example shown below and also as explained in Figure 8-17.

Relational calculus solution
{ r.SalesperName : r IN SALESPERSON AND r.OfficeCity = 'Boston' }

In the figure, the components of the relational calculus statement are pointed out. Note the descriptions of the components as shown below:

CUSTOMER Relation

CustomerNo	CustomerName	Country
1000	Rosato Electric	U.S.A.
1010	MDZ Electric	U.K.
1050	Electric des Royal	France
1100	Mitshista Electric	Japan
1120	Jean Pierre	France

SUPPLIER Relation

SupplierNo	SupplierName	SupCountry
200	Herman Electricals	U.S.A.
205	Allied Electrics, Ltd.	U.K.
300	Akiro & Amana	Japan

PRODUCT Relation

ProductCode	ProdDesc	SupplierNo
4136	Three-way switch	205
5555	Circuit breaker	200
5678	Junction box	300
6543	5HP Motor	300

SALE Relation

Date	CustomerNo	ProductCode	SalespersID
5-Mar	1000	4136	15
7-Mar	1010	5555	21
9-Mar	1050	5678	23
13-Mar	1100	6543	27
7-Mar	1120	5555	35
15-Mar	1000	4163	38
29-Mar	1100	6543	23

SALESPERSON Relation

SalespersID	SalesperName	SupvrID	OfficeCity
15	Peterson	42	Boston
21	Espinoza	38	Trenton
23	James	42	Boston
27	Warren	38	Toronto
35	Rolland	38	Montreal
38	Demetrius		Quebec
42	McPherson		Boston

Figure 8-18 Sample relations to illustrate solutions.

Target list. List of attributes to be included in the solution relation.

Row variable. A letter to indicate a variable quantity that represents the qualifying rows.

Qualifying statement. The part of the relational calculus solution that contains conditions for qualifying rows.

Separator. The indicator ":" separating the target list of attributes to be present in the solution relation from the rest of the relational calculus statement.

Comparison of Generic Languages

Let us conclude our discussion of the two powerful generic languages proposed by Dr. Codd with a comparison between them.

Comparison of Solutions Let us go over a few examples of relational algebra and relational calculus solutions. Use the relations presented in Figure 8-18.

Data request What are the names of the customers in France? Mark the result relation as CUSTFRANCE

Relational algebra solution
A : = SELECT (CUSTOMER: Country = 'France')
CUSTFRANCE : = A [CustomerName]

Relational calculus solution
CUSTFRANCE
{r.CustomerName : r in CUSTOMER and r.Country = 'France'}

Data request   List the names and countries of customers who bought product 5555. Mark the result relation as CUSTPROD5555.

Relational algebra solution
A : = SELECT (SALE : ProductCode = '5555')
B : = JOIN (CUSTOMER, A)
CUSTPROD5555 : = B [CustomerName, Country]

Relational calculus solution
CUSTPROD5555

{(r.CustomerName, r.Country) : r IN CUSTOMER and there exists s in SALE (s.CustomerNo = r.CustomerNo and s.ProductCode = '5555')}

Notice that you need two row variables r and s in the relational calculus solution. Note also the existence condition. A solution is available only if qualifying rows exist in relation SALE. The existence condition in a relational calculus solution is comparable to the JOIN operation in a relational algebra solution.

Procedural and Nonprocedural   What is the essential difference you have noticed between the two languages from the above solution examples? The relational algebra solution consists of a few steps of distinct operations, whereas the relational calculus solution is just a single statement. Using relational algebra, you need to determine the operations and their sequence. With relational calculus, you just state the result you require. This significant difference expresses the essential nature of the two generic languages.

Relational Algebra: Procedural Language   A procedural language is a language in which the programmer must code the steps in the proper sequence. The language allows execution of the distinct steps in the specified sequence. You have to write the procedure. You have to state how the data manipulation must be done to produce the solution.

Relational Calculus: Nonprocedural Language   When using a nonprocedural language, you do not have to specify the steps or operations, nor do you have to state the order in which the operations must be executed. You do not have to code a procedure. You do not have to state how the solution must be arrived at. You just have to state the solution you are looking for. You simply express the solution through a single solution statement.

Same Solution   The generic languages are two different methods for language implementations. Let us say you arrive at a certain solution relation for a particular data manipulation request by using an implementation of relational algebra. According to Dr. Codd, the two languages are relationally equivalent. That means that you can also arrive at the same solution relation by using an implementation of relational calculus.

Every data manipulation request that can be completed through the use of one language can be done through the use of the other language. Let us say that you write a relational algebra solution for a complex query involving several source relations. The solution is likely to contain several relational algelra operations such SELECT, PROJECT, JOIN, DIVIDE, and so on. Assume that you are able to arrive at the solution through a commercial language implementing relational algebra. Relational equivalency means that you can arrive at the solution for the same complex query in relational calculus and a proper commercial language implementation of relational calculus will find the exactly same solution.

Relationally Complete   According to the author of the relational model, the true test for whether a commercial language implementation is truly relational is straightforward. If a commercial language can produce the same results that are produced by either of the two generic languages for any query, then the commercial language is said to be relationally complete.

The property of being relationally complete is an important qualification for a language that can be used in a relational database. In other words, the commercial language must be able to perform any set of relational algebra operations, however complex the set may be. Similarly, the commercial language must be able to implement and produce the result expressed by any relational calculus statement, however complex the statement may be.

Commercial Language Implementations   Structured Query Language (SQL) has gained acceptance as the standard for the relational model. The language incorporates functions of the generic languages, although the standard SQL statement is seen to be more like a relational calculus implementation. However, specific relational algebra operations are also included in the repertoire of SQL.

Commercial database vendors include SQL as part of their database products. SQL interface is a standard component of the relational database management systems on the market. However, each vendor tries to augment SQL standards with its own proprietary enhancements. This results in a kind of incompatibility. SQL code written for one commercial DBMS may not work for another DBMS unless you refrain from using any of the proprietary revisions to SQL standards.

RELATIONAL MODEL DESIGN

From the discussion so far, you have captured the significance of the relational data model. You have understood how it stands on a solid mathematical foundation and is, therefore, a disciplined approach to perceiving data. The view of data in the form of the common two-dimensional tables adds to the elegance and simplicity of the model. At the same time, relational constraints or rules, to which the two-dimensional tables must conform, ensure data integrity and consistency.

Commercial relational database management systems are implementations of the relational data model. So, to develop and build a relational database system for your organization, you need to learn how to design and put together a relational data model. Although the model appears to be simple, how do you create a relational data model from the requirements? The previous chapters covered the details of creating data models. We went through the methods and steps for creating the object-based data model and the entity-relationship data model. Now the task is to create a relational data model, which is not the same as one of those two data models. Why do you need to create a relational data model? If you are developing a relational database system, then you require that your information requirements be represented in a relational data model first. Let us explore the methods for creating a relational data model.

Requirements for Data Model

From the previous chapters you know how to create a semantic data model from the information requirements. A semantic data model captures all the meanings and content of the information requirements of an organization. We also discussed the merit of the semantic data model. Being a generic data model, it is not restricted by the structure and format rules of the conventional data models such as hierarchical, network, or relational data models. You are now convinced that representing information requirements in the form of a semantic data model is the proper way.

Well, what are the steps between creating a semantic data model and the implementation of a relational database system for your organization? You know that the semantic data model, if created correctly, will represent every aspect of the information that needs to be found in the proposed database system. The next steps depend on the extent and complexity of your database system. Let us examine the options.

Design Approaches

Database practitioners adopt one of two approaches to design and put together a relational data model. The relational data model must, of course, truly represent the information requirements. In the simplest terms, what is a relational data model? It is a collection of two-dimensional tables with rows and columns and with relationships expressed within the tables themselves through foreign keys. So, in effect, designing and creating a relational data model reduces to creating the proper collection of two-dimensional tables.

Figure 8-19 presents the two design approaches for creating a relational data model.

Note how in one approach, you go through the steps of creating a semantic data model first and then transform the semantic model into a relational data model. The other approach appears to be a short-cut method bypassing the semantic data model. In this approach, you proceed to the task of creating the relational data model straight from the requirements definitions. Let us examine the basics of the two approaches.

Semantic to Relational Model

The first method shown in Figure 8-19 takes you through the semantic data model. In this approach, you complete the semantic data model. To create the semantic data model, you may use either the object-based data modeling technique or the

1. **Semantic Modeling Approach** (*used for large, complex databases*):
   - Create Semantic Data Model
   - Transform Semantic Model to Relational Model

2. **Traditional Approach** (*used for smaller, simpler databases*):
   - Create random two-dimensional table structures
   - Normalize the data structures

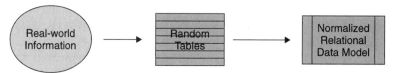

Figure 8-19   Relational data model: design approaches.

entity-relationship data modeling technique. Either of these techniques will produce a semantic data model that can be used to create the relational data model.

Here are the steps in this design approach:

- Gather the information requirements of the organization.
- Create semantic data model to truly represent the information requirements.
- Review the overall semantic data model for completeness.
- Take each component of the semantic data model at a time and examine it.
- Transform each component of the semantic data model into a corresponding component of the relational data model.
- Pull together all the components of the relational data model resulting from the transformation from the semantic data model.
- Complete the relational data model.
- Review the relational data model for completeness.

Chapter 9 elaborates on this approach to designing the relational data model. We will list the components of the semantic model and the corresponding components of the relational model. We will determine how each component of the semantic data model must be mapped to its corresponding component in the relational data model.

Traditional Method

Before the introduction and standardization of data modeling techniques, database practitioners had traditionally adopted a different method. A relational data model is, after all, a set of two-dimensional tables. Why not look at the information requirements and try to come up with the necessary tables to represent the data that would satisfy the information requirements? Why do you need an intermediary step of creating a semantic data model? Does this not appear to be a practical design approach?

Although the approach is deceptively simple, as you will note in Chapter 10, this method is subject to serious problems if the tables are not defined properly. You are likely to end up with a faulty set of tables in your relational data model, with a high potential for data corruption and inconsistency.

Dr. Codd suggested an ordered methodology for making this design approach work. After an initial set of tables is designed, you must go through a step-by-step process of normalization of the initial tables. After the normalization steps are completed, your relational data model will result in a set of tables that are free from redundancies and errors.

Here are the steps in this design approach:

- Gather the information requirements of the organization.
- Review the information requirements to determine the types of tables that would be needed.
- Come up with an initial set of tables.
- Ensure that your initial set of tables contains all the information requirements.
- Normalize the tables with a step-by-step methodology.
- Review the resulting set of tables, one by one, and ensure that none of the tables has potential redundancies or errors.
- Complete the relational data model.
- Review the relational data model for completeness.

Chapter 10 covers this approach to designing the relational data model in detail. You will recognize the need and motivation for the normalization process. We will list the normalization steps and show how to apply a normalization principle at each step. You will note how, after each step, the set of tables comes closer to being the correct set of tables and becoming part of the final relational data model.

Evaluation of the Two Methods

Naturally, when there are two ways for arriving at the same place, you must ask which path you should take. If both methods produce the same desired result, which method is more appropriate? The answers to these questions depend on the circumstances of the design process.

Note the following points about the two methods while making the choice between the two ways:

Same result. If you carry out the transformation of the semantic data model into a relational model or adopt the traditional method using normalization, you will arrive at the same relational data model. However, either method must be used carefully, making sure that every task is executed properly.

One method intuitive. In the traditional method, you are supposed to come up with an initial and complete set of tables. But how do you come up with the initial set? Using what method? There is no standard method for arriving at an initial set of tables. You have to look at the information requirements and arrive at the initial set of tables mostly through intuition. You just start with the best possible set that is complete. Then you proceed to normalize the tables and complete the relational data model.

Other method systematic. The method of creating the semantic data model first and then transforming it into the required relational data model is a systematic method with well-defined steps. The semantic data model is created through clearly defined data modeling techniques. You then take the components of the semantic data model, one by one, and transform these in a disciplined manner.

Choosing between the two methods. When can you adopt the traditional method? Only when you can come up with a good initial set of tables through intuition. If the information requirements are wide and complex, by looking at the information requirements it is not easy to discern the tables for the initial set. If you attempt the process, you are likely to miss portions of information requirements. Therefore, adopt the traditional approach only for smaller and simpler relational database systems. For larger and more complex relational database systems, the transformation method is the prudent approach. As data modelers gain experience, they tend to get better at defining the initial set of tables and choose the normalization method.

CHAPTER SUMMARY

- The relational data model is found to be superior to other earlier conventional data models such as the hierarchical and network data models.
- The relational data model, standing on solid mathematical principles, is a disciplined method for data organization, provides a simple and familiar view of data in the form of tables, and, above all, links related data elements logically and not physically.
- A relation or a two-dimensional table with rows and columns is the single modeling concept for this data model. The columns represent the attributes of the entity; the rows represent single instances of the entities.
- Relationships between tables or relations are established through foreign keys, not physical pointers.
- To provide data integrity and consistency, the set of tables in a relational model must conform to relational constraints or rules. The entity integrity rule governs the integrity of a single relation; the referential integrity rule stipulates conditions for two related tables.
- Each data item in a row or tuple of a relation must depend on the entire primary key alone, not on any other attribute in the row.
- Relational algebra and relational calculus are two generic languages for data manipulation in a relational data model. Relational algebra is a procedural language consisting of distinct operations; relational calculus, being a nonprocedural language, just specifies the solution in the form of single statements.

Commercial language implementations are based on these two generic languages.

- Two methods for creating a relational data model: transformation method, in which you create a semantic model first and then transform it into a relational model; traditional method, in which you come up with a set of initial tables and then normalize the tables to produce a correct relational model.

REVIEW QUESTIONS

1. List and explain the major strengths of the relational data model.
2. "The relational data model is based on a single modeling concept." Do you agree? Explain.
3. What is an attribute domain? Describe with an example.
4. How is the relationship between two related tables established? Explain with an example.
5. What are data integrity constraints? What purposes do they serve in a relational data model?
6. Describe the referential entity rule with an example. What is the consequence of violation of the rule in a relational data model?
7. What are functional dependencies? Explain with examples.
8. Name any six of the relational algebra operations. Give examples for any two of these operations.
9. "Relational calculus is a nonprocedural language." Explain briefly with an example.
10. What are the two methods for creating a relational data model? Under what conditions would you prefer one method to the other?

EXERCISES

1. Indicate whether true or false:
   A. In a relational data model, columns are identified by their names.
   B. Each table or relation can contain only a specified number of rows or tuples.
   C. If the foreign key value of a row in one table is equal to the primary key value of a row in another table, the two rows are related.
   D. A null value in a foreign key attribute signifies a mandatory relationship.
   E. In a relational data model, the order of the rows is insignificant but the columns must be in order, with the primary key as the first column.
   F. The foreign key attribute in one table and the primary key attribute in the related table must have the same column name.
   G. The SELECT and PROJECT operations work on single relations.
   H. The JOIN operation can operate only on union-compatible relations.

I. The existence condition in relational calculus is similar to the JOIN operation in relational algebra.

J. If a commercial language can perform every operation in relational algebra, then the commercial language is said to be relationally complete.

2. Describe the data manipulation method of relational algebra. Compare this with the relational calculus method and explain the difference. Specify a typical data query in a banking environment. Find the result for this query using both generic languages.

3. As a data modeler for a small appliance store, describe the steps you would take to create a relational data model.

4. A large manufacturer of electronic components wants to implement a relational database. Which method would you adopt to create the relational data model? Give a list of the important tables in your data model.

5. The relational data model consists of two-dimensional tables, not random tables but tables that conform to relational rules. What are these rules and properties of a relational model? Describe the rules.

CHAPTER 9

SEMANTIC DATA MODEL TO RELATIONAL DATA MODEL

CHAPTER OBJECTIVES

- Examine the data model transformation method in detail
- Understand the circumstances under which this method must be used
- Study the mapping of components from the semantic to the relational model
- Specifically, learn the transformation of relationships
- Finally, compare the two models and check out the results of transformation

Toward the end of Chapter 8, we indicated that either of two methods might be used for creating a relational data model. Model transformation method is one of these two methods. This method is a straightforward way of examining the components of your semantic data model and then transforming these components into components of the required relational data model.

Two techniques were presented for creating a semantic model. A semantic model is a generic model. The object-based data modeling technique produces a semantic model by starting out with business objects that are of interest to an organization. The more popular technique, the entity-relationship data modeling technique, also produces a semantic model by adopting a natural way of looking at information requirements. For a given set of information requirements, both techniques produce similar semantic models with comparable components. You know how the components of an object-based data model maps to the components of the entity-relationship data model.

In this chapter, you will study the transformation of the object-based data model into the relational data model. It will not be necessary to repeat the discussion to

---

Database Design and Development: An Essential Guide for IT Professionals by Paulraj Ponniah
ISBN 0-471-21877-4   Copyright © 2003 by John Wiley and Sons, Inc.

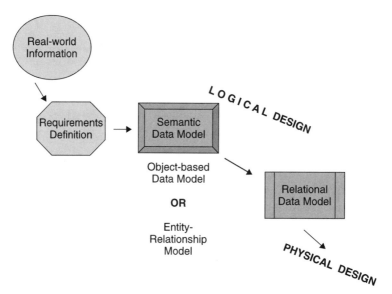

Figure 9-1   Data model transformation in the flow.

cover the transformation of the entity-relationship data model to the relational data model; the transformation principles are the same. You can easily derive them your-selves. So our concentration is on the transformation of the object-based data model. Nevertheless, while providing examples or listing data model components, we will present notations and components from both object-based and entity-relationship data models.

MODEL TRANSFORMATION APPROACH

Obviously, first you need to firm up your requirements definition before beginning any data modeling. We discussed requirements-gathering methods and contents of requirements definitions in great detail. Requirements definition drives the design of the semantic data model. Figure 9-1 shows the transition from the requirements definition phase. Note the flow from real-world information to the eventual phase of physical design. Note the model transformation activity.

Merits

Why go through the process of creating a semantic model first and then transform-ing it into a relational data model? Does it not sound like a longer route to logical design? What are the merits and advantages of the approach? Although we have addressed these questions earlier, in bits and pieces, let us summarize the merits and rationale for the model transformation approach.

Need for Semantic Model   You must ensure that your final database system stores and manages all aspects of the information requirements. Nothing must be missing from the database system. Everything should be correct. The proposed database system must be able to support all the relevant business processes and provide users with proper information. Therefore, any data model as a prelude to the proposed database system must be a true replica of the information requirements.

A semantic data model captures the true and complete meaning of information requirements. The model is made up of a complete set of components such as objects, attributes, and relationships and so is able to represent every aspect of the information requirements. If there are variations in object types or relationship types in the information requirements, a semantic data model can correctly reflect such nuances.

Limitations of Implementation Models   Consider the conventional data models such as the hierarchical, network, and relational data models. These are models that are implemented in commercial database systems. Hierarchical, network, and relational databases are offered by vendors. The conventional or implementation models are the ones that stipulate how data is perceived, stored, and managed in a database system. For example, the relational data model lays down the structure and constraints for how data can be perceived as two-dimensional tables and how relationships may be established through logical links. As such, the implementation data models address data modeling from the point of view of storing and managing data in the database system.

However, the objectives of database development are to ensure that any data model used must truly replicate all aspects of information requirements. The conventional data models do not directly perceive data from the point of view of information requirements; they seem to come from the other side. Therefore, a conventional data model is not usually created directly from information requirements. Such an attempt may not produce a complete and correct data model.

Need for Generic Model   Imagine a process of creating a conventional data model from information requirements. First of all, what is the conventional data model that is being created? If it is a hierarchical data model, then you, as a data modeler, must know the components of the hierarchical data model thoroughly and also know how to relate real-world information to these model components. On the other hand, if your organization opts for a relational data model, again you, as a data modeler, must know the components of the relational data model and also know how to relate real-world information to the relational model components.

However, data modeling must concentrate on correctly representing real-world information irrespective of whether the implementation is going to be hierarchical, network, or relational. As a data modeler, if you learn one set of components and gain expertise in mapping real-world information to this generic set of components, then you will be concentrating on capturing the true meaning of real-world information and not on variations in modeling components.

Simple and Straightforward   The attraction for the model transformation method of creating a relational model comes from the simplicity of the method. Once the semantic data model gets completed with due diligence, the rest of the process is straightforward. There are no complex or convoluted steps. You simply have to follow an orderly sequence of tasks.

Suppose your organization desires to implement a relational database system. Obviously, the information requirements must be defined properly no matter which type of database system is being implemented. Information requirements define the set of real-world information that must be modeled. A data modeler who specializes in semantic data modeling techniques creates a semantic data model based on information requirements. At this stage, the data modeler need not have any knowledge of the relational data model. All the data modeler does is to represent the information requirements in the form of semantic model components. The next straightforward step for the data designer is to review the components of the semantic data model and change each component to a component of the relational data model.

Easy Mapping of Components   An object-based data model is composed of a small, distinct set of components. It does not matter how large and expansive the entire data model is; the whole data model is still constructed with a few distinct components. You may be creating an object-based data model for a large multinational corporation or a small medical group practice. Yet, in both cases, you will be using a small set of components to put together the object-based data model. This is also true of an entity-relationship data model.

What then is the implication here? Your semantic data model, however large it may be, consists of only a few distinct components. This means that you just need to know how to transform a few distinct components. From the other side, a relational data model also consists of a few distinct components. So mapping and transforming the components becomes easy and very manageable.

When to Use This Method

When there is more than one method for creating a relational data model, a natural question arises as to how you choose to adopt one method over the other. When do you use the model transformation method and not the normalization method? In Chapter 8, we had a few hints. The model transformation method applies when the normalization method is not feasible. Let us now list the conditions that would warrant the use of the model transformation method:

Large database system. When a proposed database system is large and the data model is expected to contain numerous component pieces, the model transformation method is preferable.

Complex information requirements. Some sets of information requirements may require modeling complex variations and many types of generalization and specialization. There may be several variations in the relationships, and the attributes themselves may be of different types. Under such conditions, modeling complex information requirements directly in the relational model, bypassing the semantic data model, proves to be very difficult.

Large project. A large project requires many data modelers to work in parallel to complete the data modeling activity within a reasonable time. Each data modeler will work on a portion of information requirements and produce a partial seman-

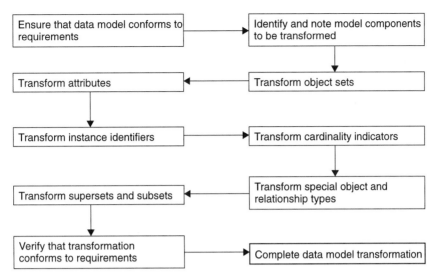

Figure 9-2   Model transformation: major steps.

tic data model. When a project is large and the data model is expected to contain numerous component pieces, the model transformation method is preferable. The partial semantic data models are integrated and then transformed into a relational data model.

Steps and Tasks

Figure 9-2 presents the major steps in the model transformation method. Study these major steps and note how each major step enables you to proceed toward the final transformation of the data model.

Critical Issues

Although the model transformation method for creating a relational data model is straightforward and generally simple, you have to be concerned about a few critical issues. In any method, there are aspects that need special attention. Let us go over the significant issues.

Need for thoroughness. It is important to be well-disciplined and thorough in performing all the steps and tasks with utmost care. Otherwise, your final relational data model is likely to miss significant portions of information requirements.

Long and tedious. In the development of a large database system, the model transformation method could be long and tedious. It could take a long time to complete all portions of the information requirements. The project team needs to stay with it and ensure that each step and each task is performed correctly.

Integration of partial models. Again, in a large project, integration of all the partial semantic data models put together by several data modelers could present a challenge. You have to make sure that all modelers adopt the same set of modeling conventions. It is a good practice to integrate all the partial semantic models first and then transform the whole semantic data model into a relational data model.

Verification with requirements. At each step, you need to check back with the information requirements and verify that the evolving semantic model is a true representation. This verification becomes especially important when the database system tends to be large.

Review for completeness. Do not neglect to make sure that all portions of the information requirements are reflected correctly and completely in the final relational data model.

MAPPING OF COMPONENTS

While creating an object-based data model, the data modeler uses the components or building blocks available in that technique to put together the data model. You studied these components in sufficient detail in Chapter 6. Similarly, to create a relational model, the building blocks are the ones available in the relational modeling technique. You reviewed these components in Chapter 8. Essentially, transforming an object-based data model involves finding matching components in the relational data model and transferring the representation of information requirements from one model to the other. Model transformation primarily consists of mapping of corresponding components from one data model to the other.

Let us recapitulate the components or building blocks for each of the two models—the semantic and the relational data models. The list of components makes it easier to begin the study of component mapping and model transformation.

Semantic data models

Object-based data model
    Object sets
    Attributes
    Identifiers
    Relationships
    Cardinalities
    Supersets/Subsets

Entity-relationship data model
    Entity Types
    Attributes
    Keys
    Relationships
    Cardinality Indicators
    Generalization/Specialization

Relational data model
    Relations or Tables
    Rows
    Columns
    Primary Key
    Foreign Key
    Generalization/Specialization

Mapping and Transformation

Just by going through the list of components, it is easy to form the basic concepts for mapping and transformation. The semantic data model deals with the things that are of interest to the organization, the characteristics of these things, and the relationships among these things. On the other hand, the relational model stipulates how data about the things of interest must be perceived and stored, how the characteristics must be represented, and how the links between related things must be established.

First, let us consider the mapping of things and their characteristics. Then we will move on to the discussion of relationships. As you know, a major strength of the relational model is the way it represents relationships through logical links. We will describe the mapping of relationships in detail and also take up special conditions. Mapping involves taking the components of the semantic data model one by one and finding the corresponding component or components in the relational data model.

Object Sets to Relations

Let us begin with the most obvious component—the object set in the object-based data model or the entity type in the entity-relationship data model. What is an object set? If *employee* is a "thing" the organization is interested in storing information about, then *employee* is an object represented in the semantic data model. The set of all employees in the organization about whom data must be captured in the proposed relational database system is the object set EMPLOYEE.

Figure 9-3 shows the mapping of the object set EMPLOYEE. The mapping shows the transformation of the object set represented in object-based data modeling notation to the relation denoted in relational data model notation.

From the figure, note the following points about the transformation from object-based data model to relational data model:

- The object set is transformed into a relation.
- The name of the object set becomes the name of the relation.
- The object instances viewed as present inside the object set box transform into the rows of the relation.
- The complete set of object instances becomes the total set of rows of the relation or table.
- In the transformation, nothing is expressed about the order of the rows in the transformed relation.

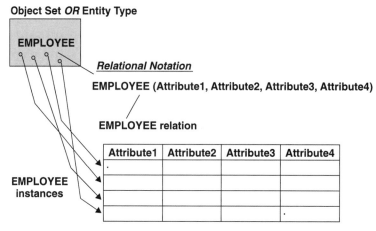

Figure 9-3   Mapping of object set or entity type.

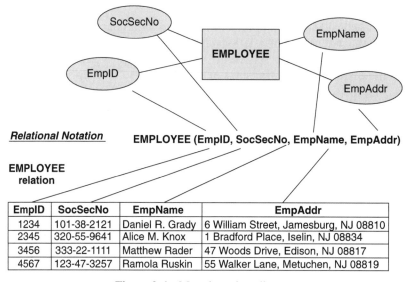

Figure 9-4   Mapping of attributes.

Attributes

Objects have intrinsic or inherent characteristics, so naturally, the next component to be considered is the set of attributes of an object. Figure 9-4 shows the transformation of attributes.

Make note of the following points with regard to the transformation of attributes:

- The attributes of an object are transformed into the columns of the corresponding relation.
- The names of the attributes become the names of the columns.
- The domain of values of each attribute translates into the domain of values for the corresponding column.

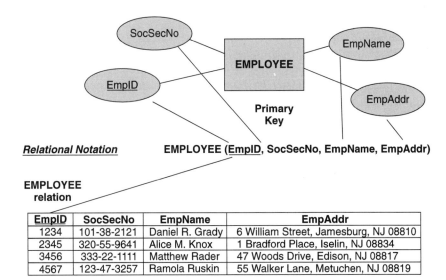

Figure 9-5   Mapping of instance identifiers.

- In the transformation, nothing is expressed about the order of the columns in the transformed relation.
- A single-valued or a derived attribute becomes one column in the resulting relation.
- If a multivalued attribute is present, this is handled by forming a separate relation with this attribute as a column in the separate relation.
- For a composite attribute, as many columns are used as the number of component attributes.

Instance Identifiers

In the semantic data model, each instance is uniquely identified by values in one or more attributes. These attributes together form the instance identifier. Figure 9-5 indicates the transformation of instance identifiers.

Note the following points on this transformation:

- The set of attributes forming the instance identifier becomes the primary key of the relation.
- If there is more than one attribute, all the corresponding columns are indicated as primary key columns.
- Because the primary key columns represent instance identifiers, the combined values in these columns for each row are unique.
- No two rows in the relation can have the same values in the primary key columns.
- Because instance identifiers cannot have null values, no part of the primary key columns can have null values.

TRANSFORMATION OF RELATIONSHIPS

The semantic data modeling techniques have elegant ways for representing relationships between two object sets. Wherever you perceive direct associations between instances of two object sets, the two object sets are connected by lines with a diamond in the middle containing the name of the relationship. How many of instances of one object set are associated with how many instances of the other? An indication about the numbers is given by cardinality indicators, especially the maximum cardinality indicator. The minimum cardinality indicator denotes whether a relationship is optional or mandatory.

You know that the relational data model establishes relationships between two relations through foreign keys. Therefore, transformation of relationships as represented in the semantic model involves mapping of the connections and cardinality indicators into foreign keys. We will discuss how this is done for one-to-one, one-to-many, and many-to-many relationships. We will also go over the transformation of optional and mandatory conditions for relationships. While considering transformation of relationships, we need to review relationships between a superset and its subsets.

One-to-One Relationships

When one instance of an object set is associated with a maximum of only one instance of another object set, we call this relationship a one-to-one relationship. Figure 9-6 shows a one-to-one relationship between the two object sets CLIENT and CONTACT PERSON.

If a client of the organization has designated a contact person, then the contact person is represented by the CONTACT PERSON object set. Only one contact person exists for a client. But some clients may not have contact persons, in which case there is no corresponding instance in the CONTACT PERSON object set. Now we can show the relationship by placing the foreign key column in the CLIENT relation. Figure 9-7 illustrates this transformation.

Observe how the transformation is done. How are the rows of the CLIENT relation linked to corresponding rows of the CONTACT PERSON relation? The values in the foreign key columns and primary key columns provide the linkage. Do you note some foreign key columns in the CLIENT relation with null values? What are these? For these clients, client contact persons do not exist. If the majority of clients do not have assigned contact persons, then many of the rows in the CLIENT relation will contain null values in the foreign key column. This is not a good transformation. A better transformation would be to place the foreign key column in the

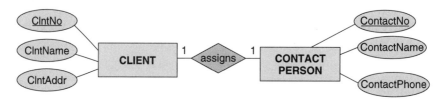

Figure 9-6 One-to-one relationship.

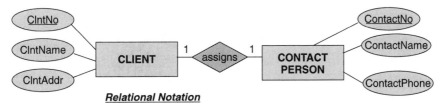

Relational Notation

CLIENT (<u>ClntNo</u>, ClntName, ClntAddr, ContactNo)
Foreign Key: **ContactNo** REFERENCES **CONTACT PERSON**
CONTACT PERSON (<u>ContactNo</u>,ContactName, ContactPhone)

CLIENT relation

<u>ClntNo</u>	ClntName	ClntAddr	ContactNo
11111	ABC Industries	6 William Street, Jamesburg, NJ 08810	234
22222	Progressive Systems	1 Bradford Place, Iselin, NJ 08834	123
33333	Rapid Development	47 Woods Drive, Edison, NJ 08817	
44444	Richard Associates	55 Walker Lane, Metuchen, NJ 08819	
55555	Quality Consulting	35 Rues Ave., E. Brunswick, NJ 08821	345

CONTACT PERSON relation

<u>ContactNo</u>	ContactName	ContactPhone
123	Mary Williams	732-345-8100
234	Winston Poyser	732-555-4000
345	Lisa Moore	732-767-5300

Figure 9-7 Transformation of one-to-one relationship.

CONTACT PERSON relation, not in the CLIENT relation. Figure 9-8 presents this better transformation.

Foreign keys links two relations. If so, you must be able to get answers to queries involving data from two related tables by using the values in foreign key columns. From Figure 9-8, examine how results for the following queries are obtained.

Who is the contact person for client number 22222? Read the CONTACT PERSON table by values in the foreign key column. Find the row having the value 22222 for the foreign key attribute.

Who is the client for contact person number 345? Read the CONTACT PERSON table by values in the primary key column. Find the row having the value 345 for the primary key attribute. Get the foreign key value of this row, namely, 55555. Read the CLIENT table by values in the primary key column. Find the row having the value 5555 for the primary key attribute.

Let us summarize the points on transformation of one-to-one relationships.

- When two relations are in a one-to-one relationship, place a foreign key column in either one of the two relations. Values in the foreign key column for rows in this table match with primary key values in corresponding rows of the related table.
- The foreign key attribute has the same data type, length, and domain values as the corresponding primary key attribute in the other table.

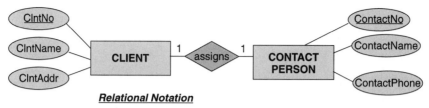

Relational Notation

CLIENT (<u>ClntNo</u>, ClntName, ClntAddr)
CONTACT PERSON (<u>ContactNo</u>, ContactName, ContactPhone, ClntNo)
Foreign Key: **ClntNo** REFERENCES **CLIENT**

CLIENT relation

ClntNo	ClntName	ClntAddr
11111	ABC Industries	6 William Street, Jamesburg, NJ 08810
22222	Progressive Systems	1 Bradford Place, Iselin, NJ 08834
33333	Rapid Development	47 Woods Drive, Edison, NJ 08817
44444	Richard Associates	55 Walker Lane, Metuchen, NJ 08819
55555	Quality Consulting	35 Rues Ave., E. Brunswick, NJ 08821

CONTACT PERSON relation

ContactNo	ContactName	ContactPhone	ClntNo
123	Mary Williams	732-345-8100	22222
234	Winston Poyser	732-555-4000	11111
345	Lisa Moore	732-767-5300	55555

Figure 9-8   Better transformation of one-to-one relationship.

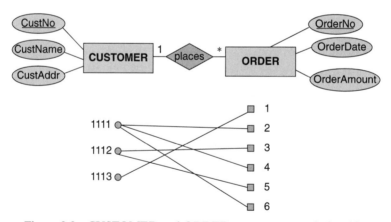

Figure 9-9   CUSTOMER and ORDER: one-to-many relationship.

- It does not really matter whether you place the foreign key column in one table or the other. However, to avoid wasted space, it is better to place the foreign key column in the table that is likely to have fewer rows.

One-to-Many Relationships

Let us begin our discussion of the one-to-many relationship by reviewing Figure 9-9. This figure shows the one-to-many relationship between the two objects CUSTOMER and ORDER.

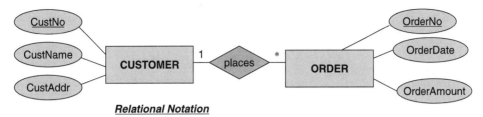

Relational Notation

CUSTOMER (<u>CustNo</u>, **CustName, CustAddr, OrderNo1, ...**)
Foreign Key: **OrderNo1, OrderNo2, OrderNo3** REFERENCES **ORDER**

ORDER (<u>OrderNo, OrderDate, OrderAmount</u>)

CUSTOMER relation

CustNo	CustName	CustAddr	OrderNo1	OrderNo2	OrderNo3
1111	ABC Industries	Jamesburg, NJ	2	4	6
1112	Progressive Systems	Iselin, NJ	3	5	
1113	Rapid Development	Edison, NJ	1		

ORDER relation

OrderNo	OrderDate	OrderAmount
1	10/1/2002	2,122.50
2	10/3/2002	3,025.00
3	10/6/02	4,111.25
4	10/17/2002	3,005.50
5	10/19/2002	7,000.00
6	10/25/02	6,540.00

Figure 9-10   Transformation of one-to-many relationship.

The figure also indicates how individual instances of these two object sets are associated with one another. You see a clear one-to-many relationship—one customer can have one or more orders. So how should you transform this relationship? As you know, the associations are established through the use of a foreign key column. But in which table do you place the foreign key column? For transforming the one-to-one relationship, we noted that you might place the foreign key column in either relation. In the same way, let us try to place the foreign key in the CUSTOMER relation. Figure 9-10 shows this transformation of a one-to-many relationship.

What do you observe about the foreign keys in the transformed relations? In the CUSTOMER relation, the row for customer 1113 needs just one foreign key column to connect to order 1 in the ORDER relation. But the row for customer 1112 seems to need two foreign key columns, and the row for customer 1111 seems to require three foreign key columns. What if there is a customer with 50 orders? How many foreign key columns are sufficient in the CUSTOMER relation? How will you search for a particular order from the several foreign keys in the CUSTOMER relation? Obviously, this transformation is not correct.

We can try another solution by placing the foreign key column in the ORDER relation instead of including the foreign key column in the other related table. Figure 9-11 illustrates the correct solution.

Examine this figure. First, you notice that there is no need for multiple foreign keys to represent one relationship. Multiple rows in the ORDER relation have the same value in the foreign key column. This indicates the several orders related to

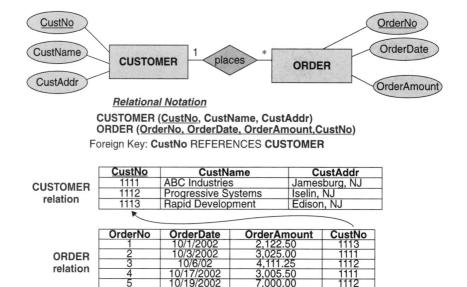

Relational Notation

CUSTOMER (<u>CustNo</u>, CustName, CustAddr)
ORDER (<u>OrderNo, OrderDate, OrderAmount,CustNo</u>)
Foreign Key: **CustNo** REFERENCES **CUSTOMER**

CUSTOMER relation

CustNo	CustName	CustAddr
1111	ABC Industries	Jamesburg, NJ
1112	Progressive Systems	Iselin, NJ
1113	Rapid Development	Edison, NJ

ORDER relation

OrderNo	OrderDate	OrderAmount	CustNo
1	10/1/2002	2,122.50	1113
2	10/3/2002	3,025.00	1111
3	10/6/02	4,111.25	1112
4	10/17/2002	3,005.50	1111
5	10/19/2002	7,000.00	1112
6	10/25/02	6,540.00	1111

Figure 9-11   Correct transformation of one-to-many relationship.

the same customer. The values in the foreign key column link the associated rows. From the figure, let us examine how queries involving data from two related tables work.

Which are the orders related to CUSTOMER number 1112? Read the ORDER table by values in the foreign key column. Find the rows having the value 1112 for the foreign key attribute.

What is the name of the customer for order number 4? Read the ORDER table by values in the primary key column. Find the row having the value 4 for the primary key attribute. Get the foreign key value of this row, namely, 1111. Read the CUSTOMER table by values in its primary key column. Find the row having the value 1111 for the primary key attribute.

Let us summarize the points on transformation of one-to-many relationships.

- When two relations are in a one-to-many relationship, place a foreign key column in the relation that is on the "many" side of the relationship. Values in the foreign key column for rows in this table match with primary key values in corresponding rows of the related table.
- The foreign key attribute has the same data type, length, and domain values as the corresponding primary key attribute in the other table.

Many-to-Many Relationships

As you know, in a many-to-many relationship, one instance of an object set is related to one or more instances of a second object set and also one instance of the second

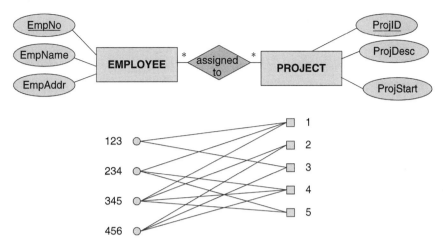

Figure 9-12 Example of many-to-many relationship.

object set is related to one or more instances of the first object set. Figure 9-12 presents an example of a many-to-many relationship.

One employee is assigned to one or more projects simultaneously or over time. Again, one project is related to one or more employees. Let us try to transform the object-based data model to a relational data model and establish the many-to-many relationship. For establishing the relationship, you have to place foreign keys. While transforming a one-to-many relationship, we placed the foreign key attribute in the relation on the "many" side of the relationship; that is, we placed the foreign key attribute in the child relation.

In a many-to-many relationship, which of the two relations is the child relation? It is not clear. Both relations participate in the relationship in the same way. Look at the associations shown in Figure 9-12. Transform the object sets into relations and place the foreign key in the PROJECT relation. Figure 9-13 shows this transformation with foreign key attributes placed in the PROJECT relation.

Note the foreign keys in the transformed relations. In the PROJECT relation, the rows for projects 1 and 4 need three foreign key columns whereas the rows for projects 2, 3, and 4 need two foreign key columns each. You get the picture. If some projects are related to many employees, as many as 50 or so, how many foreign key columns must the PROJECT relation have? Therefore, it appears that this method of transformation is not correct.

Let us determine how queries involving data from two related tables work.

Which are the projects related to employee 456? Read the PROJECT table by values in the foreign key columns. But which foreign key columns? All of the foreign columns? Right away, you note that finding the result for this query is going to be extremely difficult.

What are the names of employees assigned to project 1? Read the PROJECT table by values in the primary key column. Find the row having the value 1 for the primary key attribute. Get the foreign key values of this row, namely, 123, 234, and 345. Read the EMPLOYEE table by values in the

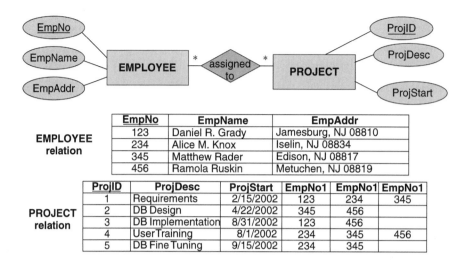

EmpNo	EmpName	EmpAddr
123	Daniel R. Grady	Jamesburg, NJ 08810
234	Alice M. Knox	Iselin, NJ 08834
345	Matthew Rader	Edison, NJ 08817
456	Ramola Ruskin	Metuchen, NJ 08819

EMPLOYEE relation

ProjID	ProjDesc	ProjStart	EmpNo1	EmpNo1	EmpNo1
1	Requirements	2/15/2002	123	234	345
2	DB Design	4/22/2002	345	456	
3	DB Implementation	8/31/2002	123	456	
4	UserTraining	8/1/2002	234	345	456
5	DB Fine Tuning	9/15/2002	234	345	

PROJECT relation

Related project-employee instance pairs: (1, 123), (1, 234), (1, 345), (2, 345), (2, 456), (3, 123),(3, 456), (4, 234), (4, 345), (4, 456), (5, 234), (5, 345)

Figure 9-13   Transformation of many-to-many relationship: first method.

primary key column. Find the rows having the values 123, 234, and 345 for its primary key attribute. Getting the result for this query seems to be workable.

Because the transformation from the first method does not work, let us try another solution by placing the foreign key columns in the EMPLOYEE relation instead of including the foreign key column in the other related table. Figure 9-14 illustrates this method of transformation.

Where are the foreign keys in the transformed relations? In the EMPLOYEE relation, the row for employee 123 needs two foreign key columns whereas the rows for employees 234 and 456 need three foreign key columns each and the row for employee 345 needs four foreign key columns. By reasoning similar to that for the first method, if an employee is related to 25 projects over time, then you need to have that many foreign key columns in the EMPLOYEE relation.

Let us examine how queries involving data from two related tables work.

Which are the projects related to employee 456? Read the EMPLOYEE table by values in the primary key column. Find the row having the value 456 for the primary key attribute. Get the foreign key values of this row, namely, 2, 3, and 4. Read the PROJECT table by values in the primary key column. Find the rows having the values 2, 3, and 4 for its primary key attribute. Getting the result for this query seems to be workable.

What are the names of employees assigned to project 1? Read the EMPLOYEE table by values in the foreign key columns. But which foreign columns? All of them? Right away, you note that finding the result for this query is going to be very difficult.

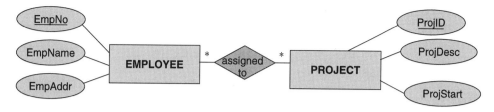

EMPLOYEE relation

EmpNo	EmpName	EmpAddr	ProjID1	ProjID2	ProjID3	ProjID4
123	Daniel R. Grady	Jamesburg, NJ 08810	1	3		
234	Alice M. Knox	Iselin, NJ 08834	1	4	5	
345	Matthew Rader	Edison, NJ 08817	4	2	1	5
456	Ramola Ruskin	Metuchen, NJ 08819	2	3	4	

PROJECT relation

ProjID	ProjDesc	ProjStart
1	Requirements	2/15/2002
2	DB Design	4/22/2002
3	DB Implementation	8/31/2002
4	User Training	8/1/2002
5	DB Fine Tuning	9/15/2002

Related employee-project instance pairs: (123, 1), (123, 3), (234, 1), (234, 4), (234, 5), (345, 4), (345, 2), (345, 1), (345, 5), (456, 2), (456, 3), (456, 4)

Figure 9-14   Transformation of many-to-many relationship: second method.

It is clear that the second method of transformation also does not work. We seem to be in a quandary. Where should you place the foreign key column—in which of the two related tables? Placing foreign key columns in either table does not seem to work. So this second method of transformation is also not correct.

Note the pairs of related primary key values shown the above figures. Each pair represents a set of a project and a corresponding employee. Look at the pairs (1,123) and (1,234). Each pair indicates a set of related rows from the two tables. For example, the pair (1,123) indicates that the row for project 1 is related to employee 123, the pair (1,234) indicates that the row for project 1 is related to employee 234, and so on. In fact, you note that the complete set of pairs represents all the associations between rows in the two tables. In other words, the set of pairs establishes the many-to-many relationship. However, the values in the pairs are not present as foreign keys in either of the two tables. In our above two attempts at transformation, the real problem is that we do not know where to place the foreign keys—in the PROJECT relation or in the EMPLOYEE relation. What if you make a separate table out of these pairs of related values and use the values in the pairs as foreign key values? Then this new table can establish the many-to-many relationship. This elegant method is the standard method for representing many-to-many relationships in the relational data model.

Figure 9-15 illustrates the correct method of transforming a many-to-many relationship. The table containing the pairs of related values of primary keys is known as the intersection table.

Note the primary key for the intersection table. The primary key consists of two parts—one part is the primary key of the PROJECT table and the other part is the primary key of the EMPLOYEE table. The two parts act as the foreign keys

Relational Notation

EMPLOYEE (EmpNo, EmpName, EmpAddr)

PROJECT (ProjID, ProjDesc, ProjStart)

ASSIGNMENT (ProjID, EmpNo)
Foreign Keys: **ProjId** REFERENCES **PROJECT**
   EmpNo REFERENCES **EMPLOYEE**

EMPLOYEE relation

EmpNo	EmpName	EmpAddr
123	Daniel R. Grady	Jamesburg, NJ 08810
234	Alice M. Knox	Iselin, NJ 08834
345	Matthew Rader	Edison, NJ 08817
456	Ramola Ruskin	Metuchen, NJ 08819

PROJECT relation

ProjID	ProjDesc	ProjStart
1	Requirements	2/15/2002
2	DB Design	4/22/2002
3	DB Implementation	8/31/2002
4	User Training	8/1/2002
5	DB Fine Tuning	9/15/2002

ASSIGNMENT relation

ProjID	EmpNo
1	123
1	234
1	345
2	345
2	456
3	123
3	456
4	234
4	345
4	456
5	234
5	345

Figure 9-15   Transformation of many-to-many relationship: correct method.

to establish both sides of the many-to-many relationship. Also, observe that each of the two relations PROJECT and EMPLOYEE is in a one-to-many relationship with the intersection relation ASSIGNMENT.

Now, let us review how queries involving data from the two related tables work.

Which are the projects related to employee 456? Read the intersection table by values in part of the primary key columns, namely, EmpNo attribute showing values for employee key numbers. Find the rows having the value 456 for this part of the primary key. Read the PROJECT table by values in its primary key column. Find the rows having the values 2, 3, and 4 for the primary key attribute. Getting the result for this query seems to be workable.

What are the names of employees assigned to project 1? Read the intersection table by values in part of the primary key columns, namely, ProjID attribute showing values for project key numbers. Find the rows having the value 1 for this part of the primary key. Read the EMPLOYEE table by values in its primary key column. Find the rows having the values 123, 234, and 345 for the primary key attribute. Getting the result for this query is straightforward and easy.

To end our discussion of transformation of many-to-many relationships, let us summarize the main points.

- Create a separate relation, called the intersection table. Use both primary keys of the participating relations as the concatenated primary key for the intersection table. The primary intersection table contains two attributes—one attribute establishing the relationship to one of the two relations and the other attribute linking the other relation.
- Each part of the primary key of the intersection table serves as a foreign key.
- Each foreign key attribute has the same data type, length, and domain values as the corresponding primary key attribute in the related table.
- The relationship of the first relation to the intersection relation is one-to-many; the relationship of the second relation to the intersection relation is also one-to-many. In effect, transformation of the many-to-many relationship is reduced to creating two one-to-many relationships.

Mandatory and Optional Conditions

The semantic model is able to represent whether a relationship is optional or mandatory. As you know, the minimum cardinality indicator denotes mandatory and optional conditions. Let us explore the implications of mandatory and optional conditions for relationships in a relational model. In our discussions so far, we have examined the relationships in terms of maximum cardinalities. If the maximum cardinalities are 1 and 1, then the relationship is implemented by placing the foreign key attribute in either of the participating relations. If the maximum cardinalities are 1 and *, then the relationship is established by placing the foreign key attribute in the relation on the "many" side of the relationship. Finally, if the maximum cardinalities are * and *, then the relationship is broken down into two one-to-many relationships by introducing an intersection relation. Let us consider a few examples with minimum cardinalities and determine the effect on the transformation.

Minimum Cardinality in One-to-Many Relationship   Figure 9-16 shows and example of a one-to-many relationship between the two object sets PROJECT and EMPLOYEE.

Note the cardinality indicators (1,1) shown next to the PROJECT object set. Intentionally, the figure does not show the minimum cardinality indicator next to EMPLOYEE. We will discuss the reason for this very shortly. What is the meaning of the cardinality indicators next to the PROJECT object set? The indicators represent the following conditions:

An employee can be assigned to a maximum of only one project. Every employee must be assigned to a project. That is, an employee instance must be associated with a minimum of 1 project instance. In other words, every employee instance must participate in the relationship. The relationship as far as the employee instances are concerned is mandatory.

Now look at the foreign key column in the EMPLOYEE table. If every employee is assigned to a project, then every EMPLOYEE row must have a value in the foreign key column. You know that this value must be the value of the primary key of the related row in the PROJECT table. What does this tell you about the foreign

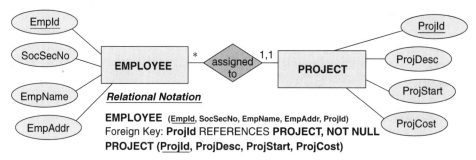

EMPLOYEE relation

EmpId	SocSecNo	EmpName	EmpAddr	ProjId
1234	101-38-2121	Daniel R. Grady	6 William Street, Jamesburg, NJ 08810	DESN
2345	320-55-9641	Alice M. Knox	1 Bradford Place, Iselin, NJ 08834	IMPL
3456	333-22-1111	Matthew Rader	47 Woods Drive, Edison, NJ 08817	DESN
4567	123-47-3257	Ramola Ruskin	55 Walker Lane, Metuchen, NJ 08819	DESN

PROJECT relation

ProjId	ProjDesc	ProjStart	ProjCost
DESN	DB Design	6/1/2000	200,000
IMPL	DB Implementation	12/15/2000	100,000
USER	User Training	10/22/2000	75,000
TUNE	DB Fine Tuning	3/1/2001	50,000

Figure 9-16   One-to-many relationship: mandatory and optional.

key column? In a mandatory relationship, the foreign key column cannot contain null values. Observe the Foreign Key statement under relational notation in the figure. It stipulates the constraints with the words "NOT NULL" expressing that null values are not allowed in the foreign key attribute.

Next, consider the optional condition. Suppose the cardinality indicators (0,1) are shown next to the PROJECT object set. Then the indicators will represent the following conditions:

An employee can be assigned to a maximum of only one project. Not every employee need be assigned to a project. That is, some employee instances may not be associated with any project instance at all. At a minimum, an employee instance may be associated with no project instance or with zero project instances. In other words, not every employee instance needs to participate in the relationship. The relationship as far as the employee instances are concerned is optional.

It follows, therefore, that in an optional relationship of this sort, null values may be allowed in the foreign key attribute. What do the rows with null foreign key attribute in the EMPLOYEE relation represent? These rows represent those employees who are not assigned to a project.

Minimum Cardinality in Many-to-Many Relationship   Figure 9-17 shows an example of many-to-many relationship between the two object sets PROJECT and EMPLOYEE.

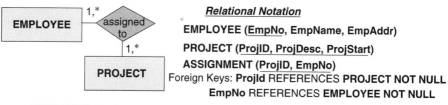

Relational Notation

EMPLOYEE (EmpNo, EmpName, EmpAddr)

PROJECT (ProjID, ProjDesc, ProjStart)

ASSIGNMENT (ProjID, EmpNo)

Foreign Keys: **ProjId** REFERENCES **PROJECT NOT NULL**

EmpNo REFERENCES **EMPLOYEE NOT NULL**

EMPLOYEE relation

EmpNo	EmpName	EmpAddr
123	Daniel R. Grady	Jamesburg, NJ 08810
234	Alice M. Knox	Iselin, NJ 08834
345	Matthew Rader	Edison, NJ 08817
456	Ramola Ruskin	Metuchen, NJ 08819

PROJECT relation

ProjID	ProjDesc	ProjStart
1	Requirements	2/15/2002
2	DB Design	4/22/2002
3	DB Implementation	8/31/2002
4	User Training	8/1/2002
5	DB Fine Tuning	9/15/2002

ASSIGNMENT relation

ProjID	EmpNo
1	123
1	234
1	345
2	345
2	456
3	123
3	456
4	234
4	345
4	456
5	234
5	345

Figure 9-17   Many-to-many relationship: minimum cardinality.

Note the cardinality indicators (1,*) shown next to the PROJECT object set and (1,*) shown next to the EMPLOYEE object set. What do these cardinality indicators represent? The indicators represent the following conditions:

An employee may be assigned to many projects.

A project may have many employees.

Every employee must be assigned to at least one project. That is, an employee instance must be associated with a minimum of 1 project instance. In other words, every employee instance must participate in the relationship. The relationship as far as the employee instances are concerned is mandatory.

Every project must have at least one employee. That is, a project instance must be associated with a minimum of 1 employee instance. In other words, every project instance must participate in the relationship. The relationship as far as the project instances are concerned is mandatory.

Carefully observe the transformed relationship described in the figure. Look at the intersection relation and the concatenated primary key of this relation. As you know, each part of the primary key forms the foreign key. Note the two one-to-many relationships and the corresponding tables showing attribute values. As discussed in the previous subsection on one-to-many relationship the foreign keys in the intersection table, that is, either of the two parts of the primary key table, cannot be nulls. You may stipulate the constraints with the words "NOT NULL" in the Foreign Key statement for the intersection table. However, the two foreign keys are part of the primary key, and because the primary key attribute cannot have nulls, the explicit stipulation of "NOT NULL" may be omitted.

Next, let us take up optional conditions on both sides. Suppose the cardinality indicators (0,*) are shown next to the PROJECT and EMPLOYEE object sets. Then the indicators will represent the following conditions:

An employee may be assigned to many projects.

A project may have many employees.

Not every employee need be assigned to a project. That is, some employee instances may not be associated with any project instance at all. At a minimum, an employee instance may be associated with no project instance or with zero project instances. In other words, not every employee instance needs to participate in the relationship. The relationship as far as the employee instances are concerned is optional.

Not every project need have an employees. That is, some project instances may not be associated with any employee instance at all. At a minimum, a project instance may be associated with no employee instance or with zero employee instances. In other words, not every project instance needs to participate in the relationship. The relationship as far as the project instances are concerned is optional.

It follows, therefore, that in an optional relationship of this sort, null values may be allowed in the foreign key attributes. However, in the way the transformation is represented in Figure 9-17, allowing null values in foreign key attributes would present a problem. You have noted that the foreign key attributes form the primary key of the intersection relation, and no part of a primary key in a relation can have null values according to the integrity rule for the relational model. Therefore, in such cases, you may adopt an alternate transformation approach by assigning a separate primary key as shown in Figure 9-18.

What do the rows with null foreign key attributes in the ASSIGNMENT relation represent? These rows represent those employees who are not assigned to a project or those projects that have no employees. In practice, you may want to include such rows in the relations to indicate employees already eligible for assignment but not officially assigned and to denote projects that usually have employees assigned but not yet ready for assignment.

Minimum Cardinality on the "Many" Side   In the above figures, we considered minimum cardinalities shown next to object sets on the "one" side of one-to-many relationships. For example, Figure 9-16 shows minimum cardinality indicator next to the PROJECT object set that is on the "one" side of the relationship. Now, let us consider the minimum cardinality indicator on the "many" side. Assume cardinality indicators of (1,*) on the "many" side next to the EMPLOYEE object set. This would indicate the following conditions:

A project may have many employees. Every project must have at least one employee. That is, a project instance must be associated with a minimum of 1 employee instance. In other words, every project instance must participate in the relationship. The relationship as far as the project instances are concerned is mandatory.

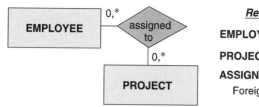

Relational Notation

EMPLOYEE (<u>EmpNo</u>, EmpName, EmpAddr)

PROJECT (<u>ProjID</u>, ProjDesc, ProjStart)

ASSIGNMENT (<u>AsmntNo</u>, ProjID, EmpNo)
    Foreign Keys: **ProjId** REFERENCES **PROJECT**
                EmpNo REFERENCES **EMPLOYEE**

EMPLOYEE relation

EmpNo	EmpName	EmpAddr
123	Daniel R. Grady	Jamesburg, NJ 08810
234	Alice M. Knox	Iselin, NJ 08834
345	Matthew Rader	Edison, NJ 08817
456	Ramola Ruskin	Metuchen, NJ 08819

ASSIGNMENT relation

AsmntNo	ProjID	EmpNo
10	1	123
11	1	234
12	1	345
13	2	345
14	3	123
15	4	234
16	4	345
17		456
18	5	

PROJECT relation

ProjID	ProjDesc	ProjStart
1	Requirements	2/15/2002
2	DB Design	4/22/2002
3	DB Implementation	8/31/2002
4	User Training	8/1/2002
5	DB Fine Tuning	9/15/2002

Figure 9-18 Many-to-many relationship: alternative approach.

Let us interpret the mandatory nature of this relationship. The mandatory condition says that, after transformation, for every primary key value in the PROJECT relation, there must be at least one row in the EMPLOYEE relation with the same value for the foreign key attribute. Such a condition is not needed in a relational model to satisfy any integrity constraints. Therefore, it is not generally shown in the relational model. Any enforcement of this mandatory condition must be implemented by other means in the database system.

Before we end this discussion, let us also consider the corresponding optional condition. Assume cardinality indicators of (0,*) next to the EMPLOYEE object set. What are the implications in the transformation to a relational data model?

What is the meaning of the cardinality indicators (0,*) next to the EMPLOYEE object set? The indicators represent the following conditions:

A project may have many employees. Not every project need have employees. That is, some project instances may not be associated with any employee instance at all. At a minimum, a project instance may be associated with no employee instance or with zero employee instances. In other words, not every project instance needs to participate in the relationship. The relationship as far as the project instances are concerned is optional.

What is the interpretation of the optional nature of this relationship? The optional condition says that, after transformation, there may be rows in the

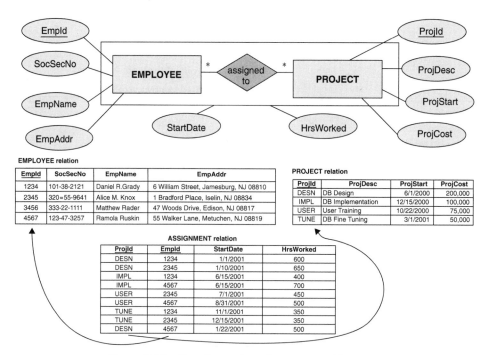

Figure 9-19   Transformation of aggregate object set.

PROJECT relation with no related rows in the EMPLOYEE relation. Again, such a condition is not needed in a relational model to satisfy any integrity constraints. Therefore, it is not generally shown in the relational model. In the relational database system, you may create PROJECT rows without creating corresponding EMPLOYEE rows without violating any integrity constraints.

Aggregate Objects as Relationships

Recall that in relationships, the participating object sets together form an aggregate object set by virtue of the relationship itself. Let us discuss how such aggregate object sets are transformed into the components of a relational data model. Figure 9-19 illustrates such a transformation of an aggregate object set ASSIGNMENT.

Note the intersection relation and the attributes shown in this relation. These are the attributes of the aggregate object set. You will note that the aggregate object set becomes the intersection relation.

Identifying Relationship

In the discussion of semantic data modeling, we studied identifying relationships. A weak entity type is one that depends on another entity type for its existence. A weak entity type is, in fact, identified by the other entity type. The relationship is therefore called an identifying relationship.

Figure 9-20 illustrates the transformation of an identifying relationship. Note especially the primary key attributes of the weak entity type.

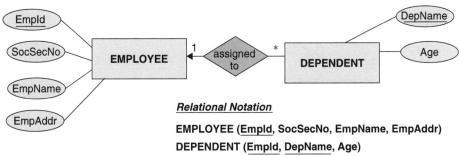

Relational Notation

EMPLOYEE (Empld, SocSecNo, EmpName, EmpAddr)

DEPENDENT (Empld, DepName, Age)

Foreign Key: **Empld** REFERENCES **EMPLOYEE**

EMPLOYEE relation

Empld	SocSecNo	EmpName	EmpAddr
1234	101-38-2121	Daniel R.Grady	6 William Street, Jamesburg, NJ 08810
2345	320=55-9641	Alice M. Knox	1 Bradford Place, Iselin, NJ 08834
3456	333-22-1111	Matthew Rader	47 Woods Drive, Edison, NJ 08817
4567	123-47-3257	Ramola Ruskin	55 Walker Lane, Metuchen, NJ 08819

Empld	DepName	Age	
1234	Mary Grady	14	DEPENDENT
1234	John Grady	11	relation
2345	David Knox	15	
2345	Jeremy Knox	13	(Weak Entity
2345	Amanda Knox	12	Type)
3456	Luke Nader	16	
4567	Anne Ruskin	10	
4567	Drew Ruskin	5	

Figure 9-20 Transformation of identifying relationship.

Supersets and Subsets

While creating semantic data models, you discover objects in the real world that are subsets of other objects. Some objects are specializations of other objects. On the other hand, you realize that individual object sets may be generalized in supertype object sets. Each subset of a superset forms a special relationship with its superset.

Figure 9-21 shows the transformation of a superset and its subsets. Note how the primary key attribute and other attributes migrate from the superset relation to the subset relations.

OUTCOME OF MODEL TRANSFORMATION

You know the phases that lead up to a relational data model. Initially, you define the information requirements. Then, you create a semantic data model based on the real-world information requirements. You may apply either of the two data modeling techniques—object-based or entity-relationship modeling—to create the semantic data model. The next step is the important transformation step. You have already studied the components and concepts of a relational data model. Now the model transformation accomplishes the creation of the relational data model.

In this section, let us review the model transformation process. We will summarize what has been covered so far in this chapter.

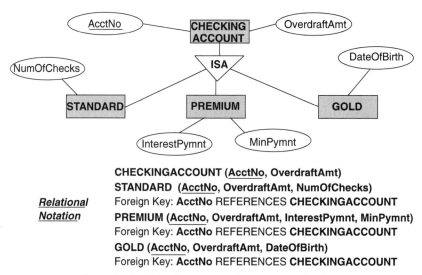

CHECKINGACCOUNT (**AcctNo**, OverdraftAmt)

STANDARD (**AcctNo**, OverdraftAmt, NumOfChecks)

Relational Foreign Key: **AcctNo** REFERENCES **CHECKINGACCOUNT**

Notation PREMIUM (**AcctNo**, OverdraftAmt, InterestPymnt, MinPymnt)

Foreign Key: **AcctNo** REFERENCES **CHECKINGACCOUNT**

GOLD (**AcctNo**, OverdraftAmt, DateOfBirth)

Foreign Key: **AcctNo** REFERENCES **CHECKINGACCOUNT**

Figure 9-21   Transformation of superset and subsets.

Comparison of Models

By now, you have a fairly good grasp of the principles of transformation of a semantic data model into a relational data model. We took each component of the semantic data model and reviewed how the component is transformed into a component in the relational model. Let us list the components of the semantic data model and note how each component gets transformed. Although most of our discussion so far in this chapter has used the semantic model with the object-based modeling technique, we list the components of the entity-relationship data model here. This will further confirm that whether your semantic data model is arrived at through object-based data modeling or entity-relationship data modeling, the transformation process is the same.

The components of the semantic data model and how they are transformed into relational data model follow:

Entity Type

Strong   Transform into relation.

Weak   Transform into relation. Include the primary key of the identifying relation in the primary key of the relation representing the weak entity type.

Attribute

Transform attribute name into column name.

Translate attribute domains into domains for corresponding columns.

Simple, single-valued   Transform into a column of the corresponding relation.

Composite   Transform into columns of the corresponding relation with as many columns as the number of component attributes.

Multivalued   Transform into a column of a separate relation.

Derived   Transform into a column of the corresponding relation.

Primary Key

Single attribute   Transform into a single-column primary key.

Composite   Transform into a multicolumn primary key.

Relationship

One-to-One   Establish the relationship through a foreign key attribute in either of the two participating relations.

One-to-Many   Establish the relationship through a foreign key attribute in the participating relation on the "many" side of the relationship.

Many-to-Many   Transform by forming two one-to-many relationships with a new intersection relation between the participating relations. Establish the relationship through foreign key attributes in the intersection relation.

Optional and mandatory conditions   Set constraint for the foreign key column. If null values are not allowed in the foreign key column, this represents a mandatory relationship. Allowing null values denotes an optional relationship. Mandatory and optional conditions apply only to the participation of the relation on the "many" side of a one-to-many relationship, that is, to the participation of rows in the relation that contains the foreign key column.

Summary of Transformation

Recall the example of the semantic data model for the teaching aspects of a university given in Chapter 7. Figure 7-22 shows an entity-relationship diagram (ERD). Let us summarize our discussion on transformation of a semantic data model by transforming the model represented by that ERD into a relational data model. Figure 9-22 shows the relational data model, the outcome of the transformation.

Go through each component of the semantic data model and check out the corresponding component in the relational data model. Note the columns for each relation. Observe the establishment of relationships through foreign key columns.

CHAPTER SUMMARY

- Transformation of the semantic data model into the relational data model is an approach with many merits for creating the relational model.
- The model transformation method applies to large database systems with complex information requirements.
- However, the model transformation method could be long and tedious and must be carried out with thoroughness and care.
- Semantic data models created by either the object-based modeling technique or the entity-relationship modeling technique may be transformed into

Relational Notation

STUDENT (<u>SocSecNo</u>, StudntName, Major)

TEXTBOOK (<u>ISBN</u>, Title, Price)

AUTHOR (<u>ISBN, Author</u>)
  Foreign Key: **ISBN** REFERENCES **TEXTBOOK**

COURSE (<u>CourseNo</u>, CourseDesc, Credits, ISBN)
  Foreign Key: **ISBN** REFERENCES **TEXTBOOK**

CLASS (<u>CourseNo</u>, <u>ClassNo</u>, RoomNo, FacultyID)
  Foreign Key: **CourseNo** REFERENCES **COURSE**
          FacultyID REFERENCES **FACULTY**

FACULTY (<u>FacultyID</u>, FacultyName, Phone, Department, Speczn)

EXAMTYPE (<u>TypeID</u>, ExamName, MinScore)

GRADE (<u>CourseNo, ClassNo, TypeID, SocSecNo</u>, Score)
  Foreign Key: **CourseNo, ClassNo** REFERENCES **CLASS**
          TypeID REFERENCES **EXAMTYPE**
          SocSecNo REFERENCES **STUDENT**

Figure 9-22   University ERD: transformation into relational data model.

relational data models in the same way by adopting similar transformation principles.

- Each component of the semantic data model transforms into one or more components of the relational data model.
- Object sets transform into relations of the relational data model; attributes transform into columns of relations.
- Relationships transform into logical links through foreign key attributes.
- In a one-to-one relationship, place the foreign key attribute in either of the participating relations; in a one-to-many relationship, place the foreign key attribute in the relation on the "many" side of the relationship; in a many-to-many relationship, break the relationship down into two one-to-many relationships with an intersection relation between them and place foreign key attributes in the intersection relation.

REVIEW QUESTIONS

1. List the major merits of the model transformation method of creating a relational data model.

2. Differentiate between a semantic data model and a conventional data model. Define the terms.

3. Explain some of the critical issues of the model transformation method.

4. List any three components of an object-based data model and describe how these are transformed into a relational data model.

5. List any two types of attributes. How are these transformed into the relational data model?

6. How is a composite instance identifier transformed into the relational data model? Provide two examples.

7. Describe the transformation of a one-to-many relationship with an example.

8. What is an intersection relation? When is it necessary? Give an example.

9. What is an identifying relationship? How is this transformed into the relational data model? Explain with an example.

10. What are supersets and subsets? Show the transformation of superset and subsets into the relational data model with a very simple example.

EXERCISES

1. Match the columns:

1. intersection relation	A. transformed into conventional data model
2. model transformation method	B. same primary key in transformed relations
3. weak entity type	C. relation
4. semantic data model	D. relation columns
5. aggregate object set	E. foreign key in either participating relation
6. entity type	F. two foreign keys
7. superset and subset	G. mandatory relationship
8. one-to-one relationship	H. good for large complex databases
9. foreign key not null	I. relation with concatenated primary key
10. composite attribute	J. additional relation

2. As the database designer of the relational database system for an automobile manufacturer, you have chosen the model transformation method to create the relational data model. Write a note to your project manager, describing the process and highlighting aspects of the method that would need special attention.

3. Describe how mandatory and optional conditions in relationships are transformed into the relational data model. Give specific examples.

4. Draw an ERD for a small farm market. Transform it into a relational data model.

5. Three data modelers worked on the semantic data model for a local bank. As a senior analyst on the project, it is your responsibility to integrate the partial data models created by the data modelers and transform the integrated data model into a relational model. Create a simple example with partial data models, and explain the process with this example.

CHAPTER 10

DATA NORMALIZATION METHOD

CHAPTER OBJECTIVES

- Understand how the normalization method creates the relational data model
- Examine this informal approach and its potential pitfalls
- Note the significance of the normalization approach
- Study the systematic steps that lead to a normalized relational data model
- Learn the fundamental normal forms in depth
- Review the higher normal forms

As you studied the model transformation method in Chapter 9, you might have had thoughts on the necessity of that method. You might have wondered why you need to create a semantic data model first and then bother to transform that model into a relational data model. If you already know that your target database system is going to be a relational database system, why not create a relational data model itself from the information requirements? These are valid thoughts. Even though you learned the merits of the model transformation method in Chapter 9, is it not a longer route for logical design?

In this chapter, we will pursue these thoughts. We will attempt to put together a relational data model from the information requirements. We will see what happens and whether the resultant model readily becomes a relational data model. If not, we will explore what should be done to make the initial outcome of this method become a good relational model.

Database Design and Development: An Essential Guide for IT Professionals by Paulraj Ponniah
ISBN 0-471-21877-4   Copyright © 2003 by John Wiley and Sons, Inc.

INFORMAL DESIGN

In a sense, this attempt to create a relational model seems to be an informal design technique. Creating a semantic data model first is a rigorous and systematic approach. On the other hand, if you want to create relational tables straight away, you seem to bypass standard and proven techniques. Therefore, first try to understand exactly what we mean by an informal design method.

Let us describe this method first. Then let us review steps that can formalize this methodology. Although the goal is to come up with relational tables in the initial attempt, you will note that the initial attempt does not always produce a good relational data model. Therefore, we need specific steps to make the initial data model a true relational model.

As you know very well, a relational model consists of relations or two-dimensional tables with columns and rows. Because our desired outcome is a true relational data model, let us quickly review its fundamental properties:

- Relationships are established through foreign keys.
- Each row in a relation is unique.
- Each attribute value in each row is atomic or single-valued.
- The order of the columns in a relation is immaterial.
- The sequence of the rows in a relation is immaterial.
- Relations must conform to entity integrity and referential integrity rules.
- Each relation must conform to the functional dependency rule.

Forming Relations from Requirements

The attempt in this method is simply to come up with relations or tables from the information requirements. Figure 10-1 explains this seemingly informal approach in a simple manner.

Note the objectives of the method. When you create a relational data model with this method, you must come up with tables that conform to the relational rules and possess the correct properties of a relational data model.

What are the steps in the creation of a proper relational model? Create an initial data model by putting together a set of initial tables. Examine this initial set of tables and then apply procedures to make this initial set into a proper set of relational tables. As you will learn in the later sections, this application of procedures to rectify problems found in the initial set of tables is known as normalization.

Of course, an obvious question is why you should go through normalization procedures. Are you not able to produce a proper set of relational tables from the information requirements in the initial attempt itself? Let us explore the reasons.

Pitfalls of Informal Design

Let us consider a very simple set of information requirements. Using these information requirements, we will attempt to create an initial relational data model and then examine the model. Creating an initial relational data model by this approach simply means coming up with an initial set of relational tables. Study the following

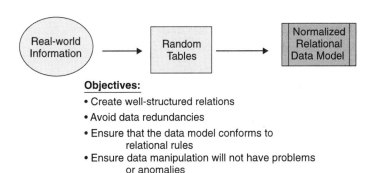

Objectives:
- Create well-structured relations
- Avoid data redundancies
- Ensure that the data model conforms to
    relational rules
- Ensure data manipulation will not have problems
    or anomalies

Steps:
- Create random tables or relations
- Normalize the tables

Figure 10-1   Informal design of relational data model.

statement of information requirements for which you need to create a relational data model:

Assignment of employees to projects

Employees work in departments. Information about the employees such as name, salary, position, and bonus amount must be represented in the data model. The model should include names of the departments and their managers. Project numbers and project descriptions are available. The model must represent the start date, end date, and hours worked on a project for each employee. New employees are not assigned to a project before they finish training.

Examine the information requirements. Clearly, your data model must represent information about the employees and their project assignments. Also, some information about the departments must be included. Compared to other real-world information requirements, the information about employee-project assignments being modeled here is very simple. With this set of information requirements, you need to come up with two-dimensional tables. Let us say that you are able to put the data in the form of tables and also express the relationships within the tables. If you are able to do this, then you are proceeding toward creating the relational data model.

Looking at the simplicity of the information requirements, it appears that all of the data can be put in just one table. Let us create that single table and inspect the data content. Figure 10-2 represents this single table showing sample data values.

Inspect the PROJECT-ASSIGNMENT table carefully. To uniquely identify each row, you have to assign EmpId and ProjNo together as the primary key. At first glance, you note that the table contains all the necessary data to completely represent the data content of the information requirements. The table contains columns and rows. Review each column. It represents an attribute, and the column name represents the name of the attribute. Now look at the rows. Each row represents one employee, a single instance of the entity represented by the table. So far, the table looks like it qualifies to be part of a relational data model.

PROJECT-ASSIGNMENT

EmpId	Name	Salary	Position	Bonus	DptNo	DeptName	Manager	ProjNo	ProjDesc	ChrgCD	Start	End	Hrs
100	Simpson	35000	Analyst	5000	3	Design	Ross	23	DB design	D100	Apr-02	Jul-02	200
140	Beeton	28000	Technician	3000	2	Operations	Martin	14	Network cabling	N140	Sep-02	Oct-02	120
160	Davis	30000	Technician	3000	4	Tech Suprt	Lucero	14	Network cabling	S160	Sep-02	Nov-02	150
								36	Network testing	S160	Nov-02	Dec-02	100
190	Berger	45000	DBA	6000	1	DB Suprt	Rawlins	45	Physical design	D190	Aug-02	Nov-02	300
								48	Space allocation	S190	Nov-02	Dec-02	80
100	Simpson	35000	Analyst	5000	3	Design	Ross	25	Reports	C100	Oct-02	Nov-02	100
110	Covino	34000	Analyst	5000	5	Analysis	Williams	31	Forms	D110	Mar-02	May-02	120
								25	Reports	D110	May-02	Jul-02	150
120	Brown	35000	Analyst	5000	5	Analysis	Williams	11	Order entry	D120	Jul-02	Sep-02	300
180	Smith	30000	Programmer	4000	6	Programming	Goldner	31	Forms	C180	Sep-02	Nov-02	250
								25	Reports	C180	Nov-02	Dec-02	200
200	Rogers	32000	Programmer	4000	6	Programming	Goldner	11	Order entry	D200	Sep-02	Oct-02	200
								12	Inventory Control	P200	Oct-02	Dec-02	200
								13	Invoicing	P200	Nov-02	Dec-02	100
100	Simpson	35000	Analyst	5000	3	Design	Ross	31	Forms	D100	Aug-02	Oct-02	150
130	Clemens	38000	Analyst	5000	3	Design	Ross	23	DB design	D130	Apr-02	Jun-02	200

Figure 10-2   Table created from information requirements.

Before proceeding further, let us have a brief explanation of the column named ChrgCD. When an employee is assigned to a project, a charge code is given for that assignment. The charge code depends on the type of work done by the employee in that assignment irrespective of his or her position or title. For example, when Simpson, an analyst, does design work in a project, a charge code of D100 is given for that assignment; when he does coding work in another project, a charge code of C100 is given for this assignment. Charge codes indicate the type of work done by an employee in the various projects.

Next, observe the projects for Davis, Berger, Covino, Smith, and Rogers. Each of these employees has been assigned to multiple projects. The resulting relational database must contain information about these multiple assignments. However, looking at the rows for these employees, these rows contain multiple values for some attributes. In other words, not all columns contain atomic or single-valued attribute values. This is a violation of the attribute atomicity requirement in a relational data model. Therefore, the random PROJECT-ASSIGNMENT table we created quickly cannot be part of true relational data model.

Let us now examine the table further and see how it will hold up when we try to manipulate the data contents. As indicated in Figure 10-1, a proper relational data model must avoid data redundancies and also ensure that data manipulation will not cause problems. When we attempt to use the data model for data manipulation, you will find that we run into three types of problems or anomalies as noted below:

Update anomaly. Occurs while updating values of attributes in the database.

Deletion anomaly. Occurs while deleting rows from a relation.

Addition anomaly. Occurs while adding (inserting) new rows in a relation.

We will discuss these anomalies in the next subsections. Try to understand the nature of these problems and how our PROJECT-ASSIGNMENT table has such problems and therefore cannot be correct. Unless we remove these anomalies, our table cannot be part of a true relational model.

Update Anomaly

If a relational two-dimensional table does not conform to relational rules, you find that problems arise when you try to do updates to data in a database based on such a table. Our data model at this point consists of the randomly created PROJECT-ASSIGNMENT table. Let us try to do an update to the data in the PROJECT-ASSIGNMENT table and see what happens.

After the database is populated, users find that the name "Simpson" is recorded incorrectly and that it should be changed to the correct name "Samson." How is the correction accomplished? The correction will have to be made wherever the name "Simpson" exists in the database. Now look at the example of data content shown in Figure 10-2.

Even in this extremely limited set of rows in the table, you have to make the correction in three rows. Imagine a database of 500 or 5000 employees. Even this is not a large database. It is not unusual to store data about many thousands of employees in a typical database. Now go back to the correction. In a large database covering a large number of rows for employees, the number of rows for PROJECT-ASSIGNMENT is expected to be high. Therefore, it is very likely that when you make the correction to the name, you will miss some rows that need to be changed. So, what is the effect of the update anomaly in this case?

Update anomaly

Results in data inconsistency because of possible partial update instead of the proper complete update.

Deletion Anomaly

Again, if the relational two-dimensional table does not conform to relational rules, you find that problems arise when you try to delete rows from a database based on such a table. Let us try to delete some data from the PROJECT-ASSIGNMENT table and see what happens.

Here is the situation. Employee Beeton leaves your organization. Therefore, it is no longer necessary keep any information about Beeton in your database. You are authorized to delete all data about Beeton from the database. Now inspect the sample database contents shown in Figure 10-2.

How is the deletion of data about Beeton carried out? Luckily, you have to delete just one row, namely, the second row in the PROJECT-ASSIGNMENT table, to get rid of all data about Beeton in the database. Now, consider another aspect of this operation. What happens when you delete this row? Data such as Beeton's EmpId, Name, Salary, Position, and his project assignment are deleted. This is fine, because this is what you intended to do.

Now examine the row as shown in the figure. When you delete this row, you not only remove data about Beeton, you also delete data about Department 2. And looking at the entire contents of the table, you notice that this is only row that has information about Department 2. By deleting this row, you also delete all data about Department 2 from the database. However, this is not your intention. Data about Department 2 have to be preserved in the database for possible future uses. But if you delete the second row, data about Department 2 are also (unintentionally) lost. Let us express the effect of deletion anomaly.

Deletion anomaly

Results in unintended loss of data because of possible deletion of data other than what must be deleted.

Addition Anomaly

We have considered the effects of updates and deletions in a two-dimensional table that is put together in a random fashion from information requirements. You have noted that these operations cause anomalies or problems. Now let us try to perform one more common data operation on this table. Try to add new data to the database.

This is the situation. A new employee, Potter, has joined your organization. As usual, the human resources department has already assigned a unique EmpId to Potter. So you need to add data about Potter to the database. However, Potter is still in training and therefore is not assigned to a project yet. You have data about Potter such as his salary, bonus, and the department in which is hired. You can add all of these data to the database.

Begin to create a row for Potter in the database. You are ready to create a row in our PROJECT-ASSIGNMENT table for Potter. You can enter the name, department, and so on. But what about the unique primary key for this row? As you know, the primary key for this table consists of EmpId and ProjNo together. However, you are unable to assign a value for ProjNo for this row because he is not assigned to a project yet. So you can have a null value for ProjNo until Potter is assigned to a project. But can you really do this? If you place a null value in the ProjNo column, you will be violating the entity integrity rule that states no part of the primary key may be null. You are faced with a problem—an anomaly concerning added new data. Data about Potter cannot be added to the database until he is assigned to a project. Even though he is already an employee, data about Potter will be missing in the database. This is the effect of addition anomaly.

Addition anomaly

Results in inability to add data to the database because of the absence of some data presently unavailable.

NORMALIZATION APPROACH

Let us review our discussion so far. We inspected the information requirements about employees, departments, projects, and project assignments. Our intention was to create a relational data model directly from the study of the information requirements. This meant creating a data model consisting of two-dimensional tables or relations that normally make up a relational data model. Because of the simplicity of the information requirements, we were able to represent all the data in a single random table. So far, this is the relational data model for us. If it has to be a good relational model, it must conform to relational rules.

You have observed that the random table PROJECT-ASSIGNMENT violates some relational rules at the outset. More importantly, when you attempt to update data, delete data, or add data, our initial data model has serious problems. You have noted the problems of update, deletion, and addition anomalies. So what is the next step? Do you simply abandon the initial data model and look for other methods? Your goal is to create a good relational model even while you attempt to do this directly from information requirements.

It turns out that by adopting a systematic methodology you can, indeed, regularize the initial data model created by the first attempt. This methodology is based on Dr. Codd's approach to normalizing the initial tables created in a random manner directly from information requirements. Before getting into the actual methodology of normalization, let us consider its merits and note how the methodology is used.

Purpose and Merits

Normalization methodology resolves the three types of anomalies encountered when data manipulation operations are performed on a database based on an improper relational data model. Therefore, after applying the principles of normalization to the initial data model, the three types of anomalies will be eliminated. The normalization process standardizes or "normalizes" the table structures. You come up with revised table structures. It is a systematic, step-by-step methodology.

Normalization

- Creates well-structured relations
- Removes data redundancies
- Ensures that the initial data model is properly transformed into a relational data model conforming to relational rules
- Guarantees that data manipulation will not result in anomalies or other problems

How to Apply This Method

As mentioned above, this normalization process is a step-by-step approach. It is not completed in one large task. The process breaks down the problem and applies remedies, one at a time. The initial data model is refined and standardized in a clear and systematic manner, one step at a time.

At each step, the methodology consists of examining the data model, removing one type of problem, and changing it to a better normal form. You take the initial data model created directly from information requirements in a random fashion. This initial model, at best, consists of two-dimensional tables representing the entire data content, nothing more or less. As we have seen, such an initial data model is subject to data manipulation problems.

You apply the principles of the first step. In this step, you are examining the initial data model for only one type of nonconformance and seeking to remove one type of irregularity. Once this one type of irregularity is resolved, your data model becomes better and is rendered into a first normal form of table structures. Then you look for another type of irregularity in the second step and remove this type of irregularity from the data model resulting from the step. After this next step, your data model becomes still better and becomes a data model in the second normal form. The process continues through a reasonable number of steps until the resulting data model becomes truly relational.

Steps and Tasks

The first few steps of the normalization methodology transform the initial data model into a workable relational data model that is free from the common types of irregularities. These first steps produce the normal forms of relations that are fundamental to creating a good relational data model. After these initial steps, in some cases, further irregularities still exist. When you remove the additional irregularities, the resulting relations become higher normal form relations.

We will discuss the fundamental and higher normal forms in the next section. However, let us just list the steps here:

Fundamental normal forms

Step 1

Examine initial data model and remove first type of irregularity.

Data model becomes a set of first normal form relations.

Step 2

Inspect data model resulting from previous step and remove second type of irregularity.

Data model becomes a set of second normal form relations.

Step 3

Inspect data model resulting from previous step and remove third type of irregularity.

Data model becomes a set of third normal form relations.

Step 4

Inspect resulting data model and remove another type of irregularity.

Data model becomes a set of Boyce-Codd normal form relations.

Higher normal forms

Step 1

Examine data model in the final fundamental normal form and remove fourth type of irregularity.

Data model becomes a set of fourth normal form relations.

Step 2

Inspect data model resulting from previous step and remove fifth type of irregularity.

Data model becomes a set of fifth normal form relations.

Step 3

Inspect data model resulting from previous step and remove domain-key irregularity.

Data model becomes a set of domain-key normal form relations.

In practice, only a few initial data models need to go through all the above steps. Generally, a set of third normal form relations will form a good relational data model. You may want to go one step further to make the model a set of Boyce-Codd normal form relations. Only very infrequently would you need to go to higher normal forms.

FUNDAMENTAL NORMAL FORMS

As explained above, normalization is a process of rectifying potential problems in two-dimensional tables created at random. This process is a step-by-step method, each step addressing and remedying one specific type of potential problem. As we proceed with the normalization process, you will clearly understand why this step-by-step approach works so well. By taking a step-by-step approach, you will not overlook any type of anomaly. And, when the process is completed, you will have resolved every type of potential problem.

In the last section, we have noted the four steps that make up the portion of the normalization process transforming the initial data model into the fundamental normal forms. After the third step, the initial data model becomes a third normal form relational data model. As already mentioned, for most practical purposes, a third normal form data model is an adequate relational data model. You need not go further. Occasionally, you may have to proceed to the fourth step and refine the data model further and make it a set of Boyce-Codd normal form relations.

First Normal Form

Refer back to Figure 10-2 showing the PROJECT-ASSIGNMENT relation created as the initial data model. You have already observed that the rows for Davis, Berger, Covino, Smith, and Rogers contain multiple values for attributes in six different columns. You know that this violates the requirement in a relational model that states each row must have atomic values for each of the attributes.

This step in normalization process addresses the problem of repeating groups of attribute values for single rows. If a relation has such repeating groups, we say that the relation is not in the first normal form. The objective of this step is to transform the data model into a model in the first normal form. Here is what must be done to make this transformation.

Transformation to First Normal Form (1NF)

Remove repeating groups of attributes and create rows without repeating groups.

Figure 10-3 shows the result of the transformation to first normal form.

Carefully inspect the PROJECT-ASSIGNMENT relation shown in the figure. Each row has a set of unique values in the columns. The composite primary key consisting of EmpId and ProjNo uniquely identifies each row. No single row has multiple values for any of its attributes. This step has rectified the problem of multiple values for the same attribute in a single row.

PROJECT-ASSIGNMENT

EmpId	Name	Salary	Position	Bonus	DptNo	DeptName	Manager	ProjNo	ProjDesc	ChrgCD	Start	End	Hrs
100	Simpson	35000	Analyst	5000	3	Design	Ross	23	DB design	D100	Apr-02	Jul-02	200
140	Beeton	28000	Technician	3000	2	Operations	Martin	14	Network cabling	N140	Sep-02	Oct-02	120
160	Davis	30000	Technician	3000	4	Tech Suprt	Lucero	14	Network cabling	S160	Sep-02	Nov-02	150
160	Davis	30000	Technician	3000	4	Tech Suprt	Lucero	36	Network testing	S160	Nov-02	Dec-02	100
190	Berger	45000	DBA	6000	1	DB Suprt	Rawlins	45	Physical design	D190	Aug-02	Nov-02	300
190	Berger	45000	DBA	6000	1	DB Suprt	Rawlins	48	Space allocation	S190	Nov-02	Dec-02	80
100	Simpson	35000	Analyst	5000	3	Design	Ross	25	Reports	C100	Oct-02	Nov-02	100
110	Covino	34000	Analyst	5000	5	Analysis	Williams	31	Forms	D110	Mar-02	May-02	120
110	Covino	34000	Analyst	5000	5	Analysis	Williams	25	Reports	D110	May-02	Jul-02	150
120	Brown	35000	Analyst	5000	5	Analysis	Williams	11	Order entry	D120	Jul-02	Sep-02	300
180	Smith	30000	Programmer	4000	6	Programming	Goldner	31	Forms	C180	Sep-02	Nov-02	250
180	Smith	30000	Programmer	4000	6	Programming	Goldner	25	Reports	C180	Nov-02	Dec-02	200
200	Rogers	32000	Programmer	4000	6	Programming	Goldner	11	Order entry	D200	Sep-02	Oct-02	200
200	Rogers	32000	Programmer	4000	6	Programming	Goldner	12	Inventory Control	P200	Oct-02	Dec-02	200
200	Rogers	32000	Programmer	4000	6	Programming	Goldner	13	Invoicing	P200	Nov-02	Dec-02	100
100	Simpson	35000	Analyst	5000	3	Design	Ross	31	Forms	D100	Aug-02	Oct-02	150
130	Clemens	38000	Analyst	5000	3	Design	Ross	23	DB design	D130	Apr-02	Jun-02	200

Figure 10-3 Data model in first normal form.

Let us examine whether the transformation step has rectified the other types of update, deletion, and addition anomalies encountered before the model was transformed into first normal form. Compare the PROJECT-ASSIGNMENT relation shown in Figure 10-3 to the earlier version in Figure 10-2. Apply the tests to the transformed version of the relation contained in Figure 10-3.

Update: Correction of name "Simpson" to "Samson"
> The correction has to be made in multiple rows. Update anomaly still persists.

Deletion: Deletion of data about Beeton
> This deletion will unintentionally delete data about Department 2. Deletion anomaly still persists.

Addition: Addition of data about new employee Potter
> Cannot add new employee Potter to the database until he is assigned to a project. Addition anomaly still persists.

So, you note that, although this step has resolved the problem of multivalued attributes, data manipulation problems still remain. Nevertheless, this step has removed a major deficiency from the initial data model. We have to proceed to the next steps and examine the effect of data manipulation operations.

Second Normal Form

Recall the discussion on functional dependencies in Chapter 8 covering the properties and rules of the relational data model. If the value of one attribute determines the value of a second attribute in a relation, we say that the second attribute is functionally dependent on the first attribute. The discussion on functional dependencies in Chapter 8 concluded with a functional dependency rule. Let us repeat the functional dependency rule:

Each data item in a tuple of a relation is uniquely and functionally determined by the primary key, by the whole primary key, and only by the primary key.

Examine the dependencies of data items in the PROJECT-ASSIGNMENT relation in Figure 10-3. You know that this relation is in the first normal form, having gone through the process of removal of repeating groups of attributes. Let us inspect the dependency of each attribute on the whole primary key consisting of EmpId and ProjNo. Only the following attributes depend on the whole primary key: ChrgCD, Start, End, and Hrs. The remaining nonkey attributes do not appear to be functionally dependent on the whole primary key. They seem to functionally depend on one or another part of the primary key.

This step in the normalization process deals specifically with this type of problem. Once this type of problem is resolved, the data model becomes transformed to a data model in the second normal form. In other words, the condition for a second normal form data model is as follows:

If a data model is in the second normal form, no nonkey attributes may be dependent on part of the primary key.

Therefore, if there are partial key dependencies in a data model, this step resolves this type of dependencies. Here is what must be done to make this transformation.

Transformation to Second Normal Form (2NF)

Remove partial key dependencies.

If you look at the other attributes in the PROJECT-ASSIGNMENT relation in Figure 10-3, you will note that the following attributes depend on just EmpId, a part of the primary key: Name, Salary, Position, Bonus, DptNo, DeptName, and Manager. The attribute ProjDesc depends on ProjNo, another part of the primary key. These are partial key dependencies. This step resolves partial key dependencies. Now look at Figure 10-4 that shows the resolution of partial key dependencies. The relations shown in this figure are in the second normal form.

Note how the resolution is done. The original relation has been decomposed into three separate relations. In each relation, to make sure that each row is unique, duplicate rows are eliminated. For example, multiple duplicate rows for employee Simpson have been replaced by a single row in the EMPLOYEE relation.

Decomposition is an underlying technique for normalization. If you go carefully through each of the three relations, you will be satisfied that none of these has any partial key dependencies. So this step has rectified the problem of partial key dependencies. But what about the types of anomalies encountered during data manipulation?

Let us examine whether the transformation step has rectified the types of update, deletion, and addition anomalies encountered before the model was transformed

EMPLOYEE-PROJECT

EmpId	ProjNo	ChrgCD	Start	End	Hrs
100	23	D100	Apr-02	Jul-02	200
140	14	N140	Sep-02	Oct-02	120
160	14	S160	Sep-02	Nov-02	150
160	36	S160	Nov-02	Dec-02	100
190	45	D190	Aug-02	Nov-02	300
190	48	S190	Nov-02	Dec-02	80
100	25	C100	Oct-02	Nov-02	100
110	31	D110	Mar-02	May-02	120
110	25	D110	May-02	Jul-02	150
120	11	D120	Jul-02	Sep-02	300
180	31	C180	Sep-02	Nov-02	250
180	25	C180	Nov-02	Dec-02	200
200	11	D200	Sep-02	Oct-02	200
200	12	P200	Nov-02	Dec-02	200
200	13	P200	Nov-02	Dec-02	100
100	31	D100	Aug-02	Oct-02	150
130	23	D130	Apr-02	Jun-02	200

PROJECT

ProjNo	ProjDesc
23	DB design
14	Network cabling
36	Network testing
45	Physical design
48	Space allocation
25	Reports
31	Forms
11	Order entry
12	Inventory Control
13	Invoicing

EMPLOYEE

EmpId	Name	Salary	Position	Bonus	DptNo	DeptName	Manager
100	Simpson	35000	Analyst	5000	3	Design	Ross
140	Beeton	28000	Technician	3000	2	Operations	Martin
160	Davis	30000	Technician	3000	4	Tech Suprt	Lucero
190	Berger	45000	DBA	6000	1	DB Suprt	Rawlins
110	Covino	34000	Analyst	5000	5	Analysis	Williams
120	Brown	35000	Analyst	5000	5	Analysis	Williams
180	Smith	30000	Programmer	4000	6	Programming	Goldner
200	Rogers	32000	Programmer	4000	6	Programming	Goldner
130	Clemens	38000	Analyst	5000	3	Design	Ross

Figure 10-4   Data model in second normal form.

into the first normal form. Compare the relations shown in Figure 10-4 to the previous version in Figure 10-3. Apply the tests to the transformed version of the relations contained in Figure 10-4.

Update: Correction of name "Simpson" to "Samson"

The correction has to be made only in one row in EMPLOYEE relation. The update anomaly has disappeared.

Deletion: Deletion of data about Beeton

This deletion will unintentionally delete data about Department 2. Deletion anomaly still persists.

Addition: Addition of data about new employee Potter

You can now add new employee Potter to the database in EMPLOYEE relation. Addition anomaly has disappeared.

So you note that, although this step has resolved the problem of partial key dependencies, still some data manipulation problems remain. Nevertheless, this step has removed a major deficiency from the data model. We have to proceed to the next steps and examine the effect of data manipulation operations.

Third Normal Form

After transformation to the second normal form, you note that a particular type of functional dependencies is removed from the preliminary data model and that the data model is closer to becoming a correct and true relational data model. In the previous step, we removed partial key dependencies. Let us examine the resulting data model to see whether any more irregular functional dependencies still exist. Remember the goal is to make each relation in the data model into a form where each data item in a tuple is functionally dependent only on the full primary key and nothing but the full primary key.

Refer to the three relations shown in Figure 10-4. Let us inspect these relations one by one. The attribute ProjDesc functionally depends on the primary key ProjNo. So this relation PROJECT is correct. Next look at the relation EMPLOYEE-PROJECT. In this relation, each of the attributes ChrgCD, Start, End, and Hrs depends on full primary key EmpId, ProjNo.

Now examine the relation EMPLOYEE carefully. What about the attributes Position and Bonus? Bonus depends on the position. Bonus for an Analyst is different from that for a Technician. Therefore, in that relation, the attribute Bonus is functionally dependent on another attribute Position, not on the primary key. Look further. How about the attributes DeptName and Manager? Do they depend on the primary key EmpId? Not really. These two attributes functionally depend on another attribute in the relation, namely, DptNo.

So what is the conclusion from your observation? In the relation EMPLOYEE, only the two attributes Name and Salary depend on the primary key EmpId. The other attributes do not depend on the primary key. Bonus depends on Position; DeptName and Manager depend on DptNo.

This step in normalization process deals with this type of problem. Once this type of problem is resolved, the data model is transformed to a data model in the third normal form. In other words, the condition for a third normal form data model is as follows:

> If a data model is in the third normal form, no nonkey attributes may be dependent on another nonkey attribute.

In the relation EMPLOYEE, dependency of the attribute DeptName on the primary key EmpId is not direct. The dependency is passed over to the primary key through another nonkey attribute DptNo. This passing over of the dependency means that the dependency on the primary key is a transitive dependency—passed over through another nonkey attribute, DptNo. Therefore, this type of problematic dependency is also called a transitive dependency in a relation. If there are transitive dependencies in a data model, this step resolves this type of dependencies. Here is what must be done to make this transformation.

Transformation to Third Normal Form (3NF)

Remove transitive dependencies.

Figure 10-5 shows the resolution of transitive dependencies. The relations shown in the figure are all in the third normal form.

Note how the resolution is done. The EMPLOYEE relation is further decomposed into two additional relations, POSITION and DEPARTMENT. In each relation, to ensure that each row is unique, duplicate rows are eliminated. For example, multiple duplicate rows for the position Analyst in the EMPLOYEE relation have been replaced by a single row in the POSITION relation.

EMPLOYEE

Empld	Name	Salary	Posnld	DptNo
100	Simpson	35000	ANLY	3
140	Beeton	28000	TECH	2
160	Davis	30000	TECH	4
190	Berger	45000	DBAM	1
110	Covino	34000	ANLY	5
120	Brown	35000	ANLY	5
180	Smith	30000	PGMR	6
200	Rogers	32000	PGMR	6
130	Clemens	38000	ANLY	3

EMPLOYEE-PROJECT

Empld	ProjNo	ChrgCD	Start	End	Hrs
100	23	D100	Apr-02	Jul-02	200
140	14	N140	Sep-02	Oct-02	120
160	14	S160	Sep-02	Nov-02	150
160	36	S160	Nov-02	Dec-02	100
190	45	D190	Aug-02	Nov-02	300
190	48	S190	Nov-02	Dec-02	80
100	25	C100	Oct-02	Nov-02	100
110	31	D110	Mar-02	May-02	120
110	25	D110	May-02	Jul-02	150
120	11	D120	Jul-02	Sep-02	300
180	31	C180	Sep-02	Nov-02	250
180	25	C180	Nov-02	Dec-02	200
200	11	D200	Sep-02	Oct-02	200
200	12	P200	Nov-02	Dec-02	200
200	13	P200	Nov-02	Dec-02	100
100	31	D100	Aug-02	Oct-02	150
130	23	D130	Apr-02	Jun-02	200

PROJECT

ProjNo	ProjDesc
23	DB design
14	Network cabling
36	Network testing
45	Physical design
48	Space allocation
25	Reports
31	Forms
11	Order entry
12	Inventory Control
13	Invoicing

DEPARTMENT

DptNo	DeptName	Manager
3	Design	Ross
2	Operations	Martin
4	Tech Suprt	Lucero
1	DB Suprt	Rawlins
5	Analysis	Williams
6	Programming	Goldner

POSITION

Posnld	Position	Bonus
ANLY	Analyst	5000
TECH	Technician	3000
DBAM	DBA	6000
PGMR	Programmer	4000

Figure 10-5 Data model in third normal form.

Again, you will note that decomposition is a basic technique for normalization. If you carefully go through each of the relations, you will be satisfied that none of these has any transitive dependencies—one nonkey attribute depending on some other nonkey attribute. So this step has rectified the problem of transitive dependencies. But what about the types of anomalies encountered during data manipulation?

Let us examine whether the transformation step has rectified the other types of update, deletion, and addition anomalies encountered before the model was transformed into first normal form. Compare the relations shown in Figure 10-5 to the previous version in Figure 10-4. Apply the tests to the transformed version of the relation contained in Figure 10-5.

Update: Correction of name "Simpson" to "Samson"

The correction has to be made only in one row in EMPLOYEE relation. Update anomaly has disappeared.

Deletion: Deletion of data about Beeton

Removal of Beeton and his assignments from EMPLOYEE and EMPLOYEE-PROJECT relations does not affect the data about Department 2 in DEPARTMENT relation. Deletion anomaly has disappeared from the data model.

Addition: Addition of data about new employee Potter

You can now add new employee Potter to the database in EMPLOYEE relation. Addition anomaly has disappeared.

So you note that this step has resolved the problem of transitive dependencies and the data manipulation problems, at least the ones we have considered. Before we declare that the resultant data model is free from all types of data dependency problems, let us examine the model one more time.

Boyce-Codd Normal Form

Consider the EMPLOYEE-PROJECT relation in Figure 10-5. Think about the ChrgCD attribute. A particular charge code indicates the specific employee's role in an assignment. Also, each project may be associated with several charge codes depending on the employees and their roles in the project. The charge code is not for the project assignment. The attribute ChrgCD does not depend on the full primary key or on a partial primary key. The dependency is the other way around.

In the EMPLOYEE-PROJECT relation, EmpId depends on ChrgCD and not the other way around. Note how this is different from partial key dependency. Here a partial key attribute is dependent on a nonkey attribute. This kind of dependency also violates the functional dependency rule for the relational data model.

This step in normalization process deals with this type of problem. Once this type of problem is resolved, the data model is transformed to a data model in the Boyce-Codd normal form. In other words, the condition for a Boyce-Codd normal form data model is as follows:

If a data model is in the Boyce-Codd normal form, no partial key attribute may be dependent on another nonkey attribute.

Here is what must be done to make this transformation.

Transformation to Third Normal Form (3NF)

Remove anomalies from dependencies of key components.

Figures 10-6 and 10-7 show the resolution of the remaining dependencies. The relations shown in both figures are all in the Boyce-Codd normal form.

Note how the resolution is done. The EMPLOYEE-PROJECT relation is decomposed into two additional relations, CHRG-EMP and PROJ-CHRG. Note that duplicate rows are eliminated when the additional relations are formed.

Again, note that decomposition is a basic technique for normalization. The final set of relations in Figures 10-6 and 10-7 is free from all types of problems resulting from invalid functional dependencies.

HIGHER NORMAL FORMS

Once you transform an initial data model into a data model conforming to the principles of the fundamental normal forms, most of the discrepancies are removed. For all practical purposes, your resultant data model is a good relational data model. It will satisfy all the primary constraints of a relational data model. The major problems with functional dependencies are resolved.

EMPLOYEE

EmpId	Name	Salary	PosnId	DptNo
100	Simpson	35000	ANLY	3
140	Beeton	28000	TECH	2
160	Davis	30000	TECH	4
190	Berger	45000	DBAM	1
110	Covino	34000	ANLY	5
120	Brown	35000	ANLY	5
180	Smith	30000	PGMR	6
200	Rogers	32000	PGMR	6
130	Clemens	38000	ANLY	3

PROJECT

ProjNo	ProjDesc
23	DB design
14	Network cabling
36	Network testing
45	Physical design
48	Space allocation
25	Reports
31	Forms
11	Order entry
12	Inventory Control
13	Invoicing

DEPARTMENT

DptNo	DeptName	Manager
3	Design	Ross
2	Operations	Martin
4	Tech Suprt	Lucero
1	DB Suprt	Rawlins
5	Analysis	Williams
6	Programming	Goldner

POSITION

PosnId	Position	Bonus
ANLY	Analyst	5000
TECH	Technician	3000
DBAM	DBA	6000
PGMR	Programmer	4000

Figure 10-6   Data model in Boyce-Codd normal form – part 1.

EMPLOYEE-PROJECT

EmpId	ProjNo	Start	End	Hrs
100	23	Apr-02	Jul-02	200
140	14	Sep-02	Oct-02	120
160	14	Sep-02	Nov-02	150
160	36	Nov-02	Dec-02	100
190	45	Aug-02	Nov-02	300
190	48	Nov-02	Dec-02	80
100	25	Oct-02	Nov-02	100
110	31	Mar-02	May-02	120
110	25	May-02	Jul-02	150
120	11	Jul-02	Sep-02	300
180	31	Sep-02	Nov-02	250
180	25	Nov-02	Dec-02	200
200	11	Sep-02	Oct-02	200
200	12	Nov-02	Dec-02	200
200	13	Nov-02	Dec-02	100
100	31	Aug-02	Oct-02	150
130	23	Apr-02	Jun-02	200

CHRG-EMP

ChrgCD	EmpId
C100	100
C180	180
D100	100
D110	110
D120	120
D130	130
D190	190
D200	200
N140	140
P200	200
S160	160
S190	190

PROJ-CHRG

ProjNo	ChrgCD
23	D100
14	N140
14	S160
36	S160
45	D190
48	S190
25	C100
31	D110
25	D110
11	D120
31	C180
25	C180
11	D200
12	P200
13	P200
31	D100
23	D130

Figure 10-7   Data model in Boyce-Codd normal form – part 2.

We want to examine the resultant data model further and check whether any other types of discrepancies are likely to be present. Occasionally, you may have to take additional steps and go to higher normal forms. Let us consider the nature of higher normal forms and study the remedies necessary to reach these higher normal forms.

Initial table

Executive	Department	Committee
Jones	Administration	Planning
	Finance	Technology
	Info. Technology	
Cooper	Marketing	R & D
	Personnel	Recruitment
	Production	

Initial relation

Executive	Department	Committee
Jones	Administration	Planning
Jones	Finance	Planning
Jones	Info. Technology	Planning
Jones	Administration	Technology
Jones	Finance	Technology
Jones	Info. Technology	Technology
Cooper	Marketing	R & D
Cooper	Personnel	R & D
Cooper	Production	R & D
Cooper	Marketing	Recruitment
Cooper	Personnel	Recruitment
Cooper	Production	Recruitment

Figure 10-8   Multivalued dependencies.

Fourth Normal Form

Before we discuss the fourth normal form for a data model, we need to define the concept of multivalued dependencies. Consider the following assumptions about the responsibilities and participation of company executives:

- Each executive may have direct responsibility for several departments.
- Each executive may be a member of several management committees.
- The departments and committees related to a particular executive are independent of each other.

Figure 10-8 contains data in the form of an initial data model to illustrate these assumptions. The first part of the figure shows the basic table and the second part the transformed relation.

Note that for each value of Executive attribute, there are multiple values for Department attribute and multiple values for Committee attribute. Note also that the values of Department attribute for an executive are independent of the values of Committee attribute. This type of dependency is known as multivalued dependency. A multivalued dependency exists in a relation consisting of at least three attributes A, B, and C such that for each value of A, there is a defined set of values for B and another defined set of values for C, and furthermore, the set of values for B is independent of the set of values for C.

Now observe the relation shown in the second part of Figure 10-8. Because the relation indicating the relationship between the attributes just contains the primary key, the relation is even in the Boyce-Codd normal form. However, by going through the rows of this relation, you can easily see that the three types of anomalies—update, deletion, and addition—are present in the relation.

This step in normalization process deals with this type of problem. Once this type of problem is resolved, the data model is transformed to a data model in the fourth normal form. In other words, the condition for a fourth normal form data model is as follows:

RESPONSIBILITY

Executive	Department
Jones	Administration
Jones	Finance
Jones	Info. Technology
Cooper	Marketing
Cooper	Personnel
Cooper	Production

MEMBERSHIP

Executive	Committee
Jones	Planning
Jones	Technology
Cooper	R & D
Cooper	Recruitment

Figure 10-9   Data model in fourth normal form.

If a data model is in the fourth normal form, no multivalued dependencies exist.

Here is what must be done to make this transformation.

Transformation to Fourth Normal Form (4NF)

Remove multivalued dependencies.

Figure 10-9 shows the resolution of the multivalued dependencies. The two relations are in the fourth normal form.

When you examine the two relations in Figure 10-9, you can easily establish that these relations are free from update, deletion, or addition anomalies.

Fifth Normal Form

When you transform a data model into second, third, and Boyce-Codd normal forms, you are able to remove anomalies resulting from functional dependencies. After going through the steps and arriving at a data model in the Boyce-Codd normal form, the data model is free from functional dependencies. When you proceed further and transform the data model into a fourth normal form relation, you are able to remove anomalies resulting from multivalued dependencies.

A further step transforming the data model into fifth normal form removes anomalies arising from what are known as join dependencies. What is the definition of join dependency? Go back and look at the figures showing the steps for the earlier normal forms. In each transformation step, the original relation is decomposed into smaller relations. When you inspect the smaller relations, you note that the original relation may be reconstructed from the decomposed smaller relations. However, if a relation has join dependencies and if we are able to decompose the relation into smaller relations, it will not be possible to put the decomposed relations together and recreate the original relation. The smaller relations cannot be joined together to come up with the original relation. The original relation is important because that relation was obtained directly from information requirements. Therefore, in whatever ways you may decompose the original relation to normalize it, you should be able to go back to the original relation from the decomposed relations.

Figure 10-10 shows a relation that has join dependency. Note the columns in the relation shown in the figure.

This relation describes the materials supplied by suppliers to various buildings that are being constructed. Building B45 gets sheet rock from supplier S67 and

BUILDING-MATERIAL-SUPPLIER

BuildingID	Material	SupplierNo
B45	Sheet Rock	S67
B45	Ceiling Paint	S72
B51	Sheet Rock	S72
B51	Shower Stall	S67
B93	Ceiling Paint	S75

Figure 10-10   Relation with join dependency.

ceiling paint from supplier S72. Suppose you have a constraint that suppliers may supply only certain materials to specific buildings even though a supplier may be able to supply all materials. In this example, supplier S72 can supply sheet rock to building B45, but to this building B45, only supplier S67 is designated to supply sheet rock. This constraint imposes a join dependency on the relation. However, the way the relation is composed, it does support the join dependency constraint. For example, there is no restriction to adding a row (B45, Sheet Rock, S72). Such a row would violate the join constraint and not be a true representation of the information requirements.

This step in normalization process deals with this type of problem. Once this type of problem is resolved, the data model is transformed to a data model in fifth normal form. In other words, the condition for a fifth normal form data model is as follows:

If a data model is in the fifth normal form, no join dependencies exist.

Here is what must be done to make this transformation.

Transformation to Fifth Normal Form (5NF)

Remove join dependencies.

Figure 10-11 shows the resolution of the join dependencies. The three relations are in the fifth normal form.

Note something important in the relations shown in the figure. If you join any two of the three relations, the result will produce incorrect information, not the true real-world information with the join dependency. To arrive at the correct original real-world information with the join dependency constraint, you have to join all three relations.

Domain-Key Normal Form

This normal form is the ultimate goal of good design of a proper relational data model. If a data model is in the domain-key normal form (DKNF), it satisfies the conditions of all the normal forms discussed so far. The objective of DKNF is to make one relation represent just one subject and to have all the business rules expressed in terms of domain constraints and key relationships. In other words, all rules could be expressly defined by the relational rules themselves.

BUILDING-MATERIAL

BuildingID	Material
B45	Sheet Rock
B45	Ceiling Paint
B51	Sheet Rock
B51	Shower Stall
B93	Ceiling Paint

MATERIAL-SUPPLIER

Material	SupplierNo
Sheet Rock	S67
Ceiling Paint	S72
Sheet Rock	S72
Shower Stall	S67
Ceiling Paint	S75

BUILDING-SUPPLIER

BuildingID	SupplierNo
B45	S67
B45	S72
B51	S72
B51	S67
B93	S75

Figure 10-11   Data model in fifth normal form.

EMPLOYEE (EmpID, EmpName, SkillType, TrainerID)

TRAINER (TrainerID, TrainerName, Location, SubjectArea)

> **Business rule:**
> An employee can have many trainers, but only a specific trainer for each skill type. A trainer can train only in his or her subject area.

Figure 10-12   Relations not in DKNF.

Domain constraints impose rules on the values for attributes—they indicate restrictions on the data values. In DKNF, every other rule must be expressed clearly in terms of keys and relationships without any hidden relationships. Consider the relations shown in Figure 10-12 and also note the accompanying business rule.

How do you know if the relations are in DKNF? You cannot know this until you are aware of the business rule. From the business rule, you understand that an employee can have multiple skill types. Therefore, the primary key EmpId of the EMPLOYEE relation cannot be unique. Furthermore, trainer is related to skill type, and this is a hidden relationship in the relation. There must also be an explicit relationship between skill type and subject area.

Figure 10-13 resolves these discrepancies and expresses the business rule and the relationships correctly. The resultant data model is in DKNF.

NORMALIZATION SUMMARY

Let us go back and review the normalization approach covered so far. Compare this approach with the method of creating a semantic data model first and then transforming the semantic data model into a relational data model. Consider the merits and disadvantages of either method. Also, think about the circumstances and con-

EMPLOYEE (<u>EmpID</u>, EmpName)

TRAINING (<u>EmpID</u>, <u>SkillType</u>, TrainerID)
Foreign Keys: **TrainerID** REFERENCES **INSTRUCTOR**
          EmpID REFERENCES **EMPLOYEE**

INSTRUCTOR (<u>TrainerID</u>, TrainerName, Location, SubjectArea)
Foreign Key: **SubjectArea** REFERENCES **TRAINING**

Figure 10-13   Data model in domain-key normal form.

ditions under which one method is preferable to the other. You notice that both methods finally produce a true and correct relational data model. In the final relational data model, every single relation or table represents just one object set or entity type. In each relation, every attribute is functionally dependent on the full primary key and only on the full primary key.

As you know, the data model transformation method is a more straightforward approach. Systematically, you create partial semantic data models by applying standard techniques. You then integrate all the partial data models to produce the consolidated semantic model. After this step, you transform the consolidated semantic model into a final relational data model. Although straightforward, the data model transformation method might take longer to come up with the final relational data model.

On the other hand, the normalization approach starts out with an intuitive initial data model. If you cannot begin with an intuitive initial data model that reflects the real-world information requirements completely, then this method will not work. That is why this normalization approach is difficult when the real-world information requirements are large and complex. If you are able to start with a good initial data model, then it is a matter of rendering the initial data model into a successive series of normal forms. Each step brings you closer to the true relational data model. Observe, however, that each step in the normalization process is defined well. In each step, you know exactly the type of problem you have look for and correct. For example, to refine the data model and make it a first normal form data model, you remove repeating groups of attributes. To refine the data model and make it a second normal data model, you look for partial key dependencies and rectify this problem.

Review of the Steps

When we discussed the normalization steps, we grouped the steps into two major sets. The first set of steps deal with the refinement of the data model into the fundamental normal forms. The second set of steps relate to higher normal forms. As mentioned above, if you complete the first set of steps, then for a vast majority of cases your resulting data model will be truly relational. You need not proceed to the second set of steps to produce higher normal forms.

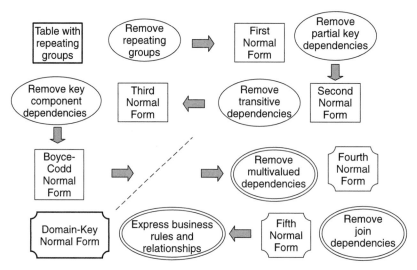

Figure 10-14   Normalization summary.

What exactly do you accomplish in the first set of steps refining the data model into the fundamental normal forms? In the relational data model, for every relation, each attribute must functionally depend only on the full primary key. There should not be any other type of functional dependencies. Update, deletion, and addition anomalies are caused by incorrect functional dependencies within a relation. Once you complete the first set of steps to produce the fundamental normal forms, all problems of invalid functional dependencies are removed.

The second set of normalization steps considers other types of dependencies. Such dependency problems are rare in practice. For that reason, the fundamental normal forms are more important.

Figure 10-14 summarizes the normalization steps. Note the two sets of steps producing the two types of normal forms—fundamental normal forms and higher normal forms. In each step, you tackle one and only one type of problem. The result in each step is a progression toward the final true relational data model.

Critical Issues

Before we end our discussion of the normalization approach, it is worthwhile to list a few critical issues to be concerned about. Give careful consideration to the following points.

- Remember that the normalization method begins with an intuitive data model.
- If the scope of the real-world information is too large or complex and you are not able to create a complete initial data model intuitively, then do not pursue this method.
- Each normalization step focuses on only one type of problem. Make sure you look for the appropriate type of problem in each step.
- The normalization process follows a predefined sequence of steps. Follow the steps in sequence for best results.

- Decomposition of a relation into more than one relation or table is the general technique in each step. Make sure that you do not lose any information when decomposing a table into multiple tables.
- Furthermore, at each step, you must be able to recreate the original set of relations from the set of decomposed relations. This will ensure that you did not lose any information in the normalization step.
- At the end of each step, it is a good practice to verify that the update, deletion, and addition anomalies are eliminated in each of the resulting relations.

Normalization Example

In Chapter 7, we discussed the information requirements for the teaching aspects of a university and developed an entity-relationship diagram as shown in Figure 7-22. The diagram represents the semantic data model. Later, in Chapter 9, we transformed that semantic data model into a relational data model as shown in Figure 9-22. This was the data model transformation method for producing a true relational data model.

Let us take the same example of information requirements for a university and adopt the normalization approach to create a true relational model. First, create an initial set of random tables intuitively from the information requirements. Figure 10-15 shows this initial data model.

Information Requirements

SocSecNo	
StudntName	
ClassNo	
RoomNo	
CourseDesc	
Credits	
FacltyName	
Speczn	
Department	
Phone	
TextbookTitle	
Author	Possibility of multiple authors
Price	
ExamName	Multiple exams for each student in a class
StudntScore	
Score	
MinScore	
Major	

Initial Set of Random Tables

SocSecNo	StudntName	ClassNo	RoomNo	CourseDesc	Credits	FacltyName	Speczn	Department	Phone

BookTitle	Author	Price	ExamName	Score	Grade	Major

Figure 10-15   University information: initial set of random tables.

SocSecNo	StudntName	ClassNo	RoomNo	CourseDesc	Credits	FacltyName	Speczn	Department	Phone	Major

ISBN	Title	Price

ISBN	Author

TypeID	ExamName	MinScore	SocSecNo	ClassNo	Score

SocSecNo	StudntName	Major

ClassNo	RoomNo	CourseDesc	Credits	FacltyName	Speczn	Department	Phone

ClassNo	CourseNo	RoomNo	FacultyID

CourseNo	CourseDesc	Credits	ISBN

FacultyID	FacltyName	Speczn	Department	Phone

TypeID	ExamName	MinScore

CourseNo	ClassNo	TypeID	SocSecNo	Score

Figure 10-16 University information: normalization steps.

Next, examine each table and go through the normalization steps one by one. Figure 10-16 illustrates the normalization steps. Note carefully the outcome from each step.

Figure 10-17 presents the final relational data model as a result of the normalization process. Compare this with the relational data model in Figure 9-22 arrived at through the data model transformation method.

CHAPTER SUMMARY

- The normalization method of creating a relational data model is an informal design methodology.
- In this method, you intuitively create an initial data model from information requirements and normalize it into a relational data model.
- An initial data model created through intuition contains potential anomalies relating to updates, deletes, and addition of data.
- The normalization approach consists of systematically examining the initial data model, removing the causes for anomalies, and transforming the data model into a true relational data model. The approach consists of definite, sequential steps.
- Each step removes one type of irregularity in the initial data model and transforms the model into a distinct normal form.
- The first four steps transform the initial data model into fundamental normal forms. Transformation into these fundamental normal forms removes

STUDENT

SocSecNo	StudntName	Major

TEXTBOOK

ISBN	Title	Price

AUTHOR

ISBN	Author

COURSE

CourseNo	CourseDesc	Credits	ISBN

CLASS

ClassNo	CourseNo	RoomNo	FacultyID

FACULTY

FacultyID	FacltyName	Speczn	Department	Phone

EXAMTYPE

TypeID	ExamName	MinScore

GRADE

CourseNo	ClassNo	TypeID	SocSecNo	Score

Figure 10-17 University information: final relational data model.

irregularities resulting from incorrect functional dependencies in the original relations.

- In practice, after the initial data model goes through the first four steps for fundamental normal forms, the resultant data model becomes truly relational and suitable for completing the logical design. No further normalization steps are usually necessary.
- The next three steps remove irregularities resulting from other types of incorrect dependencies in the original relations. These steps transform the data model into higher normal forms.
- The normalization method of creating a relational data model is difficult when the real-world information you are trying to model is large and complex.

REVIEW QUESTIONS

1. "The method of creating a relational data model seems to be an informal design technique." Discuss briefly.
2. Describe briefly the process of creating an initial data model from real-world information requirements. Why is this initial data model potentially incorrect?
3. "An update anomaly occurs when values of attributes are updated in a database." Explain with an example.

4. What is an addition anomaly in a database? Give an example.

5. Normalization is a systematic, step-by-step methodology. Describe how it is such a methodology.

6. When is a relation not in the second normal form? Give an example. How do you transform it into second normal form relations?

7. What are transitive dependencies in a relation? How do you remove transitive dependencies?

8. What is the Boyce-Codd normal form (BCNF)? Under what condition is a relation in BCNF?

9. What are multivalued dependencies? Explain with an example.

10. What is your understanding of the domain-key normal form? Why do you think this normal form is the ultimate goal of good design of a proper relational data model?

EXERCISES

1. Indicate whether true or false:

   A. Informal design of a relational data model starts with random tables created intuitively.

   B. Deletion anomaly prevents all deletion of data from a database.

   C. Each normalization step removes only one type of irregularity.

   D. When partial key dependencies are removed, a relation is in third normal form.

   E. In most cases, the first four normalization steps for fundamental normal forms are sufficient to produce a truly relational data model.

   F. A relation has transitive dependencies when every attribute is not functionally dependent on the full primary key.

   G. A relation in Boyce-Codd normal form is practically free from incorrect functional dependencies.

   H. If a data model is in fourth normal form, no multivalued dependencies exist.

   I. Join dependency in a relation is the same as multivalued dependency.

   J. Decomposition of a relation into more than one relation is the general technique in each step of the normalization process.

2. Describe the circumstances under which the normalization method is preferable to the data model transformation method for creating a relational data model. If you are the database designer for a florist business, which method will you adopt? Why?

3. List the fundamental normal forms. Describe the type of irregularity each step removes in arriving at the fundamental normal forms.

4. You are asked to create a small relational database to manage customer orders for a small business manufacturing standard vacuum cleaner parts. Create and initial data model through intuition for the Customer Order database. Normalize the initial data model and produce the final relational data model.

5. You are the senior database specialist in the database project of a large home improvement store responsible for implementing a relational database. Make assumptions and list the objects and relationships you need to include in your data model. Review the scope and complexity of the task and choose the appropriate method for creating the relational data model. Explain why you would choose either the data model transformation method or the normalization method.

PART V

DESIGN AND IMPLEMENTATION

CHAPTER 11

COMPLETING THE LOGICAL DESIGN

CHAPTER OBJECTIVES

- Understand the place and significance of logical design in the database development life cycle (DDLC)
- Study how data modeling fits in with logical design
- Review the various steps necessary to complete logical design
- Focus on logical design for the relational data model
- Learn how to document the logical design effort

In Chapter 4, while covering the database development life cycle (DDLC), we briefly discussed the design phase. The ultimate goal of a database development project is to have proper data content and structures in the database system. You must make sure that all the necessary real-world information requirements for your organization are correctly included in the database system. Before you determine how to do this and create a design, you need to know exact details about the real-world information—its exact nature and extent and how the information is used to run the business. You find out the details during the requirements definition phase. Once you have the details of all the information requirements, somehow you have to represent all of this in your design of the database system.

How do you keep data in the database? Data are stored in physical storage in the form of records, blocks, and files. Therefore, to properly store data in the database, you need to design the files, blocks, and records. This part of the design phase relates to the physical design of the database. Physical design must consider the stipulations of the DBMS selected for your organization. The selected DBMS lays down conditions, rules, and formats for the file structures.

Database Design and Development: An Essential Guide for IT Professionals by Paulraj Ponniah
ISBN 0-471-21877-4   Copyright © 2003 by John Wiley and Sons, Inc.

Logical design precedes the physical design activity. In the logical design activity, you create a conceptual design, not in terms of physical files, blocks, and records, but in terms of how data are perceived by the users and developers. If the target DBMS is relational, data are perceived as two-dimensional tables. For a hierarchical DBMS, data are seen as being organized in the form of hierarchical segments. In a network database environment, data are perceived as network nodes. The tables, segments, or nodes do not represent how data are physically kept in data storage—they just indicate how we perceive data as being organized. Logical design consists of the tasks necessary to arrive at the design of the tables, segments, or nodes, depending on the type of target DBMS.

SIGNIFICANCE OF LOGICAL DESIGN

Think back to the days of designing file-oriented data systems before the database era. Considering the business processes, the analyst would prepare the layouts for the master files and the transaction files. For an order entry application, the analyst would design the order master file and order transaction file. He or she then defined the necessary index files. This was the extent of the data design. No separation of data design into logical design and physical design existed. In fact, such separation did not make sense in a file-oriented data environment.

Although this was the best available design approach at that time, two problems were encountered. The first problem related to the lack of data independence. Every time changes in business conditions warranted revisions to data structures, the design of the file layouts had to be changed. The design changes affected the physical storage of data. The second problem referred to lack of simplicity for users in understanding the data. Users could not comprehend the technical details of physical file layouts. They need to perceive and understand data in simpler ways. They can easily perceive data as tables, segments, or nodes—not expressed in terms of data blocks, records, fields, storage addresses, and so on.

Logical Structure Versus Physical Structure

Database management systems provide means for separating the logical structure and manipulation of data from their physical representation in computer hardware. The relational revolution further confirmed the need for the separation of the logical structure from the physical structure. Logical data design simply covers the tasks necessary for creating the logical structure as distinct from the physical structure.

Before proceeding further, try to get a clear picture of what we mean by the logical and physical structures. Consider a small database system consisting of data about customers, orders, and details of orders. This is a very simple database just for the sake of illustration of the difference between the logical and physical structures. Figure 11-1 illustrates this example and distinguishes between the logical and physical structures.

This figure illustrates the logical and physical structures implementing the database system based on relational technology. If the database system were to be based on the hierarchical data model, the logical and physical structures would be differ-

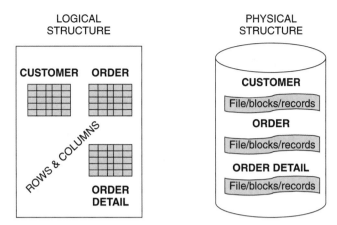

Figure 11-1   Logical and physical structures.

ent. Note that the logical structure is based on the conventional data model adopted for the implementation. The physical structure is determined by the specific DBMS used for the particular conventional data model.

Logical Design Phase in DDLC

Let us retrace the steps discussed so far in the development of a database system. Quickly review the DDLC steps from the beginning and note where logical design phase fits in the DDLC. After initial planning and feasibility study, you launch requirements analysis and definition. You have to determine exactly what information is required to be contained in the final database system. You have gone through the process of creating a generic data model to truly represent the real-world information requirements. You already know the necessity for creating a generic data model first. You know that only a generic data model unrestricted by any constraints can truly represent all the details of real-world information.

After the creation of a generic data model, what comes next? You know that a generic semantic data model created through a data modeling technique such as the E-R modeling technique has no flavor of the relational, hierarchical, or network approaches. If you are developing a relational database, your semantic data model must be transformed into a relational data model. What is the relational data model at this stage of the development? It does not represent how data are to be stored in the final database system. Then what does it represent? It indicates the logical structure, at a conceptual level, of the data perceived as two-dimensional tables. Figure 11-2 shows the place of logical design phase in DDLC.

What is the logical design phase? It is the set of tasks in DDLC intended for the design of the logical structure. Observe the presentation in Figure 11-2. Note the illustration of logical design phase for the small orders database above.

Why This Phase Is Necessary

Imagine a situation in which you plan to bypass the logical design phase and go directly to the physical design phase from requirements definition. You will be

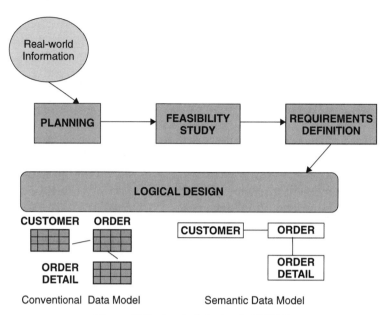

Figure 11-2 Logical design in DDLC.

taking the semantic data model and transforming it into the physical design. You will be designing files and records based on the features of the hardware. Your issues and concerns will be centered more on hardware features than on the information requirements. As hardware changes occur, your design will have to be modified.

Let us say that you are designing a relational database system by adopting this plan of bypassing the logical design. You need to define the files and records for data elements determined in your requirements definition phase. You are not going to think in terms of relational tables, but only about designing files and records. How are you going to ensure that your files will be free from data redundancy and that they will conform to the relational rules? How are you going to ensure that your files will be free from update, deletion, and addition anomalies? Remember, the relational model rests on the understanding that data may be perceived as two-dimensional, relational tables. Relational DBMSs work on this premise.

This logical design phase is essential for the following reasons:

- The output of the logical design phase represents data as perceived as tables, segments, or nodes—the way data are considered in the relational, hierarchical, and network models.
- Users do not understand the output of the physical design phase in the form of hardware files, records, and so on. Tables, segments, or nodes are better understood.
- Logical design enables data independence, a crucial advantage of the database approach.
- The design effort becomes easier and more manageable when you separate it into logical and physical design phases.

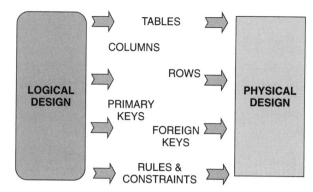

Figure 11-3 Output from logical design as input to physical design.

- In the logical design phase, you can focus on designing the tables, segments, or nodes without being bogged down by hardware considerations.

Input to Physical Design

When you finish the logical design phase, you produce a representation of the information requirements in the form of tables, segments, or nodes. If you are designing for the relational data model, your output from the logical design phase consists of two-dimensional tables with their columns and rows. The logical design phase takes the database development effort to this stage.

However, you know that data do not exist as tables, or segments, or nodes in physical storage. Therefore, to implement the target database system, you have to define the representation of data in formats that are suitable for physical storage. How do you accomplish the design of the physical structure? The output of the logical design phase serves as the input to the physical design phase. In the physical design phase, you take each table from the output of the logical design phase and transform it into file and record layouts.

Figure 11-3 illustrates how the output from the logical design phase is used as input to the physical design phase. Note the components of the logical design output. Also, observe once again how design is simplified by separating it into logical and physical design phases.

Ensuring Design Completeness

When you are near the end of the logical design phase, usually it is a good place in DDLC to ensure that the design is complete. You started from the real-world information that needs to be represented in the target database system. You gathered requirements and defined the content, extent, and scope of the information requirements. On the basis of the requirements definition, you created a semantic data model to represent the real-world information. Then you transformed the semantic data model into a relational data model. If your target database system were hierarchical or network, you would have transformed the semantic data model into a hierarchical or network data model. If you had adopted the traditional method of

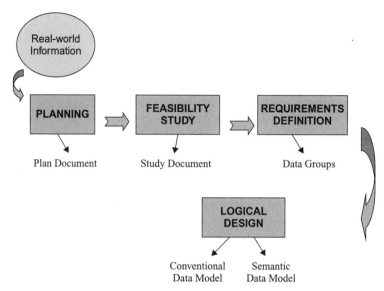

Figure 11-4   DDLC steps up to logical design.

designing the relational data model, you would have created it with the data normalization method. In any case, you now have a relational data model. Figure 11-4 recapitulates these steps.

Having gone through these distinct steps, how are you sure that the output of the logical design phase truly and completely represents the real-world information? Has something been missed along the way? Has something been misrepresented in the transition from step to step? Especially if the database project is large with multiple analysts working in each step of DDLC, there are more chances of things going wrong. So, this is a good stage in DDLC to pause and ensure the completeness and correctness of the design. Adjustments can be made with comparative ease at this point rather than after defining the files and records in the physical design phase.

Go back and review the outputs from all the steps leading up to this point and adjust the logical design accordingly. Pay attention to the following critical factors in your review:

- Real-world information requirements could create variations in the way business objects and the relationships among these are perceived in your organization. Ensure that your semantic data model represents all the nuances of the information requirements in your particular environment.
- Semantic data modeling techniques have all the necessary components to represent every aspect of real-world information. Become familiar with the features and purposes of the data model components and employ these suitably.
- If the scope of the information requirements for your organization is large and complex, your database project team will be dividing up the data modeling task. The team will be creating partial data models. Ensure that nothing gets lost

when consolidating the partial data models into the global semantic data model.

- When the semantic data model is transformed into the appropriate conventional data model—relational, hierarchical, or network—ensure that none of the essential properties of the conventional data model is overlooked.
- If your target database is relational, make sure that the transformed data model conforms to all the relational rules and constraints.

DATA MODELING IN LOGICAL DESIGN

Think of logical design phase as consisting of two distinct steps—creation of the semantic data model and transformation of the semantic data model into the desired conventional model. Sometimes, semantic data modeling is taken to be part of the requirements definition phase, perhaps considering the semantic model as the output of the requirements definition phase. We would rather place semantic data modeling in the logical database design phase. Both the semantic and the conventional data models are conceptual or logical models. They are conceptual representations of real-world information requirements.

Also, the skills needed for semantic data modeling and for gathering and defining information requirements are not the same. Analysts working on the requirements definition phase must possess special proficiency in analyzing business operations, reviewing business processes, and interviewing users to gather the requirements. Data modelers must have expertise in modeling techniques and knowledge of leading CASE tools.

Steps for Completing Logical Design

In the previous section, we listed a number of critical factors to be concerned about in the logical design process. Essentially, steps for completing the logical design relate to the fulfillment of these factors. Semantic data modeling is the beginning of the logical design phase. We have covered semantic data modeling in elaborate detail in earlier chapters. You know the components of a semantic data model; you are very familiar with data modeling techniques. Let us trace the steps to complete the logical design from the semantic data model.

Figure 11-5 shows a semantic data model for a small florist business. Note the components in the data model diagram. Observe the entities, attributes, and relationships. As this exercise is meant just to illustrate the steps for completing the logical design, we are not considering all the possible entities and attributes for a typical florist business. Let us begin with this data model and complete the logical design.

We will consider the relational data model as the conventional data model while studying the steps for completing the logical design. Similar steps are applicable if the conventional data models were to be hierarchical or network. Here are the obvious basic steps to complete the logical design from the semantic data model:

- Represent entities in the conventional data model.
- Represent attributes in the conventional data model.

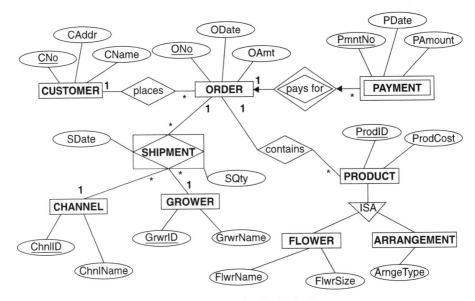

Figure 11-5   ERD for florist business.

- Represent relationships in the conventional data model.
- Include the necessary rules and constraints in the conventional data model.
- Review conventional data model for completeness.

Representing Entities

Figure 11-6 illustrates the representation of entities in the relational data model for the florist business. Note how each entity is represented by a relation or table in the relational data model.

Representing Attributes

Figure 11-7 illustrates the representation of attributes in the relational data model for the florist business. Note how the representation is done as columns for attributes. Also, observe how entity identifiers or primary keys are represented in the tables.

Representing Relationships

Figure 11-8 illustrates the representation of relationships in the relational data model for florist business. As you know, relationships are represented through foreign keys in the relational data model. Note the foreign key columns in the appropriate tables. CustNo is a foreign key column in the ORDER relation. Also, observe the foreign key columns in the PAYMENT, SHIPMENT, FLOWER, and ARRANGEMENT relations.

CUSTOMER

·			

ORDER

·			

PAYMENT

·			

CHANNEL

·			

GROWER

·			

SHIPMENT

·			

PRODUCT

·			

FLOWER

·			

ARRANGEMENT

·			

Figure 11-6   Representing entities for florist business.

CUSTOMER

CustNo	CustAddr	CustName
·		
		·

ORDER

OrdrNo	OrdrDate	OrdrAmt
·		
		·

PAYMENT

OrdrNo	PmntNo	PmntDate	PmntAmt
·			
			·

CHANNEL

ChnlID	ChnlName
·	

GROWER

GrwrID	GrwrName
·	

SHIPMENT

OrdrNo	ChnlID	GrwrID	ShipDate	ShipQty
·				
				·

PRODUCT

ProdID	ProdCost
·	

FLOWER

ProdID	ProdCost	FlwrName	FlwrSize
·			
		·	

ARRANGEMENT

ProdID	ProdCost	ArngeType
·		
		·

Figure 11-7   Representing attributes for florist business.

CUSTOMER

CustNo	CustAddr	CustName
.		
		.

ORDER

OrdrNo	OrdrDate	OrdrAmt	CustNo
.			
			.

PAYMENT

OrdrNo	PmntNo	PmntDate	PmntAmt
.			
			.

CHANNEL

ChnlID	ChnlName
.	

GROWER

GrwrID	GrwrName
.	

SHIPMENT

OrdrNo	ChnlID	GrwrID	ShipDate	ShipQty
.				
				.

PRODUCT

ProdID	ProdCost
.	

FLOWER

ProdID	ProdCost	FlwrName	FlwrSize
.			
			.

ARRANGEMENT

ProdID	ProdCost	ArngeType
.		
		.

Figure 11-8   Representing relationships for florist business.

Rules and Constraints

This step in the logical design includes representation of the following in the relational data model:

- Reduction of many-to-many relationships into multiple one-to-many relationships
- Representation of foreign keys as additional columns
- Indication of optional and mandatory relationships through minimum cardinality indicators

Once this step is completed, logical design comes to an end, to be followed by physical design.

DESIGN FOR THE RELATIONAL DATA MODEL

Before going through the completion of the logical design for the relational data model, let us recapitulate the basic features of the relational model. This refresher will help you appreciate the special requirements for going through this phase of completing the logical design. Here is a recapitulation of the significant properties of the relational data model.

- In the relational data model, data are perceived as in two-dimensional tables that conform to relational rules and constraints.
- A table represents a single entity type or business object set.
- Each row in a table representing an object refers to one instance of that object set.
- Each column in a table refers to an attribute of the object set. Data values in all the columns for a row denote the values of the attributes for that single object.
- Each row in a table is unique. The primary key value identifies each row uniquely.
- Each value of every attribute is atomic from a certain domain.
- The order of the columns in a relation is immaterial; the sequence of the rows is insignificant.
- No part of the primary key of any tuple in a relation can have a null value (entity integrity rule).
- The value of a foreign key in a table must either be null or be one of the values of the primary key in the related table (referential integrity rule).

Relation as the Single Design Concept

While completing the logical design for your relational database, keep the following fundamental notion as the main focus:

> The underlying design concept for a relational data model is the two-dimensional table or relation.

All of the logical design rests on the premise that data is formulated and perceived as two-dimensional tables. Within each table you have columns and rows. Columns and rows are used to express the different aspects of each business object represented by a table or relation. One or more columns are designated as the primary key for the relation. Every relationship among the tables is established by the values in a column known as the foreign key. All of the real-world information requirements are expressed as a complete set of two-dimensional tables with columns and rows.

What is the implication of stressing the fundamental design concept for the relational data model? When you complete the logical design and produce the logical schema for your relational database system, the logical schema essentially consists of table descriptions. The relational schema contains a list of all the tables. For each table, you include the column names, and for each column you provide the descriptions and data types. You indicate the primary key columns for each table. You add the foreign key columns to establish each relationship among the tables. Then you

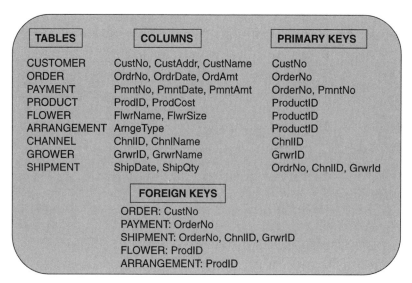

Figure 11-9   List of logical design components for florist business.

note the relational constraints about the applicable columns in each table. In short, the logical schema is nothing but descriptions of the relational tables.

Logical Design Components

In the previous section, we discussed a florist business and covered the representation of individual components. Let us pull the separate representations of individual components together and list the complete set of logical design components. Figure 11-9 displays such a list.

Note each component. Again, note how every component is part of the underlying design concept—the two-dimensional table or relation.

Logical Schema

Creating and defining the logical schema essentially completes the logical design phase. The logical schema for the relational data model contains the representation and descriptions of the relational tables. Let us take the complete relational data model for the florist business and define the logical schema. Each table in the relational data model must be defined. Every column in each table must be expressed in the logical schema.

Figure 11-10 displays the logical schema for the relational data model representing the information requirements for the florist business. We have used standard relational notation to express the schema. Data definition languages are used to define the schema to the data dictionary.

Carefully note the definition for each table in the logical schema. Also, for each table, observe how the columns are defined. Make a note of the definition of relational constraints in the schema.

CUSTOMER (CustNo, CustAddr, CustName)

ORDER (OrdrNo, OrdrDate, OrdrAmt, CustNo)
Foreign Key: **CustNo** REFERENCES **CUSTOMER** ON DELETE CASCADE

PAYMENT (OrdrNo, PmntNo, PmntDate, PmntAmt)
Foreign Key: **OrdrNo** REFERENCES **ORDER**

PRODUCT (ProdID, ProdCost)

FLOWER (ProdID, ProdCost, FlwrName, FlwrSize)
Foreign Key: **ProdID** REFERENCES **PRODUCT**

ARRANGEMENT (ProdID, ProdCost, ArngeType)
Foreign Key: **ProdID** REFERENCES **PRODUCT**

CHANNEL (ChnlID, ChnlName)

GROWER (GrwrID, GrwrName)

SHIPMENT (OrdrNo, ChnlID, GrwrID, ShipDate, ShipQty)
Foreign Key: **OrdrNo** REFERENCES **ORDER**
ChnlID REFERENCES **CHANNEL**
GrwrID REFERENCES **GROWER**

Figure 11-10   Relational schema for florist business.

Special Considerations

Before declaring that the logical design phase is complete, you need to examine each statement in the logical schema carefully. This is the basis for defining the physical files, records, fields, and restrictions. The logical schema, therefore, must truly define and represent the real-world information requirements. Here is a list of special considerations in verifying the logical schema for the relational model:

- Ensure that the logical schema defines each and every table in the relational model.
- Define each table and its columns with meaningful names. Remember, these names will be used for accessing tables and the columns.
- For each column, define appropriate data types and data lengths.
- If there are any edits to be specified for specific columns, do so clearly for these columns.
- If any column may not contain null values, express this clearly.
- Clearly indicate the columns that make up the primary key for each table. Primary keys cannot contain null values.
- Show the foreign key columns distinctly. Indicate the table to which a foreign key establishes a relationship.
- Ensure that all intersection tables are clearly defined with proper primary key and foreign key columns.
- Indicate the columns for which duplicate values are not allowed in the table.

- Express the referential integrity constraints for each relationship in terms of how to handle additions and deletion of related rows.

DOCUMENTATION OF LOGICAL DESIGN

Let us go back and review the role of documentation in the database development life cycle. In the requirements definition phase, analysts skilled in interviewing techniques and analysis of business operations complete the study of information requirements. After the requirements definition phase comes the design phase. The first part of the design phase consists of the logical design activity. At this stage, data modelers and database designers enter the scene in the database development life cycle. These professionals possess different sets of skills and training. However, they have to pick up from where the analysts leave off and build on the outputs from the requirements definition phase. What enables the data modelers and database designers to embark on the design phase? The answer is the documentation produced during the requirements definition phase. Whenever you switch gears and move into the next phase in the database development life cycle, you need adequate documentation to proceed further.

What happens at the end of the logical design activity? Data modelers and designers complete the semantic data model. If your target database system is relational, the semantic data model is transformed into a relational data model. If the designers adopt the traditional approach, they design the relational tables, normalize the structures, and produce the relational data model. At this point, the logical design step is deemed to be complete. What happens next? The database administrators take up the project and proceed to the next step, namely, physical design. How can they perform their physical design tasks? Again the answer is the documentation produced during the logical design step. Proper documentation enables the database administrators to correctly perform the physical design. As you complete the logical design, ensure that adequate documentation exists and that the outputs are clearly identified.

Logical Design Outputs

What are the major outputs from the logical design step? These outputs are generated from the tasks in the logical design activity. The first major set of tasks center on the creation of the semantic data model. Next, you have the mapping of the components of the semantic data model to those of the relational data model. The outputs from the logical design step must, therefore, include the semantic data model and the transformation of the semantic data model into the relational data model.

Here is a summary of the logical design outputs:

- Partial semantic data models represented in standard format
- Methodology for consolidating partial semantic data models
- Consolidated semantic data model diagram with detailed descriptions

- Mapping of each individual component of the consolidated semantic data model to one or more components of the relational data model
- Completion of the relational data model schema, expressed with standard conventions and notations
- List of any special considerations

Usage of Outputs

The outputs from the logical design step serve both users and database developers. This point in the database development life cycle is a good time to review the semantic data model diagram with the key users and get their further confirmation. In the requirements definition document, the users get the initial knowledge of how real-world information requirements are reviewed and captured. But the semantic data model crystallizes the representation of real-world information requirements in a clearer manner. You can walk the key users through the semantic model diagram, explain how the model is a true replica of real-world information, and relate the components of the model to the business processes in which the users are engaged.

When the data modelers and designers review the consolidated semantic model diagram, they can ensure that nothing is missed from the requirements definition. The completeness of the model is the confirmation of one major step in the database development life cycle.

Database administration function is more concerned with the completeness of the relational schema. This forms the basis for the physical design. In addition, database administrators also need information for defining the data views to the database management system. As you recall, each data view is the portion of the database in which a particular user group is interested. The data views form the external schemas. All the data views combined together make up the complete logical schema.

Use of CASE Tools

CASE (Computer-Aided Software Engineering) tools offer major benefits during the logical design step in the database development life cycle. You can use drag-and-drop techniques to create semantic data models. The ease of use of most of the data modeling tools provides enormous advantages and saves considerable time for data modelers in completing their tasks. The software tools generate the outputs in the form of E-R diagrams, supporting the standard methods for data modeling.

In addition to providing facilities for creating semantic data models, most of the CASE tools contain features known as forward engineering and backward engineering.

Forward Engineering. As soon as a generic semantic data model is created with the CASE tool, you can use this feature to transform the logical data model into a physical data model for the target database system. The database administrator can use this powerful feature to take the physical schema generated by the forward engineering feature and define the database in the data dictionary of the target DBMS.

Backward Engineering. This feature is the converse of forward engineering. Assume that your new database system includes data already part of some earlier databases in the organization. The database designers and analysts need to get details of the data structure in the older databases. They can get the physical schema of those databases and transform back into generic logical data model. The backward engineering feature of CASE tools accomplishes this.

Let us summarize the major benefits of CASE tools:

- Provide data modelers with toolbox capabilities to create the semantic data model with utmost ease.
- Provide adequate documentation for use by database analysts and developers to communicate among themselves and with users.
- Give a simple, clear picture of the information requirements in the form of a semantic data model diagram.
- Provide forward engineering feature, greatly reducing the effort of the database administrator in defining the physical schema.

Documentation Outline

When a logical design document is issued, you arrive at the conclusion of the logical design step in the database development life cycle. Therefore, it is important that the results of all the steps leading up to the finish of the logical design process are reviewed and confirmed with key users. The issuance of the logical design document marks the beginning of the physical design and leads into the concluding phases of implementation and ongoing maintenance.

Here is a suggested outline for the logical design document. Review the outline, amend it, and adapt it for your specific database project.

Introduction. State the overall scope and content of the logical design step. Include an executive summary.

Semantic data modeling technique. Describe the data modeling technique adopted—object-based or entity-relationship modeling or any other.

CASE tool features. If a CASE tool is used for the logical design, highlight the important features of the tool and its use in the logical design.

Partial semantic data models. List the partial data models. Describe why and how the real-world information requirements are separated out for partial data modeling.

Consolidated semantic data model. Include the consolidated data model diagram. Include descriptions of the various components.

Relational schema of logical model. Include the schema definition of the logical data model.

Data views. Derive and present the subschemas for all the data views of individual user groups.

Physical data model. If you use a CASE tool and are able to forward engineer, include the physical data model.

Special issues. List any special issues, considerations, and assumptions.

Confirmation of logical design. Describe the procedure used for having the logical data model reviewed with user groups. State the results of the reviews and any special requests for revisions.

CHAPTER SUMMARY

- The logical data structure represents how data are perceived; in a relational data model, logically, data are perceived as two-dimensional tables.
- The physical data structure refers to how data are stored in physical storage.
- The logical data design phase in DDLC defines the logical structure of data. This phase is a prerequisite for physical design.
- Users understand the logical structure of data better than physical structures. The logical design phase is necessary to produce the logical structure that can be used to communicate with users.
- The design effort is easier and more manageable when it is divided into logical design and physical design.
- The outputs of the logical design phase are used as inputs in the physical design phase.
- The first part of the logical design phase consists of creating a semantic data model truly representing real-world information requirements.
- In the second part of the logical design phase, the generic semantic data model is transformed into the desired logical data model. To implement a relational database system, the semantic data model is transformed into a relational data model.
- Entities, attributes, relationships, and rules and constraints are represented in the target relational data model.
- CASE tools offer major benefits during the logical design phase.
- The issuance of the logical design documentation marks the conclusion of the logical design phase and the commencement of the physical design phase.

REVIEW QUESTIONS

1. Distinguish between logical data structures and physical data structures.
2. Explain briefly the difference between logical and physical data structures in a relational database system.
3. Describe briefly how and where logical design fits in the database development life cycle (DDLC).
4. List any three reasons why the logical design phase is necessary.
5. "The output of the logical design phase forms the input to the physical design phase." Explain briefly.
6. Completing the logical design phase involves ensuring design completeness. List any four critical factors for consideration in the review for design completeness.

7. What are the two major activities in the logical design phase?

8. Instead of considering the creation of a semantic data model as part of the logical design, can this considered as part of the requirements definition phase? If you do so, what are some of the advantages and disadvantages?

9. How are CASE tools useful in the logical design phase? List any three major benefits.

10. List the major contents expected to be part of logical design documentation.

EXERCISES

1. Match the columns:

1. output of logical design	A. data as segments
2. logical schema	B. files, blocks, records
3. data views	C. consists of two-dimensional tables
4. consolidated semantic model	D. input to physical design
5. hierarchical data model	E. transformation of semantic data model
6. CASE tools	F. representation at conceptual level
7. logical design of relational DB	G. useful for communicating with users
8. second part of logical design	H. translate into subschemas
9. physical data structure	I. simplify data modeling
10. logical data model	J. represents all relevant information

2. You are the senior analyst in the database project building a relational database for a large bank. Write a memorandum to the CIO explaining the significance of the logical design phase and describe the major activities in that phase.

3. As the project manager for the database project for an insurance company, what special measures will you take to ensure the completeness of the design by end of the logical design phase?

4. Create a semantic data model for a small bakery and transform the semantic data model into a relational data model. Produce the logical schema.

5. Describe the forward and backward engineering features found in most CASE tools. As the lead database designer for a fast-food chain, describe how you propose to use these features of your CASE tool.

CHAPTER 12

THE PHYSICAL DESIGN PROCESS

CHAPTER OBJECTIVES

- Study the transition to physical design from logical design
- Understand how physical design conforms to the target DBMS
- Learn the physical design process for the relational database
- Discuss storing of data on physical storage
- Examine various indexing techniques to improve data access
- Identify special performance considerations

With Chapter 11, our discussions on logical design have to come to a state of completion. You now know the purpose of the logical design process; you have reviewed the steps, and you have learned the steps and tasks of the process. First, you model the information requirements by creating a semantic data model. Then you complete the logical design process by transforming the semantic data model into a conventional data model such as the relational, hierarchical, or network data model. Because the relational data model is superior to the others and because it is widely used, we emphasized the relational data model in our discussions. You have also studied two data modeling techniques for creating a semantic data model—the object-based data modeling and entity-relationship data modeling techniques.

Remember that a semantic data model is a generic data model. It has no relational, hierarchical, or network flavor. A semantic data model does not consist of tables with rows and columns; only a relational data model does. Only when you move from a semantic data model to a conventional data model such as the

Database Design and Development: An Essential Guide for IT Professionals by Paulraj Ponniah
ISBN 0-471-21877-4   Copyright © 2003 by John Wiley and Sons, Inc.

relational data model, do you represent and perceive data as being contained in two-dimensional tables or relations.

From the relational data model we proceed to the physical design to represent the information requirements in physical hardware storage. Semantic and conventional data models are logical data models; these are conceptual data models. They are conceptual representations, not representations of how data are actually stored. Actual data are going to reside on physical storage, and physical design stipulates how, where, and which data are stored in physical storage. This chapter covers the physical design of relational database systems. The emphasis is exclusively on relational databases. When we discuss any aspect of physical design, assume that the discussion refers to relational databases.

INTRODUCTION TO PHYSICAL DESIGN

For a moment, think of the logical design process in terms of its output. Take, for instance, the logical design of a relational database system. At the end of the process, you arrive at a set of two-dimensional tables or relations. In the standard notation, you represent the set of relations, indicating the columns, primary keys, and foreign keys. This is the output from the logical design. The output is still at a conceptual level, not at the practical and physical level for storing actual data.

To store and manage data on physical storage, the representation of the logical design must be transformed into a representation for actual data storage. Why is this necessary? Computer systems do not store data in the form of tables with columns and rows; they typically store data in a different way. Computer storage systems store data as files and records. Physical design is the process of implementing the database on physical storage. Therefore, in the physical design process, you are concerned with the features of the storage system on which your database will reside. Furthermore, you are also concerned with the functions, features, and facilities of the DBMS selected to manage your database.

Figure 12-1 illustrates the transition to physical design in the DDLC. Note the place of physical design in the overall design process.

Logical to Physical Design

Logical design produces a data model in one of the standard conventional models. For the purpose of our discussions here, we will focus on the relational data model as the chosen conventional model. Although logical design is independent of any particular DBMS and details of physical hardware and systems software, physical design must necessarily take these into account. Physical design has to be tailored to a target DBMS. The features of the host computer system must be used to shape the output of the physical design process. The physical designer must know how the target DBMS works and must be very familiar with the capabilities and working of the host computer system.

So in physical design, the last stage of the database design process, your objective is to proceed from the logical design to implement the database system as a set of records, files, and other data structures on physical storage. When doing this, you

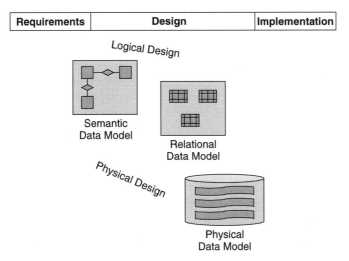

Figure 12-1 Physical design in the overall design process.

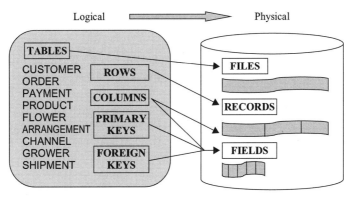

Figure 12-2 Logical design to physical design.

want to ensure adequate performance levels and provide for security and data integrity. You want to design your data structures on storage in such a way as to safeguard against any data loss.

Let us get back to the logical design for the florist business discussed in Chapter 11. How do you make the transition from this logical design to the physical design for the database to support the business? What are the overall components of the physical design? How do the components of the logical design map to those of the physical design? Figure 12-2 portrays the transition to physical design from logical design.

Examine the mapping of the components between logical design and physical design. As a result of the logical design, you have tables or relations with columns and rows for each table. These are the data as represented in the logical model for a relational database system. Now, in physical storage, you have files and records within files. How do you map relations, columns, and rows to files and records? Do you store one relation per file? Or is it more efficient to store several relations in one computer file? Are there advantages if you intend to store related rows from two relations in one file? What happens when the database system grows in size and more transactions begin to access the system? Decisions such as these make up the physical design process. We will consider all the relevant issues and describe the goals and tasks of physical design.

Goals and Design Decisions

Of course, the main objective of physical design is the implementation of the logical design on physical storage. Only then can you begin to store data in the target database and provide for its usage by users. Although this objective appears to be straightforward, when designing the data structures to be stored you need to be concerned with certain crucial issues.

If the way you store data in storage makes data retrieval cumbersome and inefficient, your physical design lacks quality and usefulness. If your data storage method is not compatible with the features of the host system and is difficult for the target DBMS to work with, then again your physical design becomes ineffective. Therefore, let us consider the main goals and decision issues.

Physical Design Goals   Two major goals stand out for the physical design process. All tasks must be conditioned to achieve these goals.

Database performance. Your physical design must ensure optimal performance. This means, as data are retrieved from storage, retrieval must be as fast as possible. Again, when a piece of data is written on storage, it must be done as quickly as possible. Fast data operations constitute a major goal. In terms of physical storage, this translates into minimizing the time for each input/output (I/O) operation. This concern for database performance must continue as usage intensifies after the initial deployment. The physical design must be open and flexible to accommodate all future adjustments for continued better performance.

Data management. As data are stored in your database systems and begin to be used, you now have a vital resource to be managed well and protected. Your physical design must enable effective management of the database. This may involve grouping of tables to be managed as a collection for the purpose of backup and recovery. This may require setting up of proper data views for individual user groups and protecting the database from unauthorized usage.

In addition to the two major goals of database performance and data management, let us list a few other underlying objectives in the physical design process. Consider the following:

Scalability. As the usage of the database system continues to increase, you must ensure that the physical design enables upward scalability of the system. When you need to consider upgrades to hardware, operating system, and the DBMS itself, the physical design must be able to adapt itself to the enhancements.

Openness and flexibility. Business conditions do not stay static but keep changing all the time. What happens when business conditions change? These changes must be reflected in your database system so that it can support business operations adequately. On the basis of the changes, the logical data model will change and evolve. How should this affect the actual implementation of the database system? The physical design must be open and flexible enough to accommodate revisions to the logical design.

Security. Safeguarding and protecting the database system from unauthorized access is accomplished through the physical design. You must ensure that the security features in the physical design provide thorough and comprehensive protection.

Ease of administration. Administrative details include database backup, recovery from failures, and ongoing space allocation. The physical design must ensure easy administration with simple and straightforward features.

Physical Design Decisions Initially and on an ongoing basis, the following design issues require serious consideration and appropriate decisions:

- Features, functions, and options supported by the target DBMS
- Features and capabilities of host computer system
- Disk storage configuration
- Usage of data—access patterns and access frequencies
- Data volumes—initial volumes and growth rates
- Hardware and software—initial setup and ongoing upgrades

Physical Design Components

When you finish with the physical design phase, what collective set of components do you expect to produce? At the end of physical design, what is the set of components that are expected to emerge? What major components make up the physical design of your database system? Here is a list of the essential components:

File organization   For each file in the physical model, the method or technique for arranging the records of the file on physical storage

Indexes   Types and list of index files to improve data access

Integrity constraints   Constraints or rules in the form of data edit rules and business rules; rules for enforcement of referential integrity on inserts and deletes

Data volumes   Sizing for each data and index file

Data usage   Analysis of expected data access paths and access frequencies

Data distribution   Strategy for providing data to users by means of centralized, partitioned, or replicated database systems

Physical Design Tasks

To understand the significance of the physical design components, we need to discuss the tasks that produce these components. As we go through the physical design tasks, you will note how these tasks take into account the target DBMS and physical storage. The features of the DBMS and the configuration of physical storage structures affect and influence the physical design to a large extent.

Consider the following list of major tasks in the physical design process:

Translate global logical data model into physical data model for the target DBMS Design files conforming to DBMS and physical storage configuration for the base relations in the global logical data model. Include integrity constraints—data edit rules, business rules, and constraints for referential integrity.

Design representation on physical storage Analyze potential transactions. Determine organization for each file. Choose secondary indexes. Establish other performance improvement techniques. Estimate storage space requirements.

Design security procedures Design user views to regulate usage of data elements by select user groups. Design data access rules.

Use of Data Dictionary

The data dictionary records the components of the design phase. In the logical design phase for a relational database system, you determine all the relations that comprise the logical data model. Now in the physical design phase, you conform your representation to the features of the selected DBMS, the physical hardware, and the systems software configuration to come up with the set of physical files. You also determine index files and other performance improvement strategies. Furthermore, you include the integrity constraints.

Types of Information The data dictionary or catalog is used to record all of the data about the contents of your database system. The following is a list of the types of information contained in the data dictionary or catalog:

Relations Relation names, number of attributes in each relation

Attributes Attribute names within each relation, data type and length for each attribute, value domain for each attribute

Indexes Index names, names of corresponding relations, index types, index attributes for each index

Constraints Data edit rules, business rules, referential integrity constraints

Users Names of authorized users, user groups, accounting information about users, passwords

Data views Names of the views, definition of each data view

Security Authorization for individual users or user groups through data views

Statistical Number of tuples in each relation, data usage statistics

Space Management Storage space allocation for database and files in terms of database records, disk extents, disk block management parameters, storage method for each relation—clustered or nonclustered

Defining Design Components As noted above, the data dictionary contains definitions for all the design components. As you know, the language used for defining these components is known as Data Definition Language (DDL). For the relational data model, SQL (Structured Query Language), which has evolved as the standard, contains a DDL component. Let us take a specific example of a logical data model and express the definitions for the data dictionary with SQL.

First, this is a partial data model consisting of just four relations. The data model represents the information requirements for the assignment of workers to building construction. Figure 12-3 shows the semantic data model and the relational data model denoted with standard notation.

Figure 12-4 lists the SQL statements used for defining the data model in the data dictionary.

Note the following statements in the figure:

- Definition for each relation with CREATE TABLE statement
- Definition of attributes with their data types, data lengths, and value domains
- Default values for selected attributes
- Primary key statements
- Foreign keys to represent the relationships

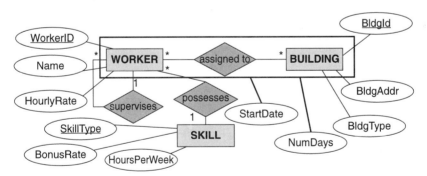

WORKER (<u>WorkerId</u>, Name, HourlyRate, SkillType, SupvId)
Foreign Keys: **SkillType** REFERENCES **SKILL**
         SupvId REFERENCES **WORKER**

Relational
Notation   BUILDING (<u>BldgId</u>, BldgAddr, BldgType)

SKILL (<u>SkillType</u>, BonusRate, HoursPerWeek)

ASSIGNMENT (<u>WorkerId</u>, <u>BldgId</u>, StartDate, NumDays)
Foreign Keys: **WorkerId** REFERENCES **WORKER**
         BldgId REFERENCES **BUILDING**

Figure 12-3 Logical model for building construction.

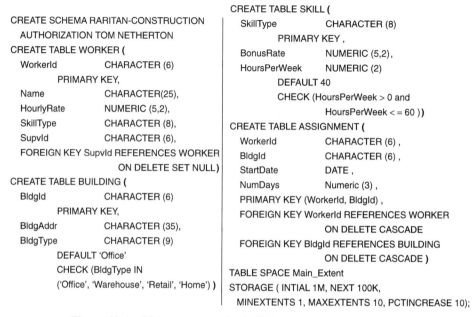

Figure 12-4   SQL statements for building construction data model

- Data edits with CHECK statements
- Referential integrity constraints
  - ON DELETE SET NULL (set foreign key value to be null when corresponding parent entity is deleted)
  - ON DELETE CASCADE (if a parent entity is deleted, cascade the delete and delete child entity as well)
- Storage statement indicating disk space extents

DATA STORAGE AND ACCESS

Physical design is the process of implementing the database on physical storage. Therefore, a close look at data storage mechanisms and the methods of data access will help you get a better understanding of physical design. What are the various levels of data storage? How are data organized as physical files that reside on physical storage? When a user requests for a particular set of data from the database system, how do different software and hardware layers execute the request? What are the implications of data storage management in the physical design process?

We will cover the various aspects of storage management and trace the handling of data requests. Data are stored as records within file blocks. We will explore the nature of file blocks and understand how block management is part of the physical design process. Records may be arranged in files in a variety of ways. Considering the major access patterns, records must be arranged with the most optimal method. This is called file organization, and we will review the major file organizations.

Storage Management

Data in a relational table may be taken as a collection of records. For example, consider a relational table containing customer data. Each row in the CUSTOMER relational table refers to one specific customer. All the columns in each row refer to the attributes of the particular customer. A table consists of rows, and each row may be considered as a record. Thus customer data contained in the CUSTOMER relational table are a collection of customer records.

Data in physical storage are kept as blocks. A block of data spans a given number of physical disk tracks. A physical file has a certain number of disk blocks allocated to it. For example, the customer file could be allocated 100 blocks. How much space is then allocated to the customer file? That depends on how big the block size is. File blocks may be specified in multiples of the block size determined in the operating system. If the operating system determines the block size to be 2K, then you may have file blocks with sizes of 2K, 4K, and so on.

From the perspective of the higher levels of data storage software, data reside in physical storage as files containing data blocks. Getting back to our customer table example, customer records will reside in the blocks of the customer file. Depending on the block size and the size of the customer records, a certain number of records may be stored in one block. All of the customer records stored in the various blocks make up the customer file. Figure 12-5 illustrates how records are stored in file blocks. The figure also shows how file blocks are related to the storage sectors of the storage medium.

DBMS and the operating system work together to manage the file blocks. They continuously keep track of which blocks are filled up and which ones have room for more records. They monitor the blocks that are being requested to be fetched and those that are already fetched and in use. Storage management encompasses all tasks to manage the movement of data in file blocks.

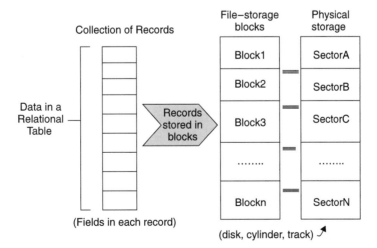

Figure 12-5 Data records in file storage blocks.

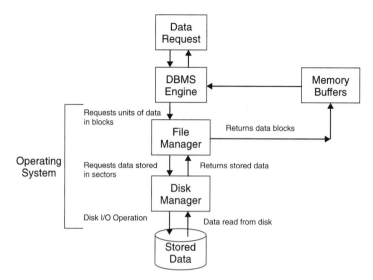

Figure 12-6 How physical data are accessed.

Access of Physical Data

Before proceeding further, you need to understand how data are accessed and fetched from physical storage. You need to know the significance of arranging data in file blocks. A block is the unit of data transfer from physical storage into main memory. Typically, a block of data is fetched from the physical storage device in one input/output (I/O) operation.

Assume that a request is made to obtain the data of customer number 12345678 from storage. You know that the data record for this customer resides in one of the blocks of the customer file. How is the requested customer data retrieved? First, the DBMS determines the particular block on which this customer record resides. Then the DBMS requests the operating system to fetch the specific block. Figure 12-6 illustrates the operation for fetching the specific block. The figure also shows how the request is processed through different software and hardware layers. Note that data are fetched into main memory as blocks and not as individual records.

Files, Blocks, and Records

A quick recapitulation of the essential points covered we have covered so far:

- Data are stored as files in physical storage.
- A file is made up of data blocks.
- A block contains a certain number of records.
- A block is the unit of transfer for reading data from physical storage or for writing to physical storage.
- Data are retrieved as blocks from physical storage into main memory.

Block Addressing Block addressing is the general technique for database records. Suppose that a file of data is allocated n blocks and that each block can hold up to m records. That means the file may contain up to a maximum of $(m \times n)$ records. Each record gets placed in a specific block. To read or write to a specific record, the DBMS addresses the block in which the record must reside. This is determined according to the way the file is organized. When a record is deleted from a block, the space occupied by the record in the block is freed up. As more and more records are deleted, the block may contain a number of fragmented empty spaces.

Figure 12-7 indicates the contents of a storage block.

Let us review the figure. Note the block header and the important information the header holds. The holes shown in the figure are empty spaces resulting from deletion of records from the block. The holes are chained together by physical addresses so that the system software can look for appropriate contiguous empty space for inserting a new record in a block.

Note the size of each hole. Let us say that a new record of size 1.3K has to be inserted in the block. The system software searches for an empty space large enough in the block to store this record. Now the first hole has enough space, and so the record gets stored there. Let us now say that another record of size 1.8K has to be inserted in the block. Neither of the two remaining holes has contiguous space large enough for this second record. Where will the system software insert the block?

The system software chooses one of the two predefined options:

1. Because there is no single hole large enough, place the entire new record in the overflow block. Therefore, when the need to retrieve the record arises, the system software will first look for it in the original block and then proceed to the overflow block.

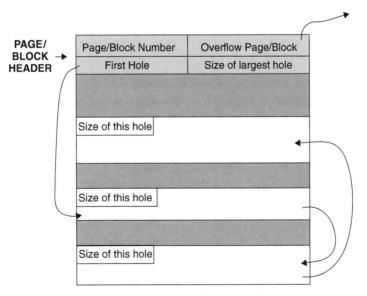

Figure 12-7   Contents of a storage block.

2. Place part of the new record in the original block and the rest of the record in the overflow block. The two parts of the records are chained together by physical addresses.

You must already have realized the imposition of system overhead while writing or reading when either the whole record or part of the record is placed in the overflow block. Block chaining and record chaining come with a price. Therefore, block management becomes significant.

Block Size   As you know, the file block is the unit of data transfer between disk storage and main memory. The goal is to be able to transfer large volumes of data from disk storage in a few I/O operations. How can you accomplish this? It would seem that if you make the block size large, you fit more records in a block and therefore move a greater number of records in fewer I/O operations. Let us consider the option of making the block size large.

First, make sure your operating system does not fix the block size. If the operating system supports a certain fixed block size and does not allow larger file blocks, then this option of using large block sizes is not open to you. Usually, file block sizes are allowed to be defined in multiples of the operating system block size. If this is the case in your environment, take advantage of this option.

Each block contains a header area and a data area. The data area represents the effective utilization of the block. The header has control information, and the size of the header does not change even if the data area becomes larger. For a small block, the header utilizes a larger percentage of the total block size. As a percentage of the total block size, the header utilizes a small percentage of a large block.

What are the effects of having large blocks?

- Decrease in the number of I/O operations
- Less space utilized by block headers as percentage of total block size
- Too many unnecessary records retrieved in the full block even when only a few records are requested for

You cannot arbitrarily keep on increasing the block size assuming that every increase results in greater efficiency. If the data requests in your environment typically require just a few records for each request, then very large block sizes result in wasteful data retrievals into memory buffers. What will work is not the largest block size, only the optimal block size. Determine the optimal block size for each file on the basis of the record sizes and the data access patterns.

Block Usage Parameters   Consider the storage and removal of records in a block. As transactions happen in the database environment, new records are added to a block, using up empty space in the block; records get deleted from a block, freeing up space in the block; records change their lengths when they are updated, resulting in either using up more space in the block or freeing up some space in the block. DBMSs provide two methods for optimizing block usage. In the various commercial DBMSs, these block usage parameters may go by different names. Nevertheless, the purpose and function of each block usage parameter are the same. Let us examine these parameters and understand how they work.

Block Percent Free   This parameter sets the limits on how much space is reserved in each block for expansion of records during updates. When a record has variable length fields, it is likely to expand when transactions update such fields. Also, a record is likely to expand when null values of attributes are replaced with full data values.

Let us take a specific example of this block usage parameter: PCTFREE 20

This means that 20% of each block is left empty for the records in the block to expand into when updates to the records take place. Assume a file with records having many variable length fields subject to many frequent updates. Then you should allocate enough empty space in each block for updated records to occupy. The Block Percent Free parameter, in such a case, must be set at a high level to allow a larger percentage of each block to be left empty. However, if you set the parameter at too high a level, large chunks of blocks may be reserved unnecessarily and wasted.

Block Percent Used   Block management by the DBMS involves keeping track of blocks ready and available for insertion of new records. DBMS can do this efficiently only if it marks a block as available for new records only when the block is fairly empty. This reduces the overhead for managing too many "free" blocks. The Block Percent Used parameter sets an indicator when a block is ready and available for new records.

Take a particular example of this block usage parameter: PCTUSED 40

What is the meaning of this parameter? It is like a watermark below which the usage of a block must dip before new records are allowed to be inserted in the block. Only when space used in a block falls below 40%, can new records be accepted in the block. Obviously, deletion of records keeps changing the actual percentage of the block being used at a given time. If, at a given time, the percentage of the block used is 41%, leaving 59% free, new records are still not allowed to be inserted into the block. If a record deletion causes the percent block used to go down to 39%, new records are allowed to be inserted into the block. If a file is fairly volatile, with many deletions and insertions of records, then set this parameter as low as possible.

File Organization

Go back to Figure 12-5 showing how a physical file contains data records. A file is an arrangement of records, and these records are spread over the storage blocks allocated to that file. Data records reside in the database as records arranged in files. Before proceeding further about how records may be arranged in a file, let us review the major operations on records stored in a database.

Here are the main types of operations:

Insert. Add a record to the database. Identify the file and the block within the file, and insert a record in the block.

Delete. Identify the file and the block where the record resides. Delete the record from the block and free up the space.

Equality selection. Fetch only the records where the value of a specific attribute equals a given value.

Range selection. Fetch only those records where the value of a specific attribute is within a given range of values.

Scan. Full file scan. Fetch all the records in a file.

How can you arrange the records in a file? Whether you keep the records in a certain sequence of values of a specific attribute or just throw the records into the file in a random fashion, the arrangement of records in a file affects the types of data operations listed above. The arrangement of records in a file determines how each record gets stored in storage blocks. Therefore, how you arrange the records in a file becomes important and influences efficiency of data access. The database administrator must choose the right arrangement of records in each file.

DBMSs support several methods for arranging records in a file. File organization refers to the way records are arranged in a file. There are three basic file organizations: heap, sequential, and hash. Each file organization affects the database operations in a certain way. Let us examine each of the basic organizations and note the circumstances for which each organization is best suited.

Heap or Pile Organization

- Records placed in the order of creation
- No ordering of records
- Usually single file for each relational table
- New record inserted on last block of file
- Inserting records very efficient
- Searching very inefficient—linear search from beginning to end of file
- Deleting leaves wasted space in the block
- Useful for collecting and storing data for later use
- Good for database backup and transportation of data
- Best if most common operation is full file scan

Sequential Organization

- Records sorted on some search key field—only one search key field per file
- Records placed in sequence or chained together in the order of data values in search key field
- Allows records to be read in search key order
- Fast retrieval in search key order
- Inserting consecutive records takes place in the same block or overflow blocks
- Deletion leaves wasted space in the block

- Searching for random records inefficient
- Best if most common operation is range selection

Hash or Direct Organization

- A hash function computes addresses based on values in specified field
- Hash function specifies the block where a record must be placed
- Search for record in a block done in memory buffer
- Very fast retrieval for random data
- Inserting specific record fast and direct
- Deletion leaves wasted space in the block
- Not good for sequential retrieval
- Best if most common operation is equality selection
- Hashing can cause collisions when many records hash to the same block
- Methods for resolution of collisions (linear probing or multiple hashing)

Figure 12-8 illustrates the problem of collisions in direct file organization. In this figure, you will note that a very simple hashing function is used—the last two digits of the employee social security number are used to indicate the storage address for the employee record. Employee 102-49-2121 comes on board, and his record gets stored in Block 21. Then employee 352-11-3421 joins the company and the hash algorithm calculates the storage address as 21, but Block 21 is already filled

Figure 12-8   Direct file organization: resolution of collisions.

up. Therefore, DBMS does linear probing and sequentially searches for the next available empty block. That happens to be Block 36, and the employee record for 352-11-3421 is stored there. In the same way, when employee 246-15-4721 joins the company, her record gets stored in the next available empty block, namely, Block 63. Instead of linear probing, another method for resolving collisions is to find the appropriate address by means of applying multiple hash functions. The data records that hash to the same storage address are known as synonyms in direct file organization.

Now imagine that you want to retrieve the record for employee 246-15-4721. You apply the hash function and determine that the record must be found at address 21. However, the record is not in that block; the block contains record for employee 352-11-3421. So how does the DBMS find the record for 246-15-4721? Does it have to search through all blocks sequentially? That would be very inefficient. The DBMS maintains a synonym chain to link all the records that hash to the same block address. This is a list of pointers linking the blocks in which the synonyms are stored. Therefore, when record for 246-15-4721 is not found at address 21, the DBMS follows the synonym chain and locates the record at address 63.

Linking of Related Data Elements

In the previous section, we mentioned pointers and linking of storage units. The storage blocks where synonyms are stored need to be linked together by physical addresses. Frequently in physical implementation of databases, you will come across the need to link records by means of physical addresses or pointers. You will observe the need for physical pointers when we discuss indexes a little later in this chapter. Therefore, let us briefly discuss how related data elements are linked together in physical storage.

You link two records by placing the physical address of one record as part of the other record itself. These addresses placed in records to connect other records are known as pointers. The list of records linked together forms a linked list. You may link records within the same file through intrafile pointers; similarly, you may link records in more than one file through interfile pointers.

Figure 12-9 shows a file in which the records are connected to form a linked list.

In the example illustrated in the figure, the file consists of 10 records apparently stored in a random sequence. How can you arrange the records in the sequence of serial numbers without moving the records? You can accomplish this by forming a linked list of the records connecting the records in serial number sequence. Note that the address in each record points to the next record in serial number sequence. Also, observe the arrows pointing to the consecutive records in the linked list. The last record in the sequence does not have to point anywhere and therefore contains a *null* address in the pointer field.

What types of addresses are the addresses shown in the above figure? Are these the actual addresses of the physical storage locations? The addresses may be of one of two types.

Absolute addresses. Each record in the linked list contains the actual physical address to point to the next record.

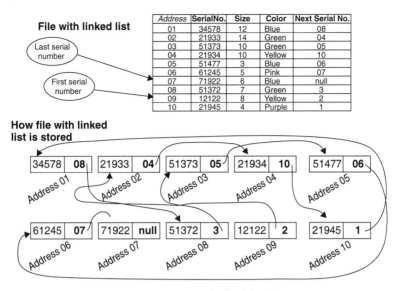

Figure 12-9   File with a linked list.

- Absolute addresses are device-dependent. If you need to reorganize the file or move the file to a different storage medium, you have to change all the addresses in the linked list. This could be a major disadvantage.
- On the other hand, absolute addresses provide a fast method for retrieving records in the sequence of the linked list. You fetch each record, get the address of the next record, and use that address directly to get the next record, and so on.

Relative addresses.   Each record in the linked list contains a relative address, not the actual physical address, to point to the next record. The relative address of a storage location is a number indicating the relative offset of the location from the beginning of the storage device.

- Relative addresses are device-independent. If you need to reorganize the file or move the file to a different storage medium, you do not have to change the addresses in the linked list.
- On the other hand, data storage and retrieval are slower with relative addresses. Every time you want to store or retrieve a record, you have to calculate the actual physical address from the relative address. You have to contend with address-resolution overhead.

RAID Technology Basics

Currently, in most organizations, disk storage devices form the primary media for databases. Because storage management is part of the physical design considerations, we need to discuss the nature of disk storage devices. Although disk storage devices have improved tremendously over the past decade, still they have two inherent problems. First, despite major advances, disk storage is still slow for data movement compared to the other hardware components such as main memory and the processor. Second, disk storage devices have more mechanical parts compared to the other components. Therefore, disk storage devices are more prone to failures.

RAID (redundant array of inexpensive disks) technology addresses these two problems as follows:

- Improve performance through data striping. Stripe or spread data across several disks so that storage or retrieval of required data may be accomplished by parallel reads across many disks. When data is stored on a single disk unit, you may need sequential reads, each sequential read waiting for the previous one to finish.
- Improve reliability by storing redundant data to be used only for reconstructing data on failed units.

We will now examine how RAID technology provides these improvements. In today's database environment, the use of RAID technology has become essential.

Performance Improvement   Data striping enables an array of disks to be abstracted and viewed as one large logical disk. While striping data across disks, you take a specific unit of data and store it on the first disk in the array, then take the next unit of data and store it on the next disk in the array, and so on. These units of data are called striping units. A striping unit may be one full disk block, or it may even be one single bit. The striping units are spread across the array of disks in a round-robin fashion. Let us say that the data you want to stripe across 6 disks in an array consists of 24 striping units. These 24 units of data are striped across the disks beginning from the first disk, going to the last disk, and then wrapping around. Figure 12-10 illustrates the storage of the 24 striping units on the 6 disks.

Now assume that you want to retrieve the first five striping units in a certain query to the database. These units will be read in parallel from all the first five disks in just the time taken to read one unit of data. Striping units of data across the disk array results in tremendous reduction in data access times.

Reliability Improvement   The greater number of disks in an array, the better the access performance is likely to be. This is because you can retrieve from more disks in parallel. However, having more disks also increases the risk of failure. In RAID technology, redundant parity data written on check disks enable recovery from disk failures. Therefore, in the RAID system, over and above the data disks, you need additional check disks to store parity data. Let us see how the parity data stored in the check disks are used for recovery from disk failures.

How Parity Works   Assume that a disk array consists of eight disks. Now, consider the first data bit on each of these eight disks. Review the 1s and 0s written as the first bit on each disk. Let us say that five of these first bits are 1s as follows:

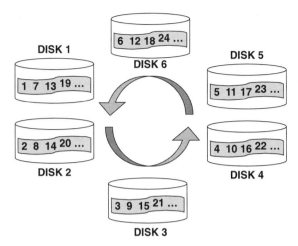

Figure 12-10   Striping units of data across a disk array.

1   0   1   1   0   1   0   1

The first parity bit written on the check disk depends on whether the total number of 1s written as the first bit on the data disks is odd or even. In our case, this number is 5. Because the number 5 is odd, the first parity bit is written as 1. If the number were even, the first parity bit would be written as 0.

When a disk failure occurs, you must be able to recover from the failure. You must be able to recreate the contents of the failed disk. Let us assume that the fourth disk failed. After the failure, the recovery mechanism counts the number of 1s in the first bit positions of all the disks other than the failed disk. This number of 1s is 4—an even number. Now examine the first parity bit on the check disk. It is 1. Therefore, because of the way parity bits are written and because the number of 1s in the first bit position of the remaining disk is even, the first bit of the failed disk must have been 1. In this manner, by looking at the data in the remaining disks and reviewing the parity data, the data in the failed disk may be completely recovered. RAID systems may be implemented at different levels. The number of check disks needed to write parity data depends on the RAID level.

RAID Levels   Let us discuss the implementation at different RAID levels for data on four data disks. The disk array will then consist of these four data disks and a certain number of check disks for parity data. As far as storage of data is concerned, the check disks do not contribute to space utilization for data storage; the check disks contain redundant data.

Level 0—Nonredundant

- Just data striping
- Best write performance
- Reliability still a problem
- RAID system consists of 4 data disks and no check disks
- Effective space utilization 100%

Level 1—Mirrored

- Keeps 2 identical copies of data
- Write block on one disk followed by write block on second disk
- Does not stripe data across disks
- Most expensive
- No improvement in reading data
- RAID system consists of 4 data disks and 4 check disks
- Effective space utilization 50%

Level 0 + 1—Striped and Mirrored

- Combines features of Levels 0 and 1
- RAID system consists of 4 data disks and 4 check disks
- Effective space utilization 50%

Level 2—Error-Correcting Codes

- Single-bit striping
- Even small unit of read requires reading all 4 disks
- Good for large workloads, not for small
- RAID system consists of 4 data disks and 3 check disks
- Effective space utilization 57%

Level 3—Bit-Interleaved Parity

- Only 1 check disk needed
- Need to identify failed disk through disk controller
- Performance similar to Level 2
- Most expensive
- No improvement in reading data
- RAID system consists of 4 data disks and 1 check disk
- Effective space utilization 80%

Level 4—Block-Interleaved Parity

- Block as striping unit
- Check disk written for each data write
- RAID system consists of 4 data disks and 1 check disk
- Effective space utilization 80%

Level 5—Block-Interleaved Distributed Parity

- Improves on Level 4
- Parity blocks distributed uniformly over all disks

- Best overall performance
- RAID system consists of 5 disks of data and parity
- Effective space utilization 80%

INDEXING TECHNIQUES

Take the example of an employee file consisting of data records where each data record refers to one employee. If this is a file for a large organization, the employee file may contain thousands of records stored on a huge number of storage blocks. Depending on the file organization, to search for the record of a particular employee you may have to search through several blocks. You have to search through a large file with perhaps huge records. How can you make your search more efficient?

Imagine another file that contains index records with just two fields—one having the key values of the employee records and the other storing addresses of the data records. Each index record points to the corresponding data record. So when you want to search for an employee record with a particular key value, you do not go directly to the employee file to search for the record. First, you go to the other smaller file, search for the record with the desired key value, find the address of the record in the employee file, and then fetch the record from the employee file. This is the principle of indexing. The smaller file containing the key values and data addresses is the index file.

Figure 12-11 illustrates the principle of indexing. Note the data file and the index file.

The figure shows two types of indexes.

Dense Index. There is an index record for each data record.

Sparse Index. There is an index record for each block, not for each data record.

In Figure 12-11, the index file contains values of the primary key in the employee file. An index file may be created based on any attribute in the data file. Indexes created on the primary key are known as primary indexes. Indexes created on any other field are called secondary indexes. Consider a few of the fields in the employee record: EmployeeNo, JobCode, DeptNo, SkillType.

To speed up data access based on EmployeeNo, a primary index created on the primary key field of EmployeeNo may be used. Now suppose you have data access requests based on SkillType. If you want to retrieve all employees whose SkillType is "Programming," you have to retrieve each employee record and gather all the records with this SkillType. Instead of this method, if you have an index file created based on SkillType, then you can speed up your data access.

Figure 12-12 indicates the usage of primary and secondary indexes for data access to the employee file. Note how, in the case of the primary index, one index value points to one target data record. In secondary index files, one index value may point to several target data records. For example, there could be several employees with the SkillType "Programming."

DENSE INDEX					DATA FILE	
INDEX FILE						
						Page/Block
EA10	1				Employee record EA10	
EH06	1				Employee record EH06	1
EH15	1				Employee record EH15	
EH38	2				Employee record EH38	
EM22	2				Employee record EM22	2
EM42	2				Employee record EM42	
EQ33	3				Employee record EQ33	
ER45	3				Employee record EQ45	3
ES33	3				Employee record ES33	

SPARSE INDEX					DATA FILE	
INDEX FILE						
						Page/Block
					Employee record EA10	
					Employee record EH06	1
EH15	1				Employee record EH15	
EM42	2				Employee record EH38	
ES33	3				Employee record EM22	2
					Employee record EM42	
					Employee record EQ33	
					Employee record EQ45	3
					Employee record ES33	

Figure 12-11 Data and index files.

Primary Index
One Index Value ==> One Target Record Address
Secondary Index
One Index Value ==> Addresses of Multiple Target Records

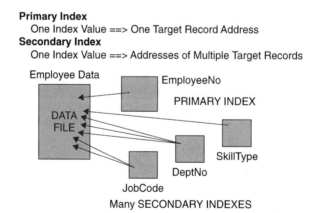

Figure 12-12 Primary and secondary indexes for employee file.

Primary Indexes

For primary indexes, one index record points to one data record. That means there will be as many index records as there are data records. How can you best arrange the index records in the index file to optimize data access? First, consider searching for a specific data record under three different options—directly from the data

Search for
data with key
value 60

Data File

Address	Key	Data
01	48	....
06	34	....
11	21	....
12	8	....
15	3	....
23	81	....
44	60	....

Random Index

Key	Address
48	01
34	06
21	11
8	12
3	15
81	23
60	44

Sorted Index

Key	Address
3	15
8	12
21	11
34	6
48	1
60	44
81	23

Figure 12-13   Primary index search.

file, with an index file with index records arranged in a random manner, or with an index file with index records arranged in the order of the primary key values. Figure 12-13 shows these three options with key values and addresses.

Suppose your intention is to search for a data record with key value 60. It takes seven I/O operations to search the data file directly. When you arrange the index records randomly in the index file, it takes the same number of I/O operations. However, when you arrange the index records sequentially in the index file in the order of the key values, the I/O performance is slightly better, at six I/O operations.

How can we improve the performance even more? Suppose you start your search on the index file at the middle of the index file, that is, at the record with index value 34. Compare the key value of 60 you are searching for with the value 34 at the middle of the index file. Because the value 60 is greater than 34, then key value 60 must be in the second half of the index file. Then go to the middle of the second half and get the index record. In our example, this index record happens to be the one with value 60 and, therefore, our search is over with just two I/O operations.

Step back and observe how we are able to improve the performance in this type of search. We divide the index entries in a binary fashion and compare the search value with the index value at the middle of the file. Immediately we are able to determine in which half of the file the key value lies. We then proceed to that half and compare the key value with the index at the middle of the selected half. This process of binary divisions continues and speeds up the search process. This technique, known as binary search, cuts the number of searches to find the desired index record.

Binary Search

The binary search method utilizes a binary search tree. The index entries are logically arranged in the form of an inverted tree, where the root is at the top. The root

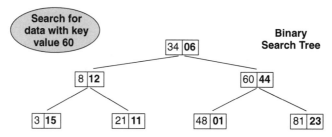

Figure 12-14 Binary search tree.

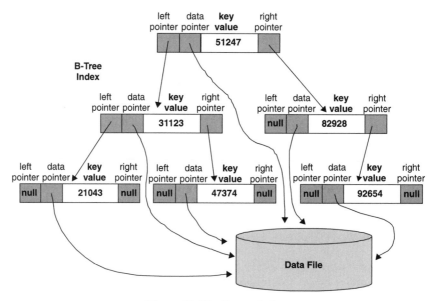

Figure 12-15 B-tree index.

represents the index entry at the middle of the index file. Figure 12-14 presents a binary search tree for the example considered here.

Primary indexes adopt binary search techniques by arranging the index records as nodes in a binary search tree. The lines pointing outward from each node represent pointers to the other nodes on either side. The search for an index record always begins at the root node and then proceeds to the right or the left by following the appropriate pointers.

B-Tree Index

Figure 12-15 shows the contents of each node in a B-tree index and illustrates how the pointers trace the search for a particular record.

Each node contains two pointers for pointing to the index records on the left and right sides. A node also contains a pointer to where the data for the particular key value resides on data storage. These pointers are actually storage addresses. For

Option1:

JobCode	Address
101	19
101	67
101	89
111	33
111	58
211	26
211	45
211	98
321	37
321	76
445	53
445	54

Option 2:

JobCode	Address1	Address2	Address3
101	19	67	89
111	58	33	
211	26	98	45
321	76	37	
445	53	54	

Option3:

JobCode	Address of first
101	19
111	58
211	26
321	76
445	53

Figure 12-16 Secondary indexes.

example, trace the search for the data record with key value 92654. Start the search at the root node containing index value 51247. The search key value 92654 is greater than 51247. Therefore, follow the right pointer from the root and go to the index record with key value 82928. The search value 92654 is greater than 82938, so follow the right pointer from this index record and go to the index record with key value 92654. This is the index record you are looking for. Pick up the data pointer from this index record and go to the data record.

B-tree indexes come with a few important variations. Nevertheless, the indexing principle is the same. Most DBMSs automatically create B-tree indexes for primary keys. The DBA need not explicitly create primary indexes.

Secondary Indexes

Secondary indexes are built on any fields other than the primary key. A secondary index may contain more than one field. Figure 12-16 indicates three options for creating index file records. The figure presents indexes built on the field JobCode in the employee file.

Option 1: One index entry in secondary index file for each value-address pair. The index file contains as many records as the data file. Retrieval of index value 101 results in retrieval of 3 index records and then retrieval of corresponding 3 data records.

Option 2: One index entry in secondary index file for each value with a list of address entries. The index file contains a lower number of records than the data file. Retrieval of index value 101 results in retrieval of just 1 index record and then retrieval of corresponding 3 data records. If there are too many distinct data records for the same index value, this option will not work.

Option 3: One index entry in secondary index file for the first value-address pair, with a pointer in the data record to the next target data record, and so on.

The index file contains a lower number of records than the data file—only 1 index record for each index value. Retrieval of index value 101 results in retrieval of just 1 index record, retrieval of the first corresponding data record, and then retrieval of the other 2 data records by following the pointers in the data records.

Bitmapped Indexing

Bitmapped indexes are ideally suitable for low-selectivity fields. A field with low selectivity is one that consists of a small number of distinct values. If there are only six different job codes for employee data, then JobCode is a low-selectivity field. On the other hand, Zip is not a low-selectivity field; it can have many distinct values.

A bitmap is an ordered series of bits, one for each distinct value of the indexed column. Let us review a sales file containing data about sales of appliances. Assume that the field for Color has three distinct values, namely, white, almond, and black. Construct a bitmap with these three distinct values. Each entry in the bitmap contains three bits. Let us say, the first bit refers to the value white, the second to almond, and the third bit to black. If a product is white in color, the bitmap entry for that product consists of three bits where the first bit is set to 1, the second bit is set to 0, and the third bit is set to 0. If a product is almond in color, the bitmap entry for that product consists of three bits where the first bit is set to 0, the second bit is set to 1, and the third bit is set to 0. You get the picture. Now, please study the bitmapped index example shown in Figure 12-17.

The figure presents an extract of the sales file and bitmapped indexes for the three different fields. Note how each entry in an index contains the ordered bits to represent the distinct values in the field. An entry is created for each record in the sale file. Each entry carries the address of the record.

How do the bitmapped indexes work to retrieve the requested rows? Consider the following data retrieval from the sales file:

> Select the records from sales file
>   Where Product is "Washer" and
>   Color is "Almond" and
>   Division is "East" or "South"

Figure 12-18 illustrates how Boolean logic is applied to find the result set based on the bitmapped indexes shown in Figure 12-17.

As you observe, bitmapped indexes support data retrievals using low-selectivity fields. The strength of this technique rests on its effectiveness when you retrieve data based on values in low-selectivity fields. Bitmapped indexes take significantly less space than B-tree indexes for low-selectivity fields.

On the other hand, if new values are introduced for the indexed fields, bitmapped indexes have to be reconstructed. Another disadvantage relates to the necessity to access the data files all the time after the bitmapped indexes are accessed. B-tree indexes do not require data file access if the requested information is already contained in the index file.

Extract of Sales Data

Address or Rowid	Date	Product	Color	Region	Sale ($)
00001BFE.0012.0111	15-Nov-00	Dishwasher	White	East	300
00001BFE.0013.0114	15-Nov-00	Dryer	Almond	West	450
00001BFF.0012.0115	16-Nov-00	Dishwasher	Almond	West	350
00001BFF.0012.0138	16-Nov-00	Washer	Black	North	550
00001BFF.0012.0145	17-Nov-00	Washer	White	South	500
00001BFF.0012.0157	17-Nov-00	Dryer	White	East	400
00001BFF.0014.0165	17-Nov-00	Washer	Almond	South	575

Bitmapped Index for Product Column
Ordered bits: Washer, Dryer, Dishwasher

Address or Rowid	Bitmap
00001BFE.0012.0111	001
00001BFE.0013.0114	010
00001BFF.0012.0115	001
00001BFF.0012.0138	100
00001BFF.0012.0145	100
00001BFF.0012.0157	010
00001BFF.0014.0165	100

Bitmapped Index for Color Column
Ordered bits: White, Almond, Black

Address or Rowid	Bitmap
00001BFE.0012.0111	100
00001BFE.0013.0114	010
00001BFF.0012.0115	010
00001BFF.0012.0138	001
00001BFF.0012.0145	100
00001BFF.0012.0157	100
00001BFF.0014.0165	010

Bitmapped Index for Region Column
Ordered bits: East, West, North, South

Address or Rowid	Bitmap
00001BFE.0012.0111	1000
00001BFE.0013.0114	0100
00001BFF.0012.0115	0100
00001BFF.0012.0138	0010
00001BFF.0012.0145	0001
00001BFF.0012.0157	1000
00001BFF.0014.0165	0001

Figure 12-17   Bitmapped indexes.

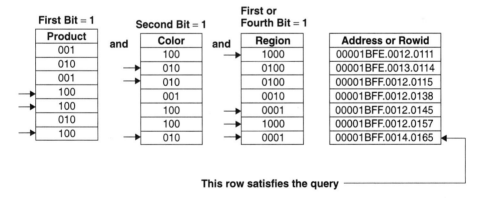

Figure 12-18   Data retrieval with bitmapped indexes.

OTHER PERFORMANCE CONSIDERATIONS

Indexing is by far the widely used and most effective method for performance improvement in a database system. In addition to the primary indexes automatically created by the DBMS, the database administrator can create secondary indexes based on other fields in the various files. Both primary indexes and secondary indexes serve well in improving performance.

In addition to indexing, a few other options are available to enhance data access performance and to improve storage management. We will now explore some of these other improvement techniques. Some of these techniques may readily apply to your particular database system. A few others may have universal applicability. Study the techniques as we discuss them and try to determine their applicability to your environment.

Clustering

Consider two relational tables common in most database environments—the ORDER table and the ORDER DETAIL table. Typically, the details of each order are retrieved along with order data. Most of the typical data access to order information requires retrieval of an order row from the ORDER table together with rows from the ORDER DETAIL table for that order. Let us see if we can improve data access performance in such situations when rows from two tables are usually retrieved together in one transaction. How can we do this?

Instead of placing the rows from the ORDER table and the rows from the ORDER DETAIL table in two separate files, what if we place the rows from both tables as records in one file? Furthermore, what if we interleave the order detail records with the corresponding order records in this single file? Then, as the records in the file are allocated to storage, it is most likely that an order and its details will reside on one block. What is the big advantage of this arrangement? In one I/O operation, order and corresponding order detail records can be retrieved. This principle of interleaving related records from two tables in one file is called clustering. Figure 12-19 illustrates clustering of ORDER and ORDER DETAIL records.

If your DBMS supports data clustering, you can utilize this significant feature to improve performance. To create a cluster, you need to identify the tables whose rows must be clustered and the key columns that link those tables. The DBMS will then store and retrieve related records from the same cluster.

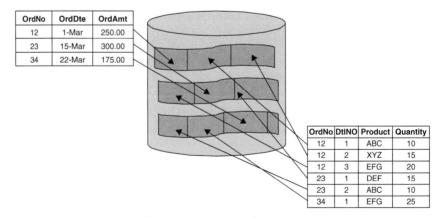

Figure 12-19 Data clustering.

Denormalization

You know clearly the significance of normalizing the tables in a relational data model. Normalization eliminates data anomalies, eliminates data redundancies, supports simpler logic, makes the design application-independent, and encourages data sharing. But, in practice, we come across cases in which strict normalization sometimes has an adverse effect on data access performance.

Consider the following cases and note how denormalization can improve data access performance.

PRODUCT-LINE (LineNo, ProductLineDesc, ...)

PRODUCT (ProductId, ProductDesc, UnitCost, ..., LineNo)

Foreign Key: LineNo REFERENCES PRODUCT-LINE

> *Very common data access:* product data along with ProductLineDesc
>
> *Normal method of retrieval:* data from both tables by joining them
>
> *Improved method:* Denormalize PRODUCT table by adding Product LineDesc so that all the required data may be obtained from only the PRODUCT table

STUDENT (StudentNo, StudentName, ...)

CLASS (ClassId, ClassDesc, ...)

ENROLLMENT (StudentNo, ClassId, ...)

Foreign Key: StudentNo REFERENCES STUDENT

ClassId REFERENCES CLASS

> *Very common data access:* enrollment with student name and class description
>
> *Normal method of retrieval:* data from both the two primary tables through joins
>
> *Improved method:* Denormalize ENROLLMENT table by adding Student-Name and ClassDesc so that all the required data may be obtained from only the ENROLLMENT table

Although there are no specific rules on when to denormalize, you must exercise sufficient caution before attempting to denormalize. Here are some general guidelines.

Many-to-many relationships. Add nonkey attributes whenever joining of the three tables to get data from the two primary tables is too frequent in your environment.

One-to-one relationships. Even when one table has a lower number of rows, if matching rows in these tables occur most of the time, consider combining the two tables into one.

One-to-many relationships. Add only the most needed attribute from the table on the "one" side to the table on the "many" side.

Fragmentation

When some tables in your database system are huge, with many attributes and a large number of rows, it is not easy to manage and administer their storage requirements. Huge tables need special considerations for improving data access. You can manage a huge table if you partition it in the best possible manner.

In some cases, part of the data in a huge table may be used less frequently than the rest of the data. Then you may want to partition the more frequently used data and store it on fast storage. In other cases, some parts of a huge table may be used primarily by one user group and the rest used by other user groups. In such cases, you may partition the table by user groups.

In the relational data model, a table may be partitioned and stored in multiple files in the following ways.

Horizontal Partitioning   Split the table into groups of rows. This type of partitioning is appropriate for separating the data for user groups in geographically dispersed areas. Horizontal partitioning is also applicable for separating active data from old data.

Vertical Partitioning   Split the table into groups of columns. This type of partitioning is appropriate if some columns are used more frequently than others. Vertical partitioning is also applicable if certain sets of columns are used by different user groups.

Figure 12-20 indicates how a CUSTOMER table may be partitioned horizontally or vertically.

Memory Buffer Management

The buffer manager is the software component responsible for bringing blocks of data from disk to main memory as and when they are needed. Main memory is partitioned into collections of blocks called buffer pools. Buffer pool slots hold slots for blocks to be transferred between disk and main memory. The buffer pool slots must be managed efficiently to influence data access performance. Buffer pool slots must be made available by clearing the data that are no longer required for processing. The buffer manager must be able to keep track of buffer usage properly so as to be able move the necessary volumes of data between disk and main memory efficiently.

Proper buffer management improves data access performance. You may set the DBMS parameters to accomplish this objective. You may improve performance in the following ways:

- Allocating the right number of memory buffers so that only the needed data are kept in the buffers and the needed data are retained in the buffers for the right length of time.
- Determining the right buffer sizes so that the buffers are of optimum sizes—large enough to accommodate the needed data and small enough not to waste buffer space.

CUSTOMER data file

CustomerNo	Name	Address	Phone	CreditCde	Balance
2235	Rolland				
5598	Williams				
6699	Jones				
7755	Hathaway				
9655	Cervino				
0089	Cuccia				
0109	Harreld				
0412	McKeown				

Horizontal Partitioning

CustomerNo	Name	Address	Phone	CreditCde	Balance
2235	Rolland				
5598	Williams				
6699	Jones				
7755	Hathaway				
9655	Cervino				

CustomerNo	Name	Address	Phone	CreditCde	Balance
0089	Cuccia				
0109	Harreld				
0412	McKeown				

Vertical Partitioning

CustomerNo	Name	Address	Phone
2235	Rolland		
5598	Williams		
6699	Jones		
7755	Hathaway		
9655	Cervino		
0089	Cuccia		
0109	Harreld		
0412	McKeown		

CustomerNo	CreditCde	Balance
2235		
5598		
6699		
7755		
9655		
0089		
0109		
0412		

Figure 12-20   Horizontal and vertical partitioning.

- Taking advantage of special features of the DBMS such as prefetching of blocks that are likely to be needed for the next processing.

Preconstructed Joins

Consider three related tables for a product distributing business: CUSTOMER, PRODUCT, and SALE. The CUSTOMER table contains data about each customer. The PRODUCT table contains data about each product. The SALE table contains data such as date of sale, product sold, manufacturer of product, customer number, sale representative identification, and so on.

Assume that a large number of data retrieval requests require data from all three of these tables. How will these data retrieval requests be satisfied? For every such request, the three tables must be joined and then the requested data have to be retrieved. In such situations, joining these tables for every request causes big overhead and slows the data retrievals. Is there an alternative to these numerous joins?

Suppose you do the joins before hand and preconstruct another table as a directory containing join-attribute values with pointers to the CUSTOMER and PRODUCT table rows. If you do that, then all the corresponding data requests can

CUSTOMER
relation

Storage Address	CustNo	CustName
10	123	Customer1
11	234	Customer2
12	345	Customer3
13	456	Customer4
14	567	Customer5

PRODUCT
relation

Storage Address	ProdNo	ProdDesc
20	1	Prod1
21	2	Prod2
22	3	Prod3
23	4	Prod4
24	5	Prod5

SALE
relation

Storage Address	SaleDte	CustNo	ProdNo	Units
30	2/1/2003	345	1	25
31	2/15/2003	234	3	35
32	2/15/2003	567	3	40
33	2/22/2002	123	5	45
34	2/24/2002	123	4	60

Directory with
join-attribute
values

CustNo Value	Addr to CUSTOMER	Addr to PRODIUCT
123	10	24
123	10	23
234	11	22
345	12	20
567	14	22

Figure 12-21 Preconstructed join directory table.

be made against this new table first and then followed by retrievals from the base tables. Figure 12-21 illustrates this method of performance improvement.

You should use this method for large primary tables where joins on the fly are expensive in terms of performance overhead. However, if you create too many preconstructed join tables, you may be propagating too much data redundancy. Every time you add new rows to the participating tables, you have to insert new rows in the directory table. This additional processing may offset any advantage gained with the preconstructed join table.

CHAPTER SUMMARY

- Physical design is the final stage in the design process.
- Physical design implements the database on physical storage.
- When you make the transition from logical design to physical design, you map the components of one to those of the other.
- Database performance and data management form the primary focus of physical design.
- Physical design components: file organization, indexes, integrity constraints, data volumes, data usage, and data distribution.
- Physical design major tasks: translate global logical model into physical model, design representation on physical storage, and design security procedures.
- Data dictionary or catalog records the components of the design phase.
- Data is stored as files in physical storage; a file consists of data blocks; a block contains records; typically, a record is a row of a relational table.

- A block is the unit of transfer of data between physical storage and the main memory of the computer system; block addressing is the general technique for finding records.
- Three major file organizations: heap, sequential, and hash.
- RAID technology improves data retrieval performance and reliability of disk storage.
- Indexing with primary and secondary indexes forms the primary method for performance improvement of database systems.
- Other performance considerations include data clustering, denormalization, data fragmentation, memory buffer management, and preconstructed joins.

REVIEW QUESTIONS

1. List the primary goals of the physical design process. Which ones are the most important?
2. Describe very briefly the physical design components.
3. What are the major physical design tasks?
4. How is the data dictionary used to record the contents of the database system? What are the types of information stored in the data dictionary?
5. Describe how rows of a relational table are stored in physical storage.
6. What is your understanding of file organization? What are the major types of file organizations?
7. How does RAID technology improve reliability of disk storage?
8. What is a B-tree index? Explain with a simple example.
9. What is data clustering? How does it improve data access performance?
10. Distinguish between horizontal and vertical partitioning. State the conditions under which each option is useful.

EXERCISES

1. Indicate whether true or false:
   A. Physical design may ignore the features of the target DBMS.
   B. Proper physical design ensures improved database performance.
   C. File organization refers to how blocks are allocated to files.
   D. A row in a relational table is the unit of data transfer from physical storage.
   E. Sequential file organization is best if the most common operation is range selection.
   F. Data striping in RAID technology improves disk reliability.
   G. You can build a secondary index only on certain fields in the file.
   H. Denormalization increases data redundancy but improves data access performance.
   I. Most DBMSs automatically create primary indexes.

     J. Absolute addresses in linked lists provide faster data retrieval than relative addresses.

2. You are the database administrator in the database project for a department store. Name any six relational tables that will be part of the logical design. Describe how you will allocate storage for these tables and how you will assign the data to physical files.

3. Explain how you can improve data access performance by adjusting block sizes and block usage parameters.

4. What is hash or direct file organization? How are the records organized in the file? Explain the problem of collisions in this method of file organization and describe how collisions are resolved.

5. What is bitmapped indexing? When is it effective? Show, with a simple example, how bitmapped indexes speed up data access.

CHAPTER 13

SPECIAL IMPLEMENTATION
CONSIDERATIONS

CHAPTER OBJECTIVES

- Study the role of languages in the implementation of a data model
- Discuss in detail SQL, the relational standard
- Learn how SQL is used for data definition, manipulation, maintenance, and control
- Review examples of simple and complex queries in SQL
- Examine how a query is optimized and executed
- Understand the various aspects of database deployment

When you review the phases of the database development life cycle (DDLC), physical design is the last stage in the design phase. In Chapter 12, we discussed physical design in considerable detail. You learned how to transform the logical model into the physical model of a relational database system. You studied how the physical model conforms to the target DBMS and the configuration of the computer system where the database has to reside.

Once physical design is completed, you are ready to implement the database system. Implementation brings all the efforts during the different phases of DDLC to culmination. You have moved from the generic data model to the relational model. You know that both of these form the logical data model. After that stage, you moved to the physical model, taking into account the features of the DBMS and the computer system. The data models must be implemented as the resultant database management system.

First, try to understand the significance and meaning of implementing the data model. Find out why we need languages for implementation. We need languages

Database Design and Development: An Essential Guide for IT Professionals by Paulraj Ponniah
ISBN 0-471-21877-4   Copyright © 2003 by John Wiley and Sons, Inc.

for defining the data structures, for manipulating the data, and for maintaining the data. Structured Query Language (SQL) has evolved as the standard to fulfill these needs.

Implementation includes tasks required to move from an earlier data system to the new database system. Existing data from the current system have to be converted over to the new system. Furthermore, you need applications in the new environment that will tap into the new database system. Also, you need a proper strategy to deploy the database and distribute the data wherever they are needed.

Implementation considerations include the optimal processing of data queries. Data retrieval involves execution of queries in the most optimal way. Our discussion of implementation considerations will not be complete without an examination of query processing.

IMPLEMENTATION LANGUAGES

You carry out the implementation of a database system through languages. You know that language is a medium for communication and serves as a link. Just think about programming languages. Programming languages enable user transactions to be communicated to the computer systems. They therefore contain structures to indicate the logic, components to denote the data requirements, and methods to organize the flow of control.

Database implementation languages also serve to interpret and communicate database transactions to the DBMS and to the database system. In practice, because they support distinct functions, database implementation languages must have distinct features specially intended for the required functions. Several implementation languages have evolved for the relational data model; however, SQL has become the accepted standard.

Even though the name of the language implies that SQL is intended just for queries, the language has all the components to support the various aspects of implementation. In the following sections of this chapter, you will observe the distinct features of SQL and understand how it is a complete language for implementation of the relational data model.

Meaning of Model Implementation

At the outset, let us describe what we mean by implementing a data model as a database system. Consider a relational data model. The logical data model consists of relations or tables, tuples or rows indicating individual entities, columns showing the attributes, primary keys, and foreign keys. In the physical data model you find these components transformed into files, blocks, records, indexes, and constraints. So what do we mean by implementing the data model?

Implementation serves two primary purposes—storage of data and usage of data. As you know, these are the two basic aspects of a database system. Users need to access and use data; you need to store the data in a database for this purpose. A data model represents the information requirements for an organization. When you implement a data model, you make provisions to store the information content represented by the data model and also enable the stored information to be used.

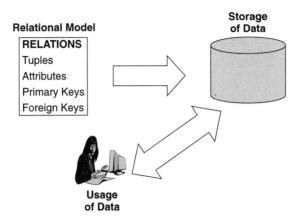

Figure 13-1   Aspects of data model implementation.

Figure 13-1 illustrates these two major aspects of implementing a data model as a database system. Note the model components on the left side of the figure and see how implementation of the data model provides for data storage and data usage.

Role of Languages

How is the implementation of a data model as a database system accomplished? Accomplishing the implementation includes storage of data and usage of data. You need a method, a medium, a language component for providing for each of the aspects of implementation. You must have a language component to support data storage; you need a component to enable the usage of data. In addition to these two primary requirements, there must be language components for some other aspects as well.

Let us review each of these aspects of model implementation and note the desired features of the language components. Note how each component serves a distinct purpose and understand how all these language components together make the implementation of the data model happen.

Defining Data Structure   To store data, you need to define the data structure to the database management system. Data definition for the relational data model includes defining the logical model components as well as physical model components. The data definition language (DDL) module supports the storage of data in the database system.

Figure 13-2 shows the features of the DDL component and illustrates how this component enables data storage.

Data Retrieval   Once the data structure is defined and the data are stored in the database, we need a language component to enable usage of the data. Data access is part of the overall ability to manipulate the data in the database. This part of the data manipulation language (DML) component enables retrieval of data from the

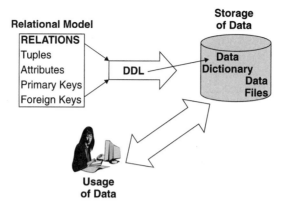

Figure 13-2 DDL component.

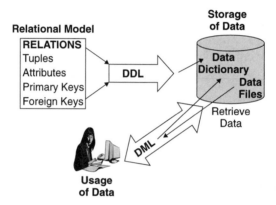

Figure 13-3 DML component: data access.

database system. Data access provides for retrieval of relevant portions of data based on various criteria.

Figure 13-3 indicates those features of DML that deal with data access.

Data Maintenance Data access and retrieval are just one part of data manipulation. The other parts include adding new data, deleting unwanted data, and revising data values as necessary. The data maintenance part of DML allows the maintenance of the data in the database.

Figure 13-4 presents the features of DML that are relevant to data maintenance in a database system.

Data Control "Usage of data in the database" implies controlled usage under proper authorization. There must be one language component to ensure proper data control. The data control language (DCL) enables data security and control through methods for proper access for authorized users. Authorization must include opening

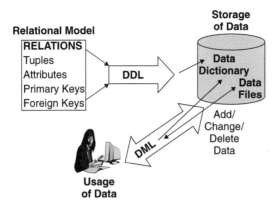

Figure 13-4   DML component: data maintenance.

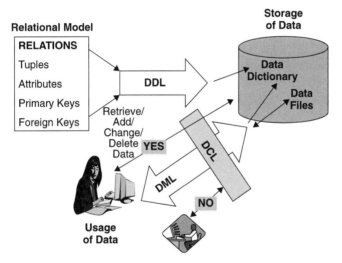

Figure 13-5   DCL component.

the database to authorized users not only for data retrieval, but also for adding, changing, or deleting data.

Figure 13-5 shows the features of the DCL component and how this component supports authorized data manipulation.

Languages for the Relational Model

As mentioned above, SQL has established itself as the preferred language for the relational model. Before we discuss SQL in detail in the next section, it is worthwhile to briefly introduce a few other commercial languages that support the relational data model. This introduction will give you some insight into the purpose and features of the language components that support the various aspects of data model implementation.

Queries on ORDER relation

Print all order numbers for Customer "Robert Smith"

OrdrNo	OrdrDate	OrdrAmt	CustName
P.			Robert Smith

Find the order numbers and order dates of all orders with amounts more than $750

OrdrNo	OrdrDate	OrdrAmt	CustName
P.	P.	>750	

Find the order numbers and order amounts of all orders not for "Bill Jones"

OrdrNo	OrdrDate	OrdrAmt	CustName
P.		P.	NOT Bill Jones

Figure 13-6   QBE queries.

Query-by-Example   Query-by-example (QBE) adopts a visual approach to implementing the data model through templates. You enter an example value into the template for data retrieval. Queries are expressed as examples that are provided through the language.

QBE was developed in early 1970s at IBM's Watson Research Center. Later, the QBE data manipulation language component was used in IBM's Query Management Facility (QMF). Today, many relational DBMSs including Microsoft ACCESS and IBM's Paradox use QBE in one form or another.

In QBE, you use a skeletal two-dimensional table to express your query. Queries are in the form of tables, not free-form text with statements or commands. You fill in a skeletal table with example rows. An example row consists of example data elements and constants. The result of the query is also presented as a table.

Figure 13-6 shows examples of QBE queries.

QBE has provisions to perform the following:

- Indicate conditions for data retrieval through the use of condition boxes
- Display results taking values from several database relations
- Order the display of result rows
- Perform aggregations
- Data maintenance—deletion, insertion, and update

Quel   Developed at the University of California, Berkeley, Quel was introduced as the implementation language for the Ingres database system. Three basic types of clauses exist: range of, retrieve, and where. The underlying structure resembles that of relational calculus.

You can express most of the queries just by using these three standard clauses. The first clause, "range of" declares a tuple or row variable taking on values of tuples in a certain relation. The next clause, "retrieve" serves to indicate the values of selected attributes from the declared relation that must be found in the result. The "where" clause sets the conditions and constraints for the data retrieval.

Examine the following Quel queries and note the basic constructs.

Query: List the names of the customers in Japan.
range of r **is** *customer*
retrieve unique *r.customer-name* **where** *r.customer-country* = 'Japan'
Query: List the names and countries of customers who bought product 2241.
range of r **is** *customer*
range of s **is** *sale*
retrieve unique *(r.customer-name, r.customer-country)*
where *s.product-id* = '2241' **and** *r.customer-id* = *s.customer-id*

Quel has provisions to perform the following functions, all functions being structured in a similar basic format:

- Perform arithmetic aggregate functions such as count, sum, average, maximum, minimum, and so on
- Execute simple and complex queries
- Data maintenance—deletion, insertion, and update
- Do set operations

Datalog As you know, a nonprocedural language simply states the desired solution without writing out a set of procedural statements to arrive at the result. You have seen that relational calculus is a generic nonprocedural language. In the same way, Datalog is a nonprocedural query language developed based on Prologic, a logic-programming language. In a Datalog query, the user simply describes the desired information without writing a detailed procedure on how to obtain that information.

A Datalog program is made up of a set of rules. A Datalog view defines a view of a given relation. You may consider a view as a subset of the given relation. Figure 13-7 illustrates the definition of a Datalog view and the description of a Datalog query. Notice the nonprocedural nature of the language.

SQL: THE RELATIONAL STANDARD

Designed and developed at IBM Research in the early 1970s as the language interface for an experimental relational database, SQL has become the accepted relational standard. Consider the DBMS of any relational database vendor. You will find that every vendor has adopted the standard version of SQL and added some embellishments. It is even doubtful that the relational data model would have gained such popularity and acceptance without SQL.

SQL makes the transition from one relational DBMS to another easy. Businesses that move into relational databases from hierarchical or network database systems

VIEW DEFINITION:

Define a view relation v1 containing order numbers, order dates, and order amounts for customer "Bill Jones" with order amount greater than $1,000

V1 (A, B) :=   ORDER (A, B, C, "Bill Jones"), C > 1000

QUERY

Retrieve order numbers, order dates, order amounts for customer "Bill Jones"

? V1 (A, B) :=   ORDER (A, B, C, "Bill Jones")

QUERY

Retrieve order numbers, order dates, order amounts for order with amounts less than $ 150"

? V1 (A, B) :=   ORDER (A, B, C), C < 150

Figure 13-7   Datalog view and query.

or from file-oriented data systems may select an initial relational DBMS. As the organizations gain experience and desire to move forward to another, more robust relational DBMS, SQL makes the transition possible.

SQL is a command-driven, declarative, nonprocedural language serving as DDL, DML, and DCL. With SQL you can define database objects, manipulate data, and exercise data control. You can write SQL code as free-form text. The structure of the commands consists of standard English words such as CREATE, SELECT, FROM, WHERE, DROP, and so on. The language may be used by DBAs, analysts, programmers, and even end users with equal ease—a language easy to learn, but perhaps not so easy to master.

Let us now begin an in-depth discussion of SQL—its features, history and evolution, major commands, and usefulness. You will learn how to use facilities in SQL to define data structures, manipulate data, compose queries, provide data control, and manage data. You will also study examples of simple and complex queries written in SQL. Nevertheless, this coverage of SQL is not meant to be a detailed reference guide. You are encouraged to continue your study of SQL with the aid of books specifically intended for that purpose.

Overall Features

SQL is a comprehensive database or model implementation language mostly based on tuple relational calculus. The language also includes some relational algebra operations. It combines features and functions both for definition of data structures and for usage of data in the database. The widespread use and acceptance of SQL enables it to evolve and become more robust.

Because the underlying construct is based on relational calculus, a nonprocedural language, there is no sequencing of the commands in SQL. An SQL query is simply written as a solution statement declaring the outcome desired from execution of the query. How the result is formatted and presented to the user is left outside of SQL. In SQL you find only definitional and manipulative commands. You do not have flow of control commands—no if-then-else navigation within SQL code. Therefore, SQL has to be embedded in a host language to provide flow of control. The host language constructs provide the flow of control logic and also the presentation of results on GUI screens or reports.

Major Aspects of SQL

- *Data definition language component*—for creation, deletion, and modification of definitions for relational tables and user views; for creation and dropping of indexes (as provided in commercial versions); for specifying integrity constraints
- *Data manipulation language component*—consisting of a query language based on relational calculus and some relational algebra
- *Data maintenance facility*—to insert, modify, or delete rows from relational tables
- *Security control*—to grant or revoke access privileges to users
- *Transaction control*—commands specifying beginnings and endings of transactions with explicit locking by some implementations for concurrency control
- *Embedded SQL*—providing calls from host languages
- *Dynamic SQL*—for constructing and executing queries dynamically at run time
- *Triggers*—actions coded as program modules executed by DBMS whenever changes to the database meet conditions stipulated in the trigger
- *Client/server adaptation*—for client application programs to connect to an SQL database server
- *Remote access*—access of relational database over a network

Brief History and Evolution

It all began in the early 1970s when Dr. E. F. Codd of IBM's San Jose Research Laboratory proposed the relational data model. IBM developed a prototype DBMS called System R to validate the feasibility of the relational data model. D. Chamberlin, from the same laboratory, defined a language called the Structured English Query Language as the language interface for System R. This language came to be known as SEQUEL. However, SEQUEL owes its beginning to another language called SQUARE (Specifying Queries as Relational Expressions), designed to implement relational algebra with English, which formed the basis for the development of SEQUEL. Development of SEQUEL, later known as SQL (pronounced as *es-que-el*), formed the high point of the relational model projects at San Jose.

In the late 1970s, Oracle became the first commercial implementation of a relational DBMS based on SQL. INGRES followed shortly thereafter as an implementation of relational DBMS with QUEL as the interface language. IBM's first commercial DBMS on the relational data model known as SQL/DS appeared in 1981 for DOS/VSE environments, and in 1982 for the VM/CMS environments. Subsequently, in 1983 IBM introduced DB2 for MVS environments. Now the relational DBMS of every vendor is based on SQL. Each vendor provides all the standard features of SQL. Each vendor also provides additional features of its own, called extensions to standard SQL. Vendors attempt to distinguish their SQL versions with these extensions.

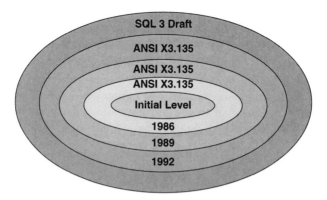

Figure 13-8 SQL: evolution of standards.

Evolution of Standards Both the American National Standards Institute (ANSI) and the International Standards Organization (ISO) have adopted and standardized SQL over the years. Figure 13-8 shows the evolution of SQL as standardization continues. Note how each new level adds and consolidates features.

Highlights of Each Version

ANSI X3.135—1986
Definition of language constructs: verbs, clauses, operators, syntax
Details of functions left to the discretion of implementers

ANSI X3.135—1989
Integrity enhancement
Support for primary and foreign key

ANSI X3.135—1992 (SQL 2)
Language enhancements
Detailed definitions for existing functions

SQL 3 Draft
Object-oriented capabilities

Data Definition in SQL

When you design a database system, you proceed through the logical and physical phases. The components developed in these phases form the basis for your database system. For the database management system (DBMS) to manage the database content, the components of the logical design and the physical design must be defined to the DBMS. In a relational database system, you have to define the logical structures in terms of tables, columns, and primary keys. You need to relate the tables and rows to physical files, blocks, and records. These also must be defined to the DBMS.

Data definition language serves to define the logical and physical components to the DBMS. You know that the definitions are recorded in the data dictionary of the DBMS. The data definition language component of SQL makes it possible to define the logical and physical components of the relational data model to the DBMS.

Definition of Database Objects   SQL provides functions to define and create database objects. In addition to the provision of statements to define and create the overall schema consisting of the complete set of relations in the database, SQL provides statements for the specification of the following for each relation:

- Schema and name for the relation
- Security and authorization
- List of attributes
- Data type and domain of values for each attribute
- Primary and foreign keys
- Integrity constraints
- Indexes
- Structure on physical storage medium

Here is a list of the major data definition statements in SQL:

CREATE SCHEMA	Define a new database schema for the set of relations or tables
DROP SCHEMA	Remove the definition and contents of an existing database
CREATE TABLE	Define a new table with its columns
ALTER TABLE	Add or delete columns to an existing table
DROP TABLE	Remove the definition and contents of an existing table
CREATE VIEW	Define a logical data view consisting of columns from one or more tables or views
DROP VIEW	Remove an existing view
CREATE DOMAIN	Define a domain name with certain a data type (domain name to be used later to define the data types of attributes)
ALTER DOMAIN	Change the data types of a defined domain
DROP DOMAIN	Remove a defined domain
CREATE INDEX	Define an index on one or more columns
DROP INDEX	Remove an existing index

SQL-based database management systems usually provide additional definition features as noted below:

CREATE SYNONYM	Define an alternative name for a table or view (usually an abbreviation or acronym to reduce the number of key strokes for referring to the table or view)
DROP SYNONYM	Remove a defined synonym
LABEL	Define a column heading for an attribute when results are displayed
COMMENT	Provide remarks or comments for table columns (stored as part of the table in the data dictionary)

Data Types   SQL supports a variety of data types for the table columns representing the attributes. In the database, legal values may be entered for each column based on the declared data type. The standard versions of SQL allow for accepted data types; in addition, specific vendor implementation may have additional data types or some variations of a standard data type.

The following is a list of the common SQL data types:

Character data

CHAR(n)	Alphanumeric character data of fixed length n
VARCHAR (n)	Alphanumeric character data of variable length up to a maximum length of n

Numeric data

DECIMAL (m,n)	Signed number, where m is the total number of digits including the sign and n is the number of digits to the right of the decimal point
INTEGER	Large positive or negative whole numbers up to 11 digits
SMALLINT	Small positive or negative whole numbers up to 5 or 6 digits
FLOAT (m)	Floating point number represented in scientific notation with specified precision of at least m digits

Date/time data

DATE	Calendar date showing year, month, and day in a prescribed format (year/month/day, month/day/year, or day/month/year)
TIME	Hour, minute, second with time zone

Interval data

INTERVAL	Representation of periods of time

Bit data

BIT (n)	Bit string of fixed length n

Logical data

LOGICAL	"True" or "False" values

SQL Data Definition Example   You have now gone through the various SQL statements available for defining database objects. You have also noted the provisions to indicate the different data types for values to be stored in the database. Let us put what we have covered so far in a practical example. In Figure 11-5, you studied an entity-relationship diagram for a florist business. Also, Figure 11-10 presents the relational schema for that business. We will refer to those figures and create data definitions with SQL statements. While doing so, we will provide examples of most of the data definition statements listed above.

Carefully observe all the statements now shown in Figure 13-9. This figure presents the definition of the schema with the tables, columns, indexes, and so on for

```
CREATE SCHEMA RAINBOW-FLORIST
      AUTHORIZATION Amanda-Russo;
CREATE DOMAIN ItemIdentifier CHARACTER (4) DEFAULT "ZZZZ"
      CHECK (VALUE IS NOT NULL);
CREATE TABLE CUSTOMER (
      CustNo                    CHARACTER (8),
      CustAddr                  CHARACTER (45),
      CustName      CHARACTER (35),
      PRIMARY KEY (CustNo) );
CREATE TABLE ORDER (
      OrdrNo                    CHARACTER (8),
      OrdrDate                  DATE,
      OrdrAmt                   DECIMAL (9,2)  NOT NULL,
      CustNo                    CHARACTER (8),
      PRIMARY KEY (OrdrNo),
      FOREIGN KEY (CustNo) REFERENCES CUSTOMER (CustNo)
                  ON DELETE CASCADE );
CREATE TABLE PAYMENT (
      OrdrNo                    CHARACTER (8),
      PmntNo                    CHARACTER (4),
      PmntDate                  DATE,
      PmntAmt                   DECIMAL (9,2)  NOT NULL,
      PRIMARY KEY (OrdrNo, PmntNo),
      FOREIGN KEY (OrdrNo) REFERENCES ORDER (OrdrNo) );
CREATE TABLE PRODUCT (
      ProdID                    ItemIdentifier,
      ProdCost                  DECIMAL (5,2)  NOT NULL,
      CHECK (ProdCost < 100.00 AND ProdCost > 1.00),
      PRIMARY KEY (ProdID) );
```

```
CREATE TABLE FLOWER (
      ProdID                    ItemIdentifier,
      ProdCost                  DECIMAL (5,2)  NOT NULL,
      FlwrName                  CHARACTER (25),
      FlwrSize                  SMALLINT,
      PRIMARY KEY (ProdID),
      FOREIGN KEY (ProdID) REFERENCES PRODUCT (ProdID) );
CREATE TABLE ARRANGEMENT (
      ProdID                    ItemIdentifier,
      ProdCost                  DECIMAL (5,2)  NOT NULL,
      ArngeType                 CHARACTER (15),
      PRIMARY KEY (ProdID),
      FOREIGN KEY (ProdID) REFERENCES PRODUCT (ProdID) );
CREATE TABLE CHANNEL (
      ChnlID                    ItemIdentifier,
      ChnlName                  CHARACTER (35),
      PRIMARY KEY (ChnlID) );
CREATE TABLE GROWER (
      GrwrID                    ItemIdentifier,
      GrwrName                  CHARACTER (35),
      PRIMARY KEY (GrwrID) );
CREATE TABLE SHIPMENT (
      OrdrNo                    CHARACTER (8),
      ChnlID                    ItemIdentifier,
      GrwrID                    ItemIdentifier,
      ShipDate                  DATE,
      ShipQty                   INTEGER,
      PRIMARY KEY (OrdrNo, ChnlID, GrwrID),
      FOREIGN KEY (OrdrNo) REFERENCES ORDER (OrdrNo),
      FOREIGN KEY (ChnlID) REFERENCES CHANNEL (ChnlID),
      FOREIGN KEY (GrwrID) REFERENCES GROWER (GrwrID) );
```

Figure 13-9   Florist business: data definition in SQL.

the florist business. Walk through each data definition statement, note its purpose, and see how it is constructed.

Data Retrieval in SQL

Whereas data manipulation in SQL deals with accessing and fetching desired data from a relational database, data maintenance in SQL relates to the adding, deleting, and changing of data. SQL provides commands for both types of data handling—data retrieval and data maintenance. The SQL query is used to fetch data from a relational database. Let us therefore begin our discussion on data manipulation by examining the SQL query format.

The basic structure of an SQL query expression consists of three simple clauses or commands: SELECT, FROM, and WHERE. Take a simple example. Let us say that you want to list all sales persons working out of the Los Angeles office. For this purpose, you need to write a query in SQL to retrieve the data about all the sales persons from those rows in the SALESPERSON table where the SalesOffice column contains the value "Los Angeles." Here is this simple query in English:

What are the names of the sales persons in the Los Angeles office?

Now let us write the query using the data manipulation language (DML) component of SQL.

> **SELECT** SalespersonName
> **FROM** SALESPERSON
> **WHERE** SalesOffice = 'Los Angeles'

SELECT   This clause contains the list of columns from the base table to be projected into the result relation. An asterisk (*) in the clause indicates projec-

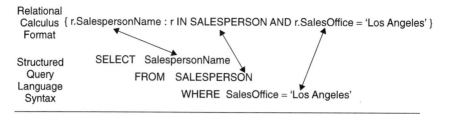

SELECT– *Lists the columns from base tables to be projected into the result relation.*
FROM – *Identifies tables from which columns will be chosen.*
WHERE – *Includes the conditions for row selection within a single table and
conditions between tables for joining*

Figure 13-10   Query in relational calculus and in SQL.

tion of all columns from the base table. The operation corresponds to the
project operation of relational algebra.

FROM   This clause identifies the table or tables from which rows and columns
will be chosen. The operation corresponds to the Cartesian product operation
of relational algebra.

WHERE   This clause includes the conditions for row selection within a single
table or for joining two tables. The clause corresponds to the select or join
operations of relational algebra.

Figure 13-10 shows the correspondence between the components of a relational
calculus expression and the basic structure of an SQL query. Note how the query
for the names of sales persons from the Los Angeles office is shown in the relational
calculus format and with SQL query syntax.

In addition to the three basic clauses, SQL provides a few optional clauses as
follows:

GROUP BY   To form groups of rows with the same values in given columns
HAVING   To filter the groups of rows subject to a given condition
ORDER BY   To specify the order of the rows in the result

SELECT, the most common clause in SQL, may contain specifications as to the
selection of the columns to be presented in the result set. These specifications are
indicated by the following keywords:

DISTINCT   To eliminate duplicates in the result
ALL   To state explicitly that duplicates must not be eliminated
AS   To replace a column or attribute name in the table with a new
name

In a later subsection, we will consider several examples of SQL queries—both
simple and complex. Let us now indicate the general format of the SQL query and
move on.

SELECT	[DISTINCT|ALL] {*|[column-name [AS new-name], [.....], ...}
FROM	table-name [alias], ...
WHERE	condition
GROUP BY	column-list HAVING condition
ORDER BY	column-list

Data Maintenance in SQL

As discussed thus far, SQL provides you with facilities to define the database objects and to retrieve data once they are stored. But you know that the data in a database keep changing all the time. If you have a customer database table, you need to add more rows to the table as and when your organization gets new customers. If your database has a table for customer orders, new rows must be added to this table almost daily. Whenever changes are made to any of the rows in the customer or order tables, you need to update the relevant rows. After a period of time, you may want to delete the old orders and archive them on a separate storage medium. In this case, you must be able to delete selected rows from the orders table. All of these actions form part of data maintenance. Every database is subject to continual data maintenance.

SQL provides three commands to perform data maintenance. Let us discuss each command and understand it with some examples.

Adding Data

SQL Command

INSERT

Function

Add a new row to a table using the given values for the columns, or add one or more rows to a table using the result of a query.

Examples

1. Add a new row into the EMPLOYEE table with the supplied values for all columns.
   INSERT INTO EMPLOYEE
   VALUES   (1234, 'Karolyn', 'Jones', '733 Jackie Lane, Baldwin Harbor, NY 11510', '516-223-8183', 'Senior VP', 95000, 'MGR')
2. Add a new row into the EMPLOYEE table with the supplied values for most of the columns, leaving some column values as NULL.
   INSERT INTO EMPLOYEE
   VALUES   (3344, 'Robert', 'Moses', '142 Crestview Drive, Long Branch, NJ 08835', NULL, NULL, 40000, 'STF')
3. Add new rows into the MANAGER, selecting managers from the EMPLOYEE table.

```
INSERT INTO MANAGER
    SELECT *
        FROM EMPLOYEE
            WHERE EmployeeCode = 'MGR'
```

Modifying Data

SQL Command

UPDATE

Function

Change values in one or more columns of specified rows by replacing current values with supplied constants or with results of calculations.

Examples

1. Change last name in a specified row in EMPLOYEE table with supplied value.
    ```
    UPDATE EMPLOYEE
        SET LastName = 'Raj'
            WHERE EmployeeNo = 1234
    ```
2. Increase the salary of all managers by 5%.
    ```
    UPDATE EMPLOYEE
        SET Salary = Salary * 1.05
            WHERE EmployeeCode = 'MGR'
    ```
3. Modify multiple columns in a specified row in EMPLOYEE table with supplied values.
    ```
    UPDATE EMPLOYEE
        SET EmployeePosition = 'Asst. Supervisor', Salary = 60000, EmployeeCode = 'SPR'
            WHERE EmployeeNo = 3344
    ```

Deleting Data

SQL Command

DELETE

Function

Delete one or more specified rows from a table.

Examples

1. Delete all rows from the MANAGER table.
    ```
    DELETE FROM MANAGER
    ```

2. Delete one specific row from the EMPLOYEE table.
   DELETE FROM EMPLOYEE
      WHERE EmployeeNo = 3344
3. Delete from EMPLOYEE table those rows for staff earning less than 25000.
   DELETE FROM EMPLOYEE
      WHERE EmployeeCode = 'STF' and Salary <25000

Data Control in SQL

A relational database management system controls access to the database based on three concepts: user identifier, data ownership, and access privileges. The database administrator assigns a user identifier and password to each authorized user for signing onto the database system. A user with a proper user identifier performs every action on the database. Access privileges indicate which database objects a user may access and what actions he or she may perform. Chapter 16 explores this topic of database security in greater detail.

In a relational database, every object has an owner. The user identifier indicates the owner as defined in the AUTHORIZATION clause during schema definitions. Initially, only the owner has all access privileges to the database objects. When an authorized user creates a table using the CREATE TABLE statement, the user automatically becomes the owner of the table, receiving all access privileges to that table. Later, the owner may give access privileges to other authorized users.

SQL provides two commands for controlling access to the relational database. The database administrator has these commands to give access privileges to individuals or groups of users and to take away the privileges as soon as the privileges are to be removed. Access privileges permit users to perform various actions on tables or views. The privileges include:

SELECT	Permission only to retrieve data from a table or view
INSERT	Permission to add new rows into a table
UPDATE	Permission to modify the contents of a table
DELETE	Permission to remove rows from a table
REFERENCES	Permission to reference columns of a named table in integrity constraints

INSERT, UPDATE, and REFERENCES may be restricted to specific columns in the applicable table.

Providing Access Privileges

SQL Command

GRANT

Function

Give access privileges on database objects to specific users.

Examples

Use the following tables for the examples:

DEPARTMENT (DeptNo, DeptName, DeptLocation)
EMPLOYEE (EmployeeNo, FirstName, LastName, Address, Phone, Employ-
eePosition, Salary, EmployeeCode, DeptNo)
Foreign Key: DeptNo REFERENCES DEPARTMENT

1. Give permission to Rogers to read all of EMPLOYEE table.
   GRANT SELECT
     ON EMPLOYEE
       TO Rogers
2. Give Miller and Rodriguez full privileges to the DEPARTMENT table.
   GRANT ALL PRIVILEGES
     ON DEPARTMENT
       TO Miller, Rodriguez WITH GRANT OPTION
3. Give Chen read and update privileges on specific columns in EMPLOYEE table.
   GRANT SELECT, UPDATE (FirstName, LastName, Address, PhoneNo)
     ON EMPLOYEE
       TO Chen

Removing Access Privileges

SQL Command

REVOKE

Function

Remove access privileges previously granted to database objects from users.

Examples

Use the same DEPARTMENT and EMPLOYEE tables for the following examples:

1. Remove from all users the privilege to delete DEPARTMENT table rows.
   REVOKE DELETE
     ON DEPARTMENT
       FROM PUBLIC
2. Remove from Miller all privileges on DEPARTMENT table.
   REVOKE ALL PRIVILEGES
     ON DEPARTMENT
       FROM Miller
3. Remove from Chen update privileges on EMPLOYEE table.
   REVOKE UPDATE
     ON EMPLOYEE
       FROM Chen

Queries

Let us now examine a few examples of queries. First, let consider simple queries, mostly deriving results from single database tables. These will increase your grasp of the basic query statements in SQL. After that, we will go over a few examples of more advanced queries where the results need to be obtained from more than one table. There you will become familiar with queries within queries. The technique of using subqueries enables a complex query to be broken down into simple queries to produce the desired result.

Do not assume that the examples here form a complete set of all possible types of queries. The intention here is to provide you with a good introduction to SQL queries. Any standard SQL reference guide will provide you with a more comprehensive coverage of all types of queries.

Simple   The queries in these examples are based on the data model for a university we considered in earlier chapters. As you are already familiar with this data model, let us use it to illustrate the following query types. Go back and review the following figures from earlier chapters:

Figure 7-22   ERD: university teaching aspects
Figure 9-22   University ERD: transformation into relational data model

1. **Find the name of the course with course number 10971.**
   SELECT CourseDesc
     FROM COURSE
       WHERE CourseNo = '10971'

2. **Find the names of students with computer science major.**
   SELECT StudntName
     FROM STUDENT
       WHERE Major = 'Computer Science'

3. **List all data for faculty member John Saunders.**
   SELECT *
     FROM FACULTY
       WHERE FacltyName = 'John Saunders'

4. **Find all the majors for which students have enrolled.**
   SELECT DISTINCT Major
     FROM STUDENT

5. **Find the maximum and minimum price of prescribed textbooks.**
   SELECT MAX (Price), MIN (Price)
     FROM TEXTBOOK

6. **Add 5 points to minimum score for mid-term examination.**
   SELECT MinScore, (MinScore+5)
     FROM EXAMTYPE
       WHERE TypeId = 'MIDTERM'

7. **Print the total number of faculty members in the English department.**

   SELECT "The total number of faculty members in", Department, "is"
   COUNT (FACULTY)
      FROM FACULTY
         WHERE Department = 'English'

8. **Find the number of credits for the course with course number 10971.**

   SELECT Credits
      FROM COURSE
         WHERE CourseNo = '10971'

9. **List students by social security number in a given class with total score greater than given number.**

   SELECT SocSecNo, ClassNo, SUM (Score)
      FROM GRADE
         WHERE ClassNo = '11223344'
            GROUP BY SocSecNo, ClassNo
               ORDER BY SocSecNo, ClassNo
               HAVING SUM (Score) > 60

10. **Find the students who have not yet declared a major.**

    SELECT SocSecNo, StudntName
       FROM STUDENT
          WHERE Major IS NULL

11. **Find the names and phone numbers of faculty members with specialization in data systems.**

    SELECT FacltyName, Phone
       FROM FACULTY
          WHERE Speczn LIKE 'Data%'

Advanced   These examples of advanced queries are based on the relational data model for a medical center as shown in Figure 13-11. In these queries, observe how subqueries are used to obtain the desired results.

1. **List the services billed to patient whose number is 224466.**

   SELECT SERVICE.ServiceCode, ServiceDesc
      FROM SERVICE, BILLING
         WHERE SERVICE.ServiceCode = BILLING.ServiceCode and
         PatientNo = 224466

2. **List the services billed to patient whose number is 224466. (Alternative query.)**

   SELECT SERVICE.ServiceCode, ServiceDesc
      FROM SERVICE
         WHERE ServiceCode =
            (SELECT ServiceCode FROM BILLING
               WHERE PatientNo = 224466)

PATIENT (<u>PatientNo,</u> PatientName, DOB, AdmissionDate, DischargeDate)

DOCTOR (<u>DoctorID,</u> DoctorName, DoctorPhone)

SERVICE (<u>ServiceCode,</u> ServiceDesc)

TREATMENT (<u>PatientNo, DoctorID,</u> TreatmentDesc)
Foreign Key: **PatientNo** REFERENCES **PATIENT**
            DoctorID REFERENCES **DOCTOR**

BILLING (<u>PatientNo, ServiceCode,</u> BilledAmount)
Foreign Key: **PatientNo** REFERENCES **PATIENT**
            ServiceCode REFERENCES **SERVICE**

Figure 13-11   Relational data model: medical center.

3. **List those patients who have been charged more than the average for service SCAN.**

SELECT DISTINCT PatientNo
  FROM BILLING
    WHERE ServiceCode = 'SCAN'
    And BilledAmount >
    (SELECT AVG (BilledAmount)
      FROM BILLING
        WHERE ServiceCode = 'SCAN')

4. **List those patients who have been charged for XRAY and SCAN.**

SELECT DISTINCT PatientNo
  FROM BILLING B1
    WHERE EXISTS
    (SELECT *
      FROM BILLING B2
        WHERE B1.PatientNo = B2.PatientNo and
          B1.ServiceCode = 'XRAY' and
          B2.ServiceCode = 'SCAN')

5. **List all patients who have been charged the same for XRAY and SCAN.**

SELECT PatientNo, PatientName
  FROM PATIENT
    WHERE PatientNo IN
    (SELECT PatientNo
      FROM BILLING
        WHERE ServiceCode = 'XRAY' and
          BilledAmount = ALL
      (SELECT BilledAmount

        FROM BILLING
            WHERE ServiceCode = 'SCAN'))

6. Obtain a list of all billings including those patients for whom no billings have been done until now.

SELECT BILLING.PatientNo, PatientName, BilledAmount
    FROM BILLING, PATIENT
        WHERE BILLING.PatientNo = PATIENT.PatientNo
UNION
SELECT PatientNo, PatientName, 0
    FROM PATIENT
        WHERE PatientNo NOT IN
            (SELECT PatientNo
                FROM BILLING)

Summary of SQL Query Components

Having reviewed various types of SQL queries, let us summarize the different query components. Figure 13-12 provides a summary of the main clauses, operators, and built-in functions that are part of typical SQL queries.

Database Access from Application Program

The queries discussed in the previous subsection illustrate one method of using SQL. We have covered the interactive use of SQL. To obtain the desired results from the database, you write SQL code in the database environment. The commercial database systems support SQL and execute the SQL statements interactively. The end of the SQL code, usually signified by a semi-colon (;), triggers the

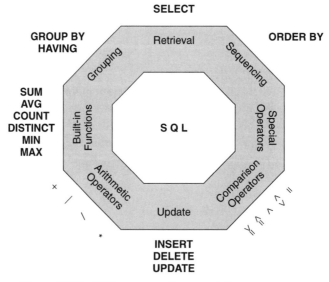

Figure 13-12 SQL query and manipulation components.

execution of the SQL statements; no other code in any programming language is necessary. However, the results are displayed or printed only in certain standard formats.

What if you are writing an application program with the necessary logic in a programming language such as Visual Basic, C, C++, COBOL, Ada, and so on, and want your program to access a relational database? SQL is the standard language for relational database access. How can your application program interface with the database using the facilities of SQL? The following two methods provide database access to an application program.

Embedded SQL In this approach, SQL statements are included directly in the source code of the application program. At the points in the application program where database access is necessary, SQL statements are embedded into the program. The application program directly accesses the database using SQL statements. A special precompiler replaces the SQL statements in the application programs written in a host programming language with database functions.

Figure 13-13 shows a sample program written in C with embedded SQL. Observe how standard SQL statements are embedded at the appropriate points in the program.

Application Programming Interface (API) In this alternative approach, the application programmer is provided with a set of standard functions that can be invoked or called from the application program. This type of call-level interface allows the application program to access the database. These APIs enable the application program to access the database as do the embedded SQL statements in the other approach. However, this approach does not require any precompilation of the program.

An initial function call in the application program establishes the connection to the database. Then, at the point in the program where database access is required, a call is made to the appropriate database function to process the relevant SQL statements passed on in the call.

Figure 13-14 illustrates how an application program uses an SQL call-level interface (CLI).

Although this approach does away with precompilation, unfortunately, each database vendor's API is specific to that vendor's DBMS. This is the case even though all the calls result in the execution of standard SQL statements. No standards institution has established a common interface. However, Microsoft's Open Database Connectivity (ODBC), a SQL-based API, has become the industry standard.

QUERY PROCESSING

As you have seen, SQL provides a high-level data manipulation language to write queries and obtain the desired data from a relational database. You construct a query with SQL statements. You can either execute a query interactively or embed a query in a host language for execution at appropriate points in the application program. Query processing is a major consideration in the implementation of database systems.

```
EXEC SQL BEGIN DECLARE SECTION ;
        int depno ;                              /* department number */
        int empno ;                              /* employee number */
        varchar depname (20) ;                   /* department name */
EXEC  SQL END DECLARE ;
/* SQL communication area and declaration of exceptions */
EXEC  SQL INCLUDE SQLCA ;
EXEC  SQL WHENEVER NOT FOUND GOTO errA ;
EXEC  SQL WHENEVER SQLERROR GOTO          errB ;


/* MAIN PROGRAM */
main ( )
{
        empno = 5555 ;
        strcpy (depname.arr, "FINANCE") ;
        dname.len = strlen (depname.arr) ;

        EXEC SQL SELECT DeptNo INTO    :depno
        FROM DEPARTMENT
        WHERE         DeptName =    :depname ;

        EXEC SQL UPDATE EMPLOYEE
        SET DeptNo =  :depno
        WHERE EmployeeNo =  :empno ;

        printf ("Transfer of employee %d to department %s complete. \n",
                      empno, depname.arr) ;

        EXEC SQL COMMIT WORK ;
        exit (0) ;

        errA:
                    printf ("Department named %s not found.  \n, dname.arr) ;
                    EXEC SQL ROLLBACK WORK ;
                    exit (1)

        errB:
                    printf ("SQL error – no updates to database made. \n") ;
                    EXEC SQL ROLLBACK WORK ;
                    exit (1)
}    /* -------- END -------- */
```

Figure 13-13   Sample program with embedded SQL.

What happens when you write and run an SQL query? How are the various SQL statements executed? Are they verified by the DBMS before execution begins? Are they executed in the order in which the statements are translated? If so, will the natural sequence in the way a query is written be the optimal method for execution?

In earlier database systems like the hierarchical or network database systems, the application programmer writing a query in a procedural language was able to determine and direct the flow of the execution steps. A nonprocedural language such as SQL does not consist of sequential execution steps; the programmer is not in control of how a query must be executed. So it becomes the responsibility of the DBMS to examine each query, analyze it, and come up with the best possible sequence and plan for its execution. The optimal plan for the execution of a query must have

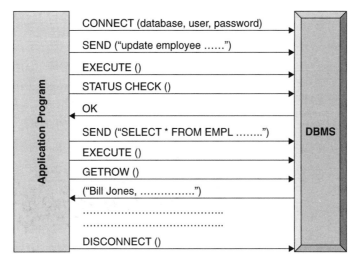

Figure 13-14 Sample program with SQL CLI.

minimum cost in terms of resource utilization and must result in minimum response time for the query.

Relational DBMSs translate a nonprocedural SQL data request into an optimal execution plan using computer science optimization techniques. We will briefly examine the various steps necessary to parse, analyze, prepare an optimal query plan, and execute an SQL query. You will gain an insight into the mechanics of query processing and understand how various components of a relational DBMS work together to process a query. Query optimization and execution techniques are major and extensive topics. For our purposes, we need not go into the complexities of the methods and algorithms. You need a broad and general view of the topics.

Query Processing Steps

Consider what happens to a query once it is written and presented for execution. What are the distinct steps, and what functions does DBMS carry out in each of these steps? How do these steps finally produce the result of the query in an optimal manner?

Let us begin with a diagram. Figure 13-15 highlights the major steps and indicates the functions in each step.

Note the following highlights of each step shown in the figure and the functions of each DBMS component:

Scanning. Carefully examine the text of the query and identify the language components such as SQL keywords, names of relations, names of attributes, built-in functions, and operators.

Parsing. Verify that the query syntax conforms to SQL syntax grammar.

Validating. Check and validate relation and attribute names and verify the semantics of the query.

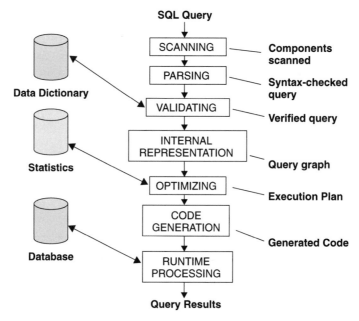

Figure 13-15 Query processing steps.

Internal representation. Create an internal representation or data structure for the query in the form of a query tree or query graph. Usually this data structure consists of translations of query components into relational algebra operations forming a query tree or query graph.

Optimizing. Examine alternative execution strategies for the query, choose an optimal strategy, and produce an execution plan.

Code generation. Generate code for executing the plan produced by the optimizer.

Runtime processing. Run the query code, compiled or interpreted, to produce the query result.

The Query Optimizer

In a relational database system, the query optimizer plays a vital role by enhancing performance a great deal. If every query is translated and executed in the haphazard manner in which it is written, database access tends to be slow and overall performance suffers. User productivity diminishes in such an environment.

Figure 13-16 presents the overall function of the query optimizer.

First, the query optimizer must analyze the query and determine the various ways in which the query may be executed. In the best of conditions, the query optimizer must consider every possible way a query may be executed. Let us say that a query consists of just three operations: SELECT, JOIN, and PROJECT. Even this simple

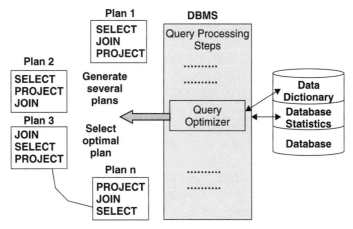

Figure 13-16   Query optimizer: overall function.

query may be executed in six different sequences. In practice, however, queries contain several operations with complex selection and join conditions. Therefore, it is not practical to review every possible way a query may be executed. Query optimizers only consider a feasible subset of all the possible ways.

Next, the query optimizer must have a proven method for choosing the best execution strategy from the competing strategies. The optimizer adopts an optimization technique to evaluate each execution plan. On the basis of the optimization technique, the optimizer selects the best possible query plan.

We will briefly scrutinize two common techniques used by the query optimizer for selecting the optimal execution plan. One technique adopts a heuristic approach; the other approach utilizes cost comparisons. These techniques examine the query tree for each of the possible ways a query may be executed and then select the tree that represents the optimal execution plan.

Heuristic Approach

If you consider a single query, it can be transformed into several different distinct sets of relational algebra operations. Each set of these operations comprises a relational algebraic expression. When you are able to transform a single query into several distinct algebraic expressions, in effect, all these expressions are equivalent and expected to produce the same result. Now the question arises: Which of the several algebraic expressions will produce the result in the most optimal manner using the minimum resources and consuming the least time?

As a consequence of parsing the query, an initial query tree representing the SQL query is constructed. This version of the query tree just represents the initial transformation of the query into a relational algebraic expression without any optimization. The optimizer must now transform this initial relational algebraic expression or its representation as a query tree into a more efficient expression or tree. The process of transformation continues until the most efficient expression or tree emerges.

How does the optimizer proceed to refine the query tree and make it more and more efficient? In the heuristic approach, the optimizer applies heuristic rules to convert the initial tree into a more efficient tree in each step. Therefore, this approach is also known as rule-based optimization.

Here are a few examples of good heuristic practices for making an initial relational algebraic expression or query tree more efficient:

- Perform selection operations first. This means moving selection operations down the query tree. Again, apply the most restrictive selection operation earliest.
- Combine a Cartesian product operation and a subsequent selection operation and replace them with a join operation.
- Perform projection operation as early as possible. This means moving projection operation down the query tree.
- Compute repeating expressions once, store the result, and reuse the result.

Now, let us see how rules such as these are applied in the heuristic approach. Use Figure 13-11 to consider the following query:

```
SELECT   PatientName
FROM     PATIENT P, TREATMENT T, DOCTOR D
WHERE    DoctorName = "Ruby Ross"
         AND D.DoctorID = T.DoctorID
         AND P.PatientNo = T.PatientNo
         AND DOB > 12DEC1952
```

Figures 13-17 and 13-18 illustrate the consecutive steps in the transformation process of the query trees for this query using the heuristic approach.

Follow optimization steps 1 through 5. Note how, in step 1, the initial query tree will produce a large result set from the PRODUCT operations on the PATIENT, DOCTOR, and TREATMENT relations. Therefore, this initial query tree is very inefficient. Note, however, that the query needs only one row from the DOCTOR relation and only those PATIENT relation rows where the date of birth is after Dec. 31, 1952. So the next version of the query tree, in step 2, moves the SELECT operations down to be executed first. A further improvement, in step 3, is achieved by switching the order of these two SELECT operations because the SELECT operation on DOCTOR relation will retrieve only one record. Proceed further and examine the improvements in steps 4 and 5.

Cost-Based Optimization

In the heuristic approach, the optimizer applies a number for rules to arrive at the optimal query tree for execution. The optimizer selects the appropriate rules for a particular query and applies the rules in the proper sequence as the process of query tree transformation continues. At the end of each step when a more efficient query tree emerges, you do not know exactly how much better the newer version of the

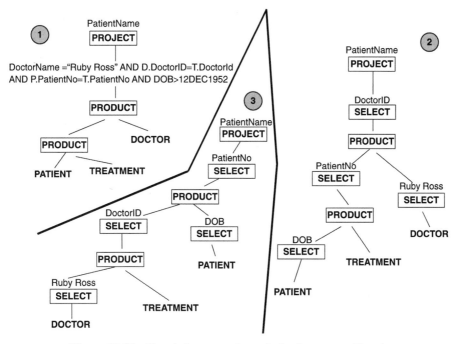

Figure 13-17   Heuristic approach: optimization steps—Part 1.

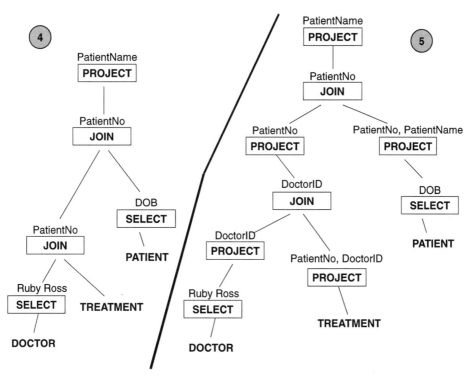

Figure 13-18   Heuristic approach: optimization steps—Part 2.

query tree is. The optimizer does not compare any numbers between tree versions to justify each transformation step.

On the other hand, the underlying principle in cost-based optimization is the ability to compute cost of resources for each version of the tree, compare the costs, and then choose the tree version that is optimal. However, you know that each query may be represented by an enormous number of versions of the query tree. It is not, therefore, practical to compute the costs for every possible version of the query tree and make the comparisons. The query optimizer limits the number of versions of the query tree by rejecting the unpromising ones.

For computing query costs, the optimizer must determine the cost components of a query and the actual calculation of cost for each component. We will briefly examine these two aspects of cost-based optimization before moving on to another topic.

Cost Components   Although the cost for accessing data storage constitutes the primary cost for query execution, the total cost includes the following factors:

Cost to store data. For storing any intermediate result sets during query execution—could be substantial for queries involving large data volumes.

Cost to access data storage. For searching and reading data blocks from disk storage with or without indexes and for writing data blocks to disk storage.

Cost for sorting and merging data. For sorting and merging during query execution and for performing any heavy-duty computations.

Cost for memory buffers. For allocation and usage of numerous and large memory buffers.

Cost for data transmission. For data communication between user machine and database server, wherever these are.

Cost Computation   In the calculation of the cost for query execution, the cost of data access is by far the largest element. Reduction of the cost of data access through query optimization produces the biggest payoff. Query optimizers basically concentrate on selection of the best query plan by comparing costs of data access.

The data access cost for a particular query depends on a number of factors. If the query accesses a CUSTOMER table, pertinent data for cost calculation include information about the number of rows in the table, number of data blocks for that relation, indexes, and so on. The query optimizer has to get these statistics to compute data access costs every time a query is executed. Query execution will incur a large overhead if the optimizer has to spend too much time to calculate the costs for many alternative plans every execution.

Therefore, this approach to query optimization is more suitable for compiled queries where calculations and optimization could be done at compile time and the resulting code based on optimal execution plan is stored. Then at runtime, recalculation and reoptimization are not necessary every time the query is run. For interpreted queries, all of this calculation has to be redone every time the query is run.

What about the statistics for calculating the costs? Where are they stored? Typically, the data dictionary or system catalog stores the following statistics to be used for cost calculation:

Data cardinality. Number of rows for each relational table.

Data volume. Number of data blocks for each relational table.

Index cardinality. Number of distinct values for each index.

Index height. Number of nonleaf levels in each B-tree index.

Index range. Current minimum and maximum values of the key for each index.

As you know, day-to-day database transactions will be affecting these statistics for each relation continually. The number of rows of a particular relation is likely to change, as are other statistics about the relation. As the statistics change, so does the calculation of the access costs for queries on given relations. If the statistics for a given relation have to be changed by every relevant transaction, such an arrangement will slow the transactions down. Therefore, the general practice is to run special utility jobs for updating the statistics. When the statistics are updated, any affected, compiled queries must be reoptimized

To examine the principles of cost-based optimization, let us consider a query discussed above.

    SELECT SERVICE.ServiceCode, ServiceDesc
      FROM SERVICE, BILLING
        WHERE SERVICE.ServiceCode = BILLING.ServiceCode and
          PatientNo = 224466

Figure 13-19 presents two versions of the query tree for executing this query. Note the differences between the two tree versions. Even with a cursory examination, the cost of running version 1 of the query is seen to be much larger because of the large product operations. Cost-based optimizers calculate the costs for performing each operation as you move up the query tree. The cost for each type of operation depends on a number of factors including the types of indexes available. Just note how the query optimizer first comes up with a reasonable set of query tree options and then decides on the optimal tree after calculating the costs of executing each tree version. The details of how these cost calculations are performed are beyond the scope of our discussion.

DATABASE SYSTEM DEPLOYMENT

Let us trace back and find our place in the database development life cycle. The life cycle begins with planning and feasibility study. Then you gather the information requirements and produce the requirements definition document. Next, in the design phase, you complete the logical design followed by the physical design of the

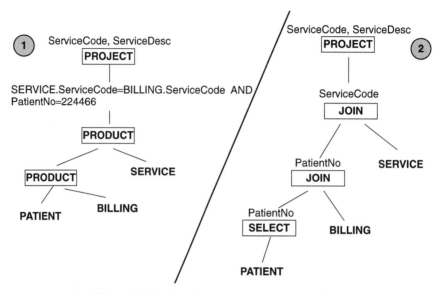

Figure 13-19   Sample query: query tree versions.

database system. We covered physical design in sufficient detail in Chapter 12. Now you are ready for implementation and deployment of the database system.

In the deployment phase, you make the database system ready and available to users. The final database system must contain data to satisfy the information requirements as defined in the requirements definition phase and then used to perform the logical and physical design.

We will now review the major tasks for deployment. Access to the database through application programs must be established. Storage space for files must be allocated. Data dictionary entries must be made. Database files must be populated with initial data. Let us highlight the major tasks and also discuss special issues relating to implementation and deployment of the database system.

Deployment Tasks

Let us continue from the end of the physical design step of the design phase. As you will note, the design has been verified and now you are ready to implement the physical design as the database system. We will list and highlight the major deployment tasks. In later subsections, we will also consider special issues relating to the deployment phase.

Here is a list of major deployment tasks:

Install DBMS. As you know, the physical design took the target or selected database management system into consideration. Now, set all the initial parameters and complete the installation of the selected DBMS.

Build data dictionary. Using the data definition facility provided in the selected DBMS—usually a version of SQL—create the data dictionary entries to define the relations, attributes, key constraints, indexes, and other constraints.

Provide application interfaces. Install and test software interfaces to provide links for application programs written in host languages to access the database.

Complete final testing. Test a final set of queries and application programming interfaces. Obtain user acceptance.

Complete data conversions. Special programs are written to convert data from the old data systems in the organization and to populate the new database. Complete testing of the data conversion programs.

Populate database. Use the outputs of the data conversion programs to populate the new database. Special programs may have to be written to use these outputs and add data to the new database. Alternatively, you may use these outputs to create sequential files with exact layouts of the database tables. Such files are called load image files. DBMS provides utility programs to load the database with the initial data from load image files. Initial data loading may be inordinately long if you create all the indexes during the load process. It is customary to suspend creation of indexes during the load process and to create the indexes after the loading is complete.

Build indexes. After the initial data load, build primary and secondary indexes.

Get user desktops ready. Install all system and other software needed at each desktop. Deployment of the database may become an opportunity to upgrade user desktops. Test each user machine including logging on to the database system.

Complete initial user training. Train users on database concepts, the overall database content, and the access privileges. If applicable to your environment, train power users in creating and running queries.

Institute initial user support. Set up support to assist users in basic usage and to answer questions on database access and performance.

Deploy in stages. Consider opening up the database system in well-defined stages to the various user groups. This approach is especially recommended if this is the first database system for the organization.

Implementation in Centralized Architecture

Earlier computer systems based on mainframes centralized all transaction processing. User applications were run on mainframes; database functionality was provided in a centralized architecture. User terminals connected the users to the mainframe and the centralized database systems. These terminals did not possess innate processing power; they were just display terminals. Data manipulation was done remotely at the mainframe, and the results were propagated to the display terminals.

Figure 13-20 illustrates a centralized DBMS architecture.

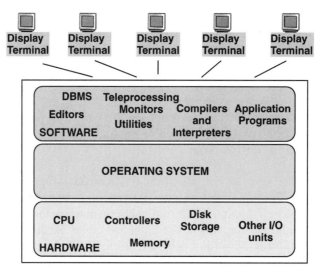

Figure 13-20   Centralized DBMS architecture.

Implementation in Client/Server Architecture

You are probably familiar with client/server computing. However, let us first review the client/server computing model and briefly describe its features. Here is a broad description:

- Client/server architecture implies cooperative or distributed processing. Two or more systems are linked through network connections.
- There could be one or many servers on the network—print server, file server, communications server, and relational database server. However, to the user signing on to the computer system, the system appears to be a unified system.
- The client system executes some parts of the application and provides the user interface. The client system requests services from the various servers.
- The server system provides services requested by client systems. Typically, a relational DBMS engine runs on a server machine.

Figure 13-21 illustrates a simple client/server architecture at the logical level. Note the various client machines attached to a communications network in a centralized configuration.

Although many database management systems started out as mainframe versions, now every vendor has adapted its DBMS for client/server architecture. User interface and application programs used to reside on the mainframe computer system. Now, these are the first programs to be moved to the client side in a client/server configuration. Query and transaction processing performs on the server side. The database component resides on the server side.

In a typical client/server setup, application programs and user interface software run on the client machines. When an application program on the client side requires a database access, it establishes a connection to the DBMS on the server side. When

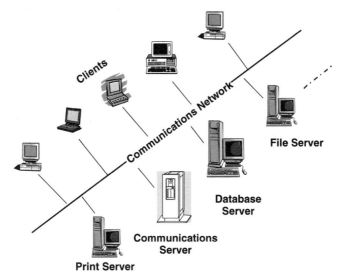

Figure 13-21 Logical client/server architecture.

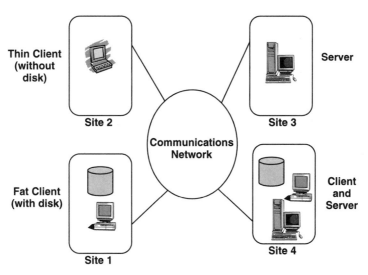

Figure 13-22 Physical client/server architecture configurations.

both client and server machines have the necessary software, ODBC, the current standard, provides an Application Programming Interface (API) to call the DBMS from the client side. Most DBMS vendors provide ODBC drivers for their databases. Query results are sent to the client machine, which formats and displays the results as necessary. Similarly, JAVA client programs can access the DBMS through another interface known as JDBC.

Figure 13-22 provides a sample of physical client/server architecture configurations. Note the different configurations at various sites.

CHAPTER SUMMARY

- Database implementation includes definition of data structures, enabling of database usage, optimal processing of data requests, and other ancillary tasks to prepare users.
- Languages are essential for implementation of a database system. These languages serve two primary purposes—storage of data and usage of data.
- The data definition language (DDL) component defines the data structures and supports the storage of data.
- The data manipulation language (DML) component enables data retrieval and data maintenance. Data maintenance consists of addition, deletion, and modification of data.
- Earlier relational languages include Query-by-Example (QBE), Quel, and Datalog. These languages contain DDL and DML components.
- Structured Query Language (SQL), a command-driven, declarative, nonprocedural language, has evolved as the standard for relational database systems.
- Both ANSI and ISO have adopted and standardized SQL. The process of standardization and enhancing SQL continues.
- As a DDL, SQL provides statements for the specification of logical and physical components for the relational database. SQL supports a variety of data types.
- Data retrieval in SQL is accomplished through an SQL query made up of three simple clauses or commands—SELECT, FROM, and WHERE.
- SQL has provisions to grant and revoke data access privileges to users. Access privileges may be granted to users to perform only specific functions such as data retrieval, data addition, data update, and so on.
- Data access from an application program to a relational database is generally accomplished in two ways: embedding SQL statements in host language programs or using an application programming interface (API) consisting of standard database functions.
- Query processing consists of several steps including the important step of optimizing the query. Two common approaches for query optimization are heuristic or rule-based optimization and cost-based optimization.

REVIEW QUESTIONS

1. What is the meaning of implementation of a data model? Which two primary purposes are accomplished by implementation?
2. How do languages enable implementation of a data model? What is the role of languages in implementation?
3. Distinguish the functions: data retrieval, data maintenance, and data control.
4. List any four of the overall features of SQL.
5. Name any five data definition statements in SQL. Describe the purpose of each.

6. List and explain any four data types supported by SQL.

7. What are the three primary clauses in an SQL query? Describe the function of each clause.

8. How is data modification done in SQL? Describe with an example.

9. List the steps in query processing. Describe the tasks carried out in two of these steps.

10. What is cost-based query optimization? How does the optimizer compute costs?

EXERCISES

1. Match the columns:

1. query validating	A.	eliminate duplicates in result
2. delete row	B.	rule-based
3. distinct specification in SQL	C.	directly access database
4. QBE	D.	call-level interface to database
5. float	E.	verify relation names
6. index height	F.	verify query semantics
7. heuristic query optimization	G.	data type in SQL
8. API	H.	used by query optimizer
9. query parsing	I.	data maintenance function
10. embedded SQL	J.	adopts a visual approach

2. Create a relational data model for a doctor's office consisting of the following objects: PATIENT, DOCTOR, VISIT, SERVICE, and BILLING. Using SQL, code data definition statements to create the schema for this database.

3. Write five different SQL queries using the above DOCTOR database. Explain the functions of the SQL statements in each of the queries.

4. Write five different SQL data control commands granting and revoking access privileges to the above DOCTOR database. Explain the purpose of each command.

5. You are the database administrator in a database project for an airline company. Write a memo to your project manager describing the functions of the query optimizer of your DBMS. Discuss the two common approaches, and state your preference with reasons.

PART VI

DATABASE ADMINISTRATION AND MAINTENANCE

CHAPTER 14

OVERVIEW OF ADMINISTRATION FUNCTIONS

CHAPTER OBJECTIVES

- Appreciate the importance of administering the database environment
- Study the goals and objectives of administration
- Distinguish between two aspects of administration—data and database
- Learn the major responsibilities of data and database administration
- Examine skills and training needed for the administration roles
- Ascertain the administration responsibilities throughout the database development life cycle

Think of an organization with a database system. When you consider any organization supported by a database system, you cannot imagine the system functioning without the services of a database administrator (DBA). Well, who is a DBA and what kind of specialized administration does he or she perform?

A database environment brings with it a set of new technologies and new functions. Many of these are specialized functions. The DBMS (database management system) that supports a database system is sophisticated software. You need special knowledge and skills to install and operate a DBMS. Designing the data structures, organizing them, and managing storage space for them call for special training. One or more specially trained personnel must be available to administer the database environment.

We will examine the evolution of the DBA role in database systems. You will study the objectives and responsibilities of the administrative role. The administrative role, in one form or another, continues to be necessary throughout the life cycle

Database Design and Development: An Essential Guide for IT Professionals by Paulraj Ponniah
ISBN 0-471-21877-4   Copyright © 2003 by John Wiley and Sons, Inc.

of a database system. You will walk through the life cycle phases and observe the administrative tasks required in each phase.

This chapter is intended as an overview of all administration functions. The chapter will highlight the various responsibilities and tasks and the significance of administration functions. In a general way, we will explore the significance of administration and establish why it is indispensable for a database system. Then we will discuss the special skills and knowledge required for those responsible for administration functions. We will look at the specific tasks necessary for administration during every phase of database development, deployment, and even after deployment.

Among these responsibilities are a few that are of crucial importance. Although this chapter introduces database administration and provides you with a broad overview, we will cover the important functions more extensively in separate chapters. Database administration extends to maintaining the integrity of the database. The data content should be correct and consistent. Chapter 15 deals exclusively with data integrity. Chapter 16 covers database security. Safeguarding the database is a prime responsibility of administration. The issues of who gets data access privileges and to what extent must be carefully managed.

The administration functions do not cease when the database project is completed and the database system is up and running. Ongoing maintenance is a vital part of administration. You will learn about ongoing maintenance in Chapter 17, which is completely devoted to that topic.

SIGNIFICANCE OF ADMINISTRATION

Many organizations made the transition to database systems from their file-oriented data systems in the 1970s and 1980s. Usage of database software, laying out the files, keeping the data consistent and correct, safeguarding the data content from unauthorized users, ensuring continued availability of the data system to users—these and many other tasks in the file-oriented environment were no match for those in the by far more sophisticated database environment.

Each user group owned, managed, and controlled its own data files. The advent of database systems changed the dispersed nature of control and management. The database system, because of its ability to share data among various user groups, prompted centralized coordination. The database moved control and administration functions from local units to the center of an organization. Someone, or some role, must exercise centralized control and coordination.

In the 1970s, we see the emergence of this new role for administration of the database system. Information technology professionals had to be specially trained for this new role and were entrusted with the administration of the database environment. As database management systems became more and more sophisticated, database vendors welcomed the emergence of the specially trained administrator. They needed people with special knowledge and skills within their client organizations with whom they could communicate on a technical level.

Although in earlier database implementations, organizations realized the need for the role for administration of the database system, specialists called DBAs did not appear right away. Initially, the systems programmer and the technical support group took on the additional responsibility of administration of the database system. The need for special training and knowledge became more and more evident. Organizations began to train technical analysts and project leaders already in database projects. These professionals were given training in the particular DBMS and allocated additional responsibilities to carry out administration functions. As DBMSs and databases moved toward greater sophistication, the need for specialists with sole administration responsibilities became evident. Now most organizations with database systems have DBAs set apart for a distinct role. In many companies, the administration functions are split between data administration and database administration. Let us explore these administration functions further and cover wider ground.

Essential Need for Administration

You now have a broad idea of how the role of DBA emerged and why it is necessary in a database environment. You understand that the database environment is more complex and more sophisticated than earlier file-oriented data systems and therefore needs someone or some group, properly trained, to manage and administer it. Given the intricacies of modern DBMSs, you appreciate why special training and knowledge have become necessary to understand these software systems.

Let us get more specific and list the reasons why a specialized administration function is absolutely essential in a database environment. Reviewing these reasons will enable you to understand how the administration function continues throughout the life cycle of a database system. You will gain insight into the types of skills and training needed to strengthen data and database administration specialists for carrying out their responsibilities.

In Chapter 2, we presented the components of the database environment in Figure 2-2. We will use that figure to place the administration function in the database environment and to observe how and where an administrator fits in. Figure 14-1 illustrates the role and place of administration in the database environment. Carefully note the various components of the database environment and notice how administration fits in and interacts with these components.

Now let us move on to the list of major reasons for the essential need to have a distinct administration role in the database environment.

Centralized Coordination   Note the change in an organization with a database system. The database system promotes information sharing; it shares information with many departments and users. Pieces of corporate data are no longer owned or administered by individual departments. The shared resource belongs to the entire enterprise; it is not the property of a single group. This radical change in responsibility and ownership calls for centralized control and administration. A centralized administration role must be established to assume this responsibility.

Data, a Vital Asset   Every organization now considers its database system to be highly important. Just like other assets of cash, inventory, or equipment, corporate data are regarded as a significant asset for an organization. The corporate controller manages and controls the company's finances. Similarly, there ought to be a custo-

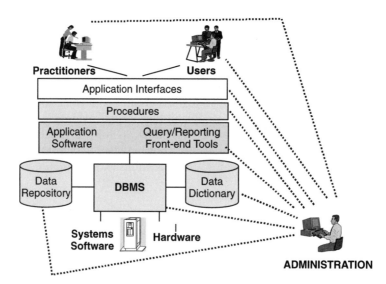

Figure 14-1 Administration in the database environment.

dian for corporate data. This custodian must develop procedures to manage and control the data asset of an organization. A specialized group or person must assume direct responsibility for the organization's data resource.

Protection of Data If data is a significant corporate asset, then they must be safeguarded from unauthorized access. Authorized users must be given the necessary access privileges to the applicable data elements. Only authorized users must be permitted to access the database. The organization must establish a clear and reliable security policy. The policy must be carefully reviewed and put into practice. In a large establishment, this is an extensive responsibility. Such a responsibility can be entrusted only to people with knowledge of the data needs of every user group in the organization.

Uniform Standards Consider the definitions and naming of data elements in an organization with a database system. Assume that there is a data element called *account* in a bank's database. Now this data element, being part of the database, is shared and used by the bank's staff in the various departments. What does the data element *account* mean? Does it refer to savings accounts, checking accounts, or loan accounts? Does it denote the balance amount in the account? If so, how large is the account field?

Because the data elements in a database are shared among various departments, it becomes all the more necessary to standardize data names, data definitions, and data types. You need someone responsible for instituting corporate-wide standards.

Sophisticated DBMSs The sophistication of commercial DBMSs continues to increase as the organization's database expands to serve new information needs. DBMS enables an organization to set up the database, to define the structures, to incorporate constraints and rules, to grant access privileges to authorized users, to back up the data content, to safeguard the data from concurrent updates, and so on. Now, with the Internet, data warehousing, and analytical processing, the scope and usage of database systems have expanded tremendously.

How can organizations make use of the remarkable power and range of today's DBMSs? Only by having a group or an individual fully trained in particular DBMSs. The DBA in an organization must have expertise in the particular commercial DBMS that manages its database system.

Data Integrity A database is only as good as the integrity and correctness of the data it contains. If the data are incorrect or inconsistent, then the worth of the database is greatly diminished. For example, if the database in a large medical center shows the room numbers of the inpatients and if you do not find the patients in the room numbers shown by the database system, then the database is worthless as far as patient locations are concerned.

Data integrity in a database may be compromised in a number of ways. If proper edits are not instituted, incorrect data creep in. In a relational database, if entity integrity and referential integrity are not enforced, data may get out of line. When concurrent transactions attempt to update the same data elements simultaneously, without proper concurrency controls, the data elements may be left with incorrect values.

The administration role in a database environment has the serious responsibility of preserving data integrity. The administrator must accomplish this through proper edits, constraints, and concurrency controls. He or she needs special training and knowledge in data integrity methods.

Data Availability Modern enterprises depend on the information contained in their operational databases to run their day-to-day businesses. Profitability, competitive edge, and even the very survival of many businesses rest heavily on the strength of their database systems. Organizations need their database systems to be up and available all the time. 24/7 operation is especially critical for global organizations with user locations spread out worldwide.

Can you imagine an airline reservation system down even for a few minutes? What about the databases in banks and financial institutions? Can these be down for even short durations? Think of the databases supporting defense applications and government departments. Continuous availability of the corporate database is a critical requirement. Apart from scheduled downtime for maintenance, an organization's database must always be available to users in today's business environment.

What can go wrong, and why would database systems become unavailable? Many types of hardware and software malfunctions can interrupt availability. The organization has to recover quickly from such disruptions and make the database accessible again. We will consider database recovery in greater detail in Chapter 15. Right now, realize that recognizing malfunctions and taking suitable actions to recover the database are intricate functions. An organization needs specially trained professionals to perform such complicated functions.

Resource Management Many types of hardware and software resources work together to make the database system of an organization functional. You need proper hardware infrastructure with powerful database servers. A robust operating system that can support parallel processing of data access requests must be present. Disk storage based on RAID technology has become the norm for storage of today's databases. Most companies also need data communications hardware and software for the database to be in operation. In addition, middleware to support remote operations is also in order for the database environment.

The DBMS works with the operating systems and the communication systems. Specialists in database products need to work with systems programmers and technical support groups to manage the various resources in the database environment. You can therefore see the need for people specialized in resource management to carry out the necessary functions.

Tuning for Efficiency   Typically when a new database system is installed in an organization, usage of the database steadily expands. Usage patterns themselves change. New users come on board. More sophisticated applications are added. Over time, the efficiency of the database begins to slide and data access times start to rise. Transaction response times are crucial in most environments.

What must be done when the database slows down and the response becomes sluggish? The symptoms must be analyzed, the changes in the usage patterns must be reviewed, and the usage of resources must be examined. It is likely that new indexes are necessary and that some existing indexes may have to be dropped. The process of fine-tuning is a complex analytical task, and an organization needs specialists to perform this task.

Administration Objectives

From the previous subsection you are now convinced that someone or some group, specially trained, must be responsible for the administration of the database environment in an organization. You have seen several reasons for this essential need. What are the major objectives of the administration function? What is this function intended to accomplish in the database environment?

Let us summarize the main goals and objectives:

Enterprise information requirements. Analyze business needs and determine the information requirements to plan and conduct the organization's business.

Data integration. Consolidate information requirements and define standards.

Information framework. Plan for the database system; determine hardware and system software upgrades; select DBMS.

Physical implementation. Assist in the logical design; perform physical design; implement and deploy database system.

Data quality. Ensure correctness, validity, and consistency of the database system.

Data security. Enable data access to authorized users; protect database system from unauthorized use.

Data availability. Ensure that data is available to users from the database system—whenever data are required, whatever data are required, and however data are required.

Data system performance. Ensure continued acceptable performance levels of the database system.

Examine the major goals listed. Think of the types of skills and training needed to perform the administration function. As you scrutinize the activities and tasks required to accomplish the goals and objectives, you will conclude that persons performing the administration function must have both managerial and technical skills.

For example, the tasks for determining enterprise information requirements involve a lot of coordination and organization. The tasks for establishing the information framework require more planning and coordination than working with highly technical details.

On the other hand, the tasks for physical implementation and ensuring system performance suggest more technical details than planning and coordination. Ensuring that the database system is quickly recovered from malfunctions and made available to users within a short time also involves more technical skills than managerial acumen.

Consider the goal of data security. Who gets authorized, for what purposes, and to access which data items—these are matters of planning and organization. But how to set up the authorization is more technical than managerial in nature.

On the basis of these considerations, many organizations realize that administration of a database system is not for a single group but needs two groups of specialists. So they are dividing up the administration function between two groups of professionals. One group, adopting the more managerial aspects, has come to be known as the data administration group; the other, taking on the more technical responsibilities, is known as the database administration group.

Figure 14-2 illustrates the division of responsibilities between data administration and database administration.

Although the bifurcation of responsibilities between data administration and database administration is gaining ground, not all organizations with databases have clear-cut divisions. Nor do most organizations have two distinct groups handling data administration and database administration tasks. Many small to medium-sized

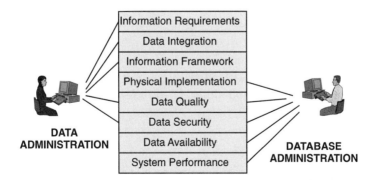

Figure 14-2   Data administration and database administration.

companies have only database administrators, who perform most of the data administration functions as well. Analysts and project leaders pitch in and perform any remaining data administration functions.

In the following subsections, we will explore the nature of data administration and database administration functions. For the rest of this chapter, even though we discuss these two functions separately, remember that in many organizations you will only find DBAs and no group designated as data administrators (DAs). Although in these organizations the functions are combined as the responsibility of DBAs, for the purpose of our discussions, it is worthwhile to consider the functions separately. In this way, our discussions will be complete.

Data Administration

As already mentioned, data administration is more of a managerial function to manage and control the database environment. The DA practices all the key elements of management in his or her involvement in the database environment—planning, coordination, execution, control, and communication. The DA is generally responsible for policies and procedures. The DA is like a custodian of corporate data resource. He or she is intimately involved in planning the various aspects of the database environment.

In some large enterprises, a group of professionals form the data administration group. The group—not a single individual—assumes the data administration role. Nevertheless, whether a single individual or a group has the responsibility for data administration, the role is still the same and the same tasks are performed.

Here is a typical list of functions of data administration:

- Establish corporate-wide data requirements.
- Ascertain future requirements.
- Communicate with users on data ownership and data control policies.
- Set up centralized control over the data resource.
- Play a leading role in planning for the database system—what data to collect, how to store data, and how to promote data usage.
- Plan for hardware and system software upgrades to support the new database system.
- Organize education for users on database technology and its great advantages.
- Establish realistic expectations and set guidelines to measure user satisfaction.
- Standardize data names, data types, and definitions for universal use.
- Establish standards and procedures for data integrity.
- Institute data security policy.
- Constantly communicate with IT management, corporate management, user departments, the DBA, and other IT professionals on plans, policies, and procedures.

Database Administration

The database administration role comprises a different set of responsibilities. Although the DBA participates in database planning, coordination and planning are not primary responsibilities. The DBA gets the technical work done. The DBA's role of getting down to technical details is evident throughout the development and implementation of the database system.

Typical functions for the database administration role are as follows:

- Participate in the selection of the DBMS.
- Define requirements for hardware and system software upgrades to accommodate the new database.
- Work with the DA on data standards to conform to the provisions in the target DBMS.
- Perform physical design of the database system.
- Liaise with the database vendor and install the DBMS.
- Set up data dictionary entries in coordination with the DA.
- Create user accounts and maintain data access authorizations.
- Manage database backup and recovery.
- Monitor and tune database performance.
- Coordinate with the database vendor and plan for upgrades.
- Provide DBMS-specific information to analysts and database designers.

SKILLS AND RESPONSIBILITIES

You have grasped the significance of the administration functions in a database environment. You have understood why these functions are absolutely essential not only to initiate a database system but also to keep it going in an organization. We reviewed the broad objectives of administration. You have also learned the essential difference between data administration and database administration. Because of the enormous importance of administration functions in a database environment, let us focus on these from slightly different perspectives.

You have noted the need for a DA and also for a DBA. How are they different, and why do you need both roles? What specific roles do these two types of administrators assume in a database environment? What major responsibilities do the DA and DBA fulfill?

By now you must assume that, given the significance and specialty of data administration and database administration functions, the DA and DBA have to be given specialized training and must acquire extraordinary skills. It is true that these professionals must possess specialized knowledge and have expertise in management and technical areas. We will elaborate on these as we proceed.

Administrative Roles

As you must have understood by now, the administrative roles assumed by the DA are more pronounced in the earlier stages of the database development life cycle. The early phases need a corporate-wide view of the organization's data, more intense planning, and coordination among the various departments who intend to be benefited by the database. On the other hand, the administrative roles of the

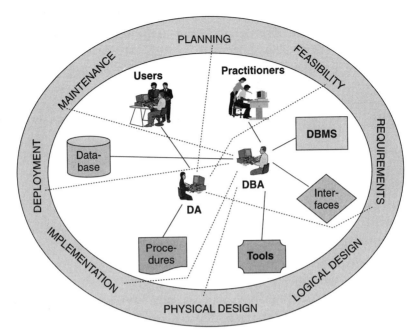

Figure 14-3   Administrative roles.

DBA begin their effect in later phases of the database development life cycle. Only in the later stages do you tend to get more and more technical.

Figure 14-3 depicts the administrative roles of the DA and those of the DBA.

Note the phases of the life cycle shown in the periphery of the figure. Also, observe the major components of a database environment. See how the administrative roles prove to be useful in the various phases and note how the DA and DBA play out these significant roles. It is important to observe how the DA and the DBA must work together in a highly cooperative manner.

Especially note the illustration of the following specific roles in the figure.

Data administrator. Planner, analyst, organizer, coordinator, communicator, liaison with users, controller.

Database administrator. Designer, technical expert, technical advisor, tester, security expert, database tuner.

Areas of Responsibility

Let us now look at the DA and DBA from another angle. Consider the major areas of responsibilities. Who is primarily responsible for specific activities and areas? How are the two functions meshed together for effective design and development of the database system?

We list here the areas of responsibilities without tying them to particular phases of the database development life cycle. In a later section, we will enumerate the tasks of the DA and DBA in the development phases, one by one. At this point, let us consider answers to broader questions. What are the responsibilities of the DA? What responsibilities fall under the DBA's jurisdiction? We will consider how the DA and DBA share the responsibilities for achieving the major goals of administration. For these major goals, let us demarcate the areas of responsibility.

Data Administrator

Information requirements. Coordinate requirements gathering activities. Liaise with user departments to analyze business needs and determine the information requirements, current and future. Develop an enterprise-wide overall data model. Determine information types and content to be included in the database system.

Data integration and design. Identify and reduce data redundancy among various departments. Define data names, types, and formats; establish standards. Approve all modifications to data characteristics. Coordinate preparation for data dictionary entries. Estimate current and future data volumes. Review logical design and ensure that all requirements are included.

Information framework. Plan for database environment. Review feasibility studies. Coordinate determination of hardware and system software upgrades. Coordinate selection of any productivity software for administration, data definitions, data design, and performance monitoring. Participate in selection of DBMS.

Physical implementation. No direct responsibility for physical design or DBMS installation. Ensure that all of the original information requirements are included in the final database system. Oversee verification of file conversions for initial population of database. Coordinate user training.

Data quality. Establish data quality standards. Coordinate with users on quality assurance practices. Define data ownership and responsibilities of user departments. Determine edits and constraints to be included in database system.

Data security. Establish security policy and procedures. Ensure that legal security and privacy requirements are satisfied.

Data availability. Liaise with users on usage and requirements for database availability; work out details of scheduled database maintenance with users and get their cooperation.

Data system performance. Establish database performance levels based on user expectations.

Database Administrator

Information requirements. No direct responsibility. Provide file layouts and data definitions from current data systems to DA and other interested professionals on the project team.

Data integration and design. No direct responsibility. Provide advice on possible data types and formats.

Information framework. Evaluate different DBMSs and participate in the final selection. Determine hardware and system software upgrades for the proposed database system; examine compatibility with selected DBMS. Evaluate productivity software from a technical viewpoint.

Physical implementation. Perform physical database design. Prepare disk storage and allocate space for database components. Install DBMS. Complete data dictionary entries in cooperation with DA. Load data from file conversions for initial population of database. Assist other IT professionals in project team in testing and verification of loaded data. Assist in user training.

Data quality. Incorporate edits and constraints through the facilities of the selected DBMS. Add all the necessary entity integrity and referential integrity constraints. Include proper controls such as locking mechanisms to eliminate problems from concurrent database updates.

Data security. Grant and revoke data access privileges to authorized users on the basis of established security policy. Monitor database access to detect unauthorized access.

Data availability. Back up database at regular intervals. Establish and test database recovery through the use of log files. Follow recommended maintenance schedule.

Database system performance. Monitor disk space usage and allocate additional space as and when necessary. Continuously monitor database usage; create or drop indexes according to changing access patterns. Perform DBMS upgrades. Recommend hardware and system software upgrades based on increased usage.

Skills, Knowledge, and Experience

Having examined the roles and responsibilities of the DA and the DBA in a number of ways and from different perspectives, you must now have a reasonable idea of the types of skills and expertise required to perform these administration functions. Once again, be guided by the general focus of each function. The DA is more of a managerial type than a technician; the DBA is more of a technical expert than an overall manager. That does not, however, imply that the DA is devoid of any technical knowledge or that the DBA has no managerial tasks at all.

Let us summarize the types of skills, knowledge, and experience needed for the two administration functions.

Data Administrator Must be able to see the big picture and perceive the overall information requirements. Must have strong appreciation of the significance of information as a corporate asset. Should be able to communicate effectively with all levels of users and information technology professionals. Must possess good people skills and be respected in the user community. Must have the ability to prepare short-term and long-term plans. Should be able to think through issues and establish policies and procedures for areas such as database usage, data ownership, data quality, and data security. Must be user-oriented rather than technology-oriented. Prior experience in managing application projects in a database environment could form a good foundation.

Database Administrator   Must possess expertise in physical design of database systems. Expected to have prior experience as a DBA in a similar organization. Should possess thorough knowledge of database implementation and deployment. Must have intimate knowledge of the selected DBMS. Knowledge and background in systems programming and technical support are very helpful. Must have acute problem-solving and trouble-shooting skills. Should have the ability to share technical knowledge about database systems and the particular DBMS with other information technology professionals on the project team—required to be a good team player. Must be knowledgeable in issues of concurrency control and database recovery. Should be flexible and dedicated to work and resolve problems in emergency situations at odd hours.

Interaction with Users and Practitioners

In the next sections, we will walk through the phases of the database development life cycle and summarize the tasks and responsibilities of the DA and DBA. This will provide a good conclusion to the discussion of the important topic of administration of the database environment.

Before proceeding to summarize the tasks and responsibilities, let us pause to observe the interaction of the DA and DBA with users and database practitioners. These administrators must interact with other people in a number of ways to carry out their responsibilities. Figure 14-4 highlights their interaction with users and information technology professionals. Note how the figure shows the various users at different levels and technology professionals by their job functions. Also, observe how the figure indicates the interaction with each group of people.

DURING DEVELOPMENT

We will now summarize the tasks and responsibilities of the DA and DBA in each of the phases of the development and implementation of the database system. Chapter 4 covered the various phases of the database development life cycle. Please go back to that chapter and quickly review the activities and tasks in every phase.

We will list the tasks in each phase in which the DA and DBA assume key roles. First, consider their participation in each phase. Figure 14-5 provides a broad indication of their participation.

In each of the following sections, we have listed the significant tasks in which the DA and DBA assume substantial responsibilities. Against each task, the function that plays a significant role is indicated. Note each task and also who is more involved in that task.

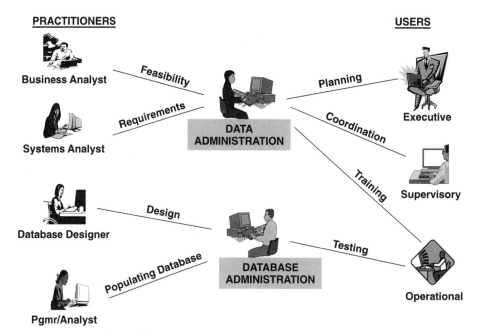

Figure 14-4 Interaction with users and practitioners.

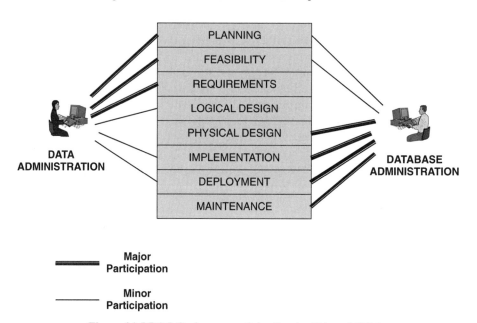

Figure 14-5 DDLC phases: participation by DA and DBA.

Planning and Feasibility Study

In these phases, the DA assumes a significant role. These phases set the tone for the entire project, and, therefore, as custodian of the organization's data, the DA is there to ensure that none of the overall data concerns are overlooked.

The DBA may sit in on the planning meetings as a technical advisor, but it is too early to define the needed DBMS features. In the feasibility study phase, the DBA assists in determining upgrades to the current infrastructure and calculation of costs.

DA	Understand business goals and objectives.
DA	Interpret organization's business plan for information requirements.
DA	Assess business opportunities and risks.
DA	Classify user groups for determination of data needs.
DA	Gauge user expectations.
DA	Determine data ownership issues.
DA	Develop enterprise information strategy and overall database environment.
DA/DBA	Make preliminary estimate of data volumes.
DBA	Assess the readiness of technological infrastructure and estimate costs for upgrade.
DA/DBA	Do preliminary skills review and estimate costs for training and additional personnel.
DBA	Establish criteria for DBMS selection.
DA	Match benefits against costs and prepare justification for database system.

Requirements Definition

The DA takes more active responsibilities in the requirements definition phase. The DBA's role in this phase is to be available as a technical advisor and database expert.

DA	Provide insight into overall business operations to analysts.
DA	Consolidate and integrate information requirements.
DA	Establish clear data definitions.
DA	Express business rules.
DA	Establish constraints and rules to validate data.
DA/DBA	Prepare data dictionary entries for data elements.
DA	Ascertain data usage patterns and access frequencies.
DA	Prepare list of users to be authorized and their data access requirements.
DA	Liaise with users to provide operational documents to analysts.
DBA	Provide layouts of current data files for analysts.
DA/DBA	Determine file conversions to switch over to new database system.
DBA	Estimate hardware storage space requirements.

Logical Design

The data modelers and database designers are active in this phase. They perform almost all the tasks of modeling and logical design. The DA assumes the role of a facilitator and establishes liaison with user groups. The DBA continues in the role of technical advisor to the project team on database concepts. Although not related to logical design, normally during this time frame, the DA and the DBA participate in finalizing the selection of the DBMS.

DA	Interpret and review data models with users.
DA	Ensure that logical data model is complete in terms of entities and relationships.
DA	Ensure that logical data model conforms to information requirements.
DA	Relate logical data model to individual user groups and establish user views.
DBA	Provide technical advice to data modelers and designers.
DBA	Install and maintain CASE tools needed for data modeling and design.
DBA/DA	Complete selection of DBMS.

Physical Design

The DBA is almost exclusively responsible for this phase. Here and there, the DA is available to answer questions or clarify any user requirements. While listing the tasks for physical design, implementation, and deployment, we have assumed the implementation of a relational database system. However, the tasks for any other type of conventional database system will be similar to these.

DBA	Transform logical design into physical design.
DBA	Determine file organization for various tables.
DBA	Determine indexes and clustering of tables.
DBA	Map physical storage to files and set data blocks.
DBA	Establish storage management parameters.
DBA	Review user views.
DBA	Review entity and referential integrity constraints.
DBA	Review data edits and business rules to be implemented through DBMS.
DBA/DA	Review and complete list for data dictionary entries.

Implementation and Deployment

All the database project members participate in final implementation and deployment. This is the culmination of all of the effort, and everyone has a stake in the success. Nevertheless, the DBA plays a key role in implementation and deployment. He or she is responsible for bringing the whole effort to a successful conclusion, and the significance of this role cannot be overemphasized. Review the following list and you will grasp the importance of the role.

DBA	Install selected DBMS.
DBA	Install application interfaces.
DBA	Define files for various tables.
DBA	Define indexes and clustering of tables.
DBA	Allocate physical storage to files and set data blocks.
DBA	Define storage management parameters.
DBA/DA	Define user views.
DBA	Define entity and referential integrity constraints.
DBA	Define data edits and business rules in data dictionary.
DBA/DA	Complete data dictionary entries for all definitions.
DBA/DA	Grant user privileges.
DBA/DA	Test backup and recovery.
DBA	Set concurrency control criteria.
DBA/DA	Complete final testing.
DBA/DA	Complete data conversions.
DBA	Perform initial data loads.
DBA/DA	Complete initial user training.
DBA/DA	Initiate initial user support.

AFTER DEPLOYMENT

Administration tasks do not end with the deployment of the initial version of the database system. They continue in several ways. The DBA continues to have many responsibilities. He or she has to keep the database up and running with optimum efficiency. In the postdeployment phase, the DA mostly gets involved when new data requirements emerge or when the service levels decrease.

In each of the following sections, we have listed the significant tasks and indicated the involvement of the DBA and DA.

Ongoing Functions

The DBA continues to perform many maintenance functions on an ongoing basis. These are mainly routine maintenance functions, and the DA is rarely involved in these activities.

DBA	Monitor database usage by gathering statistics.
DBA	Monitor usage by various user groups.
DBA	Police and detect unauthorized database access.
DBA	Watch space utilization and expand disk extents as data volume increases.
DBA	Organize and ensure periodic backups.
DBA	Create and maintain recovery log files.

DBA   Conduct periodic database recovery tests.

DBA   Reorganize files as and when necessary.

DBA   Schedule regular database maintenance.

DBA   Assist analysts and programmers in resolving database-related application problems.

DBA   As necessary, import external data into the database system or export data from the database.

DBA/DA   Grant and revoke access privileges as conditions change.

Maintenance of Service Levels

In a database environment, as the number of users increases and the patterns of data usage change, service levels tend to deteriorate. The database system becomes sluggish, and database transactions are apt to slow down. The DBA has the prime responsibility of maintaining and improving service levels.

DBA   Gather statistics to monitor database performance.

DBA   Add indexes and drop indexes based on changes in usage patterns.

DBA   Perform other performance improvement techniques as necessary.

DBA   Revise memory buffering as necessary.

DBA   Verify concurrency control procedures and revise when needed.

DBA   Work with application programmers to tune database access routines in application programs.

DBA   Recommend and install productivity and efficiency software tools.

Enhancements to Database System

This is a common feature of every database environment. Vendors continue to fix problems in the current version of the DBMS and also produce new versions with sustained regularity. The DBA interacts with the database vendor and assumes a primary role in enhancing the database system.

DBA   Apply software patches and enhancements to existing DBMS version received from vendor.

DBA   Install version upgrades to DBMS.

DBA   Organize testing of DBMS version upgrades.

DA   Liaise with users to test enhancements to database system.

DBA   Recommend and test infrastructure upgrades and enhancements to storage system.

Growth and Change

After deployment, the database grows in a few different ways. The data volume continues to increase as rows are added to the database tables. As business conditions change additional database tables become necessary. Even in existing tables, the need arises to add more columns. Growth and change are basic realities in a database environment. The administration functions need to manage growth and change in the database environment. Both the DA and the DBA share responsibilities in managing growth and change.

DA	Review changes to business conditions and plan for growth.
DA	Institute change management procedures for routine enhancements to existing tables and indexes.
DBA	Make changes to existing tables according to change management procedures.
DA/DBA	Develop procedures to archive old data and set up the archival system.
DBA	Use data compression techniques to conserve disk storage space and data communication costs in a distributed database environment.
DBA	Benchmark and recommend infrastructure upgrades.
DBA	Examine and recommend newer technologies such as parallel processing or RAID for data storage.
DBA	Coordinate with technical support group to evaluate processor capacity at regular intervals.

CHAPTER SUMMARY

- With the transition to more sophisticated database systems beginning in the 1970s, new roles for administration emerged.
- In a database environment, administration has become essential to have centralized coordination, protect the vital asset of data, adopt enterprise-wide uniform standards, understand and make use of sophisticated DBMSs, and make quality data available whenever, wherever, and however necessary.
- Administration in a database environment tends to be both managerial and technical—data administration is more managerial and database administration is more technical.
- The data administrator, as custodian of corporate data, is involved in planning, setting standards, coordinating and communicating with users, and establishing policies and procedures.
- The database administrator, as technical expert, implements and deploys the database system by providing data integrity, data security, and continued maintenance.
- Skills, training, and experience of the data administrator: ability to perceive the big picture, knowledge in methods for planning and coordination, capacity to communicate effectively, a user orientation rather than a technical one, and prior experience in managing application projects in a database environment.
- Skills, training, and experience of the database administrator: expertise in physical database design, deep knowledge of the selected DBMS, qualities of a team player, acute problem-solving and trouble-shooting skills, flexibility in being available, and prior experience or training as a database administrator.

- The data administrator assumes a major role in the earlier phases of the database development life cycle such as planning, feasibility study, and requirements definition.
- The database administrator assumes primary responsibilities in physical design, implementation, deployment of the database system, and ongoing maintenance.

REVIEW QUESTIONS

1. Give any four reasons why data administration and database administration are essential in a database environment.
2. Why is data a vital asset to an organization? How do the administrators protect this vital asset?
3. "The sophistication of modern DBMSs makes the DBA role essential." Explain.
4. Describe how the roles of the data administrator and database administrator are different.
5. List any five typical functions of data administration.
6. Name any five typical functions of database administration.
7. List four types each of skills needed by the data administrator and the database administrator.
8. List any four important functions of the data administrator in database planning and requirements definition phases.
9. Name any four significant functions of the database administrator in physical design and implementation phases.
10. List the major tasks of the data administrator and the database administrator after deployment of the database system.

EXERCISES

1. Indicate whether true or false:
   A. Every database environment must have both DA and DBA.
   B. DA is responsible for uniform standards.
   C. For data protection, DBA establishes policies and DA executes them.
   D. Sophistication of the DBMS needs specially trained DBAs.
   E. DA is responsible for managing physical resources such as disk storage.
   F. DBA liaises with database vendor.
   G. DA plays an important role in database planning.
   H. DBA interprets and reviews logical data models with users.
   I. DBA is responsible for backup and recovery of the database.
   J. DA has absolutely no responsibilities after database deployment.

2. You are the project manager of a database project. Draft a note to the CIO of your organization listing the skills, knowledge, and experience to be considered in hiring a data administrator.

3. Describe the qualifications for a DBA position in a large manufacturing company. Indicate which qualifications are absolutely necessary, desirable, or good to have.

4. As a DBA in a medical center, briefly describe your major functions during development and after deployment of the database system.

5. "DA and DBA functions are not that different; they need not be separate in a database environment." Do you agree or disagree? Support your assertion with reasons.

CHAPTER 15

DATA INTEGRITY

CHAPTER OBJECTIVES

- Learn what data integrity is and why it is extremely important
- Note the nature and significance of a database transaction
- Study the meaning of ACID properties of transactions and appreciate why a database system must preserve these
- Understand concurrent transactions and the types of problems they could cause
- Discuss serializability and recoverability of transactions
- Examine various methods of concurrency control
- Classify the potential types of failures in a database environment and review recovery concepts
- Survey logging and log-based recovery techniques
- Inspect shadow paging and its role as a recovery method

Take the case of a banking database system. Consider this scenario. Assume that one of the bank's customers wants to transfer $50,000 from his or her savings account to the his or her checking account to cover a check issued for an important deal. The check bounces, and on investigation the bank discovers that although $50,000 was deducted from the customer's savings account the amount was not added to the checking account. The bank loses an important but irate customer. Why? What has happened?

That database transaction transferring the amount from savings to checking accounts did not leave the database in a consistent state. Only one part of the trans-

Database Design and Development: An Essential Guide for IT Professionals by Paulraj Ponniah
ISBN 0-471-21877-4   Copyright © 2003 by John Wiley and Sons, Inc.

action updated the savings account database table; the other part meant to update the checking account database table failed. The database became inconsistent as far this customer's accounts were concerned.

Data integrity means absence of inconsistent data. The data in the database must be correct, valid, and accurate at all times. None of the transactions that update the database can leave the database in an inconsistent state. Transactions must preserve consistency; they must not corrupt the correctness and validity of the database.

In a typical database environment, thousands of transactions interact with the database and many of these update data. Concurrent transactions may attempt to update the same data element simultaneously. A database is also vulnerable to several types of failures. In such unsettling circumstances, the database system must maintain data consistency, correctness, and validity.

First, we will explore the nature of a proper transaction and its requisite properties for data integrity. We will examine how improper executions of transactions could cause problems, and we will review solution options. We will also discuss failures of the database caused by external elements and present methods to recover from such failures.

TRANSACTION PROCESSING

Consider the database systems that support businesses like airlines, banking, finance, and retail. These are large transaction processing systems. Transactions in the tens of thousands interact with databases for airline reservations, banking operations, supermarket sales, credit card processing, stock buying and selling, and so on. Such critical database systems must be available at all times and must provide fast response times for hundreds of concurrent users. Some of these transactions just read the database and display data, but most of the transactions perform some type of updating.

A database system is susceptible to two major types of problems. First, concurrent transactions attempting to update the same data item may affect one another adversely and produce incorrect and inconsistent results. Second, hardware or software malfunctions could cause failures of the database and ruin its content. Concurrency control and recovery from failures form the foundation for maintaining data integrity.

Transaction Concepts

Let us get back to the example of transfer of funds from a savings account to a checking account. Figure 15-1 illustrates the execution of this transaction.

First, note that this transaction would be part of an application program usually written in a high-level language. For a transaction, the terminal points are marked with BEGIN and COMMIT statements. Consider a transaction as a unit of an application program. A program consists of one or more transactions. When you execute a program, you may be executing many transactions. Next, observe that in the example shown of a transaction, although the transaction is considered as one unit, it has two database updates—one to update the savings account record and the other to update the checking account record. Before the execution of the

Application Program

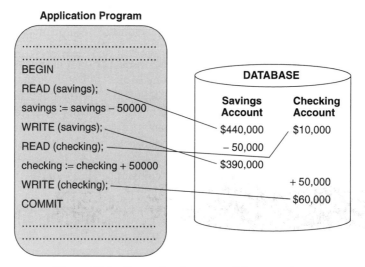

Figure 15-1   Example of a successful transaction.

Application Program

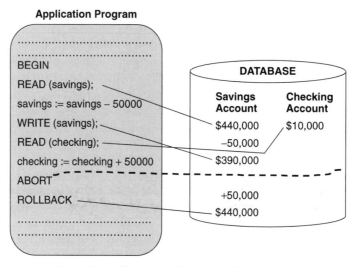

Figure 15-2   Example of an aborted transaction.

transaction, the combined total amount in both accounts is $450,000; after the completion of the transaction, the combined total amount is still the same, preserving data consistency.

Now assume that some program malfunction occurs immediately after the update to the savings record but before the update to the checking record. The program detects the malfunction and rolls back the effect of the update to the savings record. Figure 15-2 shows the action of the transaction in this case. Note the BEGIN and ROLLBACK statements demarking the start and end of the transaction.

In the successful execution of the transaction in the first case, the database is taken from an old consistent state to a new consistent state. When program aborts and the effects of incomplete updates are rolled back, the database is restored to its old consistent state. In either case, the transaction leaves the database in a consistent state.

Let us now summarize the key points of a database transaction:

- A transaction is an atomic unit of work.
- A transaction must leave the database in a consistent state; it must either be completed in its entirety or not all.
- The database management system cannot detect the beginning and end points of each individual transaction within an application unless the boundary points are marked by specific statements.
- Data manipulation languages provide specific statements of BEGIN, COMMIT, ABORT, and ROLLBACK that can be included in the application program. The BEGIN statement signifies the start of a transaction; COMMIT the end of a transaction after successful database updates; ROLLBACK the end of a transaction after rolling back the effects of unsuccessful database updates.
- When a transaction completes, two outcomes are possible—a new consistent state of the database or partial database updates rolled back and the database restored to its old consistent state.
- Transactions of the same program cannot be nested. Only while a transaction is in progress can COMMIT and ROLLBACK commands be performed.
- Each transaction must be executed only once as written, not repeatedly.
- If the start and end of transactions are not marked with specific statements, the database management assumes the beginning and end of the entire program as the start and end points of the transactions within the program.

Properties of Transactions

You must already have noticed that database transactions need to behave in a certain way to preserve data consistency, correctness, and validity. Unless transactions execute properly, users cannot trust the data in the database. They cannot depend on the database system to provide them with correct and consistent information.

Analyzing the required behavior of database transactions, we come up with four basic, essential properties that each database transaction must possess. The acronym ACID refers to these fundamental properties: A for atomicity, C for consistency, I for isolation, and D for durability. When a transaction has these four properties, it will maintain the consistency, correctness, and validity of a database. Let us examine and describe these properties.

Atomicity   A transaction is said to be atomic if it executes all of its database updates or none at all. An atomic transaction is considered to be one complete unit of work—either the entire work in the unit gets done or the bad effects of no part of the work are left behind in the database.

The transaction management component of the database management system (DBMS) handles atomicity.

Consistency This property of a transaction preserves database consistency. If a transaction executes successfully and performs its database updates properly, the database is transformed from one consistent state to another consistent state.

Preservation of database consistency also results from the other three properties of a transaction.

Isolation For the user, a transaction must appear as though it executed by itself without interference from any other concurrent transaction. In practice, however, many concurrent database transactions execute simultaneously. For performance reasons, operations of one transaction are interleaved with operations of other transactions. However, the database system must guarantee the effects of database updates for every pair of concurrent transactions to be as though one transaction executed from beginning to end and then the second started, or vice versa. Transactions must execute independently, and intermediary or partial results of incomplete transactions must be transparent to other transactions.

The concurrency control component of the DBMS handles isolation.

Durability The effects of database updates by successfully completed transactions must be permanent in the database. Even if and when there are subsequent failures, the effects must persist in the database.

The recovery management component of the DBMS handles durability.

Let us revisit the example of the transfer of funds from savings to checking accounts. Look at Figures 15-1 and 15-2 again. If you name the transaction T1, then the coding shown below may represent the transaction:

```
T1:    BEGIN
       READ (savings);
       savings := savings – 50000;
       WRITE (savings);
       READ (checking);
       checking := checking + 50000;
       WRITE (checking);
       COMMIT
```

Walk through the ACID requirements for transaction T1 and note how database integrity is preserved.

Atomicity. As shown in Figures 15-1 and 15-2, the initial values of *savings* and *checking* before T1 started are 440000 and 10000, respectively. Figure 15-1, which presents the successful completion of T1, represents the case in which all database updates are performed and the transaction is executed in its entirety. Figure 15-2 presents a database failure after WRITE (*savings*) operation. In this case, the transaction management component ensures atomicity by removing the effect of WRITE (*savings*). The effects of all operations of a transaction are left in the database or none at all. This is the requirement of the property of atomicity.

Consistency. The consistency requirement in this case is that the combined total of savings and checking balances must be $450,000. From Figure 15-1, you will note that the combined total is the same at the start as well as at the end of the transaction. Figure 15-2 similarly shows the combined total to be same at the start and end of the transaction. Whether the transaction reaches a successful end or is aborted, consistency of the database is maintained.

Isolation. To understand the property of isolation, consider another transaction, T2, that simply makes a deposit of $30,000 to the savings account. Now assume that T1 and T2 execute concurrently and that the database operations of T1 and T2 are interleaved. If T1 executes first, the balance in the savings account is $390,000. If T2 follows, at the end of T2 the balance in the savings account is $420,000. Now reverse the order. If T2 executes first, the savings balance is $470,000. If T1 follows, at the end of T1 the savings balance is $420,000. The property of isolation requires that even if the database operations of T1 and T2 are interleaved, the final savings balance is still $420,000 as if the two transactions executed independently without any interference between them.

Durability. Look again to Figures 15-1 or 15-2. At the successful end of the transaction shown in Figure 15-1, the checking balance is $60,000 and the savings balance is $390,000. Figure 15-2 shows these amounts as $10,000 and $440,000 respectively. If transaction T1 executed successfully, the values of $60,000 and $390,000 must persist in the database. Even after a hardware failure or a system failure, if there are no intervening transactions affecting these balances, these values must persist.

Transaction States

As a transaction proceeds through its various operations, it passes through several states. Each state marks a transition point where some specific action takes place or which signals a specific stage in the processing. You know that the database system is a transaction-processing environment. To understand and appreciate the types of data integrity problems and possible solution options, you need a good understanding of transaction processing. This means that you need to trace through the different states of a transaction, clearly comprehend the significance of each state and also what happens between two consecutive states, and understand the branch points. The recovery manager of the DBMS keeps track of the operations of each transaction.

Figure 15-3 illustrates the various operations and the state of the transaction at the end of each operation.

Here is a list of operations and states as shown in the figure:

BEGIN	Marks the beginning of the transaction. Transaction enters *active* state.
READ	Transaction performs read operation. Transaction remains in *active* state.
WRITE	Transaction performs write (insertion or update or deletion) operation. Transaction remains in *active* state.

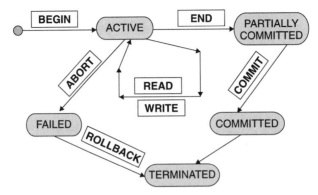

Figure 15-3 Operations and states of a transaction.

END	Indicates end of transaction read or write operations. Transaction proceeds to *partially committed* state.
COMMIT	Signifies successful end of transaction so that any database updates can be safely confirmed or committed to the database. Updates cannot be undone. Transaction moves to *committed* state and finally reaches the *terminated* state.
ABORT	Indicates failure of transaction so that effects of any database updates must be undone. Transaction proceeds to *failed* state from either *active* state or *partially committed* state depending on the nature of the failure.
ROLLBACK	Indicates that the recovery manager needs to roll back database updates and restore database to prior consistent state. After rollback, transaction reaches the *terminated* state.

Processing of Transactions

According to C. J. Date, an eminent database expert, "The fundamental purpose of the database system is to carry out *transactions*." As already mentioned, a database system is a transaction-processing environment. The database is there to support processing of transactions.

In the process of supporting transactions, what is the impact of transactions on the database itself? How do the users consider transactions? What purpose do transactions serve for reading and changing database content? Let us go over a few important aspects of transactions.

Transaction Structure   Typically, a transaction consists of three major phases:

Input phase	Receive messages and parameters to carry out the necessary interaction with the database.
Database interaction	Perform database read or write.

Output phase	Provide messages to be passed along regarding the successful or unsuccessful completion of the database interaction. Retrieve and provide data for completion of the application program. or update database as needed.

Transaction Types   From the point of view of database interactions, transactions fall into two broad types:

Read-only transactions. These do not change the database content. Therefore, any number of read-only transactions can share the database content simultaneously.

Update transactions. These change the database content. Therefore, while processing update transactions, conflicts could arise among simultaneous transactions attempting to update the same data items.

Single-User Environment   Personal database systems are single-user environments. Concurrent transactions and resulting concurrency problems are typically absent in such an environment. However, different types of hardware and software failures could cause data integrity problems.

Multi-User Environment   Most database systems are multiuser environments. In such environments, concurrent transactions are the norm. Concurrent transactions could give rise to transaction conflicts.

Concurrency Control   A multiuser environment requires effective measures and techniques for concurrency control. Each transaction must perform independently as though it were executing in isolation. Concurrent transactions must employ locking mechanisms to prohibit other transactions attempting to update the same data items.

Data Granularity   A database is a collection of named data items intended to be shared among multiple users. When multiple users need to update the same item, the data item must be locked by one transaction while it goes through the database interaction phase. How many data items do you lock and prevent other users from updating? Just specific fields, specified rows, or the whole table? Data granularity, in this context, refers to the level and scope of database content that needs to be locked at a given time.

Dependability   When user requests are processed as transactions, the users expect the transactions to preserve the integrity of the database. Processing of concurrent transactions in parallel must be transparent to the users.

Availability   The database must be kept available to the users as and when needed. Even after system and hardware failures, the database must be quickly restored to a stable and consistent state.

Integrity Considerations

As you have seen, the transaction-processing database system is subject to potential integrity problems. Users may be exposed to inconsistent, incorrect, and invalid data. Integrity functions in the database management system must be able to preserve the integrity of the database by performing the following actions:

- Monitor and scrutinize all transactions, especially those with database updates
- Detect any data integrity violations by transactions
- If a violation is detected, take appropriate action such as
  - Rejection of the operation
  - Reporting of the violation
  - Correction of error condition, if possible

Specific components exist in the DBMS for preserving database integrity. Figure 15-4 presents an overview of integrity components. Each component performs a particular set of functions.

While processing concurrent transactions in a database environment, the operations of different transactions interleave with one another. Integrity problems might arise because of such interleaved processing of transactions. We will discuss concurrency control in detail in subsequent sections.

Database failures result in potential integrity problems. The transactions that are in flight during a disk crash may not complete all the database updates. They may not have a chance to roll back the incomplete updates. We will examine database failures in depth in another subsequent section.

Here, let us turn our attention to a few other types of integrity problems and look at the solution options. For our discussion, we will adopt a very common example of a suppliers and parts database schema. Figure 15-5 presents the relational tables of the suppliers and parts database.

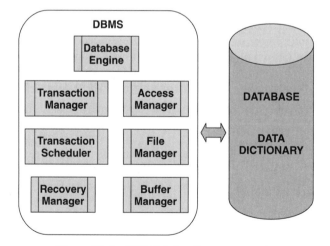

Figure 15-4 DBMS integrity components.

SUPPLIER

SupplierID	SupplierName	SupplierStatus	SupplierCity	ShipCode

PART

PartNo	PartName	PartColor	PartWeight

SUPPLY

SupplierID	PartNo	Quantity

SHIP-METHOD

ShipCode	ShipDesc	UnitCost

Figure 15-5   Suppliers and parts database.

Domain Integrity   Recall the DDL statements defining a relational schema. Each attribute has an underlying domain; the attribute can take values only from a specific domain of values and can only be of a particular data type. When a transaction inserts or updates a row in a particular table, the values of the attributes added or changed must conform to the domain values of the attributes. If they do not, then the transaction attempts to violate domain integrity rules. Violations of domain integrity rules are more common than you might imagine, and they must be addressed to preserve database integrity.

Figure 15-6 shows the DDL statements for defining the relational database schema for the suppliers and parts database.

Note the following examples of domain integrity rules as indicated in the schema definition. The transaction manager of the DBMS must detect any attempted violation and reject the transaction with a message. In some cases, the system may substitute default values and allow the transaction to proceed.

Data types.   Each attribute must conform to the defined data type.

Null values.   Null values are not allowed for the attribute SupplierName.

Allowable values.   Only certain values are allowed for the attribute SupplierStatus.

Range values.   Values for PartWeight must fall within the given range.

Missing values.   Substitute a given color if value of PartColor is missing.

Referential Integrity   Refer to Figure 15-6 and note the ON DELETE clauses. These specify conditions for enforcing referential integrity constraints. Also, note the NOT NULL conditions for foreign keys. These specify actions to preserve

```
CREATE SCHEMA PARTS-SUPPLY
        AUTHORIZATION McMillan;
CREATE DOMAIN ItemIdentifier CHARACTER (4) DEFAULT "ZZZZ"
        CHECK (VALUE IS NOT NULL);
CREATE TABLE SUPPLIER(
        SupplierID                      ItemIdentifier,
        SupplierName                    CHARACTER (35) NOT NULL,
        SupplierStatus                  CHARACTER (2),
                    CHECK (SupplierStatus IN '10', '20', '30', '40'),
        SupplierCity                    CHARACTER (25),
        ShipCode                        CHARACTER (6),
        PRIMARY KEY (SupplierID),
        FOREIGN KEY (ShipCode) REFERENCES
        SHIP-METHOD(ShipCode)
                    ON DELETE SET NULL);
CREATE TABLE PART (
        PartNo                          CHARACTER (8),
        PartName                        CHARACTER (25),
        PartColor                       CHARACTER (15)
                                        DEFAULT 'RED',
        PartWeight                      DECIMAL (5, 2)  NOT NULL,
        CHECK (PartWeight < 900.00 AND PartWeight > 99.00),
        PRIMARY KEY (PartNo));

CREATE TABLE SHIP-METHOD (
        ShipCode                            CHARACTER (6),
        ShipDesc                            CHARACTER (25),
        UnitCost                            DECIMAL (5, 2)
                                            NOT NULL,

        PRIMARY KEY (ShipCode) );
CREATE TABLE SUPPLY (
        SupplierID                          ItemIdentifier,
        PartNo                              CHARACTER (8),
        Quantity                            INTEGER,
        PRIMARY KEY (SupplierID, PartNo),
        FOREIGN KEY (SupplierID) REFERENCES SUPPLIER (SupplierID)
                    ON DELETE CASCADE,
        FOREIGN KEY (PartNo) REFERENCES PART (PartNo)
                    ON DELETE CASCADE);
```

Figure 15-6   Schema definition: suppliers and parts.

referential integrity. The integrity subsystem of the DBMS handles attempted referential integrity violations.

Business Rules   The integrity subsystem can also enforce business rules through stored procedures and triggers. A stored procedure is a named module of code defining a business rule and specifying the action to be taken in case of attempted violation. A trigger is a special type of stored procedure. A trigger module can be made to fire when a particular type of insert, update, or delete takes place. Figure 15-7 presents a sample trigger.

CONCURRENT TRANSACTIONS

The database environment supports processing of transactions, several of which may interact with the database at the same time. Transaction T1 may start at a certain

```
CREATE      TRIGGER  PARTWEIGHT
BEFORE                            INSERT, UPDATE (PartWeight)
ON                                        PART
FOR EACH ROW
DECLARE
              BigPartWeight                          PART.PartWeight%type   ;
BEGIN
              SELECT PartWeight        INTO        BigPartWeight
              FROM PART
              WHERE PartName = 'BigPart'    ;

              IF        :new.PartWeight > BigPartWeight        AND
                        :old.PartName < > 'BigPart'            THEN
                        RAISE APPLICATION ERROR (-20200,
                        'Part cannot have overweight'   )  ;
              ENDIF  ;
END  ;
```

Figure 15-7   Sample trigger module.

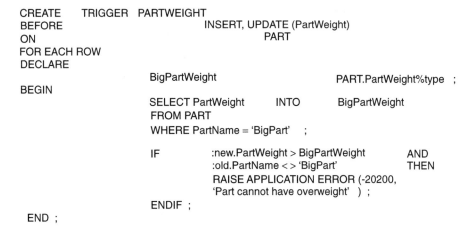
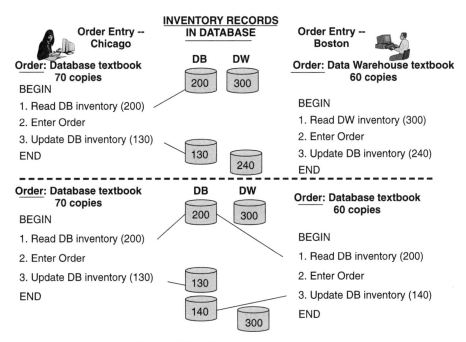

Figure 15-8   Concurrent transactions.

time and start executing. Within microseconds, a second transaction, T2, may start execution from another place and interact with the database. Transaction T2, with fewer reads and updates, may finish sooner, and transaction T1, although started earlier, may end later. These are concurrent transactions or transactions that interact with the database simultaneously. Transaction T1 may read and update a particular record in the database, while T2 may read and update an altogether different record. On the other hand, both may need to read and update the same record.

Figure 15-8 presents these two cases: In the first case, T1 reads and updates the inventory record for database textbook and T2 reads and updates the inventory record for data warehousing textbook; in the second case, both transactions need to read and update the inventory record for database textbook.

Note the two cases carefully. In both cases, transactions T1 and T2 execute simultaneously. Observe the second case and see why this case gives rise to a potential problem. In the second case, both transactions need to read and update the same record, namely, the inventory record of database textbook. Instead of allowing transactions T1 and T2 to execute concurrently, let the system allow transaction T1 to execute independently first from beginning to end and then start transaction T2 and allow T2 also to execute from beginning to end. If this is done, you will not have an integrity problem even though both transactions read and update the same record.

Motivation for Concurrency

The question naturally arises: Why not execute transactions sequentially and avoid potential integrity problems? Note that in the above two cases, because the two transactions are permitted to execute concurrently, the read and write operations within the two transactions can be interleaved. How does this help? Does not this interleaving of operations cause integrity problems? Let us examine possible reasons for allowing transactions to execute concurrently.

Remember that a database system is a transaction-processing environment and any method to speed up the overall processing is highly welcome in such an environment. A database system exists to support the processing of transactions—every effort to accelerate transaction processing deserves top priority.

A transaction consists of CPU processing and I/O operations. While one transaction waits for I/O, CPU can process another transaction. In this manner, parallelism of the overall process can be achieved. You have noted this type of parallelism in the above example. This is the primary motivation for concurrent transactions.

Here is a list of major benefits of transaction concurrency:

· Overall increase in system throughput
· Reduced response times
· Simultaneous sharing of data
· Executing a short transaction and a long transaction concurrently allows the shorter transaction to finish quickly without waiting for the longer transaction to end
· Avoids unpredictable delays in response times

Concurrency Problems

Perhaps you are now ready to accept that there are potential benefits of allowing the concurrent processing of transactions. Especially in a large transaction-processing environment and in an environment with long-running transactions, concurrent transaction processing seems to be inevitable.

You are already aware of potential integrity problems when two or more concurrent transactions seek to read and write the same database item. In this case, we say that the two concurrent transactions are in conflict. Two operations on

TIME	T1 -- Chicago Order:	T2 -- Boston Order:	INVENTORY
	DB 70 copies	**DB 60 copies**	
t1	BEGIN T1		200
t2	READ inventory	BEGIN T2	200
t3	inventory = inventory – 70	READ inventory	200
t4	WRITE inventory	inventory = inventory – 60	130
t5	COMMIT	WRITE inventory	140
t6	END	COMMIT	140
t7		END	140

Figure 15-9 Concurrent transactions: lost update.

the same database item conflict with each other if at least one of them is a write operation.

When two transactions execute concurrently, the operations of one transaction interleave with the operations of the other transaction. So it becomes obvious that, to avoid integrity problems, all types of interleaving of operations may not be allowed.

Three potential problems arise when operations of concurrent transactions are interleaved: the lost update problem, the problem resulting from dependency on uncommitted update, and the inconsistent summary problem. We will discuss these problems individually. If concurrency has to be allowed in transaction processing, then these problems must be resolved. Before considering solution options, try to get a clear understanding of the nature of the three types of problems.

Lost Update   In this scenario, an apparently successful database update by one transaction can be overridden by another transaction. Figure 15-9 repeats the second case presented in the Figure 15-8. Here, both of transactions T1 and T2 read and write the inventory record for database textbook.

Note the apparent successful update by transaction T1 writing out the inventory balance as 130. Transaction T2, however, overwrites the inventory balance as 140, which is incorrect.

Dependency on Uncommitted Update   Just as in the previous case, the operations of transactions T1 and T2 interleave. Transaction T2 starts slightly later after both read and write operations of T1 are completed but before the update is committed to the database. However, transaction T1 aborts for whatever reason and rolls back. Figure 15-10 presents this case.

Why does this case present an integrity problem? Transaction T2 is allowed to see the intermediate result of transaction T1 before the update is committed. So transaction T2 starts out with the uncommitted value of 130 and comes up with the final result of 70. That would be correct if transaction T1 had not aborted and rolled back its update.

Inconsistent Summary   In this case, each transaction does not both read and write. One transaction reads several records while the second transaction, interleaved with the other transaction, updates some of the records being read by the first transaction. Figure 15-11 illustrates this situation.

TIME	T1 -- Chicago Order:	T2 -- Boston Order:	INVENTORY
	DB 70 copies	DB 60 copies	
t1	BEGIN T1		200
t2	READ inventory		200
t3	inventory = inventory − 70		200
t4	WRITE inventory	BEGIN T2	130
t5		READ inventory	130
t6	ROLLBACK	inventory = inventory − 60	70
t7	END	WRITE inventory	70
t8		COMMIT	70
t9		END	200

Figure 15-10 Concurrent transactions: uncommitted dependency.

TIME	T1 -- Count books on DB, DW, VB	T2 -- update inventory for DB, DW	DB	DW	VB	SUM
t1	BEGIN T1		200	250	300	
t2	sum = 0	BEGIN T2	200	250	300	0
t3	READ DB inventory	READ DB inventory	200	250	300	0
t4	sum = sum + DB inventory	DB inventory = DB inventory − 70	200	250	300	200
t5	READ DW inventory	WRITE DB inventory	130	250	300	200
t6	sum = sum + DW inventory	READ VB inventory	130	250	300	450
t7		VB inventory = VB inventory − 60	130	250	300	450
t8		WRITE VB inventory	130	250	240	450
t9	READ VB inventory	COMMIT	130	250	240	450
t10	sum = sum + VB inventory	END	130	250	240	690
t11	COMMIT		130	250	240	690
t12	END		130	250	240	690

Figure 15-11 Concurrent transactions: inconsistent summary.

Transaction T1 simply reads the inventory records of the books on the database, data warehousing, and Visual Basic to find the total number of these books in the warehouse. In the meantime, T2 reads and updates two of these records—one after it is read by T1 and another before it is read by T1. Note the error in the summary reads and the final sum arrived at the end of transaction T1.

Transactions and Schedules

The foregoing discussions clearly establish the need for concurrency control techniques that can preserve data integrity even while allowing interleaving of operations belonging to different transactions. But before you can appreciate the concurrency control techniques, you need to study the operations of concurrent transactions as they impact the database.

From the point of view of the database, a transaction is simply a list of operations such as BEGIN, READ, WRITE, END, COMMIT, and ABORT. In concurrent executions of different transactions, these operations are interleaved. The READ of one transaction may be followed by the READ of another transaction. After that, you may have the WRITE of the first transaction, and so on. These operations interact with the database. If you observe the operations over a certain time interval, you note a series of operations belonging to various concurrent transactions interacting with the database. How these operations of different transactions are scheduled—in what sequence and at which intervals—has a direct bearing on data integrity. Proper scheduling would result in preservation of integrity.

Let us review a few concepts about scheduling.

Schedule. Consists of a sequence of operations in a set of concurrent transactions where the order of the operations of each transaction is preserved.

Serial schedule. Operations of different transactions are not interleaved. Leaves database in a consistent state.

Nonserial schedule. Operations of different transactions are interleaved.

Complete schedule. A schedule that contains a COMMIT or ABORT for each participating transaction.

Cascadeless schedule. A schedule is said to be cascadeless, that is, to be avoiding cascading rollbacks, if every transaction in the schedule reads only data items written by committed transactions.

Figure 15-12 explains the definitions using the operations of two transactions, T1 and T2. Note each example and understand the significance of the variations in the schedule.

Now you will readily conclude that, given the operations of even four transactions, you can arrange the operations in different ways and come up with many

SCHEDULE

T1	T2
READ (A)	
A := A + 100	READ (A)
WRITE (A)	A := A - 50
READ (B)	WRITE (A)
B := B + 200	READ (B)
WRITE (B)	B := B - 100
	WRITE (B)

COMPLETE NON-SERIAL SCHEDULE

T1	T2
BEGIN	
READ (A)	BEGIN
A := A + 100	READ (A)
WRITE (A)	A := A - 50
READ (B)	WRITE (A)
B := B + 200	READ (B)
WRITE (B)	B := B - 100
COMMIT	ABORT
END	ROLLBACK
	END

COMPLETE SERIAL SCHEDULE

T1	T2
BEGIN	
READ (A)	
A := A + 100	
WRITE (A)	
READ (B)	
B := B + 200	
WRITE (B)	
COMMIT	
END	
	BEGIN
	READ (A)
	A := A - 50
	WRITE (A)
	READ (B)
	B := B - 100
	WRITE (B)
	COMMIT
	END

CASCADELESS SCHEDULE

T1	T2
BEGIN	
READ (A)	
A := A + 100	
WRITE (A)	
COMMIT	BEGIN
END	READ (A)
	A := A - 50
	WRITE (A)
	COMMIT
	END

Figure 15-12 Transactions and schedules.

different schedules. In fact, the number of possible schedules for a set of n transactions is much larger than $n(n - 1)(n - 2)\ldots\ldots3.2.1$. With just five transactions, you can come up with more than 120 different schedules. Some of these possible schedules preserve data integrity—many do not.

Obviously, all the possible serial schedules preserve data integrity. In a serial schedule, the operations of one transaction are all executed before the next transaction starts. However, serial schedules are unacceptable, because they do not promote concurrency. Concurrent processing of transactions is highly desirable. So, what types of nonserial schedules are safe to preserve data integrity? In what types of schedules is there no interference among the participating transactions? This leads us to the discussion of serializability and recoverability.

Serializability

A serial schedule, although leaving the database in a consistent state, is inefficient. However, a nonserial schedule, although improving efficiency, increasing throughput, and reducing response times, still has the potential of leaving the database in an inconsistent state. So the question is whether you can find an equivalent schedule that will produce the same result as a serial schedule. This new schedule must still be nonserial, to allow for concurrency of transaction execution, but behave like a serial schedule. Such a schedule is known as a serializable schedule.

Serializability finds nonserial schedules that allow transactions to execute concurrently without interference and leave the database in a consistent state as though the transactions executed serially.

Serializable Schedule   Consider a schedule S of n transactions with interleaving operations. Schedule S is defined to be serializable if it is equivalent to some serial schedule of the same n transactions. Two schedules are equivalent if they produce the same final state of the database. A serializable, complete schedule leaves the database in a consistent state.

Figure 15-13 illustrates the equivalence between a given serializable schedule and a serial schedule.

Ordering of Operations   In serializability, ordering of read and write operations is important. Consider the following cases for two concurrent transactions, T1 and T2:

- If both T1 and T2 only read a specific data item, there is no conflict; therefore, order of the operations is not important.
- If T1 and T2 read or write completely different data items, there is no conflict; therefore, order of the operations is not important.
- If T1 writes a specific data item and T2 reads or writes the same data item, conflict arises; therefore, order of the operations becomes important.

Forms of Equivalence   When two consecutive operations in a schedule belonging to different transactions both operate on the same data item, and if at least one of the two operations is a write, then the two operations are in conflict. Therefore,

T1	T2
BEGIN	
READ (A)	
A := A + 100	
WRITE (A)	
READ (B)	
B := B + 200	
WRITE (B)	
COMMIT	
END	
	BEGIN
	READ (A)
	A := A – 50
	WRITE (A)
	READ (B)
	B := B – 100
	WRITE (B)
	COMMIT
	END

SERIAL SCHEDULE

T1	T2
BEGIN	
READ (A)	
A := A + 100	
WRITE (A)	
	BEGIN
	READ (A)
	A := A – 50
	WRITE (A)
READ (B)	
B := B + 200	
WRITE (B)	
COMMIT	
END	READ (B)
	B := B – 100
	WRITE (B)
	COMMIT
	END

**EQUIVALENT
SERIALIZABLE SCHEDULE**

Figure 15-13   Equivalence of a serial and a serializable schedule.

it follows that, if two operations do not conflict, we can swap the order of the operations to produce another schedule that is equivalent to the original schedule.

Consider Schedule-1 as shown Figure 15-14.

Look for sets of two operations that do not conflict and swap the operations within each set. After swapping we arrive at Schedule-2 as shown in Figure 15-15.

Closely examine Schedule-2. You can see that Schedule-2 is a serial schedule obtained by swapping nonconflicting operations. Because Schedule-2 is obtained by swapping nonconflicting operations in Schedule-1, Schedule-1 and Schedule-2 are said to be conflict equivalent.

Conflict serializability

A schedule is conflict-serializable if it is conflict equivalent to a serial schedule.

Let us relax the equivalence conditions slightly and establish the concept of two schedules being view equivalent. Two schedules, Schedule-1 and Schedule-2, are view equivalent if the following conditions are satisfied:

- For a particular data item, if T1 reads the initial value of the data item in Schedule-1, then T1 must also read the initial value of the same data item in Schedule-2.
- For a particular data item, if T1 reads that data item in Schedule-1 and that value was produced by T2, then T1 must also read the data item in Schedule-2 that was produced by T2.

T1	T2
BEGIN	
READ (A)	
A := A + 100	
WRITE (A)	
	BEGIN
	READ (A)
	A := A − 50
	WRITE (A)
READ (B)	
B := B + 200	
WRITE (B)	
COMMIT	
END	READ (B)
	B := B − 100
	WRITE (B)
	COMMIT
	END

SCHEDULE-1
NON-SERIAL SCHEDULE

Figure 15-14   Example of a nonserial schedule.

T1	T2
BEGIN	
READ (A)	
A := A + 100	
WRITE (A)	
	BEGIN
	READ (A)
	A := A − 50
READ (B)	
B := B + 200	
	WRITE (A)
WRITE (B)	
COMMIT	READ (B)
END	B := B − 100
	WRITE (B)
	COMMIT
	END

WRITE (A) of T2 does
not conflict with
READ (B) of T1.
Therefore, these two
operations are
swapped.

SCHEDULE-2
OBTAINED BY
TRANSACTION SWAPPING

Figure 15-15   Schedule obtained by operation swapping.

T1	T2
BEGIN	
READ (A)	
A := A + 100	
WRITE (A)	
READ (B)	
B := B + 200	
WRITE (B)	
COMMIT	
END	
	BEGIN
	READ (A)
	A := A - 50
	WRITE (A)
	READ (B)
	B := B - 100
	WRITE (B)
	COMMIT
	END

SCHEDULE-1
SERIAL SCHEDULE

T1	T2
BEGIN	
READ (A)	
A := A + 100	
WRITE (A)	
	BEGIN
	READ (A)
	A := A - 50
	WRITE (A)
READ (B)	
B := B + 200	
WRITE (B)	
COMMIT	
END	READ (B)
	B := B - 100
	WRITE (B)
	COMMIT
	END

SCHEDULE-2
VIEW EQUIVALENT TO
SCHEDULE-1

T1	T2
	BEGIN
	READ (A)
	A := A - 50
	WRITE (A)
	READ (B)
	B := B - 100
	WRITE (B)
	COMMIT
	END
BEGIN	
READ (A)	
A := A + 100	
WRITE (A)	
READ (B)	
B := B + 200	
WRITE (B)	
COMMIT	
END	

SCHEDULE NOT
VIEW EQUIVALENT TO
SCHEDULE-1

Figure 15-16 View equivalent schedules.

- For a particular data item, the transaction that performs the final write of that data item in Schedule-1 must be the same transaction that performs the final write of that data item in Schedule-2.

The above conditions ensure that each transaction reads the same values for the particular data item in both schedules and that both schedules produce the same final state of the database.

Figure 15-16 presents two schedules that are view equivalent.

View serializability

A schedule is view-serializable if it is view equivalent to a serial schedule.

In the next section, we will examine concurrency control options that establish serializability of schedules. When serializable schedules execute, we derive both benefits: (1) concurrent processing of transactions by interleaving operations and (2) preservation of database integrity.

Recoverability

In our discussion on serializability, we considered schedules that are serializable and therefore acceptable for preserving database consistency. The assumption had been that no transaction failures occur during concurrent executions of transactions. You know that this is not quite true. Concurrent transactions are as vulnerable to failures as serial executions. So we need to take into account the effect of transaction failures during execution of concurrent transactions.

T1	T2
BEGIN	
READ (A)	
A := A + 100	
WRITE (A)	
	BEGIN
	READ (A)
	COMMIT
READ (B)	END
B := B + 200	
WRITE (B)	
....	
....	

NON-RECOVERABLE SCHEDULE

T1	T2
BEGIN	
READ (A)	
A := A + 100	
WRITE (A)	
	BEGIN
	READ (A)
READ (B)	
B := B + 200	
WRITE (B)	
COMMIT	
END	COMMIT
	END

RECOVERABLE SCHEDULE

Figure 15-17   Nonrecoverable and recoverable schedules.

Suppose transactions T1 and T2 are executing concurrently. Assume that T1 fails for some reason. Then the effects of its interaction with the database must be rolled back. If T2 had read a data item updated by T1 and used the value for some processing, then T2 must also be aborted and rolled back. Only then is the schedule containing the operations of T1 and T2 a recoverable schedule.

Figure 15-17 shows an example of a schedule that is nonrecoverable and another equivalent schedule that is recoverable.

Here are some ways of describing the concept of a recoverable schedule:

- In a recoverable schedule, once a transaction is committed it should never be rolled back
- A schedule S is recoverable if no transaction T in S commits until all transactions that have written an item that T reads have committed.
- In a recoverable schedule with transactions T1 and T2, if T2 reads a data item previously written by T1, then the commit of T1 must precede the commit of T2.

CONCURRENCY CONTROL

We have discussed the need for concurrent processing of transactions. You have understood that allowing transactions to process concurrently with interleaving operations could result in conflicts between transactions interacting with the same data item in the database. We covered transaction schedules in sufficient detail. You have also realized that serializable and recoverable schedules would preserve database consistency and enable recovery from transaction failures.

Now let us consider solution options for addressing problems resulting from the concurrent processing of transactions. Concurrency control is the process of allowing and managing simultaneous operations of transactions without conflicts or interference. Without concurrency control techniques, simultaneous processing of transactions is not possible.

Broadly, there are two basic approaches to concurrency control: one is a pessimistic or conservative approach and the other is an optimistic approach. The pessimistic approach takes the view that you must take every precaution to prevent interference and conflicts among concurrent transactions. Such preventive measures involve heavy overhead in transaction processing. In the optimistic approach, you assume that interference and conflicts among concurrent transactions are rare and that therefore enormous system overhead for preventing conflicts is not warranted. Instead, you take action as and when such infrequent conflicts do arise.

The pessimistic or conservative method makes use of concurrency control protocols that ensure serializability. One set of protocols relate to locking of data items; the other set relate to timestamping of transactions. We will discuss both concurrency control techniques. We will also cover the optimistic approach to concurrency control. You will learn about the applicability of these techniques to specific database environments.

Lock-Based Resolution

Why do conflicts arise while transactions process concurrently? Think of the underlying reason. The operations in a schedule interact with the same data item; they need to read or write or do both operations on the same data item. We reviewed the three types of problems that can be caused by concurrent processing above.

An obvious method to ensure serializability is to require that operations interact with a particular data item in a mutually exclusive manner. While one transaction is accessing a data item, no other transaction must be allowed to modify that data item. Allow a transaction to perform an operation on a data item only if the transaction holds a lock on that data item.

Locking and Locks   Locking is a preventive procedure intended to control concurrent database operations. When one transaction performs database operations on a data item, a lock prevents another transaction from performing database operations on that data item. Locking is meant to ensure database consistency and correctness. Unlocking is the function of releasing a lock on a data item so that other transactions may now perform database operations on that data item.

A lock is simply a variable associated with a data item. This variable indicates the status of a data item as to whether or not it is open for any operation to be performed on it. A binary lock constitutes a simple locking mechanism. It can have two values representing the locked or unlocked states of a data item. For example, if the value of the lock variable for a data item is 1, the data item is locked and may not be accessed; if the value is 0, the data item is unlocked and available for access. A binary lock enforces mutual exclusion of transactions. In the database environment, the lock manager component of the DBMS keeps track of locks and exercises control over data items.

Locking Schemes   Binary locking is a straightforward locking scheme. The locking rules are simple: At most only one transaction can hold a lock on a particular data item; if a transaction holds a binary lock on a data item, it has exclusive control over the data item until the lock is released. But a transaction-processing database environment needs more sophisticated locking schemes. If transaction T1 just needs to read a data item, it does not have to lock the data item from another transaction T2 that also just wants to read the data item. Let us explore the locking schemes commonly available in database management systems.

Two basic types of locks are available:

Exclusive lock. Also referred to as a write lock and indicated as an X-lock, this locking mechanism provides exclusive control over the data item. When a transaction holds an X-lock on a data item, no other transaction can obtain a lock of any type on the data item until the first transaction releases the X-lock.

Shared lock. Also referred to as a read lock and indicated as an S-lock, this lock type allows other transactions to share the data item for access. While a transaction T1 holds an S-lock on a data item, another transaction T2 can also acquire an S-lock on that data item, but T2 cannot obtain an X-lock on that data item until all shared locks on the data item are released. When a transaction acquires an S-lock on a data item, it is allowed to read the data item but not to write to that data item.

Let us consider locking and unlocking of a data item D by a transaction T using X- and S-locks. The locking scheme provided by the DBMS works as follows:

1. T must acquire an S-lock(D) or X-lock(D) before any read(D) operation in T.
2. T must acquire an X-lock(D) before any write(D) operation in T.
3. T need not request an S-lock(D) if it already holds an X-lock (D) or an S-lock(D).
4. T need not request an X-lock(D) if it already holds an X-lock (D).
5. T must issue an unlock(D) after all read(D) and write(D) operations are completed in T.

Locking Levels   In our discussion on locking, we have mentioned locking a data item. What is a data item? What is the unit of data we need to lock and unlock? Naturally, the granularity size of data a transaction needs to lock depends on the intention and scope of the transaction. DBMSs support multiple levels of granularity for locking. Figure 15-18 shows a hierarchy of locking levels provided for a database system.

When multiple transactions execute concurrently, some may need to lock only at the record level and a few at the field level. Transactions very rarely need to lock at the entire table level in normal transaction processing. The entire database is hardly ever locked by a single transaction. Multiple granularity level protocols are flexible to allow locking at different levels even for transactions in a single schedule.

Lock Management   The DBMS must ensure that only serializable and recoverable schedules are permitted while processing concurrent transactions. No operations of committed transactions can be lost while undoing aborted transactions. A

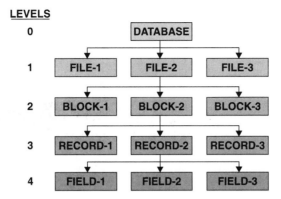

Figure 15-18   Hierarchy of locking levels.

locking protocol is a set of rules to be followed by transactions and enforced by the DBMS to enable interleaving of database operations.

The lock manager component of the DBMS keeps track of all active locks by maintaining a lock table. Usually, a lock table is a hash table with the identifier of the data item as the key. The DBMS keeps a descriptive record for each active transaction in a transaction table, and this record in the transaction table contains a pointer to the list of locks currently held by the transaction. Generally, the lock table record for a data item contains the following: the number of transactions currently holding a lock on the data item (more than one possible in shared mode), the nature of the lock (S or X), and a pointer to a queue of lock requests for the data item. The lock manager responds to lock and unlock requests by using the lock table records and the queues of lock requests.

Let us briefly trace how the lock manager handles lock and unlock requests. Assume a transaction T making lock and unlock requests on a data item D.

- If T requests an S-lock(D), the queue of lock requests is empty, and D is not currently in X-mode, the lock manager grants S-lock(D) and updates the lock table record for D.
- If T requests an X-lock(D) and no transaction currently holds a lock on D indicated by an empty queue of lock requests, the lock manager grants X-lock(D) and updates the lock table record for D.
- Otherwise, the lock manager does not grant the request immediately and adds the request to the queue for D (T is suspended.) When a transaction that was holding D aborts or commits, it releases all locks. When a lock is released, the lock manager updates the lock table record for D and inspects the lock request at the head of the queue for D. If the lock request at the head of the queue can be granted, the lock manager wakes up the transaction (T) at the head of the queue and grants the lock.

When a transaction requests a lock on a data item D in a particular mode and no other transaction has a lock on the same data item in a conflicting mode, the lock manager grants the lock. Now, follow the sequence of a set of lock requests on data item D and observe the predicament of one of the transactions:

T1 has S-lock(D)—T2 requests X-lock(D)—T2 waits—T3 requests S-lock(D)—T3 acquires S-lock(D)—T2 still waits—T4 requests S-lock(D)—T4 acquires S-lock(D)—T2 still waits

In this situation, we say that T2 is in starvation mode, unable to acquire a lock and proceed with its operations. Starvation of transactions can be avoided if lock requests are handled with the following rules:

- When a transaction T requests a lock on a data item D in a particular mode, grant the lock provided
  - There are no other transactions holding a lock on D in a mode that conflicts with the mode of the lock request by T, and
  - There is no other transaction Tn waiting for a lock on D, where Tn made its lock request earlier than T.

Application of Lock-Based Techniques

Lock-based concurrency control techniques depend on proper management and control of locking and unlocking of data items. Before a transaction attempts to perform a database operation, the transaction must request a lock on the data item. A management facility in the DBMS must grant the lock if the data item is not already locked by another transaction. Only after receiving a lock on a data item, may a transaction proceed to perform a database operation. After completion of the database operation, the lock on the data item must be released.

Simple Locking Let us now turn our attention to the application of locking and unlocking in a few examples and appreciate the significance of concurrency control protocols. We will begin with a simple binary locking scheme. Revisit the example of concurrent transactions for accessing inventory record of database textbooks. Figure 15-19 illustrates a simple locking protocol for two concurrent transaction accessing inventory record of database textbooks.

Let us refer to the inventory record accessed as data item D. In the simple locking scheme shown in the figure, every transaction T must obey the following plain set of rules:

1. T must issue lock(D) before any read(D) or write(D) in T.
2. T must issue unlock(D) after all read(D) and write(D) are completed in T.
3. T will not issue unlock(D) unless it already holds a lock on D.

The lock manager will enforce these rules. If you look at the figure closely, you note that a transaction T holds the lock on D between the initial locking and the final unlocking. In this simple concurrency control protocol, only one transaction can access D during any period. Two transactions cannot access D concurrently. In practice, this protocol is too restrictive. What if two concurrent transactions just want to read D? Even then, this protocol will delay one transaction until the other completes. Therefore, we need to employ both S-locks and X-locks. With S-locks, you can allow multiple transactions with only read operations to proceed concurrently.

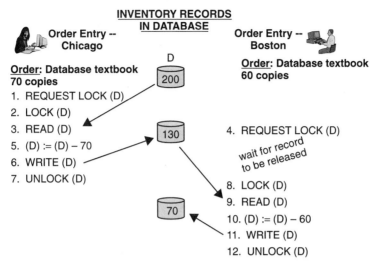

Figure 15-19   Example of simple locking with binary locks.

Figure 15-20   Example of locking with S- and X-locks.

Locking with S- and X-Locks   Let us consider another example, already mentioned in earlier sections, about two transactions accessing the inventory records of database and data warehousing textbooks. In this example, each of the two transactions makes adjustments to inventory numbers. Figure 15-20 presents the application of S- and X-locks to this example.

The first part of the figure lists the operations of the two transactions T1 and T2. The inventory records of database and data warehousing textbooks are indicated as D1 and D2 in the illustration. Note the initial values for D1 and D2. The second part of the figures shows a serial schedule with T1 followed by T2. Note the final values for D1 and D2 produced by this serial schedule. The other serial schedule with T2 followed by T1 produces a different set of values for D1 and D2. The last part of the figure shows an interleaved execution of T1 and T2 with S- and X-locks. Note the set of values for D1 and D2 produced by this interleaved schedule.

Review the execution of T1 and T2 as shown in the figure. Locking and unlocking as shown in the figure follow the rules stipulated earlier about S- and X-locks. Nevertheless, the execution of T1 and T2 as illustrated in the figure does not produce the correct final results. You can easily see that the schedule consisting of T1 and T2 as presented in the figure is nonserializable. Binary locks or S- and X-locks, just by themselves, do not guarantee serializability. We need to adopt a specific set of rules or protocol to ensure serializability. We need to adopt a two-phase locking protocol to obtain the correct final results.

Two-Phase Locking (2PL) Two-phase locking guarantees serializability. This protocol is based on the assumption of all transactions being made to obey the following rules:

1. Before performing any operation on any database object the transaction must first acquire a lock on that object.
2. After releasing a lock, the transaction never acquires any more locks.

Adherence to these rules ensures that all interleaved executions of those transactions are serializable. In the two-phase locking protocol, all locking operations precede the first unlock operation in a transaction. Once a transaction issues an unlock, it cannot obtain any more locks.

According to the concepts of this protocol, every transaction may be divided into two phases: first a growing or expanding phase and then a second shrinking phase.

- In the growing phase, the transaction acquires all the necessary locks but does not release any of them. Each lock may be an S- or X-lock, depending on the type of database access. If upgrading of locks is permitted, upgrading can take place only in this phase. (Upgrading means changing an S-lock to an X-lock.)
- In the shrinking phase, the transaction releases all the locks. Once the transaction releases the first lock, it cannot acquire any new lock. If downgrading of locks is allowed, downgrading can take place only in this phase. (Downgrading means changing an X-lock to an S-lock.)

Now, let us get back to our example of concurrent transactions accessing inventory records of database and data warehouse textbooks. Figure 15-21 presents the operations in T1 and T2 rearranged so that each transaction follows the two-phase locking protocol. Any schedule with T1 and T2 will be serializable. When every transaction in a schedule follows 2PL, the schedule is serializable. 2PL enforces seri-

T1 and T2 following 2PL

T1	T2
LOCK-S (D2)	LOCK-S (D1)
READ (D2)	READ (D1)
LOCK-X (D1)	LOCK-X (D2)
UNLOCK (D2)	UNLOCK (D1)
READ (D1)	READ (D2)
(D1) := (D1) + (D2)	(D2) := (D2) + (D1)
WRITE (D1)	WRITE (D2)
UNLOCK (D1)	UNLOCK (D2)

Figure 15-21 Transactions following 2PL.

TIME	T1 -- Chicago Order: DB 70 copies	T2 -- Boston Order: DB 60 copies	DB
t1	BEGIN T1		200
t2	LOCK-X (DB)	BEGIN T2	200
t3	READ (DB)	LOCK-X (DB)	200
t4	(DB) := (DB) – 70	.... wait	200
t5	WRITE (DB)	.... wait	130
t6	UNLOCK (DB)	.... wait	130
t7	COMMIT	READ (DB)	130
t8	END	(DB) := (DB) – 60	130
t9		WRITE (DB)	70
t10		UNLOCK (DB)	70
t11		COMMIT	70
t12		END	70

Figure 15-22 Two-phase locking: resolution of lost update problem.

alizability. Carefully inspect the lock and unlock operations in T1 and T2 to ensure that each of these transactions follows 2PL.

Before we proceed further, go back and review Figures 15-9, 15-10, and 15-11, which presented the three major problems of concurrent transactions—lost update, uncommitted dependency, and inconsistent summary. You can address these three problems by applying the two-phase locking protocol. Figure 15-22 illustrates how 2PL resolves the lost update problem presented earlier in Figure 15-9. 2PL also resolves the other two problems of uncommitted dependency and inconsistent summary.

Deadlock: Prevention and Detection

Review lock-based concurrency control protocols including 2PL. Although 2PL ensures serializability, it is still subject to a different problem. Refer back to Figure 15-21 showing the two transactions T1 and T2, each of which follows 2PL. In the first phase, each transaction acquires all the locks it needs and performs its database operations. While each transaction is acquiring the necessary locks, it is possible that the first transaction may have to wait for a lock held by a second transaction to be released and vice versa. Refer to Figure 15-23 portraying a situation in which transactions T1 and T2 are deadlocked although they attempt to conform to 2PL.

TIME	T1 -- Chicago Order:	T2 -- Boston Order:	DB	DW
	DB 70 copies	DW 45 copies		
	DW 65 copies	DB 60 copies		
t1	BEGIN T1		200	150
t2	LOCK-X (DB)	BEGIN T2	200	150
t3	READ (DB)	LOCK-X (DW)	200	150
t4	(DB) := (DB) – 70	READ (DW)	200	150
t5	WRITE (DB)	(DW) := (DW) – 45	130	150
t6	LOCK-X (DW)	WRITE (DW)	130	105
t7	.... wait	LOCK-X (DB)	130	105
t8	.... wait	.... wait	130	105
t9	.... wait	.... wait	130	105
t10		.... wait	130	105

Figure 15-23 Transactions in deadlock.

A cycle of transactions waiting for locks to be released is known as a deadlock. Two or more deadlocked transactions are in a perpetual wait state. 2PL or any other lock-based protocol, by itself, cannot avoid deadlock problems. In fact, 2PL is prone to cause deadlocks whenever the first phases of two or more transactions attempt to execute simultaneously.

First, let us look at two obvious solutions to resolve deadlocks:

Deadlock prevention protocol. Modify 2PL to include deadlock prevention. In the growing phase of 2PL, lock all required data items in advance. If any data item is not available for locking, lock none of the data items. Either lock everyone of the needed data items or none at all. If locking is not possible, the transaction waits and tries again. The transaction will be able to lock all data items as and when all become available. The solution, although workable, limits concurrency a great deal.

Ordering of data items. Order all lockable data items in the database and ensure that when a transaction needs to lock several data items, it locks them in the given order. This is not a solution that can be implemented through the DBMS. The programmers need to know the published order of lockable items. It is not a practical solution at all.

In practice, these two solutions are not feasible. One solution seriously limits the advantages of concurrent transaction processing. The other is impractical and too hard to implement. We have to explore other possibilities. Ask a few questions about your current or proposed database environment. How frequently do you expect concurrent transactions to process the same data item simultaneously? What are the chances? How large is your transaction volume? What kind of overhead can your environment tolerate for resolving deadlocks?

If deadlocks are expected to be very rare, then it is unwise to take a sophisticated approach to prevent deadlocks. You might do well to have a method for detecting the rare deadlocks and deal with them as and when they occur. Deadlock detection and deadlock prevention are commonly used schemes for resolving deadlocks. Deadlock detection has wider acceptance and appeal.

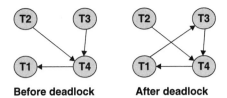

Before deadlock   After deadlock

Figure 15-24 Wait-for graph: before and after deadlock.

Deadlock Detection If transactions are generally short and each transaction usually locks only a few data items, you can assume that deadlocks are quite infrequent in such environments. Then you can let deadlocks happen, detect them, and take action. What is the resolution when a deadlock is detected? On the basis of a chosen set of criteria, the system is allowed to abort one of the contending transactions. Of course, before the DBMS can take this action, it must first be able to detect that two or more transactions are in a deadlock.

Here are the common methods for detecting deadlocks:

Wait-for graph. The DBMS maintains a wait-for graph with a node for each currently executing transaction. If transaction T1 is waiting to lock data item D that is currently locked by T2, draw a directed line from node T1 to node T2. When T2 releases the locks on the data items T1 is waiting for, drop the line from T1 to T2 in the graph. Figure 15-24 shows a sample wait-for graph before and after deadlock. When the wait-for graph has a cycle, the DBMS detects a deadlock. Two major issues arise with this deadlock detection approach. First, how often should the DBMS check the wait-for graph? Common methods are based on the number of currently executing transactions or based on the waiting times of several transactions. The second issue relates to choosing the transactions for aborting. Tip: Avoid aborting long-running transactions or transactions that have already performed many write operations.

Timeouts. The DBMS assumes a deadlock if a transaction is waiting too long for a lock and aborts the transaction. A predefined period is used as the waiting time after which a transaction is subject to be aborted. This is a simpler scheme with very little overhead.

Deadlock Prevention If most of the transactions in a database environment run long and update many data items, deliberately allowing deadlocks and aborting the long-running transactions frequently may not be the acceptable approach. In such environments, you must adopt deadlock prevention schemes and avoid deadlocks.

Deadlock prevention or avoidance schemes are based on the answer to the question of what should be done to a transaction proceeding toward a possible deadlock. Should the transaction be put on hold and made to wait, or should it be aborted? Should the transaction preempt and abort another possible contending transaction?

Each transaction is given a logical timestamp, a unique identifier assigned to each transaction in chronological sequence of the start times of transactions. If transaction T1 starts earlier than transaction T2, Timestamp (T1) < Timestamp (T2). The earlier transaction has the smaller value of the timestamp.

Two schemes are available for deadlock prevention, both using transaction timestamps for taking appropriate action. Assume that transaction T1 is attempting to lock data item D that is locked by transaction T2 with a conflicting lock.

Wait-die. (1) T1 is older than T2. Timestamp (T1) < Timestamp (T2). T1 is permitted to wait. T1 waits. (2) T1 is younger than T2. Timestamp (T1) > Timestamp (T2). Abort T1 and restart it later with the same timestamp. T1 dies.

Wound-wait. (1) T1 is older than T2. Timestamp (T1) < Timestamp (T2). Abort T2 and restart it later with the same timestamp. T1 wounds T2. (2) T1 is younger than T2. Timestamp (T1) > Timestamp (T2). Allow T1 to wait. T1 waits.

Both schemes end up aborting the younger transaction. It can be easily shown that both techniques are deadlock-free. However, both schemes may abort some younger transactions and restart them unnecessarily even though these younger transactions may never cause a deadlock.

In wait-die, the older transaction waits on the younger transaction. A younger transaction requesting a lock on a data item locked by the older transaction is aborted and restarted. Because transactions only wait on younger transactions, no cycle is generated on the wait-for graph. Therefore, this scheme prevents deadlock.

In wound-wait, the younger transaction is allowed to wait on the older one. An older transaction requesting a lock on a data item locked by the younger transaction preempts the younger transaction and aborts it. Because transactions only wait on older transactions, no cycle is generated on the wait-for graph. Therefore, this scheme prevents deadlock.

Timestamp-Based Resolution

From our discussion on lock-based concurrency control, you have perceived that use of locks on the basis of 2PL ensures serializability of schedules. Locking of data items according to 2PL determines the order in which transactions are made to execute. A transaction waits if the data item it needs is already locked by another transaction. The order of execution of transactions is implicitly determined by such waits for locks to be released. Essentially, the ordering of transaction execution guarantees serializability.

There is another method in use to produce the same effect. This method does not use locks. Right away, because of the absence of locks, the problem of deadlocks does not occur. This method orders transaction execution by means of timestamps. Lock-based protocols prevent conflicts by forcing transactions to wait for locks to be released by other transactions. However, transactions do not have to wait in the timestamp method. When a transaction runs into a conflict, it is aborted and restarted. The timestamp-ordering protocol also guarantees serializability.

How are timestamps used to determine the serializability order? If Timestamp(T1) < Timestamp(T2), then the DBMS must ensure that the schedule produced by timestamp ordering is equivalent to a serial schedule where T1 precedes T2.

Timestamps The DBMS assigns a unique identifier to each transaction as soon as it is submitted for execution. This identifier is used as the timestamp for that transaction to be used for ordering transaction executions. If transaction T2 is submitted after transaction T1, Timestamp(T1) < Timestamp(T2).

DBMSs use two common methods for assigning timestamps:

- Use a logical counter that is incremented each time its value is assigned to a transaction when the transaction arrives at the system. The logical counter is reset periodically to an initial value.
- Use the current date and time value of the system while making sure that no two transactions are given the same timestamp value.

Besides timestamps for transactions, timestamp ordering also needs timestamps for data items. Two timestamp values are associated with a data item D as indicated below:

Read-timestamp(D)— Indicates the timestamp of the largest timestamp of the transactions that successfully read D, that is, the timestamp of the youngest transaction that read D successfully.

Write-timestamp(D)— Indicates the timestamp of the largest timestamp of the transactions that successfully wrote D, that is, the timestamp of the youngest transaction that wrote D successfully.

Read- and write-timestamps for data item D are updated whenever newer transactions read or write D, respectively.

Basic Timestamp Ordering Recall transaction executions using 2PL. The protocol makes a schedule serializable by making it equivalent to some serial schedule. The equivalent serial schedule is not necessarily representative of the order in which transactions entered the system. However, in the case of timestamp ordering, the equivalent schedule preserves the specific order of the transactions.

The timestamp ordering protocol examines each read and write operation to ensure that they are executed in strict timestamp order of the transactions. Here is how the protocol works for a transaction T in relation to a data item D:

(1) T issues read(D)
  (a) Timestamp(T) < Write-timestamp(D)
     T asks to read D that has already been updated by a younger or later transaction. This means that an earlier transaction T is asking to read D that has updated by a later transaction. T is too late to read the previous outdated value. Values of any other data items acquired by T are likely to be incompatible with the value of D.
     Reject read operation. Abort T and restart it with a new timestamp.
  (b) Timestamp(T) > = Write-timestamp(D)
     T asks to read D that has been updated not by a later transaction.

Execute read operation. Set Read-timestamp(D) to the larger of Read-timestamp(D) and Timestamp(T).

(2) T issues write(D)

(a) Timestamp(T) < Read-timestamp(D)
T asks to write D that has already been read by a younger or later transaction. This means that a later transaction is already using the value of D and it would be incorrect to update D now. T is too late to attempt to write D.
Reject write operation. Abort T and restart it with a new timestamp.

(b) Timestamp(T) > Write-timestamp(D)
T asks to write D that has been updated by a younger or later transaction. This means that T is attempting to override the value of D with an obsolete value.
Reject write operation. Abort T and restart it with a new timestamp.

(c) Otherwise, when (a) and (b) are not true
Execute write operation. Set Write-timestamp(D) to Timestamp(T).

To illustrate the basic timestamp-ordering protocol, let us consider two transactions T1 and T2 concurrently accessing savings and checking account records. T1 wants to read the two records, add the balances, and display the total. T2 intends to transfer $1,000 from a savings account to a checking account. Assume that T2 is submitted after T1 so that Timestamp(T1) < Timestamp(T2). Figure 15-25 presents the functioning of the timestamp-ordering protocol.

The basic timestamp-ordering protocol ensures conflict serializability. It produces results that are equivalent to a serial schedule where transactions are executed in their chronological order. In other words, the executions of operations would be as though all operations of one transaction are executed first, followed by all operations of another transaction that are executed next, and so on, with no interleaving of operations. A modification of the basic timestamp-ordering protocol affords greater potential for concurrency. We discuss this in the next subsection.

Thomas's Write Rule Consider concurrent transactions T1 and T2 accessing data item D. Assume that T1 starts earlier than T2 so that Timestamp(T1) < Time-

Transaction T1

T1
READ (SAV)
READ (CHK)
SUM := (CHK) + (SAV)
DISPLAY SUM

Transaction T2

T2
READ (SAV)
(SAV) := (SAV) – 1000
WRITE (SAV)
READ (CHK)
(CHK) := (CHK) + 1000
WRITE (CHK)
SUM := (CHK) + (SAV)
DISPLAY SUM

Execution under timestamp ordering protocol

TIME	T1	T2	CHK	SAV	SUM
t1	READ (SAV)		2000	15000	
t2		READ (SAV)	2000	15000	
t3		(SAV) := (SAV) – 1000	2000	15000	
t4		WRITE (SAV)	2000	14000	
t5	READ (CHK)		2000	14000	
t6		READ (CHK)	2000	14000	
t7	SUM := (CHK) + (SAV)				17000
t8	DISPLAY SUM				
t9		(CHK) := (CHK) + 1000	2000	14000	
t10		WRITE (CHK)	3000	14000	
t11		SUM := (CHK) + (SAV)			17000
t12		DISPLAY SUM			

Figure 15-25 Timestamp-ordering protocol.

stamp(T2). The schedule consisting of the operations of T1 and T2 is shown below in time sequence:

| T1: | Read(D) | | Write(D) |
| T2: | | Write(D) | |

Let us apply the timestamp-ordering protocol to the schedule:

Read(D) of T1 succeeds.
Write(D) of T2 succeeds.
When T1 attempts to perform Write(D), Timestamp(T1) < Write-timestamp(D) because Write-timestamp(D) was set to Timestamp(T2).
Therefore, Write(D) of T1 is rejected and the transaction must be aborted and restarted with a new timestamp.

Examine the application of the protocol carefully. The timestamp-ordering protocol requires the rejection of T2 although it is unnecessary. See what has happened to D. T2 had already written D; the value T1 wants to write to D will not be required to be read. Any transaction Tn earlier than T2 attempting to read D will be aborted because Timestamp(Tn) < Write-timestamp(D). Any transaction Tn with Time-stamp(Tn) > Timestamp(T2) must read D as written by T2 rather than the value of D written by T1. Therefore, the write operation of T1 may be ignored.

What you have reviewed here leads us to a modified version of the timestamp-ordering protocol in which certain obsolete write operations may be ignored. The modified version has no changes for read operation. The modified version for write operation of the timestamp-ordering protocol incorporates Thomas's Write Rule as follows:

T issues write(D)

(a) Timestamp(T) < Read-timestamp(D)
T asks to write D that has already been read by a younger or later transaction. This means that a later transaction is already using the value of D and it would be incorrect to update D now. T is too late to attempt to write D.
Reject write operation. Abort T and restart it with a new timestamp.

(b) Timestamp(T) > Write-timestamp(D)
T asks to write D that has been updated by a younger or later transaction. This means that T is attempting to override the value of D with an obsolete value.
Ignore write operation.

(c) Otherwise, when (a) and (b) are not true
Execute write operation. Set Write-timestamp(D) to Timestamp(T).

Optimistic Techniques

Review the types of processing done while using lock-based or timestamp-ordering protocols. Before each database operation gets performed, some verification has to be done to ensure that the operation will not cause a conflict. This results in system overhead during transaction execution through locking or time-stamping and slows the transaction down. In database environments where conflicts among transactions are rare, such additional overhead is unnecessary. In these environments, we can adopt different techniques based on this optimistic assumption. Because no locking is involved optimistic techniques allow greater concurrency.

In optimistic concurrency control techniques, no checking is done during transaction execution; verification is put off until a validation phase. In this later phase, a check determines whether a conflict has occurred. If so, the transaction is aborted and restarted. Restarting may be time-consuming, but it is assumed that in database environments where conflicts are rare, aborting and restarting will also be sufficiently infrequent. Restarting is still tolerable compared to the overhead of locks and timestamps.

The system keeps information for verification in the validation phase. During execution, all updates are made to local copies. If serializability is not violated, a transaction wishing to commit is allowed to commit and the database is updated from the local copy; otherwise, the transaction is aborted and restarted later. The optimistic protocol we are studying here uses timestamps and also maintains Write-sets and Read-sets for transactions. The Write-set or Read-set for a transaction is the set of data items the transaction writes or reads.

Let us study the three phases of an optimistic concurrency control technique:

Read Phase. Extends from the start of a transaction until just before it is ready to commit. The transaction performs all the necessary read operations, stores values in local variables, and stores values in local copies of data items kept in transaction workspace.

Validation Phase. Extends from the end of the read phase to when the transaction is allowed to commit or is aborted. The system checks to ensure that serializability will not be violated if the transaction is allowed to commit. For a read-only transaction, the system verifies whether data values read are still the current values. If so, the transaction is allowed to commit. If not, the transaction is aborted and restarted. For an update transaction, the system determines whether the transaction will leave the database in a consistent state and ensure serializability. If not, the transaction is aborted and restarted.

Write Phase. Follows a successful verification in the validation phase. Updates are made to the database from the local copies.

The system examines reads and writes of the transactions in the validation phase using the following timestamps for each transaction T:

Start(T)	Start of execution of T
Validation(T)	Beginning of validation phase of T
Finish (T)	End of T, including write phase, if any

For a transaction T to pass the verification in the validation phase, one of the following must be true:

(1) Any transaction Tn with earlier timestamp must have ended before T started, that is, $Finish(Tn) < Start(T)$.

(2) If T starts before an earlier Tn ends, then
   (a) Write-set(Tn) is not the same as Read-set(T), and
   (b) Earlier transaction Tn completes its write phase before T enters its validation phase, that is, Start(T) < Finish(Tn) < Validation(T).

Rule 2 (a) above ensures that values written by an earlier transaction are not read by the current transaction. Rule 2 (b) guarantees that the write operations are performed serially, not causing conflicts.

DATABASE FAILURES AND RECOVERY

So far, we have concentrated on problems emanating from concurrent processing of transactions and how concurrent processing could cause data integrity problems. If concurrent transactions are not processed according to specific concurrency control protocols, they are likely to leave the database in an inconsistent state.

We now turn our attention to data integrity problems that arise because of various types of failures. Recall the definition of a transaction as a unit of work that must be completed successfully to maintain database consistency. You know that in a large database environment a continuous stream of transactions is accessing the database all the time. What happens in such an environment if there is a sudden crash of the disk where the database resides? Just at the moment when disaster strikes, several transactions could be in flight, unable to complete successfully and resulting in serious data inconsistency problems. The effects of the partially executed transactions must be cleaned up, and the database should be restored to a consistent state.

We begin by surveying the types of failures that could cause data integrity problems and examine some ideas on how to recover from these types of failures. Specific recovery techniques address particular types of failures and how to recover from them. We will explore these recovery techniques. Recovering from failures and keeping the database system correct and consistent are primary requirements in a modern organization.

Classification of Failures

A database system is subject to a variety of failures. When a database system fails for one reason or another, the processing of transactions stops and the database is rendered unusable. The action that follows to recover from the interruption and make the database functional depends on the type of failure. The database and operating system software automatically handle some error conditions. Other error conditions need special actions. Depending on the severity of the failure, it may take a while for the recovery process to complete.

Let us list the types of failures and try to classify them. The list describes each type of failure and also indicates the nature of the recovery process.

Transaction error. Malfunction of a transaction caused by exception conditions such as integer overflow, divide by zero, bad input, data not found, resource limit exceeded, and so on. These are usually handled in the application program. The program is coded to detect such conditions and take appropriate action. Most of the time, the transaction aborts and rolls back partial database updates. Usually, these errors are not considered database system failures; these are local exceptions at the transaction level.

System error. In this type of failure, the database system enters an undesirable state such as a deadlock or overflow on some system file or resource. The database system is unable to continue processing. In such cases, the database may or may not be corrupted. The cause for the error must be determined and corrected before restarting the database.

System failure. This includes failure of hardware, data communication links, network components, operating system software, or the DBMS itself. Hardware failure is usually failure of main memory losing volatile storage. The cause for the failure must be ascertained and corrected. The effects of partial database updates of transactions in process at the instant of failure must be resolved before restarting the database system.

Disk failure. This is usually a head crash caused by the disk head crashing into the writing surface of the disk. The extent of the damage must be ascertained, and the disk has to be discarded if the damage is extensive. The database must be restored on another disk from a backup copy and recovered from copies of transactions up to the point of failure. Also, the effects of partial database updates of transactions in process at the instant of failure must be resolved before restarting the database system.

Physical failure. This type comprises a variety of problems including power loss, power surge, fire, disk overwrites, and so on. Full recovery from such a failure depends on the exact nature of the cause.

Human error. You may include a number of problems in this group such as operator error, carelessness, sabotage, and theft. Recovery options vary and are difficult.

Recovery Concepts

One of the major concerns about recovering from failures relates to the transactions in progress at the time of a failure. These in-flight transactions do not have a chance to complete, and the recovery mechanism must address the partial updates to the database by these transactions. Let us consider one such transaction in progress at a time of failure. Figure 15-26 shows the transaction in progress at the instant of failure.

To preserve the consistency of the database, either the effects of the partial updates must be removed or the updates must be completed. How can we achieve this? If the system keeps information about all the intended updates of the transaction, then the system can use that information either to back out the effects of the partial updates or to complete the remaining updates. If the partial updates are backed out, the database is restored to the prior consistent state. On the other hand, if the remaining updates are completed correctly, the database is taken to a new

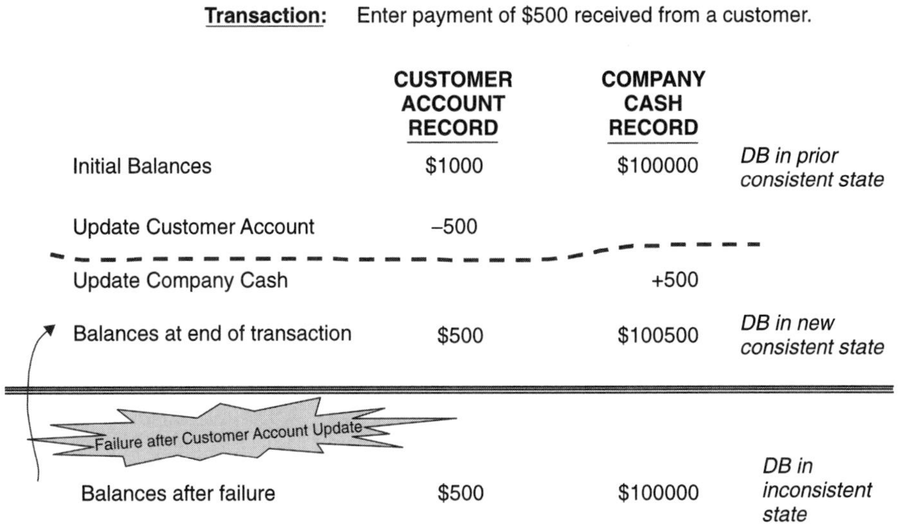

Transaction: Enter payment of $500 received from a customer.

	CUSTOMER ACCOUNT RECORD	COMPANY CASH RECORD	
Initial Balances	$1000	$100000	DB in prior consistent state
Update Customer Account	−500		
Update Company Cash		+500	
Balances at end of transaction	$500	$100500	DB in new consistent state
Failure after Customer Account Update			
Balances after failure	$500	$100000	DB in inconsistent state

Figure 15-26   Transaction in progress at time of failure.

consistent state. Again, remember that in this example we have considered only one transaction in progress. In practice, many transactions are normally in progress at the time of a failure. The effects of partial database updates by all of the in-flight transactions must be addressed.

The underlying principle for recovery is redundancy. Keep enough redundant data to enable recovery. This includes keeping backup copies of the database and a file of copies of the updates since the last backup. A transaction is the basic unit of recovery in case of failures. The recovery system must be able to recover the effects of transactions in progress—for all of them, one by one. The recovery manager of the DBMS must be able to guarantee the properties of atomicity and durability.

To summarize, a DBMS must provide the following facilities for recovery from failures:

- A backup mechanism to create periodic backup copies of the entire database
- Journalizing or logging facilities to maintain an audit trail of transactions and database changes
- A checkpoint facility for the DBMS to suspend all processing, from time to time, and synchronize its files and journals
- A recovery manager module to bring the database to a consistent state and resume transaction processing

Logging

Please go back to the example shown in Figure 15-26. You note that the failure interrupts the transaction and stops it before it can complete successfully. You quickly realize that you could easily bring the database to a consistent state if only you had information about the updates intended by the transaction. Using the information

Log File	CUSTOMER ACCOUNT RECORD	COMPANY CASH RECORD	
Balances after failure	$500	$100000	*DB in inconsistent state*
Recovery (making transaction atomic):			
Option 1 - backout DB updates	+500		*DB stays in prior consistent state*
Balances at end of recovery	$1000	$100000	
Option 2 - complete all DB updates		+500	*DB brought to new consistent state*
Balances at end of recovery	$500	$100500	

Figure 15-27   Log file.

about the intended updates, you can do one of two things. You can either back out the effects of partial update and restore the database to its prior consistent state or you can apply the incomplete update and move the database forward to a new consistent state. But where can you get the information about the intended updates? What if you store this information in another file apart from the database itself? The transaction can write information about the update on this file in addition to updating the database. Such a file is called a log, journal, or trail file. Figure 15-27 demonstrates the use of a log file for the transaction shown in Figure 15-26.

Logging is a principal component in the database recovery process. Most database systems adopt log-based techniques for recovery from failures. The log file keeps track of all operations of transactions that change values of data items in a database. The file is kept on secondary storage such as a disk and used for recovery from failures. Initially, the recent log records are kept in main memory and then forced out to secondary storage. By this approach, processing of each transaction need not wait on the I/O to write log records to disk. Periodically, the contents of the log file on disk are transferred to a tape or other archival medium for safekeeping. Let us examine the types of records written on the log file.

Writing Log File Records   Every log record receives a unique identifier called the log sequence number to identify the specific transaction. Usually, log sequence identifiers are in increasing order, as required by some recovery techniques. Each record relating to a transaction has this unique identifier. The DBMS writes a log record for each of the following actions:

- Start of a transaction
- Read of a data item (not required in all recovery techniques)
- Update of a data item
- Insertion of a data item
- Deletion of a data item

- Commit
- Abort

Types of Log File Records   Recovery requires a few pieces of important information about each transaction and the data items the transaction intends to update. Therefore, a log file keeps different types of records to trace the operations of each transaction. Each record type is identified in the log file. A log record contains a transaction identifier and a record type indicator. Each record is also date and time-stamped. Here is a list of the record types. The record types shown are for a transaction T performing operations on data item D.

(T, BEGIN)
> Marks the start of T.

(T, D, value)
> Indicates the read operation and contains the value of D read from database.

(T, D, old value, new value)
> Indicates an update, insertion, or deletion operation. A record indicating an insertion contains the new value (after image field). For update, the old and new values (before and after image fields) are present in the log record. For deletion, the log record has the old value (before image field).

(T, COMMIT)
> Marks the commit point of T.

(T, ABORT)
> Marks the abort operation for T.

Checkpoint

By now, you have realized that the recovery manager of the DBMS needs to read through the log file, first to identify the transactions that were in progress at the time of a failure and then to use the information from the log records for actually performing the recovery process. The recovery manager has to search through the log records. In a large database environment, there are thousands of transactions daily and many of these perform update operations. So in the event of a recovery, the recovery manager is compelled to go through thousands of log records to redo or undo partial database updates and restore the database to a consistent state. Two difficulties arise:

- The recovery process will be too long because of the time taken for the recovery manager to process thousands of log records.
- On the basis of the recovery technique adopted, the recovery manager is likely to unnecessarily redo many updates to the database that had already taken place. This will further extend the recovery time.

What if the DBMS periodically marks points of synchronization between the database and the log file? Checkpoint records may be written on the log file with date- and timestamps. These points of time indicate that completion of all database updates up to that point are confirmed. In this scenario, the recovery manager is relieved of the task of reading and processing the entire log file; it only needs to process log records from the latest checkpoint found on the log file.

Through the use of the recovery manager you can determine how often to take a checkpoint. While taking a checkpoint, the system has to be paused to perform the necessary actions of synchronization. Too frequent checkpoints, therefore, interrupt transaction processing. On the other hand, if the checkpoints are too far apart, the recovery process is likely to become longer. So a proper balance is necessary. The recovery manager can be made to take a checkpoint at the end of a certain number of minutes or at the end of a given number of transactions.

Actions at a Checkpoint At each checkpoint, the DBMS performs the following actions:

- Temporarily suspend executions of transactions.
- Force-write all modified main memory buffers to the database on secondary storage.
- Write a checkpoint record on the log file. A checkpoint record indicates the transactions that were active at that time.
- Force-write the log entries in main memory to secondary storage.
- Resume transaction executions.

Log-Based Recovery Techniques

Assume that a failure has not destroyed the database but has caused inconsistency problems in the database. Transactions in progress at the time of the failure could not complete their database updates and commit. These partial updates rendered the database inconsistent. In such a failure, the recovery process has to undo the partial updates that have caused inconsistency. Sometimes, it is also necessary to redo some updates to ensure that the changes have been completed in the database. The recovery manager utilizes the before and after images of the update operations as found in the log to restore the database to a consistent state.

Two common methods available for log-based recovery are referred to as the deferred updates technique and the immediate updates technique. Both techniques depend on the log records for recovery. They differ in the way updates are actually made to the database in secondary storage.

Deferred Updates Technique In this technique, a transaction does not update the database until after the transaction commits. This means that the transaction defers or postpones updating the database until after all log entries are completed. The writing of log records precedes any database update.

Consider a transaction T, performing database operations, and the DBMS writing log records for the transaction. Let us trace the actions of T.

1. When T starts, write a (T, BEGIN) record on the log file.
2. When T issues a write operation to data item D, write a (T, D, old value, new value) record on the log file. For the deferred updates technique, the old value

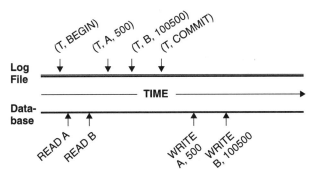

Figure 15-28   Logging with deferred updates.

or before image is not necessary. Do not write to the data item D in the database memory buffers or to the database itself yet.

3. When the transaction is about to commit, write (T, COMMIT) record on the log file. Write all log records for the transaction to secondary storage and then commit the transaction.

4. Perform actual updates to the database from the log records.

5. If T aborts, write (T, ABORT) record on the log file. Do not perform any writes to the database. (Recovery process will ignore all log records.)

Figure 15-28 is a simple illustration of the deferred updates technique for transaction T updating two data items, A and B. Note the chronological order of the log records and database updates.

If a failure occurs, the recovery system scrutinizes the log file to identify the transactions in progress at the time of failure. Beginning from the last record in the log file, the recovery system goes back to the most recent checkpoint record. The recovery system needs to examine only the log records in the interval from that checkpoint and to take action to restore the database to a consistent state.

Assume that T is possibly one of the transactions in progress. So the log records for T will be on the log file in the interval from the most recent checkpoint to the end of the file. The log records for T will be among the records the recovery system will examine for recovery. It will take action based on the log records for T using the logic indicated below:

CASE 1:   Both (T,BEGIN) and (T,COMMIT) present on the log.
Failure occurred after all log records were written.
Cannot be sure whether all database updates were completed.
However, the log file contains all records for T.
So the log records for T can be used to update the database.
USE LOG RECORDS TO UPDATE DATABASE.
DATABASE BROUGHT TO NEW CONSISTENT STATE.

CASE 2:   (T,BEGIN) present but (T,COMMIT) not present on the log.
Failure occurred before any database updates were made.
No updates were completed on database.

Cannot be sure whether all log records are written.
So, the log records cannot be used to update the database.
IGNORE LOG RECORDS.
DATABASE STAYS IN PRIOR CONSISTENT STATE.

Immediate Updates Technique The deferred updates technique holds off all database updates until a transaction reaches its commit point. The immediate updates technique speeds up the processing by applying database updates as they occur without waiting for the entire transaction to arrive at the commit point. This may make a significant difference in a long transaction with many updates. The writing of log records is interleaved with database updates.

Again, consider a transaction T, performing database operations, and the DBMS writing log records for the transaction. Let us trace the actions of T.

1. When T starts, write a (T, BEGIN) record on the log file.
2. When T issues a write operation to data item D, write a (T, D, old value, new value) record on the log file. For the immediate updates technique, both old and new values or before image and after image are necessary.
3. Write the update to the database. (In practice, the update is made in the database buffers in main memory and the actual update to the database takes place when the buffers are next flushed to secondary storage.)
4. When the transaction commits, write (T,COMMIT) record on the log file.
5. If T aborts, write (T, ABORT) record on the log file. (Recovery process will use log records to undo partial updates.)

Figure 15-29 is a simple illustration of the immediate updates technique for transaction T updating two data items, A and B. Note the chronological order of the log records and database updates.

If a failure occurs, the recovery system scrutinizes the log file to identify the transactions in progress at the time of failure. Beginning from the last record in the log file, the recovery system goes back to the most recent checkpoint record. The recovery system needs to examine only the log records in the interval from that checkpoint and to take action to restore the database to a consistent state.

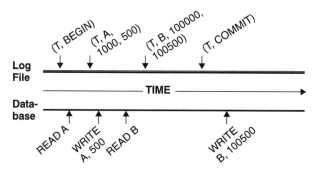

Figure 15-29 Logging with immediate updates.

Assume that T is possibly one of the transactions in progress. So the log records for T will be on the log file in the interval from the most recent checkpoint to the end of the file. The log records for T will be among the records the recovery system will examine for recovery. It will take action based on the log records for T using the logic indicated below:

CASE 1:   Both (T,BEGIN) and (T,COMMIT) are present on the log
             Failure occurred after all log records were written.
             Cannot be sure whether all database updates were completed.
             However, the log file contains all records for T.
             So the log records for T can be used to update the database.
             USE LOG RECORDS TO UPDATE DATABASE WITH AFTER IMAGE VALUES. DATABASE BROUGHT TO NEW CONSIS TENT STATE.

CASE 2:   (T,BEGIN) is present but (T,COMMIT) is not present on the log.
             Cannot be sure exactly when failure occurred.
             Failure could have occurred before updating B or both B and A.
             Cannot be sure whether all log records are written.
             However, available log records may be used to undo any database updates.
             USE AVAILABLE LOG RECORDS TO UNDO DATABASE UPDATES WITH BEFORE-IMAGE VALUES.
             DATABASE STAYS IN PRIOR CONSISTENT STATE.

Shadow Paging

The log-based recovery techniques, however effective, come with some substantial overhead. The DBMS must maintain log files. Depending on the circumstances of the failure, the recovery process can be long and difficult. Shadow paging is an alternative technique for database recovery. This technique does not require log files, nor is this recovery process as long and difficult as that of log-based techniques. However, it is not easy to extend shadow paging to an environment with concurrent transaction processing. Still, shadow paging has its use under proper circumstances. We will quickly review the concepts of shadow paging. A detailed discussion is not within our scope here.

The underlying principle in shadow paging is the consideration of the database as a set of fixed-size disk pages or blocks. A directory or page table is created to point to database pages. If the database has n pages, the directory has n entries. Directory entry number 1 points to the first database page, entry number 30 points to the 30th database page, entry number 75 points to the 75th database page, and so on. Unless the directory is too large, the directory is kept in main memory during transaction processing. All database reads and writes pass through the directory. During the life of a transaction, two directories are maintained, the current page table or current directory and the shadow page table or shadow directory. The current directory points to the current set of database pages.

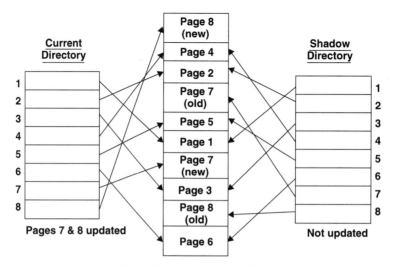

Figure 15-30 Example of shadow paging.

Transaction Execution Let us illustrate the concept of database pages and the two directories. Figure 15-30 shows an example of shadow paging. Refer to the figure and follow the actions during transaction execution.

Here is the list of actions:

Transaction starts execution.
    Current directory is copied to shadow directory.
    During transaction execution shadow directory is not modified.
Transaction performs a write operation (say to page 7 and 8 of the database).
Disk pages (page 7 and 8) are copied to unused disk pages.
    Update is performed in the new disk pages.
    Current directory is modified to point to new disk pages.
    Shadow directory still points to the old disk pages.
To commit the transaction:
    Ensure that all buffer pages in main memory changed by the transaction are written to disk.
    Write current page table to disk.
    Change disk address of the shadow directory to that of the current directory.

Recovery Let us say that a failure occurred during the execution of the above transaction. During execution, the shadow directory still points to the prior status of the database pages. The following actions are taken for recovery:

- Discard the current directory.
- Free the modified pages.
- Reinstate the shadow directory as the current directory.

Although shadow paging is simple and straightforward, and avoids the overhead associated with log-based recovery, it has a few disadvantages as listed below:

- The simple version of shadow paging does not work in database environments with concurrent transaction processing. In such environments, the technique must be augmented by logs and checkpoints.
- The shadow paging technique scatters around the updated database pages and changes page locations. If pages contained related data that must be kept together in a particular database system, then shadow paging is not the proper technique for that system.
- When a transaction commits, the old pages must be released and added to the pool of unused pages. In a volatile environment with numerous updates, constant reorganization becomes necessary to collect the dispersed free blocks and keep them together.
- The process of migration between current and shadow directories itself may be vulnerable to failures.

A Recovery Example

We have reviewed the types of failures that can cause problems in a database environment—some serious enough to damage the entire database and some resulting in database inconsistencies for a few data items. Serious failures take a lot of effort and time to recover and restore the database. We examined a few major techniques for recovery from failures. You have understood the use of logging and how log-based recovery techniques work. You now know the significance of taking checkpoints and the purpose of the checkpoint records on a log file. You have learned the role and importance of database backups.

Let us look at an example of how to recover and restore a database to the latest consistent state after a system crash that has damaged the database contents on disk. You have to begin the recovery from the latest available full backup of the database and do forward recovery. Figure 15-31 presents a comprehensive example of the process.

Observe the timeline in the top half of the figure and note the backup and logging activities shown. Note the points on the timeline when different events take place. The bottom half of the figure indicates how the various log files are used to recover from the crash. Observe how each file is used to bring the status of the database forward up to the point of the crash.

CHAPTER SUMMARY

- Data integrity in a database includes data consistency, correctness, and validity.
- A database system is prone to two kinds of problems: Concurrent transactions may cause data inconsistency, and hardware or software failures may ruin its contents.

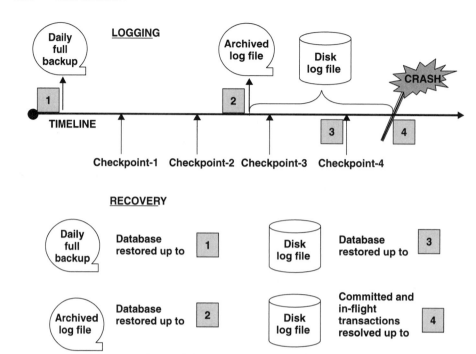

Figure 15-31   A database recovery example.

- A proper transaction must have the properties of atomicity, consistency, isolation, and durability(ACID).
- Operations or actions performed by a transaction: BEGIN, READ, WRITE, END, COMMIT, ABORT, ROLLBACK.
- Major benefits of transaction concurrency: increased system throughput, reduced response times, simultaneous sharing.
- Three primary types of concurrency problems: lost update, dependency on uncommitted update, inconsistent summary.
- A schedule is a set of interleaved database operations of concurrent transactions. A serializable schedule leaves the database in a consistent state.
- Lock-based techniques resolve concurrency problems. A transaction may hold a shared or exclusive lock on a data item.
- The two-phase locking protocol guarantees serializability. However, two-phased locking or any other lock-based scheme cannot avoid deadlock situations.
- Deadlock prevention and deadlock detection are two methods for deadlock resolution.
- The timestamp-ordering protocol also resolves transaction concurrency problems. This scheme does not depend on locks.
- Common types of database failures: system error, system failure, disk failure, physical failure, human error.

- A log file keeps information necessary for recovery from failures. Two log-based recovery techniques: deferred updates technique and immediate updates technique.

- Shadow paging, which does not utilize logging, is a less common method for recovery from database failures.

REVIEW QUESTIONS

1. What are the four essential properties of a database transaction? Describe any one.

2. List the major operations of a transaction.

3. What is domain integrity? State a few domain integrity constraints or rules.

4. Why is concurrent processing of transactions important in a database environment? Describe any one type of concurrency problem.

5. Distinguish between a serial schedule and a serializable schedule. Give an example.

6. What are S-locks and X-locks? Describe their purposes in transaction processing.

7. How is timestamp-based concurrency control different from lock-based techniques?

8. What are the major types of database failures? Briefly describe each.

9. What are the two common log-based database recovery protocols? List their similarities and differences.

10. What are the advantages and disadvantages of shadow paging?

EXERCISES

1. Match the columns:

1. transaction commit	A. no rollback of committed transaction
2. trigger	B. database and log synchronization
3. concurrent transactions	C. used for deadlock prevention
4. serial schedule	D. leaves database in consistent state
5. recoverable schedule	E. used for deadlock detection
6. wound-wait scheme	F. special type of stored procedure
7. wait-for graph	G. desired property of database transaction
8. checkpoint	H. confirm database updates
9. isolation	I. no interleaved operations
10. atomic transaction	J. increased system throughput

2. Define lock-based concurrency control. Why does simple locking not establish serializability? Describe the two-phase locking protocol and show how this technique ensures serializability.

3. As the database administrator for a local bank, which method of deadlock resolution will you adopt? Describe the two common methods and explain the reasons for your choice.

4. What are optimistic concurrency control techniques? In what types of database environments are these techniques applicable?

5. As the database administrator for an international distributor of electronic components, write a general plan for recovery from potential database failures. Describe the type of facilities you will look for in a DBMS for recovery.

CHAPTER 16

DATABASE SECURITY

CHAPTER OBJECTIVES

- Establish the goals and objectives of a database security system
- Examine potential security problems and review solution options
- Understand the principles and applications of access control
- Distinguish between authentication and authorization and learn how these are performed in a database system
- Study encryption and its application to databases
- Review special security considerations such as security of statistical databases and the use of views for database security

Think of a storage place for a manufacturing organization where it keeps all the important raw materials required for making its products. The organization uses these materials to run its production. Various types of materials form parts of different products. Some types of materials are more critical and sensitive to the production process. The organization cannot perform its day-to-day operations without access to the materials. Will the organization allow anyone to walk into the storage facility off the street and have access to the materials? Unless the place is properly secured, unauthorized persons can enter and steal or destroy the materials. Not even all authorized persons may be permitted access to all parts of the storage area. Sensitive and critical materials must be off-limits to most people.

For a modern organization, its database system is even more significant than many other types of assets. Many organizations such as financial institutions and

Database Design and Development: An Essential Guide for IT Professionals by Paulraj Ponniah
ISBN 0-471-21877-4   Copyright © 2003 by John Wiley and Sons, Inc.

travel companies cannot survive even a single day without their database systems. Any type of destruction of or unauthorized access to the database system has serious impact. Obviously, an organization must ensure that its database system is adequately guarded against accidental breaches of security or theft, misuse, and destruction through malicious intent.

Every organization must protect its database system from intentional and unintentional threats. To do so, it must employ both computer-based and other types of controls. The DBMS must include a proper security system to protect the database from unauthorized access.

SECURITY ISSUES

What are we trying to protect by ensuring database security? What levels of information need to be safeguarded and how? What are the types of problems and threats that deserve special attention? Can we distinguish between threats from outside and internal threats? Do these require different types of protection mechanisms? What are the solution options? How is protection of privacy related to database security?

Let us address these broad questions before getting into specific access control techniques. Many organizations are opening up their database systems for access over the Internet. This openness results in great advantages but, at the same time, makes the database system vulnerable to threats from a much wider area. Web security demands special attention.

Goals and Objectives

Specifically, what are we trying to protect? How are we planning to protect? These questions form the basis for discussions on database security. Let us consider the primary goals and objectives. Figure 16-1 provides an overview of the security system for a database.

Note the following three broad goals of database security highlighted in the figure.

• Denial of access to the database by unauthorized users
• Guarantee of access to all authorized users
• Protection of privacy of data

In a broad sense, you understand database security and what protection means. However, let us get into specific objectives. What are the particular objectives to deal with individual types of threats? Here is a list of specific objectives of a security system:

Shield from destruction. Shield the database from fire or any other such disaster.

Safeguard from theft. Safeguard the database from malicious schemes of competitors or profiteers to steal the data content.

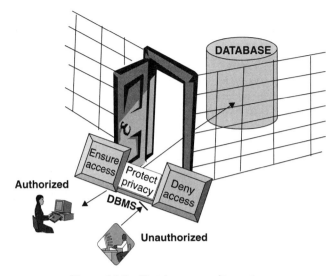

Figure 16-1 Database security system.

Defense from vandalism. Defend the database from the attempts of ingenious, disgruntled professionals intending to tamper with and vandalize the database.

Provide safety from fraud. Keep the database safe from persons with intentions to commit fraud or to misuse its contents .

Shelter of privacy. Shelter the privacy of individuals and institutions about whom data reside in the database.

Identification of users. Be able to positively identify authorized users.

Authorization of users. Guarantee access to authorized users.

Scope of authorization. Be able to authorize individual users for specific portions of the database as needed.

Levels of authorization. Provide individual users with particular authorization levels to read, update, add, or delete data.

Monitoring of usage. Be able to monitor access by authorized users to keep audit trails for tracing actions.

Security Problems

Many aspects of security problems require attention in a database environment. Legal, social, and ethical aspects are involved. Does the person requesting for particular information have a legal right to that piece of information? Also, there are policy questions about who decides on what types of access authorizations must be granted to whom and when. Operational and administrative aspects need to be considered. How do you allocate passwords, maintain them, and preserve confidentiality?

What about physical controls to prevent problems? Should workstations and servers be guarded with physical lock-and-key schemes? Are hardware controls available in your environment to be used for database security? Are there security schemes in the operating system itself? Finally, what are the security provisions in your DBMS, and to what extent can your environment take advantage of these provisions?

To come up with solution options, first it will be worthwhile to classify the types of security problems likely to be encountered. When you are able to classify the threats, you will be able to find solutions to each type of problem. Broadly, we may classify the types of security exposure in a database environment as follows:

Natural disasters. Fire, floods, and other such catastrophes.

Human carelessness. Unintended damage caused by authorized users, especially while running jobs in batch.

Malicious damage. Sabotage, vandalism, actions of malicious programmers, technical support staff, and persons performing database administration functions.

Crime. Theft, embezzlement, industrial espionage, and employees selling a company's secrets and data for mailing lists.

Privacy invasion. Casual curiosity, data lookup by competitors, obtaining data for political or legal reasons.

Let us put together the components of the problems of database protection and summarize the potential threats. Figure 16-2 presents a summary of threats to database security. Note each component showing the type of threat and its source.

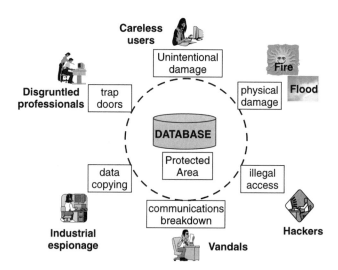

Figure 16-2 Threats to database security.

Solution Options

We have looked at the types of potential threats to a database system. Various types of sources pose different threats. How do you make provisions to protect your database system? When you consider each type of threat or problem, adopt a three-level approach to problem resolution:

- Minimize the probability of the problem happening. Establish enough protection rings to enclose the database system. Take all the necessary protective measures and institute strong deterrents.
- Diminish the damage if it happens. If an intruder manages to penetrate the outer layer of protection, make it progressively difficult to cut through the inner layers. Guard the most sensitive portions of the database with the most stringent security measures.
- Devise precise recovery schemes. If a vandal manages to destroy some parts of the database, have a tested method to recover from the damage. If a fire destroys your database, plan to be able to restore from a copy stored off-site.

When you examine the types of threats, you will notice that most of the recovery solutions must be a combination of general control procedures and computer-based techniques. Let us explore the nature of these two types of solution methods.

General Control Procedures These are matters of broad security policy and general procedures. Although these procedures deal with the security of the database in a computer system, most of these do not involve the direct use of computers. Many of these relate to planning and policy-making. Some are physical controls, and a few others involve outside agencies. The following is a list of such security measures.

Physical controls. Include physical access to buildings, monitoring of visitors at entrances and exits, and guarding of workstations and servers.

Human controls. Safeguard against threats from information system professionals and specialists by proper security clearance to work on sensitive data.

Control of equipment. Includes secure placement of equipment such as laptops loaded with sensitive data and printers that are designated to print critical data.

Security through outside agencies. Refers to third-party storage areas to keep backup copies of database and outside installations that can be used for disaster recovery.

Contingency Plans. Intended to be adopted in case of fire or bomb alerts. Plans must include designation of responsibilities and procedures for recovery.

Security Policy. An essential element of the security system to address the scope of the security schemes, the duties and responsibilities of employees, the procedures to be followed, and disciplinary action in the event of noncompliance with policy and procedures.

Computer-Based Techniques   Now let us turn our attention to the types of countermeasures that are executed through the use of the computer system including the DBMS. Here is a list of the major techniques:

Authorization of users. Includes authentication of authorized users and granting of access privileges to them.

Tailoring authorization through views. Defining user views to have the ability to authorize users for specific portions of the database.

Backup and recovery. Creation of backup copies of the database at regular intervals and also testing and implementing recovery procedures.

Protection of sensitive data. Use of encryption technology to protect sensitive data.

All DBMSs have security systems to guarantee database access to authorized users. Commonly, these security mechanisms are referred to as discretionary and mandatory security mechanisms. Let us define the scope of this division:

Discretionary security mechanisms. Used for granting and revoking data access privileges to users for accessing specific parts of a database in any of the access modes of read, update, add, and delete.

Mandatory security mechanisms. Used for establishing security at multiple levels by classifying users into distinct groups and grouping data into distinct segments and, thereafter, assigning access privileges for particular user groups to data segments.

From our discussions so far, you must have concluded that database security is critical but also difficult. You must look toward enforcing database security at different levels. Security mechanisms must exist at several layers such as within the database system itself, at the level of the operating system, the network, the application, the hardware, and so on. Figure 16-3 clearly illustrates the layers of control for database security.

Privacy Issues

Businesses and government agencies collect and store large volumes of information about customers, suppliers, distributors, and employees. Data privacy concerns those kinds of information that relate to individuals and external organizations that are part of the company's database. Who owns this information—the company that has the database or the individuals and organizations to whom the information relates? Who can access this information? Can this information be sold to others? What are the regulations?

Data privacy fits into data security in an unorthodox manner. Data security is generally thought of as the protection of a company's data from unauthorized access. Who authorizes access, and who decides on how and to whom access must

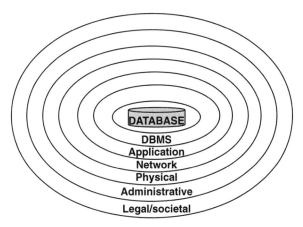

Figure 16-3   Database security: layers of control.

be granted? Of course, the company does this because it is deemed that the company owns the data in the database. In the same way, data privacy may be thought of as protecting information about employees, customers, suppliers, and distributors from unauthorized access. Who decides on this authorization? Naturally, the owners must make the decision. Who are the owners—the company or those about whom information is collected and stored?

Privacy issues are becoming more and more sensitive in North America, as they have been in Europe for some time. Legislation about privacy and confidentiality of information varies from region to region. Some basic rights are available to those about whom data is retained in corporate databases. Individuals and institutions may inquire about what information about them is stored and may demand to correct any information about them. Privacy concerns escalate with the widespread use of the Internet. Although formal regulations may not be adequate, organizations are ethically obliged to prevent misuse of the information they collect about individuals and third-party institutions.

Web Security

While discussing database security, it is important to mention security mechanisms as they relate to the DBMS and the Web. We will discuss these security options in Chapter 19, which is dedicated to the topic of the database and the Web. Security options include firewalls, proxy servers, digital signatures, and so on.

ACCESS CONTROL

Essentially, database security rests on controlling access to the database system. Controlling physical access forms one part of database security. The other major part consists of controlling access through the DBMS.

Let us consider two primary dimensions of access control. One dimension of access control deals with levels of data access. A single user or a category of users may be granted access privileges to database objects at various levels of detail. Another dimension of access control refers to the modes or types of access granted to a single user or to a category of users. How do you grant access privileges to a single user or user category? This leads to the two basic approaches to access control.

As noted above, the DBMS provides two basic approaches to access control: discretionary control and mandatory control. Discretionary access control refers to the granting of privileges or rights to individual users. Although discretionary access control is fairly effective, it is possible for an unauthorized user to gain privileges through an unsuspecting authorized user. Mandatory access control is more effective in overcoming the defects of discretionary access control.

We will first discuss how data access control pertains to levels of database objects and access types or modes. Data levels and access types form a grid, and access privileges may be granted at the intersections of data levels and access types. Our discussion will continue on the mechanisms for granting access privileges under the discretionary or mandatory access control approaches. In this section, you will also study the two important topics of authentication and authorization of users.

Levels and Types of Data Access

Let us grasp the significance of data levels for the purpose of granting access privileges. Consider the following database relation containing data about a worker in a construction company:

WORKER (<u>WorkerId</u>, Name, Address, City, State, Zip, SuperId, WageRate)

Examine the following list of possible ways of granting of access privileges to a specific user:

- User has unlimited access privileges to the entire WORKER relation.
- User has no access privileges of any kind to any part of the WORKER relation.
- User may only read any part of WORKER relation but cannot make any changes at all.
- User may read only his or her row in the relation but cannot change any columns in that row.
- User may read only his or her row in the relation but can change only the Name and Address columns.
- User may read only the WorkerId, Name, Address, and SuperId columns of any record but can change only the Name and Address columns.
- User may read only the WorkerId and WageRate columns of any record but can modify the WageRate column only if the value is less than 5.00.
- User may read all columns of any record but can modify the WageRate only if the SuperId column value is the value of WorkerId of that user.

The above list is in no way exhaustive. Yet you can readily observe that a general method of security enforcement must possess a great range and flexibility. A flexible security system in a DBMS must be able to grant privileges at the following data levels:

   The whole database
     Individual relation; all rows and all columns
       All rows but only specific columns of a relation
       All columns but only specific rows of a relation
         Specific rows and specific columns of a relation

Now let us move on to the consideration of modes or types of data access. You are familiar with access types or modes of create, read, update, and delete (sometimes indicated by the acronym CRUD). Let us expand the list of access types to include all types:

Insert or Create. Add data to a file without destroying any data.

Read. User may read and copy data from the database into the user's environment through an application program or a database query.

Update. Write updated values.

Delete. Delete and destroy specific data objects.

Move. Move data objects without the privilege of reading the contents.

Execute. Run a program or procedure with implied privileges needed for the execution.

Verify Existence. Verify whether a specific database object exists in the database.
   You have noted the various access types and also the levels of data eligibility based on which access privileges may be granted. What is your observation from this discussion? What are the implications? You can easily realize the immense flexibility needed for giving access privileges. Although numerous variations are possible, most commonly access privileges are granted to single relations in the CRUD modes.

Discretionary Control

As mentioned above, in this approach, individual users are granted privileges or rights to access specific data items in one or more designated modes. On the basis of the specification of privileges, a user is given the discretion to access a data item in the read, update, insert, or delete modes. A user who created a database object automatically derives all privileges to access the object including the passing on of privileges to other users with regard to that object.
   While discussing SQL data control examples in Chapter 13, we introduced the SQL commands for granting and revoking access privileges. This is how SQL supports discretionary access control. Now we will explore the fundamental concepts of discretionary access control and go over a few more examples.

Basic Levels There are two basic components or levels for granting or revoking access privileges:

Database Objects   Data item or data element, generally a base table or view
Users   A single user or a group of users identifiable with some authorization identifier

With these two components, access privileges may be granted as shown in the following general command:

GRANT privileges ON database object TO users

At the level of *users,* access privileges include the following:

CREATE privilege   To create a database schema, a table or relation, or a user view
ALTER privilege   To alter and make changes to schema such as adding or eliminating columns
DROP privilege   To delete a table or view
SELECT privilege   To retrieve data
MODIFY privilege   To add or insert, update, or delete data
REFERENCES privilege   To define foreign keys and reference columns in another table

At the level of *database objects*, the access privileges listed above apply to the following:

Base table   All data in the table or relation
View   All data defined in the virtual relation or view
Column   Data in the specified column only

Authorization Matrix We can think of the two levels of *users* and *database objects* forming a matrix for the purpose of granting access privileges. Set the users as columns and the database objects as rows. Then in the cells formed by the intersection of these columns and rows we can specify the type of privilege granted.

Figure 16-4 presents an example of a type of authorization matrix. Note how this type of presentation makes it easy to review the access privileges in a database environment.

Owner Account Each database table or relation has an owner. This user account that created the table possesses all access privileges on that table. The DBA can assign an owner to an entire schema and grant the appropriate access privileges. The owner of a database object can grant privileges to another user. This second user can then pass along the privileges to a third user and so on. The DBMS keeps track of the cycle of granting of privileges.

SUBJECT or USER	DATABASE OBJECT	PRIVILEGE	CONSTRAINT
Rogers	Department record	Modify	None
Miller	Department record	Create	DeptNo NOT EQUAL 101
Chen	Employee record	Select	None
Goldstein	Employee record	Create	None
Jenkins	Department record	Modify	Address ONLY
Gonzales	Employee record	Drop	EmployeePosition = 'Staff'

Figure 16-4   Authorization matrix.

Here is an example of a cycle of privileges passed along from Rogers, who is the owner of table EMPLOYEE:

By Rogers	GRANT ALL PRIVILEGES ON EMPLOYEE TO Miller WITH GRANT OPTION
By Miller	GRANT ALL PRIVILEGES ON EMPLOYEE TO Chen WITH GRANT OPTION
By Chen	GRANT ALL PRIVILEGES ON EMPLOYEE TO Williams WITH GRANT OPTION
By Rogers	GRANT SELECT ON EMPLOYEE TO Goldstein WITH GRANT OPTION
By Goldstein	GRANT SELECT ON EMPLOYEE TO Rodriguez WITH GRANT OPTION
By Rogers	REVOKE ALL PRIVILEGES ON EMPLOYEE FROM Miller CASCADE

Figure 16-5 illustrates this cycle of privileges with an authorization graph. Note how the privileges are passed along and how the revoking of privileges with cascade option works.

REFERENCES Option   The REFERENCES privilege is not the same as the SELECT privilege. Let us take an example. Suppose Nash is the owner of the DEPARTMENT table as indicated below:

DEPARTMENT (<u>DeptNo</u>, DeptName, DeptLocation)

Nash can authorize Miller to create another table EMPLOYEE with a foreign key in that table to refer to the DeptNo column in the DEPARTMENT table. Nash can do this by granting Miller the REFERENCES privilege with respect to the DeptNo column. Note the EMPLOYEE table shown below:

EMPLOYEE (<u>EmployeeNo</u>, FirstName, LastName, Address, Phone, Employee Position, Salary, EmployeeCode, DeptNo)

Foreign Key: DeptNo REFERENCES DEPARTMENT

If Miller loses the REFERENCES privilege with respect to the DeptNo column in the DEPARTMENT table, the foreign key constraint in the EMPLOYEE

After all granting of privileges

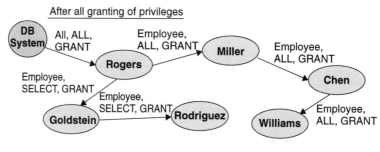

After revoking of privileges from Miller by Rogers with cascade option

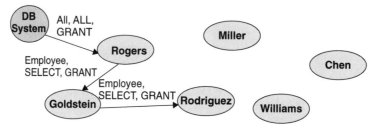

Figure 16-5   Authorization graph.

table will be dropped. The EMPLOYEE table itself, however, will not be dropped.

Now suppose Miller has the SELECT privilege on the DeptNo column of the DEPARTMENT table, not the REFERENCES privilege. In this case, Miller will not be allowed to create the EMPLOYEE table with a foreign key column referring to DeptNo in the DEPARTMENT table.

Why not grant Miller the SELECT privilege and allow him to create the EMPLOYEE table with a foreign key column referring to the DeptNo column in the DEPARTMENT table? If this is done, assume that Miller creates the table with a foreign key constraint as follows:

EMPLOYEE (EmployeeNo, FirstName, LastName, Address, Phone, Employee Position, Salary, EmployeeCode, DeptNo)

Foreign Key: DeptNo REFERENCES DEPARTMENT ON DELETE NO ACTION

With the NO ACTION option in the foreign key specification, Nash is prevented from deleting rows from the DEPARTMENT table even though he is the owner. For this reason, whenever such a restrictive privilege needs to be authorized, the more stringent privilege REFERENCES is applied. The SELECT privilege is therefore intended as permission just to read the values.

Use of Views

Earlier we had discussions on user views. A user view is like a personalized model of the database tailored for individual groups of users. If a user group, say, in the marketing department, needs to access only some columns of the DEPARTMENT and EMPLOYEE tables, then you can satisfy their information requirements by creating a view comprising just those columns. This view hides the unnecessary parts of the database from the marketing group and shows them only those columns they require.

Views are not like tables in the sense that they do not store actual data. You know that views are just like windows into the database tables that store the data. Views are virtual tables. When a user accesses data through a view, he or she is getting the data from the base tables, but only from the columns defined in the view.

Views are intended to present to the user exactly what is needed from the database and to make the rest of the data content transparent to the user. However, views offer a flexible and simple method for granting access privileges in a personalized manner. Views are powerful security tools. When you grant access privileges to a user for a specific view, the privileges apply only to those data items defined in the views and not to the complete base tables themselves.

Let us review an example of a view and see how it may be used to grant access privileges. For a user to create a view from multiple tables, the user must have access privileges on those base tables. The view is dropped automatically if the access privileges are dropped. Note the following example granting access privilege to Miller for reading EmployeeNo, FirstName, LastName, Address, and Phone information of employees in the department where Miller works.

```
CREATE VIEW MILLER AS
    SELECT EmployeeNo, FirstName, LastName, Address, Phone
        FROM EMPLOYEE
            WHERE DeptNo =
                (SELECT DEPARTMENT.DeptNo
                    WHERE DEPARTMENT.DeptNo =
                        EMPLOYEE.DeptNo AND
                        (EMPLOYEE.LastName = 'Miller' )) ;

GRANT SELECT ON MILLER TO Miller;
```

SQL Examples

In Chapter 13, we considered a few SQL examples on granting and revoking of access privileges. Now we will study a few more examples. These examples are intended to reinforce your understanding of discretionary access control. We will use the DEPARTMENT and EMPLOYEE tables shown above for our SQL examples.

DBA gives privileges to Miller to create the schema:

GRANT CREATETAB TO Miller;

Miller defines schema, beginning with create schema statement:

CREATE SCHEMA EmployeeDB AUTHORIZATION Miller; (other DDL statements follow to define DEPARTMENT and EMPLOYEE tables)

Miller gives privileges to Rodriguez for inserting data in both tables:

GRANT INSERT ON DEPARTMENT, EMPLOYEE TO Rodriguez;

Miller gives Goldstein privileges for inserting and deleting rows in both tables, allowing permission to propagate these privileges:

GRANT INSERT, DELETE ON DEPARTMENT, EMPLOYEE TO Goldstein
   WITH GRANT OPTION;

Goldstein passes on the privileges for inserting and deleting rows in the DEPARTMENT table to Rogers:

GRANT INSERT, DELETE ON DEPARTMENT TO Rogers;

Miller gives Williams the privilege to update only the salary and position columns in the EMPLOYEE table:

GRANT UPDATE ON EMPLOYEE (Salary, EmployeePosition) TO Williams

DBA gives Shady privilege to create tables:

GRANT CREATETAB TO Shady;

Shady creates table MYTABLE and gives Miller privilege to insert rows into MYTABLE:

GRANT INSERT ON MYTABLE TO Miller;

Mandatory Control

Discretionary access control provides fairly adequate protection. This has been the traditional approach in relational databases. A user either has certain access privileges or he or she does not. The discretionary access control method does not support variations based on the sensitivity of parts of the database. Although the method is sufficient in most database environments, it is not bulletproof. An ingenious professional can drill holes into the protection mechanism and gain unauthorized access.

Note the actions of user Shady indicated in the last few statements of the previous subsection. Shady has created a private table MYTABLE of which he is the owner. He has all privileges on this table. All he has to do is somehow get sensitive data into MYTABLE. Being a clever professional, Shady may temporarily alter one of Miller's programs to take data from the EMPLOYEE data and move the data into MYTABLE. For this purpose, Shady has already given privileges to Miller for inserting rows into the MYTABLE table. This scenario appears as too unlikely and contrived. Nevertheless, it makes the statement that discretionary access control has its limitations.

Mandatory access control overcomes the shortcomings of discretionary access control. In the mandatory access control approach, access privileges cannot be granted or passed on by one user to another in an uncontrolled manner. A well-defined security policy dictates which classes of data may be accessed by users at which clearance levels. The most popular method is known as the Bell–LaPadula model. Many of the commercial relational DBMSs do not currently provide for mandatory access control. However, government agencies, defense departments, financial institutions, and intelligence agencies do require security mechanisms based on the mandatory control technique.

Classes and Clearances   The mandatory access control model is based on the following components:

Objects   Database objects such as tables, views, rows, and columns
Subjects   Users, programs, and modules that need access privileges
Classes   Security classes for objects
Clearances   Security clearances for subjects

Each database object is assigned a security class. Typical classes are (TS) top secret, (S) secret, (C) confidential, and (U) unclassified. The data sensitivity sequence is as follows: TS > S > C > U. Each subject is assigned clearance for a specific security class. We may represent these by the following notation:

Class (O)   Security class for an object O
Class (S)   Security clearance for a subject S

How Mandatory Control Works   The model enforces two basic restrictions on all reads and writes:

1. ***Simple Security Property***
   Subject S is not permitted to have read access to an object O unless Class (S) $\geq$ Class (O).

2. ****-Property (Star Property)***
   Subject S is not permitted to have write access to an object O unless Class (S) $\leq$ Class (O).

Look at the first property, which is fairly intuitive. This property allows a subject to read an object only if the subject's clearance level is higher than or equal to that of the object. Try to understand what the second property is meant to prevent. The second property prohibits a subject from writing to an object in a security class lower than the clearance level of the subject. Otherwise, information may flow from a higher class to a lower class. Consider a user with S clearance. Without the enforcement of the star property, this user can copy an object in S class and rewrite it as a new object with U classification so that everyone will be able to see the object.

Get back to the case of Shady trying to access data from the EMPLOYEE table by tricking Miller. The mandatory access control method would spoil Shady's plan as follows:

- Classify EMPLOYEE table as S.
- Give Miller clearance for S.
- Give Shady lower clearance for C.

Shady can therefore create objects of C or lower classification. MYTABLE will be in class C or lower. Miller's program will not be allowed to copy into MYTABLE because

Class (MYTABLE) < Class (Miller), violation of star property.

SPECIAL SECURITY CONSIDERATIONS

We have covered several topics on database security so far. You know the common types of security threats. You have explored solution options. You have reviewed the two major approaches to database access control—discretionary and mandatory. Before we finish our discussion of the significant topics, we need to consider just a few more.

In our discussion on granting access privileges, we have been referring to individual users or user groups that need access privileges. Who are these users, and how do you identify them to the database system? This is an important question we need to address. Another obvious question is, Where is the DBA in all of these database security provisions, and what is the role of the DBA? Finally, we will inspect what are known as statistical databases and consider special security problems associated with these.

Authorization

The security mechanism protecting a database system is expected to prevent users from performing database operations unless they are authorized to do so. Authorization for data access implies access control. We have discussed discretionary and mandatory access control approaches. Let us now complete the discussion by touching on a few remaining topics.

Profiles To authorize a subject that may be a user, a group of users, a program, or a module, an account is assigned to the subject. Let us confine our discussion to a subject who is a user. User Samantha Jenkins is eligible to have access to the human resources database. So first, Jenkins must be assigned an account or user-identification.

The DBMS maintains a user profile for each user account. The profile for Jenkins includes all the database objects such as tables, views, rows, and columns that she is authorized to access. In the user profile, you will also find the types of access privileges such as read, update, insert, and delete granted to Jenkins.

Alternatively, the DBMS may maintain an object profile for each database object. An object profile is another way of keeping track of the authorizations. For example, in the object profile for the EMPLOYEE table, you will find all the user accounts that are authorized to access the table. Just like a user profile, an object profile also indicates the types of access privileges.

Authorization Rules The user profile or the object profile stipulates which user can access which database object and in what way. These are the authorization rules. By examining these rules, the DBMS determines whether a specific user may be permitted to perform the operations of read, update, insert, or delete on a particular database object. You have already looked at an example of an authorization matrix in Figure 16-4. This matrix tends to be exhaustive and complex in a large database environment.

Many DBMSs do not implement elaborate information matrices as presented in Figure 16-4 to enforce authorization rules. Instead, they adopt simpler versions to implement authorization rules. Authorization rules may be represented as an autho-

PRIVILEGE	Department Record	Employee Record
Read	Y	Y
Update	N	N
Insert	N	Y
Delete	N	N

Authorization Rule
Subject: Samantha Jenkins

PRIVILEGE	Samantha Jenkins (password JNK271)	Will Rogers (password WRG346)
Read	Y	Y
Update	N	N
Insert	Y	N
Delete	N	N

Authorization Rule
Object: Employee Record

Figure 16-6   Implementation of authorization rules.

rization table for either subjects or users. On the other hand, an authorization table for objects can also do the job. A DBMS may implement authorization rules through either of the two tables or both.

Figure 16-6 presents both options for implementing authorization rules. Note how you can derive the same rule authorizing Samantha Jenkins to access the EMPLOYEE table with read and insert privileges.

Enforcing Authorization Rules   We have authorization rules in an authorization matrix or in the form of authorization tables for users or objects. How are the rules enforced by the DBMS? A highly protected privilege module with unconstrained access to the entire database exists to enforce the authorization rules. This is the arbiter or security enforcer module, although it might not go by those names in every DBMS. The primary function of the arbiter is to interrupt and examine every database operation, check against the authorization matrix, and either allow or deny the operation.

The arbiter module goes through a sequence of interrogations to determine the action to be taken about an operation. Figure 16-7 provides a sample interrogation list.

Suppose after going through the interrogation sequence, the arbiter has to deny a database operation. What are the possible courses of action? Naturally, the particular course of action to be adopted depends on a number of factors and the circumstances. Here are some basic options provided in DBMSs:

- If the sensitivity of the attempted violation is high, terminate the transaction and lock the workstation.
- For lesser violations, send appropriate message to user.
- Record attempted security breaches in the log file.

TEST	INTERROGATION	ACTION	
		YES	NO
1	Unconditional access to all relations in request?	GRANT	
2	Any relation in request unconditionally prohibited?	DENY	Next test
3	Unconditional access to all attributes in request?	GRANT	
4	Any attribute in request unconditionally prohibited?	DENY	Next test
5	Unconditional access to all groups of attributes in request?	GRANT	
6	Any group of attributes in request unconditionally prohibited?	DENY	Inform user

Figure 16-7   Arbiter interrogation list.

- Monitor for continued attempts of security breaches by same user for possible censure.

Authentication

Let us return to the authorization of access privileges to Samantha Jenkins. The authorization matrix contains security authorization rules for her. When she attempts to perform any database operation, the DBMS, through its arbiter module, can verify authorization rules as applicable and either allow or deny the operation. When Samantha Jenkins signs on to the database system with her user-id, in effect, she declares that she is Samantha Jenkins. All authorization she can have relates to the user known to the system as Samantha Jenkins.

Now when she signs on with her user-id and declares that she is Samantha Jenkins, how does the system know that she is really who she says she is? How can the system be sure that it is really Samantha Jenkins and not someone else signing on with her user-id? How can the system authenticate her identity? Authentication is the determination of whether the user is who he or she claims to be or declares he or she is through the user-id.

It is crucial that the authentication mechanism be effective and failsafe. Otherwise, all the effort and sophistication of the authorization rules will be an utter waste. How can you ensure proper authentication? Let us examine a few of the common techniques for authentication.

Passwords. Passwords, still the most common method, can be effective if properly administered. Passwords must be changed fairly often to deter password thefts. They must be stored in encrypted formats and be masked while being entered. Password formats need to be standardized to avoid easily detectable combinations. A database environment with highly sensitive data may require one-time-use passwords.

Personal information. The user may be prompted with questions for which the user alone would know the answers such as mother's maiden name, last four digits of social security number, first three letters of the place of birth, and so on.

Biometric verification. Verification through fingerprints, voiceprints, retina images, and so on. Smartcards recorded with such biometric data may be used.

Special procedures. Run a special authentication program and converse with the user. System sends a random number m to the user. The user performs a simple set of operations on the random number and types in the result n. System verifies n by performing the same algorithm on m. Of course, m and n will be different each time and it will be hard for a perpetrator to guess the algorithm.

Hang-up and call-back. After input of user-id, the system terminates the input and reinitiates input at the workstation normally associated with that user. If the user is there at that customary workstation and answers stored questions for the user-id, then the system allows the user to continue with the transaction.

Role of the DBA

The database administrator plays a pivotal role in security administration. Along with user representatives and senior management staff including the DA, the DBA develops a security policy appropriate for the environment. The DBA is the central authority executing the security policy by setting up user accounts and granting access privileges. The DBA has a user account that has extensive access privileges on all of the database objects.

Let us summarize the responsibilities of the DBA.

Creation of new accounts. Assign user-id and password to each user or group of users.

Creation of views. Create user views as needed for the purpose of tailoring security provisions for specific user groups.

Granting of privileges. Grant access privileges for users or user groups to perform database operations on database objects in accordance with security policy.

Revocation of privileges. Cancel access privileges originally assigned to users or user groups.

Assignments of security levels. Assign user accounts to proper security classification for mandatory access control. Designate security levels to database objects.

Maintenance of audit trail. Extend log file record to include updates with user-ids.

Statistical Databases

Statistical databases pose a great and interesting challenge in the matter of data security. Statistical databases are usually large databases intended to provide statistical information and not information about individual entities. Statistical databases may contain data about large populations of entities.

A census database contains information about the people in specific geographic areas. The database system of a large international bank holds information about the savings and checking account activities of significant strata of the population. Databases of large financial institutions contain profiles of investors. Databases used in data warehousing and data mining may be considered as statistical databases in some significant sense.

Need for Data Access   Statistical databases serve critical purposes. They store rich data content providing population statistics by age groups, income levels, household sizes, education levels, and so on. Government statisticians, market research companies, and institutions estimating economic indicators depend on statistical databases. These professionals select records from statistical databases to perform statistical and mathematical functions. They may count the number of entities in the selected sample of records from a statistical database, add up numbers, take averages, find maximum and minimum amounts, and calculate statistical variances and standard deviations.

All such professionals need access to statistical databases. However, there is one big difference between users of an operational database needing access privileges and professionals requiring access privileges to a statistical database. Users of an operational database need information to run the day-to-day business—to enter an order, to check stock of a single product, to send a single invoice. That is, these users need access privileges to individual records in the database. On the other hand, professionals using statistical databases need access privileges to access groups of records and perform mathematical and statistical calculations from the selected groups. They are not interested in single records, only in samples containing groups of records.

Security Challenge   So what is the problem with granting access privileges to professionals to use a statistical database just the way you would grant privileges to use any other type of database? Here is the problem: The professionals must be able to read individual records in a select sample group for performing statistical calculations but, at the same time, must not be allowed to find out what is in a particular record.

For example, take the case of the international bank. The bank's statisticians need access to the bank's database to perform statistical calculations. For this purpose, you need to grant them access privileges to read individual records. But, at the same time, you cannot allow them to see Jane Doe's bank account balance. The challenge in the case of the bank is this: How can you grant access privileges to the statisticians without compromising the confidentiality of individual bank customers?

Perhaps one possible method is to grant access privileges to individual records because the statistician needs to read a group of records for the calculations but restrict the queries to perform only mathematical and statistical functions such as COUNT, SUM, AVG, MAX, MIN, variance and standard deviations.

Although this method appears to be adequate to preserve the confidentiality of individual customers, a clever professional can run a series of queries and narrow the intersection of the query result to one customer record. This person can infer the values in individual rows by running a series of ingenuous queries. Each query produces a result set. Even though only statistical functions are permitted, by combining the different results through a series of clever queries, information about a single entity may be determined. Figure 16-8 illustrates how, by using different predicates in queries from a bank's statistical database, the bank balance of a single

Query A:

SELECT COUNT (*) FROM CUSTOMER

WHERE CustCity = 'Any City' AND CustGender = 'F' AND
        IncomeLevel = 'High"

Query B:

SELECT AVG (Balance) FROM CUSTOMER

WHERE CustCity = 'Any City' AND CustGender = 'F' AND
        IncomeLevel = 'High"

If result from Query A is 1, then Query B gives the account balance for the specific customer.

If result from Query A is 2 or 3, issue additional queries by including statistical functions of MAX, MIN, SUM to get a precise range for the account balance for the specific customer.

Figure 16-8   Ingenuous queries isolating individual records.

customer Jane Doe may be determined. Assume that the infiltrator knows some basic information about Jane Doe.

Solution Options   Safeguarding privacy and confidentiality in a statistical database proves to be difficult. The standard method of granting access privileges does not work. In addition to discretionary and mandatory techniques, other restrictions must be enforced on queries.

Here is a list of some solution options. None of them is completely satisfactory. Combinations of some of the options seem to be effective. Nevertheless, protection of privacy and confidentiality in statistical databases is becoming more and more essential.

Only statistical functions.   Allow only statistical functions in queries.

Same sample.   Reject series of queries to the same sample set of records.

Query types.   Allow only those queries that contain statistical or mathematical functions.

Number of queries.   Allow only a certain number of queries per user per unit time.

Query thresholds.   Reject queries that produce result sets containing fewer than n records, where n is the query threshold.

Query combinations.   The result set of two queries may have a number of common records referred to as the intersection of the two queries. Impose a restriction saying that no two queries may have an intersection larger than a certain threshold number.

Data pollution.   Adopt data swapping. In the case of the bank database, swap balances between accounts. Even if a user manages to read a single customer's record, the balances may have been swapped with balances in another customer's record.

Introduce noise. Deliberately introduce slight noise or inaccuracies. Randomly add records to the result set. This is likely to show erroneous individual records, but statistical samples produce approximate responses quite adequate for statistical analysis.

Log queries. Maintain a log of all queries. Maintain a history of query results and reject queries that use a high number of records identical to those used in previous queries.

ENCRYPTION

We have discussed the standard security control mechanisms in detail. You studied the discretionary access control method whereby unauthorized persons are kept away from the database and authorized users are guaranteed access through access privileges. You have also understood the mandatory access control method, which addresses some of the weaknesses of the discretionary access control scheme. Now you are confident that these two standard schemes provide adequate protection and that potential intruders cannot invade the database.

However, the assumption is that an infiltrator or intruder tries to break into the system through normal channels by procuring user-ids and passwords through illegal means. What if the intruder bypasses the system to get access to the information content of the database? What if the infiltrator steals the database by physically removing the disks or backup tapes? What if the intruder taps into the communication lines carrying data to genuine users? What if a clever infiltrator runs a program to retrieve the data by breaking the defenses of the operating system?

The normal security system breaks down in such cases. Standard security techniques fall short of expectations to protect data from assaults bypassing the system. If your database contains sensitive financial data about your customers, then you need to augment your security system with additional safeguards. In today's environment of electronic commerce on the Internet, the need for dependable security techniques is all the more essential. Encryption techniques offer added protection.

What is Encryption?

Simply stated, encryption is a method of coding data to make them unintelligible to an intruder and then decoding the data back to their original format for use by an authorized user. Some commercial DBMSs include encryption modules; a few others provide program exits for users to code their own encryption routines. Currently, encryption techniques are widely used in applications such as electronic fund transfers (EFT) and electronic commerce.

An encryption scheme needs a cryptosystem containing the following components and concepts:

- An encryption key to code data (called plaintext)
- An encryption algorithm to change plaintext into coded text (called ciphertext)

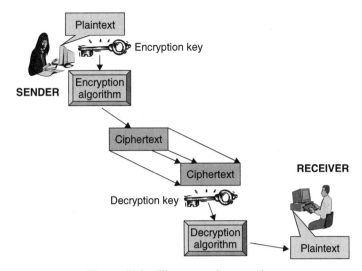

Figure 16-9   Elements of encryption.

- A decryption key to decode ciphertext
- A decryption algorithm to change ciphertext back into original plaintext

Figure 16-9 shows the elements of encryption. Note the use of the keys and where encryption and decryption take place.

The underlying idea in encryption dictates the application of an encryption algorithm to plaintext where the encryption algorithm may be accessible to the intruder. The idea includes an encryption key specified by the DBA that has to be kept secret. Also is included a decryption algorithm to do the reverse process of transforming ciphertext back into plaintext.

A good encryption technique, therefore, must have the following features:

- Fairly simple for providers of data to encrypt
- Easy for authorized users to decrypt
- Does not depend on the secrecy of the encryption algorithm
- Relies on keeping the encryption key a secret from an intruder
- Extremely difficult for an intruder to deduce the encryption key

Just to get a feel for an encryption scheme, let us consider a simple example before proceeding further into more details about encryption. First, we will use a simple substitution method. Second, we will use a simple encryption key. Let us say that the plaintext we want to encrypt is the following plaintext:

ADMINISTRATOR

Simple Substitution   Use simple substitution by shifting each letter in the plaintext to three spaces to the right in the alphabetic sequence. A becomes D, D becomes G; and so on. The resulting ciphertext is as follows:

```
DGPLQLVWUDWRU
```

If the intruder sees a number of samples of the ciphertext, he or she is likely to deduce the encryption algorithm.

Use of Encryption Key   This is a slight improvement over the simple substitution method. Here, let us a use a simple encryption key stipulated as "SAFE." Apply the key to each four-character segment of the plaintext as shown below:

```
ADMINISTRATOR
SAFESAFESAFES
```

The encryption algorithm to translate each character of the plaintext is as follows:

Give each character in the plaintext and the key its position number in the alphabetic scheme. The letter "a" gets 1, the letter "z" gets 26, and a blank in the plaintext gets 27. Add the position number of each letter of plaintext to the position number of the corresponding letter of the key. Then apply division modulus 27 to the sum. This calculation means dividing a number by 27 and using the remainder to applying to the algorithm. Use the number resulting from the division modulus 27 to find the letter to be substituted in the ciphertext.

Let us apply the algorithm to the first position in our plaintext.

Plaintext letter	A	Key letter	S
Position number	1	Position number	19

Sum of position numbers = (1 + 19)
Result of division modulus 27 = 20 divided by 27, remainder 20

Letter in position 20 is T. Therefore, the first letter "A" in the plaintext is substituted by "T" in the ciphertext.

After doing all the substitutions, the ciphertext reads as follows:

```
TESNFJYYbBYTb
```
                              (b indicates a blank)

Now compare the ciphertexts produced by the two methods and note how even a simple key and fairly unsophisticated algorithm could improve the encryption scheme.

Original plaintext	ADMINISTRATOR
Ciphertext using simple substitution	DGPLQLVWUDWRU
Ciphertext using simple key	TESNFJYYbBYTb

Encryption Methods

Three basic methods are available for encryption:

Encoding. Most simple and inexpensive method. Here, for important fields, the values of are encoded. For example, instead of storing the names of bank branches, store codes to represent each name.

Substitution. Substitute, letter for letter, in the plaintext to produce the ciphertext.

Transposition. Rearrange characters in the plaintext using a specific algorithm.

Usually a combination of substitution and transposition works well. However, techniques without encryption keys do not provide adequate protection. The strength of a technique depends on the key and the algorithm used for encryption and decryption. However, with plain substitution or transposition, if an intruder reviews sufficient number of encoded texts, he or she is likely to decipher.

On the basis of the use and disposition of encryption keys, encryption techniques fall into two categories.

Symmetric Encryption This technique uses the same encryption key for both encryption and decryption. The key must be kept a secret from possible intruders. The technique relies on safe communication to exchange the key between the provider of data and an authorized user. If the key is to be really secure, you need a key as long as the message itself. Because this is not efficient, most keys are shorter. The Data Encryption Standard (DES) is an example of this technique.

Asymmetric Encryption This technique utilizes different keys for encryption and decryption. One is a public key known openly, and the other is a private key known only to the authorized user. The encryption algorithm may also be known publicly. The RSA model is an asymmetric encryption method.

Data Encryption Standard

This technique, designed and developed by IBM in 1977, was adopted by the National Bureau of Standards as the official Data Encryption Standard (DES). Since then, various industry agencies have adopted DES. The technique uses a single key for both encryption and decryption. The key has to be kept secret from potential intruders. Similarly, the encryption algorithm must not be publicly known. The algorithm consists of character substitutions and transpositions or permutations.

Figure 16-10 illustrates this single-key encryption technique.

How it Works DES divides plaintext into blocks of 64 bits each. A 64-bit key is used to encrypt each block. Although the key is 64 bits long, effectively, it is only a 56-bit key because 8 bits are used as parity bits. Even with 56 bits in a key, there are 2^{56} possible distinct keys. So there are a huge number of choices for establishing a key.

Encryption takes place in the following sequence:

- Apply an initial permutation to each block using the key.
- Subject each transformed or permuted block to a sequence of 16 complex substitution steps.
- Finally, apply another permutation algorithm, the inverse of the initial permutation.

The decryption algorithm is identical to the encryption algorithm, except that the steps are in the reverse order.

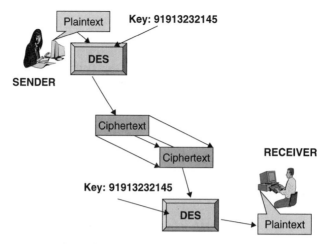

Figure 16-10 DES: single-key encryption.

Weaknesses Despite the complexity of the encryption algorithm and the sophistication of key selection, DES is not universally accepted as absolutely secure. Critics point out the following deficiencies:

- 56-bit keys are inadequate. With the powerful and special hardware available now, they are breakable. Even such expensive hardware is within the reach of organized crime and hostile governments. However, 128-bit keys are expected to be unbreakable within the foreseeable future. A better technique known as PGP (pretty good privacy) uses 128-bit keys. Another possible remedy is double application of the algorithm at each step.
- Users must be given the key for decryption. Authorized users must receive the key through secure means. It is very difficult to maintain this secrecy. This is a major weakness.

Public Key Encryption

This technique overcomes some of the problems associated with the DES technique. In DES you have to keep the encryption key a secret, and this is not an easy thing to accomplish. Public key encryption addresses this problem. The public key as well as the encryption algorithm need not be kept secret. Is this like locking the door and making the key available to any potential intruder? Let us examine the concept.

The widely used public key encryption technique was proposed by Rivest, Shamir, and Adleman. It is known by the acronym RSA. The RSA model is based on the following concepts:

- Two encryption keys are used—one public and the other private.
- Each user has a public key and a private key.
- The public keys are all published and known openly.
- The encryption algorithm is also made freely available.

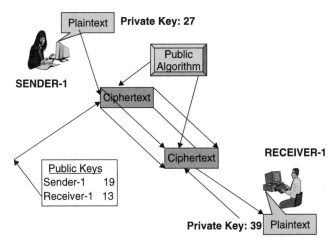

Figure 16-11   RSA: public key encryption.

- Only an individual user knows his or her private key.
- The encryption and decryption algorithms are inverses of each other.

Figure 16-11 illustrates this public key encryption technique.

How it Works   Consider the following scenario:

Data provider U1 wants to share data with authorized user U2.
U2 has a public key P2 and a private key R2.
U1 uses the public key P2 of U2 to encrypt the data and transmits the data to U2.
U2 uses the private key R2 to decrypt the data.

If data have to be transmitted securely, it must be extremely difficult for any intruder to deduce the private key from the publicly known public key and the encrypting algorithm. The RSA model stands on the premise that it is virtually impossible to deduce the private keys. This premise rests on the following two facts:

- A known efficient algorithm exists for testing whether or not a given number, however large, is a prime number.
- No known efficient algorithm exists for determining the prime factors of given number, however large.

Incidentally, one of the authors of the RSA technique had estimated that testing whether a given 130-digit number is a prime or not would take about 7 minutes on a fast computer. On the other hand, if you have a large number obtained by multiplying two 63-digit prime numbers, then it would take about 40 quadrillion years on the same machine to determine the prime factors of the product!

The public key encryption technique treats data as a collection of integers. The public and private keys are reckoned for an authorized user as follows:

- Choose two large, random prime numbers n1 and n2.
- Compute the product of n1 and n2. This product is also known as the limit L, assumed to be larger than the largest integer ever needed to be encoded.
- Choose a prime number larger than both n1 and n2 as the public key P
- Choose the private key R in a special way based on n1, n2, and P

[If you are interested, R is calculated such that R * P = 1, modulo (n1–1) * (n2–1).]

The limit L and the public key P are made known publicly. Note that the private key R may be computed easily if the public key P and the prime numbers n1 and n2 are given. However, it is extremely difficult to compute the private key R if just the public key P and the limit L are known. This is because finding the prime factors of L is almost impossible if L is fairly large.

Data Exchange Example   Let us consider the use of public key encryption in a banking application. Here are the assumptions:

- Online requests for fund transfers may be made to a bank called ABCD. The bank's customer known as Good places a request to transfer $1 million.
- The bank must be able to understand and acknowledge the request.
- The bank must be able to verify that the fund transfer request was in fact made by customer Good and not anyone else.
- Also, customer Good must not be able to allege that the request was made up by the bank to siphon funds from Good's account.

Figure 16-12 illustrates the use of public key encryption technique showing the banking transaction. Note how each transfer is coded and decoded.

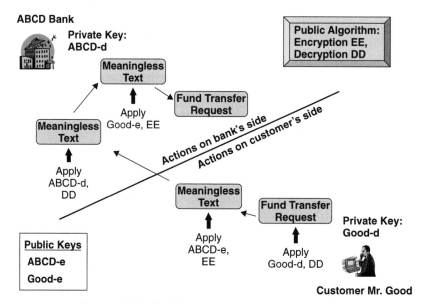

Figure 16-12   Public key encryption: data exchange.

CHAPTER SUMMARY

- An organization's database, being a vital asset, must be protected from unintentional and intentional threats by an effective security system.
- The security system must safeguard a database against theft, vandalism, and fraud; it must preserve the privacy of those about whom data is stored; it must also guarantee proper access privileges to authorized users.
- General security procedures include controls in the physical environment, prevention of malicious acts, and securing of equipment. A strong security policy must guide the procedures. Contingency plans are absolutely necessary.
- Computer-based security measures: protection through authorizing only those who have to be given database access, tailoring access provisions through user views, backup and recovery procedures, and safeguarding of sensitive data by encryption.
- Discretionary access control relates to granting access privileges to authorized users for accessing specific data items on prescribed access modes. Mandatory access control classifies database objects by levels of criticality, assigns security clearance levels to subjects such as users, and matches object levels to subject clearances for providing access.
- Statistical databases pose a special security challenge for protecting privacy. A number of solution options have been proposed.
- Encryption of data provides protection from intruders who attempt to bypass the normal access control mechanisms. The encryption method codes data to make them unintelligible to an intruder and then decodes the data back to original format for use by an authorized user.
- The encryption technique involves encryption and decryption keys along with encryption and decryption algorithms. Symmetric encryption uses the same key for both encryption and decryption; asymmetric encryption uses different keys.
- The Data Encryption Standard (DES) is a single-key encryption technique requiring that the encryption key be kept secret.
- In the public key encryption technique, a public key and a private key are used. The public key is openly available, whereas the private key is chosen and kept secret by the authorized user.

REVIEW QUESTIONS

1. List the major goals and objectives of a database security system. Which ones are important?
2. What are the types of general access control procedures in a database environment?
3. What is data privacy? What are some of the privacy issues to be addressed?
4. What is discretionary access control? What are the types of access privileges available to users?
5. Describe an authorization graph with an example.

6. Name the components of a mandatory access control model.
7. Distinguish between security authorization and authentication.
8. What purposes do statistical databases serve? Name any four types of options to preserve individual privacy in a statistical database.
9. What are the important characteristics of a good encryption technique?
10. Compare DES with the public key encryption technique and list the differences.

EXERCISES

1. Indicate whether true or false:
   A. Discretionary access control provides better protection than mandatory access control.
   B. Biometric verification is an authentication procedure.
   C. Statistical databases have potential data privacy problems.
   D. In the DES encryption technique, the encryption key may be made public.
   E. In the RSA encryption technique, two encryption keys are used.
   F. Simple security restriction relates to discretionary access control.
   G. An authorization graph shows the cycle of how access privileges are passed along.
   H. The DROP VIEW command destroys the data represented in the user view.
   I. The DBMS maintains a profile for each user.
2. As a data security consultant for a large department store, prepare a draft outline of a security policy document.
3. You are the DBA for an airline company. Group the users in your company by functional roles. Indicate four major database tables for the company. Prepare a sample authorization matrix showing user groups, database tables, and access privileges.
4. Explain how user views can be used as security tools. Provide three examples.
5. Choose one of the encryption techniques: DES or RSA. Describe, by means of a simple example, how data is exchanged by using the technique.

CHAPTER 17

ONGOING MAINTENANCE AND GROWTH

CHAPTER OBJECTIVES

- Understand the critical need for ongoing maintenance of the database system
- Note the routine maintenance activities that must continue
- Examine the importance of regular database backups and recovery procedures
- Study how continuous monitoring and gathering of statistics take place
- Appreciate how performance monitoring enables provision for growth
- Review the use of benchmarks and how these help assess the status of the database system
- Note the various aspects of growth and enhancements in a database environment
- Comprehend the significance of performance tuning
- Learn how to tune the various components of a database system

Let us say that you are part of the project team implementing a database system for your company. Perhaps you are the database administrator. The project team has worked through the database development project cycle from planning through implementation and deployment of the database system. The project is successful, and the system is up and running. Everyone is happy; the project team and the DBA can now stop working on the database system. Is this not true?

From Chapter 14 on database administration, you definitely know that the database development life cycle does not simply terminate as soon as you deploy your database system. Maintenance activities just get started at that point and continue as long as the database system is in operation. The database administra-

Database Design and Development: An Essential Guide for IT Professionals by Paulraj Ponniah
ISBN 0-471-21877-4   Copyright © 2003 by John Wiley and Sons, Inc.

tor has the primary responsibility during this continuous period of maintenance and growth.

Within a few short weeks after deployment, you will note an increase in the usage of the database system. In an operational environment, growth does not materialize in just more transactions in the initial applications. Newer applications get developed to take advantage of the database system. The project team, especially the DBA, must be able to provide for the growth.

After deployment, the database system must be closely monitored. Although the usage pattern and frequency of usage could mostly be anticipated, you will see variations very soon after deployment. You will understand that the project team could not foresee every aspect of the usage. So the DBA must carefully monitor usage on an ongoing basis.

In a typical database environment, new users will need authorizations to access the database. Access privileges may have to be changed for the current authorized users. As and when users leave an organization, their access privileges must be revoked immediately. Security administration becomes an important ongoing responsibility of the DBA.

As soon as a database system is deployed and made ready for use, the system is open to potential failures. Safeguarding against failures is an essential ongoing activity. Proper backup and recovery procedures constitute a basic responsibility in the postdeployment period.

Figure 17-1 provides a comprehensive overview of the ongoing maintenance activities in a database environment.

In the previous chapters, we have touched on these activities. Now in this chapter, we will get into more details on the significant activities. One such activity is ongoing tuning of the database for performance. We will consider how various components are tuned so that the database system may perform at optimal performance.

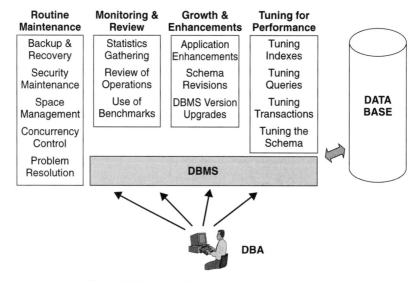

Figure 17-1 Overview of ongoing maintenance.

ROUTINE MAINTENANCE

Just like a mechanical system or any other type of system, to keep the database system working, the database administrator must perform routine maintenance functions. These are not for addressing major problems or recovery from failures. On a day-to-day basis, routine maintenance functions ensure that the components are working well. Routine maintenance functions keep the database performing at the current level without coming to a halt. Let us consider a few key routine maintenance activities.

Backup and Recovery

It does not matter to what extent a database system is safeguarded, in practice failures do occur and they destroy the system partially or completely. Whatever may be the cause of the failure—fire, unintentional or intentional action by people, power failure, or mechanical malfunctions of hardware devices—the DBA must plan and provide for a method to recover and restore the database to a consistent state.

Backing up the database at frequent intervals is obviously an effective, straightforward technique to help in the recovery process. As you know, backup files alone cannot restore the database to the current state if a failure occurs much later than when the latest backup was taken. You know that other files such as the transaction log file are also necessary to bring the database to its most current state.

Recovery System   A complete recovery system consists of the following functions and components:

Backup capability. Create backup copies of the entire database at specified intervals. Most database installations create backups at least once a day, usually after the nightly batch update jobs are completed.

Backup files are kept on tape cartridges or optical media other than the disk medium on which databases usually reside. It is customary to keep at least three generations of the backup files, just in case the latest backup file cannot be read during the recovery process. Also, it is advisable to store backup files at an off-site location.

Journalizing capability. Create log files containing details of all transactions since the last full backup of the database. As discussed in a previous chapter, log file records contain before and after images of the database objects that were accessed by individual transactions. The records also keep the timestamp and disposition of each transaction.

Checkpoint capability. Create checkpoint records on the log file to speed up the recovery process. While recovering, the recovery manager module may need to go back only up to the most recent checkpoint record.

Recovery capability. The DBMS should provide a recovery manager module to restore the database to the most recent possible state from the backup and log files.
Figure 17-2 presents the components of the database recovery system.

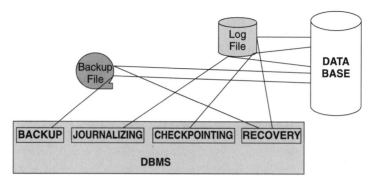

Figure 17-2 Database recovery system.

Routine Backup and Recovery Activities Let us now summarize the routine activities for backup and recovery. Here are the major tasks:

- Schedule regular backups, at least once a day, more often if the nature of your database content warrants it. Find a suitable time window on the computer system to perform the backups. If frequent full backups are not feasible, have a combination of full and partial backups. Partial backups may be hot backups while the database is up and running. Recovery is more difficult with partial backups. Have a good tape management system to make sure that backup tapes are not scratched before their expiration dates.
- Ensure that logging is properly done and that all the necessary details are written in the log records. Partial backups are more difficult for recovery. Monitor the space allocation on disk for the log file so that it does not get filled up before the next archival. Periodically archive the disk log file on other media such as tape cartridges or optical devices. Keep archived log files in safe custody.
- Monitor the frequency of writing checkpoint records. Writing checkpoint records results in system overhead. Adjusting the frequency is a balance between such system overhead and saving time during recovery.
- Review your disaster recovery plan on a regular basis. Have a regular schedule to test the recovery process. This will validate your backup files and the log files. Also, if and when database failure occurs, you will be prepared with a tested procedure.

Recovery Methods How recovery must be performed depends on the nature of the failure, the availability of backup and log files, and the extent of the damage. In failures resulting from disk crashes, depending on how badly the disk gets destroyed, you may have to discard the current devices and use newer or other available ones.

In Chapter 15, Figure 15-31 presented a comprehensive database recovery example. We will now review the applicability of recovery methods to different types of failures. The underlying principle in recovery involves restoring the database to a consistent state as close to the time of failure as possible. The recovery process must be short, fast, and easy.

First, let us explore three standard recovery methods.

Restore and reprocess. This is the simplest of the recovery methods. You take the latest available backup tape and copy it down to the disk extent. From that point, apply or process all the transactions up to the time of failure. Let us say that you create backup tapes every night at 11 P.M. Suppose a failure occurred around 3 P.M. today. You take last night's backup and use it to recreate your database. Then you redo all on-line and batch transactions that executed between 11 P.M. last night up to 3 P.M. today. Although simple and straightforward, this method is not usually acceptable. The time and effort to reprocess all the transactions from the time of the latest backup may be too great. Next, to bring the database to the exact state it was before the crash, you need to reprocess the transactions in the same order they were processed before.

Backward recovery or rollback. In this case, the latest backup tape and the log file are used for recovery. As pointed out in the previous method, the backup tape created last night at 11 P.M. is first used to create the database as it was at that time. Then the recovery manager of the DBMS runs to process the transactions from the log file. All completed transactions found in the log file are applied to the database created by copying the backup file. For transactions in flight or incomplete because of the failure, the before images of data items are applied. All the incomplete transactions must be sorted out and reprocessed.

Forward recovery or rollforward. This is similar to rollback except that, wherever possible, incomplete transactions are completed from the available after images of data items found on the log file. The database is first recreated from the backup file, and then the completed transactions from the log file are applied to the database. The database is then brought forward with any available after images in the log file for the in-flight transactions.

Figure 17-3 shows these three recovery methods. Note the use of the backup and log files in each case.

Applicability to Failure Types   When do you apply these recovery modes? Are there any circumstances under which restore and reprocess method can apply? When is forward recovery more appropriate?

Figure 17-4 lists the types of failures and also suggests the recovery method suitable for each type.

Security Maintenance

In Chapter 16 on database security, you studied the significant techniques relating to protecting the database system. As you know, discretionary access controls deal with granting and revoking access privileges to individual users and user groups. Mandatory access control is more stringent, with security classes for database objects and security clearances for users. Here we want to list the types of activities that must be routinely performed as part of the ongoing maintenance.

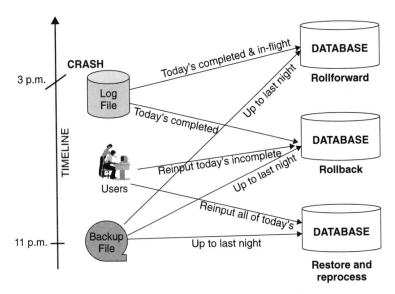

Figure 17-3 Database recovery methods.

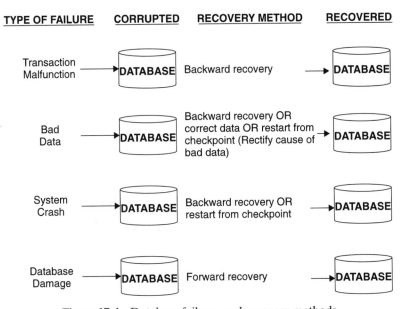

Figure 17-4 Database failures and recovery methods.

Initially, the DBA authorizes users with access privileges. The initial setup usually enables the users to get started with the new database system. However, very soon, changes to the access privileges are warranted. Here are some of the reasons for revisions to access privileges:

- Access privileges must be revoked immediately for people who leave the organization.
- Access privileges must be granted to new employees. This may take the form of a preliminary set of privileges as soon as an employee joins the organization and upgraded privileges soon after the initial orientation and training.
- When staff members move from one region to another or from one division to another, their responsibilities change. Consequently, their access privileges must be revised.
- When employees get promoted to greater responsibilities, their need to access information also changes. Their access privileges need revisions.
- User groups or departments pick up additional responsibilities or shed some current responsibilities. If group authorizations are in place, these will need upgrades or downgrades.
- For organizations using mandatory access controls, database objects may be reclassified because of the changes in the sensitivity of the data content of these objects. In these cases, the security clearances of users may need to be revised.

In large organizations where there are numerous staff movements, security administration takes up substantial time. Special security administrators are employed in such organizations to keep the security authorizations current.

The following is a list of the types of routine security functions in a database environment after deployment:

- Create new user accounts and assign passwords to new eligible employees.
- Grant fresh set of access privileges to new eligible employees.
- Upgrade or downgrade access privileges to existing employees.
- Create, revise, or drop user groups or roles.
- Create views for the purpose of tailoring access privileges to specific users or user groups.
- Deactivate user accounts of terminated employees.
- Revoke access privileges of terminated employees.
- Drop views that are no longer needed for security and other purposes.
- Revise security classes for database objects and security clearances for users if your organization uses mandatory access control.

Space Management

If you are a DBA, every morning you will be monitoring the space utilization of your production database files. You cannot let any production files get completely filled up and stop any transaction from completing for want of space in the middle of the day. Space management is a continuous activity for the DBA.

Some authorized users are also allowed to create test database tables and a few temporary, private tables. Frequently, these tables are not dropped even long after their purposes are served. Review of such obsolete tables and removing them also forms part of routine maintenance.

Here are the routine activities relating to space management:

- Monitor space utilization of all production files regularly.
- Expand disk space for files reaching the end of the allocated space.
- Archive database records not needed for regular, current use. Maintain archived tape files in a safe place.
- Whenever needed, bring back archived tape files, restore them on a special instance of the database, and allow users to use the data.
- Drop one-time, obsolete tables and recover disk space.
- Allocate space quotas to authorized users for creating one-time temporary tables. Revise or remove quotas as and when necessary.

Concurrency Control

Chapter 15 covered concurrent processing of transactions and methods for controlling concurrency from producing adverse effects. You have noted the need for concurrency and also studied the locking techniques needed to prevent problems associated with concurrent transactions. Although database management systems provide adequate lock management, the DBA must still keep monitoring locks and potential deadlock situations. Routinely, the DBA has options to manage and adjust concurrency control techniques.

Usually, a DBMS provides utility scripts to check the current state of a database. When a database system is running slowly and two or more transactions are waiting in deadlock situations, the DBA can run the script and find out what locks are held and which transactions are waiting. This facility usually provides the following information that can be used to resolve deadlocks:

- Transactions that have another transaction waiting on a lock and are not themselves in a wait state
- DDL locks held and requested (DDL locks prevent changes to database definitions while a transaction is executing.)
- DML locks held and requested (DML locks relate to read/write locks in shared and exclusive modes.)
- All locks held or requested
- Transactions that are waiting for database locks and transactions that are currently holding locks
- Locked database objects and the transactions that are currently accessing them

The locking mechanisms of most DBMSs work well. However, if some transactions do not lock at the lowest level of database objects needed by them, deadlock situations could result. Manual intervention by the DBA becomes routinely necessary. After finding out the transactions that are caught in deadlock situations, the DBA has the option of terminating one or more transactions in deadly embrace, thus enabling the waiting transactions to proceed.

Problem Resolution

The DBA is involved in detection and resolution of certain problems on an ongoing basis. Here are a few major problem resolution tasks.

System malfunctions. When the database system stops functioning because of some type of malfunction of the operating system or the DBMS itself, the DBA takes a core dump of the main memory and registers for determining the nature of the problem. The dump is taken before restarting the database system.

Follow-up and coordination. Typically for system malfunctions, the DBA has to seek outside help from the vendors of the operating system and the DBMS. The DBA sends the core dump to the outside vendors. He or she needs to follow up and coordinate the problem resolution with the vendors.

Application of fixes. Usually vendors of the operating system or the DBMS supply code to fix or patch up the system malfunctions. The DBA applies the fixes under appropriate conditions and tests the solutions.

Transaction failures. Whenever any transaction does not execute successfully and aborts, the DBA gets involved in determining the cause of the problem and finding a resolution. Transactions abort for many reasons such as bad data, incorrect coding, or some external conflict.

User support. The DBA and other project team members provide support to the users of the database system by providing clarifications, educating the users on database concepts, and resolving any of their database problems. The DBA is part of the user support loop.

MONITORING AND REVIEW

After deployment of the database system, in addition to performing routine maintenance tasks, the DBA continues to inspect system performance. The project team continues to monitor how the new database system matches up with the requirements and stores the desired information content. The DBA constantly examines the various factors that affect system performance. He or she needs to know the growth trend and whether the database will be able to scale up. The DBA also has to keep the database performing at an optimal level to process transactions efficiently.

How can the DBA and other project team members assess performance levels and be assured of providing for growth? Of course, they need information about how well the database is operating and how smoothly could it accommodate growth. They need statistics about current performance. They need to review various aspects of the design and development of the database system.

Statistics are indicators whose values provide information on how the database is operating. These indicators present growth trends. You will understand how well the database server functions. You will gain insights into how well applications perform in the new database environment.

How do you monitor and collect statistics about the database environment? Two common methods apply to the collection process. Sampling methods and event-driven methods are generally used. The sampling method measures specific aspects of database activity at regular intervals. You can set the duration of the interval. For example, if you want to record the number of active transactions every 20 minutes, this method will produce the numbers three times every hour. The sampling method has minimal impact on system overhead. In the event-driven method, recording of statistics happens only when a specified event takes place, not at regular intervals. If you want to monitor growth of an index table, you can set the monitoring mechanism to record the event every time an update is made to the index table. We will elaborate on these methods a little later. First, you must appreciate the purpose of database monitoring and what monitoring is expected to accomplish.

Purpose of Monitoring

After deployment, actual use of the new database system reveals unanticipated difficulties and factors. During implementation, the project team plans according to the expected usage and access patterns. Not even extensive testing could expose all the variations. Only after the database is sufficiently exercised by the users can the DBA gain real insights.

Actual use for a reasonable period, with execution of all types of transactions, exposes bottlenecks affecting performance. Perhaps the size of the memory buffers constricts the flow of transactions. It is possible that the initial index plan for a particular table hinders quick access instead of speeding up the transactions. All such bottlenecks surface as the database is used more and more. Therefore, ongoing monitoring and collection of statistics becomes important.

At a high level, two major purposes prompt database monitoring and collection of statistics:

- Discerning the growth pattern, estimating additional resources, and planning for future needs
- Tuning the database system for performance

At a more detailed level, database monitoring enables the DBA and other concerned members of the project team to accomplish the following:

- Identify and analyze performance problems in the database system configuration or in the applications using the database system.
- Utilize early warning systems to be alerted to potential problems.
- Discover exception conditions based on defined threshold values.
- Wherever possible, automate corrective actions in response to detected problems.
- Define additional requirements of statistics to be produced in addition to system defaults.
- As and when changes are made to the database system after deployment, assess the effects of the changes.

The Monitoring Process

Above we briefly mentioned two common methods for monitoring the performance and the state of the database system. Now let us get into more details. Let us generalize the two methods as snapshot monitoring and event monitoring. Let us examine how the monitoring process works in each case.

Snapshot Monitoring   This method provides a snapshot or picture of the current state of activities in the database system. Suppose you have a problem that is occurring right now. Then you would want a snapshot of the database activities at this moment. If a transaction executes for an inordinately long time, you may want to take snapshots at short intervals to monitor how the transaction is progressing and discover bottlenecks.

You may start the monitoring process and direct the system to take snapshots at specified intervals. At these intervals, snapshots of performance variables are recorded. You may define performance variables on the entire database, a specific table, a disk space for tables, or other similar database objects.

Some systems let you gather cumulative numbers wherever applicable from the start of the monitoring to the current snapshot. Snapshot monitoring systems can also provide comparisons of performance variables at different snapshot points. The comparisons may also be presented in the form of graphs that can display performance trends, peaks, and valleys.

Typical snapshot monitoring systems have graphical interfaces that let you take the following types of actions:

- Set sampling frequency of performance snapshots
- View results of performance computations
- Define threshold values and alert actions
- Generate alerts and view results of alert actions

Event Monitoring   With an event monitor, you capture information about transient events you cannot normally monitor through snapshot monitoring. An event monitor lets you monitor events such as deadlocks, completion of a transaction, execution of a particular statement in application code, an insert to a database table, and so on. In addition, you can also receive details about the monitored event. You can know how long a transaction took to complete, how much processor time was used by the transaction, and how many I/Os were necessary.

The details about an event are stored in an event file that can be analyzed by running an analyzer facility, usually as part of the event monitoring system. Details generated by event monitors may be used to manage and tune database systems in the following ways:

- Analyze deadlocks, review locks in participated transactions, and correct lock requests.
- Monitor usage at application level and provide usage accounting.
- Tune long-running transactions by monitoring operations such as reads and writes within the transactions.
- Analyze usage trends, predict future needs, and improve capacity planning.
- Analyze data collected on usage of buffer pools, table areas, and tables.

Gathering of Statistics

While gathering statistics, crucial items to monitor include disk space, free space left for tables, number of users, memory usage, and I/O performance. You should also monitor database usage by individuals, trace data accesses, and database update patterns. Let us list the main types of statistics to be collected. Some of these are automatically collected and stored by the DBMS itself. For others, you have to use monitoring systems.

- Sizes of individual tables
- Number of active tables
- Number of distinct values in table columns
- Number of times a particular query is submitted and completed successfully or unsuccessfully within a period
- Execution times for different phases of queries and transactions
- Storage statistics (tablespaces, indexspaces)
- Number of times DBMS is looking for space in blocks or causes fragmentation
- I/O device performance statistics—total times for read/write operations
- Query processing statistics—execution times, wait times, times for optimization and preparation, I/Os
- Transaction processing statistics—execution times, wait times, times for optimization and preparation, I/Os
- Lock processing statistics—rates of issuing different types of locks
- Logging statistics—log file activity
- Indexing statistics—index creation and accesses
- Input/output usage by user
- Count of authorized users
- Number of read and write operations executed during a set interval
- Number of completed transactions during a set interval
- Audit trail details for selected activities
- Number of page faults during a prescribed interval
- Number of times buffers full condition reached during a given interval
- Profiles of CPU usage during each day

Review of Operations

In addition to monitoring the database system and collecting statistics, the DBA and other team members must continue to review the operations on an ongoing basis. They will be able to spot trends and changes by means of such reviews.

Review the following:

- For each query, tables accessed, attributes used for selection conditions, attributes used for join conditions, and attributes whose values are retrieved
- For each update transaction, type of operation (insert, write, or delete), attributes used in selection conditions, and attributes whose values are changed

- Expected frequencies of individual queries
- Anticipated frequencies of individual transactions
- Time constraints
- Uniqueness constraints in database tables
- Indexes for each tables
- Validity of primary and foreign keys

Use of Benchmarks

As the number of users increases, the size of the database becomes larger, the scope of the applications expands, and the complexity of database operations intensifies, the DBMS tends to become inadequate to provide acceptable performance. Queries and transactions slow down. Conflicts among concurrent transactions escalate, resulting in locking problems. Routine maintenance becomes more and more time-consuming and difficult. You may begin to consider upgrading the DBMS or, perhaps, even replacing it with a more robust one.

How do you go about making decisions to upgrade or replace the existing DBMS? Performance benchmarks provide metrics that can be used for making upgrade or replace decisions. You may apply benchmark tests to the existing DBMS to check how inadequate it has become in the current environment. Also, bench-mark tests can be used to justify upgraded versions or new DBMSs considered as replacement.

Benchmarks quantify performance. They allow for variations in database environments. Individual tasks cannot measure performance satisfactorily. You need a collection of tasks to be used to quantify performance. Such a collection or suite of tasks constitutes a performance benchmark. Typically, benchmarks measure performance as transactions per second (tps). Also, they tie in with costs and compute price/performance ratios ($/tps).

Benchmarks defined by the Transaction Processing Council (TPC) are well known and are used more than some other benchmarks from industry. Other proprietary benchmarks proposed by individual vendors are not very useful because they are not universal. Let us examine the TPC benchmarks.

TPC-A. First in a series of benchmarks. Defined in 1989, it measures performance (tps and $/tps) in typical OLTP or operational environments. Simulates a standard bank application with a single type of transaction similar to cash withdrawal and deposit at a teller station, updating three tables, and adding an audit trail record in another table. Measures end-to-end performance of the system including performance at the workstation and on the data communications devices.

TPC-B. Similar to TPC-A, but it measures only the core performance of the DBMS and the OS by themselves. Not a measure for end-to-end performance. Used less widely than TPC-A.

TPC-C. More complex set of database operations than TPC-A or TPC-B. Based on the model of an order entry transaction performing operations to enter order, deliver order, record payment, monitor stock levels, and verify order status.

TPC-D. Not applicable to OLTP systems. Designed for decision support systems such as OLAP systems. Consists of a set of 17 queries in SQL, with some complex SQL features such as aggregation.

When using a particular benchmark, try to understand what it measures, in what context, and in which environment. Is the selected benchmark meaningful to your environment? How well does the benchmark apply to your workload?

GROWTH AND ENHANCEMENTS

Let us assume that the deployment of a database system by your project team is a great initial success. What can you expect in the next six months to a year after deployment? Initial success makes a database system dynamic and vibrant. You can be sure of sharp growth and a demand for additional applications using the database. The benefits of data integration and data sharing will result in greater collaboration among departments.

As users begin to use the initial applications more and more, you will notice substantial increase in data volumes. When the users realize the advantages of the database system, they will demand additional applications. Executives and managers will request new types of applications to provide summary information. Requests for enhancements to the initial applications will come in as a continuous stream.

Business conditions change. Your organization might expand into newer regions, and the users in these new areas would need access to the database. Progressive companies expanding through acquisitions need to have their database enlarged to accommodate additional data. These types of changes also result in revisions and enhancements to the database schema itself.

After a successful deployment of the database system, you must expect growth, revisions, and enhancements. And you must be prepared to manage the growth and enhancements. You must have procedures in place to handle the expansion of the database. We will consider ongoing growth and enhancements by first listing a few practical tips. Then we will cover application enhancements and schema revisions. Finally, we will discuss upgrades to the DBMS.

Ongoing Growth and Enhancements

The underlying principle is to anticipate growth and be prepared. If growth and enhancements are not properly managed, the adverse results will show up as user frustration and loss of productivity. Here are a few tips for managing growth and enhancements:

- Constantly monitor increases in data volumes. Observe the trends and be prepared to have additional disk space at short notice.
- Discourage users, programmers, and analysts from having their own private database tables in the development or test environment. If allowed, very soon these go out of control. All tables must be created through the DBA.
- The entire production database must be under the control of the DBA. Do not permit anyone else to create production tables.

- Have a regular schedule for archiving historical data. Operational systems usually do not need historical data to be available on-line from the database.
- The greater the number of users in an organization, the greater is the need for a fully streamlined procedure for security authorizations. The procedure should ensure strict screening of eligible users, prompt authorizations wherever needed, and immediate revoking of privileges of terminated employees.

Application Enhancements

At the time of deployment of the database system, you have initial applications utilizing data from the database. Users access the database through these applications. Application enhancements include revisions to the initial applications. The revisions may just be enhancing the GUI screens with additional fields or adding new screens. Very often, the enhancements take the form of newer phases of the initial applications. When the database is deployed in an organization for the first time, it is customary to bring the users into a database environment with preliminary versions of the initial applications. Then as the users get more and more accustomed to database concepts, additional versions are implemented.

More involved enhancements relate to brand new applications. For example, the database may be deployed to serve primarily as a repository for an initial order processing application. When this application is pronounced a success, it is quickly followed by an inventory control application. After the inventory control application, another new application may be implemented.

Enhancements have two major requirements. First, application developers need a development or test database environment for testing the changes. This environment is separate from the production database environment. The DBA is responsible for creating and maintaining the test environment. Second, enhancements to the initial applications and development of new applications involve revisions to the database schema. Depending on the nature of the enhancements or the new applications, the revisions could be extensive. We will deal with issues relating to the test environment first. In the next subsection, we will cover schema revisions.

Test Environment   We mentioned creating an entire test or development database environment for the purpose of implementing enhancements to applications. Why do you need a separate environment? Does this not involve much effort and resources to have a separate environment operational? Why not accommodate the testing of revisions in the production database environment itself?

You will find that a separate environment becomes necessary not just for enhancements. A separate environment is needed even for resolving problems that arise from time to time. Imagine that an application program that has been in use for some time aborts suddenly. You need to diagnose the problem, fix it, and have the user resume processing. The program execution must have tried to go through one of the paths not taken until now. You need test data with proper conditions to determine the reason for the problem and resolve it. You cannot add suitable test data in the production database and corrupt it. You need a separate test database environment.

Let us list a few significant issues relating to the test or development database environment.

Initial creation. Create the initial test database system by copying the production schema. The test system will start out as a replica of the production system.

Data from production. Move a sufficient number of rows from production tables to corresponding test tables. It is not practical to have the entire contents of the production database copied into the test database. However, you must have enough data to support adequate testing of application enhancements. Have a suite of special programs to select related records from various files. For example, if you select 1000 rows from the customer table, you must select the related orders, not random ones, to populate the orders table. Also, the suite of programs will usually have programs to copy full reference and code files. For example, you would want to copy the entire product file because the selected orders may contain many sets of products.

Test data. In addition to selected data moved from the production database, from time to time, special test data need to be created to test specific conditions. Have programs ready for creating special test data.

Test database operation. The production database is up and running every day during the designated hours. Should the test database be also up and running every day? Most companies discover the necessity of keeping the test database up every day to support the testing of application enhancements. Similar to the production job that is used to start the production database every day, a test start-up job is created to point to the test database files.

Test database maintenance. While test versions of application programs access the test database, very often, program malfunctions corrupt the database. As the test versions of the programs are still being tested, they are not free from error conditions. After some time, the test database gets so corrupted that it becomes useless for further testing. Therefore, periodically, you have to reload the test database from the production database and recreate any special test data.

Duration of test system. Is there a life span for the test database? Should it be kept indefinitely? Almost all organizations with database systems carry a test system indefinitely. However, the composition and data content are likely to keep changing.

Test program versions. Ensure that the test program versions are restricted to access only the test database and never the production database. Only after the programs are fully tested and approved, should they be promoted to access the production database.

Recovery. When failures occur in the test environment, should the test database be restored? Usually, this is not done except when you want to test your recovery procedure. Otherwise, simply refresh the test database with selected production data and proceed.

Schema Revisions

Application enhancements generally require revisions to the database schema. Depending on the type and extent of application enhancements, schema revisions may comprise the following kinds of revisions:

- Changes to data types or sizes of individual attributes
- Additions of new columns to individual tables
- Additions of new tables
- Deletions of any redundant columns
- Changes to uniqueness constraints
- Inclusion of new foreign keys

The revisions to the database schema are first made in the test database environment, tested, and only then applied to the production schema. Figure 17-5 illustrates how schema revisions are implemented.

Here are a few practical suggestions with regard to schema revisions:

Approval for revisions. All revisions to database schema must be subject to serious consideration and approval. Scrutinize the revisions and ensure that they do not violate any standards. Extensive revisions must be treated with great care as if they are part of the overall design.

Procedure for revisions. Have a formal procedure establishing the method for requesting, testing, validating, and approving the revisions. Include the users concerned as part of the process. Identify the responsibilities and assign relevant tasks to the DBA, programmers, analysts, and user representatives. Each revision must follow the prescribed procedure.

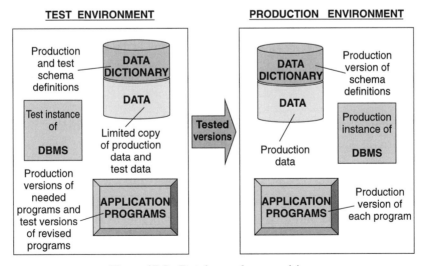

Figure 17-5   Database schema revisions.

Testing revisions. Revisions are tested through test versions of application programs. Have queries ready to view data changes in the database. Ensure that referential integrity and other constraints are not violated.

Revisions promoted to production. When test versions of application programs are promoted to production, the corresponding schema revisions must also be moved to the production environment. Have a good approval procedure for the move to production. For major revisions involving creation of new tables, you will be required to populate the new tables with initial data.

Fallback procedure. When you promote test versions of application enhancements and the corresponding schema revisions to production, if you run into unforeseen problems after the move to production, have a fallback procedure to revert to the previous state of the schema. However extensive testing could have been, there is always a slight chance of revisions not working properly; safeguard against such mishaps with a good fallback procedure.

DBMS Version Upgrades

From time to time, your database vendor will announce upgrades to the DBMS. Some of these newer versions contain fixes to problems noticed in the earlier versions. Most of the newer versions provide enhancements and better ways of managing the database versions. Many of the recent upgrades to relational DBMS focus on the merging of database and Internet technologies. Whether or not enhancements in the upgraded versions are directly beneficial to your environment, eventually you will be forced to move up to the latest version. Vendors usually discontinue supporting older versions of DBMSs after a designated period.

Version upgrades cause potentially serious interruption to the normal work unless they are properly managed. Good planning minimizes the disruption. Vendors try to pressure their customers into upgrades on their schedules based on their new releases. If the timing is not convenient for you, resist the initiatives from the vendor. Schedule the upgrade at your convenience and based on when your users can tolerate interruption.

The DBA takes primary responsibility in installing DBMS version upgrades. But others from the database and application project teams as well as user representatives assist with the testing. Here is a brief list of major tasks associated with DBMS version upgrades:

- Coordinate with vendor for assistance during the upgrade process
- Ensure that new version is fully tested by the vendor and free from any errors
- Prepare test database system to install new version
- Configure the new version with proper initialization parameters
- Revise database start-up job, if necessary
- Create a test plan and review the plan with other team members and users
- Compile list of programs to be tested with test conditions and assign responsibilities for testing
- Verify and approve test results

- Install new version in production and perform a dry run
- Run selected programs and queries in production before turning over new version for use

TUNING FOR PERFORMANCE

During the design and implementation phases, all the facts and statistics are not available. The designers and developers go by the information obtained while gathering requirements. As users begin to use the database after deployment, new usage patterns emerge. Over time, usage patterns change. Also, the size of the database increases. Ongoing tuning for performance becomes an essential activity.

In a database environment, problems and bottlenecks affect the performance at four levels: (1) the hardware level, primarily the data storage devices, (2) the level of the operating system that enables the actual interface with the storage devices, (3) the level of the DBMS that manages the database, and (4) the level of the applications that execute transactions and queries. Therefore, any effort at tuning must include considerations at all these four levels. The DBA coordinates the tuning activity, taking primary responsibility for tuning the DBMS. The technical support personnel perform the tuning of the operating system and deal with hardware configurations. Applications staff such as programmers and analysts get involved in applications tuning.

Figure 17-6 illustrates the nature of tuning the database environment at different levels.

Tuning the database environment involves looking at various aspects of performance. The following is just a sample of the factors to be considered while tuning for performance:

- Database configuration parameters
- Disk block utilization parameters
- Memory buffer pools

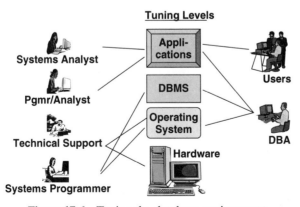

Figure 17-6 Tuning the database environment.

- Prefetching of data pages
- Locking patterns
- Logging overhead
- Memory allocation
- Disk space allocation
- Storage device read/write mechanisms

Goals and Solution Options

Three broad goals prompt the tuning effort in a database environment:

- Improve overall system throughput
- Reduce response times for transactions and queries
- Speed up applications

Bottlenecks Performance is generally affected by constrictions or bottlenecks in one or a few components. Removing bottlenecks produces the greatest benefit. A database environment is like a complex queuing system. Bottlenecks in queuing systems can slow down and even halt movement. In the same way, bottlenecks in a database system can slow down the execution of queries and transactions. Before undertaking a formalized tuning effort, first try to discover bottlenecks and eliminate them.

Figure 17-7 presents a database environment as a queuing system and demonstrates how bottlenecks can make transactions and queries sluggish.

Tuning Options Performance tuning is an elaborate topic. Getting into too detailed a discussion is beyond our scope here. We will consider three areas for per-

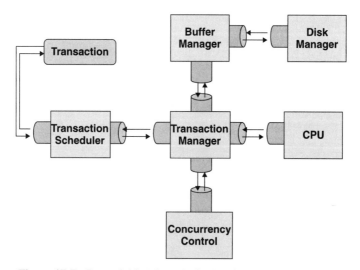

Figure 17-7 Potential bottlenecks in the database environment.

formance tuning: indexes, transactions and queries, and schema. Before that, let us first state some obvious examples of tuning options at the four levels.

Hardware level. This is the lowest level at which tuning activities may be performed. If the bottleneck is at the storage devices, some solution options are to add disks or use improved configurations such as RAID technology. If main memory buffer size is a restriction, try to add more memory. If the processor is a bottleneck, upgrade to a faster processor.

Operating system level. Look into page sizes and block sizes. Consider the block usage parameters and overhead to maintain overflow blocks. Review page faults and page swapping.

DBMS level. Scrutinize and adjust buffer sizes, checkpoint intervals, and deadlock resolution methods.

Applications level. Review the schema, tune indexes, and improve data access schemes. At every possible opportunity, employ stored procedures for which syntax checking, validation, optimization, and compilation have all been done already.

Tuning Indexes

As you know, proper indexes speed up processing considerably. Indexes are the most effective means to improve performance. After deployment, with users settling down in their usage patterns, and with the availability of statistics, indexes may be tuned successfully. Some queries may run long for lack of indexes; certain indexes may not be utilized at all; a few indexes may cause too much overhead because the attributes used for indexing are too volatile.

DBMSs provide trace facilities to sketch out the flow of operations in a query or transaction. Use the trace on a query or a transaction to determine the indexes used. Verify whether the indexes are appropriate. If not, revise the indexing.

The following is a list of general guidelines for tuning indexes:

- If queries are running slow, create appropriate indexes.
- If transaction updates are problems, reevaluate the indexes and ensure that there are not too many indexes suggesting inefficient execution paths to the optimizers.
- Make sure that proper indexing technique is defined for each index. For queries with selections based on ranges of values, B-tree indexing is appropriate. Hash indexing is best for selections based on exact values.
- Periodically reorganize and rebuild indexes to minimize overflow chains and reclaim empty space. Without reorganization, indexes, especially B-tree indexes, carry too much wasted space because of deletions.
- Optimizers depend on updated statistics about the database content such as number of rows, number of distinct values for attributes, and so on. When there is a choice of indexes for a table, the optimizer selects the right index based on

the statistics. Therefore, run the database utility program frequently to keep the statistics reasonably up to date.

- Drop redundant indexes.
- Add new indexes as suggested by changes in access patterns.
- For a multiattribute index, verify and ensure that the order of the attributes as defined in the index is appropriate for most of the processing using that index.

Tuning Queries and Transactions

When users run applications, they access the database through queries and transactions. Queries perform read operations; transactions execute update, insert, and delete operations. When transactions perform update, insert, and delete operations, most of the time they deal with single records. However, queries may read one record or a complete group of records based on a set of selection criteria. The selection may also involve join operations. Therefore, tuning queries constitutes the most significant effort in the overall performance tuning.

As you have seen above, the query optimizer provided in the DBMS intercepts each query and optimizes the query execution with a proper plan of execution. Usually, you can get an indication that a query does not perform efficiently when you note the following:

- The query issues too many disk I/Os.
- The query plan shows that the relevant indexes are not being used.

When you observe these symptoms, take appropriate action. Sometimes rewriting long-running queries may speed them up. Some DBMSs allow the use of hints to the optimizer. Hints are suggestions to the optimizer to use an index other than what it normally picks for a query when more than one index is available for a database table.

Do not hesitate to run the database utility program provided for asking to explain the plan used by the optimizer. Verify that the query is using the index you expect it to use. Also, make sure the optimizer of your DBMS works well for all types of queries and transactions. Some optimizers are found to perform poorly under the following conditions:

- Selection condition has null values
- Selection condition involves arithmetic or string expressions

Let us close with a few comments on the impact of concurrency on the overall performance.

- In an environment with a high volume of transactions, excessive locking is expected. Such excessive locking hurts performance.
- Duration of locking also affects performance because of transactions waiting for locks to be released.

- Placing of data and indexes across multiple disks, as in a RAID configuration, helps speed up concurrent transactions.
- In environments with a high volume of transactions, B-tree indexes themselves may be the bottlenecks. Change indexing techniques in such cases.

Tuning the Schema

Sometimes, you will find that the design of the conceptual and the physical schema does not meet the objectives of the evolving workload. In that case, the schema itself must be examined. You may consider changing the file organizations and allocation of database records to physical files. Changing the conceptual or logical schema requires substantial effort and time.

Here are a few options to be considered while examining the logical schema for the purpose of revisions:

- Decide to settle for third normal form (3NF) relations instead of further normalization into Boyce-Codd normal form (BCNF). The more you normalize a data structure, the more decomposed the relations become. Data access to retrieve a piece of information will have to extend to extra relations. For all practical purposes, 3NF proves to be adequate.
- Data retrieval patterns may indicate that some parts of a table are more frequently accessed than others. Splitting the table appropriately speeds up processing in such cases. Opt for horizontal or vertical partitioning.
- Denormalize in certain situations. For example, if the DEPARTMENT table and the EMPLOYEE table are in a one-to-many relationship and the DepartmentName attribute is required in most queries, it is worthwhile to denormalize the EMPLOYEE table. Repeat the DepartmentName attribute in the EMPLOYEE table. Such controlled redundancies improve efficiency.

CHAPTER SUMMARY

- The database development life cycle does not terminate as soon as you deploy the database system. Ongoing maintenance just gets started and continues as long as the database is in operation.
- The project team members, especially the DBA, must provide for growth and keep the database system tuned for top performance.
- Routine maintenance includes the following: regular backups and preparation for recovery from possible failures, administration of security, storage space management, concurrency control, and problem resolution.
- In large organizations, security maintenance is a major ongoing activity.
- The DBA and other responsible professionals need to monitor the database environment continually for growth planning and tuning the database for performance.

- Two common methods used for monitoring the database environment and collecting statistics: (1) snapshot monitoring by taking samples of performance indicators at defined intervals, and (2) event monitoring by capturing details about transient events.
- Monitoring systems collect statistics on a large variety of indicators such as table sizes, number of active database tables, execution times of different operations in transactions, storage allocations, lock processing details, database usage by authorized users.
- In addition to monitoring and collecting statistics, also review the status of basic components of the database system—indexes, transaction frequencies, uniqueness constraints, and so on.
- Benchmarks quantify performance of the database environment, particularly the DBMS. Benchmarks defined by the Transaction Processing Council are commonly used.
- Growth in a database environment takes the form of increase in data volume, multiplication of the number of users, enhancements to applications, and schema revisions.
- The DBA and the project team must create and maintain a test database environment for ongoing application development and for testing error corrections.
- On a regular basis the DBA, with the assistance of other team members, tunes the database for efficient performance. Tuning requires usage of statistics about the working of the various components.
- Tuning options relate to four levels of the overall environment: hardware, operating system, DBMS, and application. Three significant areas for tuning: indexes, queries and transactions, and the schema itself.

REVIEW QUESTIONS

1. "The DDLC does not terminate with the deployment of the database system." Explain.
2. What are the major activities of routine maintenance in a database environment?
3. Name the three standard recovery methods. Briefly describe any one method.
4. List any six types of routine security functions.
5. What are the types of details available to the DBA to resolve deadlocks? Generally, what actions does the DBA take?
6. What is snapshot monitoring? Briefly list the types of statistics you can gather through snapshot monitoring.
7. What are benchmarks? How are benchmarks useful in a database environment?
8. List any five major tasks associated with DBMS version upgrades.
9. What are the major factors for consideration while tuning the database system for performance?
10. Name any five general guidelines for tuning indexes.

EXERCISES

1. Match the columns:

1. restore and reprocess	A. continues after deployment
2. DDL locks	B. reduce recovery time
3. schema tuning technique	C. part of concurrency control
4. space management	D. measured by benchmark tests
5. checkpoints	E. simple recovery method
6. DDLC	F. uses database statistics
7. staff transfers	G. denormalization
8. monitoring locks	H. revisions to access privileges
9. query optimizer	I. prevent untimely schema changes
10. transactions per second	J. drop obsolete tables

2. As the DBA of a local department store, discuss the components of a backup and recovery system. Write a detailed procedure for regular backups and for testing recovery from different types of failures.

3. Six months after deployment of the database system in your organization, users notice sharp increases in the response times as the day progresses into the afternoon. Describe the steps you would take to diagnose the problems. What types of statistics would you look into? Suggest some solution options.

4. Assume that your organization has over 5000 employees who need access privileges to the database system. As the project manager, you are responsible for setting up an ongoing security administration process. Prepare a detailed plan, outlining all aspects and defining responsibilities.

5. Prepare a detailed task list for installing a version upgrade of the DBMS. Indicate the sequence of the tasks, the responsibilities, and user involvement.

PART VII

ADVANCED DATABASE TOPICS

CHAPTER 18

DISTRIBUTED DATABASE SYSTEMS

CHAPTER OBJECTIVES

- Understand the fundamental principles of distributed database systems
- Appreciate the motivation and goals for distributing data
- Examine the various types, configurations, and methods for data distribution
- Note how the client/server architecture enables distributed database systems
- Study the features and functions of a distributed database management system (DDBMS)
- Explore the principle of transparency and grasp its significance
- Learn the implications of query and transaction processing

Refer back to the evolution of database systems in the early 1970s from file-oriented data systems. Each application had its own set of files; each group of users accessed the files pertinent to their applications. As business conditions changed and the demand for information sharing escalated, file-oriented systems became inadequate. Each user group could not work in isolation. For the overall benefit of the organization, all user groups needed to share information and collaborate with one another to achieve the corporate business goals. Decentralization by applications in file-oriented systems no longer served useful purposes. A centralized database system emerged, and users could share information from the integrated database and work together. By the late 1980s, many organizations possessed huge, centralized databases. Tremendous growth in computing technology made this transition possible.

Database Design and Development: An Essential Guide for IT Professionals by Paulraj Ponniah
ISBN 0-471-21877-4   Copyright © 2003 by John Wiley and Sons, Inc.

What has happened in the business scene since then? More and more corporations have become global in their operations. Business opportunities outside the local areas have provided growth and profitability. Think of the local bank where you opened a checking account about 10 years ago. To survive and be profitable, the bank has probably extended into a few more states and perhaps has even become international. Let us say that your progressive bank has become global and has opened branches in London, Paris, Tokyo, and Hong Kong in addition to a large number of domestic offices. The Paris branch primarily serves French customers. The users in the Paris branch access the data from the bank's database. But most of the data they need is about the local customers. Does it make sense for the Paris branch to go all the way to the centralized database stored in New York to access data about French customers?

All organizations expanding through mergers, acquisitions, and consolidations because of competitive pressures face similar questions. Each local office seeks autonomy, data ownership, and control for better service to its customers. The trend is to distribute the corporate data across the various dispersed locations so that each location can efficiently access the data it needs for running its portion of the overall business. This pattern of decentralization is not the same type of decentralization that existed in the case of the old file-oriented system. At that time, the decentralization based on applications perpetuated dispersal of redundant data with no information sharing. What you observe now is different. Database is being decentralized with geographic separation of data, but logical unity and integrity are preserved for proper information sharing—one logical database, but data not stored in just one location.

How is this becoming possible? Distributed database systems are emerging as a result of the merger between two major technologies: database and network. Recent advances in data communications and standardization of protocols such as Ethernet, TCP/IP, and ATM, along with the ubiquity of the Internet, promote physical distribution of corporate data across global locations yet preserving the integration and logical unity.

Database vendors have not yet come up with "pure" distributed database systems as envisioned in research studies. The technology is slowly maturing. Vendors are developing systems based on the client/server approach and the concept of a collection of active heterogeneous, geographically dispersed systems. But the momentum is strong and sustained.

FUNDAMENTAL PRINCIPLES

How is the push for decentralization of corporate data to be accomplished? Remember, the storing of relevant portions of the data has to be at each of the various geographic locations; but at the same time, users at each location must be able share data with users at any and all of the locations. Physical separation but logical integration—that is the underlying premise.

Examine this premise. What this implies is that when a user executes a query or a transaction accessing some data from the database, the user must be able to do so without knowing where the data resides and how it is going to be retrieved. The distribution of the data across the locations must be transparent to the user. The user need not be concerned while coding his or her query. This distributed data independence is, in fact, a natural extension of the principles of logical and physical data independence.

Pursue further the consideration of a transaction executed from a certain location. The transaction may operate on pieces of data stored at different locations. If the transaction completes successfully and commits, then all changes to data by the transaction must persist; if the transaction aborts, none of the changes must remain in the database. In other words, the atomicity of the transaction in the distributed environment must be ensured as if it executed in a centralized database system.

Let us define a distributed database system. We will explore a few fundamental concepts and then review the goals of distributed database systems. That will lead into a review of the advantages and disadvantages.

What is a Distributed Database?

Let us begin with a standard definition:

A distributed database

is a related collection of shared data of an organization along with the description of that data, logically integrated and interrelated, by physically distributed across locations over a computer network.

Figure 18-1 shows an illustration of a distributed database.

A distributed computing system consists of a number of processing units interconnected by a communications network. These processing units need not be homogeneous, but they have to cooperate with one another in processing queries and

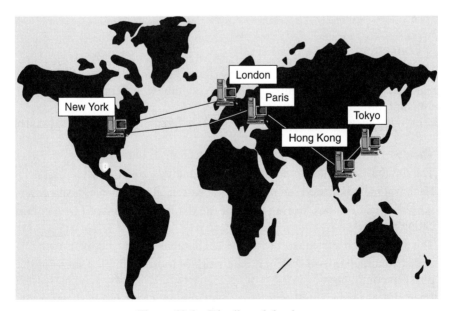

Figure 18-1   Distributed database.

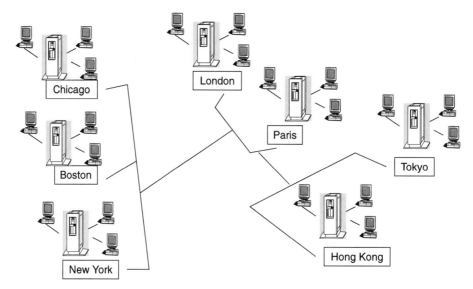

Figure 18-2   Distributed database system for a bank.

transactions. A distributed database is not stored in its entirety at a single physical location but spread across several locations on a computer network.

Let us also give a formal definition for a distributed database management system (DDBMS).

A DDBMS

is a software system that manages the distributed database and makes the distribution of data transparent to users.

Basic Concepts

Let us go over the basic concepts of a distributed database system by considering an example. Figure 18-2 presents a distributed database system for a bank that has domestic and international branches.

Observe the figure, note the following, and understand the underlying concepts:

- The distributed database system is a single, logical database.
- The database is split into a number of fragments.
- Each fragment is stored separately at a location, also known as a site or a node.
- All the sites or nodes, storing parts of the database, are linked by a communication network.
- The data at each site constitute a physical database managed by its own DBMS.
- A distributed database system is a network of loosely coupled sites not sharing physical components.
- Each site has substantial autonomy over the data and rarely depends on any type of centralized control or service.

- A distributed database system may be thought of as a collaboration of participating remote sites storing parts of the logical database.
- Each site, however, may participate in transaction execution when the transaction needs to access data from that site.
- Applications at a site not requiring data from any other sites are known as local applications. Applications that do need data from other sites are called global applications. If all applications at every site are local applications, then there is no necessity for a DDBMS.

Motivation and Goals

At the beginning of this chapter, we discussed broadly the evolution and purposes of distributed database systems. Let us now formalize the motivation for these systems. Why distributed databases? Here are the major reasons.

Efficient access of local data. In many global organizations or in those with a number of geographically dispersed locations, most of the database operations are on the local data. Maintaining the pertinent data at the local site allows efficient and immediate access to local data.

Improved customer service. Global organizations must be flexible enough to meet the needs of local customers. Each location, although part of the overall organization, must primarily look after the customers at that location. Local ownership and control of the local data are essential.

Enhanced reliability. If the computer system at one site fails or if the communication link between two locations goes down, presumably the other sites can continue working. Furthermore, if replication techniques are used to store copies of the same data at more than one site, then other operating sites may still supply the required data.

Availability of global data. Each site in a global organization, although autonomous, is still part of the overall organization. Therefore, users at a site would require data from other sites as well through their global applications. Global data must also be available at every site.

Advantages and Disadvantages

You have been introduced to the concept of distributed database systems. You have understood the motivation that has guided the development of these systems. Let us review a list of advantages provided by distributed database systems. From the list of advantages, you will note that, in practice, distributed database systems are fulfilling the aspirations that prompted their development. These systems also have a few disadvantages.

We will get into in-depth discussions of distributed data systems in the next sections. We will cover the components, the types, and the configurations. DDBMSs have to be more sophisticated than DBMSs. You will learn about

DDBMS—its functions and features. Later, we will consider all aspects of processing queries and transactions in a distributed database environment. But, before covering all of these, first let us summarize the advantages and disadvantages, and then move on.

Advantages Here is the list of major advantages:

Suitable structure. A modern enterprise has users in dispersed locations who need to access primarily local data and, less frequently, global data. Now note the structure of a distributed database with data spread across dispersed locations and yet any data available from anywhere. This structure is well suited for many of today's corporations.

Desirable local autonomy. Users at each site can have autonomy in owning and controlling their local data.

Preserved shareability. Data sharing, a principal motivation for database systems, is still available in a distributed database. All data in the distributed database may be shared by users at all sites.

Improved availability. If the computer system where a centralized database resides goes down, all the data become unavailable to users. However, in a distributed environment, only the part of the data that resides in the failed site becomes unavailable.

Enhanced reliability. Reliability ensures continuous operation of a database system. Even when one site is down, other sites can continue operation, and, in special circumstances, other sites may pick up the operations of the failed site until it is restored.

Better efficiency. As you know, users at each site demand local data much more than global data. Local data may be accessed quite efficiently.

Reduced transmission costs. For global enterprises, compared to centralized databases, distributed databases incur lower data communication costs.

Easier growth. A distributed database provides for modular growth. When a new office is opened at a remote location, simply add a new site or node in your distribution network.

Disadvantages Note the following potential disadvantages presented by distributed database systems. However, it is expected that, as distributed database products mature and become more robust, some of the disadvantages are likely to be less troublesome.

Increased complexity. Making the nature of distribution transparent to users, fragmenting and replicating of data, routing of queries and transactions—all these and other similar issues add to the complexity of distributed database systems.

More complex design. The design of a distributed database system, at both the logical and physical levels, is more complicated than that of a centralized database system.

Difficult integrity control. Distributed query and transaction processing, despite the benefits they offer, are more prone to problems relating to concurrency conflicts, deadlocks, and recovery from failures.

Involved security systems. Security protection must be duplicated at every site.

Added maintenance cost. Maintenance cost must increase to include maintenance of local computer systems, local DBMSs in addition to the overall DDBMS, and the communications network.

Lack of standards. Standards for data communications and data access, critical in distributed database environments, are only emerging now at a slow pace.

Limited acceptance. Despite the numerous advantages, general-purpose distributed database systems are not widely used. Therefore, there is not much industry experience.

DISTRIBUTED DATABASES

When you decide to distribute the corporate data and spread it across the various locations, you are faced with a number of design and implementation issues. You need to plan what type of distributed system you must have. How about the database software at each location? Then how are you going create segments of data and determine which segment gets stored in which location? The next consideration relates to the features necessary in the overall database software to manage the distribution. What about moving data from one site to another whenever needed? What are the characteristics of the communications network?

We will explore these issues in this section. You will learn about the variations available for distributing data and managing data at each site. You will examine the components of DDBMS. You will note implementation options and review design issues.

Types and Configurations

Let us begin by looking at a basic configuration. Figure 18-3 shows a plain distributed database environment.

Look at the figure and note the following points that indicate what components and features are needed in the configuration to make it a distributed database environment.

- At each location, also known as site or node, there is a computer system.
- Local data are stored at each site.

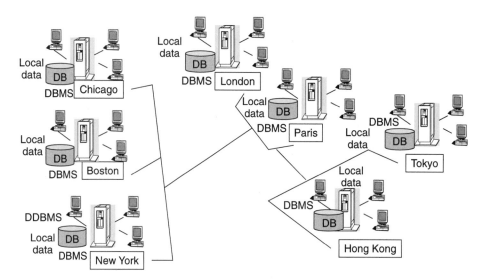

Figure 18-3 Basic distributed database configuration.

- Each site needs database software to manage its local data.
- Each site must have autonomy to own, control, and manage its data and operations.
- Each site must also collaborate with any other site that needs data stored at this site.
- Similarly, each site must also be able to access data from any other site.
- There must be some overall database software to enable cooperation among sites for data access.

Considering these factors, we find that distributed database systems fall into two major types: homogeneous and heterogeneous systems. Figure 18-4 illustrates how these two types are configured in addition to showing a centralized database system for comparison.

Homogeneous Systems The first feature of a homogeneous system is the degree of homogeneity and the second feature is the degree of autonomy. In a homogeneous system, all sites use identical software.

The server at each site uses the same DBMS as that in every other site. Clients at every site use identical software for data access. Each local DBMS is allowed to function as a stand-alone database management system, thus providing local autonomy.

Heterogeneous Systems In this case, different sites run under the control of different DBMSs. However, the sites are connected in such a manner to enable data access across different sites. A heterogeneous system, also known as a multidatabase system, provides a high degree of local autonomy. Because a heterogeneous system consists of a federation of autonomous database systems, it is also called a federated multidatabase system.

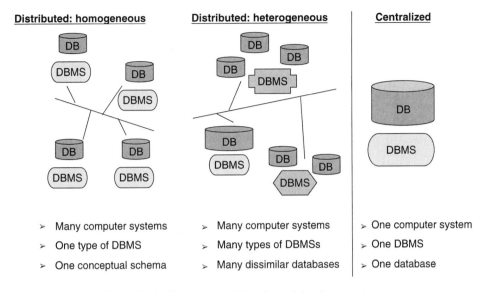

Figure 18-4   Two types of distributed database systems.

A configuration may be heterogeneous in several ways. The global schema must reconcile the variations. Heterogeneity can be manifested as follows:

Different data models. You may have relational databases at a few sites, and some hierarchical or network databases at other sites. In organizations with old legacy systems still in full operation, this configuration may be a practical method for implementing distributed database systems. However, you will have to deal with variations in data representations.

Different constraints. Different models implement data integrity constraints in different ways. For example, the referential integrity constraint in relational models governs relationships between entities in the relational model.

Different naming conventions. Each database may name the same data item in different ways, assigning different data types.

Different data content. The same data element may have different attributes at different sites.

Different data languages. Each site may have its own data definition and data manipulation languages.

DDBMS

The DDBMS constitutes the software that manages the distributed database as a logical whole. Although parts of the data are stored at different sites and managed as local data through the local database management system, DDBMS envelops all of the parts of data at different sites and provides global data access.

When managing global data access, a primary goal for DDBMS is transparency. All aspects of data distribution must be transparent to the users. Users at any site must not be concerned about the location of the data requested by them, nor should they need to know how the data are obtained. Because of the significance of transparency, a later section covers the topic in detail. Let us now examine the components of DDBMS and see how they fit together.

Architecture and Components   As you know, for a centralized database, the DBMS supports three schema levels:

- External schema representing the set of user views of the database
- Conceptual schema representing the entire database
- Internal schema consisting of the physical representation of the entire database as files, blocks, and records

These are clearly identifiable and applicable to all centralized database systems. In the case of distributed database systems, however, variations on the types of schemas are possible. We will present two such variations, one for a homogeneous system and the other for a heterogeneous or federated system.

Homogeneous system: schema levels   Figure 18-5 shows a configuration with the following schemas:

- A collection of global external schemas
- A single global conceptual schema
- A fragmentation schema

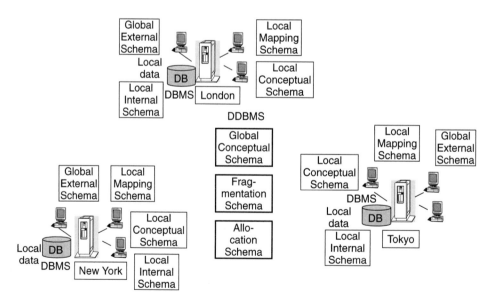

Figure 18-5   Homogeneous system: schema levels.

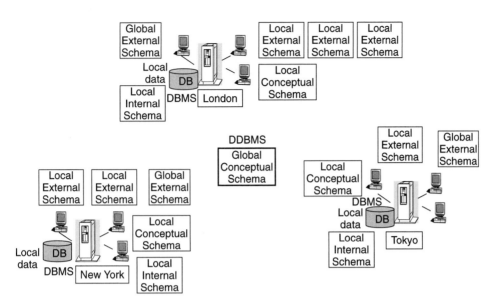

Figure 18-6   Heterogeneous system: schema levels.

- An allocation schema
- For each site, a set of local mapping schema, local conceptual schema, local internal schema

The global conceptual schema logically describes the entire database. It is a union of all the local conceptual schemas. Global external schemas represent user views containing data from different sites. The local mapping schema maps portions of data allocated to different sites to the local external schemas.

The fragmentation schema indicates how data are divided up through partitioning or replication. The allocation schema indicates where fragmented parts are to be located. We will cover fragmentation and allocation further in a later subsection.

Heterogeneous system: schema levels   Figure 18-6 shows a configuration with the following schemas:

- A collection of global external schemas
- A single global conceptual schema
- For each site, a set of local external schemas
- For each site, a local conceptual schema
- For each site, a local internal schema

The global conceptual schema in this case is not necessarily a complete union of all the local conceptual schemas. It is a subset of the collection of all the local schemas. It consists of only those parts of the local data that each site agrees to share.

Functions and Features As a starting point, a DDBMS must have the features and functions of a regular database management system. In addition, a DDBMS is responsible for keeping track of the data allocations, routing data access requests to appropriate sites, and transmitting results correctly to the requesting sites.

Here is a summary of the additional functions and features of a DDBMS:

- Enable data fragmentation and allocation to different sites
- Extend system catalog or data dictionary functions to keep track of how data are distributed
- Manage distributed query processing including query optimization, translation of data access requests between sites, and routing of requests and results
- Manage distributed transaction processing including translation of data access requests between sites, routing of requests, and processing of database operations
- Provide concurrency control to maintain consistency of data replicated in multiple locations
- Provide locking and resolve deadlocks in a multisite database system
- Provide distributed database recovery from failures of individual sites and data communication links

Catalog Management As you know, the data dictionary, also known as the system catalog or system directory, holds information for the system to translate high-level requests for database objects from queries and transactions into appropriate low-level operations to be executed on physical data items. Usually, the system catalog in a DBMS contains the usual schema information, security authorizations, statistical data, programs, integrity constraints, and so on.

This type of information in a system catalog, although useful, is hardly sufficient in a distributed database environment. The system ought to know how database relations are fragmented and which parts of the relations reside where. For a given database object, the system catalog must record at which site or multiple sites the object is stored. The catalog must also enable the system to refer to the object using the correct name, taking into consideration the site where it was created and where it is stored now.

We will consider two fundamental issues about catalog management: where to keep the catalog and how to name the database objects. First, about the placement of the catalog, a few possible approaches are indicated:

At a central site. Only one copy exists in the system, and that is held at a single central site. All sites other than where the catalog is kept do not have full autonomy. Each site will have to inform the central site of any schema changes relating to local data at the site. Even for referring to local data at the sites, they have to go to the central site. Another more serious concern: What happens when the centralized site goes down? The catalog will become unavailable, virtually halting all database operations.

Full catalog at all sites. A full copy of the catalog is kept at every site. This approach addresses the vulnerability of losing the whole catalog when the central site goes down. However, this does not solve the local autonomy problem. Every change to a local catalog must be broadcast to all sites.

Partial catalog at every site. Each site is responsible for its own data; each site maintains its own catalog for the local data. In this case, the total catalog is the union of all partial catalogs maintained at all the sites. This option provides site autonomy. For operations on local data, it works well. However, for requests for global data, the system must go to other sites to get the catalog entries.

Optimal approach. This is a combined approach that removes the vulnerability of a central site and also ensures site autonomy. Each site maintains the catalog for the local data. The catalog at the birth site of a relation, that is, where the relation was created, keeps track of where copies of the relation are held and also precise details of what parts of the relation are held at these other sites.

Now, let us look at the issue of naming database objects. Consider a relation called CUSTOMER. In a centralized database, there can be only one relation with that name. However, in a distributed database system, it is possible for two or more sites to have objects called CUSTOMER whose contents and purpose may not be same. If the CUSTOMER relation at a given site is kept purely local and private, then no other site will be referring to that relation. However, as you can imagine, in a distributed environment users in many sites would want to share the information contained in the CUSTOMER relation. So how do you name business objects? How does the DDBMS know which CUSTOMER table is required?

Database objects are assigned names with four components:

Creator Id   ID of user who created the database object (user ID unique within the site)

Creator Site Id   ID of site at which object was created (sites have unique IDs across entire system)

Local Name   name of object assigned by creator (unique within objects of this type created by this user at the birth site)

Birth Site Id   ID of site at which object is initially stored (sites have unique IDs across entire system)

Here is an example of an object following these principles:

MILLER @ MUNICH – ORDER @ PARIS

The name refers to the database object with the local name ORDER created by MILLER of the MUNICH site, with ORDER stored initially at the PARIS site.

How does a user refer to this object in a query? The user at a given site may refer to the object using the global name with all four of its components. As you know, this is cumbersome; you cannot expect users to refer to objects by their global names. The general practice is to define a synonym for the global name of the object. Each site will maintain a set of synonym tables for users at that site. If MARY at the LONDON site needs to refer to the above ORDER relation, an entry will be made in a synonym table at the LONDON site for MARY to refer to the ORDER relation as M-ORD. Mary's queries will use the simpler name of M-ORD. When we mention queries here, we do not confine data access requests only to queries. The discussion applies equally to all transactions.

Network Component

Effective implementation of a distributed database depends on a good data communications network. A distributed database system is built over a communications network. The various sites have to be linked up properly so that pertinent portions of the database may be stored at the respective sites. The communications network must enable efficient flow of data from one site to another.

Data communications have made great progress over the past few years. We are not purely interested in the various communications protocols and their specifications. However, we want to examine a few aspects of data communications as they pertain to distribution of data in a distributed database environment. Two major aspects are of importance from this standpoint: the linking of sites and the routing of data.

Linking of Sites   On the basis of whether the sites to be linked are within a short distance or further apart, data communications networks are classified as follows:

Local area network (LAN). Designed for connecting computers within the same premises.

Wide area network (WAN). Intended for linking computers or LANs at vast distances from one another.

Figure 18-7 presents a comparison of the important features of LAN and WAN arrangements.

Routing of Data   Routing implies choosing a path on the network for the movement of data. For this purpose, we may design a network either as a point-to-point network or a broadcast network. For sending a single message to more than one site in a point-to-point network, the sending site must send separate messages to each of the receiving sites. In a broadcast network, the ID of the destination site is attached as a prefix to the message. Virtually each message is sent around so that all sites may listen in. The site for which the message is intended picks up the message.

Configuration Options   Figure 18-8 shows the common options for configuring a network for a distributed database. The nature of the organization, the distribution of data, and the data access pattern dictate the choice of the configuration.

Let us quickly review the configurations.

Fully connected. Each site is connected to every other site. Highly reliable and flexible, but expensive.

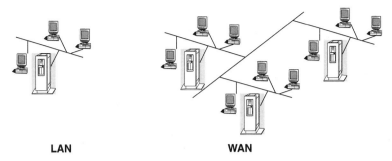

LAN   **WAN**

• Covers short distances   • Covers long distances

• Covers short distances   • Covers long distances

• Simple Protocol   • Complex Protocol

• Network managed locally   • Network managed by carriers

• Regular topologies   • Irregular topologies

• Links collaborating systems   • Links disparate systems

• Low data rate   • High data rate

• Low error rate   • High error rate

• Broadcasting common   • Point-to-point connections

Figure 18-7   LAN and WAN: features.

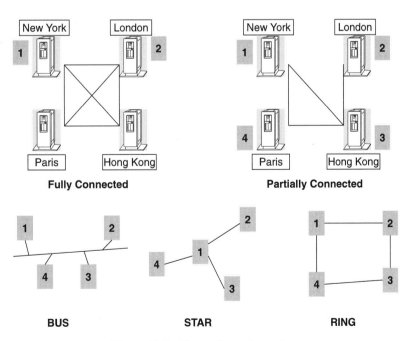

Figure 18-8   Network configurations.

Partially connected. Only certain sites are linked. Sites with high volumes of data traffic are usually connected. Less expensive than fully connected configuration.

Bus. All sites connected to a backbone link. Simple, easily extendable, and cost-effective. Useful in small network with low traffic volumes.

Star. Used for connecting sites with the use of the concept of a central site. The configuration fails if the central site goes down.

Ring. Connects sites in a closed loop. Generally used for high-performance networks.

Data Distribution

All along we have been saying that parts of the database are stored and managed at the various sites of an organization. We looked at the levels of schemas that must be present at the sites for representing the database. We also discussed the network configurations that could enable moving of data between sites as needed. Now the question remains, How exactly do you break up the database into portions that can be kept at different sites? How do you divide the data content and distribute it among the sites?

Two basic methods are commonly used to break up the database for the purpose of distribution among the sites. Our discussions will be based on the relational data model. Nevertheless, the principle applies equally well to the other data models such as hierarchical or network. Let us consider just one relation, an EMPLOYEE relation, to present the methods.

Figure 18-9 illustrates the following two methods using the EMPLOYEE relation as the contents of the database:

- Data fragmentation
- Data replication

Data Fragmentation   When using the data fragmentation or data partitioning method, you break up a relation into smaller fragments or partitions in one of two ways. Look at the data in the EMPLOYEE relation. What is the data content made of? Rows and columns. You know the significance of rows and columns in a relation. How can you partition the relation into fragments? You can break up the relation horizontally into groups of rows or vertically into groups of columns. You can then store these fragments at the various sites.

Horizontal fragmentation   Each fragment consists of a subset of rows or tuples of a relation. How can you use this method to create fragments from the EMPLOYEE relation? Let us say that three sites exist on your distributed system network—New York, London, and Milan. Naturally, the Milan site would be interested in dealing with the Italian employees, the London site with the British employees, and the New York site with the American employees. So it makes sense to break up the

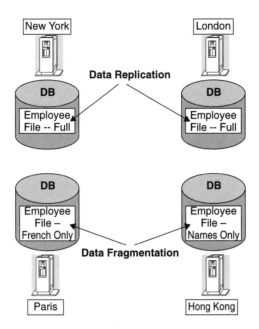

Figure 18-9   Data fragmentation and data replication.

EMPLOYEE relation into subsets of rows relating to employees in these three regions.

Figure 18-10 demonstrates horizontal fragmentation. Note how the subsets are stored at the three sites.

Vertical fragmentation   Each fragment consists of a subset of columns of a relation. Each subset must also contain the key column in addition to the other selected columns. Sometimes, a tuple-ID is added to each tuple to uniquely identify it. How can you use this method to create fragments from the EMPLOYEE relation? Let us say that for your organization the human resources functions are localized in Boston and the accounting functions, including payroll, are localized in New York. When you examine the columns of the EMPLOYEE relation, you will note that there are a few columns that are of interest only for payroll and the remaining columns are desirable for the human resources division. Break up the EMPLOYEE relation into two subsets of columns to be stored at the two sites.

Figure 18-11 demonstrates vertical fragmentation. Note how the subsets are stored at the two sites.

Advantages and disadvantages   Fragmentation improves efficiency in data access. Data fragments are stored at the sites where they are used most. Local query and transaction performance gets better. At the same time, you get enhanced data security because it is easier to protect the local data.

On the other hand, when any site needs data from other sites for any types of queries or transactions, access speeds become inconsistent. Queries on global data

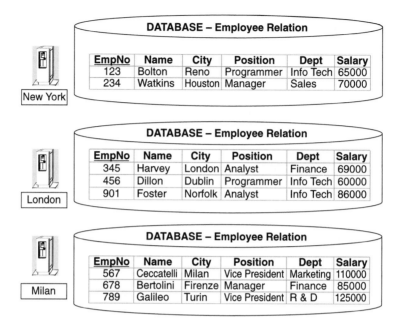

Figure 18-10   EMPLOYEE relation: horizontal fragmentation.

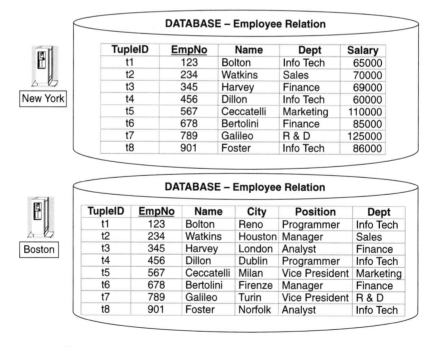

Figure 18-11   EMPLOYEE relation: vertical fragmentation.

DATABASE – Employee Relation

EmpNo	Name	City	Position	Dept	Salary
123	Bolton	Reno	Programmer	Info Tech	65000
234	Watkins	Houston	Manager	Sales	70000
345	Harvey	London	Analyst	Finance	69000
456	Dillon	Dublin	Programmer	Info Tech	60000
901	Foster	Norfolk	Analyst	Info Tech	86000

New York

DATABASE – Employee Relation

EmpNo	Name	City	Position	Dept	Salary
123	Bolton	Reno	Programmer	Info Tech	65000
234	Watkins	Houston	Manager	Sales	70000
345	Harvey	London	Analyst	Finance	69000
456	Dillon	Dublin	Programmer	Info Tech	60000
901	Foster	Norfolk	Analyst	Info Tech	86000

London

DATABASE – Employee Relation

EmpNo	Name	City	Position	Dept	Salary
567	Ceccatelli	Milan	Vice President	Marketing	110000
678	Bertolini	Firenze	Manager	Finance	85000
789	Galileo	Turin	Vice President	R & D	125000

Milan

Figure 18-12   EMPLOYEE relation: replication.

run a lot slower than queries on local data. Also, fragmentation presents a problem with failures. When one site fails, the data at that site become inaccessible throughout the organization.

Data Replication   Suppose that, in your environment, every site needs the full EMPLOYEE relation. What is the best method of providing for users at every site? Keep a full copy of the relation at every site. Then every user in the organization can have fast and easy access to employee data. The data replication method means that we store either full copies of a relation or copies of appropriate fragments at several sites. Figure 18-12 illustrates data replication. Observe the copies stored at different sites.

Advantages and disadvantages   Replication improves data availability. If one of the sites containing a copy of a relation goes down, another copy may be accessed from another site. In full replication, because each site gets a full copy, the data constitute local data at every site. Therefore, you can get fast response to queries against the relation at every site.

However, in practice, implementation of replication is complex, especially for keeping all the copies synchronized whenever updates take place. Also, if each site stores a full copy of a large relation with thousands of rows and several columns, storage requirements for the distributed database can be quite extensive.

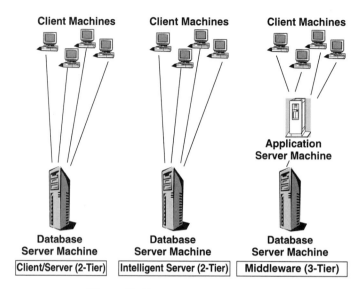

Figure 18-13 Architectural options.

Synchronous and asynchronous replication In our example of replication of the EMPLOYEE relation, suppose some transaction at the London site wants to update the copy of the relation at a certain time. How do we include the effects of the update in all the copies? One method is for the transaction to update all copies of the EMPLOYEE relation before it commits. This method is known as *synchronous replication*. If there are too many copies spread around at different sites, then update transactions will take a long time to synchronize all copies and commit.

Instead of updating all copies each time an update transaction executes, we can wait to update the copies at a later time. This method is called *asynchronous replication*. At specific intervals, copies of modified relations are updated. Obviously, anyone using a copy that has not yet been updated will not obtain the correct results. Many commercial systems implement this method.

Architectural Options

Let us now turn our attention to options for the types of computing architectures that are used for implementing distributed databases. You know that data are distributed among several sites of an organization. You have also learned the techniques for dividing the database and distributing the fragments to the various sites. You have examined the communications network options for linking the sites. What types of architectures are suitable at the sites?

We will explore three common options. Figure 18-13 presents the three options. Note how data access is provided in each option. We will now briefly describe the three architectural options.

Client/Server Architecture (Two Tier) As an information technology professional, you are familiar with client/server systems. Let us examine how this architecture works for distributed database systems in very simple terms. At each site you have a database server machine and as many client machines as needed. The server on one tier and the clients on the other tier form this two-tier architecture. The server and the clients are usually linked on a LAN.

The following briefly describes how a two-tier system may apply to distributed databases.

- The server performs all database functions. Based on query requests, the server retrieves the requested data and passes them on to the requesting client. It also updates the database as required by executing transactions.
- The client manages the user interface, interprets queries and transactions, and routes them to the appropriate servers. When data is received from the server, the client presents the information to the user. If a query requires data from multiple sites, the client breaks up the query into appropriate subqueries and routes each subquery to the proper server. When results are received from multiple servers, the client consolidates the result sets and presents the consolidated result to the user.

The two-tier architecture clearly demarcates the functions of the server and the client. Each side can be suitably configured for high performance. The server can be made robust enough with sufficient memory, storage, and computing power to carry out its database functions. But, when you look at the configuration of the client, it must also be powerful and have software to interpret queries, create subqueries, and route them properly. And every client machine must be so configured. This is not an inexpensive option.

Intelligent Server Architecture (Two Tier)   This is also a two-tier option. Let us go over this option and inspect how this can work in a distributed database environment. As in the previous case, at each site you have a database server machine and as many client machines as needed. The server on one tier and the clients on the other tier form this two-tier architecture. The server and the clients are usually linked on a LAN.

The server and the clients serve the following functions.

- The server performs all database functions. Based on query requests, the server retrieves the requested data and passes them on to the requesting client. It also updates the database as required by executing transactions. If a query requires data from multiple sites, the server breaks up the query into appropriate subqueries and routes each subquery to the proper server. When results are received from multiple servers, the local server consolidates the result sets and sends the merged result to the requesting client.
- The client manages the user interface, receives query and transaction input, and sends them to the local server at that site. When data are received from the server, the client presents the information to the user.

Although the two-tier architecture clearly demarcates the functions of the server and the client, we have just shifted some functions to the server from the clients. This relieves the clients from being too heavy. However, now the servers must perform routing and consolidation functions in addition to the large array of database functions. This option is slightly less expensive because we have to duplicate routing and consolidation functionality only on the servers, not on the numerous clients.

Architecture with Middleware (Three Tier) This is a practical and efficient approach to relieve the server and the clients of the additional routing and consolidation functionality. You create a middle tier between the server and client tiers. You install software, called middleware, with routing and consolidation capability in the middle tier. Let us review how this architecture works for distributed database systems. At each site you have a database server machine, a middleware machine, and as many client machines as needed. The server on one tier, the clients on the other tier, and the middleware on the third tier form this three-tier architecture. The server, middleware, and the clients are usually linked on a LAN.

The following briefly describes how a three-tier system may apply to distributed databases.

- The server performs all database functions. Based on query requests, the server retrieves the requested data and passes them on to the middle-tier. It also updates the database as required by executing transactions.
- The client manages the user interface, interprets queries and transactions, and routes them to the middle tier. When data are received from the middle tier, the client presents the information to the user.
- The middle tier examines each query and routes it to the appropriate server. If a query requires data from multiple sites, the middle tier breaks up the query into appropriate subqueries and routes each subquery to the proper server. When results are received from multiple servers, the middle tier consolidates the result sets and sends the consolidated result to the requesting client.

The three-tier architecture proves to be a straightforward and efficient option. The machines at each tier can be configured correctly for the functions they intend to support. In practice, the systems tend to be multitier systems with other tiers such as application servers added to the mix.

Design and Implementation Issues

By now, you are proficient at the design and implementation process for centralized database systems. You are quite familiar with the phases of the database development life cycle. After the initial planning and feasibility study phases, you move into the requirements definition phase. For developing distributed database systems, you do the same thing. The requirements definition phase forms the basis for the design and implementation phases.

In the requirements phase, you gather information requirements for performing logical and physical design. While designing a centralized database, you know that the entire database will reside in one location, perhaps on a single database server. This, however, is not the case with a distributed database. You do not store all the data in one place. This is a major difference you encounter while designing and implementing a distributed system.

Therefore, your design should include considerations for placement of data at the various sites. How can you make the design and implementation decisions on what parts of data must be kept at which points? Of course, you need to find out the usage patterns and match them up with data content. This expands the scope of your requirements definition phase. In that phase, you must gather details to address two basic issues:

- How to fragment the database
- How to allocate fragments to sites

We will address these issues for a relational data model. Let us list a few suggestions on these issues and indicate some design and implementation steps:

- On the basis of the requirement definition, proceed through the design phase and come up with a global schema for the entire database. This schema will include all the relations.
- Next comes the decision point on how to divide the database and then which segments to store where. Once you are able to determine the location of parts of the data, then the local schema at each site will represent the part of the data stored at that site.
- Consider each relation for the possibility of fragmenting it horizontally or vertically.
- When you are examining a potential subset for fragmentation, evaluate data sharing as it applies to the subset. Determine which site is likely to use the subset most. If you can establish the site that is expected to use the subset most, then assign the fragment to that site.
- Sometimes a number of sites are likely to use a subset or a complete relation with almost equal frequency. If so, consider full or partial replication and place copies at all such sites.
- Decisions on fragmentation and replication are never easy and clear-cut. That is why a lot of preliminary work must be done in the requirements definition phase itself. Analysts and designers must "know" their data extremely well.
- Remember that usage access patterns change over time. Business conditions change. New applications are added. The initial set of applications is enhanced. So the data allocation plan must be reviewed periodically after deployment and adjusted as necessary.
- Another key factor in the allocation plan is the placement and management of the global system catalog. Consider alternatives.

Figure 18-14 presents an example of a data allocation scheme. Note how the database is fragmented and fragments are placed at different sites. Also note the replicated copies stored at different sites.

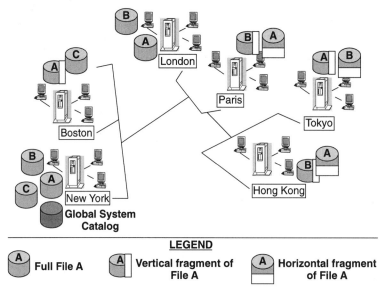

LEGEND

Figure 18-14   Sample data allocation scheme.

TRANSPARENCIES

When we introduced DDBMS in an earlier section, we mentioned in passing that a primary goal for DDBMS is transparency. We will now describe the concept further. Please note the motivation for transparency and why it must be a primary goal for DDBMS.

Transparency: Key Ideal

By now, you have realized that a distributed database is a lot more complicated than a centralized database in design, implementation, architecture, and software support. By and large, the complexity arises out of the way data are distributed across various sites. When a user initiates a query or an application executes a transaction performing database operations, should the user or the application be concerned about how and where the data are stored, how data will be accessed, and by exactly what means the results must be consolidated and presented? Not at all.

The DDBMS must insulate users from these complexities. The DDBMS must make the data locations and access routes transparent to users. Data access and processing must appear to the users as though all data are stored at one site. The overall ideal goal the DDBMS must strive for is to portray a distributed database to users as though it is a centralized database.

The DDBMS may provide transparencies at different levels. The actual techniques used by the DDBMS to provide for each level of transparency are quite intricate. We will not get into all the technical details. Instead, we will broadly discuss each level of transparency so that you can appreciate its purpose and significance.

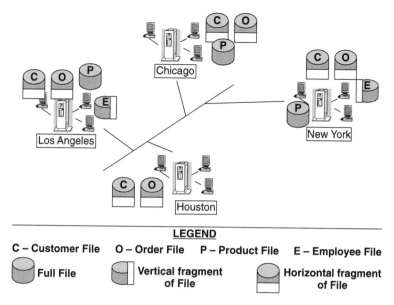

Figure 18-15   Sample distributed database system.

For the purpose of our discussion, let us assume a distributed database system with four sites at New York, Los Angeles, Chicago, and Houston. The database consists of four relations: CUSTOMER, ORDER, PRODUCT, and EMPLOYEE. Figure 18-15 presents this sample distributed database system and indicates how the data are distributed. Using the figure, let us examine the levels of desired transparencies.

Note the four relations and observe how they are fragmented. The CUSTOMER and ORDER relations are partitioned horizontally, and each site stores the partitions pertinent to it. The EMPLOYEE relation is partitioned vertically. The partition relating to human resources functions is kept in Los Angeles, and that relating to payroll is stored in New York. The PRODUCT relation is replicated, and full copies are stored in New York, Los Angeles, and Chicago. Houston has only occasional sales.

Fragmentation Transparency

You have noted how the database is divided and parts are allocated to the various sites. However, a user at any site does not know whether the database is stored in its entirety or is divided into parts. For example, let us say that a user in Chicago wants a report showing the complete details of all employees. The user query is submitted as though employee data are stored as whole. You know that all employee data are not kept together and that the EMPLOYEE relation is partitioned vertically. The DDBMS enables the query to execute by retrieving the information from both vertical partitions and to produce a consolidated result.

This is fragmentation transparency. The DDBMS hides the complexities of how the horizontal and vertical partitions are created. It makes the partition scheme completely transparent to the user.

Replication Transparency

You know that the PRODUCT relation is replicated and that full copies are stored in three sites. Assume that a user in Houston wants a product list. When the query is submitted, the user has no knowledge of whether there is one copy or more copies of product. In fact, the user need not be concerned. The DDBMS hides the details of replication from the user and provides replication transparency.

The DDBMS knows that there is no local copy of product data in Houston. So it selects a copy from one of the other three sites, enables the query to execute, and produces the result. When there are copies at multiple sites, the DDBMS chooses the best possible candidate that will execute the query efficiently. This takes in consideration network traffic and other factors. If one of the sites, namely, Los Angeles, is not operational at that time, the DDBMS will go to other sites even though they are further away by comparison.

Location Transparency

Through the property of location transparency, the DDBMS hides from the user the details of where parts of the database are stored. To the user, it appears as though all data are stored at the local site. How many sites there are and how the database is spread to any sites—these are totally transparent to the user.

For example, assume that the Chicago site is given the responsibility of analyzing all the orders for the past six months. A user in Chicago charged with this responsibility submits a query to retrieve selected data from the entire ORDER and CUSTOMER relations. You know that these two relations are partitioned horizontally and the data are spread across all sites. However, the query from the Chicago user need not be concerned about where all of these data are coming from. The DDBMS hides all the distribution details from the query. The coding of the query is exactly as though it is coded for a centralized database. The DDBMS enables data to be retrieved from all the partitions at different sites and consolidated to produce the result.

Network Transparency

In an earlier subsection, we discussed the various methods of configuring the communications network. We looked at LANs and WANs. We mentioned fully connected and partially connected networks. We also considered a few topologies such as bus, star, and ring. Now suppose that a user in New York needs to create a confidential employee report printing full details. Should the user be concerned whether New York and any other site that may store employee data are connected directly? Should the network configuration affect the way the user query must be coded?

The DDBMS makes the data communications network, its protocols, and its configuration transparent to the user. The user does not even need to be concerned whether there is a network at all. The user's query will be coded as though all data will be retrieved locally without any complex networks to support the retrieval.

Naming Transparency

While covering catalog management above, we dealt with the naming of database objects in a distributed database system. As in a centralized database, database objects in a distributed database must also have unique names. You have noted how the names are made unique. You attach three different identifiers to the local name of the object to make the name unique.

The DDBMS hides the complications of extending the local object names from the users. User queries can refer to database objects by local names. DDBMS provides naming transparency through a method of using synonyms. Please refer back to the subsection on catalog management.

Failure Transparency

You know that, in a centralized database system, a transaction must preserve its atomicity and durability. That is, in the event of failures, either every operation of a transaction is completed successfully or none of the operations of the transaction is completed at all. Then atomicity of transactions is maintained. Furthermore, if a transaction completes successfully and commits, no failure should be able undo any database update performed by the committed transaction. The database changes must be durable.

A distributed database environment is vulnerable to other types of failures related to communication links. The DDBMS ensures that atomicity and durability of a transaction will still be protected in the distributed environment as well. This property is failure transparency.

DISTRIBUTED PROCESSING

The complexities of processing queries and transactions in a distributed database environment far exceed those in a centralized database system. When a query is submitted in a distributed database system, the DDBMS has to take into account a number of factors to prepare an optimal query plan to execute the query. Do the data elements needed by the query reside locally at that site? If not, are the data elements stored elsewhere? Are the data elements parts of fragments? Is there any replication scheme to be considered? If so, which is the optimal copy to be used? Similar questions arise while processing transactions that perform insert, update, and deletion operations.

Concurrency control gets more complicated in a distributed environment. Where do you keep the locks? What types of locking protocols are effective? How do you resolve deadlocks? Could transactions from multiple sites be in a deadlock situation? Recovery from failures poses greater challenges as well. What happens when a site fails? Can the other sites keep operating while the failed site is recovered?

We will consider the essential basics in this section. We will highlight the underlying complexities and present how distributed processing is generally performed. We will present some recovery methods. However, more than cursory coverage of

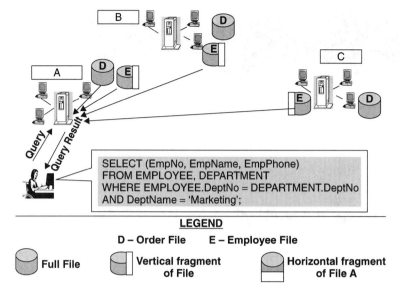

Figure 18-16   Query processing example.

the topic of distributed processing is beyond our scope. Nevertheless, you will survey and learn the fundamental principles and concepts.

Query Processing

For the sake of simplicity, let us say that our tiny distributed database consists of just the following two relations and the system comprises only three sites at A, B, and C.

DEPARTMENT (<u>DeptNo</u>, DeptName, DeptLocation, DeptManager)

EMPLOYEE (<u>EmpNo</u>, SocSecNo, EmpName, EmpAddr, EmpPhone, Salary, DeptNo)

Foreign Key: DeptNo REFERENCES DEPARTMENT

Figure 18-16 illustrates one version of the data distribution showing some fragments and replicas at the three sites. Also, note the typical query.

Query Transformation   Let us take a very simple query to list all the rows of the DEPARTMENT relation, submitted by a user at site A.

SELECT *
　　FROM DEPARTMENT

How is this simple query processed? That depends on the fragmentation and replication schemes used for distributing the data. Depending on the distribution, the DDBMS must transform the query into subqueries, execute each subquery at the appropriate place, combine the results through union or join operations, and present the result to the requestor. While decomposing a query and executing subqueries the optimizer examines the options and chooses the most optimal execution. Let us consider some possible scenarios of query decomposition.

Horizontal Partitioning   Assume that the DEPARTMENT relation is partitioned horizontally into three fragments, DEP-H-A, DEP-H-B, DEP-H-C, with each site storing the appropriate fragment. The DDBMS may transform the query into three subqueries: Subquery-A, Subquery-B, Subquery-C. For example, Subquery-A is as follows:

SELECT *
   FROM DEP-H-A

We are neither getting into the exact technical details of how the DDBMS looks up the system catalog and transforms the original query nor getting into the exact format of the query. However, please note the principles of query transformation. The DDBMS processes Subquery-A at the local site A and dispatches the other two subqueries to sites B and C, respectively. When the results are received from sites B and C, the results are consolidated through union operation and presented to the user at site A.

Vertical Partitioning   Assume that the DEPARTMENT relation is partitioned vertically into two fragments, DEP-V-B and DEP-V-C, with each site storing the appropriate fragment. The DDBMS may transform the query into two subqueries: Subquery-B, Subquery-C. For example, Subquery-B is as follows:

SELECT *
   FROM DEP-V-B

No department data are stored at the local site of the user. The DDBMS dispatches the two subqueries to sites B and C, respectively. When the results are received from sites B and C, the results are consolidated through union operation and presented to the user at site A.

Hybrid Partitioning   In this case, assume that the DEPARTMENT relation is first partitioned horizontally into two fragments, DEP-H-A and DEP-H-BC, and that site A stores fragment DEP-H-A. Fragment DEP-H-BC is portioned further vertically into two vertical partitions, DEP-H-BC-V-B and DEP-H-BC-V-C, stored at sites B and C, respectively. The DDBMS may transform the original query into three subqueries, each executing on the appropriate fragments at sites A, B, and C. The results from sites B and C are first put together through a join operation, and then the result of this join is combined with the result from site A through a union operation.

Replication   Let us consider one case with replication. Assume that the DEPART-MENT relation is not partitioned but replicated. Full copies are stored at sites B and C. In this case, the DDBMS must choose between sites B and C based on optimum processing conditions. Let us say that site C is chosen. The DDBMS transforms the query to execute on the copy at site C, changing the name of the relation to the local name at site C. The result of the query is received at site A and presented to the user there. No union or join operations are necessary.

What we have considered here simply illustrates the principle of query transformation, decomposition, and routing. The details are involved. Again, the DDBMS has a number of options to transform and decompose a query based on the partitioning and replication schemes. It makes the determination based on query optimization techniques by considering all costs in the distributed database environment.

Nonjoin Queries   In the above subsection, we considered a very simple query and reviewed the query transformation process. Let us go over a few more queries with selection criteria, but without any explicit joins. We will present a few cases and make general comments on the nonjoin queries.

Example 1

Query from site B: List of employees from departments with department numbers 24 and 43.

Data distribution: EMPLOYEE relation partitioned horizontally. Employees with department number 24 at site A and those with department number 43 at site C.

Action by DDBMS: Transform query incorporating local database object names, execute query at sites A and C, receive results at site B, combine results through union operation.

Example 2

Query from site A: List of employees from department number 31.

Data distribution: EMPLOYEE relation partitioned horizontally. Employees with department number 31 at site B and all others at site C.

Action by DDBMS: Recognize that data for employees from department number 31 are stored at site B. Transform query incorporating local database object names, execute query at site B, receive results at site A.

Example 3

Query from site B: Find the average salary of employees from departments with department numbers 24 and 43; average computed taking employees from both departments together.

Data distribution: EMPLOYEE relation partitioned horizontally. Employees with department number 24 at site A and those with department number 43 at site C.

Action by DDBMS: Recognize that averages cannot be computed individually at each of the sites A and C and combined by union operation. Transform query into two subqueries, one for site A and the other for site C. Change the queries to compute count of employees and sum of salaries. From these two queries, receive sum of salaries and count of employees at each site. Now calculate average by adding up the sums of salaries and dividing by the total number of employees. This case illustrates the potential complexity of some query transformations.

Example 4

Query from site B: List all data for employees from departments with department numbers 24 and 43.

Data distribution: EMPLOYEE relation first partitioned vertically, keeping salary data for all employees at site B. The rest of the data in the relation partitioned horizontally. Horizontal partition for employees with department number 24 at site A and those with department number 43 at site C.

Action by DDBMS: Recognize the hybrid partitioning scheme. Transform and decompose query into three subqueries. Execute two subqueries appropriately at sites A and C where horizontal partitions are stored. Receive results at B, and put the results together through union operation. Execute the other subquery at B. Combine this result with earlier consolidation of results from sites A and C through union operation.

Join Queries   Processing of queries with join conditions in a distributed database environment can be quite complicated and difficult. The complexity varies with the manner in which base relations are distributed across the sites. Many of the typical queries in any database environment contain join conditions. For optimizing join queries, the DDBMS has to examine a large number of processing options.

Let us take a simple example and scrutinize the processing options. We will use the following relations for our example. This discussion is modeled after a presentation by C. J. Date, an acknowledged database expert and an eminent author, in his book mentioned in the References section.

PROJECT (<u>ProjNo</u>, ProjDesc, ProjManager, ProjLocation)

EMPLOYEE (<u>EmpNo</u>, SocSecNo, EmpName, EmpAddr, EmpPhone, Salary, DeptNo)

ASSIGNMENT (<u>ProjNo</u>, <u>EmpNo</u>, HoursWorked)

Foreign Keys: ProjNo REFERENCES PROJECT

  EmpNo REFERENCES EMPLOYEE

Assume that database is distributed to two sites, A and B, as follows:

At site A   PROJECT relation (500 rows)

  ASSIGNMENT relation (50,000 rows)

At site B   EMPLOYEE relation (10,000)

Manager Jones wants to know the names of employees on his projects who make more than $100,000.

> **SELECT** E.EmpName
> **FROM** PROJECT P, EMPLOYEE E, ASSIGNMENT A
>   **WHERE** P.ProjNo = A.ProjNo
>   **AND** E.EmpNo = A.EmpNo
>   **AND** P.ProjManager = 'Jones'
>   **AND** E.Salary > 100000

This is not a very complicated query. As you know, in terms of relational algebra, the result is obtained by two select operations, two union operations, and one project operation. In a centralized database system, all of these operations are performed on the database at a single site. That is not the case with a distributed database system. There are numerous ways that data can be moved around to perform these operations in the most optimal manner. The DDBMS is expected to examine these ways and choose the least expensive option.

Even in our simple distributed database system with just three relations and three sites, several options are conceivable. Just to give you an idea of the complexity of join query processing, let us list a few options. After the result is obtained, the result is transmitted to the site where manager Jones is. Review the following list:

- Perform select operation at site B on EMPLOYEE for salary > 100000. Move result to site A. Complete all remaining operations at site A.
- Move entire EMPLOYEE relation to site A. Perform all operations at site A.
- Perform join operation on PROJECT and ASSIGNMENT relations at site A. Perform select operation on the result for 'Jones.' For each of the rows in this selection, send a message to B to check whether the corresponding EMPLOYEE row shows salary > 100000. Get responses back from B. Select only such EMPLOYEE rows. Perform project operation and obtain final result.
- Move PROJECT and ASSIGNMENT relations to site B. Perform all operations at site B.
- Perform select operation at site A on PROJECT relation for 'Jones.' Perform join operation on this result and ASSIGNMENT relation at site A. Perform select operation at site B on EMPLOYEE relation for salary > 100000. For each of the selected rows send a message to site A to verify whether the selected row relates to 'Jones.' Select only such rows. Perform project operation and obtain final result.
- Perform join operation on PROJECT and ASSIGNMENT relations at site A. Perform select operation on result for 'Jones.' Move result to site B. Complete remaining operations at site B.

The total data transmission time for each of these options can be computed based on the number of rows in each relation, the number of qualifying rows in the EMPLOYEE and PROJECT relations, the size of the records, and data transfer rates between the sites.

Optimization Considerations From our discussion in the previous subsection, you realize how complex query optimization would be in a distributed database environment. The more intricate the data distribution, the more complicated query optimization turns out to be. You have seen how, even in a very simple example of EMPLOYEE, PROJECT, and ASSIGNMENT relations distributed across two sites, several plausible options exist for query processing. Can you imagine how these would be multiplied in a real-life distributed database environment?

We discussed earlier the issues and factors involved in optimizing queries in a centralized database system. We need to include the challenges caused by the following additional factors in a distributed database environment:

- Scope, extent, and composition of the data fragmentation scheme
- Data replication scheme requirement decisions on which copies to use
- Options for performing primitive operations on the data fragments at different sites
- Creation and execution of subqueries
- Consolidation of results of subqueries
- Transmission of final result to the requesting user
- Network configuration and data transmission costs
- Necessity for the DDBMS to preserve the autonomy of local DBMSs

Transaction Processing

Consider a transaction in a centralized database system. Each transaction performs database operations as an atomic unit of work. In its execution, a transaction may perform operations on several database objects. Even as a transaction proceeds through its execution reading, updating, inserting, and deleting database items, it executes in a manner such that its ACID properties are maintained.

In a distributed database system, the parameters of transaction execution do change. A transaction must execute in such a manner as to preserve its ACID properties. Either all the updates the transaction makes to database items take place, or none at all. Still, as in the case of a centralized environment, a transaction must leave the overall distributed database in a correct and consistent state whether it commits or aborts. A transaction in a distributed environment is expected to perform as efficiently as in a centralized environment.

One major difference, however, is that all the data objects a transaction operates on may not be at a single site in a distributed environment. In fact, in almost all cases of transactions, they operate on database objects dispersed across different physical locations. Figure 18-17 provides a transaction processing example.

In this example, a transaction has to perform updates to employee records stored at three sites. The DDBMS must coordinate the execution of the transaction in cooperation with the local DBMSs at the three sites. Let us trace the execution of the transaction.

- Transaction requests locks or whatever other means available in the local DBMSs to gain shared or exclusive control over the database objects accessed.

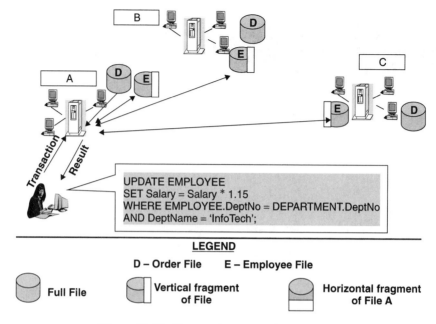

UPDATE EMPLOYEE
SET Salary = Salary * 1.15
WHERE EMPLOYEE.DeptNo = DEPARTMENT.DeptNo
AND DeptName = 'InfoTech';

LEGEND

D – Order File   E – Employee File

Full File   Vertical fragment of File   Horizontal fragment of File A

Figure 18-17 Transaction processing example.

- Completes database transactions of reads, writes, and so on.
- When ready to commit, sends "prepare to commit" message to all cooperating DBMSs where the database objects reside.
- Also, sends "prepare to commit" message to all other sites where replicated copies of the updated database objects are held.
- All sites where database updates are being made and those sites with replicated copies send back response messages to transaction initiating site (each response is either "ready to commit" or "not prepared to commit, aborted").
- The execution protocol may allow a transaction to commit only if all participating sites can commit or may permit a transaction to commit if a sufficient number of sites can commit. The coordinating transaction examines the responses and determines the course of action.
- If the coordinating transaction decides to commit, it issues a "commit" message to participating sites.
- Coordinator waits for "commit" responses from participating sites. When all responses are received, coordinator completes processing of the transaction.
- Sends "commit complete" message to participating sites.

If the coordinating transaction decides to abort, it issues messages to abort to all participating sites. The sequence to abort and roll back at every participating site and to complete the abort process is similar to the sequence following the decision to commit.

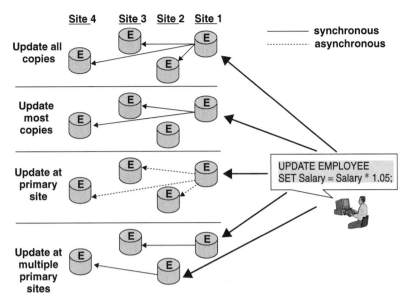

Figure 18-18   Update propagation techniques.

Update Propagation to Replicas   In an earlier subsection on replication, we briefly mentioned two major methods for keeping replicated copies of database objects synchronized when updates take place. We covered synchronous and asynchronous replication techniques with an example of updates to an EMPLOYEE relation replicated at different sites. Now let us explore the topic a little further and study a few techniques. Figure 18-18 illustrates four common techniques.

Note the following brief descriptions of the update propagation techniques.

1. *Update all copies*

   This is a synchronous replication method. Locking is managed centrally. The central lock manager coordinates all local lock managers. All copies of the database object are updated before the transaction commits. This method imposes excessive overhead on the central site. This site has to handle all the traffic to coordinate the locking and unlocking tasks.

2. *Update most copies*

   This method is a slight variation of the synchronous replication method. As the central or coordinator site prepares to update its copy synchronously, it issues update requests to all sites where replicated copies are held. If sufficient number of sites respond positively, the coordinator completes the update process. This is similar to majority voting to authorize a process. A number of schemes exist to determine how many sites constitute a majority in a given situation.

3. *Update at primary site*

   One site is designated as the primary site where updates take place. The replicated copy at the primary site is called the primary or master copy. All other copies at other sites are secondary copies. Only the primary copy is updated synchronously. Transactions cannot update secondary copies. The primary site propagates the updates to secondary copies at a later time. This method reduces the type of traffic at the central site in synchronous replication. Still, the primary site is subject to heavy traffic. Another shortcoming of this method relates to the fact that only data at the primary site are absolutely correct at all times; the other sites are constantly being synchronized with the primary site.

4. *Update at multiple primary sites*
   All or most of the sites holding replicated copies are designated as primary sites. Each of these designated sites is the primary site for some portion of the database being replicated. By spreading the responsibility around, the traffic at each primary site becomes reduced and manageable. However, this method adds another task to the transaction—for each update, the primary site must first be identified before the transaction can proceed.

Concurrency Control

In the above discussion on transaction processing, we concentrated on the execution of a single transaction and how the execution gets coordinated across participating sites. Now let us introduce other transactions and examine concurrency control in a distributed database environment. Concurrency control becomes more complex in a distributed database environment because two or more concurrent transactions may be attempting to simultaneously update two or more copies of the same database object. Therefore, a concurrency control technique must take into account the fragmentation, replication, and data allocation schemes and also how replicated data are being kept synchronized.

Recall the concept of serializability discussed when we were dealing with concurrency control in a centralized database system. If two transactions execute one after the other, this is serial execution. If the effects on the database produced by two concurrent transactions are the same as though they executed serially, then the concurrency control techniques ensure serializability. Locking mechanisms in distributed database systems are also based on the same principle. The concurrency control protocol dictates how locks are obtained and released. In our previous discussion on transaction processing, we ignored locking and unlocking issues and confined the discussion to propagation of updates. Now let us examine lock management in a distributed database environment. Which site manages the locks?

Lock Management   Locking and unlocking functions are generally handled in the ways indicated below. As you will note, each option has its advantages and disadvantages.

Locking at primary site.   One site is chosen as a primary, central site where locks are held. The lock manager at this site is responsible for all locking and unlocking functions. This is a straightforward option. However, transaction processing at any site will halt if the primary site is down. The whole system is dependent on a particular site being operational.

Locking primary copy. One of the replicated copies of a database object is selected as the primary copy. Locking and unlocking of any copy of the object is the responsibility of the lock manager at the site where the primary copy is held. In this option, if the primary copy is held in one site and the locking is for a copy at a different site, the processing of the relevant transaction requires it to communicate not just to the site where the read or update is intended to take place, but also to the site where the primary copy is held. However, all transaction processing need not stop if one site goes down.

Locking distributed copies. The lock manager at each site is responsible for locking and unlocking of all database objects at that site. When a transaction wants to lock a copy of a database object, it need not communicate with another site just for the locking and unlocking.

Deadlock Resolution   Chapter 15, covering the important topic of data integrity, discusses deadlock resolution in a centralized database environment. In that chapter, you learned about the two methods for resolving deadlocks as part of concurrency control: deadlock prevention and deadlock detection.

Recall that deadlock prevention, a more involved technique, is generally applicable to environments where transactions run long and the number of update transactions far exceeds the number of queries that contain read-only operations. A typical database environment used for operating an organization's business generally has an even mixture of update transactions and read-only queries. Furthermore, not too many conflicts arise among concurrent transactions because the applications are streamlined and updates are orderly.

Deadlock detection, on the other hand, is simpler to implement. One of the contending transactions is forced out, and the deadlock gets resolved. The DBMS uses a wait-for graph to detect a deadlock situation and aborts one of the transactions, based on defined criteria, if a deadlock is sensed. You have studied how the DBMS maintains wait-for graphs and uses the technique to detect deadlocks. The other method used by DBMSs to detect deadlocks relies on a timeout technique.

In practice, deadlock detection with wait-for graphs is widely used. In Chapter 15, we discussed this deadlock detection scheme with wait-for graphs for the centralized database system. Now let us reexamine the scheme and note its applicability to the distributed database environment.

In a centralized database environment, there is only one site for the database and the wait-for graph is maintained and used at that site. Transactions execute at only one site. However, in a distributed database environment, transactions operate on database objects at multiple sites. When you inspect the concurrent transactions executing at a single site, some of these emanated from other sites and the rest were initiated locally. Maintenance of wait-for graphs—where and how—poses the greatest challenge.

Let us begin with the idea of each site maintaining a wait-for graph. As you know, the nodes of the graph represent all transactions, both local and otherwise, waiting on local database objects held by other transactions. Assuming a two-site distributed database system, Figure 18-19 presents an example of wait-for graphs at the two sites.

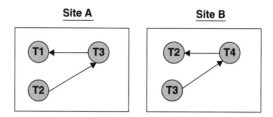

Figure 18-19   Example of local wait-for graph.

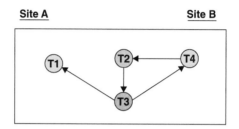

Figure 18-20   Example of global wait-for graph.

Study the two local wait-for graphs carefully. Observe that transactions T2 and T3 appear in both wait-for graphs. That means that these two concurrent transactions wait for database objects at both sites. You note each graph by itself it does not show a cycle, and, therefore, indicates that no deadlock has occurred. But what happens when you combine the two graphs and look at the union of the two? Figure 18-20 presents the global wait-for graphs combining the two individual graphs.

The global wait-for graph readily discloses a cycle in the graph and, therefore, a deadlock condition. But the DDBMS could discern and detect a deadlock only when the local wait-for graphs are combined. How could the wait-for graphs be organized and maintained to detect every deadlock without fail? Let us explore two major schemes for organizing wait-for graphs in a distributed database environment.

Centralized Scheme   At specified short intervals, transmit all local wait-for graphs to a centralized site, nominated as the deadlock coordinator. A global wait-for graph is generated at the coordinator site by taking the union of all local wait-for graphs. If the global wait-for graph discloses any cycles, the DDBMS detects a deadlock and takes action. When the DDBMS detects a deadlock and decides on a victim transaction to be aborted, the coordinator informs all concerned sites about who the victim is so that all sites may abort the transaction and roll back any database changes.

Figure 18-20 is an example of a global wait-for graph generated at a deadlock coordinator site.

Occasionally, an additional transaction may be aborted unnecessarily after a deadlock has been detected and a victim chosen. For example, in Figure 18-20 suppose that the DBMS at site A has decided to abort T2 for some unrelated reason

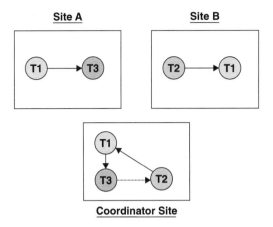

Figure 18-21   Example of a false cycle.

and, at the same time, the coordinator has picked T3 as the victim to be aborted. Then both T2 and T3 will be rolled back, although it is enough that T2 alone is aborted.

Also, sometimes false cycles may be sensed and deadlock resolution may be started unnecessarily. For example, refer to Figure 18-21 illustrating a false cycle in the global wait-for graph. False cycles indicate phantom deadlocks.

Let us say that T3 releases the resource it is holding in site A. A message to "delete" arrow from T1 to T3 is sent to the coordinator. At the same time, assume that T3 requests for a resource held by T2 at site B. This results in an "insert" arrow from T3 to T2 message to be sent to the coordinator. If the "delete" message arrives at the coordinator site a little later than the arrival of the "insert" message, a false cycle is recognized, causing unnecessary initiation of deadlock resolution.

Distributed Scheme   As the name of this scheme implies, no global wait-for graph exists at a designated central site. Every site maintains its own wait-for graph. The collection of all the wait-for graphs at the various sites forms the total graph for the distributed database system. If at any time a deadlock is encountered, it is expected that it will show up in at least one of the several wait-for graphs. This is the underlying principle of the distributed scheme.

A wait-for graph under this scheme differs from that under a centralized scheme in one component. A wait-for graph under the distributed scheme contains one extra transaction TO representing transactions that hold resources in other sites. For example, an arrow T1→TO exists in a graph if T1 is waiting for a resource held in another site by any transaction. Similarly, the arrow TO→T1 represents that any transaction at another site is waiting for a resource in the current site held by T1. Figure 18-22 represents the wait-for graphs at sites A and B when you add transaction TO to the wait-for graphs shown in Figure 18-19.

If a local wait-for graphs records a cycle not involving the TO transaction, then you know it represents a deadlock condition. However, what does a cycle with TO transaction as part of it represent? It only implies the possibility of a deadlock, not

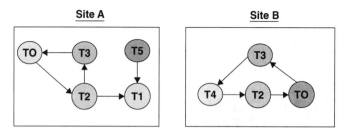

Figure 18-22   Local wait-for graphs with TO transaction.

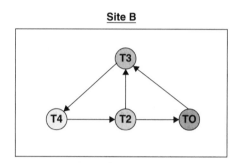

Figure 18-23   Updated local wait-for graph showing deadlock condition.

a certainty. The deadlock detection algorithm in the distributed scheme must ascertain whether a deadlock really exists. Let us see how the algorithm works.

Consider the local wait-for graphs shown in Figure 18-22. At site A, the deadlock detection algorithm senses a cycle containing a TO transaction. On analysis, a determination is made that T3 is waiting for a resource at site B. Site A sends a message to site B with information about the cycle. Site B updates its wait-for graph with the information from site A and creates the wait-for cycle shown in Figure 18-23.

The updated wait-for graph at site B displays a cycle without TO as part of it, indicating a definite deadlock. The technique described here enables you to understand the general idea behind the distributed scheme of wait-for graphs just enough for the scope of our study here.

Distributed Recovery

As expected, recovery from failures has added dimensions of complexity. A distributed database environment faces new kinds of failures not found in centralized systems. One or more remote sites may go down, and these may be the sites at which subqueries or subtransactions are executing. The DDBMS must continue to operate the other sites while the failed sites are brought back up. The communication network forms a major component in the distributed system, and the communications network, completely or in part, may fail and cause interruptions.

When the recovery manager software completes recovery, the distributed database, all parts of it and the replicas, must be left in a consistent and correct state. In a distributed database environment, typically a transaction gets divided into sub-transactions and executed at different sites. So each subtransaction must behave like a complete transaction within a site. To preserve the atomicity of the entire trans-action, either all subtransactions should commit or none at all. Whether any failure occurs or not, the atomicity and durability properties must be ensured. These are ensured by means of a proper commit protocol. The method for a centralized environment must be enhanced. The two-phase commit is commonly used as the standard for the distributed environment.

As you know, in a centralized database system the log file contains all the details that can be used to recover from failures. In a distributed database system, each site maintains a separate log file. These log files contain details of the actions performed as part of the commit protocol in addition to the operations of the transactions as in a centralized system. Recovery from failures in a distributed environment depends on such additional details.

We will briefly discuss the commit protocol and the recovery process. We will provide a summarized discussion without getting into too much technical detail. The site from which a transaction originates is known as the coordinator site for the transaction, and all other sites where subtransactions of the original transaction execute are called subordinate or participant sites.

Two-Phase Commit Protocol (2PC)   As the name implies, actions in this proto-col take place in two phases: a voting phase and a decision or termination phase. The underlying principle is that the coordinator decides to commit a transaction only when all participants vote to commit.

Now let us walk through the execution of a transaction while adopting the protocol.

Voting Phase   The user transaction completes processing and decides to com-mit. Write *begin-commit* record in the log file. Send *prepare* message to each participant.

Termination Phase   On receiving a *prepare* message, each participant is either ready to commit or abort based on local conditions. Each participant either writes a *ready-commit* record in the local log file and returns a *ready-commit* message to the coordinator or writes an *abort* message in the local log file and returns an *abort* message to the coordinator.

Case 1. Any participant returns an *abort* vote based on local processing.

Write *abort* record in the log file. Send *global-abort* message to each participant. The participant writes an *abort* record in the local log file and sends an *acknowl-edgement* to the coordinator. The coordinator, on receiving all *acknowledgement* messages, writes *end-transaction* record in its log file.

Case 2. All participants return *ready-commit* votes.

Write *commit* record in the log file. Send *global-commit* message to each partic-ipant. The participant writes a *commit* record in the local log file, commits the sub-transaction, releases all locks, and sends an *acknowledgement* to the coordinator.

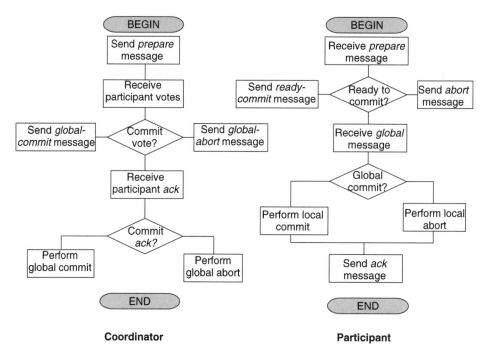

Figure 18-24 Two-phase commit: action states.

The coordinator, on receiving all *acknowledgement* messages, writes *end-transaction* record in its log file.

While these actions take place, the coordinator and the participants go through four states as illustrated in Figure 18-24.

Recovery Consider a site coming back up after a crash. The recovery process of the DDBMS gets initiated, and it reads the local log file. It takes suitable recovery actions by processing all the log records for the transactions that were executing the two-phase commit protocol at the time of the crash. Note that this site could have been the coordinator for some of these transactions and a participant for others.

The following indicates the recovery process in a general manner. This is not a detailed discussion. Assume that transaction T is one of those for which the recovery process applies.

Case 1. Commit or *abort* record exists in the log file.

If *commit* record exists, redo T; if *abort* record exists, undo T. If this site happens to be the coordinator for T, resend *commit* or *abort* message to all participants because there may be other site or link failures. When *acknowledgements* are received back from all participants, write *end-transaction* record in the log file.

Case 2. Prepare record exists, but no *commit* or *abort* record in the log file.

This site is a participant. Find coordinator site from *prepare* record and contact coordinator for status of T. If coordinator responds with a *commit* message, write corresponding log record, and redo T. If coordinator responds with an *abort* message, write corresponding log record, and undo T. Then write *end* log record for T.

Case 3. No *prepare*, *commit*, or *abort* record in the log file.

Abort and undo T. Write end log record for T. In this case, we safely assume the site could not have voted to commit T before the crash.

Three-Phase Commit Protocol (3PC)   Think of the effect of a crash on the participants if the coordinator fails. In the above discussion of transaction T, participants that have voted to commit cannot decide on the course of action—whether to commit or abort—until the coordinating site recovers. That means T is blocked. However, the active participants can talk to one another and check whether at least one of them has an *abort* or *commit* log record.

The three-phase commit protocol is intended to avoid blocking even if the coordinator site fails during recovery. This protocol postpones the decision to commit until it is ensured that a sufficient number of sites know about the decision to commit. The idea is that these participant sites could communicate among themselves and find out about the decision to commit or abort, even if the coordinator site fails. Here, briefly, is how the protocol works:

- Coordinator sends prepare message to each participant.
- When coordinator receives *ready-commit* messages back from all participants, it sends out *precommit* messages instead of *commit* messages.
- When coordinator receives back sufficient number of *acknowledgements* back from the participants, it writes a *commit* record in its log file and sends out *commit* messages.

CHAPTER SUMMARY

- Distributed database systems are emerging as a result of the merger of two major technologies: database and network.
- A distributed database features geographic separation of data but preserves logical unity and integrity. Each data fragment is stored at the site where it is most frequently used.
- A distributed database management system (DDBMS) is a software system that manages the distributed database and makes the distribution transparent to the user.
- Motivation and goals of a distributed system: efficient access of local data, improved customer service, enhanced reliability, availability of global data. A distributed system offers several advantages but also has a few shortcomings.
- Two broad types of distributed database systems: homogeneous, in which all sites run under the same DBMS; heterogeneous, in which a different DBMS may manage the data at each site.
- For a distributed database, DDBMS supports several schema levels: global external, global conceptual, data fragmentation, data allocation, local external, local conceptual, and local internal.

- The system catalog or data dictionary resides in one place for a centralized database. However, for a distributed database, a few options are available for placing the catalog: at a central site, at all sites fully or partially, and a hybrid option.
- Data distribution methods: data fragmentation (horizontal and vertical partitioning) and data replication.
- Computing architectural options: two-tier client/server, two-tier intelligent server, and three-tier architecture with middleware.
- Design and implementation issues focus on fragmentation and allocation of data to the various sites.
- The key motivation for the DDBMS is transparency or hiding complexities of data distribution and making it transparent to users. Transparencies provided at different levels: fragmentation, replication, location, network, naming, and failure.
- A query in a distributed environment typically gets divided into subqueries and executed at the sites where the pertinent data are stored. Numerous additional factors must be considered for query optimization.
- Transaction execution and propagation of updates to various replicas are more difficult. Lock management and concurrency control pose many challenges.
- The two-phase commit protocol (2PC) is the industry standard to enable distributed recovery.

REVIEW QUESTIONS

1. Briefly describe the basic concepts of a distributed database system.
2. List five advantages and five disadvantages of distributed databases.
3. Compare and contrast homogeneous and heterogeneous systems.
4. What are the options for storing the system catalog or data dictionary?
5. Name any three of the network configurations for a distributed database system. Describe one of these.
6. What is data fragmentation? Describe it using an example of a CUSTOMER relation.
7. Name three types of transparencies provided by a DDBMS. Describe any one.
8. List the four common techniques for update propagation.
9. Describe the essential differences between centralized and distributed schemes for using wait-for graphs.
10. What is the underlying principle of the two-phase commit protocol?

EXERCISES

1. Indicate whether true or false:
    A. In a distributed database system, each site must have autonomy to manage its data.

   B. In a three-tier architecture, middleware performs the database functions.

   C. Location transparency relates to how data are fragmented for storing at locations.

   D. Hybrid data partitioning combines horizontal and vertical partitioning methods.

   E. Locking primary copy technique—all locks for all database objects are kept at one site.

   F. A global wait-for graph is created at the coordinator site.

   G. The two-phase commit protocol requires a transaction to commit in the voting phase.

   H. Atomicity and durability properties of a transaction must be preserved in a distributed database environment.

   I. A heterogeneous system must have a different DBMS at every site.

   J. The ring network configuration connects sites in a closed loop.

2. An international bank has 10 domestic sites and 6 international sites. A homogeneous distributed database system supports the bank's business. Consider options to distribute the customer data and customer account data among the bank's sites. Also, discuss the schema definitions at the various levels for the distributed database.

3. Using an example, describe synchronous and asynchronous data replication in a distributed database environment.

4. How are locks for concurrency control managed in a distributed database? Discuss the options.

5. You are the senior DBA for an international distributor of electronic components with 60 domestic sales offices and 10 international offices in the European Union countries. Develop a very general plan for a distributed database system. Without getting into technical details, include data distribution strategy, network configuration, system architecture, concurrency control techniques, and recovery methods.

CHAPTER 19

DATABASE SYSTEMS AND THE WEB

CHAPTER OBJECTIVES

- Comprehend the enormous significance of the merging of database and Web technologies
- Gain a broad understanding of the interaction between the two technologies
- Initially, have a quick review of the Internet and the World Wide Web
- Examine the motivation for union of database systems and the Web
- Recognize the advantages and shortcomings of Web-database integration
- Review various integration approaches
- Consider a few security options

What is the most dominant phenomenon in computing and communications that arose in the 1990s? Undoubtedly, it is the Internet with its unique information delivery mechanism, the World Wide Web. In just a little more than 10 years since its origin in 1989, the World Wide Web has become the most powerful data content repository and information delivery system. It is estimated that at the beginning of the year 2000, about 50 million households worldwide were using the Internet. In five short years, by the end of 2005, this number is expected to grow 10-fold.

The Web changes everything, as they say. It has changed the way people shop, run their business, collect information, read the news headlines, make travel arrangements, invest in stocks, buy a new home, chat with others, study, and entertain themselves. The earlier websites began as storage places for web pages that could be served up to anyone who would request them. These static pages are no

Database Design and Development: An Essential Guide for IT Professionals by Paulraj Ponniah
ISBN 0-471-21877-4   Copyright © 2003 by John Wiley and Sons, Inc.

longer adequate for today's environment. Web users need to react to the information these pages present and use the data content interactively. Mere storage of information as rigid web pages does not serve the purposes of today's users. Information content has to be stored in databases managed by powerful DBMSs to provide interactive access in a fast and reliable manner. Electronic commerce has made the database the centerpiece of its operations over the Internet. The productive integration of Web and database technologies has emerged.

In this chapter, we will concentrate particularly on the combined application of Web and database technologies. We will consider the types of computing architecture that promote the use of database systems in delivering information on the Web. We will specifically review some of the common approaches that make the integration of the two technologies happen. Although we will begin with a brief overview of the Internet and the Web, this is just background information, not the main focus. The primary emphasis is how database and Web technologies are made to work together.

WEB TECHNOLOGY: A REFRESHER

Let us first set the stage for our coverage of database systems in the Web environment. How do Web and database technologies merge and work together? How is a user interacting with a website able to retrieve web pages and input parameters and to access a database that drives the applications? What type of system architecture supports access of web pages and data from a database at the same time?

Our main discussion is concerned about such questions. But to put those questions in proper perspective, let us begin with an examination of a few basic concepts of the Internet and the Web. For information technology professionals in today's environment, this has to be just a brief review. After beginning with the basics, we will quickly walk through the languages for the Web and the data communications protocol for moving web pages around.

The Internet and the Web

Very simply stated, the Internet is a collection of interconnected networks separately owned by government, commercial, industrial, educational, and research organizations. In addition to these organizations, internet service providers (ISPs) are also connected to the network. With this interconnection, the Internet is able to provide a number of services including e-mail, transfer of files, conferencing, and chat with others with the same interests. The Internet had its experimental beginning in the late 1960s. Here is a very brief history.

- **Late 1960s:** U.S. Department of Defense project ARPANET (Advanced Research Projects Agency NETwork) set up to build networks that would stay up even if some sections of the network go down because of any catastrophe.
- **1982:** TCP/IP (Transmission Control Protocol and Internet Protocol) adopted as the standard communications protocol for ARPANET. TCP ensures correct delivery of messages. IP manages sending and receiving information packets based on a four-byte destination address (IP number).

- **1986:** NSFNET (National Science Foundation NETwork) created after responsibility for the technology was transferred to NSF.
- **1995:** NSFNET no longer the backbone for the Internet. A complete commercial system of backbones replaced it.

Strength and Simplicity of the Web Consider the hundreds of thousands of computer systems connected over the Internet. Think of all the information residing in those systems in the form of pages spread across as connected pieces of information. The World Wide Web is a simple mechanism for exploring this huge volume of information scattered across the Internet.

As you know, information on the Web is presented in the form of pages containing multimedia components such as graphics, video and audio clips, and pictures in addition to text. A web page may also contain connections or hyperlinks to other pages. This is a clever way of navigating through the Web and browsing information on pages irrespective of the computer systems in which they reside.

When you examine the computer systems connected on the Web, you note the systems performing one of two roles. Servers are the computer systems storing information in the form of web pages; clients, usually known as browsers, are those requesting information in the form of web pages. The common language used for creating Web documents is known as HyperText Markup Language (HTML). Browsers on the Web interpret HTML and display the requested web page. The set of rules or protocols governing the transfer of Web documents between browsers and servers is known as HyperText Transfer Protocol (HTTP). A Web document or its component is identified by an address stipulated as a Uniform Resource Locator (URL). We will briefly discuss HTTP, URL, and HTML. We will also cover the usage of Web technology in intranets and extranets.

But first refer to Figure 19-1 illustrating the fundamental layout of the Web environment. Note the components and how the Internet provides the network connection.

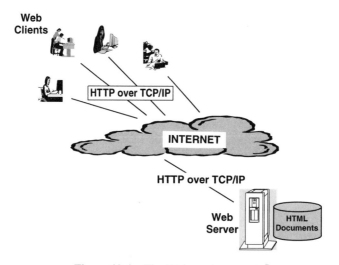

Figure 19-1 The Web environment.

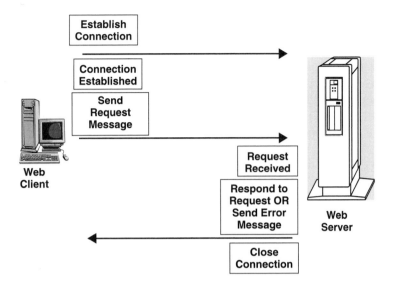

Figure 19-2   Stages of an HTTP transaction.

HyperText Transfer Protocol (HTTP)

HTTP is a simple, object-oriented protocol governing the exchange of hypertexts written in HTML on the Web. The protocol stipulates how clients and servers can communicate and exchange information. This protocol was developed especially for the Web. Its simplicity is its strength. HTTP may be thought of as a great equalizer; it allows you to create HTML documents on any computing system and deliver them in a consistent way to any other system. If a server can deliver the document, any browser can view it the way you created it.

With HTTP, exchange of information takes places in four stages or phases. An HTTP transaction operates on a request-response method. Figure 19-2 presents the stages of an HTTP transaction.

Here is a brief description of the actions in the four stages:

Connection. The client establishes connection with the identified Web server. You may note the status line of most browsers indicating this action in the status line as "connecting to . . . ." If client cannot establish the connection, nothing more happens. The connection attempt times out.

Request. If the connection is established, the client sends a request message to the Web server. The request includes information about the transmission protocol being used with the version number, the object requested, and how the server must respond to the request.

Response. The Web server sends the requested HTML document to the client indicating the protocol being used. If the server cannot fulfill the request, it sends back an error message. As soon as the document is received, the browser launches the appropriate software to display its text and the multimedia components.

Close. The server closes the connection.

The simplicity of the protocol mainly comes from its property of being stateless. What does this mean? As soon as the server closes the connection, nothing is retained in the server about the transaction. The server does not remember any prior requests. Once the connection is closed, the memory about the transaction is completely erased. When you request a document, the server does not know who you are, whether this is your first request, or whether you are at the website for the fiftieth time. This property, however, requires very simple logic. There is no need for elaborate software, and the clients and servers can run lean without holding extra memory and storage for old requests.

A big challenge in using HTTP is its inability to keep track of the state of your interaction with the server. The state indicates information about who you are and about your request or visit. Maintaining state means remembering prior information as the user at the client system moves from page to page at the website at the server system.

Being stateless, HTTP, by itself, cannot apply to database transactions. Database transactions need the concept of a session during which interactions between the client and the database can take place. Some schemes are available for maintaining state information: store it in cookies, encode it in the links, send it in the form of hidden variables, and store it on the Web server. However, these schemes have limitations. As you will see later, server functionality must be extended for database transactions to execute on the Web.

Uniform Resource Locator (URL)

URLs act like addresses to any definable resource on the Internet. They are all-purpose reference mechanisms for the Internet. URLs are the basis for HTTP and the Web. They are used to define addresses on the Web where documents or resources can be found based on their location. Any line from one document to another is coded in the form of a URL.

A URL is written with a simple syntax consisting of the following parts:

Protocol or scheme. The way or method to exchange data on the Internet (HTTP, FTP, Telnet, etc.)

Host. The host computer or the server on which the data resource is located

Port. Port number if the requested service is not located at the default port of the host system

Path. Path name on the host where the resource is to found

A URL, therefore, is a string of characters composed of these components. Here are a few examples of URLs:

> http://wiley.com/author/format.html
> ftp://raritanval.edu/documents/dbdesign/syllabus.txt
> telnet://iitf.doc.gov

HyperText Markup Language (HTML)

HTML is a simple language for marking up and tagging a document so that it can be published, that is, made available on the Web. It is known as a markup language because you can add marks to regular text; these marks carry special meanings for a Web browser indicating how the document must be formatted and presented. The flexibility and strength of HTML come from its being platform-independent.

HTML uses tags to mark the structure of a document. The label of a tag is enclosed with the "<"and">" characters. For example, <HEAD> is a tag indicating the start of the page heading. Each structure begins and ends with a tag. The heading structure begins with the <HEAD> tag and ends with the </HEAD> tag.

Parts of an HTML Document   Without going into too much detail, let us quickly review the parts of an HTML document. The document consists of elements that form its structure.

Head Elements   These are used to indicate the properties of the whole document, such as title, links denoting connections to other documents, and the base URL of the document. This element is not displayed to the user as part of the document but contains information about the document that is used by browsers.
Example: Selected Notes of Databases and the Web

Body Elements   These are used to indicate the text in the body of the document. Unlike the head elements, the body elements are displayed by browsers. There are many different body elements. Just a few samples of body elements follow.

Headings

Standard HTML supports up to six levels of headings.
Example: <H2>DBMS-Web Integration</H2>

Anchors

These are used to mark the start and end of hypertext links.
Example: <A HREF=http://www.wiley.com/author/instructions.html> </A>

Paragraph marks

These are used to define paragraph breaks.
Example: The paragraph mark defines a page break. It is placed at the end of a paragraph. <P>

Line breaks

These are used to indicate the start of a new line.
Example: The HTML School
            100 Main Street
            Anytown, XX 12345

```
<HTML>
<HEAD>
<TITLE> Data Warehousing Fundamentals: A Comprehensive Guide for IT Professionals </TITLE>
</HEAD>
<BODY> background=serenity.jpg
<H2> Welcome to the Home Page of our data warehousing textbook. Review the table of contents. Look at the sample chapters. Get
a complete inside into the unique presentation. Above all, get practical and useful knowledge that can propel your career into new
heights. For further information, please contact John Wiley & Sons, world-renowned publisher of superb technical books. <BR>
<A HREF="http://wiley.com/dw001/book/toc.html">TABLE OF CONTENTS <BR>
</A>< HREF="http://wiley.com/dw001/book/chapter1.html">1. The Compelling Need for Data Warehousing <BR>
</A>< HREF="http://wiley.com/dw001/book/chapter2.html">2. Data Warehouse: The Building Blocks<BR>
</A>< HREF="http://wiley.com/dw001/book/chapter3.html">3. Trends in Data Warehousing<BR>
</A>< HREF="http://wiley.com/dw001/book/chapter4.html">4. Planning and Project Management<BR>
</A></P>
<P>We would love to hear your comments. Happy to serve you.
</BODY>
</HTML>
```

Figure 19-3 Sample HTML coding.

Graphic Elements All modern browsers display in-line graphics embedded in an HTML page. The source of the image is indicated by the term "SRC" in the coding for the graphic element. Browsers not capable of handling graphics will display a text string based on the "ALT" attribute.

Example: <IMG SRC="ABCD.logo.gif" ALT="ABCD Logo">ABCD Company

Figure 19-3 shows a sample coding for an HTML document. Note how the various elements are combined to create the document.

Static and Dynamic Web Pages An HTML document is stored in a file on the server and displayed by the browser. Every time you request for the web page, you will see the same information. The content of the page stays intact; it does not change. If the information on a particular web page must be changed, then the document must be recoded and the revised version must be stored in the file on the server. Such web pages are static web pages.

When HTML was first introduced, its features included text and graphics as well as the embedding of hypertext links. This itself was a dramatic achievement for distributing and presenting information over the Internet. Even though the web pages were static, HTML revolutionized the use of the Internet. However, as the use of the Web expanded, the limitations of static web pages became apparent. Users want exchange of information to be interactive. Users need the ability of servers to respond to user inputs and produce web pages according to the inputs. Users need dynamic web pages.

A dynamic web page changes every time it is accessed. Dynamic HTML is a term applied to a collection of technologies that make HTML documents more dynamic and interactive. In addition to having the standard features of a static web page, a dynamic web page can return the results of a database query. For example, you can complete a form and send it as an input to the server. The server must then return results based on your input. Furthermore, a dynamic web page may be customized on the basis of user preferences.

To implement dynamic web pages, servers will have to generate hypertext based on the requests received. Consider database transactions. These transactions such as insert, update, and delete effect changes in the database. A database is dynamic—changing. Similarly, as database technology is integrated with Web technology, dynamic web pages become a requirement. In the later sections of this chapter, we will explore some of the major methods for making web pages dynamic.

Beyond HTML

Even with this brief introduction of HTML, you must have noted the striking simplicity of HTML. It is a simple language. Its simplicity has made Web publishing so widespread within a short period. HTML follows straightforward rules so that it can be easily incorporated in editing tools. A programmer can generate hypertext through these tools even without a full knowledge of HTML. The ease of use of HTML is probably one of the chief reasons for the phenomenal growth of the Web.

A language meant to be simple must necessarily adopt a small set of rules. HTML does this. The simplicity of HTML is both its strength and weakness. Consider the following list of inadequacies:

- HTML follows a set of restrictive rules.
- HTML is an application of the Standard Generalized Markup Language (SGML) that is based on a set of restrictive rules.
- HTML lacks flexibility. It cannot be used for simple and complex documents with equal ease.
- HTML is not able to describe complex documents.
- HTML is more focused on content presentation than on content description. HTML tags stipulate how the content must be presented; they say little about the meaning of the content.
- HTML is not a descriptive language.
- With just head and body elements, different types of documents such as abstracts, summaries, chapters, reference sections, and bibliographies cannot all be described adequately.

What is the solution? Perhaps more types of tags must be added to HTML. But how many new types of tags would satisfy all the numerous requirements? A method of defining user tags may be a solution. What was needed is a language with extended capabilities, a language beyond HTML—a more flexible and extensible language. Such a language is XML (eXtensible Markup Language). XML focuses on content description. Let us look at the major benefits. We are not getting into the details of XML components here. That is not the purpose of this chapter. For more information on XML, you may refer to a wide assortment of good books on the subject.

Major beneficial features of XML include:

Flexible. Capable of handling a simple home page or a large document such as *War and Peace.*

Extensible. Extended capabilities to enable you to define your own XML elements. You can define your own tags to suit your particular needs in the type of document you are publishing.

Structured. Although flexible and extensible, XML's structured approach helps conformance to rules—not a free-for-all method.

Descriptive. XML elements concentrate on meaning of the contents, not on their presentation. The elements can describe what they contain, allowing intelligent handling of the content by other programs.

Portable. When you define your own tags, how are you going to pass on the definitions and syntax of those tags to others? XML provides simple facilities to produce files capturing the rules of your elements and tags so that your documents can be read properly.

Intranets and Extranets

Consider the ease with which you can publish web pages and exchange e-mails over the Internet. The Internet provides low-cost transmission of information. The concept of exchanging information using Internet and Web technologies need not necessarily be confined to a specific set of users. All you need is the set of components: a server, a browser, and a set of applet-based applications for exchanging information. An organization needs the ability to exchange information among internal users; it also needs information to be made available to a selected set of outsiders such as distributors, suppliers, and customers.

So why cannot the same paradigm for exchanging information with the public over the Internet be extended to exchanging information with internal employees and external business partners? Intranets and extranets are the solution options.

Intranet   From the time the term "intranet" was coined in 1995, this concept of a private network has gripped the corporate world. An intranet is a private computer network based on the data communications standards of the public Internet. An intranet may be thought of as a set of websites belonging to an organization and accessible only to internal users. Information exchange happens within the firewall and, therefore, is more secure. You can have all the benefits of the popular Web technology and still manage security better on the intranet. Intranets are less expensive to build and manage.

Extranet   The Internet and the intranet have been quickly followed by the extranet. An extranet is not completely open like the Internet, nor it is restricted to internal use like an intranet. An extranet is an intranet that is open to selective access by outsiders. From your extranet, you can look outward to your customers, suppliers, and other business partners. For the purpose of security, access over the extranet must be controlled through security mechanisms such as valid user names and passwords. The Internet itself serves as the communications infrastructure. Web technology provides the means for publishing information. Tracking packages at the FedEx site and checking balances at your bank's site are examples of extranet applications.

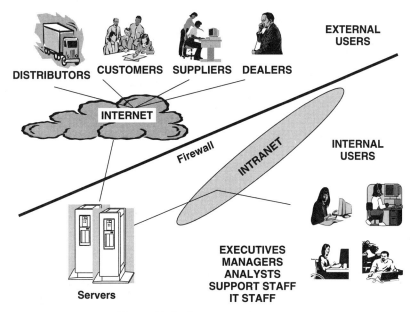

Figure 19-4   Intranet and extranet.

Figure 19-4 illustrates the concepts of intranets and extranets. Note the firewall and how information exchange takes places within and outside the firewall. Note also how the Internet provides the means for data communications.

Let us summarize a few major benefits of intranets and extranets:

- With a universal browser, users will have a single point of entry of information.
- Minimal training is required to access information. Users are already familiar with the use of a browser.
- Universal browsers run on any computer system.
- Web technology opens up multiple information formats such as text, images, graphics, charts, audio, and video.
- It is easy to keep the data content updated for access on the intranet and the extranet. Usually, there will be one source for a particular piece of information.
- Opening up limited corporate information on the extranets fosters better business partnerships and improves customer service.
- Deployment and maintenance costs are low compared to implementing communications networks run on proprietary protocols. The Internet and the Web are standardized.

WEB-DATABASE INTEGRATION

The Web is the cornerstone of electronic commerce. All you have to do is sign on to the Internet and search for any product or service. You will get a huge list of businesses offering that product or service. It is hard to believe that, not long ago, any type of commercial activity was strictly forbidden on the Internet. Now the Web is where you go to shop for thousands of products and services. There are also many special interest business sites.

Every airline, every bank, every auction house, every computer vendor, every car dealer, every database company—the list goes on and on—has its presence on the Web. Think of all the companies in the entertainment business, all those in the travel business—these alone can fill up page after page when you search for them.

How do these companies operate their businesses? How do you look for prices? When you place an order and make a payment, where are the details of your order stored? What is behind all of the commercial activity on the Web? Databases form the underlying foundation for electronic commerce. Database and Web technologies must mesh together to make electronic commerce possible. Let us now examine this integration of the two technologies.

Motivation for Integration

Imagine that you wish to shop for books on French cooking on the Internet. You browse the various sites and find an electronic bookstore that has a wide selection of books on that topic. You ask for a list of books. You narrow down your choice to three books. You want to look at what the reviewers have said about these books. You check the prices and any available discounts. You add them to your electronic shopping cart. You indicate your preferred method of shipping. The website adds shipping charge and sales tax, completes the calculations, and displays the total amount due. You pay with your credit card. The transaction is complete; you have placed your order.

How does the transaction get processed? When the website displays the list of books on French cooking, from where does it get the data? When the site shows you the prices and shipping charges, from where does it display this data? When you finish your order, where do the details of your order get stored? That merchant's database.

It makes the greatest sense to take the information stored in an organization's database and selectively allow access to the information to those visiting its website on the Internet, intranet, or extranet. Here are a few obvious but compelling reasons for integration of an organization's database with its website:

- Fixed or static Web documents do not allow customized information display. Every time data are updated, the static document becomes outdated.
- Trying to reenter data stored in an organization's database on HTML documents constitutes an enormous waste of time.
- The database can be used to create web pages to reflect the current data values.
- Customers and internal users can get up-to-date information from the database.
- Business partners can receive up-to-date information on product data such as prices and availability directly from the database.
- Order entry and fulfillment transactions can interact directly with the database. The older method of buying products on the Web required taking an order on

a form, sending the form by e-mail to a person in the organization, and that person keying in the data into the database through a separate application.

Requisites for Integration

How can Web-database integration be brought about? How can the Web be made a platform to provide users with interfaces into the database? Naturally, database vendors are working on proprietary solutions, but organizations are looking for generic solutions without restricting themselves to single-vendor options.

Review the following list of requisites of organizations for integrating their databases with their Web presence.

- Overcome the stateless nature of a Web transaction and provide continuous sessions for users to interact with the database.
- Provide secure access to the database.
- Allow session-based and application-based authentication of users.
- Protect the database from a transaction destroying the database updates made by another concurrent transaction over the Internet.
- Provide connectivity to the database, independent of the DBMS.
- Provide connectivity to the database, independent of proprietary Web browsers or servers.
- Offer a solution that utilizes all the standard features of DBMSs.
- Present an open architecture for the database system to be operable by a variety of technologies.
- Provide an interface to the database that is scalable as the volume of Web transactions rises.
- Enable access to the database guaranteeing acceptable performance.
- Offer the ability to administer the interface efficiently in a cost-effective manner.
- Allow the interface to work with productivity tools.

Architecture for Integration

Think of a simple database query. A customer picks a product sold over the Internet and wants to know the price. At one end is the browser, where the customer is establishing contact with the website. At the other end is the company's database, where the price for the selected product is stored. Make the connection between the browser at one end and the database server at the other end.

The browser and the Web server exchange information over the Internet with HTTP. The server transmits a form to the browser, and the user selects a product on the form and indicates a request for the price. The transmission of this request from the browser to the Web server takes place. What must the next link be in the communication chain?

For the request to be fulfilled by the DBMS, it must be translated from HTML into SQL for relational databases. The request in SQL must be transmitted to the DBMS at the database server to retrieve the price for the product, possibly from the

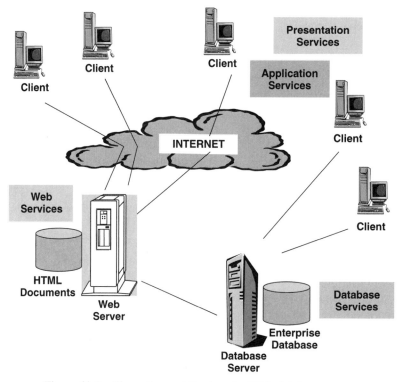

Figure 19-5   Three-tier architecture for Web database access.

product table in the relational database. The product information must be incorporated into an HTML document for the server to transmit to the browser. This has to
be done in a secure environment. Importantly, it must be done as though it is part of
a single session. This is because the user will probably complete the order and transmit it back to the server for further processing and recording in the database.

Let us design a suitable architecture for the type of processing needed for the
simplest of queries described here. Consider the traditional two-tier client/server
architecture with the client at the first tier and the database server at the second
tier. In this architecture, the client handles the presentation services and the database server performs the database services. Although for a simple query, the two-
tier architecture may be satisfactory for access over the local network, we need at
least one more tier to accommodate the Web server for access over the Internet.
Figure 19-5 shows such a three-tier architecture.

When the complexity of application services and logic increases, the need for a
separate application server becomes apparent. The browser interacts with the Web
server based on HTTP; if static HTML pages are requested, the Web server delivers these to the browser. If dynamic web pages with database content are needed,
the Web server passes on the request to an application server. The application server
interacts with one or more data sources to assemble a response. If there is a request
for database services, it is sent to the database server. When the responses to the
data sources are completed, the application server assembles a consolidated
response in the form of web pages and responds to the browser.

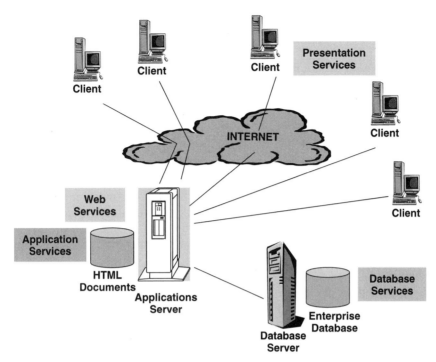

Figure 19-6   Architecture with application server.

Figure 19-6 shows this architecture with the inclusion of the application server.

Observe the services offered at each tier. However, note that the separation into a distinct application server may just be logical so that it may be deemed to reflect additional functionality of the Web server itself. Therefore, in our further discussions, we will construe the application server functionality to be part of the Web server itself.

Advantages and Disadvantages

Before proceeding to explore options for integrating Web and database technologies, let us summarize the advantages and disadvantages of such integration. This discussion will further strengthen your appreciation of the need for the integration.

Advantages   Web documents are files. In a sense, storing information in Web documents tends to be a file-oriented approach. Contrast this with storing information in databases and using databases for providing information. All the advantages of a database approach become available when you integrate database technology in the Web environment.

More specifically, here are few significant advantages.

Popular interface. Using and accessing information through a web page has become widespread. Everyone knows how to access and use a web page. It is a familiar and intuitive method for information access and navigation.

Simple interface. HTML pages do not present complexity or difficulty for either users and developers. Most pages provide a simple interface to the database.

Accessibility. With browsers being platform-independent, data from the database may be provided in the form of a dynamic web page for access to anyone using any type of client system.

Standardization. A database application providing information through web pages adheres to HTML standards. Therefore, a user needs very little training for switching among different database applications.

Single interface. The browser becomes the single interface mechanism for the user to access data stored in a database or information stored in static web pages.

Network transparency. In the Web environment, the network is basically transparent to the user, simplifying database access.

Easily upgradeable. By separating out logic and database services from the client machines, upgrading and administration of multiple platforms in an organization become easier.

Innovative services. Organizations are able to provide services and information in innovative ways to reach potential customers.

Disadvantages   Web-database integration is not without a few disadvantages. Although strong reasons drive the effort to make the database available over the Web, a few disadvantages give rise to some concerns.
   Here is a list of some difficulties that need to be overcome.

Security. Security concerns top the list. Most of the users of a company's website are anonymous, and therefore proper user authentication and secure data transmission require special attention.

Reliability. The Internet, compared to an enterprise's own network, is slow and unreliable. You cannot be sure whether or not the requested information is delivered. Organizations continue to depend on their intranets for critical data.

HTML easy, but limited. Although easy and simple, HTML is limited when it comes to supporting any large and intricate database application.

HTTP limitation. The stateless nature of the protocol requires elaborate methods to provide the continuous sessions needed in a database application.

Performance. Poor performance and slow responses could become real problems because many of the scripts used in the Web environment are written in interpreted, not compiled, languages.

Inadequate tools. The tools for developing database applications to run in the Web environment are immature and lack many significant functionalities.

INTEGRATION APPROACHES

We have reviewed the motivation for integrating Web and database technologies. We have explored architectural options. We have considered the advantages and disadvantages. Now that you are convinced of the importance of the integration, let us look at the feasibility of such an integration. We will now examine the leading approaches for Web-database integration.

Common Gateway Interface (CGI)

You are now familiar with the basic functionalities of the browser and the Web server. The browser can request for Web documents stored in files, and the server can dispense these precoded HTML documents to the browser. The Web server can read files but cannot write to them. The Web server is intended to read HTML documents but not data from multiple types of sources. Apart from providing static web pages, the Web server cannot customize web pages or satisfy a request for data from a database.

Consider a simple Web application. A simple form is presented to the browser for the user to fill in the name and address. All that is required is for the name and address to be stored at the website and a confirmation message sent back to the user addressing him or her by the first name. The Web server by itself is not equipped to complete even such a simple transaction.

Some other interface is needed to receive the name and address details from the browser, store those details in a database, embed the user's first name in a web page, and send back the page to the user. A program is needed to interface with the database and store the name and address. The Common Gateway Interface (CGI) is such an interface and a specification for programs to accomplish such tasks.

What is CGI? CGI is a standard method for interfacing Web applications to sources of data. Programs written under CGI specification can retrieve web pages, access database records, build web pages on-the-fly, send e-mails, and so on. A CGI program can read and write data files; the Web server can only read them. A browser sends information to the server, and the server passes on the information to a CGI program that sends its output to the server, which in turn sends the requested information to the browser. A CGI program does not communicate with the browser directly but through the Web server. CGI is a standard method for a Web server and a CGI program to communicate. CGI defines the standard for a browser to communicate through the server with a CGI program executing on the server machine.

Figure 19-7 illustrates the CGI methodology. Note how CGI provides a generic, standard method to interface with multiple types of data sources.

A CGI program may be written in any of the different programming languages such as C/C++ or Perl. With regard to processing logic, a CGI program is just like any other program. The essential difference lies in the way a CGI program receives information from the Web server and sends information back to the server. CGI programs are generally referred to as scripts.

When a URL from the browser points to a HTML page in a file, the Web server fetches that page and sends it to the browser. On the other hand, if a URL points to a program, the server starts that program. Let us say that the URL from the

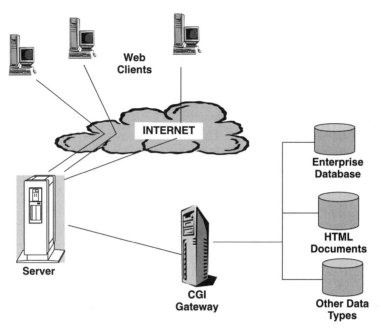

Figure 19-7   The CGI methodology.

browser points to a CGI script, then the Web server prepares certain environment variables to indicate the state of the server, directs the browser input to the script's STDIN, and launches the script. At the completion of its execution, the script places its output in its STDOUT. The server passes on the output in the script's STDOUT to the browser. STDIN and STDOUT are mnemonics for standard input and standard output, two predefined data stream or file handlers for each process. The CGI specification calls for the Web server to pass information to a script through its STDIN and to receive information from a script through its STDOUT.

Just one more detail about the information sent back from the execution of the CGI script is worthwhile to note. The server does not know what type of output is being sent to the browser from the execution of the CGI script. The CGI script could have created a plain text file, a text file with graphics, an image file, and so on. This information about the nature of the output must be communicated to the browser. So a CGI script includes a header with information about the type of page contents.

How CGI works   Let us consider how CGI applies to a Web environment and trace the execution of a Web transaction.
Here are the broad steps:

1. The browser displays an HTML page containing an input form.
2. The user enters data into the form and clicks the submit button.
3. Sometimes, a script in the browser itself may perform client-side editing and validation of the data filled into the form.
4. The browser decodes the URL and contacts the server.

5. The browser requests the file containing the HTML page from the server.
6. The server translates the URL into a path and file name.
7. The server notes that the URL points to a program and not a static file.
8. The server prepares the environment, creates the environment variables, places user input in STDIN, and launches the script.
9. The script begins execution, reads the environment variables, and gets input from STDIN.
10. At the conclusion of the execution, the script sends proper headers to STDOUT.
11. The script places its output in STDOUT.
12. The script terminates.
13. The Web server recognizes the termination of the script and closes the connection to the browser.
14. The browser displays the output from the script.

Advantages of CGI   CGI has become the de facto standard for communication of external applications with Web servers. The following is a listing of advantages offered by CGI.

Generic interface. Provides a generic interface between Web servers and user-designed applications accessing various types of data sources.

Simplicity. The only requirement for any program to be CGI-compliant is to conform to the method for passing information to and from the script.

Coding in any language. CGI programs may be coded with any of the several programming languages.

Server independence. A CGI program can be written in such a way that it will execute without modification on any server running on the same operating system.

Platform independence. A CGI program can be kept portable by using a commonly available language and avoiding platform-specific code.

Problems with CGI   CGI scripts tend to impose a heavy burden on Web servers. The scripts are separate programs. The server process must initiate a new task for every CGI script launched. Consider an enormously popular website. The Web server will be launching numerous scripts for execution. Each task initiated by every script uses system resources such as memory, disk space, and slices of processor time. When many scripts have to execute almost simultaneously, the server can be quickly bogged down. When scripts become large and complex, they take longer to load and execute.

The Web server may also become a serious communications bottleneck. The communication between a client and the database server must always go through the Web server. The problem gets worse as the number of simultaneously executing scripts increases. Every time a request is made by a Web client to a database server and every time a result is conveyed by the database server to the client, the Web server must convert an HTML document into data or vice versa.

A CGI-based approach lacks efficiency and does not provide transaction support. Essentially, this approach is not able to shake off the limitation of statelessness of HTTP. Even repeated requests from the same user require logon and logout every time.

CGI and Web-Database Integration To what extent does CGI enable the integration of the database into the Web environment? How exactly does CGI support database applications on the Web?

Take the example of a user filling in a form on a web page at the client side. The browser transfers the information to the Web server, which in turn passes on the information to the CGI script while launching it. Suppose the scenario is like this: The Web server sends the blank web page containing the form to the browser to display the blank form to the user. The transaction is completed, and the server ends the connection. The form is expected to be filled in and sent back to the Web server so that the server can pass on the information to the CGI script for further action. However, if the user does not complete the mandatory fields on the form, the CGI script is unable to display a warning box and refuse to accept the incomplete input on the form. Applications of this nature require extending interaction with the users. The difficulties caused by the statelessness of HTTP persist even when adopting CGI.

For simple direct queries against the database, CGI seems to be useful. CGI provides a useful interface to the database server. For example, if you want to know the current status of the parcel you sent through a shipping company, you can log on to the company's website, type in your tracking number and send it to the Web server. The tracking number is supplied to the CGI script, and the script is launched. The CGI program retrieves the current status of the parcel from a database and sends the information to the browser through the Web server. If the transaction is meant to end here without any further interaction, then CGI is helpful. CGI provides a generic way to interface with the database server and send back the information to the browser. The Web browser, just by itself, could not accomplish this. To get around fundamental problems arising out of the stateless nature of HTTP, some methods other than CGI must be explored.

As you have already noted, performance could be a major concern while working with CGI. Each request requires an additional process to be created. This places an enormous overhead on the server when the number of on-line requests peaks during the day.

Application Programming Interface (API)

To overcome the performance problems encountered while adopting CGI, one approach is to extend the functionality of Web servers. Servers can be changed and enhanced to provide application programming interfaces. Such enhancements or extensions are known as non-CGI gateways. An application programming interface (API) offers an interfacing technique between the Web server and a database application at the back end based on shared objects and dynamic linking. This technique avoids the need to create a separate process for each execution of a script, as in the case of CGI.

Here are the major advantages of server extensions through APIs:

- Scripts performing database operations are loaded as part of the server; therefore, back-end applications can fully utilize the input and output functions of the server.
- Only one copy of the application script needs to be loaded and shared among multiple requests to the server from browsers.
- Through an authentication layer asking for user ID and password, in addition to the browser's own security schemes, the web page or website may be protected.
- Passes information out to browsers in additional ways, not possible by unextended servers.
- Tracks more information by logging incoming and outgoing activities at the server.

However, the API approach poses certain difficulties. It is a lot more complex than the CGI method. Using APIs effectively calls for special programming knowledge and skills. Adding proprietary APIs may introduce potential risks. The normal functioning of the server is being changed, and that could introduce unknown problems. The most practical difficulty relates to portability. APIs are completely proprietary and therefore reduce the portability of the server using such APIs.

Web-Database Integration: CGI vs. API   Both CGI and API extend the functionality of the Web server so that back-end database applications may communicate with the browser through the server. Although these approaches tend to produce similar results, they essentially differ in the way each approach makes the communication possible and in the efficiency with which they accomplish it. Let us summarize these two points.

Communication Method   CGI establishes communication in a restrictive manner. A CGI program can communicate with the server according to specifications through one or more variables. It executes when the Web server interprets a request from the browser and launches it. After execution, the CGI script returns the results to the server. That is the way a CGI program can communicate—take information from the Web server and return information to the server. Only the server can send the information to the browser.

Contrast this to how communication is carried out in the API approach. An application program can intercept information sent by the browser to the server before the server even reads the information. The program can revise the intercepted information and send the information, as revised, back to the browser without the direct involvement of the browser. Additionally, an API-based program can also perform operations based on requests from the server just as a CGI script can.

Performance   API-based extensions run as part of the server; they are loaded into the same address space as the Web server. As you know, for each execution of a

CGI script, a separate process needs to be created on the server. The API approach consumes a great deal less memory and performs a whole lot better than running CGI scripts.

Server-Side Includes (SSI)

When a browser requests for a file, the Web server just fetches the file based on the URL and simply sends the file over to the browser. Normally, the server just verifies that the user is authorized to receive the file and simply hands over the file without looking at it.

Typically, graphics are included in the web page and sent to the browser. It is the browser that scans the web page received, scans and interprets the contents, and takes action. This process of scanning and interpretation, known as parsing, usually takes place on the client side of the system.

If the server can be made to do the parsing of the web page before it sends it on to the browser, then we can make the server take action based on what the server finds on the web page. Instead of the server blindly passing on a web page to the browser, the server can parse and interpret the page first. This process of the server doing the parsing is called server-side include (SSI).

Initially, SSI was used to include other files in addition to the one requested in the web page sent to the browser. This information to include other files is embedded in the web page. The server parses the web page first, notes the indication to include other files, and then includes the other files as part of the information sent back to the browser. Under SSI, generally, the end result conveyed to the browser is in the form of text.

SSI commands are embedded like comments within regular HTML pages. Therefore, like comments, all SSI commands begin with the characters <!—# and end with the characters — >. The following command directs the inclusion of the file containing the current address in a web page:

<!—# include file = "currentaddress.htm — >.

Embedding SSI commands as comments makes it easy to implement SSI. HTML pages with SSI commands are still portable. Any server that does not support SSI does not parse and interpret the commands; it simply passes on the commands to the browser; the browser simply ignores the commands as though they are comments.

Each vendor of Web servers may implement SSI in a proprietary fashion. There is no standard governing SSI; each vendor is free to implement SSI as it chooses. However, most vendors follow the basic SSI specifications outlined by NCSA, which maintain these general rules.

As you have noted, with SSI, you can include files in a Web document. But SSI can accomplish many other actions. You can include special commands to report the size of a file or the date when it was last modified. You may require the current date to be presented. You may embed a special command to send an e-mail to a given address.

Although you accomplish a number of different actions with SSI, what we are interested is database integration with the Web and how SSI enables this integration. A special SSI command relates to the execution of a subprogram similar to a CGI script. On parsing and recognizing this command, a Web server can initiate the execution of a subprogram and include its result in the web page to be delivered to the browser. And this subprogram can be a script to access a database, perform database operations, and produce results from the database.

Cookies

As we have mentioned several times in our previous discussions, HTTP is a stateless protocol. But for interactive applications such as database applications, the application program must know whether a transaction is part of an interactive session. As you know, under HTTP, the Web server maintains no state information. That is, when a user contacts a website through an URL submitted at the client site using a browser, the Web server does not know whether this is the user's first visit or thirtieth visit.

For example, in an electronic shopping encounter, the application program must know which shopping cart belongs to whom. Let us say that the database table representing a shopping cart with three items so far stores the user's name and password that came in as part of the registration. Now the user returns to the website through the browser to add a fourth item. Because of the stateless nature of HTTP, the server has no idea whether the user has returned for a fourth time or this is a brand new first visit. Any CGI script interfacing with the database server cannot receive any state information from the Web server.

Let us stop the discussion right here. Imagine that when the user returns to the website, the CGI script is able to request the browser for a file stored at the browser site containing user registration information. Suppose from the registration file received, the script is able to determine that the user is the same person with a virtual shopping cart with three items. Then this file stored at the browser end somehow is able to maintain state to the extent required by the shopping cart application. This small text file stored on the Web client system is known as a cookie (just called cookie for no valid reason). More formally, these files are referred to as persistent client state HTTP cookies. A cookie may persist at a client site for many months or even years.

How Cookies Work The use of cookies makes CGI scripts more interactive. A cookie is a small file created by a CGI script and stored at the browser site. In its simplest form, a cookie consists of a name-value pair. A developer may choose any such pair to create a cookie. More advanced implementations include expiration dates and restrictions on which Web pages can see the cookie as part of the cookie definition.

In our electronic shopping example, when the user visits the website to begin shopping, the CGI script creates a cookie, perhaps consisting of name and password as the name-value pair, and sends it to the user's browser. The browser receives the cookie and stores it on the hard drive at the client site. At a later time, when the user goes back to add items to the shopping cart, the CGI script requests for the cookie from the client side and compares with the registration information stored in the database during the previous visit. Based on the results of the comparison, the interaction proceeds further.

Some Limitations Usually, a special cookie file stores cookies on the user's computer system. Therefore, cookies are vulnerable to the whims of the user's actions. Accidentally or willfully, the user may delete the cookie file. Again, if the cookie file is not large enough or if the browser imposes restrictions on the size and number of cookie files, older cookies may be overwritten with later ones. Also, if you switch browsers, the cookies stored by the earlier browser will be lost.

Another drawback relates to name and password information stored in a cookie file. This information is usually not encrypted and therefore could cause serious problems. As a user, you are not aware of the cookies being stored on your computer's hard drive. Some browsers may be configured to alert users when cookies are being stored. Some browsers allow you to prevent any cookies from being set on your computer system at all.

Use of Java Applications

As most IT professionals know, Java is a proprietary programming language developed by Sun Microsystems. Java has been designed and developed to be completely portable. It is a "write-once, run anywhere" language. A few attributes of Java are that it is simple, object-oriented, distributed, interpreted, robust, secure, architecture-neutral, portable, high-performance, multithreaded, and dynamic.

Java's portability represents its greatest strength. It is machine-independent. For most programming languages, first you need to establish the processor and operating system on which the completed program will be running. After compiling, the linker must prepare the executable object file with components from the operating system libraries. The whole process is different for a Java program.

The Java compiler generates a file of bytecodes, called a class file. These are instructions of the Java Virtual Machine (JVM). JVM does not physically exist; however, JVM (interpreter and runtime system) may be ported to any kind of computer. You can load a class file to any computer with JVM. The Java program will run on the JVM of that computer. Therefore, a Java program is totally portable. Figure 19-8 presents the components of the Java programming environment.

Well, what has the portability of Java to do with Web computing? Currently, all available browsers have embedded JVM. Therefore, a Java program can run any computer with a browser. That includes an enormous number of and many types of computer systems. Java is generally accepted as the preferred programming language for applications on the Web. Using Java, you can build Web applications, called applets, and server applications, known as servlets.

Applets. These are Java programs that are embedded in an HTML page. A Java-enabled browser executes an applet. The browser applies its own JVM interpreter to execute the bytecode of an applet. Applets are generally written to enhance the user interface and add dynamic content to HTML pages.

Servlets. These add functionality to Web servers. Whereas an applet executes on the browser, a servlet runs on the server. A servlet may connect to database servers, process the application, and return the results in a web page.

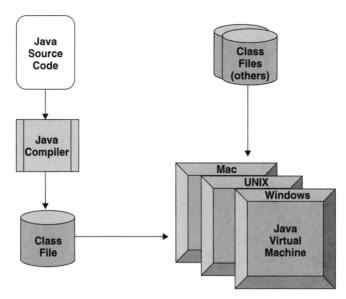

Figure 19-8   Java programming environment.

JDBC   JDBC (Java Database Connectivity) bases its structure on ODBC (Open Database Connectivity), commonly used to provide interfaces between application programs and any type of ODBC-compliant database systems. JDBC is the most effective approach for Java programs to access relational database systems. JDBC allows you to write Java programs that would work with any database system that has a JDBC driver. The driver provides a uniform interface to a Java program irrespective of the type of database system. Most database vendors offer JDBC drivers for use with their products.

The JDBC method involves two components for the API—one on the side of the program and the other on the side of the database server. A Java program can use the JDBC API to establish a connection to the database server through a pure Java JDBC driver at the database server side.

Here are the common options for the connectivity:

Driver with Direct Connection   In this method, the pure Java JDBC driver establishes a direct connection with the database server. JDBC calls are converted into the network protocol used by the DBMS, enabling a direct call from the client machine to the database server. This seems to be a practical approach for database access on the organization's intranet.

Driver Connecting Through Middleware   In this method, JDBC calls are converted into the protocol of the middleware vendor and subsequently translated into the DBMS protocol by the middleware server. Because the middleware provides connectivity to a number of database systems, this method has flexibility.

The JDBC-ODBC Bridge   This method provides JDBC access through ODBC drivers. ODBC code is required to be loaded on a client machine that adopts this

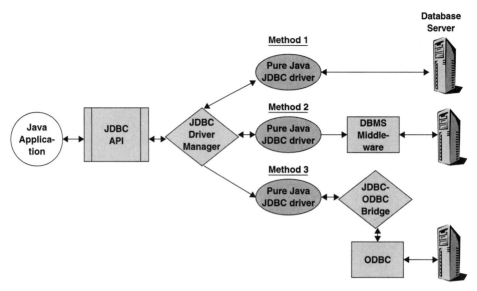

Figure 19-9 JDBC approaches.

approach. Because ODBC has become the de facto standard for database access, this is a popular method.

Figure 19-9 illustrates these three approaches of using JDBC. In each case, note the layers through which interface between a Java application program and a database system is established.

Use of Scripting Languages

This is another method for providing database functionality to browsers and servers. JavaScript from Netscape and JScript from Microsoft are the commonly used scripting languages. JavaScript resembles Java in its structure. Another popular scripting language is VBScript from Microsoft. The syntax of VBScript is more like that of Visual Basic than Java.

A script written in any of these languages may be embedded in the HTML and downloaded every time the page is accessed. The scripting languages are interpreted, not compiled. Therefore, they are well suited for small applications.

Scripts executing on the browser have objectives similar to applets written in the Java language. Figure 19-10 presents a comparison between client-side JavaScript and Java applets.

JavaScript on the Server Side On the server side, JavaScript can perform the functions related to database operations, as listed below:

- Establish connection to a database.
- Begin database query or transaction.
- Retrieve data requested in the query or perform database operations included in the transaction such as inserts, updates, or deletes.

	Java Applets	Java Script
Code Generation	Compiled on server	Interpreted by client
HTML integration	Separate – accessed from HTML documents	Integrated and embedded in HTML documents
Data typing	Strong typing	Loose typing
Binding	Static binding	Dynamic binding
Object technology	Object-oriented – with classes and inheritance	Object-based – no classes or inheritance
Updates	No automatic write to hard disk	No automatic write to hard disk

Figure 19-10   Java applets and JavaScript: comparison.

- Commit or abort and roll back a transaction according to the conditions.
- Display results of a query.
- Where necessary, access multimedia content from the database in the form of BLOBs (binary large objects).
- Terminate connection from the database.

Database Tools

We have examined various techniques of integrating databases into the Web environment. We covered different techniques for extending browser and server functionalities to access databases on the Web. Let us now briefly consider a few third-party tools that enable the creation of Web applications and linking them to databases. Only a few tools work with any type of database systems. Some of them are proprietary, geared toward specific DBMSs. Therefore, the tool you would want to use depends on a few significant factors such as:

- The database you are using
- The platform where your Web server and database server are running
- The technique for database access—CGI or proprietary API
- Cost considerations
- Maturity of the tool
- Vendor stability

Now, let us selectively review a few tools without getting into details. The discussion is simply meant to pique your interest and prompt you to be open to the possibility of using such tools in your database environment.

ColdFusion   Created by Allaire, ColdFusion enables the writing of scripts within an HTML document. ColdFusion executes the scripts and returns results within the HTML document. The tool works with every Web server running on Windows NT and interfaces with every SQL engine using ODBC.

Figure 19-11 presents the working of ColdFusion.

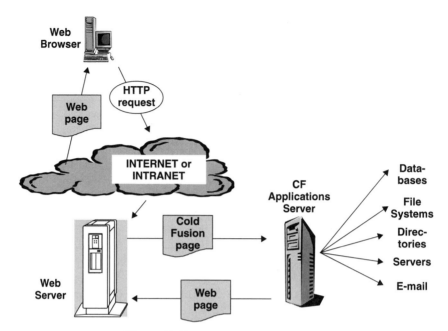

Figure 19-11 How ColdFusion works.

Active Server Pages The Active Server Platform is Microsoft's response to server-side application development. You can develop on the server side with HTML, scripts, and software modules such as Java applets and ActiveX server components. Several Microsoft server technologies, including Transaction Server and Proxy Server, are available to implement applications.

You can develop Active Server Pages (ASP) with the same set of components used for client-side scripting. This means that you can combine Java applets and Active Server components within your ASP script using scripting languages such as JavaScript, Jscript, or VBScript.

Browser Capabilities Component (BCC) and Active Data Object (ADO) are two important precreated and tested components that are used widely. With BCC you can detect the type of browser and create the kind of HTML pages the browser can handle. ADO, a more useful component, works with your server-side scripts and enables you to access databases and embed the query results in a dynamic web page.

The following indicates the sequence of actions:

Server-side Active Server Page script communicates an SQL query to ADO.

ADO passes query to database server.

Database server processes query.

Database server sends query results to ADO.

ADO returns query results to the ASP script.

Script uses query results to generate dynamic web page and sends it to browser.

Other Tools Here are few other tools that are also available for Web-database integration. The names of the tools and the website addresses are indicated below.

PHP	http://www.php.net/
W3-mSQL	http://www.hughes.com.au/software/w3-msql.htm
MsqlPerl	ftp://Bond.edu.au/pub/Minerva/msql/Contrib/
MsqlJava	http://mama.minmet.uq.oz.au/msqljava/
WDB	http://arch-http.hq.eso.org/wdb/html/wdb.html
Web/Genera	http://gdbdoc.gdb.org/letovsky/genera/
MORE	http://rbse.jsc.nasa.gov:81/DEMO/
DBI	http://www.hermetica.com/technologia/DBI/
DBGateway	http://fcim1.csdc.com/

SECURITY OPTIONS

In Chapter 16, we discussed database security in detail. We covered security administration. You are aware of the security risks and the general methods of protecting the organization's database system. Now, when your database is integrated with the Web, the security concerns intensify. The Internet is traditionally an open network. The underlying protocols, TCP/IP and HTTP, are not designed for security. Any packet-sniffing software can easily retrieve sensitive data from the open network.

First, we will explore the types of security vulnerabilities and the challenges. After that, we will broadly examine a few significant security options.

Significance of Protection

Several times so far we have reviewed examples from electronic shopping. After filling the virtual shopping cart, let us say, the user is ready to pay with a credit card. When the user enters the credit card data and finishes the transaction, data transmission to the server begins. The credit card details are part of the transmission. Any ordinary packet-sniffing software can detect the details and siphon out the information. In the Web environment, protection must be addressed at different levels.

At Each Tier   Information transmitted over the public network moves around and halts at each of the tiers in a three-tier architecture. Protection of information must be addressed at the client, at the Web server, and also at the database server. This requires the use of suitable techniques and security products.

Special Concerns at Client Machine   As you have seen, in the Web environment, information transmitted to the client may contain executable code. An HTML page transmitted to the browser may have embedded JavaScript or VBScript or one or more Java applets. These are coming from, perhaps, an unknown server and are likely to cause damages including the following on the client machine:

- Corrupt data.
- Delete or reformat entire disks.
- Steal user identification and password, and impersonate user in other computer systems on the client machine.

- Download confidential and sensitive data.
- Disrupt output devices.
- Lock up resources and render them unavailable to authorized users.
- Shut down the system totally.

Information Exchange Challenges Security protection must ensure that sending and receiving information over the Internet conform to the following safeguards:

- Information specifically transmitted from one person to another is not available to anyone else.
- Information is not modified in transmission.
- The receiver of information is sure that it actually came from the sender as identified.
- The sender is sure that the receiver is authentic.
- The sender is unable to deny that he or she sent the information.

Firewalls, Wrappers, and Proxies

This is a set of defense mechanisms to protect data that are vulnerable over the Internet. Let us briefly survey these.

Firewall A firewall may be implemented with software, hardware, or both. It is meant to prevent unauthorized access to a private network. Most commonly, a firewall is used for protecting an organization's intranet from the Internet by keeping unauthorized users outside. All messages from outside the intranet are intercepted and checked.

Figure 19-12 illustrates the placement of firewall in conjunction with an intranet. Note how users are grouped within and outside the firewall.

Let us discuss how firewalls provide protection.

An IP Packet This is the basic unit for moving information across a TCP/IP network. All information exchange consists of a set of IP packets. The address components in each packet that ensure proper delivery are destination IP address, protocol, destination port number, source IP address, and source port number.

A Network Session A session may be thought of as comprising a set of IP packets sent between the initiation and completion of a request. Therefore, a set of IP packets with the same address information represents a session. A given network application may extend to several sessions to perform its service.

Standard Firewall Services Three major services are usually provided:

Access control. Using information filtered about an IP packet or a network session and matching it against the security policy of the organization, the firewall decides to let the packet pass or deny passage.

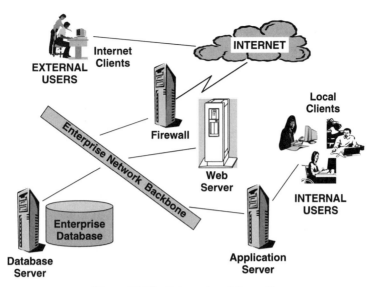

Figure 19-12   Intranet and firewalls.

Activity logging. A good firewall system logs all successful and failed attempts through it. This information is valuable for tracking any intruders and determining the extent of any inflicted damage.

Alarm function. In some firewall systems, the administrator can set an alarm to trigger a special event if an intruder tries to gain access to sensitive data.

Firewall Filtering Techniques   The following are common techniques offered:

Packet filter. Matches key fields within an IP packet against defined rules and either passes the packet on or drops it. Dropped packets are discarded. Because packet filters have no concept of the session, this method is vulnerable to spoofing. Also, packet filters are difficult to configure.

Session filter. Retaining information on all active sessions through the firewall, a session filter determines whether packets flowing in the opposite direction belong to an approved connection. A session filter also performs session auditing.

Application-Level Gateway. This is a mechanism to apply interception rules to specific applications such as Telnet or FTP services.

Circuit-Level Gateway. This is a high-level protection mechanism applied when a TCP connection is made. Once the connection is authorized, packets can flow between computer systems without further verifications.

Wrappers   Although firewalls are effective in keeping intruders from outside, they can do very little to prevent unauthorized access from within. Wrappers form the second line of defense. A wrapper runs as a surrounding layer of software, wrapping around other software.

For example, if a user is attempting to do a file transfer to you through FTP, the user will first get a wrapper that would then engage FTP. The wrapper is transparent to the user. Wrappers offer a lot of flexibility. Wrappers can act like firewalls and can refuse access based on the user sign on. Also, wrappers can give indications on how the security system is working because they log all accesses. Another interesting use for wrappers is the creation of blind alleys that can help trap intruders.

Proxy Servers   A proxy server is a computer system placed between a browser and a Web server. The proxy server intercepts all requests to the server and determines whether the request can be approved. First, the proxy server makes a determination of whether it could fulfill the request by itself. If not, and if the request is legitimate, the proxy server passes on the request to the Web server.

By saving the results of requests for a certain period, a proxy server is able to fulfill requests without sending them to the regular Web server. In this way, proxy servers can improve performance.

Proxy servers can effectively hide the actual location of data. For example, proxy servers can point to other proxy servers. The actual data can sit far away from the server itself. A local or remote browser connects to a server. But the server can forward the request to another server, and the second server can forward the request to a third server, and so on. The client cannot know where exactly the data come from.

A separate proxy server can be assigned to each major service such as Telnet, FTP, and so on. By doing this, you can route requests accordingly and distribute server loads to different physical machines. In addition to the benefit of data hiding, you also benefit from reduced load on the servers.

Digital Signatures and Digital Certificates

First, try to understand what a message digest algorithm is. Take a message in the form of an arbitrary string and generate a fixed-length string of bits, called a digest of the original message. An algorithm that can generate such a digest is known as a message digest algorithm. No two messages can generate the same digest. The digest gives no clues about the original message. We now proceed to the application of message digests.

Digital Signatures   Similar to regular handwritten signatures, digital signatures can be used to verify the origin of a message. A digital signature consists of two parts: a bit string computed from the data that are being signed and the private key of the signatory (an individual user or an organization).

Here are the main features of digital signatures:

- You can verify the authenticity of a digital signature by applying a computation based on the corresponding public key of the user.
- No one can forge a digital signature provided the private key has been kept secret, as required.

- A digital signature is computed for the data that are signed. So a particular digital signature cannot be alleged to be for some other data.
- A signed piece of information cannot be changed. Otherwise, the digital signature will not apply to the piece of information any longer.

Parts of some digital signatures are generated by using message digest algorithms.

Digital Certificates These refer to another security mechanism. A recognized Certificate Authority (CA) issues digital certificates.

Let us say that Mary wants to send a secure electronic message to Bob. She applies to the CA for a digital certificate. The CA issues an encrypted digital certificate containing Mary's public key and additional identification information. The CA's own public key is widely known through printed documents or on the Internet. Mary sends the digital certificate as an attachment to the electronic message to Bob. In this arrangement, the recipient of a message confirms the proper receipt of the message by means of a response.

What happens next?

Bob receives the message and the digital certificate. He uses the CA's public key, decodes the digital certificate, verifies that it was really issued by the CA, and gets the sender's public key and identification encrypted in the certificate. Bob can send back an encrypted response to Mary. In effect, Bob is able to verify that the message that appeared to have been sent by Mary really was from her.

Digital certificates have their application in monetary transactions such as large fund transfers. In this security scheme, you must have noted that the CA plays a key role acting as an intermediary between the sender and the recipient of a message. What if a fraudulent person tries to forge or pose as someone else or tries to bribe the CA? Other additional restrictions exist to thwart the deceptive schemes of the cleverest imposter.

Kerberos In passing, let us note the use of Kerberos in security administration. Kerberos is a secured server keeping user names and password in strictest confidentiality. It provides one central security server for all data and network resources. In a sense, Kerberos provides a function similar to that of the Certificate Authority—authenticate a user. Incidentally, the term Kerberos refers to a three-headed monster in Greek mythology that guards the gate of Hell.

SET and SST

Have you ever provided your credit card information on the Internet? The Secure Electronic Transactions (SET) protocol governs the processing of credit card transactions over the Internet. It is an open, interoperable standard created jointly by Visa, MasterCard, Microsoft, and a few other organizations. The protocol ensures security for credit card transactions and keeps these simple.

To ensure privacy requirements, the actions in a transaction are split in such a way that neither the merchant nor the credit card company has all the pieces of the information about the transaction. SET uses digital certificates for certifying a credit cardholder as well as for confirming the relationship between the merchant and the credit card company.

Visa and Microsoft, major players in the development of SET, have since provided Secure Transaction Technology (SST). This technology enables bank payments over the Internet to be secure.

SSL and S-HTTP

Netscape developed the Secure Sockets Layer (SSL) protocol for transmitting private documents over the Internet in a secured manner. Many websites use this standard to obtain confidential information such as credit card numbers. The protocol prevents tampering, forgery, and eavesdropping by unauthorized persons.

SSL is layered between services like FTP, Telnet, and HTTP and the TCP/IP connection sessions. It guarantees a secure connection between a client and a server. Once a secure connection is established, the server can transmit any amount of confidential information to the client over the safe connection. SSL verifies that the client and server networks are valid, provides data encryption using a private key encryption method, and ensures that the message does not contain any embedded commands or programs.

Secure HTTP (S-HTTP) offers a different method to transmit data securely from the server to the client. This protocol, a revised version of HTTP, allows single messages to be transmitted securely. Enterprise Integration Technologies (EIT) developed S-HTTP.

SSL and S-HTTP both enable secure transmission of confidential information over the Internet—SSL establishes a safe connection, and S-HTTP safeguards individual messages. Therefore, one method complements the other. In effect, both technologies offer the following functions:

- Enable authentication between a browser and a server
- Allow website administrators to control access selectively over specific services
- Permit a browser and a server to share confidential information while keeping others away from the protected transmission
- Ensure reliability of transmitted information, preventing accidental interruption or corruption

Java Security

You know that Java applets, embedded in a web page and transmitted from the Web server to the browser, execute on the client machine. This is unlike a known program executing on your computer. As a user on the client machine, you may not know where the executable code is coming from. Perhaps, if the applet needs local resources to execute, it will ask for permission through the browser. You may grant permission or deny permission to execute. But even if you know the source of the web page containing the applet, you cannot be completely sure. Nevertheless, you must allow a useful applet to execute and still maintain a level of trust. Network applications cannot be operational if you unequivocally deny permission to any outside programs to do useful work on your client machine. This is the crux of Java security.

What can be done? Are there any guidelines to permit applets to execute on the client machine but ensure that no damages are caused? The following are general guidelines:

- List all possible scenarios of malicious actions that could cause damages.
- Analyze and reduce the list into a basic set of wicked actions.
- Design an architecture and language protection mechanism that prevent the basic set of malicious actions.
- Test and prove that the architecture and the language are secure.
- Include flexibility in the design to accommodate any additional type of malicious actions.

Let us try to list the common types of damages that may be caused by malicious actions.

- Applet starts a process that depletes all system resources and brings the client machine to a halt.
- Application locks the browser.
- Applet tampers with the browser's Domain Name Service (DNS).
- Applet destroys other applications trying to load.
- Applet damages or deletes files on the client machine.
- Installs back door access into your network for future unauthorized entry.
- Accesses confidential files and give access privileges to other unauthorized users.
- Assumes your identity and impersonates you for the purpose of attacking other computer systems.

What about the major strength of Java—its portability? If a Java program can run on any computing platform, obviously, Java security cannot rely on security provisions in any operating system. So, safety and security provisions in Java have to be self-contained. Security and safety are, therefore, integral parts of the design of the language. The sandbox concept ensures that no undependable, malicious program can gain access. For this purpose, Java security is implemented using three components: class loader, bytecode verifier, and security manager. Figure 19-13 illustrates Java security implementation.

The three components work together and ensure the following safeguards:

- Only the proper classes are loaded.
- Each class is in the proper format.
- Undependable classes are not permitted to execute dangerous instructions.
- Undependable classes are not allowed to access system resources.

Class Loader A Java-enabled or Java-aware browser invokes the class loader to verify the format and load the incoming applet. The class loader defines a namespace for the particular web page. An executing JVM allows multiple class loaders

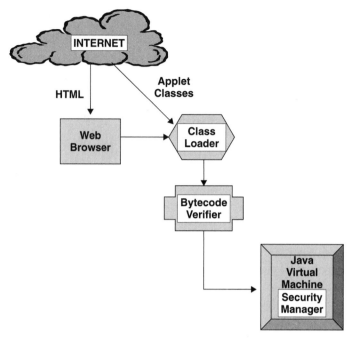

Figure 19-13   Java security.

to be active simultaneously, each with its own namespace. Classes loaded as part of one applet are not allowed to access other classes, although these can access classes in standard Java libraries.

Namespaces are organized in a hierarchical manner, allowing JVM to organize classes based on the origin—local or remote. A class loader does not permit a class from a less protected namespace to replace a class with a more protected name-space. Consider the file system's I/O primitives. These are defined in a local Java class. Therefore, the file system's I/O primitives cannot be invoked or replaced by classes from outside the local machine.

Bytecode Verifier   The JVM does not allow an applet to run before the bytecode verifier checks its bytecode completely. The bytecode verifier makes the assumption that the code is designed to crash the system and intends to violate security. From this perspective, the bytecode verifier conducts a series of checks, including the execution of a sophisticated theorem prover to negate its assumption. The theorem prover ensures that the applet does not forge pointers, bypass access restrictions, or perform illegal conversion of objects.

Specifically, verification by the bytecode verifier ensures the following:

- Compiled code is correctly formatted.
- Internal stacks will not overflow or underflow—traditionally how programmers breach security.
- No illegal conversions, such as integer to pointer, will occur.
- Bytecode instructions are correctly typed.

- Every class member access is valid.
- The applet cannot create disasters in its own namespace.

Security Manager The security manager performs the final set of checks. The security manager is responsible to preserve thread integrity—to ensure that code in one group of threads does not interfere with code in another group, even if the two groups belong to the same parent applet.

The security manager watches out for dangerous operations that could cause potential damages. The security manager monitors such operations closely. Every time the applet wants to perform any such operation, it must gain permission from the security manager. Specifically, the security manager must concur with attempts by the applet to access any of the following:

- Network communications
- Protected information including the hard drive or private data
- Programs and processes at the level of the operating system
- The class loader
- Libraries of Java classes

Generally, an applet is prevented from the following actions:

- Loading libraries
- Defining method calls
- Starting other programs on the client
- Reading or writing files on the client machine
- Making network connections to machines other than the one from where the applet emanated

CHAPTER SUMMARY

- Static web pages are no longer adequate for today's information requirements; Web and database technologies had to be integrated.
- The basics: the Internet is a collection of interconnected networks; a URL acts as an address on the Web; you use HTML to create web pages; HTTP is the object-oriented protocol for exchanging web pages.
- A static web page displays the same information every time it is accessed; a dynamic web page customizes and shows changed content based on requests.
- HTML is simple and straightforward but has many inadequacies. XML overcomes the deficiencies and provides a better solution.
- An intranet is a private network based on the communication standards of the public Internet. An extranet is open to selective access by users outside an organization.
- The Web has become the cornerstone of electronic commerce. Databases are the centerpieces of electronic commerce. Web-database integration makes electronic commerce possible.

- CGI is a common approach for integrating Web and database technologies.
- APIs extend the functionality of the Web server and enables Web-database integration more efficiently than CGI.
- With SSI, you can include files in a Web document; SSI can also accomplish other functions including special commands.
- Cookies make CGI scripts more interactive. A cookie is a small file created as a CGI script and stored at the browser site.
- Using Java language, you can build Web applications called applets and server applications known as servlets.
- JDBC is an effective approach for Java programs to access relational databases.
- Security options for Web-based databases: firewalls, wrappers, and proxies. Other security mechanisms: digital signatures, digital certificates, SET, SST, SSL, and S-HTTP.
- Java language offers security through three components: class loader, bytecode verifier, and security manager.

REVIEW QUESTIONS

1. Name the four stages or phases of information exchange under HTTP.
2. Compare and contrast static and dynamic web pages.
3. What are intranets and extranets? List any three of their major benefits.
4. List any six types of routine security functions.
5. State any four reasons for integrating an organization's database with its website.
6. Are there any disadvantages of Web-database integration? If so, list any three.
7. What is CGI? List its main advantages.
8. What is an API? How is it different from CGI?
9. How do scripting languages enable the provision of database functionality to browsers and servers?
10. Describe very briefly the three security components of Java.

EXERCISES

1. Match the columns:
   1. URL   A. hide actual location of data
   2. SSI   B. Java's security component
   3. cookie   C. tool for Web-database integration
   4. servlets   D. Internet reference address
   5. ColdFusion   E. Web-enabled private network
   6. wrappers   F. server parses and interprets a web page
   7. proxy servers   G. add functionality to Web servers

8. SSL   H. second line of security mechanism
9. class loader   I. small file stored at browser site
10. intranet   J. guarantees secure connection

2. Describe the major features of HTML. What are its advantages and disadvantages?

3. Describe briefly any three approaches to Web-database integration. Compare their relative merits and shortcomings.

4. What are firewalls? Describe their purpose and functions.

5. A major manufacturing company producing passive electronic components wants to place its database on its extranet for use by its distributors to check stock and place orders. Prepare a general plan for implementing the integration of Web and database technologies at this company. List all the major technologies to be used for the integration.

CHAPTER 20

TRENDS IN DATABASE TECHNOLOGY

CHAPTER OBJECTIVES

- Get a broad, general overview of the current trends in database technology
- Understand the motivation for going beyond relational DBMSs
- Study the concepts of object orientation in information storage and retrieval
- Note how relational and object technologies are merging into object-relational systems
- Survey the use of database technology to provide business intelligence
- Explore the leading trends in special applications of database technology

Where is the database industry heading? What are the hot research interests? What are the new demands for information? Are organizations hungry for new types of information? Are the purposes and usage of information in the modern enterprise changing? If so, in what ways? What are the leading trends? Having gone through the evolution of data systems and having studied database design and development so far, you would like to explore answers to these questions. Database technology is vibrant and dynamic. It is adapting to the newer paradigms. The technology continues to evolve to address newer information requirements. In this chapter, you will examine these exciting trends; you will understand the leading areas of innovation and progress.

Although we have reviewed data models other than the relational model, our main focus has been on relational database systems. For very good reasons, too. Relational database systems still hold a large share of the database market; most enterprises have adopted them; their strengths and features still make them

Database Design and Development: An Essential Guide for IT Professionals by Paulraj Ponniah
ISBN 0-471-21877-4   Copyright © 2003 by John Wiley and Sons, Inc.

superior compared to earlier data systems. Nevertheless, with newer types of applications, relational database systems tend to fall short on some types of information requirements. For applications dealing with multimedia and spatial data, the relational model is not quite adequate. The relational model limits the types of data that can be defined and used. For engineering, scientific, office information, and high-volume data retrieval systems, we need a more flexible and powerful model than the relational model. The trend is toward extending the functionality of relational database systems or going with a different orientation of data definitions and rules for storage and retrieval. Object-oriented database systems and object-relational systems have emerged to address the inadequacies of relational systems.

Another significant area of interest in business circles relates to business intelligence. Traditionally, for two decades or more, database systems helped organizations run their day-to-day business. With amplified complexity of business conditions and increased data volumes, today's organization cannot perform its business functions without database systems. Although information provided by current database systems supports organizations in running everyday operations, these systems cannot provide information in a form suitable for making strategic decisions. Strategic decisions deal with major and far-reaching issues that help companies set directions, make plans, and improve profitability. Database systems are being adapted and used in business intelligence applications such as data warehousing, data mining, and online analytical processing.

Database systems have also evolved to meet very specific requirements and to be fitted with very specific functionalities. These are special-purpose or special-function database systems. Such database systems, built with special properties and functions, include parallel databases, active databases, intelligent databases, and so on. There are also database systems intended for special purposes or special needs: multimedia databases, mobile databases, geographic databases, and so on. We will cover these kinds of specialized trends.

OBJECT-ORIENTED DATABASES

Let us begin with a broad definition. We may generally describe object orientation as follows: software modeling and development methods that simplify construction of complex systems with individual, reusable components. A main attraction of object orientation consists of the ability to construct applications with standard, reusable components.

What then are object-oriented databases? Object-oriented databases integrate object orientation with database technology. Object orientation enables a more precise, truer depiction of real-world objects. Therefore, object-oriented databases provide a better representation of real-world information requirements than earlier data systems. As you will see, object orientation allows a developer to hide the details of implementation, concentrate on true representation, and share objects usefully. Object-oriented databases combine the features of object orientation such as abstract data typing and distinctive object identities with database capabilities such as persistence, transaction processing, concurrency control, recovery, security, and performance.

Object-oriented databases evolved to address some of the limiting features of relational databases. Although relational databases serve well for many purposes, their specific limitations need to be addressed. Here are a few of the problems that object-oriented databases are intended to address:

- Although recent versions of relational database systems support BLOBs (binary large objects), generally they can handle only limited data types. This is no longer adequate in today's environment. Object-oriented database systems include additional data types. Furthermore, you can also have user-defined data types.
- Object-oriented systems also support user-defined functions. In fact, object orientation combines the definition of data and processes.
- In the relational data model, each normalized relation does not necessarily symbolize a real-world entity completely. You may have to combine two or three normalized relations to actually represent a single entity. The object-oriented data model improves the representation of real-world entities.
- The relational model represents entities and relationship by using a single modeling construct—a relation or table. Although this appears to simplify the representation, in reality, it is difficult to show the distinction between entities and relationships just by using a single modeling construct. You cannot express the distinction with distinguishable constructs. Object-orientation enhances the semantic nature of the data model by providing distinct meanings in the constructs.

Basic Concepts

Several features of object orientation make the concept complete and useful. However, three basic notions lay the foundation for the concept. These are data abstraction, object identity, and inheritance. Most of the data manipulation and data modeling in object-oriented database systems rests on these fundamental notions. Let us begin with these notions. If you have not been exposed to object-orientated concepts, please pay special attention.

Data Abstraction   Think of trying to define and describe an object. The first aspect of an object relates to what the object is. The second aspect of an object is what the object does. A set of operations may be applied to it for changing its state.

For example, consider an object known as EMPLOYEE. You can describe this object using its characteristics such as name, address, date of birth, salary, and so on. A set of values for these attributes defines the current state of the object. Now you can apply an operation on the object. Let us say that this operation is that of increasing the salary by 5 percent, thereby changing the state of the object.

Apart from the important aspects of what an object is and what an object does, there are other less significant aspects such as how to implement the object in a database or for an application. The notion of abstraction refers to the process of identifying and separating out essential aspects of an object from other less important ones. This leads us to two other basic concepts.

Encapsulation. This means that you can place the important aspects within the definition of an object as in a capsule. An object, therefore, contains both the data structure and the set of operations that can manipulate it.

Information hiding. With abstraction, you can separate the external aspects of implementation from the inner details. The inner aspects of what the object is and what it does may be hidden from the external realm.

What are the effects of encapsulation and information hiding on application processing? The internal details are insulated from the external implementation and processing requirements. Therefore, you may change the internal representation and the definition of internal operations without affecting processing requirements. An object resembles a black box component that can be constructed and changed, apart from the rest of the system. Such modularization simplifies the design and development of applications.

In object orientation, abstract data types (ADTs) provide encapsulation. An object has an interface part and an internal or implementation part. Only the interface part is made visible to users and programs.

Inheritance Through inheritance an object may inherit the internal components from an entity at a higher level. For example, an object known as SalesPerson can inherit the structure representation as well as definitions of internal operations or behavior from an object called EMPLOYEE at a higher level. Even at this stage you can readily appreciate how the property of inheritance results in code sharing and structure sharing. We will cover inheritance in more depth a little later.

Object Identity The identity of an object distinguishes that single object from all other objects. Using an object identity, you can differentiate one object from another through its attributes. The notion of object identity enables one object to refer to another object or one object to contain another object. Figure 20-1 illustrates the use of object identity as applied to an airplane and its component parts.

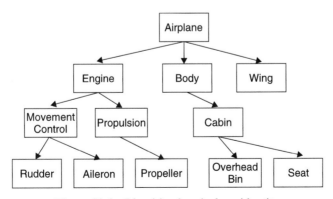

Figure 20-1   Identities for airplane identity.

Objects and Classes

The notions of object and class are keys to the understanding of object-oriented technology. An object is a single thing, and a class represents a collection of things. From this primitive definition, let us build up and review the notions in greater detail.

An Object   An object is a single, uniquely identifiable entity that consists of attributes or characteristics that describe the state of the object in the real world, as well as the actions or behavior associated with it. As noted, an object contains information about its current state. An object also holds information about the actions that can take place to change the current state of the object.

One or more attributes describe the current state of an object. The values of the attributes determine the state of an object. If you modify the value of any of its attributes, the object goes from one state to another. Attributes are also called instance variables—relating to a single object instance.

Note the following concepts with regard to objects and attributes:

Simple attribute.   A primitive type of attribute such as a string or integer that takes a literal or numeric value.

Complex attribute.   Contains a collection of objects or references to other objects.

Reference attribute.   Refers to a relationship between objects.

Complex object.   Contains one or more complex attributes

Object identifier (OID).   A system-generated identifier for identifying an object instance. An OID cannot be altered or reused; it does not depend on the state of the object; it is transparent to the user.

Figure 20-2 presents an example of attributes for an instance of the EMPLOYEE object. Note the different types of attributes and also determine why this is a complex object.

Attributes or representation	Type
EmployeeNumber	Simple, primitive
SocialSecurityNumber	Simple, primitive
EmployeeName	Simple, primitive
EmployeeAddress	Simple, primitive
EmployeePhone	Simple, primitive
Salary	Simple, primitive
DepartmentNumber	Reference (relationship with DEPARTMENT object)
Project	Complex (collection of PROJECT objects)

Figure 20-2   Attributes for employee instance.

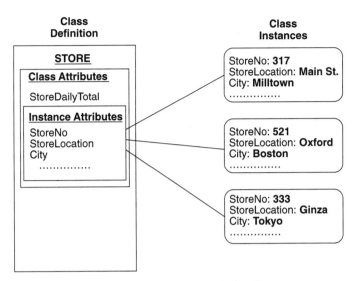

Figure 20-3   Class definition and class instances.

A Class   A class is used as a template to create objects of the same structure. Objects having the same attributes and performing the same operations can be put together as a class.

Consider a class STORE. Attributes and actions may be defined once for the class. Then all store objects can be described by the attributes and actions defined for the class STORE. Each such store object is an instance of the STORE class.

A class itself may also be considered as an object and have its own special attributes and operations. These are class attributes describing the general characteristics of the entire class. For example, StoreDailyTotal may represent the total sale amount for all the stores.

Figure 20-3 illustrates a class definition and class instances.

Methods and Messages

In our discussion on encapsulation, you have noted that an object contains both the data structure and operations or functions as a self-contained, independent package.

Methods   The functions or operations encapsulated by an object are known as methods. Methods indicate the behavior of the object. We mentioned that the current state of an object is defined by the current values of its attributes. Methods can be utilized to change the values of the attributes and thereby change the state of an object. A method in the CUSTOMER class may be defined to effect an address change to a customer instance. Another method may be stipulated to print the customer name and address.

Figure 20-4 shows the representation of the CUSTOMER class, object instances, and an example of a method defined within the class.

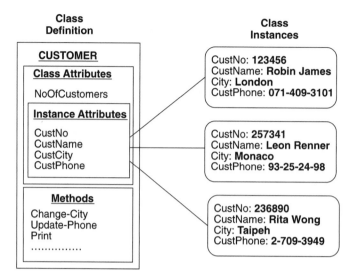

Figure 20-4   Class, class instances, and methods

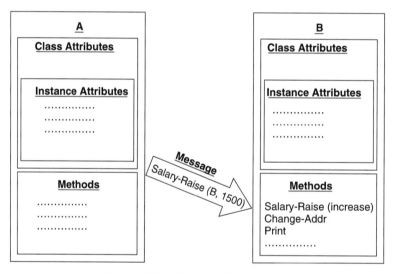

Figure 20-5   Sending of a message.

Messages   Object orientation may be considered as an object-message pattern. Objects constitute the computational set in this pattern. Messages are the means of communication between objects. Each object responds to a stipulated set of messages.

A message is a simply a request from a sender object, say A, to a receiver object, say B, asking B to execute one of B's methods. In a special case, an object A may itself be both the sender and the receiver object.

Figure 20-5 illustrates how a message is sent from one object to another so that one of its methods may be executed by the receiver.

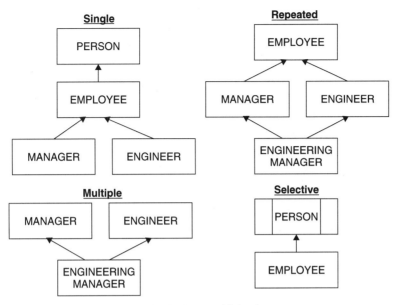

Figure 20-6   Types of inheritance.

Inheritance

Consider two classes, EMPLOYEE and MANAGER. The two classes share a number of attributes and, perhaps, a reasonable number of methods. In addition to the attributes of the class EMPLOYEE, the class MANAGER may have a few more specialized attributes. Nevertheless, the two classes are substantially similar.

A feature of object orientation, known as inheritance, allows a class to be defined as a special case of a more general class. Such special classes are called subclasses, and the general classes are called superclasses. When you form a superclass from a specialized class, the process is known as generalization. Similarly, the process of forming a subclass from a general class is called specialization. The concepts of generalization and specialization discussed here are similar to what we discussed in Chapter 6 for the object-based data model.

Inheritance may be of different forms: single, multiple, repeated, and selective. Figure 20-6 presents the various types of inheritance.

Polymorphism

This is a powerful concept in object orientation. To understand the concept, first consider the general concept of overloading. Consider any specific method defined within a class. The method has a name. Overloading allows the name of any specific method to be reused within the class or across different classes. Do you realize what this powerful technique can accomplish? Just a single message can perform different functions depending on the receiver object and the parameters passed to it. The context of the method determines its function.

Polymorphism (having many forms) is more general than overloading. Three types of polymorphism exist.

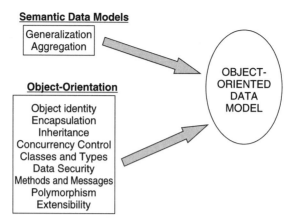

Figure 20-7   Object-oriented data model.

Operation polymorphism. Overloading is a form of operation polymorphism. With a method with one name you can have different operations performed based on the context.

Inclusion polymorphism. Relates to a method defined in one class and inherited by a subclass.

Parametric polymorphism. Uses a type as a parameter in generic type or class declarations.

Object-Oriented Data Model

When we discussed the design of a relational database, we considered the creation of a logical model. You studied the various components that make up the logical data model for traditional database systems. We also went through the steps for creating the logical model.

The detailed steps to create an object-oriented data model are beyond the scope of our discussions here. Let us just consider the features of an object-oriented data model. Basically, an object-oriented data model must represent the structure and meanings of objects defined in the context of object orientation. Figure 20-7 captures the essence of an object-oriented data model.

OODB   An object-oriented data model defines an object-oriented database (OODB). Object-oriented databases combine database capabilities with object orientation. Figure 20-8 illustrates the type of integration present in OODBs.

Vendors take different approaches for integrating object orientation and database functionality. Here are the main methods:

- Add database capabilities to object-oriented programming languages.
- Include functions provided by object orientation to existing database languages.

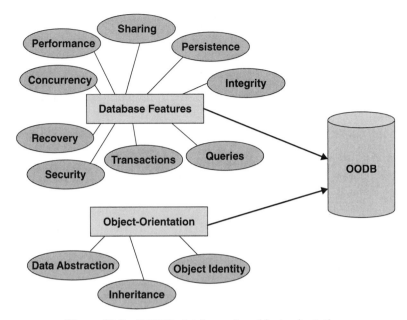

Figure 20-8   OODB: database plus object orientation.

- Take a fresh approach based on integration—not extending language to include database capabilities or the other way around.
- Embed object-oriented language for database access in host languages.
- Develop object-oriented database software for specific applications.

OODBMS   Database management systems manage the storing and accessing of data from a database implemented based on a particular data model. For doing so, DBMSs must possess a number of features and support various functions. In addition to the usual features and functions of traditional DBMSs, object-oriented database management systems (OODBMSs) must be based on object orientation also.

Here is a list of functions and features of an OODBMS.

Data model support.   Supports the object-oriented data model.

Data persistence.   Enables data created by programs to endure and persist in the database long after termination of the program.

Data sharing.   Allows data to be shared by multiple user applications.

Query processing.   Provides ad hoc query facilities on object classes and subclasses.

Transaction processing.   Enables transaction processing by ensuring atomicity of each transaction.

Concurrency control. Guarantees database consistency when transactions execute simultaneously.

Reliability and recovery. Provides the ability to recover from failures.

Security. Has facilities to protect the database from unauthorized access.

Scalability. Has capabilities to perform adequately even when data and transaction volumes increase.

Data distribution. Enables data to be partitioned and distributed among various physical locations.

Let us leave the topic of OODBMSs by listing their advantages and disadvantages.

Advantages

- Enhanced modeling of real-world information based on object orientation
- Ability to build new abstract data types
- Benefits of generalization and specialization resulting from provisions for defining superclasses and subclasses
- More feasible schema evolution because of the tight coupling between data and applications
- Ability to process transactions running for long durations without difficulty
- Capability to support sophisticated applications such as CAD and multimedia systems

Disadvantages

- O-O data model lacks solid theoretical foundation
- Complexity of OODBMS—data model slanted toward the programmer, not the end user
- Lacks the level of usage and experience of other data models
- Standards not firmed up
- Performance compromised by object-level locking for concurrency control
- No support for user views of data as in relational systems
- Security mechanisms not quite adequate

OBJECT-RELATIONAL DATABASES

As you know, relational DBMSs are more widely used than any other types of database systems. Object-oriented database systems started out to support special applications in engineering, telecommunications, and finance. Even though object-oriented databases are preferred for such applications, the extent of usage of these databases is still small compared to that of relational databases.

It appeared that organizations had to make the choice only between relational and object-oriented systems. There was no middle path. This has been changing in recent years. What seem to be needed are database systems that would allow representation of complex data types, user-defined functions to assist in processing, and user-defined operators to carry out complicated functions. SQL-92 is inadequate in this regard; so are pure object-oriented database systems.

An object-relational database system presents a viable solution for handling complex data types. It combines the capabilities of object technology with the features of data integrity, reliability, recovery, and security found in relational technology.

The Driving Forces

Users are moving to object-relational database management systems (ORDBMSs) not so much for object orientation. The need for new data types such as HTML pages, huge unstructured documents, audio, video—all of this within the relational infrastructure—is what drives the transition to ORDBMS.

Michael Stonebraker, a database expert and founder of the ORDBMS vendor Illustra, describes the characteristics of an ORDBMS. In his fundamental book, *Object-Relational DBMSs*, Stonebraker refers to a typical application at the State of California Department of Water Resources (DWR) that manages the waterways, canals, and water projects in that state. DWR maintains a library of nearly half a million pictures. DWR employees access this library several times a day. An employee would need to request for a picture by content with a query such as: show me Lake Cachuma (a Santa Barbara county reservoir) with a low water level. Despite an index system of captions and keywords, retrieval of the right picture within a reasonable time is virtually impossible. Information requirements such as this need a database system that would allow representation of complex data types and mechanisms to query and manipulate these data types.

When you group the various factors that have given rise to the object-relational system, you will note that two major forces propel ORDBMS: computerization of new types of applications and sophistication of business data processing applications. Let us consider these two driving forces.

New Types of Applications   What we notice is an ever-growing number of applications in new areas. New types of applications range in variety from satellite imaging, weather forecasting, flood control, engineering design, and bio-engineering to spatial, geographic, and temporal systems. In particular, new types of multimedia applications keep increasing in the following areas.

Web applications   Developers are loading up the World Wide Web with complex data at an amazing rate. Using the Web as a transport vehicle, Web applications require the means to run complex queries on complex data types such as multimedia objects.

Digital images   Over the next decade, X-ray, ultrasound, and other such systems are expected to store enormous amounts of data on digital storage devices. Useful

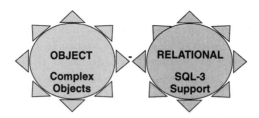

Figure 20-9   Amalgam of object/relational features.

information must be generated by managing all that digital data and combining these with textual and numerical data.

Sophistication of Business Applications   Core business applications are becoming more and more sophisticated. The continuing decline in hardware and software costs promotes the enhancement of business applications with diagrams, pictures, images, audio, and video clips.

An insurance application would add pictures to the claims database file. A manufacturing application would augment the parts inventory with intricate diagrams. An auction application would capture digital images of upscale art and move the images around preauction exhibitions worldwide. A decision support system would allow sophisticated queries on complex data.

What is an ORDBMS?

The features of ORDBMSs go well beyond those of OODBMSs and those of relational DBMSs. The features and functions result from an amalgam of the two.

Michael Stonebraker defines ORDBMSs as follows: DBMSs that support a dialect of SQL-3, include nontraditional tools, and optimize for complex SQL-3 queries are called ORDBMSs. Because these support SQL, they are relational; because they support complex data, they are object-oriented.

Figure 20-9 portrays this amalgam between object orientation and relational features.

Feature Highlights

Apart from the strengths gained from the amalgam of object and relational attributes in general, the following distinct features make ORDBMS superior to either OODBMS or RDBMS.

Base Data Type Extension   SQL-92 allows simple data types: integer, floating point number, character string, date/time, numerical, and decimal. In organizations with worldwide locations, two-dimensional data types would be required. Some useful data types would include 2-D polygon, 2-D trapezoid, 2-D ellipse, and so on.

Advanced Functions   Extensions also cover functions such as

- Contained (point, circle) returns Boolean
- Overlaps(circle, polygon) returns Boolean

Complex Operators   In addition to providing advanced functions, complex operators such as the following are also provided:

- Rotate(image, angle) returns image
- Crop (image, rectange) returns image

Create Your Own   In an ORDBMS, you can create a new base data type and define your own functions and operators.

Complex Objects   ORDBMS provides for complex objects. These objects may be composed by putting together base and user-defined data types.

Inheritance   Inheritance consists of data inheritance and function inheritance. As with base type extension and complex objects, inheritance allows you to define new data types.

Rules   In ORDBMS, the rule system is much more flexible, with the general form "on event, do action." Thus the rule system demands the ORDBMS to watch for a given event and execute the appropriate action just before or just after the event.

Managing Large Objects   Facilities are available to define and manage very large objects including audio, video, and text.

BLOB (binary large object)
CLOB (character large object)
NCLOB (fixed-width multibyte CLOB)
BFILE (binary file stored outside the database)

SQL-3: Object-Relational Support

Support features include the following:

SQL-3 provides for user-defined data types, constructors for data types, and user-defined functions and routines and also offers support for large objects and database triggers. In SQL-3, two types of objects exist: (1) row type whose instances are tuples in tables and (2) abstract data type indicative of any general type used as components of rows.

DATABASES FOR DECISION SUPPORT

The database system in an organization functions as a hub around which all business activities take place. Do you need to process an order from a customer? Do you want check inventory? Do you need to calculate the price? Do you have to check the customer's credit status? Do you want to arrange for the shipping? Do you need to bill the customer and send an invoice? Where do you get the information for all these processes? Databases, particularly relational databases, drive the day-to-day business of many organizations.

	OPERATIONAL	INFORMATIONAL
Data Content	Current values	Archived, derived, summarized
Data Structure	Optimized for transactions	Optimized for complex queries
Access Frequency	High	Medium to low
Access Type	Read, update, delete	Read
Usage	Predictable, repetitive	Ad hoc, random, heuristic
Response Time	Sub-seconds	Several seconds to minutes
Users	Large number	Relatively small number

Figure 20-10   Operational and informational systems.

Such operational applications keep businesses alive. However, executives, managers, and analysts need a different type of informational applications providing information in different formats, to review past performance, spot future trends, and make strategic decisions. Whereas operational systems enable you to make the wheels of business turn, informational systems enable you to watch the wheels of business turn. Informational systems are decision-support applications. Figure 20-10 contrasts the features of operational and informational systems.

Decision-support systems provide business intelligence to decision makers. Data warehousing, online analytical processing (OLAP), and data mining are major decision-support applications. Database systems for decision support must provide fast processing of queries, must enable sophisticated analysis along many business dimensions, and must be able to process large volumes of data.

We will broadly discuss these decision-support systems and consider their purposes, features, and functions. Specifically, we will examine the types of database systems that are needed for these applications. You will note how these database systems differ from those for operational systems. You will also observe how decision-support database systems are designed for analysis whereas operational database systems are geared for performance.

Data Warehousing

Data warehousing is a new system environment that provides strategic information for analysis and decision making. Organizations that are building data warehouses are actually building this new system environment. This new environment is kept separate from the system environment supporting day-to-day operations. A data warehouse essentially holds the business intelligence for an organization to aid its strategic decision making. Figure 20-11 shows the nature and composition of business intelligence provided by the data warehouse environment.

At a high level of interpretation, a data warehouse contains critical measurements of the business processes stored along business dimensions. For example, a data warehouse might contain units of sales, by product, by day, by customer group, by sales district, by sales region, and by promotion. Here the business dimensions are product, day, customer group, sales district, sales region, and promotion.

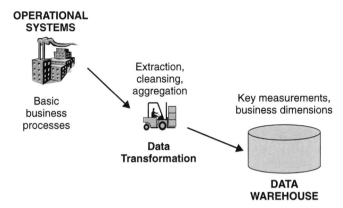

Figure 20-11   Business intelligence at the data warehouse.

From where does the data warehouse get its data? The data are derived from the operational systems that support the basic business processes of the organization. Between the operational systems and the data warehouse, there is a data staging area. In this staging area, operational data are cleansed and transformed into a form suitable to be placed in the data warehouse for easy retrieval and quick analysis.

Data Warehouse: A New Type of System Environment   You have noted that the data warehouse environment is not the same as the operational environment supporting the day-to-day business operations. Here are the defining features of the data warehouse environment:

- Database designed for analytical tasks
- Data from multiple applications
- Easy to use and conducive to long interactive sessions by users
- Read-intensive data usage
- Direct interaction with the system by the users without IT assistance
- Content updated periodically and stable
- Content to include current and historical data
- Ability for users to run queries and get results online
- Ability for users to initiate reports

So how can you define a data warehouse? The data warehouse is an informational environment that

- Provides an integrated and total view of the enterprise,
- Makes the enterprise's current and historical information easily available for decision making,
- Makes decision support transactions possible without hindering operational systems,
- Renders the organization's information consistent, and
- Presents a flexible and interactive source of strategic information.

Most of the processing in the data warehouse environment for strategic information is analytical. Four levels of analytical processing are possible:

1. Running simple queries and reports against current and historical data
2. Performing "what if" analysis is many different ways
3. Querying, stepping back, analyzing, and then continuing the process to any desired length
4. Spotting historical trends and applying them for future results

Data Warehouse: Underlying Principles

A Simple Concept   In the final analysis, data warehousing is a simple concept. It is born out of the need for strategic information; it is the result of the search for a new way to provide strategic information. The old methods using the operational computing environment, all through the last two decades, were unsatisfactory. The new concept is not to generate fresh data but to make use of the large volumes of existing data and to transform the data into forms suitable for providing strategic information.

The data warehouse exists to answer questions users have about the business, the performance of the various operations, the business trends, and about what can be done to improve the business. The data warehouse exists to provide business users with direct access to data, to provide a single unified version of the performance indicators, to record the past accurately, and to provide the ability to view data from many different perspectives. In short, the data warehouse is there to support decisional processes.

When everything is said about data warehousing, you will realize that it is really a simple concept. Take all the data you already have in the organization, clean and transform the data, and then provide useful strategic information. What could sound simpler than that?

An Environment, Not a Product   A data warehouse is not a single software or hardware product you purchase to provide strategic information. It is rather a computing environment. It is an environment where users can find strategic information. It is an environment where users are put directly in touch with the data they need to make better decisions. It is a user-centric environment.

Let us summarize the characteristics of this new computing environment called data warehouse created for the users:

- An ideal environment for data analysis and decision support
- Fluid, flexible, and interactive
- 100 Percent user-driven
- Very responsive and conducive to ask-answer-ask-again pattern
- Provides ability to discover answers to complex, unpredictable questions

A Blend of Many Technologies   Although a simple concept, data warehousing involves different functions. It involves the function of data extraction, the function of loading the data, the function of transforming the data, the function of storing

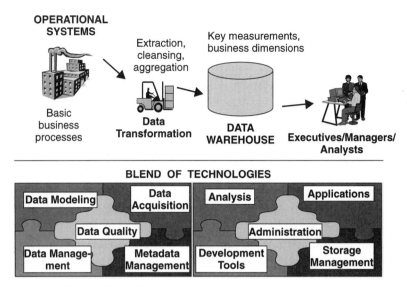

OPERATIONAL SYSTEMS

Extraction, cleansing, aggregation

Key measurements, business dimensions

Basic business processes

Data Transformation

DATA WAREHOUSE

Executives/Managers/ Analysts

BLEND OF TECHNOLOGIES

| Data Modeling | Data Acquisition | Analysis | Applications |

| Data Quality | | | Administration |

| Data Management | Metadata Management | Development Tools | Storage Management |

Figure 20-12   Data warehouse: a blend of technologies.

the data, and the function of providing user interfaces. Different technologies are therefore needed to support these functions. Figure 20-12 illustrates how various technologies blend together in the data warehouse environment.

Although many technologies are in use, they all work together in a data warehouse. The end result is the creation of a new computing environment for the purpose of providing strategic information every enterprise needs desperately. Several vendor tools are available in each of these technologies. You do not have to build your data warehouse from scratch.

Nature of the Data   It is important to consider the nature of the data in the data warehouse. How are these data different from the data in any operational system? Why does they have to be different? How is the data content in the data warehouse used?

Subject-Oriented   In operational systems, we store data by individual applications. For a banking institution, data sets for a consumer loans application contain data for that particular application. Data sets for other distinct applications of checking accounts and savings accounts relate to those specific applications. Again, in an insurance company, different data sets support individual applications such as automobile insurance, life insurance, and workers' compensation insurance.

In striking contrast, in the data warehouse, data are stored by subjects, not by applications. What are business subjects? Business subjects differ from organization to organization. These are the subjects critical for the enterprise. For a manufacturing company, sales, shipments, and inventory are critical business subjects. For a retail store, sales at the check-out counter is a critical subject.

In a data warehouse, there is no application flavor. The data in a data warehouse cut across applications.

Integrated   For proper decision making, you need to pull all the relevant data from the various applications. The data in the data warehouse come from several operational systems. Source data are in different databases, files, and data segments. These are disparate applications. The operational platforms could be different. The operating systems could be different. File layouts, character code representations, field naming conventions—all of these could be different.

In addition to data from internal operational systems, for many enterprises, data from outside sources are likely to be very important. Companies such as Metro Mail, A. C. Nielsen, and IRI specialize in providing vital data on a regular basis. Your data warehouse may need data from such sources. This is one more variation in the mix of source data for a data warehouse.

Before the data from various disparate sources can be usefully stored in a data warehouse, you have to remove the inconsistencies. You have to standardize the various data elements; you have to make sure of the meanings of data names in each source application. Before moving the data into the data warehouse, you have to go through a process of transformation, consolidation, and integration of the source data.

Time-Variant   For an operational system, the stored data contain the *current* values. In an accounts receivable system, the balance is the *current* outstanding balance in the customer's account. In an order entry system, the status of an order is the *current* status of the order. In a consumer loans application, the balance amount owed by the customer is the *current* amount. Of course, we store some past transactions in operational systems. But, essentially, operational systems reflect *current* information because these systems support day-to-day *current* operations.

On the other hand, the data in the data warehouse are meant for analysis and decision making. If a user is looking at the buying pattern of a specific customer, the user needs data not only about the current purchase but on the past purchases as well. When a user wants to find out the reason for the drop in sales in the North East division, the user needs all the sales data for that division over a period extending back in time. When an analyst in a grocery chain wants to promote two or more products together, that analyst wants sales of the selected products over a number of past quarters.

A data warehouse, because of the very nature of its purpose, has to contain historical data, not just current values. Data are stored as snapshots over past and current periods. Every data structure in the data warehouse contains the time element. You will find historical snapshots of the operational data in the data warehouse. This aspect of the data warehouse is quite significant for both the design and implementation phases.

For example, in a data warehouse containing units of sale, the quantity stored in each file record or a table row relates to a specific time element. Depending on the level of the details in the data warehouse, the sales quantity in a record may relate to a specific date, a specific week, a specific month, or a specific quarter.

The time-variant nature of the data in a data warehouse allows for analysis of the past, relates information to the present, and enables forecasts for the future.

Nonvolatile   Data extracted from the various operational systems and pertinent data obtained from outside sources are transformed, integrated, and stored in the data warehouse. The data in the data warehouse are not intended to run the day-to-day business. When you want to process the next order received from a customer, you do not look into the data warehouse to find the current stock status. The operational order entry application is meant for that purpose. In the data warehouse you keep the extracted stock status data as snapshots over time. You do not update the data warehouse every time you process a single order.

Data from the operational systems are moved into the data warehouse at specific intervals. Depending on the requirements of the business, these data movements take place twice a day, once a day, once a week, or once in two weeks. In fact, in a typical data warehouse, data movements to different data sets may take place at different frequencies. The changes to the attributes of the products may be moved once a week. Any revisions to the geographical setup may be moved once a month. The units of sales may be moved once a day. You plan and schedule the data movements or data loads based on the requirements of your users.

Not every business transaction updates the data in the data warehouse. The business transactions update the operational system databases in real time. We add, change, or delete data from an operational system as each transaction happens. You do not usually update the data in the data warehouse. You do not delete the data in the data warehouse in real time. Once the data are captured in the data warehouse, you do not run individual transactions to change the data there. Data updates are commonplace in an operational database; not so in a data warehouse. The data in a data warehouse are not as volatile as the data in an operational database. The data in a data warehouse are primarily for query and analysis.

Data Warehouse Components   Figure 20-13 presents the basic components of a data warehouse.

Let us briefly review the components illustrated in the figure.

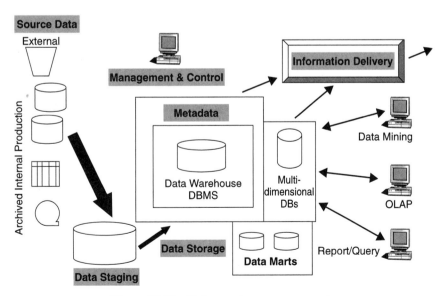

Figure 20-13   Data warehouse components.

Source Data   Source data coming into the data warehouse may be grouped into four broad categories:

Production data. Come from the various operational systems of the organization. The significant characteristic of production data is its wide disparity.

Internal data. These data relate to "private" spreadsheets, documents, customer profiles, and sometimes even departmental databases. These are internal data, parts of which could be useful in a data warehouse.

Archived data. These are the historical data separated out from current data and stored in archived media. Historical data are essential in a data warehouse.

External data. This type of data emanates from outside the organization. Many executives use performance indicators, competitor's market shares, financial parameters, and so on from outside sources.

Data Staging   This component of the data warehouse refers to the processes and the area where preparation of the data takes place. In the data staging area, data are cleansed, transformed, and prepared for loading.

Data Storage   This component includes all data storage in the overall data warehouse, data marts, and other multidimensional databases. In the top-down method of design, the overall data warehouse feeds dependent data marts. In a practical approach, a collection of conformed data marts, by themselves, constitute the organization's data warehouse.

Metadata   The metadata component in a data warehouse environment is similar to the data dictionary or system catalog of a DBMS. But the metadata component has more functions than a routine data dictionary. Metadata serves as a road map for users to navigate within a data warehouse and examine the contents.

Information Delivery   This component includes a wide variety of methods for delivery of information to users. Users obtain information on-line by e-mail or through the Internet or an intranet. Information delivery mechanisms include ad hoc reports, complex queries, multidimensional analysis, statistical analysis, data mining applications, and executive information systems.

Management and Control   This component sits on top of all other components and coordinates their services and functions within the data warehouse.

Dimensional Data Model   You are familiar with data modeling for operational or OLTP systems. We adopt the entity-relationship (E-R) modeling technique to create a data model. Operational systems possess the following characteristics:

- Capture details of events or transactions
- Focus on individual events

- Are windows into microlevel transactions
- Need data at detailed level to run the business
- Suitable only for questions at level of individual transactions
- Data consistency, nonredundancy, and efficient data storage are critical

These characteristics make E-R modeling technique appropriate for OLTP systems. The E-R modeling technique removes data redundancy, ensures data consistency, and expresses microscopic relationships.

On the other hand, data warehousing systems possess different characteristics and serve other purposes. Here is a summarized list of data warehousing features:

- Meant to answer questions on the overall processes
- Focuses on how managers view the business
- Reveals business trends
- Information centered on a business process
- Answers show how business processes are monitored and measured
- Enables measures to be analyzed and studied along several business dimensions

Fact and Dimension Tables   For modeling data warehouses, E-R modeling technique is not suitable. We need to use a different technique. For modeling data warehouses, we use the dimensional modeling technique. For a moment, consider how a manager or an analyst performs a typical analysis. For example, if an analyst wants to analyze sales, how does he or she perform the analysis? He or she needs data such as sales quantities, sales dollars, sales price, sales cost, and margin. These pieces of information are known as facts—metrics to be analyzed. How are the facts going to be analyzed?

Let us consider a typical query: How much revenue did sales of product Widget-1 to married customers generate for the past three years, in the northeast territory? In the query, the fact being analyzed is the revenue or margin. The revenue is being analyzed along four business dimensions—product, customer, time, and salesperson's territory.

The dimensional modeling technique enables us to model facts and dimensions. The result is a star schema.

STAR schema   Figure 20-14 presents a STAR schema for the subject of sales. Notice the fact table in the middle surrounded by dimension tables.

Inside the fact table, you will find all the measures or facts to be used for analysis. In each dimension table, you will find the attributes of the particular business dimension. Notice the primary keys of each table. Each dimension table is in a one-to-many relationship with the fact table in the middle. With such an arrangement in the STAR schema with the fact table in the middle, query executions are optimized.

Database Software Considerations   Examine the features of the leading commercial relational DBMSs (RDBMSs). As data warehousing becomes more preva-

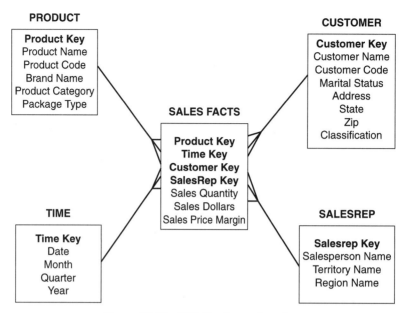

Figure 20-14   STAR schema for sales.

lent, you would expect to see data warehouse features being included in the software products. That is exactly what the database vendors are doing. Data warehouse-related add-ons are becoming parts of the database offerings. The database software that started out for use in operational OLTP systems is being enhanced to cater to decision support systems. DBMSs have also scaled up to support very large databases.

Some RDBMS products now include support for the data acquisition area of the data warehouse. Mass loading and retrieval of data from other database systems have become easier. Some vendors have paid special attention to the data transformation function. Replication features have been reinforced to assist in bulk refreshes and incremental loading of the data warehouse.

Bitmapped indexes could be very effective in a data warehouse environment to index on fields that have smaller number of distinct values. For example in a database table containing geographic regions, the number of distinct region codes is low. However, frequently queries involve selection by regions. In this case, retrieval by a bitmapped index on the region code values can be very fast. Vendors have strengthened this type of indexing.

Apart from these enhancements, the more important enhancements relate to load balancing and query performance. These two features are critical in a data warehouse. Your data warehouse is query-centric. Everything that can be done to improve query performance is most desirable. The DBMS vendors are providing parallel processing features to improve query performance. Let us briefly review the parallel processing options within the DBMS that can take full advantage of parallel server hardware.

Parallel Processing Options   Parallel processing options in database software are intended only for machines with multiple processors. Most of the current database software can parallelize a large number of operations. These operations include the following: mass loading of data, full table scans, queries with exclusion conditions, queries with grouping, selection with distinct values, aggregation, sorting, creation of tables using subqueries, creating and rebuilding indexes, inserting rows into one table from other tables, enabling constraints, star transformation, which is an optimization technique when processing queries against a STAR schema, and so on. Note that this is an impressive list of operations that the RDBMS can process in parallel.

Let us now examine what happens when a user initiates a query at the workstation. Each session accesses the database through a server process. The query is sent to the DBMS, and data retrieval takes place from the database. Data are retrieved and the results are sent back, all under the control of the dedicated server process. The query dispatcher software is responsible for splitting the work and distributes the units to be performed among the pool of available query server processes to balance the load. Finally, the results of the query processes are assembled and returned as a single, consolidated result set.

Interquery Parallelization   In this method, several server processes handle multiple requests simultaneously. Multiple queries may be serviced based on your server configuration and the number of available processors. You may take advantage of this feature of the DBMS successfully on SMP systems, thereby increasing throughput and supporting more concurrent users.

However, interquery parallelism is limited. Let us see what happens here. Multiple queries are processed concurrently, but each query is still being processed serially by a single server process. Suppose that a query consists of index read, data read, sort, and join operations; then these operations are carried out in this order. Each operation must finish before the next one can begin. Parts of the same query do not execute in parallel. To overcome this limitation, many DBMS vendors have come up with versions of their products that provide intraquery parallelization.

Intraquery Parallelization   Using the intraquery parallelization technique, the DBMS splits the query into the lower-level operations of index read, data read, join, and sort. Then each one of these base operations is executed in parallel on a single processor. The final result set is the consolidation of the intermediary results. Let us review three ways a DBMS can provide intraquery parallelization, that is, parallelization of parts of the operations within the same query itself.

Horizontal parallelism.   The data are partitioned across multiple disks. Parallel processing occurs within each single task in the query, for example, data read, which is performed on multiple processors concurrently on different sets of data to be read spread across multiple disks. After the first task is completed from all of the relevant parts of the partitioned data, the next task of that query is carried out, and then the next one after that task, and so on.

Vertical parallelism.   This kind of parallelism occurs among different tasks, not just a single task in a query as in the case of horizontal parallelism. All component query operations are executed in parallel, but in a pipelined manner. This assumes that the RDBMS has the capability to decompose the query into subtasks where each subtask has all the operations of index read, data read, join, and sort. Then each subtask executes on the data in a serial fashion. In this approach, ideally the database records are processed by one step and immediately given to the next step for processing, thus avoiding wait times. Of course, in this method, the DBMS must possess a very high level of sophistication in decomposing tasks.

Hybrid method. In this method, the query decomposer partitions the query both horizontally and vertically. Naturally, this approach produces the best results. You will realize the greatest utilization of resources, optimal performance, and high scalability.

Selection of the DBMS   Our discussions of the server hardware and the DBMS parallel processing options must have convinced you that selection of the DBMS is most crucial. You must choose the server hardware with the appropriate parallel architecture. You choice of the DBMS must match with the selected server hardware. These are critical decisions for your data warehouse.

Broadly, the following elements of business requirements affect the choice of the DBMS:

Level of user experience

If the users are totally inexperienced with database systems, the DBMS must have features to monitor and control runaway queries. On the other hand, if many of your users were power users, then they would be formulating their own queries. In this case, the DBMS must support easy SQL-type language interface.

Types of queries

The DBMS must have a powerful optimizer if most of the queries are complex and produce large result sets. Alternatively, if there is an even mix of simple and complex queries, there must be some sort of query management in the database software to balance the query execution.

Need for openness

The degree of openness depends on the back-end and front-end architectural components, and those, in turn, depend on the business requirements.

Data loads

The data volumes and load frequencies determine the strengths in the areas of data loading, recovery, and restart.

Metadata management

If your metadata component need not be elaborate, then a DBMS with an active data dictionary may be sufficient. Let your requirements definition reflect the type and extent of the metadata framework.

Data repository locations

Is your data warehouse going to reside in one central location, or is it going to be distributed? The answer to this question will establish whether the selected DBMS must support distributed databases.

Data warehouse growth

Your business requirements definition must contain information on the estimated growth in the number of users and in the number and complexity of queries. The growth estimates will have a direct relation to how the selected DBMS supports scalability.

In addition to the criteria that the selected DBMS must have load balancing and parallel processing options, we list below other key features you need to consider when selecting the DBMS for your data warehouse:

Query governor   To anticipate and abort runaway queries
Query optimizer   To parse and optimize user queries
Query management   To balance the execution of different types of queries
Load utility   For high-performance data loading, recovery, and restart
Metadata management   With an active data catalog or dictionary
Scalability   In terms of both number of users and data volumes
Extensibility   Having hybrid extensions to OLAP databases
Portability   Across platforms
Query tool APIs   For tools from leading vendors
Administration   Providing support for all DBA functions

Online Analytical Processing (OLAP)

In today's business conditions, users need to go beyond basic facilities for analysis provided by the data warehouse. Data warehousing is query-centric and designed for querying and analysis. However, in the changed and competitive business environment, users must have the capability to perform far more complex analysis in less time.

Let us quickly examine how the traditional methods of analysis provided in a data warehouse are not sufficient and perceive the nature of the more effective analytical system demanded by users.

Need for Multidimensional Analysis   Let us quickly review the business model of a large retail operation. If you just look at daily sales, you soon realize that the sales are interrelated to many business dimensions. Daily sales are meaningful only when they are related to the dates of the sales, the products, the distribution channels, the stores, the sales territories, the promotions, and a few more dimensions. Multidimensional views are inherently representative of any business model. Very few models are limited to three dimensions or fewer. For planning and making strategic decisions, managers and executives probe into business data by scenarios.

For example, they compare actual sales against targets and against sales in prior periods. They examine the breakdown of sales by product, by store, by sales territory, by promotion, and so on.

Decision makers are no longer satisfied with one-dimensional queries such as "How many units of Product A did we sell in the store in Milltown, New Jersey?" Consider the following query, which is more useful: "How much revenue did the new Product X generate during the last three months, broken down by individual months, in the South Central territory, by individual stores, broken down by promotions, compared to estimates, and compared to the previous version of the product?" The analysis does not stop with this single multidimensional query. The user continues to ask for further comparisons with similar products, comparisons among territories, and views of the results by rotating the presentation between columns and rows.

For effective analysis, your users must have easy methods for performing complex analysis along several business dimensions. They need an environment that presents a multidimensional view of data providing the foundation for analytical processing through easy and flexible access to information. Decision makers must be able to analyze data along any number of dimensions, at any level of aggregation, with the capability of viewing results in a variety of ways. They must have the ability to drill down and roll up along the hierarchies of every dimension. Without a solid system for true multidimensional analysis, your data warehouse is incomplete.

In any analytical system, time is a critical dimension. Hardly any query is executed without having time as one of the dimensions along which analysis is performed. Furthermore, time is a unique dimension because of its sequential nature. November of a year always comes after October of that year. Users monitor performance over time, as for example, performance this month compared to last month, or performance this month compared with performance in the same month last year.

Another point about the uniqueness of the time dimension is the way in which the hierarchies of the dimension work. A user may look for sales in March and may also look for sales for the first four months of the year. In the second query for sales for the first four months, the implied hierarchy at the next higher level is an aggregation taking into account the sequential nature of time. No user looks for sales of the first four stores or the last three stores. There is no implied sequence in the store dimension. True analytical systems must recognize the sequential nature of time.

Need for Fast Access and Powerful Calculations   Whether a user's request is for monthly sales of all products along all geographical regions or for year-to-date sales in a region for a single product, the query and analysis system must have consistent response times. Users must not be penalized for the complexity of their analysis. Both the size of the effort to formulate a query or the amount of time to receive the result sets must be consistent irrespective of the query types.

Let us take an example to understand how the speed of the analysis process matters to users. Imagine a business analyst looking for reasons why profitability dipped sharply in the recent months in the entire enterprise. The analyst starts this analysis by querying for the overall sales for the last five months for the entire company broken down by individual months. The analyst notices that, although the sales do not show a drop, profitability exhibits a sharp reduction for the last three months. Now the analysis proceeds further when the analyst wants to find out which countries show reductions. The analyst requests a breakdown of sales by major worldwide regions and notes that the European region reveals the reduction in profitability. Now the analyst senses that clues become more pronounced. So the analyst looks for a breakdown of the European sales by individual countries. The analyst finds that profitability is increased for a few countries and decreased sharply for some other countries and has stayed the course for the rest. At this point, the analyst introduces another dimension into the analysis. Now the analyst wants the breakdown of profitability for the European countries by country, by month, and by product. This step brings the analyst closer to the reason for the decline in the profitability. The analyst observes that the countries in the European Union show a very sharp decline in profitability for the last two months. Further queries reveal that manufacturing and other direct costs remained at the usual levels but the indirect costs shot up. The analyst is now able to determine that the decline in profitability is because of the additional tax levies on some products in the European Union countries. The analyst has also determined the exact effect of the levies so far. Strategic decisions follow on how to deal with the decline in profitability.

Now look at Figure 20-15 showing the steps through the single analysis session.

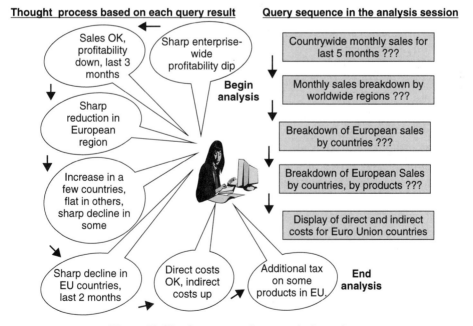

Figure 20-15   Query steps in an analysis session.

How many steps are there? Many steps, but a single analysis session. Many steps, but a single train of thought. Each step in this train of thought constitutes a query. The analyst formulates each query, executes the query, waits for the result set to appear on the screen, and studies the result set. Each query is interactive because the result set from one query forms the basis for the next query. In this manner of querying, the user cannot maintain the train of thought unless the momentum is preserved. Fast access is absolutely essential for an effective analytical processing environment.

Did you notice that none of the queries in the above analysis session included any serious calculations? This is not typical. In a real-world analysis session, many of the queries require calculations, sometimes, complex calculations. What is the implication here? An effective analytical processing environment must not only be fast and flexible, it must also support complex and powerful calculations.

What follows is a list of typical calculations that get included in the query requests:

- Roll-ups to provide summaries and aggregations along the hierarchies of the dimensions
- Drill-downs from the top level to the lowest along the hierarchies of the dimensions, in combinations among the dimensions
- Simple calculations such as computation of margins (sales minus costs)
- Share calculations to compute the percentage of parts to the whole
- Algebraic equations involving key performance indicators
- Moving averages and growth percentages
- Trend analysis using statistical methods

Features and Functions   OLAP provides users with the ability to perform multidimensional analysis with complex calculations.

Here is a summary list of features and functions of OLAP:

- Enables analysts, executives, and managers to gain useful insights from the presentation of data.
- Can reorganize metrics along several dimensions and allow data to be viewed from different perspectives.
- Supports multidimensional analysis.
- Is able to drill down or roll up within each dimension.
- Is capable of applying mathematical formulas and calculations to measures.
- Provides fast response, facilitating speed-of-thought analysis.
- Complements the use of other information delivery techniques such as data mining.
- Improves the comprehension of result sets through visual presentations using graphs and charts.
- Can be implemented on the Web.
- Designed for highly interactive analysis.

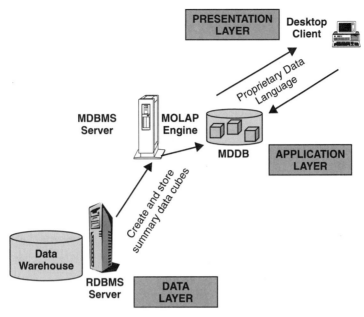

Figure 20-16 The MOLAP model.

OLAP Models OLAP systems provide multidimensionality in one of two ways: multidimensional OLAP and relational OLAP. The method of storing data differentiates the two methods. We will now examine these two methods.

The MOLAP Model In the multidimensional OLAP (MOLAP) model, data for analysis are stored in specialized multidimensional databases. Large multidimensional arrays form the storage structures. For example, to store sales number of 500 units for product ProductA, in month number 2001/01, in store StoreS1, under distributing channel Channel05, the sales number of 500 is stored in an array represented by the values (ProductA, 2001/01, StoreS1, Channel05).

The array values indicate the location of the cells. These cells are intersections of the values of dimension attributes. If you note how the cells are formed, you will realize that not all cells have values of metrics. If a store is closed on Sundays, then the cells representing Sundays will all be nulls.

Let us now consider the architecture for the MOLAP model. Please go over each part of Figure 20-16 carefully.

Note the three layers in the multitier architecture. Precalculated and prefabricated multidimensional data cubes are stored in multidimensional databases. The MOLAP engine in the application layer pushes the multidimensional view of the data from the MDDBs to the users.

Multidimensional database management systems are proprietary software systems. These systems provide the capability to consolidate and fabricate summarized cubes during the process that loads data into the MDDBs from the main data warehouse. The users who need summarized data enjoy fast response times from the preconsolidated data.

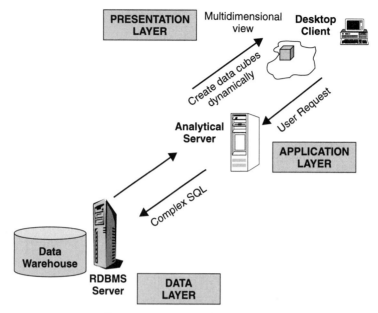

Figure 20-17   The ROLAP model.

The ROLAP Model   In the relational OLAP (ROLAP) model, data are stored as rows and columns in the relational format. This model presents data to the users in the form of business dimensions. To hide the storage structure to the user and present data multidimensionally, a semantic layer of metadata is created. The metadata layer supports the mapping of dimensions to the relational tables. Additional metadata support summarizations and aggregations. You may store the metadata in relational databases.

Now take a look at Figure 20-17. This figure shows the architecture of the ROLAP model.

What you see is a three-tier architecture. The analytical server in the middle tier application layer creates multidimensional views on the fly. The multidimensional system at the presentation layer provides a multidimensional view of the data to the users. When the users issue complex queries based on this multidimensional view, the queries are transformed into complex SQL directed to the relational database. Unlike the MOLAP model, static multidimensional structures are not created and stored.

True ROLAP has three distinct characteristics:

- Supports all the basic OLAP features and functions discussed above.
- Stores data in a relational form.
- Supports some form of aggregation.

Local storing of multidimensional cubes is a variation of ROLAP provided by vendors. This is how it works:

The user issues a query.

The results of the query get stored in a small, local multidimensional database.

The user performs analysis against this local database.

If additional data are required to continue the analysis, the user issues another query. And the analysis continues.

Data Mining

Most certainly you have heard about data mining. Most of you know that the technology has something to do with discovering knowledge. Some of you possibly know that data mining is used in applications such as marketing, sales, credit analysis, and fraud detection. All of you know vaguely that data mining is somehow connected to data warehousing. You are right. Data mining is used in just about every area of business from sales and marketing to new product development, inventory management, and human resources.

There are perhaps as many variations in the definition for data mining as there are vendors and proponents. Some experts include a whole range of tools and techniques from simple query mechanisms to statistical analysis as data mining. Others simply restrict data mining to mean knowledge discovery techniques. A workable data warehouse, although not a prerequisite, will give a practical boost to the data mining process.

Why is data mining being put to use in more and more businesses? Here are some basic reasons:

- In today's world, an organization generates more information in a week than most people can read in a lifetime. It is humanly impossible to study, decipher, and interpret all those data to find useful competitive information.
- A data warehouse pools all the data after proper transformation and cleansing into well-organized data structures. Nevertheless, the sheer volume of data makes it impossible for anyone to use analysis and query tools to discern useful patterns.
- In recent times, many data mining tools have appeared in the market that are suitable for a wide range of applications. We are seeing the maturity of the tools and products.
- Data mining needs substantial computing power. Parallel hardware, databases, and other powerful components are becoming very affordable.
- As you are aware, organizations are placing enormous emphasis on building sound customer relationships, and for good reasons. Companies want to know how they can sell more to existing customers. Organizations are interested in determining which of the customers will prove to be of long-term value to them. Companies need to discover any existing natural classifications among their customers so that the classifications may be properly targeted with products and services. Data mining enables companies to find answers and discover patterns in their customer data.
- Finally, competitive considerations weigh heavily on your company to get into data mining. Perhaps your company's competition is already into data mining.

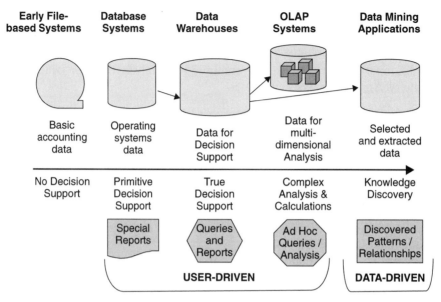

Figure 20-18 Decision support progresses to data mining.

What is Data Mining? Before getting into some formal definitions of data mining, let us try to understand the technology in a business context. Like all decision support systems, data mining delivers information. Please refer to Figure 20-18 showing the progression of decision support.

Note the earliest approach when primitive types of decision support systems existed. Next, we move to database systems providing more useful decision support information. In the 1990s, data warehouses began to be the primary valuable source of decision support information. Query and report tools assist the users to retrieve the types of decision support information they need. For more sophisticated analysis, OLAP tools became available. Up to this point the approach for obtaining information was driven by the users.

But the sheer volume of data renders it impossible for anyone to use analysis and query tools to discern all useful patterns. For example, in marketing analysis, it is almost impossible to think through all the probable associations and to gain insights by querying and drilling down into the data warehouse. You need a technology that can learn from past associations and results and predict customer behavior. You need a tool that will by itself accomplish the discovery of knowledge. You want a data-driven approach and not a user-driven one. This is where data mining steps in and takes over from the users.

Progressive organizations gather the enterprise data from the source operational systems, move the data through a transformation and cleansing process, and store the data in data warehouses in a form suitable for multidimensional analysis. Data mining takes the process a giant step further.

Knowledge Discovery Process Data mining is, therefore, a knowledge discovery process. Data mining discovers knowledge or information that you never knew existed in your data. What about this knowledge? How does it show up? Usually,

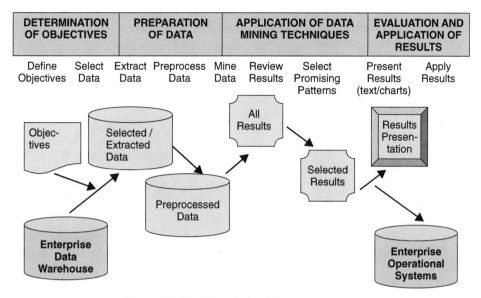

DETERMINATION OF OBJECTIVES	PREPARATION OF DATA	APPLICATION OF DATA MINING TECHNIQUES	EVALUATION AND APPLICATION OF RESULTS

Define Objectives   Select Data   Extract Data   Preprocess Data   Mine Data   Review Results   Select Promising Patterns   Present Results (text/charts)   Apply Results

Figure 20-19   Knowledge discovery process.

the uncovered hidden knowledge manifests itself as relationships or patterns. Figure 20-19 illustrates the knowledge recovery process.

OLAP Versus Data Mining   As you know, with OLAP queries and analysis, users are able to obtain results from complex queries and derive interesting patterns. Data mining also enables the users to uncover interesting patterns, but there is an essential difference in the way the results are obtained. Figure 20-20 clarifies the basic difference by means of a simple diagram.

When an analyst works with OLAP in an analysis session, the analyst has some prior knowledge of what he or she is looking for. The analyst starts with assumptions deliberately considered and thought out. In the case of data mining, however, the analyst has no prior knowledge of what the results are likely to be.

Users drive OLAP queries. Each query may lead to a more complex query and so on. The user needs prior knowledge of the expected results. It is completely different in data mining.

Data Mining in Data Warehouse Environment   Data mining fits well in the data warehouse environment. It plays a significant role in the environment. A clean and complete data warehouse forms the bedrock for data mining. The data warehouse enables data mining operations to take place. The two technologies support each other. These are some of the major factors:

- Data mining algorithms need large amounts of data, more so at the detailed level. Most data warehouses contain data at the lowest level of granularity.
- Data mining flourishes on integrated and cleansed data. If your data extracts from source systems, data transformation functions, and data cleansing proce-

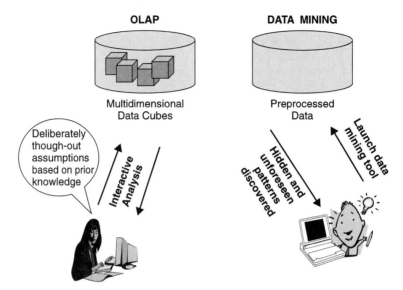

Figure 20-20   OLAP and data mining.

dures were carried out properly, your data warehouse contains data well suited to data mining.

- Already the infrastructure for data warehouses is robust, with parallel processing technology and powerful relational database systems. Because such scalable hardware is already in place, no new investment is needed to support data mining.

Let us point out one difference in the way data are used from the data warehouse for traditional analysis and data mining. When an analyst wants to analyze, say with an OLAP tool, the analyst begins with summary data at a high level. Then the analysis continues through the lower levels by means of drill-down techniques. On many occasions the analyst need not go down to the detail levels. This is because he or she finds suitable results at the higher levels for deriving conclusions. But data mining is different. Because data mining is searching for trends and patterns, it deals with lots of detailed data. For example, if the data mining algorithm is looking for customer buying patterns, it certainly needs detailed data at the level of the individual customer.

So what is a compromise approach? What is the level of granularity you need to provide in the data warehouse? Unless it is a huge burden to keep detailed data at the lowest level of granularity, strive to store detailed data. Otherwise, for data mining engagements, you may have to extract detailed data directly from the operational systems. This calls for additional steps of data consolidation, cleansing, and transformation. You may also keep light summaries in the data warehouse for traditional queries. Most of the summarized data along various sets of dimensions may reside in the OLAP systems.

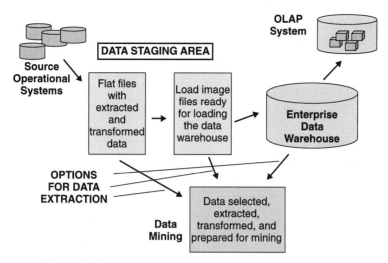

Figure 20-21 Data mining in data warehouse environment.

The data warehouse is a valuable and easily available data source for data mining operations. Data extractions for data mining tools to work on come from the data warehouse. Figure 20-21 illustrates how data mining fits in the data warehouse environment.

Note how the data warehouse environment supports data mining. Note the levels of data held in the data warehouse and the OLAP system. Also, observe the flow of data from the data warehouse for the knowledge discovery process.

Major Data Mining Techniques and Applications   Figure 20-22 shows examples of application areas, mining functions, mining processes, and techniques.

Using the figure, try to understand the connections on the basis of the following remarks:

- Data mining algorithms are part of data mining techniques.
- Data mining techniques are used to carry out the data mining functions. While performing specific data mining functions, you are involved in getting this done through mining processes.
- A specific data mining function is generally suitable to a given application area.
- Each of the application areas is a major area in business where data mining is actively used now.

LEADING TRENDS: BASIC OVERVIEW

In this section, we consider a few leading trends in database technology. This is not an in-depth coverage of each topic. The intention is just to highlight the main points and expose you to what is out there and what you should be watching for.

Application Area	Examples of Mining Functions	Mining Processes	Mining Techniques
Fraud Detection	Credit card frauds Internal audits Warehouse pilferage	Determination of variations from norms	Data Visualization Memory-based Reasoning
Risk Assessment	Credit card upgrades Mortgage Loans Customer Retention Credit Ratings	Detection and analysis of links	Decision Trees Memory-based Reasoning Neural Network
Market Analysis	Market basket analysis Target marketing Cross selling Customer Relationship Marketing	Predictive Modeling Database segmentation	Cluster Detection Decision Trees Link Analysis Genetic Algorithms

Figure 20-22   Data mining functions and application areas.

For more detailed study of any trends that pique your interest, please consult the appropriate literature. A few of the books mentioned in the Reference section will give you more information.

Parallel Databases

During the past decade, we have observed the emergence of parallel databases as a significant phenomenon. Several commercial vendors have established the feasibility of splitting large queries and running them in parallel modes. If you look at transaction processing at every organization, the enormous surge in the number and complexity of transactions becomes clear. The last 10–15 years has also experienced a great demand for decision support systems. These systems thrive on complex, multidimensional queries on large data sets. Without parallel hard-ware systems and parallel database software, decision support systems cannot be effective.

Parallel databases run on parallel hardware infrastructure. Three types of parallel architecture are commonly adopted, as illustrated by Figure 20-23.

Shared Memory

Each CPU has full access to the shared memory. Multiple CPUs are interconnected through a common network bus.

Shared Disk

Each CPU or a cluster of CPUs in a node has its own local main memory. Memory is not shared among CPUs. Communication occurs over a high-speed bus. Each node has access to the common set of disks.

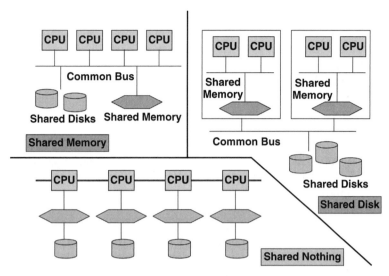

Figure 20-23   Parallel architecture options.

Shared Nothing

Each CPU has its own main memory and set of disks. Works well with an operating system that supports transparent disk access. If a table or database is located on a particular disk, access to it depends entirely on the CPU that owns it. Internode communication is through CPU-to-CPU connection.

Parallel database systems speed up queries and transactions by executing them in parallel. These systems support the following types of parallelism techniques.

I/O Parallelism   Database relations are partitioned horizontally or vertically, and the data content is spread across multiple disks. Horizontal partitioning works well for I/O partitioning. You may partition a relation into a number of horizontal partitions and distribute the partitions to disks adopting the following techniques: round-robin, hash distribution, or range partitioning.

When a query or transaction performs a retrieval of a set of rows or writing a set of rows, performing the operation in parallel becomes possible through the I/O parallelism technique. Full table scans, range selections, and value selections work differently for different methods of distribution. For example, the round-robin method is suited for sequential full table scans; value selection works well with hash distribution; range partitioning applies well to range selections.

Interquery Parallelism   This form of parallelism increases system throughput. Several queries or transactions execute in parallel. The queries are distributed among several CPUs for running in parallel. Obviously, interquery parallelism cannot be possible with single-processor systems. However, interquery parallelism does not speed up individual queries or transactions. Each query by itself takes as much time as it would in a single-processor system.

Shared-memory architecture works well for interquery parallelism. Supporting interquery parallelism in the other architectures is more difficult.

Intraquery Parallelism This method requires the dividing up of a query into its various operations. Then these individual operations of a single query may be distributed among the processors for execution in parallel. After the completion of all operations, the result sets are assembled together to produce the final result set. This method calls for pipelining the output of one operation as the input for the next.

Intraquery parallelism may be applied to a query in two ways:

Intraoperation parallelism. A transaction may consist of operations such as select, sort, project, or join. Each operation itself may be parallelized. For example, if the transaction has to sort 100,000 records, the sort itself may be split into groups of records and shared by multiple processors.

Interoperation parallelism. You can accelerate the processing of a single query by executing the various operations in parallel. Let us say that a query consists of select, sort, and join. The select operation can run on one processor, the sort on another, and the join on a third.

Hybrid Parallelism This method is a combination of interquery parallelism and intraquery parallelism.

Active Databases

Assume that you have implemented a database for your organization and one of the applications supported by the database is inventory control. Suppose your organization sells a few critical products that contribute to bulk of the revenue. Your marketing vice president is very concerned about ensuring that sufficient inventory of these critical products is always available . How can you satisfy the requirements of this executive?

If your database is a passive database, then periodically you should run queries to determine the inventory levels of these critical products. On the other hand, if your database is an active database, it can automatically alert the marketing vice president when inventory levels fall below prescribed minimum quantities. Active databases do not just store data; they can perform defined actions based on stipulated events. This concept is catching on. Many relational systems support this principle and can be used to behave as active databases.

Events that trigger actions are usually changes to data values in the database. Inserts, updates, and deletes are events that can set into action a particular response. Also, actions can be triggered by temporal events such as the arrival of a certain day or time. When an event occurs, it can initiate application of defined rules. The database system verifies the conditions of the rules and triggers appropriate actions. Rules may be applied for monitoring events. They may also be applied for enforcing integrity constraints.

Active databases work on the event-condition-action paradigm as noted below:

```
ON     event
IF     condition
THEN   action
```

Rules are stored in the database itself. The programs or modules to be executed on the occurrence of the events are also stored in the database. The programs are generally known as triggers or trigger programs. In relational databases, triggers are specialized versions of stored procedures.

Here are a few considerations for designing triggers:

- Ensure that a trigger does not create a chain reaction of triggers.
- Set priority for actions if several actions are possible for the same event.
- Depending on the nature of a particular event, set the trigger to start executing as soon as an event is sensed or immediately after an event completes.
- Address runtime errors that may result from the execution of a trigger.

Intelligent Databases

In the evolution of database systems, as of now, intelligent databases are perhaps the culmination of the search for better methods of storage and access of data. Intelligent databases provide a natural way to use them; they handle seamless movements of huge data volumes; they provide an appropriate set of user tools. Intelligent database systems integrate sophisticated technologies such as object orientation, hypermedia, expert systems, text-based searches, and online information retrieval with database technology.

Intelligent databases offer services at three levels: database engine at the foundational level, user interface at the middle level, and tools at the highest level. Figure 20-24 presents the architecture at these three levels.

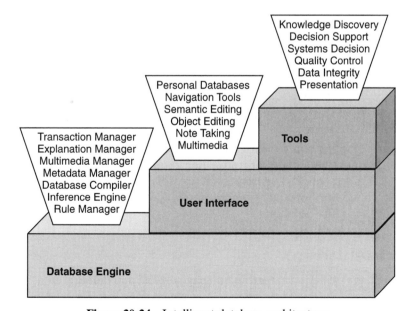

Figure 20-24   Intelligent database architecture.

Deductive Databases

Interest in deductive databases began in research establishments in the late 1970s in an effort to combine logic and database technology. During that period, the promises of artificial intelligence and expert systems attracted a lot of attention. Research projects abounded in Europe, Japan, and the U.S. Japan launched the Fifth Generation Project to encompass a number of technologies including logic systems and database technology. Research institutions proposed several experimental deductive database systems. A few commercial systems were also deployed.

Major objectives that propelled the effort included:

- Extend the relational model and develop a new type of database system.
- Improve the functionality of such a database system to perform as a deductive DBMS.
- In addition, enable the new type of DBMS to support general-purpose applications

Deductive databases combine the functionality of logic programming, methods to specify rules about data, and an inference engine. A declarative language expresses the rules. Logic similar to that used in Prolog language is applied. The inference engine performs as a deduction tool to deduce new facts from the database. Datalog, a variation of Prolog, defines the rules as they relate to relations in the database.

In a deductive database, facts and rules are specified.

Facts. Defined similar to relations in a relational database, except that attribute names are not included. A relation represents a real-world object, and its attributes attempt to describe the object, perhaps only partially. In a deductive database, the position of an attribute within the tuple determines what the value of an attribute means.

Rules. Views in a relational database system define virtual relations, not what is actually stored. In a sense, rules are like views. They specify virtual units that can be derived from the facts by applying inference techniques. Defined similar to data views in a relational database, except that attribute names are not included. Views cannot include recursive definitions; however, rules may involve recursion.

Backward chaining and forward chaining methods are used in deductive database systems to evaluate query or transaction results.

Figure 20-25 presents Prolog notation to express facts, rules, and queries. This is not an explanation of how queries work in the deductive database system—just a sample to indicate the notation.

Multimedia Databases

Traditional database systems store and manage textual and numeric data. The introduction of object-relational database systems meant a big leap forward by the inclusion of new data types. With UDTs, users can define new data types. Still this is not

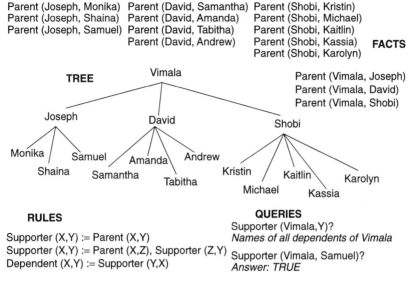

Parent (Joseph, Monika)   Parent (David, Samantha)   Parent (Shobi, Kristin)
Parent (Joseph, Shaina)   Parent (David, Amanda)   Parent (Shobi, Michael)
Parent (Joseph, Samuel)   Parent (David, Tabitha)   Parent (Shobi, Kaitlin)
                           Parent (David, Andrew)   Parent (Shobi, Kassia)   **FACTS**
                                                     Parent (Shobi, Karolyn)

TREE   Vimala

Parent (Vimala, Joseph)
Parent (Vimala, David)
Parent (Vimala, Shobi)

Joseph   David   Shobi

Monika   Samuel   Amanda   Andrew
   Shaina   Samantha   Kristin   Kaitlin   Karolyn
                       Tabitha   Michael   Kassia

RULES

Supporter (X,Y) := Parent (X,Y)
Supporter (X,Y) := Parent (X,Z), Supporter (Z,Y)
Dependent (X,Y) := Supporter (Y,X)

QUERIES
Supporter (Vimala,Y)?
Names of all dependents of Vimala

Supporter (Vimala, Samuel)?
Answer: TRUE

Figure 20-25   Prolog notation: facts, rules, queries.

enough. Modern requirements call for a more inclusive type of database system that can accommodate the ever-increasing newer types of objects.

If the number of multimedia objects is small, you can probably get by if you store the objects in a file and the descriptions in a database and somehow relate the two. Storage and retrieval based on searches can be managed without much difficulty. However, if your organization deals with a large assortment of multimedia objects, as many modern organizations do, then you need a multimedia database system.

Types of Multimedia   A multimedia database system stores and manages the following types of objects:

Text. Formatted or free-form character or numeric strings. Includes HTML pages.

Graphics. Diagrams, drawings, and charts in descriptive encoded formats.

Images. Pictures, photographs, scanned images, and so on, digitized in standard formats.

Audio. As bit strings in digitized form. Also includes structured audio with distinct components of note, tone, sound level, and duration.

Video. Sequenced photographs to be presented at precise rates.

Animation. Images or graphs in time sequence.

Mixed media. As for example, synchronized audio and video.

Issues and Challenges   Because of the variety of multimedia objects and the potential size of individual objects, multimedia databases are faced with difficult issues and challenges. Here are a few that call for serious consideration.

Modeling and design. Although all types of multimedia may be considered objects, because of the variations, creating a satisfactory database model is difficult. Design issues are also hard to address.

Storage. Even when you have to store a large number of rows in relational database systems, each individual row is of manageable size. On the other hand, multimedia database systems must store and manage individually large objects. Most databases define multimedia objects as a data type called BLOB (binary large object). Storage of large objects requires good compression techniques.

Selection and retrieval. Users must be able to retrieve multimedia objects by specifying selection conditions based on content and similarity. For example, pictures and images that are very similar must be able to be construed as the same object and retrieved.

Query type. Query formulation and execution are different from those in relational database systems, in which they are based on query languages and indexes.

Video-on-demand. Provision of this service for users by dialing into a server is gaining momentum. The server must be able to handle special types of real-time constraints and synchronization of video delivery at server and client.

Applications   Although no comprehensive commercial systems are yet available, the following types of applications will greatly benefit from multimedia database systems.

- Real-time alert, control, and monitoring
- Entertainment and travel
- Marketing and advertising
- Education and training
- Knowledge management
- Document storage and retrieval

Mobile Databases

Mobile computing has become pervasive in today's business environment. You see users with handheld devices, portable laptops, and notebooks transmitting data to databases held in remote sites. The FedEx employee, delivering a package at your front door, updates the package-tracking database from his handheld device. The cop who pulled you over on a highway verifies your driver's license against an a central database. The inventory taker at a large warehouse inputs the on-hand quantities into the main inventory database from his handheld computing system. There are many more applications of mobile computing including emergency response services, sales call assistance, and travel information services.

The enormous progress in portable computing devices and tremendous improvements in wireless communications have created a new paradigm of remote access to databases. However, a wide array of issues must be addressed before the new type of remote database access can be fully successful. We will explore the nature of mobile computing, its special needs, and the pertinent database requirements.

Nature of Mobile Computing   Mobile computing is not the same as distributed computing. Mobile users keep moving, and along with them moves the computing equipment, whereas in distributed computing, although the computing devices are dispersed, they stay in fixed locations.

The following points highlight the basic nature and considerations of mobile computing.

- Allows users to communicate with one another and perform their functions while on the move.
- Machines accessing the database do not have fixed locations or constant network addresses.
- Machines tend not to stay connected with the database server; they are off-line for long periods. Maintaining transaction consistency becomes difficult.
- Because the battery power of remote units is usually low, receiving information through separate, individual queries is not efficient.
- Most information received by remote units is through broadcasts from the database, on fixed or changeable schedules. Broadcasts are an efficient method because they can reach a large number of remote units.
- Query results sent to remote units are often dependent on the location of the user, not necessarily the current location. For example, a travel information system providing hotel and other such services must be based not on the current location of the user but on future locations.
- Downloaded data are maintained in local files to be used while working off-line. Local files need to be kept synchronized with the source data.

Mobile Computing Model and Architecture   Because of its nature, a mobile computing model must be based on a distributed architecture. Figure 20-26 presents a typical architecture.

Examine the details shown in the figure and note the descriptions mentioned below.

Fixed host   A computing device at a fixed location.

Mobile unit   Also called a mobile host, provides remote computing services.

Support station   Connects a set of fixed hosts and support stations. Support stations are also known as base stations. Base stations have wireless connections with the mobile units they support.

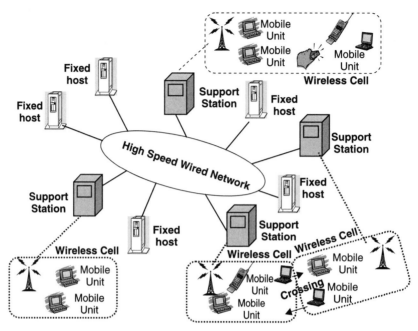

Figure 20-26 Mobile computing architecture.

Wired network   Connects a set of fixed hosts and support stations (base stations).

Communication   Support stations and fixed hosts are reachable over the wired network. Mobile hosts and support stations communicate through wireless connections.

Downlink   Used for sending data from a support station to a mobile unit.

Uplink   Used for sending data from a mobile unit to a support station.

Mobility domain   The entire domain in which a mobile unit can move.

Cell   A part of the mobility domain where wireless connectivity with the controlling support station is possible.

Movements   Mobile units move from cell to cell. When a mobile unit moves from one cell to another, a handoff procedure transfers connectivity with the mobile unit from one cell to another.

Access contiguity   Guarantees that movement from cell to cell will not affect data access.

Mobile Database Considerations   As you can observe, the database considerations for mobile computing relate many different issues not present in centralized or even distributed databases. Note the following considerations.

Types of data content   In a mobile computing environment, you can have private data owned, managed, and restricted to a single user. Public data is maintained at one unit, such as stock prices, airline fares, and so on. Public data is available for access by any user. Another type of data content may be read and updated by any user. Product inventory falls in this shared category.

Application types   Vertical applications are restricted within a cell. For example, local information about emergency services and accommodation information is valuable only within small areas. On the other hand, horizontal applications are meant for users in all cells.

Data distribution   On method is to distribute the data only among the fixed hosts and support stations, using full or partial replication techniques. This is the popular method. The other method is to distribute data among all units—fixed and mobile. Data management is more difficult in this approach.

Data synchronization   Frequently, users download relevant data from the common database and keep the downloaded data for off-line work. This adds another dimension to data management. The downloaded data must be kept synchronized with the main database.

Query processing   Query processing costs depend on the location of the mobile unit. Another consideration of query processing relates to the requirement that complete and correct query results must be provided even while the mobile unit is moving from cell to cell.

Transaction processing   A transaction emanating from a mobile unit may be executed through several support stations and perhaps on different copies of the database fragments. Traditional ACID properties of transactions do not apply to the mobile computing environment.

Recovery   Recovery from failures becomes quite involved. Failures at mobile units commonly result from battery failure. Support station failures cause routing readjustments. In this environment, recovery has to address many types of failure— mobile unit, fixed host, support station, network links, wireless links, and transactions themselves.

Geographic Databases

Geographic databases store and manage spatial data. Examples of spatial data in geographic databases include maps with political boundaries and administrative boundaries, digital satellite images showing natural contours, transportation networks, highways, rivers, and so on. These databases also hold another type of data that is nonspatial but related to the spatial data. This second type of data includes census counts, population distribution by economic factors, and sales data.

Geographic databases support a wide variety of applications. They range extensively in scope and use. Your latest automobile is probably fitted with a GPS (Global

Positioning System) unit so that you have no excuse for ever getting lost. This is an application of geographic databases.

Here is a random sample of the types of applications:

- Vehicle navigation
- Distribution of households by demographics
- Market analysis by region
- Consumption of utility services
- Distribution of economic indicators
- Pollution studies
- Water resource management
- Wildlife studies
- Soil evaluation studies
- Landscape surveys
- Parks management
- Crop and produce yield analysis

Geographic Data Formats Although geographic data cover a broad range of objects, they comprises two types. First, geographic data contain information about location or spatial objects. These are rivers, lakes, oceans, land masses, boundaries, regions, cities, towns, and so on. Next, geographic data contain information associated with these spatial units. For example, geographical data contain spatial information about the regions in the north as well as the annual rainfall statistics for these regions.

Let us formalize these two data formats in geographic databases.

Vector format Vector data are created from geometric objects such as points, lines, triangles, squares, and polygons. These are used to represent objects in two dimensions. For example, a river may be represented as a series of line segments, a region as a combination of polygons, and an exit on the highway as a point. For topological information such height and vertical contours, three-dimensional geometric objects such as cylinders, spheres, or polyhedrons may be used.

Raster format Raster data represent information associated with spatial data. Raster data constitute an array or collection of points. Each point represents a value for the information being represented. Suppose that a region is represented by a polygon—a vector format. Now you want to show the income distribution in the region. That would be done with the raster format. If a point in the raster format represents annual income level of 25,000 dollars, then you would need four points to represent 100,000 dollars at the appropriate place in the region. Raster data is kept as n-dimensional arrays where each entry is a unit representing an attribute.

Spatial Query Types How do you use geographic databases? How do you retrieve information from these databases? We are not discussing the different indexing techniques needed for geographic databases. B-tree and bitmapped indexes cannot apply here. However, let us just cover a few types of queries in a geographic database system.

Region query   Relates to whole or partial regions. Query may request for objects partially or fully inside a region. Example: Show me the rivers flowing through the state of Louisiana.

Proximity query   Requests for objects near a given place. Example: Show me the Italian restaurant nearest to the intersection of Georges Road and Fifth Street.

Intersection and union query   Requests of information obtained through intersection or union. Example: Show me the areas in the metropolitan region with low crime rate and low population density.

CHAPTER SUMMARY

- Data abstraction, inheritance, and object identity form the basis for object orientation.
- In object technology, an object is a single, uniquely identifiable entity. Objects having the same attributes and performing the same operations constitute a class. Methods indicate the behavior of an object. Messages are the means for communication between objects.
- Object-oriented database systems address some of the limitations of relational database systems. Object-oriented databases combine database capabilities with object orientation.
- Object-relational databases are emerging from a combination of object orientation and relational database technology.
- A certain set of distinct features makes ORDBMS better than RBDMS and OODBMS: base data type extension, support for complex objects, support for large objects, ability to define new data types and functions, and a flexible rule system.
- Special types of database systems provide information for decision support systems such as data warehousing, OLAP, and data mining.
- A data warehouse is a new type of system environment designed for strategic information. OLAP enables highly multidimensional analysis and complex calculations. Data mining is a knowledge discovery process uncovering patterns and relationships from data.
- Leading trends in database technology: parallel databases, active databases, intelligent databases, deductive databases, multimedia databases, mobile databases, and geographic databases.

REVIEW QUESTIONS

1. Briefly describe the concept of data abstraction in object technology.
2. Describe objects and classes with examples.
3. List the advantages and disadvantages of OODBMS.
4. Define an ORDBMS. What are its major features?

5. What is a STAR schema? How is it applicable as a data model for data warehouses?

6. Explain the need for OLAP. What are the two common OLAP models? Describe briefly any one of the models.

7. How is data mining different from OLAP?

8. What types of parallelism do parallel databases provide?

9. What are multimedia databases? Why are they essential in the modern environment?

10. What are geographic databases? List any six types of applications these databases support.

EXERCISES

1. Indicate whether true or false:

    A. In object orientation, abstract data types provide encapsulation.

    B. Methods and messages are the same in object-oriented systems.

    C. The E-R modeling technique is highly suitable for data warehouses.

    D. Parallel databases work on the event-condition-action paradigm.

    E. Deductive databases combine logic programming and an inference engine.

    F. In a mobile computing environment, fixed hosts are connected to support or base stations.

    G. In geographic databases, raster data are created from geometric objects such as points, lines, and so on.

    H. In an object-relational database environment, users can define their own data types and functions.

    I. Horizontal parallelism works best if data are partitioned across multiple disks.

    J. In a STAR schema, the fact table contains metrics for analysis.

2. Compare and contrast the functions and features of RDBMS, OODBMS, and ORDBMS.

3. Describe the basic components of a data warehouse.

4. Write a short description of data mining. List any four application areas and explain how data mining is useful in these areas.

5. You are a manager of special projects for a large distributor of canned food items. Your company distributes these products to all leading supermarket chains and other convenience stores in the northeast region of the U.S. The region is divided into many districts, each district having a team of salespersons. Plan a mobile computing system to cater to the needs of the traveling sale force. They would need customer, order, product, and inventory information from the proposed mobile database. Prepare a plan outline, considering the overall architecture, data distribution, data access requirements, and other major aspects.

APPENDICES

Legacy System Models:
Hierarchical and Network

Chapter 1 briefly introduced the hierarchical and network data models. These data models were widely used before the adoption of the relational data model. The earlier generation of data systems composed of these two data models are generally known as legacy system models. The information legacy in many enterprises is still residing on databases supporting these two data models.

As you know, the relational data model is the one that is widely used now because of its superiority and strength. Nevertheless, you need to review the earlier data models for two reasons. First, hierarchical and network databases are still in use. Second, a brief review of the earlier data models will enhance your appreciation of the relational model and its superior features.

In this appendix, we will summarize the basic concepts of the two legacy system models and provide a mapping of the semantic data model with each of the two models.

HIERARCHICAL DATA MODEL

This model is the oldest of the database models. Unlike the relational data model or the network data model, the hierarchical data model did not originate with any systematic document or research results. The network model is based on the stipulations by the DBTG of CODASYL. On the other hand, the relational model originated from the research specifications of Dr. Codd.

Database Design and Development: An Essential Guide for IT Professionals by Paulraj Ponniah
ISBN 0-471-21877-4   Copyright © 2003 by John Wiley and Sons, Inc.

The hierarchical data model, however, has been derived from IBM's Information Management System (IMS) database that has been in wide use. In an IMS database, the data structures are placed in a hierarchical top-down arrangement.

Summary of Basic Concepts

- Data is organized in the form of data segments being arranged as an inverted tree.
- Two fundamental modeling concepts make up the hierarchical data model: segment types and parent-child relational types.
- Segments are linked in parent-child relationships, as a top-down structure.
- A child segment is linked to just one parent segment whereas a parent segment may be linked to many child segments.
- A single segment, called the root segment, exists at the top of the inverted tree. The root segment does not participate as a child in any parent-child relationship.
- All other segments participate in relationships as child segments.
- A segment without any child segments is known as a leaf segment.
- For any segment type in the hierarchical tree, a single path exists from the root.
- Each segment type generally represents an entity type of the organization. Data fields in the record types denote the attributes of the entity type.
- Logical links between related segments are implemented through physical addresses (pointers) in the segment itself.

Semantic to Hierarchical Data Model

The following indicates the mapping of components of the semantic data model into components of the hierarchical data model.

Object Sets

- Object set is transformed into segment type.
- The name of the object set becomes the name of the record type. CUSTOMER object is transformed into CUSTOMER segment type.
- The object instances of an object set become the occurrences of the transformed segment type.
- The complete set of object instances becomes the total set of segment occurrences.

Attributes

- Attributes of an object are transformed into the data fields of the record type.
- The names of the attributes become the names of the data fields.
- Domain of values of each attribute becomes the domain for the corresponding data field.

- A single-valued or derived attribute is transformed into a single field.
- For a composite attribute, as many fields are used in the record type as the number of component attributes in the composite attribute.

Instance Identifiers

- The attribute or attributes forming the instance identifier maps into a set of sequence fields.
- Segment occurrences are sorted based on the values of the sequence fields.
- A sequence field may be declared to be "unique" in the sense that no duplicate values are allowed in the sequence field. This is similar to the function of a primary key.
- Only when a sequence field is defined to be "unique" it has a function similar to that of a primary key. Sequence fields may also be declared to be "non-unique."

Relationships   Each relationship in the hierarchical data model becomes a binary link between the parent and the child segment types.

One-to-One or One-to-Many Relationship

- For each object set in the semantic data model, create a segment type.
- If two object sets A and B are in a one-to-one or one-to-many relationship, create a tree structure with A as the parent segment type and B as the child segment type with link between A and B.
- The object set on the "one" side of the relationship becomes the parent segment type and the object set on the "many" side of the relationship becomes the child segment type.

Many-to-Many Relationship

- For each object set in the semantic data model, create a segment type.
- If two object sets A and B are in a many-to-many relationship, map this as two one-to-many relationships.
- Create a tree structure with A as the parent segment type and B as the child segment type with link between A and B.
- Create another tree structure with B as the parent segment type and A as the child segment type with link between B and A.

NETWORK DATA MODEL

The Conference on Data Systems Languages (CODASYL), the organization comprising of vendor representatives and user groups, developed the language COBOL. In the late 1960s, CODASYL appointed a subgroup known as the Database Task Group (DBTG) to develop standards for database systems. DBTG published a preliminary report in 1969. Based on revisions and suggestions made for improvement, DBTG published a revised version of the report in 1971.

Essentially, the network data model is based on the 1971 DBTG report. This data model conforms to a three-level database architecture: conceptual, external, and internal levels. A number of commercial database systems were developed to implement the network data model.

Summary of Basic Concepts

- Data is organized in the form of records being arranged as a network of nodes.
- Two fundamental modeling concepts make up the network data model: record types and set.
- Two record types are linked as a set. The set expresses the one-to-one or one-to-many relationship between two record types.
- A set expressing the relationship between two record types consists of a member record type and an owner record type.
- One owner record type may be part of different sets with different member record types.
- Similarly, one member record type may have multiple owner record types.
- A network consisting of one-to-one or one-to-many relationships is known as a simple network. A complex network, on the other hand, contains many-to-many relationships also.
- Each record type generally represents an entity type of the organization. Data fields in the segment types denote the attributes of the entity type.
- An instance of a set type represents one occurrence of the entity represented by the record type.
- Logical links between related records are implemented through physical addresses (pointers) in the record itself.

Semantic to Network Data Model

The following indicates the mapping of components of the semantic data model into components of the network data model.

Object Sets

- Object set is transformed into record type.
- The name of the object set becomes the name of the segment type. CUSTOMER object is transformed into CUSTOMER record type.
- The object instances of an object set become the occurrences of the transformed record type.
- The complete set of object instances becomes the total set of record occurrences.

Attributes

- Attributes of an object are transformed into the data fields of the field type.
- The names of the attributes become the names of the data fields.

- Domain of values of each attribute becomes the domain for the corresponding data field.
- A single-valued or derived attribute is transformed into a single field.
- For a composite attribute, as many fields are used in the segment type as the number of component attributes in the composite attribute.

Instance Identifiers
- The attribute or attributes forming the instance identifier maps into a set of fields termed the key of the record type.
- Record occurrences may be sorted based on the values of the key fields.
- No special significance is attached to the key fields as all navigation within the data model is through physical pointers.

Relationships   Each relationship in the network data model becomes a binary link between the owner and the member record types.

One-to-One or One-to-Many Relationship

- For each object set in the semantic data model, create a record type.
- If two object sets A and B are in a one-to-one or one-to-many relationship, connect them with A as the owner record type and B as the member record type.
- The object set on the "one" side of the relationship becomes the owner record type and the object set on the "many" side of the relationship becomes the member segment type.

Many-to-Many Relationship

- For each object set in the semantic data model, create a segment type.
- If two object sets A and B are in a many-to-many relationship, map this as two one-to-many relationships.
- Create a link record type C to contain key values of both A and B.
- Define two sets, one with A and the link record type C, the other with B and the link record type C.
- The set with A as the owner record type and C as the member record type represents one of the transformed one-to-many relationship. The set with B as the owner record type and C as the member record type represents the other transformed one-to-many relationship.

Appendix B

Codd's Relational Rules

In 1985, Dr. E. F. Codd, the acknowledged "father" of the relational data model, presented the following 12 rules that a database must obey if it is to be considered truly relational.

Rule 1: The information rule   All information in a relational database is represented explicitly at the logical level and in exactly one way—by values in tables.

Rule 2: Guaranteed access rule   Each and every datum (atomic value) in a relational database is guaranteed to be logically accessible by resorting to a combination of table name, primary key value, and column name.

Rule 3: Systematic treatment of null values   Null values (distinct from an empty character string or a string of blank characters and distinct from zero or any other number) are supported for representing missing information and inapplicable information in a systematic way, independent of the data type.

Rule 4: Dynamic online catalog based on the relational model   The database description is represented at the logical level in the same way as ordinary data, so that authorized users can apply the same relational language to its interrogation as they apply to the regular data.

Rule 5: Comprehensive data sublanguage rule   A relational system may support several languages and various modes of terminal use (for example, the fill-in-the-

Database Design and Development: An Essential Guide for IT Professionals by Paulraj Ponniah
ISBN 0-471-21877-4   Copyright © 2003 by John Wiley and Sons, Inc.

blanks mode). However, there must be at least one language whose statements are expressible, per some well-defined syntax, as character strings, and that is comprehensive in supporting all of the following items:

- Data definitions
- View definitions
- Data manipulation (interactive and by program)
- Integrity constraints
- Authorization
- Transaction boundaries (begin, commit, and rollback)

Rule 6: View updating rule   All views that are theoretically updateable are also updateable by the system.

Rule 7: High-level insert, update, and delete   The capability of handling a base relation or a derived relation (that is, a view) as a single operand applies not only to the retrieval of data but also to the insertion, update, and deletion of data.

Rule 8: Physical data independence   Application programs and terminal activities remain logically unimpaired whenever any changes are made in either storage representations or access methods.

Rule 9: Logical data independence   Application programs and terminal activities remain logically unimpaired when information-preserving changes of any kind that theoretically permit unimpairment are made to the base tables.

Rule 10: Integrity independence   Integrity constraints specific to a particular relational database must be definable in the relational data sublanguage and storable in the catalog, not in the application programs.

Rule 11: Distribution independence   The data manipulation sublanguage of a relational DBMS must enable application programs and inquiries to remain logically the same whether and whenever data are physically centralized or distributed.

Rule 12: Nonsubversion rule   If a relational system has a low-level (single-record-at-a-time) language, that low level cannot be used to subvert or bypass the integrity rules and constraints expressed in the higher-level relational language (multiple-records-at-a-time).

Appendix C

Diagramming Conventions and Symbols

Chapters 5, 6, and 7 have covered data modeling in sufficient detail. In these chapters, you were introduced to notations and symbols in use for representing business objects, attributes, relationships, and special cases of these components.

This appendix provides a summary of diagramming notations and symbols used in the entity-relationship data modeling technique. Wherever applicable, alternative notations are also shown to represent specific data model components.

Database Design and Development: An Essential Guide for IT Professionals by Paulraj Ponniah
ISBN 0-471-21877-4   Copyright © 2003 by John Wiley and Sons, Inc.

Entity Type: Strong

Entity Type: Weak

Relationship: Strong

Relationship: Weak

Attribute

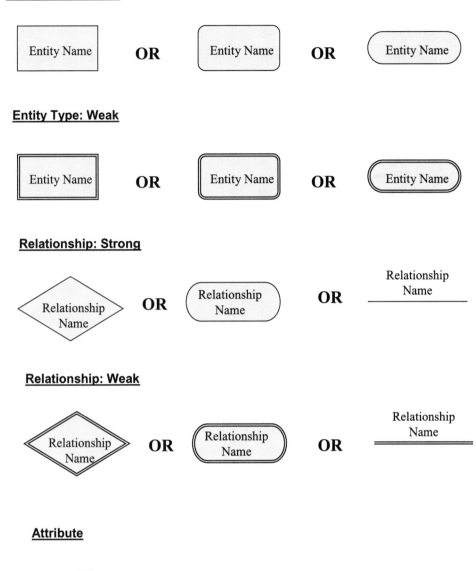

Primary Key

OR

● Attribute Name

Multi-valued Attribute

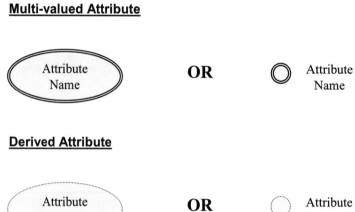

Derived Attribute

Composite Attribute

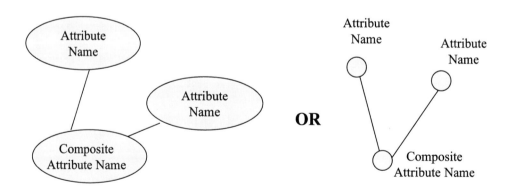

<u>Cardinality Indicators (Maximum cardinalities)</u>

ONE-TO-ONE

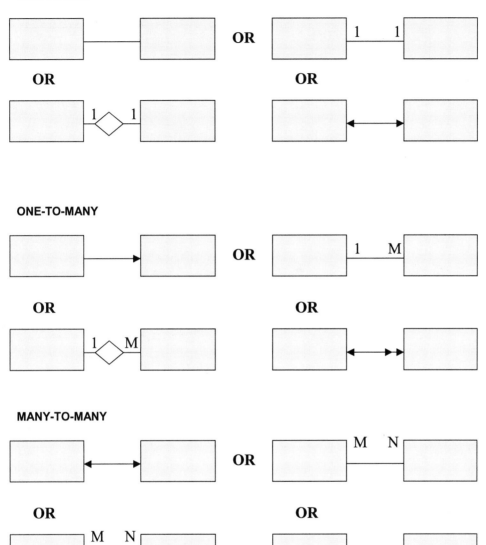

ONE-TO-MANY

MANY-TO-MANY

Cardinality Indicators (Maximum and minimum cardinalities)

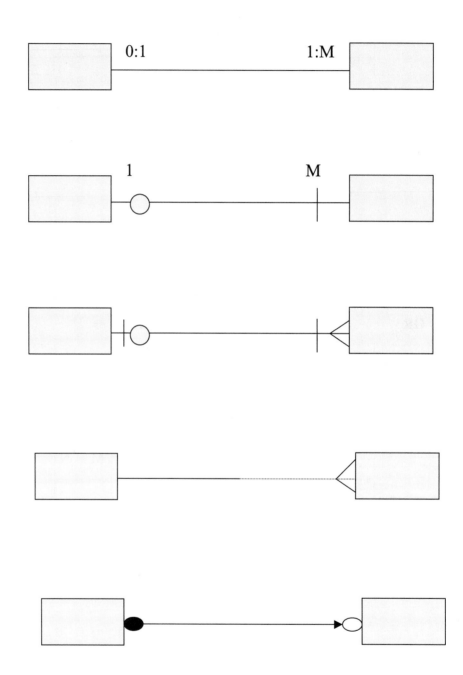

<u>Generalization/Specialization</u>

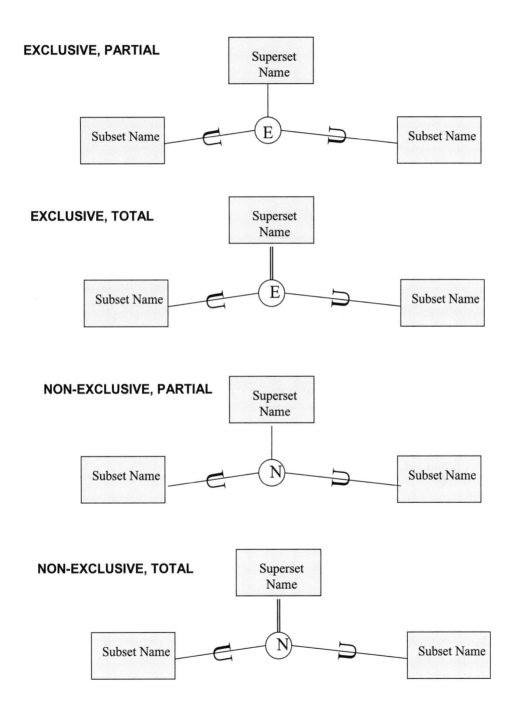

EXCLUSIVE, PARTIAL

EXCLUSIVE, TOTAL

NON-EXCLUSIVE, PARTIAL

NON-EXCLUSIVE, TOTAL

Appendix D

Use of CASE Tools

A very large array of CASE (computer-aided software engineering) tools is available to support every type of computing effort in today's environment. Over the years, the CASE tools market has matured with some leading vendors producing sophisticated tools. In today's industry, no aspect of computing seems to be beyond the scope of CASE tools. In order to give you a flavor of the wide variety, here is a brief sample of the numerous categories of CASE tools:

Analysis
Animation of mission-critical systems
Application generation for mainframe
  systems
Architecture modeling
Automated documentation
Batch code analysis
Business modeling
Business process re-engineering
Change management
Charting and graphing
Client/Server development
Code generation
Code visualization
Component modeling
Component relationship design

Cost estimation
Cross-referencing
Data collection
Data conversion
Data exchange
Data management
Data modeling
Data sharing
Database design
Database publishing
DBMS testing
Design
Diagramming and flowcharting
Flow diagram editor
Forward engineering
Full life cycle

Database Design and Development: An Essential Guide for IT Professionals by Paulraj Ponniah
ISBN 0-471-21877-4   Copyright © 2003 by John Wiley and Sons, Inc.

Function modeling	Program profiling
GUI development	Project management
Impact analysis	Prototyping
Information engineering	Rapid application development
Java development	Report generation
Metamodeling	Requirements engineering
Object modeling	Reverse engineering
Object-oriented analysis and design	Runtime error checking
Object-oriented modeling	Simulation
Performance monitoring	SQL code generation
Performance simulation	Structured analysis and design
Problem tracing	Test case generator
Process management	Test management
Process modeling	Version management

In the study of database design and development, however, we are more interested in the tools that aid in the design, development, and implementation of database systems. This appendix highlights the major features of CASE tools applicable to the database development life cycle (DDLC).

LOGICAL DATA MODELING

- Defining and naming entities and attributes
- Selecting primary keys
- Designating alternate key attributes
- Defining one-to-one and one-to-many relationships
- Resolving many-to-many relationships
- Specifying special relationship types (n-ary, recursive, subtype)
- Defining foreign keys and specifying identifying and nonidentifying relationships
- Establishing referential integrity constraints
- Completing the entity-relationship diagram (ERD)

PHYSICAL DATA MODELING (for the relational model)

- Transforming entities into tables
- Converting attributes into columns
- Assigning primary and foreign keys
- Defining data validation constraints
- Defining triggers and stored procedures for business rules
- Including triggers for INSERT, UPDATE, and DELETE to preserve referential integrity
- Set data types based on target DBMS

DIMENSIONAL DATA MODELING

- Defining fact tables
- Defining dimension tables
- Designing the STAR schema
- Designing outrigger tables (snowflake schema)
- Accounting for slowly changing dimensions
- Defining and attaching data warehouse rules
- Defining data warehouse sources
- Importing from data warehouse sources
- Attaching sources to columns

CALCULATING PHYSICAL STORAGE SPACE

- Estimating database table sizes
- Establishing volumes
- Setting parameters for space calculations

DOMAIN DICTIONARY

- Establishing standards
- Setting domain inheritances and overrides
- Creating domains
- Defining domain properties
- Changing domain properties

FORWARD ENGINEERING

- Selecting schema generation options by category
- Setting schema generation options: referential integrity, trigger, schema, table, view, column, index, and special features relating to target DBMS
- Reviewing summary information before schema generation
- Generating SQL data definition code for target server
- Executing SQL code to generate appropriate schema definitions

BACKWARD OR REVERSE ENGINEERING

- Selecting data dictionary entries of the relational database
- Selecting the file of the SQL data definition statement
- Creating the physical data model
- Creating the logical data model
- Reviewing generated data models

Appendix E

Review of Major Commercial DBMSs

All the leading commercial DBMSs briefly reviewed in this appendix provide the standard database support discussed throughout the book, especially in Chapter 2. Therefore, the standard features are not repeated here for every product.

This appendix highlights only certain significant features of each product, particularly those in the latest version of the product. Use this appendix just as a brief introduction to each DBMS. Several good books and elaborate literature are available for details of any particular DBMS. Please refer to those for further information.

The order of the products as listed here does not imply any ranking. The DBMSs are just listed in the alphabetic sequence. The suitability of any product to your situation depends on the set of requirements.

DB2

Vendor

International Business Machines Corporation

Database Product Versions and Editions

DB2, IBM's premier relational database management system delivering leading capabilities in reliability, performance, and scalability is available as the following products:

DB2 Universal Database V8.1. Relational database management system for AIX, Linux, HP-UX, Sun, and Windows.

Database Design and Development: An Essential Guide for IT Professionals by Paulraj Ponniah
ISBN 0-471-21877-4   Copyright © 2003 by John Wiley and Sons, Inc.

DB2 Everyplace. DB2 relational database and enterprise synchronization architecture for mobile and embedded devices.

DB2 Universal Database for iSeries. Combine to provide flexibility and adaptability for supporting multiple workloads.

DB2 Universal Database for z/OS and OS/390. Intended for using DB2 on the mainframe to run powerful enterprise and e-commerce applications.

DB2 Server for VSE & VM. Full-function relational database management system supporting production and interactive VM and VSE environments.

The following DB2 editions are available:

DB2 Universal Database Enterprise Server Edition

DB2 Universal Database Workgroup Server Unlimited Edition

DB2 Universal Database Workgroup Server Edition

DB2 Universal Database Personal Edition

DB2 Universal Developer's Edition

DB2 Personal Developer's Edition

Highlights of Certain Significant Features

Innovative Manageability Provision of significant automation capabilities including self-configuring, self-optimizing, and self-managing. Innovation includes Configuration Advisor providing knowledge as of a seasoned DBA, Health Center/Monitor keeping the database functioning, Memory Visualizer providing ability to dynamically see and control memory usage, advisors to deliver expert advice on index and materialized query tables, and simplified management of large-scale partitioned databases.

Integrated Information Capability to integrate information across the entire enterprise through federated Web services and enhanced XML.

Robust e-Business Foundation Inclusion of Connection Concentrator for more user scalability, dynamic configuration, online reorganization, online storage management, null and default compression, replication enhancements, and new client architecture.

Enriched Data Type Support Provision of support for spatial data, text data, and flat files via Spatial Extender, Net Search Extender, and Data Links Manager respectively.

Integrated Business Intelligence Incorporation of sophisticated business intelligence capabilities that enable information to be organized for faster and insightful queries.

Application Development Inclusion of an extensive toolkit in the developer editions for building DB2 applications.

Other Related Tools, Components, and Products

DB2 and IMS Tools support data administration, performance, application management, recovery, and replication.

DB2 Extenders manipulate multiple data types with powerful built-in functions.

DB2 related tools enable development of applications using DB2.

DB2 Intelligent Miner for Data enables mining even high-volume transaction data generated by point-of-sale, ATM, credit card, call center, or e-commerce transactions.

DB2 OLAP Server delivers analytic applications for fast, intuitive, multidimensional analysis.

DB2 Warehouse Manager provides capability for intensive and complete business intelligence applications.

INFORMIX

Vendor

International Business Machines Corporation

Database Product Versions and Editions

Informix, IBM's object-relational DBMS for data warehousing, analysis and reporting, Web content delivery, and broadcasting from a digital media library, is available as the following products:

Informix Dynamic Server (IDS). Best-of-breed, general purpose, mission-critical OLTP database software for e-business.

Informix OnLine Extended Edition. Easy OLTP for small and medium-sized businesses.

Informix SE. Zero-administration, embeddable, multiuser DBMS.

The following IDS editions are available:

Informix Dynamic Server Enterprise Edition
Informix Dynamic Server Workgroup Edition

Highlights of Certain Significant Features

Reliability Provides high reliability particularly for applications with high-performance transactions.

Online Transactions Support for complex and rigorous online transaction processing requirements.

Data Operations Maximized data operations for the workgroup and for the global enterprise.

Openness Inclusion of J/Foundation to combine the features of IDS with an open, flexible, embedded Java Virtual Machine environment.

Web Support Provision for dynamic, database-driven websites. Fully integrated with Web technology for data access over the Internet or the company's intranet.

Data Access Ability to access client information, whether on IBM or other databases.

Data Integration Capability to link together a few or even hundreds of IDS databases.

Data Replication Ability to replicate data for quick dissemination across a global organization.

Other Related Tools, Components, and Products

All Informix tools provide development aids to create powerful business applications.

All Informix DataBlades are server extensions that integrate into the core of the engine, delivering unparalleled application functionality and outstanding performance.

Informix C-ISAM provides fast and cost-effective file management technology.

Informix Extended Parallel Server (XPS) provides enterprise data warehousing.

Red Brick Warehouse enables online data warehousing.

ORACLE

Vendor

Oracle Corporation

Database Product Editions

Oracle Database is state-of-the-art in object-relational databases available in the following three editions:

Enterprise Edition. For both clustered and single-system configurations providing comprehensive features for OLTP and decision support.

Standard Edition. Low-cost alternative for small and medium-sized businesses or departments needing the power of the product without requirements for high-end options of the Enterprise Edition.

Personal Edition. Full-featured version of the database for individuals who need full compatibility with the entire Oracle database family.

Highlights of Certain Significant Features

Row Level Locking Ability to lock at the level of individual rows instead of the entire table, thereby allowing many concurrent users to access data from the same table in a multiuser environment.

Materialized Views Precomputing and storing of aggregated data to improve data access performance for common queries, thereby eliminating the need to recompute the results.

Data Partitioning Flexible partitioning of data to improve performance, availability, and manageability.

Query Optimization Proven query optimizer to determine the best data access strategy for each query, especially for the ones with complex SQL statements.

Database Clusters Clustered database with provision to scale your application on any platform with data protection comprising of fast hot failovers.

Data Protection Features Oracle Data Guard providing complete data protection scheme for all types of failures.

Single Sign-On Provision of single sign-on using interoperable certificates for authentication over Secure Sockets Layer (SSL), the Internet authentication standard.

Data Encryption Ability for selective encryption based on industry-standard DES.

Self-managing and Tuning Enhanced database management tools to automate routine DBA tasks including space, memory, and resource management as well as ongoing monitoring.

Data Replication Oracle Advanced Replication designed to support a variety of applications.

Database Clusters Clustered database with provision to scale your application on any platform with data protection comprising of fast hot failovers.

Connectivity Options Two connectivity solutions—generic connectivity and transparent gateways—providing seamless access to non-Oracle data sources.

Content Type Management   Ability to manage various types of data content for traditional, Web, and wireless applications.

Data Warehousing Support   Features including integrated OLAP, data mining functionality, and built-in data warehousing Extraction-Transformation-Loading (ETL) capabilities.

Other Major Related Products

Oracle9*i* Developer Suite and **Oracle9*i* JDeveloper** accelerate the development of all types of applications. Features include: J2EE development, Web services, XML, modeling, rapid application development (RAD), reporting, and business intelligence.

SQL SERVER

Vendor

Microsoft Corporation

Database Product Editions

SQL Server 2000 is a fully enterprise-class database product providing basic support for various types of applications including XML and Internet queries. Through data analysis and data mining capabilities integrating with familiar Microsoft Office applications, the database product provides timely business information. SQL Server 2000, a full-feature relational database product, is available in the following editions:

Enterprise Edition. Most scalable and available edition, includes the complete set of SQL Server data management and analysis features. Able to scale to the performance levels required to support large websites, enterprise OLTP applications, and data warehousing systems.

Standard Edition. Affordable option for small and medium-sized organizations, including core functionality for non-mission-critical and e-commerce solutions. Contains all XML features, all data mining, and core OLAP functionality present in the enterprise edition.

Windows CE Edition. Provides relational database management capabilities on Windows CE-based devices, with tools, application programming interfaces (APIs), and SQL grammar.

Developer Edition. Designed to allow developers build any type of application on top of SQL Server. Includes all the functionality of the enterprise edition for development and testing, but not for production deployment.

Personal Edition. Ideal option for mobile users, functionally equivalent to the standard edition in large measure.

Desktop Engine (MSDE). A redistributable version of the SQL Server relational database engine, ideal for software developers to include in their applications that use SQL Server to store data. Does not include any graphical management tools, nor any analysis capabilities such as OLAP, data mining, and data warehousing.

Highlights of Certain Significant Features

Distributed Partitioned Views   Partitioning of workload among multiple servers for additional scalability.

High Availability   Enhanced availability of business applications with the use of log shipping, online backups, and failover clusters.

Full Text Search   Management of structured and unstructured data, including searching through Microsoft Office documents.

Developer Productivity   Provision of user-defined functions, cascading referential integrity, and reuse of code through the integrated Transact SQL debugger.

XML Support   Simplification of the integration of back-end systems and data transfer across firewalls using XML.

Security   Provision of role-based security and file and network encryption.

Web Access and Hosting   Connection to SQL Server 2000 databases and OLAP cubes flexibly and ability for third-party hosting e-commerce solution with support of multiple instances.

Application Hosting   Provision of multi-instance support to take full advantage of hardware investment so that multiple applications can be run on a single server.

Data Replication   Ability to implement merge, transactional, and snapshot replication with heterogeneous systems.

Database Administration   Simplified data administration with automatic tuning and maintenance features.

Indexed Views   Provision for performance improvement from existing hardware by storing query results.

Data Warehousing Support   Provision of metadata services and data transformation services (DTS).

Advanced Querying and Analysis   Inclusion of English Query, OLAP services, closed-loop analysis, data mining, Web-enabled analysis, and clickstream analysis.

Key Technologies

Key technologies in SQL Server 2000 include: business intelligence and data warehousing, DTS, SQL Server 2000 Notification Services, SQL Server 2000 Windows CE Edition, SQL Server 2000 Enterprise Edition (64-bit), Replication, XML, MSDE.

SYBASE

Vendor

Sybase

Database Product Editions

For a number of years, Sybase has been focusing on open-architecture enterprise infrastructure software. The software solutions bridge all technology platforms and ensure that everything works together and better. Sybase offers the following three version of database software optimized specifically for the demands and complexities of individual businesses:

Sybase Adaptive Server Enterprise 12.5. Powerful data management platform designed for transaction-intensive enterprise applications, with advanced capabilities for meeting the evolving requirements of e-business.

Sybase Anywhere Studio. Comprehensive package providing data management and enterprise synchronization for rapid development and deployment of distributed e-business solutions.

Adaptive Server IQ Multiplex. High-performance relational database designed specifically to satisfy the needs of business intelligence and a new generation of scalability requirements for Web-enabled data warehousing.

Highlights of Certain Significant Features

Open Architecture   Configured to run on several computing platforms.

Content Management   Ability to support the demanding requirements of transaction-intensive, mission-critical OLTP and decision support applications.

Security and Directory Services   Specially designed package to provide complete solution for data protection and application security.

Row Level Access Control   Ability to lock at the level of individual rows providing flexible control in a multiuser environment.

Data Replication   Provision of replication server supporting replicated databases that are geographically distributed.

Navigation Server   Capability for integrating a variety of Sybase servers into a singular powerful distributed query engine for high throughput needed in complex applications.

Internet Standards   Support for all of the open Internet standards, such as XML, UDDI, and SOAP.

Tuning and Optimization   Complete SQL performance tuning and optimization solution that detects and rewrites problematic SQL.

Transition to e-Business   Special provisions in XML/XQL and EJB data management, dynamic tuning for addressing the unpredictable nature of Internet-based computing, and enhanced security features including encrypted communications.

Other Major Related Product

Industry Warehouse Studio (IWS) is an enterprise analytic infrastructure enabling the design, development, and implementation of focused business intelligence applications.

Appendix F

Database Design and
Development Summary

DATABASE DEVELOPMENT LIFE CYCLE: MAJOR PHASES
AND ACTIVITIES

Note: The major activities in each phase indicated here are at a high level. Expand these as necessary to suit the requirements of your database environment. Break down the activities into appropriate tasks.

Project Initiation

Define the scope of the proposed database system.
Establish goals and objectives.
Set values and expectations.
Prepare preliminary justification of the project.
Identify the key business objects of the organization.
Highlight the core business and primary processes in the organization.
List the basic data elements for business objects and processes.
Describe the implementation strategy.
Create a tentative project schedule.
Obtain project authorization.
Initiate project with a clear project initiation report.

Database Design and Development: An Essential Guide for IT Professionals by Paulraj Ponniah
ISBN 0-471-21877-4   Copyright © 2003 by John Wiley and Sons, Inc.

Planning

Interpret the organization's long-term plan to establish the information requirements to be included in the database system.

Consider the general goals, specific objectives, special opportunities, and challenges contained in the long-term plan.

Classify the users in the organization by responsibility levels, business functions, and geographic regions; determine the general data requirements for each user classification.

Review the business objects and the data about these to be included in the database system.

Make preliminary estimates of data volumes.

Review data ownerships across the organization.

Consider issues relating to the recruitment and training of people.

Mention contingencies for possible project failures.

Include new overhead costs.

Complete the database plan.

Feasibility Study

Study the technological feasibility in the specific areas of hardware and systems software. Establish additional needs.

Conduct a study of operational feasibility: take inventory of currently available skills and list the skills needed for the proposed database system; review the list of people with specialized skills; make recommendations for recruitment and training.

Study the economic feasibility: estimate one-time costs for hardware, systems software, database software, communications equipment and software, training, recruitment, special studies, materials and supplies; estimate ongoing costs for hardware maintenance, software upgrades, people, support system, training, materials and supplies.

List possible costs savings from the proposed database system.

Prepare broad estimates of intangible benefits.

Weigh the options for the proposed database system and make recommendations.

Prepare comprehensive feasibility study report.

Requirements Definition

Study overall business operations.

Observe all business processes.

Understand business needs for information.

Interview users and prepare interview summaries.

Study all available and relevant business documents.

Determine information requirements.

Identify data to be collected and stored.

Review data access patterns.

Establish data volumes.

Organize information requirements into data groups.

Document information requirements.

Design

Logical Design

Create semantic data model.

Form user data views from data groups defined in the requirements definition phase.

Integrate data views into the semantic data model.

Include design of the following in the semantic data model:

 Business object sets or entity types

 Relationships between objects or entities

 Generalization and specialization of objects or entities

 Any special object types and relationships

Complete the semantic data model diagram.

Create conventional data model (relational).

Select method for creating conventional data model.

If applicable, use model transformation method:

 Transform object sets into relations.

 Map attributes to columns.

 Map instance identifiers to primary keys.

 Transform relationships by including foreign keys.

If applicable, use normalization method:

 Normalize into fundamental normal forms.

 Normalize into higher normal forms.

 Consolidate normalized data structures into relational data model.

Physical Design

Transform the logical data model into the physical data model.

Map components of relations into files, data blocks, records, and file.

Set the proper file organization for each file.

Define key and other constraints.

Establish performance mechanisms.

Define primary indexes.

Define secondary indexes.

Apply data clustering techniques.
Establish horizontal or vertical partitioning of relations.

Implementation and Deployment

Install DBMS.
Define the logical and physical model in the data dictionary.
Provide application interfaces.
Complete final testing.
Populate database.
Build indexes.
Get user desktops ready.
Authorize users for database access.
Complete initial user training.
Institute initial user support.
Deploy database system in stages.

Maintenance and Growth

Grant and revoke user access privileges as necessary.
Review and maintain concurrency control measures.
Maintain ongoing database backup and recovery techniques.
Perform ongoing space management.
Resolve database problems from time to time.
Monitor database performance through gathering of statistics.
Tune indexes.
Tune queries and transactions.
Tune the schema.
Perform schema changes at all levels for ongoing growth and enhancements.
Apply DBMS version upgrades.

References

Batini, Carlo, and Stefano Ceri, *Conceptual Database Design,* San Francisco, CA: Benjamin Cummings, 1992.

Bontempo, Charles J., and Cynthia Maro Saracco, *Database Management: Principles and Products,* Upper Saddle River, NJ: Prentice-Hall PTR, 1995

Celko, Joe, *Data and Databases: Concepts in Practice,* San Francisco, CA: Morgan Kaufmann, 1999

Connolly, Thomas M., and Carolyn E. Begg, *Database Solutions: A Step-by-Step Approach to Building Databases,* Boston, MA: Addison-Wesley, 2000

Connolly, Thomas, et al., *Database Systems: A Practical Approach to Design, Implementation, and Management (Second Edition),* Boston, MA: Addison-Wesley, 1998

Date, C.J., *An Introduction to Database Systems (Seventh Edition),* Boston, MA: Addison-Wesley, 2000

Date, C.J., *An Introduction to Database Systems, Volume II,* Boston, MA: Addison-Wesley, 1983

Elmasri, Ramez, and Shamkant B. Navathe, *Fundamentals of Database Systems (Third Edition),* Boston, MA: Addison-Wesley, 2000

Fleming, Candace C., and Barbara von Halle, *Handbook of Relational Database Design,* Boston, MA: Addison-Wesley, 2000

Fortier, Paul J. (Editor), *Database Systems Handbook,* New York: McGraw-Hill, 1997

Garcia-Molina et al., *Database System Implementation,* Upper Saddle River, NJ: Prentice-Hall, 2000

Hansen, Gary W., and James V. Hansen, *Database Management and Design (Second Edition),* Upper Saddle River, NJ: Prentice-Hall, 1996

Database Design and Development: An Essential Guide for IT Professionals by Paulraj Ponniah
ISBN 0-471-21877-4   Copyright © 2003 by John Wiley and Sons, Inc.

Harrington, Jan L., *Object-Oriented Database Design,* San Francisco, CA: Academic Press, 2000

Harrington, Jan L., and Dennis Murray, *Relational Database Design,* San Francisco, CA: Morgan Kaufmann, 1998

Hernandez, Michael J., *Database Design for Mere Mortals: A Hands-On Guide to Relational Database Design,* Boston, MA: Addison-Wesley, 1997

Mattison, Rob, *Understanding Database Management Systems,* New York: McGraw-Hill, 1998

McFadden, Fred R., and Jeffrey A. Hoffer, *Modern Database Management (Fourth Edition),* San Francisco, CA: Benjamin Cummings, 1994

Muller, Robert J., *Database Design for Smarties: Using UML for Data Modeling,* San Francisco, CA: Morgan Kaufmann, 1999

O'Neil, Patrick, and Elizabeth O'Neil, *Database: Principles, Programming, and Performance (Second Edition),* San Francisco, CA: Morgan Kaufmann, 2001

Pascal, Fabian, *Understanding Relational Database,* Hoboken, NJ: Wiley, 1993

Piattini, Marlo, and Oscar Diaz (Editors), *Advanced Database Technology and Design,* Norwood, MA: Artech House, 2000

Post, Gerald V., *Database Management Systems: Designing and Building Business Applications,* New York: McGraw-Hill, 2001

Purba, Sanjiv (Editor), *Data Management Handbook,* Boca Raton, FL: Auerbach, 2000

Ramakrishnan, Raghu, and Johannes Gehrke, *Database Management Systems (Second Edition),* New York: McGraw-Hill, 2000

Reingruber, Michael C., and William W. Gregory, *The Data Modeling Handbook,* Hoboken, NJ: Wiley, 1994

Riordan, Rebecca, *Designing Relational Database Systems,* Microsoft Press, 1999

Rolland, F.D., *The Essence of Databases,* Upper Saddle River, NJ: Prentice-Hall, 1998

Schmidt, Bob, *Data Modeling for Information Professionals,* Upper Saddle River, NJ: Prentice-Hall, 1999

Silberschatz, Abraham, et al., *Database System Concepts (Third Edition),* New York: McGraw-Hill, 1999

Stephens, Ryan K., and Ronald R. Plew, *Database Design,* Indianapolis, IN: Sams Publishing, 2001

Teorey, Toby J., *Database Modeling and Design (Third Edition),* San Francisco, CA: Morgan Kaufmann, 1999

Wertz, Charles J., *Relational Database Design (A Practitioner's Guide),* Boca Raton, FL: CRC Press, 1993

Whitehorn, Mark, and Bill Marklyn, *Inside Relational Database: With Examples in ACCESS,* New York: Springer-Verlag, 1997

Glossary

Aggregate object set. A relationship among object sets itself viewed as an object set.

Anomalies. Inconsistencies or errors resulting from manipulating data in random tables containing redundant data. Three types of anomalies are encountered: update, deletion, and addition.

API (application programming interface). A functional interface, usually supplied by the operating system, that allows one application program to communicate with another program. APIs are generally implemented through function calls.

Application developer. A DBMS component that enables the creation of an application with menus, toolbars, forms, and reports.

ASCII (American Standard Code for Information Exchange). A standard code, consisting of a set of seven-bit coded characters, used for information exchange between computers and communication systems.

Atomic transaction. A transaction in which either all database actions are executed completely, or no actions are executed at all.

Attribute. An intrinsic or inherent characteristic of an entity that is of interest to an organization.

Authentication. Determination and verification of the identity of a user.

Authorization. Granting of privileges to users for accessing the database based on the established security policy of an organization.

Backward engineering. The mechanism in CASE tools to obtain the logical data model from the physical data model of a certain database.

Backward recovery. Method used to back out or undo unwanted changes to the database. The database is restored to an earlier, consistent state.

Database Design and Development: An Essential Guide for IT Professionals by Paulraj Ponniah
ISBN 0-471-21877-4   Copyright © 2003 by John Wiley and Sons, Inc.

Binary relationship. Relationship in which two object sets participate. This is the most common form of relationship between object sets.

Binary search. Widely used search technique where the data values are sorted. The search begins at the middle of the series of values and proceeds to the left or the right from the middle based on the value being searched for.

Boyce-Codd normal form (BCNF). A relation or table is in BCNF if it is already in the third normal form and no key attribute is functionally dependent on any nonkey attribute.

Bitmapped indexing. Compact, high-speed indexing method. A bitmap is an ordered series of bits, one bit for each distinct value of the indexed column.

B-tree (balanced tree). Arrangement of sorted data values in nodes forming an inverted tree with the root node at the top and an equal number of branch nodes on either side.

B-tree indexing. Common indexing technique used in most DBMSs based on a B-tree. The search begins at the root node and proceeds through the branch nodes on either side.

Buffer. Region of computer memory that holds data being transferred from one area to another. Data from database tables are fetched into memory buffers. Memory buffer management is crucial for system performance.

Business rules. Specifications based on business practices of an organization that need to be incorporated in the logical data model.

Candidate key. A single attribute or a set of attributes that uniquely identifies an instance of an object set or entity type and can be a candidate to be chosen as the primary key.

Cardinality. Cardinality of the relationship between two object sets indicates how many instances of the first object set may be related to how many of the second.

CASE (computer-aided software engineering). CASE tools or programs help develop software applications. A set of CASE tools many include code generators, data modeling tools, analysis and design tools, and tools for documenting and testing applications.

Centralized database. Database where all data is physically stored in one location.

Checkpointing. Procedure for automatically pausing database operations, committing completed transactions, and saving copies of the database at predetermined points. Database recovery may start at the latest checkpoint.

Clustering. Method for improving database performance. Related records that are likely to be accessed together are placed in the same data block.

CODASYL (Conference on Data Systems and Languages). Organization composed of hardware vendors, software vendors, and user groups. Among other efforts, famously known for the development of COBOL.

Committed transaction. Database transaction that has successfully completed all of its operations.

Composite key. Primary key made up of more than one attribute.

Concatenated key. Same as *Composite key*. Primary key consisting of more than one attribute.

Conceptual data model. Data model, independent of any specific DBMS, that represents the information requirements of an organization at a conceptual or logical level.

Conceptual object set. Set representing the types of an object, not the physical objects themselves.

Conceptual schema. Definition of a conceptual data model.

Concurrent access. Simultaneous access of the same data element in a database by two or more transactions.

Concurrency control. Method to maintain database integrity from potential problems that may result from concurrent access.

Constraint. A rule that is defined in the database. For example, the primary key or foreign key constraints on a data column imposes rules or restrictions on the data that can be entered into that column. Similarly, a business rule that DailyWageRate > 0 can be defined as a constraint in the database.

Conventional data model. See *Logical data model.*

Data administration. Responsibility for the overall planning, managing, and control of the organization's data resource. Data administration is more managerial than technical.

Data block. Records in a physical file are stored in data blocks, each block containing a specified number of records. A data block is the unit of data transfer between disk storage and main memory of a computer. Generally, one block of data is fetched or written in one I/O operation.

Data dictionary. Repository holding the definitions of the data structures in a database. In a relational database, the data dictionary contains the definitions of all the tables, columns, and so on.

Data-driven. Design and implementation of applications in a database approach are data-driven, not process-driven. The primary emphasis is on the business objects and the data about them, not on the processes.

Data fragmentation. Separation of data in the database into manageable fragments. In a relational database, a relation or table may be broken into fragments by separating the table into sets of columns or sets of rows.

Data independence. Ability in database systems to separate data descriptions from the application programs. As such, data definitions may be changed without the need to change the application programs.

Data integration. Combining of data as in a database for common use by various user groups in an organization.

Data integrity. Accuracy and consistency of the data stored in the organization's database system.

Data manipulation. Operations for altering data in the database. Data manipulation includes retrieval, addition, update, and deletion of data.

Data mining. A knowledge discovery process. Data mining algorithms uncover hidden relationships and patterns from a given set of data on which they operate. Knowledge discovery is automatic, not through deliberate search by analysts.

Data model. Representation of the real-world information requirements that gets implemented in a computer system. A data model provides a method and means for describing real-world information by using specific notations and conventions.

Data record. Data in physical files is stored as records. One record contains fields of information about one instance of an object set or entity type. A record in the customer file contains data about one customer.

Data redundancy. Duplication of data in a database.

Data repository. Storage of the organization's data in databases. Stores all data values that are part of the databases.

Data security. Protection of the database from unauthorized or fraudulent use.

Data striping. Distributing or striping data on separate physical devices for the purpose of improving performance by accessing the various segments on separate devices in parallel.

Data view. View of the database by a single user group. Therefore, a data view of a particular user group includes only those parts of the database that the group is concerned with. The collection of all data views of all the user groups constitutes the total data model.

Data warehouse. A specialized database having a collection of transformed and integrated data, stored for the purpose of providing strategic information to the organization.

Database. Repository where an ordered, integrated, and related collection of the organization's data is stored for the purpose of computer applications and information sharing.

Database administration. Responsibility for the technical aspects of the organization's database. Includes the physical design and handling of the technical details such as database security, performance, day-to-day maintenance, backup, and recovery. Database administration is more technical than managerial.

Database administrator (DBA). Specially trained technical person performing the database administration functions in an organization.

Database engine. Heart or kernel of a DBMS. Coordinates the tasks performed by the other components for storing, retrieving, and altering the data.

Database monitoring. Inspecting the performance and state of the database system. Database monitoring provides information for tuning the database for improved performance.

Database plan. Covers the activities to be performed in the various phases of the database development life cycle. Sets the tone for the database project, spells out the key activities, and provides a planning document to guide the project.

Database practitioners. Includes the set of IT professionals such as analysts, data modelers, designers, programmers, and database administrators who design, build, deploy, and maintain database systems.

Database system. Includes all the components that help define, design, build, and deploy databases. A database system not only includes hardware, systems software, DBMS, and the database, but also includes people and procedures.

DBMS (database management system). Software system to store, access, maintain, manage, and safeguard the data in databases.

DBTG (Database Task Group). A subgroup of CODASYL responsible for developing standards for DBMSs.

DCL (data control language). Language component in a DBMS to control the security of a database system. DCL is used to grant and revoke database access privileges to users.

DDBMS (distributed database management system). Software that manages a distributed database as a logical whole.

DDL (data definition language). Language component in a DBMS used for defining the data structures to the data dictionary as schema definitions.

DDLC (database development life cycle). A complete process from beginning to end, with distinct phases for defining information requirements, creating the data model, designing the database, implementing and maintaining the database.

Deadlock. A situation in which neither of two transactions can complete because each is holding exclusively a portion of data in the database that is needed by the other transaction. DBMSs contain provisions for deadlock detection and deadlock prevention.

Decomposition of relations. Splitting of relations or tables into smaller relations for the purpose of normalizing them.

Degree. The number of entity types or object sets that participate in a relationshp. For a binary relationship the degree is 2.

Denormalization. Introduction of controlled redundancy in a database, usually done for the purpose of improving data access performance.

Distributed database. A database where data is physically stored in more than one location.

DKNF (domain-key normal form). This is the ultimate goal in transforming a relation into the highest normal form. A relation is in DKNF if it represents one topic and all of its business rules are able to be expressed through domain constraints and key relationships.

DML (data manipulation language). Language component in a DBMS to perform data manipulation operations in the database.

Domain. The set of all permissible data values and data types for an attribute of an object set.

DSS (decision-support system). Application that enables users to make strategic decisions. DSSs are driven by specialized databases.

EBCDIC (Extended Binary-Coded Decimal Interchange Code). A coded character set of 256 eight-bit characters commonly used in mainframe computer systems.

Encryption. Encoding of data using key data strings so that the encrypted data becomes unintelligible to an intruder. Decryption restores the decoded data to its original form to be used by an authorized user.

Entity. A real-world "thing" of interest to an organization.

Entity instance. A single occurrence of an entity type. For example, a single invoice is an instance of the entity type called INVOICE.

ERD (entity-relationship diagram). A graphical representation of entities and their relationships.

Entity set. The collection of all entity instances of a particular type of entity.

Entity type. Refers to the type of entity occurrences in an entity set. For example, all customers of an organization form the CUSTOMER entity type.

E-R data modeling. Design technique for creating an ERD from the information requirements.

External schema. Definition of the data structures in a database that are of interest to various user groups in an organization. It is the way users view the database from outside.

Feasibility study. One of the earlier phases in the DDLC conducting a study of the readiness of an organization and the technological, economic, and operational feasibility of a database system for the organization.

Fifth normal form (5NF). A relation that is already in the fourth normal form and without any join dependencies.

File organization. Method or technique of arranging the records of a file on physical storage.

File-oriented data system. Data systems earlier than database systems were file-oriented systems depending on sequential, ISAM, and VSAM files without the benefits of database technology.

Firewall. A set of defense mechanisms to protect data that is vulnerable over the Internet.

First normal form (1NF). A relation that has no repeating groups of values for a set of attributes in a single row.

Foreign key. An attribute in a relational table used for establishing a direct relationship with another table, known as the parent table. The values of the foreign key attribute are drawn from the primary key values of the parent table.

Forms generator. A component of the DBMS to enable the creation of online forms for data input into and data display from the database.

Forward engineering. The mechanism in CASE tools to obtain the physical data model for a target database from the logical data model.

Forward Recovery. Method used to start from an earlier state of the database and apply changes. The database is brought forward to a later, consistent state.

Fourth normal form (4NF). A relation that is already in the third normal and without any multivalued dependencies.

Fragmentation. See *Data fragmentation*.

Functional dependency. The value of an attribute B in a relation depending on the value of another attribute A. For every instance of attribute A, its value uniquely determines the value of attribute B in the relation.

Generalization. The concept that some objects are general cases of other objects. The objects in the general cases are known as supersets.

Gerund. Representation of a relationship between two entity types as an entity type by itself.

Global information. Information in a distributed database that is of interest to users in all locations.

Global transaction. A transaction in a distributed database system requiring data from multiple locations for completion.

Hashing algorithm. A software routine that converts the primary key value to a storage address to store that particular record.

Hierarchical data model. A data model where the data structures are arranged in a top-down manner as in an inverted tree.

Homonyms. Two or more data elements having the same name but containing different data.

Horizontal partitioning. In a relational data model, the division of a relation horizontally as a sets of rows.

Identifier. One or more attributes whose values can uniquely identify the instances of an object set or entity type.

Identifying relationship. A relationship between two entity types where one entity type depends on another entity type for its existence. For example, the entity type ORDER DETAIL cannot exist without the entity type ORDER.

Index. A table or data structure containing sorted values of one or more columns in a given relation and the storage addresses of the rows. An index speeds up data access.

Inheritance. The property of subsets inheriting the attributes and relationships of their superset.

Internal schema. Definition of the internal structure of a database.

I/O (input/output). Abbreviation used for indicating a database read/write operation. Excessive I/Os degrade system performance.

ISAM (indexed-sequential access method). A data access method using indexes in file-oriented data systems.

IT (information technology). Covers all computing and data communications in an organization. Typically, the CIO is responsible for IT operations in an organization.

JAD (joint application development). A methodology for developing computer applications in which IT professionals and end-users cooperate and participate in the development effort.

Key. One or more attributes whose values can uniquely identify the rows of a relational table.

Local information. Information in a distributed database that is of interest to users in the local location.

Local transaction. A transaction in a distributed database system requiring data only from the local location for completion.

Lock. Mechanism to prevent access of a portion of the database by other transactions. Locks may be applied at different levels of database structures. Also, there are different types of locks such as shared or exclusive locks.

Log. A file used by the DBMS to record all database transactions. The log file is used for recovery of the database in case of failures. The log file is also known as the journal file.

Logical data model. Also referred as a conventional data model, consists of the logical data structure representing the information requirements of an organization. This data model conforms to the conventions of a class of database systems such as hierarchical, network, relational, and so on.

Logical design. Process of designing and creating a logical data model.

Model transformation. Process of mapping and transforming the components of a semantic data model to those of a logical or conventional data model.

Network data model. A data model where the data structures are arranged in a network of nodes.

Nonprocedural language. Language used for stating *what* result is required from a database transaction rather than stipulating the procedure on *how* to obtain the result.

Normal form. A state of a relation free from incorrect dependencies among the attributes. See *Boyce-Codd normal form*, *First normal form*, *Second normal form*, and *Third normal form*.

Normalization. The step-by-step method of transforming a random relation into a set of normalized relations free from incorrect dependencies and conforming to the rules of the relational data model.

Null value. A value of an attribute, different from zero or blank to indicate a missing, nonapplicable or unknown value.

Object. A physical or conceptual "thing" of interest to an organization, data about which is stored in the database.

Object-based data modeling. Data modeling method that combines the techniques of data modeling and object technology to create a semantic data model to represent the information requirements of an organization.

Object instance. A single occurrence in an object set.

Object set. Set of object instances of the same type. The CUSTOMER object set includes all customers.

ODBC (Open Database Connectivity). A programming interface from Microsoft that provides a common language interface for Windows applications to access databases on a network.

Object-relational data model. Combines the capabilities of object technology to handle complex data types and advanced relationship types with features of data integrity, reliability, and recovery found in the relational realm.

OLAP (online analytical processing). Powerful software systems providing extensive multidimensional analysis, complex calculations, and fast response times. Usually present in data warehousing systems.

Partitioning. See *Data fragmentation*.

Performance tuning. Actions usually taken by the DBA to improve the performance of the database on an ongoing basis.

Physical data model. Data model, consisting of the actual components such as data files, blocks, records, storage allocations, indexes, and so on, representing the information requirements of an organization at a physical level of hardware and system software.

Physical design. Process of designing the physical data model.

Physical object set. Set representing the physical objects themselves, not the types of objects.

Pointer. A logical or physical address of a data element in the database, usually embedded within a data record.

Primary index. An index file created with values of the primary key and corresponding addresses of the rows containing the primary key values.

Primary key. A single attribute or a set of attributes that uniquely identifies an instance of an object set or entity type and chosen as the primary key.

Procedure. Detailed steps of instructions for accomplishing a given task. In computer systems, procedures are written using programming languages.

Procedural language. Language used for stating the procedure on *how* to obtain a required result from a database transaction rather than just stating *what* result is desired.

Process. A set of tasks to accomplish a business function. In computer systems, a process produces outputs from inputs.

Process-driven. Design and implementation of applications where the primary emphasis is on the business processes rather than on the data relating to business objects.

Query. A computing function that requests data from the database, stating the parameters and constraints for the request.

Query optimizer. Part of the query processor in the DBMS responsible to enhance the query for faster processing.

Query processor. A component in the DBMS that executes queries.

RAID (redundant array of inexpensive disks). A system of disk storage where data is distributed across several drives for faster data access and improved fault tolerance.

RDBMS. A relational database management system.

Recovery manager. Software component in the DBMS that enables database backup and recovery from failures.

Referential integrity. Refers to two relational tables that are directly related. Referential integrity between related tables is established if non-null values in the foreign key attribute of the child table are primary key values in the parent table.

Relation. In relational database systems, a relation is a two-dimensional table with columns and rows, conforming to relational rules.

Relational algebra. A generic, procedural language containing well-defined operations for data manipulation in the relational data model.

Relational calculus. A generic, nonprocedural language for data manipulation in the relational data model.

Relational data model. A conventional or logical data model where data is perceived as two-dimensional tables with rows and columns. Each table represents a business object; each column represents an attribute of the object; each row represents an instance of the object.

Relational database. A database system built based on the relational data model.

Relationship. A relationship between two objects sets or entity types represents the associations of the instances of one object set with the instances of the other object set. Unary, binary, or ternary relationships are the common types depending on the number of object sets participating in the relationship. A unary relationship is recursive—instances of an object set associated with instances of the same object set. Relationships may be mandatory or optional based on whether some instances may or may not participate in the relationship.

Repeating group. A group of attributes in a relation that has multiple sets of values for the attributes.

Replication. The method of storing full or partial copies of relations at different locations in a distributed database system.

Report writer. A component in the DBMS that enables creation and running of reports.

Scalability. In a database system, the ability to support increasing numbers of users and transactions.

Schema. Definition in the data dictionary of the entire logical structure of a database.

Second normal form (2NF). A relation that is already in the first normal form and without partial key dependencies.

Secondary index. An index file created with values of the secondary key and corresponding addresses of the rows containing the secondary key values.

Secondary key. One or more attributes in a relation whose values identify a set of rows. These attributes do not constitute the primary key.

Security manager. Software component in the DBMS that controls database security and enables the granting and revoking of data access privileges to users.

Semantic data model. A generic data model that captures the true meaning of the information requirements of an organization. Does not conform to the conventions of any class of database systems such as hierarchical, network, relational, and so on. The two common data modeling techniques for creating a semantic data model are: object-based and entity-relationship.

Sequential file. In a sequential file, data records are stored in the order in which they are entered into the file. Data systems earlier than database systems used sequential files extensively.

Serializability. A set of concurrent database transactions are said to be serializable if they produce the same result as if the transactions were executed serially one after the other. Serializability is a significant requirement for concurrency control.

Space management. Administration and control of storage space for a database, usually performed by the DBA.

Specialization. The concept that some objects are special cases of other objects. The objects in the special cases are known as subsets.

SQL (Structured Query Language). Has become the standard language interface for relational databases.

Stored procedure. A software program stored in the database itself to be executed on the server based on stipulated conditions.

Subquery. A second query within a main query.

Subschema. Subsets of the full schema defining specific user views of the database.

Subset. An object that is a special case of another object known as the superset.

Superset. An object that is a general case of another object known as the subset.

Surrogate key. A unique value generated by the computer system used as a key for a relation. A surrogate key has no business meaning apart from the computer system.

Synonyms. Two or more data elements containing the same data but having different names.

Third normal form (3NF). A relation that is already in the second normal form and without any transitive dependencies—that is, the dependency of a nonkey attribute on the primary key through another nonkey attribute, not directly.

Transaction. Database operations that are executed as a unified set on the data in the database. For example, the transfer of money from the savings to the checking account involving database changes to two relations is considered as a transaction.

Transaction manager. Software component in the DBMS that enables the proper execution of transactions.

Transitive dependency. In a relation, the dependency of a nonkey attribute on the primary key through another nonkey attribute, not directly.

Tuple. A row in a relational table.

Two-phase commit. A technique for concurrency control in a distributed database environment. Commit of a transaction happens in two phases—first, the coordinating DBMS sends updates to other databases asking them to execute; next, coordinating the DBMS sends messages to commit after participating databases agree on the updates.

Vertical partitioning. In a relational data model, the division of a relation vertically as sets of columns.

VSAM (virtual sequential access method). An improved data access method in file-oriented data systems.

Weak entity. An entity that depends on another entity for its existence. For example, the entity type ORDER DETAIL cannot exist without the entity type ORDER.

INDEX